Jews of Brooklyn

Jews
of Brooklyn

EDITED BY

ILANA ABRAMOVITCH

& SEÁN GALVIN

BRANDEIS

UNIVERSITY

PRESS

PUBLISHED BY

UNIVERSITY PRESS

OF NEW ENGLAND

HANOVER & LONDON

Brandeis University Press

Published by University Press of New England,

Hanover, NH 03755

© 2002 by Brandeis University Press

Printed in United States of America

Library of Congress Cataloging-in-Publication Data

Jews of Brooklyn / edited by Ilana Abramovitch and Seán Galvin.

    p. cm.

Includes bibliographical references (p. 349).

ISBN 1-58465-003-6 (cloth : alk. paper)

1. Jews—New York (State)—New York—History.

2. Jews—New York (State)—New York—Social life and customs.

3. Brooklyn (New York, N.Y.)—Ethnic relations.

I. Abramovitch, Ilana.

II. Galvin, Séan.

F129.B7 J49 2001

974.7′23004924—dc21   2001004502

5 4 3 2 1

Leon A. Jick, 1992
The Americanization of the Synagogue, 1820–1870

Sylvia Barack Fishman, editor, 1992
Follow My Footprints: Changing Images of Women in American Jewish Fiction

Gerald Tulchinsky, 1993
Taking Root: The Origins of the Canadian Jewish Community

Shalom Goldman, editor, 1993
Hebrew and the Bible in America: The First Two Centuries

Marshall Sklare, 1993
Observing America's Jews

Reena Sigman Friedman, 1994
These Are Our Children: Jewish Orphanages in the United States, 1880–1925

Alan Silverstein, 1994
Alternatives to Assimilation: The Response of Reform Judaism to American Culture, 1840–1930

Jack Wertheimer, editor, 1995
The American Synagogue: A Sanctuary Transformed

Sylvia Barack Fishman, 1995
A Breath of Life: Feminism in the American Jewish Community

Diane Matza, editor, 1996
Sephardic-American Voices: Two Hundred Years of a Literary Legacy

Joyce Antler, editor, 1997
Talking Back: Images of Jewish Women in American Popular Culture

Jack Wertheimer, 1997
A People Divided: Judaism in Contemporary America

Beth S. Wenger and Jeffrey Shandler, editors, 1998
Encounters with the "Holy Land": Place, Past and Future in American Jewish Culture

David Kaufman, 1998
Shul with a Pool: The "Synagogue-Center" in American Jewish History

Roberta Rosenberg Farber and Chaim I. Waxman, 1999
Jews in America: A Contemporary Reader

Murray Friedman and Albert D. Chernin, 1999
A Second Exodus: The American Movement to Free Soviet Jews

Stephen J. Whitfield, 1999
In Search of American Jewish Culture

Naomi W. Cohen, 1999
Jacob H. Schiff: A Study in American Jewish Leadership

Barbara Kessel, 2000
Suddenly Jewish: Jews Raised as Gentiles

Jonathan N. Barron and Eric Murphy Selinger, editors, 2000
Jewish American Poetry: Poems, Commentary, and Reflections

Steven T. Rosenthal, 2001
Irreconcilable Differences: The Waning of the American Jewish Love Affair with Israel

Pamela S. Nadell and Jonathan D. Sarna, editors, 2001
Women and American Judaism: Historical Perspectives

Ilana Abramovitch and Seán Galvin, editors, 2001
Jews of Brooklyn

Contents

Acknowledgments

The two of us had little idea what a rich journey this would be when we agreed to edit the as-yet-inchoate project on Jewish Brooklyn for University Press of New England. *Jews of Brooklyn* presented an opportunity to get to the epicenter of the Big Kishke of American Jewish life. In the course of over three and one-half years of work, we attended academic conferences and community meetings, made new friends, talked up shopkeepers, followed up leads and leads of leads, schmoozed at *purimschpiels* and political fund-raisers, drank vodka on the boardwalk, learned the secrets of Syrian cookery, watched old Brooklyn films and TV programs, spoke to Brooklynites and former Brooklynites on three continents. We also *nudzhed* and cajoled friends, colleagues, experts, self-proclaimed mavens, and wanna-bes to interview and write for the book.

A few Brooklynites' eyes lit up in their enthusiasm for the project from the very start. Some of these, especially Jan Rosenberg, Laura Silver, and Louis Menashe, have become or remain good friends, contributing invaluable support and succor, as well as hours of work, for the project. All three also enticed their wide circles of friends, families, or colleagues to participate in the book's tasks. In this way the project's participants and connections grew, spiraling out from the center like a galactic milk bar.

Other good friends, including Emily Botein, Anita Feldman, Ellen Gruber Garvey, Justine McGovern, Sheba Meland, Lora Myers, Alan Rosen, and Renata Singer, graciously spent time interviewing or responding to drafts and suggesting materials for the book's embrace.

Other friends and colleagues who offered helpful responses and suggestions include Alice Apley, Robert Baron,

Stephen Brumberg, Jerome Chanes, Fred Ciporen, Kathy Condon, Joe Dorinson, Allen Farbman, Tracy Figueroa, Bonnie Gurewitsch, Alan Herman, Barbara Kirshenblatt-Gimblett, Alfred Gottschalk, Hal and Priscilla Grabino, Ilana Harlow, Sally Magid, Michael McQuillan, John Manbeck, Wendell Pritchett, Peter Schweitzer, Shari Segel, Jeffrey Shandler, Fred Siegel, Ethel Raim, Michael Taub, Francis P. Vardy, Florence Yudenfriend, Steve Zeitlin.

Michael Kramer generously shared his introductory remarks from the Jerusalem conference on Brooklyn.

Librarians and archivists were very helpful to us in our research, especially the staff at the Brooklyn Public Library, Brooklyn Division, and the New York Public Library, Jewish Division. We would also like to thank Brooklyn borough president Howard Golden's Office of Ethnic Affairs.

We are indebted to all the book's authors, interviewers, and the interviewees, including those whose articles did not appear in the final cut. During the course of the book project, the book's contents had a tendency to germinate and swell and grow with truly Brooklynite zeal, like the Tree of Heaven. We had more promising material than we could include in one volume and had to make difficult decisions of what to include and exclude. We had to prune constantly. There is clearly room for many more books on the Jews of Brooklyn.

Phyllis Deutsch, our editor at UPNE, inspired us with her energetic support for the project through its many phases and Middle Eastern dinners.

Other exemplary support at UPNE came from Jennifer Thomas, who coordinated much of the art and permissions, and David Bellows, who rendered the entire manuscript electronic.

We would like to thank our families for their spirited devotion during the years of extra work hours, phone calls, meetings, and excursions. And we would especially like to express our gratitude to the people of Brooklyn of all backgrounds, whose gumption made it all possible.

I. A. and S. G.

Jews of Brooklyn

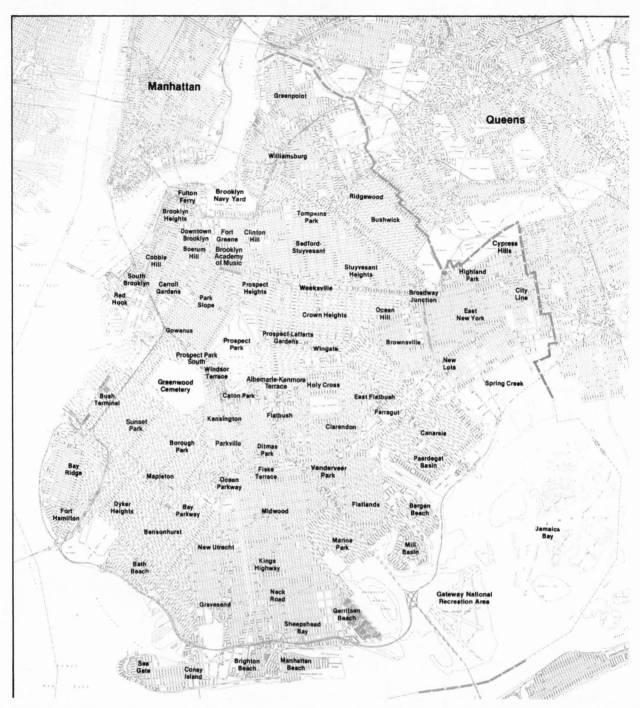

Neighborhood Map

Introduction

ILANA ABRAMOVITCH

The story of the Jews of Brooklyn has been inseparable from the development of the borough as a whole. Jewish businessmen, shop owners, politicians, rabbis, teachers, social workers, entertainers, writers, and artists, famous and not so famous, have indelibly shaped Brooklyn institutions and Brooklyn's reputation among insiders and outsiders. Capturing the breadth and scope of the contributions of individuals and communities would take volumes; capturing the feeling of Jewish Brooklyn has been the goal of this book. Juxtaposing overviews of immigrant groups, neighborhood histories, and social transformations with more intimate portraits of families and individuals, *Jews of Brooklyn* offers an illustrated chronicle—an album of text and images—that conveys the complex relationship of a people and a place.

The Jews of Brooklyn is divided into three parts, reflecting the constant flow of people into and out of the borough: "Coming to Brooklyn," "Living in Brooklyn," and "Leaving Brooklyn/Returning to Brooklyn." This division speaks to Brooklyn's dynamic position in the lives and memories of its inhabitants. While certain groups and individuals are moving in, others are leaving. While several generations are established in Brooklyn, a few "expatriates" are contemplating a return. In fifty-five chapters within these sections, scholars, journalists, and Brooklyn mavens explore what's special about Brooklyn Jewish life, past and present. There is a lot to choose from; Brooklyn Jews are at once similar to, but different, from Manhattan Jews, Brooklyn non-Jews, and all New Yorkers.

Mention Brooklyn, and everybody has an opinion. New York's most populous borough has a reputation as the city's most vivid. For decades, a good-natured stereotype set up the Brooklynite, a figure of fun in popular culture: whether for the colorful, mythical dialect "Brooklynese"[1] or for images of Brooklyn GIs in World War II movies. He was brash, ethnic, street-smart, and deeply sentimental. Popular entertainers discovered that just mentioning Canarsie or certain other Brooklyn neighborhoods could set off guffaws. In the dramatic words of author Truman Capote (1994), contented resident of pedigreed Brooklyn Heights, "[Brooklyn is a] . . . veritable veldt of tawdriness where even the *noms des quartiers* aggravate: Flatbush and Flushing Avenue, Bushwick, Brownsville, Red Hook." The old stereotypes outline a dated, yet still circulating, image of the borough, a land of white ethnic yahoos.

Actually, things have been changing for over forty years: There is a new mix of peoples in the borough. Brooklyn is now home to some 150 ethnic groups. Many old neighborhoods house new groups, be they African-Americans and Latinos, Asian immigrants, or well-heeled migrants from Manhattan and other points west. These days, a more common stereotype of Brooklyn is of hardscrabble inner-city neighborhoods. Brooklyn is largely considered the flavorful, even pungent, working-class entity lying next to its slimmer, more cosmopolitan urban partner, Manhattan.

Being from Brooklyn, with its implications of brash provincialism, cuts close to home. As the borough's president's Website brags, "Brooklyn is America's Favorite Hometown" (BRIC 2000), and there are statistics to back it up: "One out of every seven Americans was either born here, lived here once, had relatives here or got here by taking the wrong subway" (Glueck and Gardner 1991, 9). Eminent scholars Kenneth T. Jackson and Jacques Barzun raise the stakes: "As many as a quarter of all Americans can trace their ancestry to people who once lived in its 81 square miles" (Jackson 1995, xvii).

A central switchboard of the American population, Brooklyn has come to connote just about everything—or nothing. Although a big fan of Brooklyn, calling it the most real place he'd ever been in his life, Norman Mailer once paradoxically maintained that the borough was without a vital core and was not the center of anything. Other eminent authors have portrayed Brooklyn as vast and inscrutable, as in Arthur Miller's "No one can know Brooklyn, because Brooklyn is the world" (quoted in Rosen and Rosen 1999). Bernard Malamud's borough is symbolically even larger: "Brooklyn, you are the universe" (quoted in "Brooklyn" 1983). Carson McCullers: "That is one of the things I love best about Brooklyn. Everyone is not expected to be exactly like everyone else." Meanwhile, the title of Thomas Wolfe's famous story (1994) insists mysteriously that "Only the Dead Know Brooklyn."

Brooklyn is a funnel through which much of the U.S. immigrant world has whirled. This dwelling place, often temporary, of so many newcomers to the United States becomes in time a locus of memory, a place to look back at from elsewhere. The older derisive images of Brooklyn are more than counterbalanced by the fierce feelings of Brooklyn loyalists. A Brooklynite's coming of age stories are often inseparable from her or his personal attachment to Brooklyn locales, often remembered more fondly from a distance. By no means do all immigrants leave Brooklyn— many families have lived in Kings County for generations. Nonetheless, the United States, nay the world, is popu-

lated with former Brooklynites, happily living in exile, yet forever Brooklynites deep in their hearts.

Brooklyn boosters are prone to promote cohesion through nostalgic reminiscences, embracing detailed discussions of famous locales like Coney Island, Prospect Park, and the Brooklyn Bridge. Cherished neighborhood spots like DuBrow's Cafeteria, Schechter's candy store, or Erasmus Hall High School provide content for more specialized games of trivial pursuit. The quasi-mythic, much-mourned Brooklyn Dodgers still unite those who continue to trade heated opinions. Elliot Willensky's aptly titled volume, *When Brooklyn Was the World, 1920–1957*, captures the feeling of deep-rootedness that animated many who grew up in the borough's neighborhoods. A growing series of popular books and films about Brooklyn are centered in that midcentury period, viewed by many over the age of fifty as a time of greater community cohesiveness. Nostalgia for that other time feeds an endless loop of wistfulness, leaving its adherents in a perpetual state of yearning for the imagined community.

But neither Brooklyn's communities nor their representation in media images remain static. Since the 1960s, things have been changing in the neighborhoods, and popular images of Brooklyn have revealed greater violence, high-crime zones, poor schools, and interracial strife. Brooklynites are often seen as abrasive know-it-alls who live in despoiled neighborhoods and don't get along with each other. Examples, unfortunately, abound. The bitter controversy surrounding the 1968 Ocean Hill–Brownsville teachers' strike pitted Jewish schoolteachers against the black and Puerto Rican communities. This marked a public rift between Brooklynites of different ethnic and racial backgrounds who had been at least nominally allied in many neighborhood and human rights concerns (Salzman and West). Neighborhoods that had once evoked nostalgia became symbols of urban despair.

The Jews of Brooklyn are a unique subset of the residents of Kings County, its coextensive administrative entity. They have made up from 16 to 42 percent of the borough's population—an unusually high percentage when you consider that Jews have made up between 3 and 4 percent of the U.S. population. In 1990, Brooklyn Jews numbered about 420,000 out of New York City's 1.13 million Jewish inhabitants. Yet for outsiders, one of the most common stereotypes of a Brooklyn Jew features a black-clad Hasid. Brooklyn certainly is a worldwide center of Hasidism, the

Ultra-Orthodox, socially conservative movement within Judaism "distinguished by its enthusiasm for meditative prayer, joyous service of the Creator, and intellectual mystical thought" (Hassidic Discovery Welcome Center n.d.). Crown Heights houses the world headquarters of Chabad-Lubavitch, which sends out emissary couples to more than a hundred countries. There are, of course, many different Hasidic sects, and the majority of American Hasidim reside in Brooklyn. But there are Jews of all different stripes in Brooklyn.

The Jews in all the New York City boroughs share much. They live in a city with a Jewish population large enough to create a comfort zone, in which being Jewish is unremarkable. Brooklyn's diversity of Jewish communities is compounded by their density and continuity. Although the Jewish population measures its history in less than two centuries, a very short time in the Jewish chronology, it is notably strong in continuity, by North American standards. A critical mass of Jews has supported Brooklyn's rich nexus of institutional life for 150 years.

The strength of the Jewish population in Brooklyn, however, is not evenly spread throughout the borough. Jewish Brooklyn, like the Brooklyn of most of its ethnic groups, continues to be a land of neighborhoods. Brighton Beach, Flatbush, Williamsburg, among others, have had thriving local Jewish lives and institutions, each with its own particular flavor. Intense local loyalties animate inhabitants, who often express themselves in tribal defenses of boundaries, while nostalgia often overflows among those who have left. In a time when the sense of place is often weak, when franchises and globalization transform the anywhere into everywhere, Jews of Brooklyn have managed to keep the local smartly particular, as well as cosmopolitan. As Jews, they know from global, and as Brooklynites, they know from street smarts.

Arrays of choices exist as to how to express one's Jewishness, or not. This in itself distinguishes New Yorkers from most other North American communities. But significant distinctions exist between New York City's boroughs, though they are far from sealed-off entities. Brooklyn's Jewish life has shown dynamism, a constant renewal and reinvention. The more one examines Brooklyn Jewish life, the more one sees its magnetic quality. Brooklyn's Jewish community is one of the most creative in the world.

Brooklyn's Jewish life is breathtaking in its diversity. Major groupings in the borough include Jews from the former Soviet Union, from Syria, Jews of central and eastern European origin, Israeli Jews, Jews from Arab lands, Iranian Jews. There are large numbers of elderly Jews, yuppie Jews, Holocaust survivors, Orthodox, Ultra-Orthodox. . . . Within its borders, Brooklyn has contained major centers of Jewish religious, educational, and all varieties of Zionist and anti-Zionist life. In terms of individuals, Brooklyn has spawned world famous Jewish scholars, movie stars, gangsters, sports figures, politicians, scientists, directors, musicians, and opera divas.

Brooklyn has certainly produced stars, and no book on the borough would be complete without a proud listing of its famous "sons and daughters." (For example: Joan Rivers, Richard Dreyfus, Lenny Bruce, Lou Reed, Sandy Koufax, Beverly Sills, Mel Brooks, Woody Allen, Wendy Wasserstein, Paul Auster, or "Mickey" Marcus, the tough Brooklyn street kid who rose by virtue of his courage and intelligence to become Israel's first general since Judah Maccabee—nearly two thousand years.) Nevertheless, this volume's focus is on daily life, communities, and regular folks rather than celebrities. We are proud to include well-known Jewish Brooklynites, or Jews of Brooklyn origin, but they are here mostly to rub shoulders with the other kids from the neighborhood. Through a juxtaposition of essays on history and contemporary life, memoirs, interviews, and reprints, *Jews of Brooklyn* aims to capture and re-create the energy of the borough's life in the very organization of the book itself.

COMING TO BROOKLYN

New York is Babylon; Brooklyn is the true Holy City. New York is the city of envy, office work and hustle; Brooklyn is the region of homes and happiness. . . .
—Christopher Morley, 1917

The essays in this part document the arrival to Brooklyn of Jewish individuals and groups, including Germans, eastern Europeans, Syrians, Middle Easterners, Hasidim, and yuppies. This introduction historically contextualizes the early days of each group, while the next part, "Living in Brooklyn," follows some of these groups and others as they become more established in the borough.

No one knows for sure when the first Jews settled in Brooklyn, but the history of settlement is surprisingly short—almost two hundred years shorter than that of the Jews of Manhattan, whose arrival was first documented in 1654. Before 1838, Jews trod on Brooklyn ground, but only stayed for a visit. Samuel Abelow (teacher and journalist), Jewish Brooklyn's first chronicler, reports three Mr. Levys—one an auctioneer, one a variety store owner, and one a cartman—among the first Jewish names in the Brooklyn directory of 1838–39. The previous year, the first Jewish name appeared in the directory of Williamsburg, which was then an independent village. With these small beginnings the great history of Brooklyn as Jewish home begins. Asser Levy, one of the first Jewish settlers in New Amsterdam—and New York's first kosher butcher—owned substantial Brooklyn property in the 1660s and 1670s. Subsequently, Jews visited Brooklyn, participated in the Continental Army's Battle of Brooklyn, conducted business in Brooklyn, and protected its defenses during the War of 1812. Then they went back home to other places.

Brooklyn's European settlement began in the mid-1600s when the Dutch founded five towns, Breuckelen (Brooklyn), New Amersfoot (Flatlands), Midwout or Vlacke Bosch (Flatbush), New Utrecht, and Boswick (Bushwick). Lady Deborah Moody, fleeing persecution in England as well as clashes with Puritans in the Massachusetts Bay Colony, founded a sixth town, Gravesend. She was granted a land patent from New Amsterdam's governor, guaranteeing settlers the right to worship as they pleased—unique in the New World (Glueck and Gardner 1991, 15). In 1646, the Village of Breuckelen ("broken valley" or "land of brooks and marshes") was authorized by the Dutch West India Company and became the first municipality in what is now New York State. With a slow-moving pastoral beginning, Brooklyn became a city in 1834 and began incorporating the other villages and towns of Kings County throughout the nineteenth century. For only two years before 1898, when the City of Brooklyn was incorporated into greater New York City, did all the towns of Kings County become part of the City of Brooklyn.

When it started to grow, Brooklyn really grew. In the middle years of the nineteenth century, Brooklyn became the fastest-growing city in the country, with major immigration from Ireland and Germany. This is the point when Jews are first documented as settlers. Some of the first Jews in what is now Brooklyn, mostly from Bavaria and Alsace, were owners of small retail businesses. Many went into the cattle and feed business that they knew from Europe. Some became all-American cultural pioneers: Emanuel Pike, a Dutch Jewish haberdasher in downtown Brooklyn in the late 1840s, was the father of Lipman Pike, the first pro baseball player. Lists of men liable for military service during the Civil War demonstrate a substantial number of Jews by 1863.

By the late 1870s, Jews were leaders in the dry goods and garment trades, selling their wares in venues from pushcarts to the halls of great department stores, encompassing the entire range of products from shoestrings to expensive fur coats. Some created famous enterprises: Abraham Abraham was a founder in 1865 of Weschler and Abraham, which in 1893 became Abraham and Straus, or A&S, for years Brooklyn's largest department store. Inspired by the array of wonders on display in this magnificent store, Samuel Abelow, Brooklyn's Depression-era chronicler, waxed lyrical about its "best products of the most skilled workmanship in the world," which provided "a wonderful insight into the mechanical genius of the human species" (1937, 281).

Abraham Abraham, whose father was born in Bavaria, and who studied retail business in Newark with fellow clerks Benjamin Altman and Simon Bloomingdale, learned his lessons early and well, becoming a very successful businessman. Like many central European Jews of his class, he was also deeply involved in Jewish communal affairs and philanthropy. His generosity and enthusiasm were instrumental in the founding of Brooklyn Jewish Hospital, while his dedication as president of the Hebrew Orphan Asylum earned him the praise of the mayor of New York City. For Mayor William Gaynor, Abraham represented humanity at its most just and equitable. Living up to his grand name, Abraham Abraham "leads the mind back to the border line where fable closes and history begins."

Abraham's many other locales of communal leadership included the Hebrew Education Society and Temple Israel (see Seán Galvin's chapter, "First Synagogues"). As in Manhattan, Jews from central Europe and German-speaking lands established synagogues as they established themselves. According to tradition, early Jewish settlers are said to have rowed across the East River on Friday afternoons for religious services in Manhattan, staying there till after dark on the Sabbath. This often-repeated and charming tale of muscular Judaism turns out to be apocryphal. Brooklynites were much more self-sufficient, worshipping in private homes before midcentury, when they established their first congregations. In 1848, German Jews established Beth Elohim in Williamsburg and Union Fields Cemetery in Cypress Hills, close to the Brooklyn-Queens border. The synagogue later moved, amalgamated with Temple Israel, and became Union Temple, which was the leading Reform temple in Brooklyn. In 1854 a religious society was founded that became Congregation Baith Israel Anshei Emes (later, the Kane Street Synagogue). These two are considered the oldest congregations in Brooklyn.

Brooklyn, more commonly known as the City of Churches, was on its way to becoming the City of Synagogues, with more than half of all the synagogues in New York City in its terrain. There was a certain amount of fluidity in the congregations in late nineteenth-century Brooklyn, as the denominations within Judaism created and redefined themselves in North America. As the twentieth century evolved, Orthodox, Conservative, and Reform emerged as the three main religious streams. Orthodox is the most traditional and observant, while Reform has adapted most to contemporary needs. Congregants debated among themselves about their openness to the evolving practices of Reform. Many groups started out as traditional and evolved into a variety of Reform. Splinter groups broke off from congregations and reunited with like-minded worshippers in other shuls. Temple Israel had what Abelow discreetly calls "an eventful history," in which those opposed to the established orthodoxy lost out to the zeal of the newer Reform tradition. Abelow documents what might surprise a twenty-first-century Brooklynite who sees the growing influence of Orthodox institutions. In the nineteenth and early twentieth centuries, Brooklyn had a substantial number of Reform congregations, some liberal Reform; there were even Conservative synagogues in Williamsburg, now a bastion of Ultra-Orthodoxy. But as Hasia Diner (1992) documents on the national scale, many traditionalists opposed to Reform also innovated and changed the prayer services to an extent, acknowledging implicitly that Judaism would necessarily undergo some change in America.

It was in the late nineteenth century, with the influx of large numbers of immigrants, that Brooklyn transformed itself into a major urban center and a major center of Jewish life. Brooklyn in 1880 had a population of almost 600,000—an increase of more than 40 percent over the previous decade, a rapid rise in keeping with the national picture of expanding population. In 1880 New York and Brooklyn were two of twenty U.S. cities with a population of over 100,000. In 1860 there had been only nine cities of that size. And Brooklyn kept growing. The Brooklyn Bridge, completed in 1883, opened it to many newcomers, especially immigrants looking for more open spaces and affordable housing. Independent of New York City until 1898, Brooklyn was the third-largest city in the United States for nearly fifty years. Spanning 5,989 feet, the bridge connected the two major cities and spurred real estate development and commuting patterns. An icon of Brooklyn progress that continues to inspire poetry, the bridge was greeted with fascination during its fourteen-year construction, and acclaim upon its completion. Wechsler and Abraham (later Abraham and Straus) department store proclaimed: "Babylon had her hanging garden, Egypt her pyramid, Athens her acropolis, Rome her Athenaeum; so Brooklyn has her Bridge" (Snyder-Grenier 1996, 75).

Mass immigration from eastern Europe, together with advances in bridge building and transportation, helped open up larger areas of Brooklyn to Jewish settlement. The first communities were close to Manhattan. Bridges, subways, as well as energetic efforts of Jewish real estate developers brought in a large flow of occupants.

With the building of the subways and the Williamsburg (1903) and Manhattan (1909) Bridges, new neighborhoods, in the words of Abelow, "felt the magic wand of Jewish desire for improvement" (1937, 12). The construction of the Delancey Street approach to the Williamsburg Bridge (known as "Jews' Highway" by the yellow press) displaced many of Manhattan's East Side residents. German Jews who had been the first to settle in Williamsburg were joined in the early twentieth century by a vast influx of eastern European Jews and by a smaller influx of Sephardic Jews. The wealthier Germans, who had founded the first Reform temple, moved out over time to other neighborhoods, such as Greenpoint, Bedford-Stuyvesant, and streets around Prospect Park. The "uptown" Jewish community responded with fear and disdain to the eastern European Jewish masses, the "miserably darkened Hebrews" with whom "the thoroughly acclimatized American Jews . . . has no religious, social or intellectual ties."

As Jenna Joselit writes, the newer residents of Williamsburg were Jews who established Orthodox institutions, fashioning "their own home-grown notion of American Orthodoxy" that was Zionist and educationally progressive (1990, 17). Only later, in the 1930s and especially after the war, did the Hungarian Hasidim arrive en masse and insist on their own style of Ultra-Orthodoxy. Gradually, the non-Hasidic Jewish elements left the neighborhood as the anti-Zionist, distinctively garbed Satmar moved in.

The opening of the IRT subway in 1908 and subsequent lines prepared new areas for development, making outer Brooklyn more accessible. Real estate developers encouraged garment workers from the Lower East Side to move to Brownsville, a neighborhood with such dense and active Jewish life that it became known as the "Jerusalem of America." Further high-scale urban construction resulted in more transplants.

By 1927, 35 percent of Brooklyn's population were Jews. Abelow calls the "growth of the Jewish community . . . one of the most remarkable social phenomena in history" (1937, 13). Brooklyn's Jewish population grew from 100,000 in 1905 to more than 800,000 in 1930. By then a third of the borough's population were Jews, and 47 percent of all the Jews in New York City lived in Brooklyn. The tremendous growth of the Jewish population went hand in hand with industrial growth. "By 1930 Brooklyn had become, along with Chicago and Pittsburgh, one of the greatest manufacturing centers on earth. It handled 55% of all the freight of the port of NY, and it had the largest docking and terminal station in the world" (Jackson and Manbeck 1998, xxv).

The growth and density were not evenly divided among Brooklyn neighborhoods. Growth concentrated especially in Brownsville, where four thousand Jews of the early 1890s had increased by 1905 to fifty thousand. The *New York Tribune* in 1896 was calling it "a land of sweatshops and whirring sewing machines, of strange Russian baths, of innumerable dirty and tiny shops, of cows milked directly into pitchers and pails of customers at eventide, of anarchists, of Jew dancing school and of a peasant market" (Snyder-Grenier 1996, 48). By the interwar years, not much had changed in its public image, as a public schoolteacher called Brownsville, originally seen as a haven from the Lower East Side, "a cesspool of illiteracy and hooliganism" (Willensky 1986, 84).

Many Jews now immigrated directly to Brownsville instead of the Lower East Side. By the 1920s the population of Brownsville and its neighboring communities of East New York and New Lots had outstripped the Jewish settlements of the Lower East Side or Williamsburg. In 1925, Brownsville had a population that was 95 percent Jewish. It was still 80 percent Jewish in 1940, with eighty-three synagogues. Henry Roth's *Call It Sleep* includes but one story among thousands telling of eastern European Jews who traveled directly to Brownsville (the "Golden" Land of America, ironically realized here as "Bronzeville"), skipping Manhattan in their voyage to America. Through the eyes of a young child, Roth's unsentimental portrait contrasts the homey, expressive Yiddish spoken in the family with the tough, mutilated English of the street. ("Yeh? I t'ought maybe—I know sommbody wod he hoided his hand on de Futt f'om Jillai—wid a fiyuh crecker. He had id in his house so he lighded id. Den he wanned t't'row id oud f'om de windeh. So de windeh woz cluz. So he didn' know w'ea he sh't'trow id. So bang—!" [Roth 1991, 138]).

Russian Jews from the Lower East Side began settling in Borough Park in 1910. Michael Gold depicts this Jewish neighborhood, destined later to become a "New Jerusalem," in its early days. *Jews without Money* recounts how Gold's father's boss advised the family to move from the Lower East Side to his new Brooklyn suburban neighborhood. Jews with a little money were relocating to the still rural development, where a first synagogue had been established in 1903. A skeptical Gold paints a dreary picture of "half-finished skeleton buildings" and billboards shouting loud promises. "In a muddy pool where ducks paddled, another sign read: 'Why Pay Rent? Build Your House in God's Country.'" The boss's gaudy house was "bulging with bay windows and pretentious cupolas." Gold's class allegiances are rapidly made clear in his portrait of Mrs. Cohen, the boss's petulant wife, seen lounging on a sofa with a headache, "glittering like an ice-cream parlor," and looking "like some vulgar pretentious prostitute," although she was "only the typical wife of a Jewish *nouveau riche*." These were the very early days of Borough Park, long before it would become a major center of Hasidic life and one of the most vital Jewish communities in the country (Belcove-Shalin 1995, 206).

Not all Jews came from Europe. Around the same time as the big wave of immigration from eastern Europe came Jews from Syria—mostly from Aleppo—many of whom moved to Brooklyn in 1918–19 from the Lower East Side. The Syrian Jews moved as a group and set up their community in Bensonhurst, establishing their first synagogue in 1921. The Syrian Jews carried a strong identity as Syrians and have created a tight-knit community. According to the executive director of the Sephardic Community Center, Martin Maskowitz, this is "100% deliberate" (Greenberg 1999, 103). Currently the Syrian community is centered in Flatbush, Gravesend, and Bensonhurst.

An enthusiastic middle-aged Syrian member of the community explains the comfort of his community:

We still eat the same foods that our parents ate . . . we're proud of it . . . we all live around the same area . . . when you go away on vacation . . . everybody's there together

. . . easily 80% marry another Syrian. . . . The songs we sang at the *brith* [circumcision] are the songs that my parents sang, my grandparents sang, and my son knows and already learned. . . . You can close your eyes, go to any Syrian family for Friday night meal. You'll have very close to the same meal by every Syrian family. . . . Please don't change it. . . . You can't wait to go home and have that Friday night Syrian meal. (Ashkenazie 5, 18)

With the change in immigration laws after 1924, fewer Jews came from abroad to Brooklyn until World War II. Yet by 1936, Brooklyn Jewry, "which started with a cartman, a variety store keeper and an auctioneer developed into a complex, dynamic, progressive community" (Abelow 1937, 12). During and after the war, many Jews came to Brooklyn from eastern and central Europe. A large number of these were Hasidic refugees who settled in Williamsburg, Borough Park, and Crown Heights.

Today, these neighborhoods, and increasingly their surrounding areas, have become dense enclaves of Hasidic life. Neighborhoods have become transformed and are expanding, with the pressure of large families. In the decade after the war, as well as after the 1956 Hungarian Uprising, Jews of all backgrounds arrived, often to join relatives in Brooklyn. Hasidic sects are named for their town of origin in Europe. Different groups of Hasidim gravitated toward different Brooklyn neighborhoods: Satmar, Sighet, Pupa, and Klausenberg rebbes went to Williamsburg; Lubavitcher to Crown Heights; Stoliner and Bobover to Borough Park (which also attracted the smaller groups of Bostoner [of New York], Blueshover, Munkaczer, Kapishnitzer, Novominsker, Skolyer, many Ger and Belz) (Belcove-Shalin 1995). The majority of U.S. Hasidim reside in Brooklyn. The Hungarian Hasids are in the majority in Williamsburg, rapidly changing the lifestyle part of the neighborhood. By 1951, the last movie house on Lee Avenue was turned into the rebbe's residence and *besmedresh* of the Klausenbergers. Hungarian and Yiddish became the languages of the streets.

Many observers expected Hasidic life to die out, as it had suffered great losses in Europe during the Holocaust. History has shown this to be anything but true, as Hasidim since their arrival have consolidated their positions in their Brooklyn centers and thrived. Samuel Heilman, sociologist of New York Orthodox life, notes: "The Hasidim could only take root where they were allowed to take root. America offered them a fertile ground and open society, particularly New York, which allowed them to create a variety of institutions. They exist where they are allowed to, in an open society, which paradoxically offers the greatest threat" ("A Life Apart"). The lax religious observance of earlier Jewish immigrants strengthened the Hasidic commitment to strict maintenance of traditional customs, and intensified their avoidance of the attractions of mainstream American, and modern Jewish, culture. Some historians claim that the Jewish world of Europe was not actually destroyed in the Holocaust. It was merely transplanted and condensed to twenty blocks in Brooklyn. In their resistance to Americanization, these Jews remade Brooklyn in their own image, a Brooklyn that knew not the Dodgers.

The next large wave of Jewish immigrants to Brooklyn came from the former Soviet Union, starting in the early 1970s with variations through the late 1990s. Jews came not only from the western regions of the USSR but also from central Asia and the Caucasus, from former Soviet republics including Uzbekistan, Tajikistan, Azerbaijan, and Dagestan. Many former Soviet Jews settled in Brooklyn, notably in Brighton Beach, which has become known as Little Odessa by the Sea, a land of extravagant exoticism to intrepid tourists and visitors.

Smaller groups of foreign Jews came to Brooklyn around the same time as the "Russians." Middle Eastern Jews came from Arab countries in the wake of the 1967 war in Israel, while numbers of Israelis have arrived, many settling among the Middle Eastern and Sephardic Jewish communities in the region of Brooklyn's Kings Highway. The Israelis remain a relatively anonymous group in the New York Jewish mix, regarded with faint suspicion by other Jews for having abandoned the holy land to choose the Diaspora. Brooklyn's Israelis, for their part, have a tendency to regard themselves as expatriates rather than as local Brooklynites (Shokeid 1988).

The Sephardic community is as complex as the Ashkenazi: different groups of Sephardim arrived at different times from a wide dispersal. One quotation from a contemporary Brooklynite will capture some of the many layers of Jewish identity: "We're the only Sephardic temple in the Canarsie/East Flatbush area with Spanish-Turkish ritual. We specialize in Cubans. The Cuban burial society is here. Those of Turkish ancestry know Ladino, though not the Cubans. Now our emphasis is on Castilian. The Cuban Sephardim and the non-Cuban Sephardim have their problems. The non-Cuban complain that the Cubans don't do the work in support of the congregation" (Rieder 1985, 29).

Other socioeconomic shifts have precipitated the migration of American Jews to Brooklyn from Manhattan and other parts of the United States. As the real estate market has made housing in Manhattan increasingly prohibitive, many Jewish families, especially those with young children, have moved to the borough as a way to stay within New York City. For some of these Jewish families, Brooklyn gives possibilities of a family life in a house instead of a squeezed apartment. Children attend public or Jewish school because the quality of facilities in some Brooklyn neighborhoods has been maintained, along with parks and a neighborly life. Many of these couples and singles have moved into gentrifying or upscale neighborhoods closer to Manhattan, such as Brooklyn Heights, Park Slope, and Carroll Gardens, while others have moved farther into Flatbush, Kensington, and Greenpoint. The Greenpoint-Williamsburg neighborhood has become a center of housing and studios for artists because of its cheap rents and proximity to Manhattan, and it includes many young artists who happen to be Jews. More recently DUMBO (Down Under Manhattan Bridge Overpass) and Red Hook have become magnets for young artists. While most of these newcomers may not have moved into Brooklyn specifically to be in a Jewish neighborhood, many have become involved in Jewish life. They have put new energy into synagogues, Jewish schools, and other institutions.

LIVING IN BROOKLYN

You begin with the light. If you want to make Brooklyn in words or film or paint, you must see the way the sun defines the silent streets on an early Sunday morning, sculpting trees, buildings, fire hydrants, stray dogs, and wandering people with an almost perfect clarity. . . . the same luminous light quality suffuses the work of the Dutch masters. . . . those first seventeenth century Dutch settlers must have looked at this empty western end of Long Island and seen the lowlands of Holland.
—Pete Hamill, The Brooklyn Reader

The smell of a Nathan's hot dog was the equivalent of a national anthem for Brooklyn. We didn't have a borough song: we had a borough scent and taste.
—Larry King, When You're from Brooklyn, Everything Else Is Tokyo

Brooklyn startles the senses. It is luminescent and otherworldly. It is refined discernment, mystical knowledge, and juicy sausages wolfed down at a raucous amuse-ment park. Yet it has physical reality. At the southwestern end of Long Island, across the Upper Bay and East River from Manhattan, sit the eighty-one square miles of Brooklyn garlanded by water (river, bay, channel, ocean, inlet, canal) on approximately three-quarters of its perimeter. At its longest, the borough is 11.5 miles long; and it is 9.5 miles at its widest. Brooklyn has 50 miles of shoreline, including water basins and creeks; 201 miles of waterfront along the East River and Upper Bay; beach areas of more than 7 miles, and almost 6,000 acres of parkland.

In "Coming to Brooklyn" we consider the influx of population into Brooklyn. What was the experience like for Jewish inhabitants once they had become settled? How were conditions special for Brooklyn Jews? The essays in the second part, "Living in Brooklyn," consider these and related questions. One answer might begin with the density and diversity of Jewish communities. When a lot of Jews, or any group, live close together in relatively large numbers, people interact together a great deal in a wide variety of ways. They have informal interchanges as well as more organized sorts of interaction. Their nearness helps instigate and nourish a web of institutions and associations, giving rise, for example, to synagogues, schools, or mutual aid societies.

On the other hand, the diversity of the Jewish population has meant that each particular grouping has felt the need for, and had the mass to support, its own organizations. The population's composition has evolved such that many of the Jews who have remained or been drawn to Brooklyn in the postwar period are devout or deeply involved in communal life. Those less committed to their religious community have often been more upwardly mobile, moving out of Brooklyn, for example, for the suburbs.

Who can deny the centrality of its street life to Brooklyn residents? Those graced with a stoop have enjoyed the benefits of nearness to home with openness to nature and the spontaneous sway of street life. Poorer neighborhoods have a greater interplay between public and private space, as the outdoors provides a vast play area for children, a place to continue domestic tasks in company and a spot to survey and scrutinize the comings and goings of local players.

Even the most observant of Brooklyn Jews, and certainly the less traditionally religious, have created a style of acculturation to American culture. It can be seen, for example, in the growing prominence of women in public spiritual life or in the growth of Jewish affluence and adaptation to it.

These are among the most important changes in American Jewish life as a whole, while they are especially marked in dense, active communities, such as those in Brooklyn.

Certain essays in this section of the book—those, for example, by Adina Back, Henry Goldschmidt, Mark Naison, and Gerald Sorin—explore the proximity and interchange between Jewish and non-Jewish Brooklynites. Much more remains to be discussed about these complex relationships, which involve constant negotiation, cycles of peaceful coexistence and partnership as well as ongoing stresses. Occasional vituperative explosions are part of the picture. Tension and sporadic release also exist between Jews of different stripes. "Two Jews—three opinions." Nonetheless, Brooklyn Jewish neighborhood life bears an uncanny resemblance to the ideals of the New Urbanists often accused of nostalgia. They recommend compact neighborhoods that encourage pedestrian activity and public buildings—such as a library, a community center, a transit stop, and retail businesses—this could well be a description of the layout of a Brooklyn neighborhood.

Not the least important is a thread that runs throughout the essays about remembering, yearning, and nostalgia. Jewish Brooklyn is a land of memories for those whose childhoods flowered in it. As the French historian Pierre Nora has put it, "To be Jewish is to remember being Jewish." Memory is attached to a series of diasporas and old countries, each of which has left sedimentary traces.

Many of the strands evident in "Coming to Brooklyn" continue their braiding through "Living in Brooklyn," which describes Brooklyn arrivals establishing themselves as Brooklyn residents. This part of the book is the largest, as it records the effervescent yet solid state of Brooklyn Jewish life. It is divided into three sections: "Coming of Age in Brooklyn's Neighborhoods" contains rich materials, much of it in the form of personal essays, interviews, and memoirs. Most of the central figures are young, first- or second-generation Americans. While they grow up, they are learning about themselves as Jews and as Brooklynites, as local neighborhood players, creating new relationships with peers as with older generations. "Cultural Influences and Community Life" examines everyday and festive phenomena, featuring music, food, and other forms of expressive culture, not to mention those less-than-exemplary models of expressiveness, Brownsville's notorious Murder, Inc. The third section, "Jewish Institutions and Interethnic Life," examines Jewish involvement in selected Brooklyn organizations, whether educational, recrea-

tional, or informational. This section highlights some of the give and take of the relationships between people of different ethnic and racial backgrounds—through rivalry, friendship, alliances, wariness, violence, and various forms of negotiation.

"Coming of Age in Brooklyn's Neighborhoods" features articles on Brooklynites growing up during 1920–57, named the "golden age" by Eliot Willensky in *When Brooklyn Was the World*. Those who lived in that age describe local life as resembling small-town America, when everybody knew each other and there was a comfort in sameness. Elizabeth Holzman, former New York City comptroller, who grew up in Coney Island, says, "There was a great feeling of support . . . a great sense of pride for the neighborhood" (quoted in Monti 1991, 111). For neighborhood youngsters, the exciting parts of life occurred out-of-doors. Stoops, streets, alleys, parks, schoolyards, and lots were places of bonding. Larry King, the television and radio personality, has described the basic geography of a local child's life: "When we weren't at the movies or in the candy store or playing ball, we were on the stoop. The stoop was a social Mecca—at least during our early years. When we became more mature we graduated to the corner" (quoted in Monti 1991, 131).

Carole Ford, a native of Brownsville, used a shorthand method to describe her classification system of Jewish neighborhoods when she was growing up: Williamsburg was more Orthodox; Borough Park, more Zionist; her own Brownsville was basically secular. Many of the writings in this section narrate the lives of families growing up in these distinctive neighborhoods with strong Jewish populations, as well as in Brighton Beach, Crown Heights, Bensonhurst, and Flatbush. Most of these neighborhoods still have large Jewish populations, with the notable exception of Brownsville—once, ironically, the most Jewish of the neighborhoods, with a 95 percent Jewish population in 1925.

However distinguished the neighborhoods were by type, there were certain things they had in common. One thing was candy stores. Candy stores were local hangouts before the word existed. "It was like one big family gathering. A grand social event." Paul Green (in this volume) describes the constrained yet fulfilling life of his parents who ran a candy store in the 1920s and 1930s. Young and old remember candy stores as the community centers of their day. Lainie Kazan elucidates: "During my teenage years in Brooklyn, I did what all the other kids liked to do, which mainly consisted of one thing, hanging out at the local candy store" (quoted in Monti 1991, 126). The candy store, with its promise of sweets, treats, and free-form meetings provided a sheltered space, offering glimpses and encounters with characters in the local community soap opera.

Larry King jokingly exaggerates as he describes his local candy store owner as a man who had a "hate-hate relationship" with the neighborhood kids. "He referred to us all as bandits, which he pronounced ban-deets!" The local soda fountain featured the quintessential egg creams, considered "the elixir of life" (quoted in Monti 1991, 131). Egg creams, those cool froths of everything and nothing, were surely not limited to Brooklyn, nor to Jewish palates, but they certainly formed part of the camaraderie of shared delights in the golden age in the county of Kings. What is the power of the familiar joyful tastes and smells of childhood? Satisfaction is deep, touching profound pleasure centers in the brain, and ripening even more deeply in retrospect.

Many other former Brooklynites, like the chroniclers in this section of *Jews of Brooklyn*, remember fondly their childhood turf and rituals. Insiders and outsiders are essential to the creation of identity. Brooklyn Jewish youth have diligently fashioned their communal sense of self, as children do anywhere. Street, neighborhood, borough, Jewishness, type of Jewish practice, age group, or prowess are among the criteria that may determine the layers of who is an insider. The comedian Phil Silvers remembers the secret code: "Brownsville was Jewish turf. . . . A strange face in the neighborhood had to say 'bread and butter' in Yiddish fast to keep from being mangled. The Irish kids acquired remarkable Yiddish accents . . ." (quoted in Monti 1991, 194).

Power on the streets of Brownsville was Jewish, but outsiders could attain insider status if they conformed to local cultural styles. Boundaries were strictly policed and violators punished. Maintenance of distinctions continues into adult life, when insiders distinguish genuine reminiscences from the nostalgia of wanna-bes. A Brooklyn-born booster proposes a surefire way to find out if someone is truly from Brooklyn. Disk jockey "Cousin Brucie" Morrow shares his three criteria: "What is stoopball? What is hit the penny? What kind of sewer man are you? The sewer question usually exposes the impostor" (Quoted in Monti 1991, 157).

One group of insiders was the local ball team and its fans. No book on Brooklyn, Jewish or not, would be OK without mention of the Dodgers. Because so much has been written about the "Bums," this volume contains only passing reference to the revered team as it impacted on Jewish devotees. It is imperative, nonetheless, for us to attempt to describe the almost sacred zone in which the local ball team dwelt. A sampling of Jewish devotees' testimonies will capture the terms of adoration. Irv Saposnick:

> You had to be a Jewish kid to understand the appeal of the Dodgers. We related to them, I suspect, as no other ethnic group in Brooklyn could. They gave us something to identify with. We were able to use them as a magic carpet of possibility, a way out of our confinement. . . . We saw baseball in a Judaic context and followed it with religious fervor. (Frommer and Frommer 1993, 86–87)

Although inexplicably a Yankees fan, writer Ronald Sanders goes even further in revealing the ethnic symbolism of local baseball:

> [T]he Brooklyn Dodger mystique—a powerful one in any Brooklyn cultural setting—had taken a profoundly Jewish form among many of my Flatbush contemporaries. This was not only because Brooklyn and the Dodgers had come together in their eyes, as in those of America at large, to form the definitive image of a kind of funny urbanness that is above all represented by certain Jewish types, the focus of a myth of some quirky NY *shtetl* complete with cacophonous accent, bumbling chauvinism, and exaggerated eccentric mannerisms. It was also because the Dodgers were, in those days, the ultimate *schlemiels* of baseball. . . . in 1955, when the Dodgers rose up bruised and battered from their *shtetl* and won a World Series at last—and against the Yankees at last—the triumph reverberated through Flatbush like a return to Zion. (98)

One of the threads that runs through all three sections about living in Brooklyn is the evidence of a powerful working-class Jewish neighborhood life. The vitality of this group was in evidence particularly in the early part of the "golden age," the 1930s and 1940s, dwindling in the 1950s and 1960s. Many of the neighborhoods had vigorous political lives, with intense political debate and organization. Communist, socialist, and anarchist politics had large followings. It is not by chance that Margaret Sanger located the country's first birth control clinic in a tenement storefront in Brownsville. She felt that in Brownsville her work would be supported with a minimum of breaking of windows and hurling of insults. When the clinic was closed down after two weeks, Brownsville women rose to Sanger's defense. The subsequent high-profile trial and appeal led to a change in legislation, as physicians were granted the right to provide contraception for health reasons.

In an early example of a women's consumer movement, politically involved Jewish women in Brooklyn and the Bronx organized kosher meat strikes in 1935, protesting against soaring meat prices, attempting to spark the whole city into housewives' strikes. Jewish households, more dependent on their specialized butchers because of the dietary laws, were willing to fight. They succeeded in closing retail butcher shops for a week, forcing prices down and heightening political consciousness. With support from butchers' associations to the Communist Party, women "made demands on local and national government to ensure their ability to feed their families the food which physically and spiritually made them Jewish" (Wirtschafter 1998, 1).

The feisty grassroots world of Jews who were poor yet not downtrodden is remembered fondly by literary critic Alfred Kazin in *A Walker in the City*. He claims that growing up with desperately poor parents gave him a sense of what really goes on in American life that kept him from becoming a neoconservative, as many of his generation did. "Brooklyn gave me a lasting sense of the powerlessness and suffering that are endemic in our society." Kazin recounted that the most powerful early experience of his life occurred during the Depression, "when I watched my mother, who was a dressmaker at home, leading a crowd of women to put back the furniture removed during an eviction. I never got over that and never will." Apparently the action of reversing an eviction was not such a rare occurrence (see Orleck in this volume). Impresario Joe Papp (né Papirovsky) recalls how, new to Brownsville, he readily got involved in returning a family's household goods into the building. "They were putting people out on the street in the dead of winter . . . sometimes three or four children—and you could see them standing there right in front of your house, helpless, as though there had been a fire" (Epstein 1994, 38). Papp pitched in and was then invited by his new neighborhood allies to the Young Communist League. Papp explained why he joined the YCL at age sixteen:

The word Communist—which sounds so reprehensible to many people today because it's been used as a maligning word, even a death word—was a beautiful word to me. To me, in the 1930s, it represented fearlessness, a stand against appalling social conditions, a

way of creating a world that was free of injustice . . . I began to speak on street corners and at rallies about conditions on the block and to learn about the theory of communism. (Epstein 1994, 38)

The social philosophy soaked up by Brooklyn Jewish children in their homes and streets was not officially shared by the schools in which they spent a good part of their days. From the late nineteenth through the midtwentieth centuries public schools were the major Americanizing force for the children of most immigrant families. In Brooklyn, as elsewhere in New York, public school, which provided education for the vast majority of Jewish children, attempted to reshape not only the content of what they learned but also what they believed and how they behaved. The "uptown Jews" joined forces with the Protestant establishment to quickly clean up the "flagrant offenses" of foreign language and customs. Girls were taught to "make the whole world homelike."

The emphasis on American values, with ignorance and condescension toward the immigrant culture, often pushed a wedge between generations. Most children were ready to leap into the parade of mainstream American life "with flags waving, singing the marching songs—in step and in tune" (Brumberg 1986, 225). Some, like Norman Podhoretz of Brownsville, allowed a discerning and caring mentor to raise him above the crowd of "*horrible little Jewboys in the gutter,*" to be flattered, scolded, and insulted enough to undergo a complete overhaul in manners and speech (Podhoretz 1967, 10). Alfred Kazin similarly recalls: "we were supposed to be a little ashamed of what we were . . . a 'refined' . . . English was peculiarly the ladder of advancement. . . . . We were expected to show it off like a new pair of shoes" (quoted in Epstein 1994, 32).

Not only were children transformed by the public school experience, but so were the teachers. In the New York City school system—the largest public school system in the world—Jewish women started entering the profession in significant numbers in the late nineteenth century. By 1940, they constituted 56 percent of the new teaching staff, remaining the majority of the public school staff until 1960 (Moore and Hyman 1997, 1383). Active in organizing educators, Jewish women also were a significant force in union leadership. As the first professionals in their milieu, Jewish teachers brought their families into the middle classes. During the Great Depression, well-qualified people who had lost their jobs joined the ranks of teachers and brought new zeal to the profession. Many faced the dreaded "speech test": qualified teachers were not allowed to teach in public schools if they spoke with a "Yiddish intonation," according to the examiners' determination. The same strict policing of intonations was not applied to a Brooklyn accent, thus allowing gentiles with nonstandard enunciation to gain entry to the profession.

RELIGIOUS LIFE

Writers who have described neighborhood life before the 1960s reveal a time when secular and observant Jews lived side by side, sometimes even in the same family.

In between the wars, many young people experienced a taken-for-granted sense of themselves as Jews. For the most part, this experience does not point to traditional religious rigor. Selective adherence to ritual corresponds to that described in Jenna Joselit's *Wonders of America*, which details the creativity of American reinvention of Jewish culture, 1880–1950. The fact that most Jews lived in Jewish neighborhoods was often the central feature of identity. That and the family's domestic rituals, which varied considerably, according to degree of creativity and adherence to tradition. Jewish continuity switched to the family as it became more an emotional predisposition than a matter of strict ritual, "flickering to life at weekly Friday night family gatherings and yearly Passover seders." Although the majority of Brooklyn Jews may have followed this style of selective religious affirmation, not all Jewish families, by any means, fit into this pattern.

At least four other models of Jewish transmission are mentioned in "Living in Brooklyn" by Paul Green, Rivke Braitman (in Renata Singer's chapter), Jeffrey Gurock, and Henry Goldschmidt. In Green's family, *Yiddishkeit*, secular Jewish culture, was the central form of cultural expression. For his parents' left-wing group, rebellion against tradition impelled them to hold a banquet on Yom Kippur, the most solemn fast day of the Jewish ritual calendar, indicating perhaps rather more attachment to the Jewish ritual calendar than the group would likely have admitted.

Bill Mazer, sports broadcaster, credits Jewish education for his good memory: "I went to yeshiva, and anybody who goes to yeshiva who has a bad memory doesn't stay very long" ("Bill Mazer" 1978 II, 4). The less positive side of Jewish education is remembered by Phil Silvers: "The gnarled old rabbi in the prescribed gray beard and black gabardine gave private lessons in his black cellar tenement. He taught Hebrew by rote and the mumbo

jumbo of the ritual made no sense to me. By the second session I hated Hebrew and I hated the old man. He'd slap my palm with a ruler when I refused to recite . . . I ran out and never came back." Phil Silvers's childhood experience with Hebrew school was unfortunately all too common. Jeffrey Gurock documents an alternative to this. His chapter delineates major strands of Jewish education in Brooklyn life, providing valuable background to understanding the remarkable persistence of Orthodox Jewish life. Brooklyn Jews have long been innovators in Jewish education. One of the first synagogue centers was established in Brooklyn, the Brooklyn Jewish Center, "a vibrant modern amalgam of Judaism and Americanism," a creative expansion of Conservative Jewish synagogue life to include recreation and physical and spiritual development from infancy to old age. Brooklyn's synagogue center incorporating prayer, leisure, and social activities as well as Jewish education was a new model institution designed to serve the whole person, but very different from the traditional synagogue.

Between the two world wars Judaism was in crisis because of a disinterest in synagogue life among the second generation. There was, nonetheless, a small committed core whose lives revolved around Jewish schools, clubs, and synagogues. Brooklyn became a national hub of Jews dedicated to Jewish day schools. Religious-cultural Zionists with a zeal for Hebrew education connected to an ongoing Hebrew-speaking nationalist and Modern Orthodox constituency; the results were the eminent Yeshivah of Flatbush and other exemplary educational institutions. Early efforts at Hebrew education reform, including *Ivrit b'Ivrit* (Hebrew-language classroom instruction on Jewish subjects), produced results very different from Phil Silvers's school.

Rivke Braitman, a creative yet adaptive woman in a hierarchical Hasidic community, has benefited from a new atmosphere in the Ultra-Orthodox world that has promoted improvements in the schooling of girls. Yet she remembers days of greater flexibility within Hasidic life when she was growing up, when children were freer to read books of their choice and when women had an average of only three or four children each.

Three Brooklyn neighborhoods have become major Hasidic or Ultra-Orthodox communities: Crown Heights, Williamsburg, and Borough Park. The Lubavitcher Hasidim, whose world headquarters is at 770 Eastern Parkway in Crown Heights, are best known to outsiders for their outreach campaign, welcoming returnees to Judaism. They seek out nonobservant Jews, trolling the streets of major U.S. cities with their ubiquitous "Mitzvah Tanks," offering religious kits free to encourage ritual practice. Although their dynastic leader, Rabbi Menachem Schneerson, died childless in 1994, the Chabad-Lubavitch movement has continued to build its strength as it has for the past two hundred years with the inspiration of its charismatic rebbe. The movement's infrastructure has expanded nearly 30 percent since the rebbe's death, while more than 3,700 emissary couples work in more than one hundred countries in its community centers.

Williamsburg's largest group of Hasidim are the Satmars, known for their anti-Zionism, resolute lifestyle, and the largest Jewish school system in the United States. Unlike the Lubavitchers, who seek out Jews to join Hasidism, the Satmar group isolates itself from the outside world. Borough Park is a middle-class neighborhood with many Hasidic groups, of which the largest is the Bobov. The comfortable setting has re-created a sense of home for Hasidim, while most non-Hasidic Jews have left the neighborhood in droves (Belcove-Shalin 1995).

No matter what else is transmitted, family and religious observation often centers in culinary Judaism. For a Sephardic family such as the Menashes in Williamsburg, Fridays were marked by *fijon y arroz* (beans and rice). This distinguished them clearly from the world of Ashkenazi delicacies, like pastrami sandwiches, or the exotic spaghetti with ketchup, which seemed so much more cosmopolitan to the young Louis Menashe than his mother's exquisite homemade Levantine sauces. Brooklyn Jewish food, of course, has assumed wider symbolic importance as well. For a politician to succeed in New York, he/she must be seen to be eating a Nathan's hot dog.

A number of essays document the varying fortunes of Brooklyn Jews' relationships to other ethnic groups in the borough. These pieces give the reader a sense of the change in demographics and of relations between Jews and non-Jews. The Crown Heights riots and Ocean Hill-Brownsville teachers' strike pointed to, and exacerbated, the degenerating relationships between blacks and Jews. By understanding the historical processes by which each group views the other, the reader is guided to understand difficult periods in black-Jewish relations. These historical events functioned as landmarks in interethnic and interracial relations in New York City as a whole. This volume can only hint at their resonance and weight, and refer readers to further reading.

Painful flare-ups between groups again reached a peak in Crown Heights in 1991 when the accidental death of a Caribbean child, struck by a car driven by a Hasidic chauffeur, led to days of rioting, a mortal attack on a visiting Australian Jewish scholar, and endless rounds of counter-accusations between black and Jewish groups. This same incident revealed bitter feelings between Hasidic Jews in Brooklyn and "limousine Jews," liberal, assimilated Manhattan Jews accused of being ashamed of their louder, more observant coreligionists.

Mention can be made of parallel clashes between different Hasidic groups, between Jews of different denominations, as well as between Jews belonging to different political persuasions. Even the seemingly remote realm of art has brought out the antagonisms between Jews. A group of Orthodox rabbis accused Arnold Lehman, director of the Brooklyn Museum of Art, of insensitive, if not immoral, behavior in his defense of the scandalous "Sensation" exhibit in October 1999. The rabbis called on the mayor to fire him and felt it was "painful that so many Jewish people are mistakenly involved in defending Mr. Lehman's right to attack the Christian religion in this way" ("Orthodox Rabbis" 1999). Jan Rosenberg's portrait of Rabbi Robert Kaplan (in this volume) suggests one possibility of change for Brooklyn Jewish organizations in a time when white flight and upward mobility have dramatically changed the demographic pattern of many of Brooklyn's neighborhoods.

LEAVING BROOKLYN/ RETURNING TO BROOKLYN

When I first left Brooklyn and moved to California, there seemed to be something missing. . . . I especially noticed it in the evening when I would turn in for the night. It finally dawned on me . . . we lived right over the BMT subway tracks and every few minutes a train would pass under my window. . . . In a strange way you count on it. After fifteen years of going to sleep with the subway as background noise, there was suddenly a void. . . .
—Lainie Kazan (quoted in Monti 1991, 126)

The true site of nostalgia is therefore not land . . . but the loop and interminable traffic between these two lands. . . . Displacement . . . becomes the tangible home. We are all exiles in a way—from our own childhoods, our own pasts, if nothing else.
—Andre Aciman, False Papers

Since the mid-1800s, Brooklyn has been a destination for millions of Jews, but it has also been a point of departure for the upwardly mobile. Once established, families or individuals have seen fit to move elsewhere, in keeping with their newly adopted American restlessness. Having moved earlier to neighborhoods of Brooklyn to escape the crowding in their first American habitations, many Jews in the post–World War II period found themselves prosperous enough to contemplate larger accommodations with gardens, and the optimism of fresh habitations. Local destinations have included Manhattan, other outlying city areas, and the suburbs. Longer exit journeys have taken Brooklynites to California, Florida, the rest of the United States, as well as, significantly, Israel. Many Brooklynites have moved to Israel to live; the most recent group have been right-wing Orthodox bound for settlements in Israel's West Bank. Many young Orthodox Jews spend a year studying in a yeshiva in Israel. Some stay on. Brooklyn Jewish life is always in relation to some other place, a place from which one has escaped, or a place to which one will make a pilgrimage, or a place to contact at regular intervals.

"Leaving Brooklyn/Returning to Brooklyn" includes reflections on those who have moved on, why they have gone, what they have gained or lost. Since this part includes not only those who have left Brooklyn but also those who have returned, chapters here consider what the participants have regained. Included in consideration are new local conditions—"making it," changing neighborhoods, a growing right-wing Orthodoxy, the recycling of abandoned synagogues—and the exodus from Brooklyn.

You can never go home again. But many Jews return to Brooklyn, whether to visit aging relatives or the old neighborhood, to establish themselves in newly gentrified communities, or simply sightsee as tourists, or a few even to bask as celebrities. There are many ways to leave Brooklyn, not only through death or through symbolic rebirth elsewhere. There are many ways to return.

Many who grew up there could hardly wait to get out of Brooklyn. Perhaps the best-known in literature is Alfred Kazin, the literary critic, whose *Walker in the City* follows his steps as he practices leaving the borough. As Ray Goldblatt discusses, *Walker* begins with Kazin's return home to Brownsville from the symbolically distant Manhattan to revisit and write about his origins. Kazin in 1951 is looking back at memories of the Jewish world of the early 1930s. Pungent with bad smells and provincialism, it was a jarring world of clutter and noise. Everything in the surroundings was run-down, arousing the forlorn feeling of being at the margin of the city, the end of the world. Kazin

was not alone in considering Brownsville a "place that measured all success by our skill in getting away from it." He had only recently vanquished the fear that he too would become like the old women sitting on the tenement stoops in their shapeless clothing, "their hands blankly folded in each other as if they had been sitting on these stoops from the beginning of time" (6). For Kazin, leaving Brownsville, the equivalent to leaving Brooklyn, meant traveling to the real America across the bridge, into Manhattan. Manhattan, the land of culture, poise, and non-Jewish life, was the antithesis of his former life.

Another familiar figure in the literary world, known for his escape from Brooklyn, is Norman Podhoretz, for thirty-five years the editor of *Commentary* magazine. In his 1968 memoir, *Making It*, he celebrates his rise from immigrant Brooklyn to success in Manhattan. Podhoretz makes a big discovery. Growing up oblivious to the rankings and caste systems in American society, he learns, with the aid of a mentor, that "the longest journey in the world is the journey from Brooklyn to Manhattan—or at least from certain neighborhoods in Brooklyn to certain parts of Manhattan. I have made that journey . . ." (x). While his family had not long before traversed the Atlantic Ocean and established themselves in the New World of America, that journey of the immigrant generation was seen as meager compared to the new generation's arrival and acceptance into gentile, well-heeled American society. Even the company of cultivated German Jews was a remote destination.

Podhoretz's dramatic rendering, at the very least, clarifies that Brooklyn is not merely a physical, but also a class, location. Leaving Brooklyn, for the children of immigrants, is not merely moving in a horizontal direction; it is moving up. It can mean coming to feel at ease and being accepted in the wider mainstream world. There may, of course, be a price to pay. Often the move is accompanied by a desire to break with the past or by a sense of shame at humble origins. Parents and grandparents are not American enough and may be seen as figures of ridicule or, in moments more benign, viewed as archaic survivors of epic struggles. Brooklyn accents, the markers of adhesion to local community, need to be expunged. "In Dreams Begin Responsibilities," a story by Delmore Schwartz, reveals the author's need to separate himself from his past through mockery and denigration.

Brooklyn, so rapidly crowded in the twentieth century with the influx of immigrants and their children, also created the conditions for their outflow. Neighborhoods like Brownsville, once seen as alternatives to the slum conditions on the Lower East Side, promptly replicated their congestion. The immense energy and desire for improvement for the next generation of children prodded many youngsters to aim high. Americanized in the streets, in school, and increasingly through the media, younger children could not literally move on their own, but popular culture often provided a preparation for leave-taking. It provided a temporary spiritual departure.

Children's book author and illustrator Maurice Sendak vividly reveals how unappealing the pull of the past could be for a young person:

> . . . we desperately did not want to be like our parents. We wanted to be American. So there were the movies. There was Mickey Mouse, King Kong, Fred Astaire to nourish our fantasies. . . . For Brooklyn was where information about dead Jews came. About cousins my age who wouldn't have bar mitzvahs like me because they were in the ovens. They were mourning people all up and down the stairwell and crying, and photographs constantly lying on the kitchen table to remind us of what my cousins looked like. That of course, was the need, the joy of Mickey Mouse. The darkness of the theater, the idiotic face grinning at me, until I screamed like a maniac. ("Brooklyn" 1983)

Here, Brooklyn is inextricably tied to the past, to the tragedies in Jewish history—so different from the lighthearted amnesia of contemporary American life.

Prodded or protected by their parents, Brooklyn Jewish youth responded to the call of the wild side in a variety of ways, based on individual circumstances and generational opportunities. Sendak's vehement response to Mickey Mouse, "screaming like a maniac," shows explosive release through humor from the family's persistent mournfulness. The child was too young to bear the burden of the Shoah. For those with talent—self-initiated or curated by enterprising parents—the way out of the stifling past was in the insistent pursuit of creativity and, often, self-promotion.

For the less tortured, the nurturing neighborhood may have shown limited opportunities rather than haunting ghosts. Many bright, energetic youth went away to college, often in distant states, to explore a reality different from the familiar all-encompassing one in Brooklyn. This practice, so common now, was new for many immigrant families in the midtwentieth century with a limited sense of geography. For those who had traversed the Atlantic, often to join temporarily separated family members, voluntarily separating oneself from the family bosom was incomprehensible. The immigrants, or those close to their experience, were too aware of the perils of life, including anti-Semitism, to feel confident in the survival skills of their offspring.

Lynne Sharon Schwartz's novel *Leaving Brooklyn* parallels Paul Mazursky's film *Next Stop Greenwich Village*. Comical bildungsromans, they both feature suffering, talented, young people; Schwartz's hero is younger and female—Mazursky's is a slightly older male. For each of these questing youth, the yearning to leave the family nest is central—although at the same time, their parents resist accepting the fledgling flight. When Audrey, Schwartz's hero, is growing up, she finds Brooklyn stifling, a place of repression. The immigrants and children of immigrants who settled in Brooklyn did so to shield their children from the grit and violence of the city. They were very successful. Yet these young people crave unmuffled experience, a life closer to the bone. In both cases they are escaping overbearing Jewish families rather than the blandness of suburbia, a more contemporary plight.

Not all who wish to escape from Brooklyn eventually succeed. In his *Williamsburg Trilogy*, Daniel Fuchs invents characters who remain imprisoned in Brooklyn, who never succeed with the kind of uplift required to make a better life for themselves. Brooklyn pulls them down until they sink.

The numerous short pieces in "Leaving Brooklyn/Returning to Brooklyn" convey both the ambivalence of leaving and the nostalgia of return. If, for Alfred Kazin, real American life began when one crossed the Brooklyn Bridge to Manhattan (Kazin's walks are always west, out of Brownsville), Phillip Lopate offers a more sympathetic picture of growing up in working-class Williamsburg. Lopate, who experienced the vitality of Manhattan firsthand, describes his move back to Brooklyn as re-entering a "decompression chamber." Yet he is increasingly comfortable, "at home," in the changing neighborhood around Smith and Court Streets.

Other Brooklynites, like Barbra Streisand and Danny Kaye, left Brooklyn to become world-renowned celebrities. Yet the appeal of both, and especially of Streisand, is tied to how they retained, even consciously incorporated, the Brooklyn Jew in their work. In the film *Funny Girl*, Streisand's hallmark song, "People Who Need People," is staged and sung as a nostalgic ode to Jewish communal Brooklyn, a world Fanny Brice would soon relinquish for the stage and a gambling man.

Yes, some of these are rose-colored memories, but memories powerful enough to bring together, in organizations and clubs, the legions of former Brooklyn Jews who moved to warmer climes on the West Coast and in South Florida. And it is memory—rose-colored or not—that bring, to a radically different Brooklyn, the grandchildren and great-grandchildren of its former residents. As this newest generation make their homes alongside the recently arrived Orthodox, Sephardic, and Russian Jews, the cycle of Jewish life in Brooklyn renews itself into the twenty-first century.

NOTE

1. The many Brooklyn accents vary with neighborhood, age, ethnicity, educational level, etc. See George Jochnowitz's essay in this volume. Thomas Wolfe's 1935 version of the Brooklyn accent: "'How long you been livin' heah?' I says. 'All my life,' he says. 'I was bawn in Williamsboig,' he says. 'An' I can tell you t'ings about dis town you never hoid of,' he says. 'Yeah?' I says. 'Yeah,' he says" (Wolfe 1994).

REFERENCES

Abelow, Samuel P. 1937. *History of Brooklyn Jewry.* Brooklyn: Scheba.

Ashkenazie, Harry. 1978. Interview. William Weiner Oral History Archives, American Jewish Committee. III, pp. 35–40.

Belcove-Shalin, Janet, ed. 1995. *New World Hasidim: Ethnographic Studies of Hasidic Jews in America.* New York: SUNY Press.

"Brooklyn: Borough of Writers." 1983. *New York Times Book Review,* May 8.

Brooklyn Information and Culture (BRIC). 2000. Hyperlink www.brooklynx.org/tourism.

Brumberg, Stephan V. 1986. *Going to America, Going to School: The Jewish Immigrant Public School Encounter in Turn-of-the-Century New York City.* New York: Praeger.

Capote, Truman. 1994 [1959]. "A House on the Heights." *The Brooklyn Reader: Thirty Writers Celebrate America's Favorite Borough,* ed. Andrea Wyatt Sexton and Alice Leccese Powers, pp. 26–41. New York: Crown.

Chanes, Jerome A. 1995. *Antisemitism in America Today: Outspoken Experts Explode the Myths.* New York: Birch Lane Press.

Diner, Hasia R. 1992. *A Time for Gathering: The Second Migration, 1820–1880.* The Jewish People in America Series. Baltimore: Johns Hopkins University Press.

Epstein, Helen. 1994. *Joe Papp: An American Life.* Boston: Little, Brown.

Frommer, Myrna Katz, and Harvey Frommer. 1993. *It Happened in Brooklyn: An Oral History of Growing Up in the Borough in the 1940s, '50s, and '60s.* New York: Harcourt Press.

Fuchs, Daniel. 1972 [1937]. *Williamsburg Trilogy: Summer in Williamsburg, Homage to Blenholt, and Low Company.* New York: Equinox/Avon.

Glueck, Grace, and Paul Gardner. 1991. *Brooklyn: People and Places, Past and Present.* New York: Harry N. Abrams.

Greenberg, Keith Elliot. 1999. "Journey of the Syrian Jews." *Brooklyn Bridge,* September–October, pp. 100–107.

Hamill, Pete. 1994. Introduction to *The Brooklyn Reader: Thirty Writers Celebrate America's Favorite Borough,* ed. Andrea Wyatt Sexton and Alice Leccese Powers. New York: Crown.

Hassidic Discovery Welcome Center. n.d. Jewish Tours. Website: www.jewishtours.com.

Jackson, Kenneth T., ed. 1995. *The Encyclopedia of New York City.* New Haven, Conn.: Yale University Press.

Jackson, Kenneth T., and John B. Manbeck. 1998. *The Neighborhoods of Brooklyn.* New Haven, Conn.: Yale University Press.

Jacoby, Tamar. 1998. *Someone Else's House.* New York: Free Press.

Joselit, Jenna. 1990. *New York's Jewish Jews: The Orthodox Community in the Interwar Years.* Bloomington: Indiana University Press.

———. 1994. *The Wonders of America: Reinventing Jewish Culture, 1880–1950.* New York: Hill and Wang.

Kaufman, Jonathan. 1988. *Broken Alliance: The Turbulent Times Between Blacks and Jews in America.* New York: Charles Scribner's Sons.

Kazin, Alfred. 1951. *A Walker in the City.* New York: Harcourt Brace.

———. 1982. "New York City Jew." In *Creators and Disturbers: Reminiscences by Jewish Intellectuals of New York,* ed. Bernard Rosenberg and Ernest Goldstein, pp. 194–209. New York: Columbia University Press.

King, Larry, with Marty Appel. 1992. *When You're from Brooklyn, Everything Else Is Tokyo.* Boston: Little, Brown.

"A Life Apart." n.d. Oren Rudovsky, director. Video and Website www.pbs.org/alifeapart.

"Mazer, Bill." 1978. Interview. William Weiner Oral History Archives, American Jewish Committee. II, p. 114.

Miller, Rita Seiden, ed. 1979. *Brooklyn, USA: Fourth Largest City in America.* Brooklyn: Brooklyn College Press.

Monti, Ralph. 1991. *I Remember Brooklyn: Memories from Famous Sons and Daughters.* New York: Birch Lane Press.

Moore, Deborah Dash. 1981. *At Home in America: Second Generation New York Jews.* New York: Columbia University Press.

Moore, Deborah Dash, and Paula Hyman. 1997. *Jewish Women in America.* 2 volumes. New York: Routledge.

Nadell, Pamela S. 1998. *Women Who Would Be Rabbis.* Boston: Beacon Press.

"Orthodox Rabbis Demand Firing of Brooklyn Museum of Art Director Lehman." 1999. Jewish Union press release, October 11.

Podhoretz, Norman. 1967. *Making It.* New York: Random House.

Postal, Bernard, and Lionel Koppman. 1978 [1954]. *Jewish Landmarks of New York.* New York: Fleet Press.

Rieder, Jonathan. 1985. *Canarsie: The Jews and Italians of Brooklyn against Liberalism.* Cambridge, Mass.: Harvard University Press.

Ritterband, Paul. 1998. "Why Did the Brooklyn Jewish Community Survive? The Response of a Cliometrician." Paper delivered at University Conference: In and Out of Brooklyn, Jerusalem, November.

Rosen, Jonathan. 2000. *The Talmud and the Internet.* New York: Farrar, Straus & Giroux.

Rosen, Marvin, and Walter Rosen, with Beth Allen. 1999. *Welcome to Junior's Restaurant, with Recipes and Memories from Its Favorite Restaurant.* New York: William Morrow.

Roth, Henry. 1991 [1934]. *Call It Sleep.* New York: Robert O. Ballou.

Salzman, Jack, and Cornel West, eds. 1997. *Struggles in the Promised Land: Toward a History of Black-Jewish Relations in the United States.* New York: Oxford University Press.

Sanders, Ronald. 1972. *Reflections on a Teapot: The Personal History of a Time.* New York: Harper and Row.

Schwartz, Delmore. 1978 [1938]. *In Dreams Begin Responsibilities and Other Stories.* New York: W. W. Norton.

Schwartz, Lynn Sharon. 1989. *Leaving Brooklyn.* Boston: Houghton Mifflin.

Shokeid, Moshe. 1988. *Children of Circumstances: Israeli Emigrants in New York.* Anthropology of Contemporary Issues. Ithaca, N.Y.: Cornell University Press.

Snyder-Grenier, Ellen M. 1996. *Brooklyn! An Illustrated History.* Philadelphia: Temple University Press for the Brooklyn Historical Society.

Willensky, Eliot. 1986. *When Brooklyn Was the World, 1920–1957.* New York: Harmony.

Wirtschafter, Brooke. 1998. "Jewish Housewives, Jewish Bodies, Jewish Food: The Kosher Meat Boycott of 1935." Paper delivered at Seminar of American Jewish Women, New York University.

Wolfe, Thomas. 1994 [1935]. "Only the Dead Know Brooklyn." In *The Brooklyn Reader: Thirty Writers Celebrate America's Favorite Borough,* ed. Andrea Wyatt Sexton and Alice Leccese Powers. New York: Crown.

Coming to Brooklyn

A Jewish Girl in Brooklyn.
Courtesy of the Museum of Jewish Heritage—A Living Memorial to the Holocaust.
Gift of Mr. and Mrs. William Ungar.

Putting on Your Best Face

Brooklyn Jewish Studio Photography, 1881–1924

ROBERTA NEWMAN

By the twentieth century, more than a third of New York City's population was foreign-born. In Brooklyn alone, immigrants or the children of foreign-born parents made up an estimated 1,235,000 of the total population of 1,700,000 in 1912.[1] Drawn to the borough by its booming real estate market, attractive modern apartment buildings, and less congested neighborhoods, immigrants continued to leave older neighborhoods in Manhattan for Brooklyn. Some newly arrived immigrants even chose to dispense with the traditional interlude of residence on the Lower East Side and came to Brooklyn directly from Ellis Island. By 1925, Jews accounted for 36 percent of all Brooklyn residents.[2]

Those who feared the changes that immigrants might bring to a hitherto more ethnically homogenous America complained of the "'fantastic cosmopolitanism' which had submerged [New York's] original Protestant Anglo-Saxon stock." Leading cultural figures such as Henry James worried that "the newcomers were remaking New York more than it was remaking them."[3] Indeed, the thousands of new apartment buildings erected by real estate developers (many of whom were Jewish) did alter the Brooklyn skyline forever.[4] Immigrants and the children of immigrants literally and figuratively "remade" the borough once known as "the city of churches."

A 1912 pamphlet published by the Municipal Club of Brooklyn both acknowledged and sought to allay its readers' worries about the impact made by the newcomers on the borough:

> Brooklyn today impresses one more as a New England city, with a high percentage of native-born than a community composed of over fifty per cent of foreigners and children of foreign parents . . . The thoroughly American Brooklynite of the early days finds his city invaded by many from the old countries of continental Europe. He maintains the spirit of the "City of Churches," and at the same time, through the schools, through the social settlements, and the numerous other charitable and educational agencies, is making over the foreigner into the American of tomorrow. . . .[5]

As Brooklyn's old guard worried over the changing racial and ethnic character of their city, it is ironic that many of those they thought of as so different from themselves were (albeit on their own terms) preoccupied with nothing less than transforming themselves into middle-class Americans. Evidence of their aspirations can be seen in the studio portraits of the time. These formal portraits—taken by professional photographers in an era when most American families did not own cameras—are more cryptic documents than the snapshots that make up the bulk of today's family albums. Unlike candid photographs, in which people are caught "as they really are," in the settings of everyday life, studio portraits serve as socioeconomic statements about ascension into the middle class or the aspiration to do so. To a much greater degree than today's casually posed pictures, late-nineteenth- to early-twentieth-century portraits are about posterity, about self-commemoration through putting on one's "best face." They are relics of a time characterized by a much more formal aesthetic, when portrait photography was still firmly attached to the conventions of oil painting—when photography, which made formal portraiture accessible even to the poor, was a visual expression of social mobility.

Every culture reflects its own aesthetics and traditions in its photography, but to a large degree, studio portraits mask ethnicity and class. In the more formal images of bygone ages—the wedding, confirmation, baby, and family pictures of the past—few signs of ethnicity, national origin, or even of class are apparent. If we compare a portrait of a Jewish family in Brooklyn with that of a Protestant family in Ohio, we would not immediately be able to point to differences of ethnicity and class. To some extent, this is a function of our distance from and ignorance of the portrait sitters' world. Nonetheless, the studio portraits of different ethnic groups and classes are remarkably similar. It is this very absence of difference that reveals the universality of the photographic aesthetic at the turn of the century. Everyone followed the same visual conventions: the world over, people held a common idea about what a proper portrait should look like.

BECOMING AMERICANS

Despite the stereotypical image of Jewish immigrants as unsophisticated rustics, most arrived in America already familiar with modern, middle-class mores. Many came not from the ranks of the poorest Jews but from more financially secure families who could at the very least manage the cost of steamship tickets and railway passage to the port. Moreover, many eastern European Jewish immigrants were natives of large cities such as Warsaw, rather than of the small, rural *shtetlakh* that feature so prominently in the public imagination. By the 1890s, the custom of putting on one's *shabes* (Sabbath) best and sitting for

Fig. 1. B. Muckian, a Jewish immigrant, Williamsburg, 1890. It was common for recent immigrants to be photographed wearing new coats, hats, and other finery in order to demonstrate to relatives back home in Europe that they were prospering in America. Photo by Amos Silkworth, 261 Manhattan Avenue, Brooklyn. From the Archives of the YIVO Institute for Jewish Research.

one's photo portrait was a well-known ritual even in eastern Europe. Farewell portraits, taken on the eve of departure and left behind with loved ones as mementos, as well as portraits of left-behind wives and children sent to America to remind husbands of their family ties, were common.

Even in the smaller towns of eastern Europe there were professional photographers who made portraits that do not appreciably differ in style from those made in large cities or in the United States. Some places not big enough to rate a permanent studio were regularly visited by traveling photographers. These portraits present us with a very different set of images than the pictures of newly arrived immigrants made by social documentarians such as Jacob

Fig. 2. *Unidentified Jewish immigrant, Williamsburg, ca. 1890s. This woman may have commissioned her portrait in order to show off her fancy new lace collar to relatives back home in Europe. Photo by H. Caplan, 67 Manhattan Avenue, Brooklyn. From the Archives of the YIVO Institute for Jewish Research.*

Fig. 3. *Unidentified brother and sister, wearing clothes bought several sizes too big "to grow into," Tompkins Park, ca. 1890. The children's hair is beginning to grow back after having been shaved, possibly to avoid infection from one of the scalp diseases that spread frequently among city children in the summertime. Photo by A. Warshaw, 397 Bushwick Avenue, Brooklyn. From the Archives of the YIVO Institute for Jewish Research.*

Riis and Lewis Hine.[6] Riis and Hine depicted the differences and distances between poor immigrants and native-born Americans. The potential immigrants themselves invariably chose to represent themselves as respectable and middle-class.

Immigrants were acutely aware of the importance of physical appearance and fashion. One of the first things that many did after arriving here was to go out and get completely outfitted in new American clothes. Indeed, having one's photograph taken could serve as an important rite of passage for a newly arrived immigrant, allowing for a speedy (if superficial) transformation of greenhorn into middle-class American (figs. 1–3).

JEWISH STUDIO PHOTOGRAPHY IN BROOKLYN

Hundreds of photographers were active in New York City at any given time during the mass immigration era, and Brooklyn appears to have been well served by the profession. Evidence for this comes from the cardboard mounts of the studio portraits themselves. Most not only provide the names of the photographers but also give the street addresses of the photo studios (fig. 4). Card mounts from photographs in family history collections at several New York City archives suggest that at any given time, Brooklyn Jews had the pick of dozens of storefront photographers.[7] These studios were most often located on or

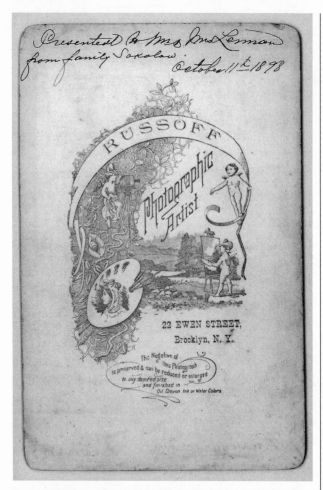

Fig. 4. Advertisement for Russoff's photographic studio on the back of one of his card mounts, Brooklyn, ca. 1898. Card mounts with generic decorations such as these could be purchased by the dozen from photographic supply businesses preprinted with the photographer's name and address. From the Archives of the YIVO Institute for Jewish Research.

near main shopping streets such as Broadway, Manhattan Avenue, and Graham Avenue in Williamsburg; Pitkin and Rockaway in Brownsville; and Tompkins Avenue in Bedford-Stuyvesant. (To judge from their predominance in collections of family photos, the Williamsburg studios of two photographers, A. Warshaw and H. Caplan, were particularly popular with Jewish immigrant families).[8] By the evidence of names alone, most of the studios that catered to a Jewish clientele seem to have been owned and operated by Jews; a few others appear to have been Gentile-owned establishments (e.g., Amos Silkworth at 261 Manhattan Avenue in Williamsburg).

The portraits and card mounts are almost the only surviving remnants of these once-thriving businesses. Apparently, very few Brooklyn photographers thought it worth their while to pay for advertisements in trade journals,

such as *Lain & Healy's Brooklyn and Long Island Business Directory*, *Uppington's Elite Directory*, or the *Almanac of the Brooklyn Daily Eagle* (the nineteenth-century equivalents of today's yellow pages).[9] Show windows and, here and there, ads in ethnic newspapers seem to have served as sufficient advertising for what were essentially small neighborhood businesses. In fact, show windows were apparently the local photographer's most effective type of advertising. Neighborhood institutions in themselves, they afforded local people the pleasant experience of seeing flattering portraits of themselves and their friends as they walked by on the way to work or shopping.[10]

IMMIGRANT GENRES

Sent to families back home in Europe, studio portraits of Brooklyn Jews functioned as compelling advertisements for the New World's middle-class consumer culture. At the same time, the portraits also furnish proof of the continuing bonds of homeland and ethnicity (figs. 5 and 6).[11]

Photography both reflected and reshaped Jewish rituals. For instance, courtship rituals were markedly different in the New World. Whereas, in the Old Country, the emphasis was on matchmakers and arranged marriages, in America, young people were increasingly in charge of choosing their own mates. Romance played a role that it hadn't for previous generations.[12] Young women, in particular, had more freedom to socialize with the opposite sex than they had had in Europe. As a Lower East Side photographer told a reporter for the *Forverts* in 1902,

> A lot of girls . . . have themselves photographed with the boys they're going out with, before they're married. Others do it on purpose, so that later on, the boy will be unable to deny that they were going out. One girl was photographed by us with 8 different boys in 2 years.
>
> In these cases, you often notice that the boy is not happy about it. He comes late on purpose and gives different excuses, but it does him no good. He's got to be photographed with her.
>
> I've got a hundred dozen of these sorts of photographs because in the couple of weeks before the pictures are ready, in the meantime they've broken up. The match is off, so the pictures remain unclaimed.[13]

Indeed, the custom of sitting for engagement, bar mitzvah, and wedding pictures was far more widespread than it had been in the Old Country (figs. 7 and 8).[14] Fancy bar

Fig. 5. Unidentified boy with long curls, Brooklyn, ca. 1900. Some Orthodox Jewish communities refrain from cutting a boy's hair until he is three years old, in deference to Rabbi Isaac Luria's dictum that "children are like trees in the field," which, according to sacred law, may not be harvested during their first three years of blooming. This photo may have been taken shortly before the boy's opshern, his ritual first haircut. Photo by A. Warshaw. From the Archives of the YIVO Institute for Jewish Research.

Fig. 6. Multigenerational Passover portrait of the Schaper family, Brooklyn, 1924. Here, a seder table has been set up in the photographer's studio. Collection of the family of Samuel and Rebecca Schnaper, Brooklyn. Photo by Eric Baum. Photo © The Jewish Museum, New York.

Fig. 8. Bar Mitzvah portrait of Seth Rubin, Bedford-Stuyvesant, ca. World War I. Photo by Dillhoff Studio, 1365 Broadway, Brooklyn. Collection of Peter Schweitzer.

Fig. 7. Unidentified bride and groom, Williamsburg, ca. 1910. Photo by H. Caplan, 67 Manhattan Avenue, Brooklyn. From the Archives of the YIVO Institute for Jewish Research.

mitzvahs and weddings were another way of proclaiming that one was American and middle-class, or at any rate up-and-coming:

All brides and grooms want to be photographed in their wedding outfits: he in his top hat and she in her white dress and veil. Most come to us by carriage before the ceremony, others come on foot dragging their bundles with them, and some come the day after the wedding, getting dressed up again in their silly costumes to get snapped. But it's a fact that 50 percent of all wedding portraits lie around at the studio for a year and sometimes 2 years before they're claimed. They spend all their money on that wedding day and become paupers as a result. They simply don't have the money to pay for the wedding pictures. A lot are simply never picked up.[15]

Another photographic item popular with Jewish immigrants was the Rosh Hashanah (Jewish New Year) portrait greeting card (fig. 9).[16] It was an American innovation to mark the High Holy Days in this way and is but one example

Fig. 9. *Hebrew/English/German Rosh Hashanah portrait greeting card, Brownsville, ca. 1915. The "candid" pose seen here is unusual and may have been devised particularly to appeal to Jewish families eager to have their children take full advantage of America's educational resources. The use of German as the third language was widespread on Rosh Hashanah portrait cards and is a vestige of the dominance of German Jews in nineteenth-century American Jewish affairs. It may also reflect the tendency of eastern European Jews to connote German with refinement and education. The makeshift photographer's stamp indicates that the owner of this studio chose to economize by not having his name embossed or engraved on his yearly supply of preprinted Rosh Hashanah portrait cards. Unidentifiable photographer, 1666 Pitkin Avenue, Brooklyn. Collection of Peter Schweitzer.*

Fig. 10. *Unidentified religious elderly Jew, Brooklyn, ca. 1920. Photo by Sol Young Studios, which had branches in Brooklyn, Manhattan, and the Bronx. From the Archives of the YIVO Institute for Jewish Research.*

of the commodification of culture and ritual as it was developing in both immigrant and general American society. In America, holidays like Christmas, Easter, Chanukah, and Passover were associated with consumer products to a degree as yet unheard of in the Old Country.[17]

Portraits of elderly parents and grandparents represent another instance of the commodification of ritual (fig. 10). Back in Europe, veneration of ancestors was traditionally expressed by visits to grave sites—but in America, immigrants were severed from ancestral graveyards. Newly es-

tablished cemeteries set off by themselves in remote areas of Long Island or New Jersey were not part of the landscape of everyday life to the same extent as back home. Now, children wanted more close at hand mementos of loved ones than distant tombstones. As one Lower East Side photographer related:

Many parents won't go to a photography studio for no money and we have to photograph them at home. It's not easy. But the overwhelming majority come in to us with their parents. The parents are dragged in reluctantly, protesting, but it does them no good. And the children have all sorts of trouble with their parents! Here, not long ago, we had one who for no money would tuck his earlocks under his skullcap, even though his children wept and begged. But it did them no good.

One father was simply tricked by his children into coming in. They told him to sit down for a while and in the mean time I snapped him. But later he realized what had happened and he wanted to hit me because I had made it so that in the next world his skin would be separate from his face.[18]

Hints that photography was becoming an aid to memory were the rotogravure photo spreads in the *Forverts*, which began to appear in 1923, a year before a new immigration law all but cut off the flow of newcomers from eastern and southern Europe. The Yiddish newspaper's illustrated section included the regularly featured "Pictures of Jewish Life and Characters" and "Portrait Studies of Jewish Women." Readers were encouraged to submit family pictures, which were then printed in the paper. The layouts often interspersed portraits from Europe with more recent pictures of immigrants in the United States.

These newspaper features simultaneously awakened the nostalgia of their readers, by encouraging them to remember their loved ones and their old hometowns through photographs, and provided them with visual markers of their own transformation into middle-class Brooklyn-Americans.

NOTES

An earlier version of this article was delivered as a paper at the Photo History X Symposium at the International Museum of Photography at George Eastman House, Rochester, New York, on October 18, 1997. I wish to thank Daniel Soyer for directing me to the 1902 articles on photographers from the *Forverts*.

1. John Creighton, "People and Population of Brooklyn," in *Brooklyn: The Home Borough of New York City* (Municipal Club of Brooklyn, 1912), p. 29. How many Jews lived in Brooklyn in the early twentieth century has not been determined. All statistics are rough estimates. See appendix in Deborah Dash Moore, *At Home in America: Second Generation New York Jews* (New York: Columbia University Press, 1981), for a discussion on the lack of reliable population statistics for Jews in New York City's boroughs prior to World War II.

2. Moore, p. 23.

3. Bayrd Still, *Mirror for Gotham: New York As Seen by Contemporaries from Dutch Days to the Present* (New York: Fordham University Press, 1994), p. 271.

4. See Leon Wexelstein, *Building Up Greater Brooklyn* (Brooklyn Biographical Society, ca. 1925), a trade publication containing biographical sketches of over one hundred Brooklyn real estate developers, of whom the overwhelming majority are Jewish.

5. Creighton, pp. 30, 32.

6. See, for example, Jacob Riis, *How the Other Half Lives* (New York: Dover Publications, 1971), and Walter Rosenblum, Naomi Rosenblum,

and Alan Trachtenberg, *America & Lewis Hine: Photographs 1904–1940* (Millerton, N.Y.: Aperture, 1977).

7. Many of the illustrations for this article have been drawn from the archives of the YIVO Institute for Jewish Research, which has an extensive collection of American Jewish family pictures. (See RG 126, Genealogy and Family History, and RG 120, Territorial Photographic Collection—United States.) Another notable New York City source for American Jewish studio portraits is the Museum of Jewish Heritage—A Living Memorial to the Holocaust.

8. The earliest of Warshaw's card mounts reveal that he (or she) operated a studio at 397 Bushwick Avenue in Williamsburg in the 1890s, but by the turn of the century had moved a few streets away to 23 Manhattan Avenue. Following the growth of new Jewish neighborhoods, he also opened additional branches on Central Avenue in Bushwick and later on Tompkins Avenue in Bedford-Stuyvesant.

9. See Lain & Healy's *Brooklyn and Long Island Business Directory* (1890–1894) and Uppington's *Elite Directory of Brooklyn* (1901–1906) at the New York Public Library, and *Brooklyn Daily Eagle Almanac* (1890–1914) at the Brooklyn Public Library.

10. "Photographs in Show Cases," *Forverts*, May 7, 1902.

11. Sometimes, they literally illustrated the ruptures caused by immigration. Composite portraits, in which pictures of family members left behind in Europe were inserted into portraits of Jewish families taken in New York, though rare, are not unknown. Such portraits symbolically reunited families separated by an ocean and were popular across ethnic lines. (See the photo collection at the Museum of the Chinese in the Americas, New York, for Chinese examples of composite family portraits). In another sort of photographic reunion, a previously made portrait of an absent or deceased family member is displayed by one of the subjects in the new portrait.

12. See Jenna Weissman Joselit, *The Wonders of America: Reinventing Jewish Culture, 1880–1950* (New York: Hill and Wang, 1994), for an extended look at the development of distinctive American Jewish rituals.

13. "At the Photographers' in the Jewish Neighborhood," *Forverts*, May 6, 1902. Translated by the author.

14. Joselit, pp. 22–28, 94–98.

15. "At the Photographers' in the Jewish Neighborhood." See also Estelle Jussim, "From the Studio to the Snapshot: An Immigrant Photographer of the 1920s," *History of Photography* vol. 1, no. 3 (July 1977), pp. 192–193, for a description of the wedding photography business on the Lower East Side in the 1920s.

16. Rosh Hashanah portraits provide the only known instances of card mounts printed in Hebrew. No card mount printed in Yiddish, the mother tongue of the overwhelming majority of the Jewish immigrants, has yet turned up. Why is difficult to determine. Yiddish was used on signs for businesses that catered to Jewish immigrant clientele, on packaging of kosher foods, and in newspaper ads, so what accounts for the absence of Yiddish on the card mounts themselves? The exclusion of non-Roman alphabets from card mounts apparently also applies for other ethnic groups. A rare exception is a mount embossed in Chinese from this period at the Museum of the Chinese in the Americas.

17. See Andrew R. Heinze, *Adapting to Abundance: Jewish Immigrants, Mass Consumption, and the Search for American Identity* (New York: Columbia University Press, 1990), and Joselit for extended looks at this topic.

18. "At the Photographers' in the Jewish Neighborhood."

First Synagogues
Rabbi A. Stanley Dreyfus and Union Temple

SEÁN GALVIN

Rabbi A. Stanley Dreyfus.
Courtesy of Seán Galvin.

Rabbi Emeritus Dr. A. Stanley Dreyfus, of Union Temple, located on Brooklyn's historic Eastern Parkway, the nation's first parkway, was asked to give a series of lectures in commemoration of the Temple's one hundred and fiftieth anniversary. When I called to ask for a copy of his lectures, he replied: "Oh, I never wrote them down. I simply spoke extemporaneously from notes."

Fortunately for me, however, he was willing to meet with me and relate the central themes of his lecture series—that the present-day congregation came together in 1848 in what was then the Village of Williamsburg; that this congregation was formally constituted in 1851 by a group of Alsatian German Jews; that in 1859 the congregation bought a former church, which served as a synagogue until 1876; that after building its synagogue on Keap Street in 1876 they moved from Orthodox to Reform; and finally, that they merged with the Temple Israel congregation in 1921 and celebrated the cornerstone-laying for their present location in 1925.

What follows is the rabbi's own synopsis of the history of the congregation, which I have filled in with some additional historical information.

Beth Elohim, the first congregation in what is now Brooklyn, was founded in the Village of Williamsburg, in 1848, by a group of nine German and Alsatian Jews who, according to the legend, had to hire a man to cross the East River in order to make a minyan for services. The year 1848 was when the revolutions began in Europe, and people fled the terrible persecutions that prevailed in Germany, France, and Czechoslovakia. "Though Jews had been living in New York since 1643, the polls show that by 1848 the Jewish population was still relatively small" (Union Temple 1999). They came anxious to establish themselves, many to the Lower East Side; some settled across the river in Williamsburg. There's no question that the congregation called Beth Elohim was formally constituted in 1851.[1] "At that time, the congregants designated as their 'synagogue' the home of Moses Kessel, on North Second Street, now known as Marcy Avenue" (Union Temple 1999). They observed their fiftieth anniversary in 1901. There were people in attendance at this jubilee who had been among the founders.

They would have been an informal organization in 1848: no rabbi, some merchants, and a few others—but people come together for worship or to establish a cemetery before they ever think of incorporating a congregation, which, such as it was, grew slowly, steadily. It was a German Orthodox community. In 1859 they bought a Lutheran church on South First Street and remodeled it into a synagogue. The oldest minutes at the temple are from the beginning of 1859.

An interesting thing occurred when the Temple was about to celebrate its one hundred and fiftieth anniversary. They asked me to give a series of talks about the history of the congregation, so my wife undertook the task of reading the old minutes. They were written in German, in Gothic script. So she has the best knowledge of these records, but they are less than interesting, because the people who kept the minutes did not relate events at Beth Elohim to the wider American Jewish community. The congregation maintained a German secular school. They wanted the children to learn German. They regarded Germany as the seat of culture, learning, and in its better days, emancipation, and they continued to offer instruction in a school with non-Jewish teachers. These were day schools before the public schools were established here in Brookyn.

In the 1870s, the congregation had a bitter debate about whether the time had come to keep the minutes in English, but the financial records, so as to avoid any fiscal malfeasance, would forever be kept in German. It is likely that that bylaw was never rescinded. The older members had grown up in the Orthodox environment, but the younger members, who grew up here, wanted to embrace the Reform movement.[2] So, in late 1869, dissenters from this group and from Baith Israel, who were attracted to Reform Judaism, withdrew from their respective congregations and incorporated as Temple Israel in 1870, at Lafayette and Bedford Avenues. Meanwhile, in 1876, the Beth Elohim congregation built a magnificent building named the Keap Street Temple, which at the time was the largest synagogue in Brooklyn.[3] This edifice was later sold in 1921 to an Orthodox congregation, and the reformers moved into central Brooklyn.

The Temple Israel congregation was established as a radical Reform congregation that accepted Rabbi Isaac Meyer Wise's Reform prayer book, *Minhag America.* They dispensed with prayer shawls and head coverings. One of the prime movers in the Temple Israel was Abraham Abraham, who became one of the founders of Abraham & Straus. He was a prominent merchant, forceful, influential, and he presided over this synagogue for some twenty years. The Keap Street Beth Elohim, Williamsburg, did not go as far as Temple Israel in accepting Reform.

Both Brooklyn congregations, Temple Israel and Beth Elohim of Williamsburg, had prominent and active members. They were active in all areas of communal endeavor. "They created various agencies of Jewish philanthropy in Brooklyn, such as the Hebrew Orphan Asylum, the Jewish Hospital, the Brooklyn Federation of Charities (which later merged with the Federation of Jewish Philanthropies), the Hebrew Education Society, the Hebrew Free Loan Society, and the Ladies' Hebrew Benevolent Society" (Union Temple 1999).

The congregants of Temple Israel built a magnificent structure in 1890, and added to it in 1891. However, the core of Reform Jews had moved away from the area of Temple Israel. Before this, Temple Israel had been considering a merger with the Congregation Beth Elohim (then on State Street and now on Garfield Place in Park Slope, not to be confused with Beth Elohim of Williamsburg). The merger fell through because Abraham Abraham insisted that no one would be required to cover his head during worship.

Temple Israel then merged with Beth Elohim in Williamsburg in 1917. The Williamsburg congregation

Union Temple, Eastern Parkway, Brooklyn. Architect's drawing from American Jewish Yearbook, vol. 28 (1926–27). Reprinted by permission of the Jewish Publication Society.

moved out of its sanctuary, sold it, and for a short time shared the Temple Israel properties, which were eventually sold, and in 1925–26 Union Temple was built. The word *Union,* of course, referred to the union of these two congregations—the former Williamsburg congregation and the Temple Israel congregation.[4] "The newly built community house was dedicated on the Eve of Sukkot in 1929. Also in 1929 Dr. Sidney S. Tedesche began his long and distinguished ministry of Union Temple" (Union Temple 1999).

When we built Union Temple, or half of it—it was never completed[5]—there was discussion of a merger of Union Temple on Eastern Parkway and Congregation Beth Elohim on Eighth Avenue and Garfield. The merger was voted upon and announced in the *Brooklyn Eagle,* but it was rescinded because some of the younger members were afraid of a loss of identity and forced a withdrawal. So they decided to raise the money to build the community house themselves, and they were quite successful.

We had about 900 families until after the war, when people flocked out of Brooklyn—to Long Island, for example—and Union Temple lost many of its congregants. When I came in 1954 there were about 750 families, and it dropped off even more from that point, especially as new congregations were founded on Long Island.

(In 1979, after leaving the pulpit at Union Temple, Rabbi Dreyfus became rabbi emeritus. He then served as director of rabbinical placement for the Central Conference of American Rabbis until 1991, when he retired. Today, "he is Director, Emeritus, of Placement for the Central Conference and is still an active and beloved faculty member at Hebrew Union College—Jewish Institute of Religion in New York" [Union Temple 1999].)

"In recent years the congregation has begun to enjoy a revitalization, the result of a revival the neighborhood, and an energetic and expanded leadership. In July of 1992, Union Temple called to the pulpit Rabbi Linda Henry Goodman, the first woman to serve as rabbi of the congregation. Rabbi Goodman is an accomplished musician and a community activist. She has been working assiduously to motivate the various constituencies of the temple toward fuller participation in the congregational family and in Jewish life in general" (Union Temple 1999). On May 15, 1999, Union Temple of Brooklyn celebrated its one hundred and fiftieth anniversary.

NOTES

1. According to Postal and Koppman, "Public worship was unknown in Brooklyn until 1851. In that year Kahal Kodesh Beth Elohim, the first Jewish congregation in Brooklyn and in all Long Island, was organized by Louis Reinhardt, Elias Adler, Isaac Mayer, Moses Kessel, and Isaac Eisman. New York's Congregation Anshe Chesed loaned the Brooklyn group its first Torah. David Barnard, Beth Elohim's first cantor, was listed in Williamsburg's 1849 directory as 'Hebrew teacher' and 'fancy grocer.' Brooklyn's earliest school was opened behind Barnard's grocery on Grand Street (Postal and Koppman 1978, 175).

2. "Temple Kahal Kodesh Beth Elohim, which must not be confused with Congregation Beth Elohim, began as an Orthodox society . . . until, in the late seventies, the younger members, led by Emil D. Mayer and Abraham J. Piddian, and assisted by the new rabbi, Leopold Wintner, succeeded in converting the congregation to Reform Judaism" (Abelow 1937, 15).

3. "A rented hall on what is now Marcy Avenue was Beth Elohim's first house of worship after it outgrew Kessell's home. Its first synagogue, erected on Keap Street in 1876, was Brooklyn's second synagogue" (Postal and Koppman 1978, 175).

4. "Union Temple, 17 Eastern Parkway, is possibly the tallest synagogue in the world. The temple is a union of Temple Israel of Lafayette and Bedford Aves., with Temple Beth Elohim (Keap Street Temple), as well as a union of the Reform Jews of the Williamsburg and Bedford sections. The temple contains, in addition to its sanctuary, an auditorium with a frescoed ceiling, social rooms, classrooms, and athletic facilities. The ceiling depicts the history of the synagogue, beginning with the Tabernacles in the Wilderness" (Postal and Koppman 1978, 192). According to Abelow, the newly built ten-story center, completed in 1926, featured "a swimming pool, a gymnasium, club rooms for all kinds of activities, a Men's club, a Sisterhood, a Hebrew school, and a beautiful synagogue that seats about 1100 people" (197, 22).

5. According to historian David Kaufman, "The architect chosen was Arnold Brunner . . . [who] designed two complimentary structures: a Neoclassical temple, and a ten-story community center building immediately adjoining. The temple was planned to seat two thousand, and was to be fronted by 'four huge marble columns,' a grand facade to visually balance the library across the street. . . . since the temple was never built (due to the stock market crash of 1929; note which building took precedence), the community center alone would serve as a 'modern synagogue'" (1999, 260).

REFERENCES

Abelow, Samuel P. 1937. *History of Brooklyn Jewry*. New York: Scheba Publishing Co.

Kaufman, David. 1999. *Shul with a Pool: The "Synagogue-Center" in American Jewish History*. Hanover, N.H. and London: University Press of New England and Brandeis University Press.

Postal, Bernard, and Lionel Koppman. 1978 [1954]. *Jewish Landmarks of New York: A Travel Guide and History*. New York: Fleet Press.

Union Temple. 1948. *A Century of Service: Union Temple of Brooklyn, Centennial Celebration, November 19th, 20th, 21st, 1948*. Brooklyn, N.Y.: Union Temple of Brooklyn.

Union Temple. 1999. *Union Temple of Brooklyn: Celebrating the Past—Building the Future, from Generation to Generation, 150th Anniversary Celebration, May 15, 1999*. Brooklyn, N.Y.: Union Temple of Brooklyn.

First Synagogues
The First 144 Years of Congregation Baith Israel Anshei Emes (The Kane Street Synagogue)

JUDITH R. GREENWALD

On January 22, 1856, "Congregation Baith Israel" was founded in Brooklyn on Myrtle Avenue at the home of a Mr. B. Ross, where, according to the articles of incorporation, "an earnest desire was manifested amongst some Jewish Residents of Brooklyn to effect the incorporation of a Congregation and Synagogue for Divine Service." This event marked the birth of one of Brooklyn's two oldest congregations and the start of the only one that has continuously served the Jewish needs of the same community in which it was first established. Attention must be paid to such a perdurable institution. What were then and are now the wellsprings of Baith Israel Anshei Emes's twelve dozen years of vitality? Its history indicates that the beliefs it kept alive were supported in each generation by dedicated individuals who exerted wise leadership and made bold decisions.

Asser Levy held property in "Bruecklen," which means marshland, in the 1660s. One Jacob Franks, a president of Manhattan's Shearith Israel, owned a summer estate in Flatbush in the mid-1770s. Jews of New York and Philadelphia fought in the Revolutionary War Battle of Long Island, and during the War of 1812, Samuel Noah, a West Point graduate, helped build defenses in Brooklyn against British attack. Yet until the midnineteenth century there was no sizable Jewish community in Brooklyn.

In the 1830s permanent Jewish settlements arose simultaneously in the City of Brooklyn, around lower Fulton Street, and in the Town of Williamsburg, to Brooklyn's north. Emanuel Pike, father of the first professional baseball player, Lipman Pike, owned a haberdashery store in downtown Brooklyn. Jews established several breweries, one of which became the famous Rheingold plant. Philip Licht founded the Eagle Fireworks Company (established 1856), which supplied signal rockets to the Union Army. The meat packing industry started along Bushwick Avenue with the opening of a kosher slaughtering house.

In these early years daily minyanim were held in homes and shops. When looking back from the vantage point of the 1930s, Jewish newspapermen wisecracked that pious Brooklyn Jews rowed across the East River each Friday to celebrate Shabbat in Manhattan synagogues.

In 1855 Williamsburg, by then grown from a town to a city, was merged into the City of Brooklyn. The merger brought with it Kahal Kodesh Beth Elohim, the predecessor of Eastern Parkway's Union Temple. Kahal Kodesh had been founded in 1851. Thus, by merger, it became Brooklyn's only synagogue. Less than a year later, however, Baith Israel was formed.

Baith Israel's founders were twelve Bavarian, Dutch, and Portuguese Jews who were dissatisfied with their weekend retreat to Manhattan and their nomadic minyanim. The members of its Committee on Incorporation were Messrs. Ehrlich, Ross, Prince, Bass, Lamm, and Tobias and Mr. Jacob Samter. Morris Ehrlich became the first of the Congregation's forty-six presidents.

After incorporating, the members outfitted a temporary synagogue in rented space at 155 Atlantic Avenue. Within five years, when the number of Baith Israel's members had increased to thirty-five families, a bold decision was made to build a sanctuary. First, two lots were purchased for $3,000 at the southeast corner of Boerum Place and State Street, near a stable of racehorses. Then building plans were drawn. On January 12, 1862, a cornerstone was laid, and by August 12, 1862, a synagogue building had been completed at a cost of $10,000. In the words of Rabbi Israel Goldfarb, the Congregation's first historian, it was "the first altar dedicated to the God of Israel" to be built on all of Long Island, for it was not until 1876 that Williamsburg's Kahal Kodesh built its own synagogue on Keap Street.

Baith Israel's members, accompanied by band music, marched proudly to their new premises and placed the Congregation's scrolls in a new holy ark, which is the same ark that continues to serve the synagogue to this day. Soon, according to legend, loud praying began to disturb racehorses in the neighboring stables.

Like many congregations of its time, Baith Israel lacked means to retain a rabbi. Regular services were led by laymen, and a chazan was hired to lead services only on Passover and the High Holidays. However, after the move to its own premises Baith Israel was in a position to retain rabbinic leaders. Among its first rabbis was Aaron Wise, father of the renowned Rabbi Stephen S. Wise and grandfather of the remarkable Justine Wise Polier. Aaron's son, Stephen S. Wise, was a distinguished rabbi and foremost Zionist leader. He founded the Free Synagogue and Jewish Institute of Religion, and served as president of both the American and World Jewish Congresses. His daughter, Justine, a prominent attorney, civic leader, and pioneering reformer, particularly under Mayor Fiorello LaGuardia, became the first woman to be appointed to serve as a judge of the New York City Domestic Relations Court.

The first innovation of the "Boerum Schule," as it was known, was the establishment of a Sunday school staffed by member volunteers. The school generated a variety of young people's clubs, a library, and a postgraduate course to train future volunteer teachers. At its peak it accommodated five hundred pupils.

Then came the Civil War. In Union Field in Cypress Hills, the Congregation's oldest burial ground, is the grave of Lieutenant Colonel Leopold C. Newman, a member who, at the age of twenty-six, fought with the Army of the Potomac. He was mortally wounded in combat at the Battle of Chancellorsville on May 2, 1863, and while on his deathbed in a Washington D.C. hospital he was visited by President Abraham Lincoln. Lt. Col. Newman, together with Morris Hess (one of Baith Israel's incorporators and its fourth president) and Joseph Goldmark, founded the Brooklyn Republican Party. Interestingly, Mr. Goldmark, a munitions maker whose factory was attacked during the draft riots, was the father-in-law of both Louis D. Brandeis, the first Jew to be appointed to the United States Supreme Court and Felix Adler, founder of the Ethical Culture Society.

A plaque in the synagogue commemorates the military service during World War I of 111 young men of the Congregation and singles out for special honor four, who, like Civil War hero Newman, made "The Supreme Sacrifice."

The secession of the South was not the only secession to affect Baith Israel. The Congregation was strictly Orthodox, and parts of its ritual began to displease members who were attracted to the new Reform movement. In 1861 a Reform contingent seceded from the synagogue and founded Beth Elohim, the Garfield Place Temple. Later, a defecting faction of Beth Elohim joined with Kahal Kodesh to form Union Temple.

By the early 1900s membership had dwindled to thirty, placing the continued existence of Baith Israel in jeopardy. The extension of mass transit to sections of east and south Brooklyn enabled Jews to move elsewhere than the downtown area. Ritual compromises made to reconcile differences of opinion between the Congregation's Orthodox and Reform factions failed to please either side. In response to Reform adherents, the Congregation had dispensed with the segregation of men and women at services, and the confirmation of girls was instituted in 1873 on Sukkot. However, when a pipe organ and mixed choir were introduced in 1904, they met with such strong disapproval from the Orthodox that they quickly were abolished.

The consensus of the remaining thirty congregants was that a more adequate building was needed to attract as many new congregants as possible, whereupon decisions were made to sell the Boerum Schule and to purchase from

Exterior of the sanctuary (north façade) of Congregation Baith Israel Anshei Emes. Photo by Ms. Laura Cooper of Tesoro Architects.

the German Evangelical Lutheran Church of South Brooklyn the Congregation's present home at the corner of Kane (then known as Harrison) Street and Tompkins Place. The purchase included a handsome complex of three buildings designed in Romanesque Revival style: a sanctuary with a capacity of 864 persons, a school building, and a connecting two-story arcade. These had been constructed by the Middle Reformed Protestant Dutch Church in 1855. Unverified hearsay has it that Samuel A. Warner, architect of the Marble Collegiate Church on Lower Fifth Avenue in Manhattan, was the architect of the complex.

The purchase of an 864-seat sanctuary and two accessory buildings on an 11,500-square-foot plot of land by a congregation of only thirty members must have been an extraordinary act. The price was $30,000, paid with donations, proceeds from sale of the Boerum Schule, and by assuming the Lutheran church's mortgage of $13,000 at 6 percent interest. On Washington's Birthday, 1905, in the presence of a large gathering of well-wishers, the holy ark and the pulpit were transported from Boerum Place and installed in the Congregation's new home.

The brave decision to acquire the Kane Street premises proved correct. Together with two other concurrent decisions, it gave Baith Israel the new lease on life it had been seeking. The first of these was the decision to hire Rabbi Israel Goldfarb, who began his sixty-year tenure at Baith Israel in 1905. Looking back in 1983, Julius I. Kahn, about whom more later, described Israel Goldfarb as a dignified and likable man "whose word was law." In writing the first history of the synagogue, Rabbi Goldfarb quite unconsciously summed up his own role in it. Commenting on the Congregation's near death in 1904, he stated, "For many years the Congregation had been without a rabbi to hold the membership together and to stimulate their interest in its work." For the subsequent sixty years he provided the positive counterpoint to this negative condition, steering the Congregation along the lines of the Conservative Jewish movement and enriching its liturgy with music. When in the 1930s the Congregation's treasury was almost depleted, Rabbi Goldfarb declined payment for his services, for which a grateful Congregation gifted to him all it had to give, burial plots in its recently acquired grounds at New Mount Carmel Cemetery in Cypress Hills.

Rabbi Goldfarb was a composer who wrote and arranged an extensive body of Jewish music for synagogue, home, and school. Together with his brother, Samuel E. Goldfarb, he composed the well-known music to the Sholem Aleichem prayer sung on Shabbat evening. He and his brother Samuel also compiled the two-volume *Jewish Songster*, a collection of Jewish liturgical and secular songs. In addition, Rabbi Goldfarb compiled *Avodath Yisro-el*, a Sabbath morning service for cantor, congregation, and choir, *Friday Evening Melodies, Song and Praise, Synagogue Melodies for the High Holidays*, and hymnals in use by the United States armed forces during World War II. Rabbi Goldfarb graduated from the Jewish Theological Seminary of America in 1902 and served there from 1920 to 1942 as professor of Jewish liturgical music. In 1949 he founded the School of Sacred Music of Hebrew Union College.

Rabbi Goldfarb conducted his first service on Shavuot 1905. On Kol Nidre in that same year Rabbi Goldfarb preached a sermon on the need for a Talmud Torah. It was organized immediately with an initial registration of ninety students. The rabbi planned the curriculum and personally instructed the new teachers in pedagogy. The Talmud Torah held classes from four to six in the afternoon, four days a week. It continued in existence until the late 1950s.

Rejuvenated by the move to Harrison Street and the arrival of Rabbi Goldfarb, the Congregation celebrated its fiftieth anniversary in November 1906 by holding a Golden Jubilee Grand Fair. It successfully increased the Congregation's financial resources and doubled the membership.

The second significant Congregation decision was the resolution to consolidate with Talmud Torah Anshei Emes, a young congregation that was outgrowing a small row house on Degraw Street. In March 1908, with great ceremony, the scrolls of the Talmud Torah were brought in carriages from Degraw to Harrison Street and were placed in Baith Israel's holy ark. A corporate resolution was adopted designating the Congregation "Baith Israel Anshei Emes" and requiring the use of that combined name form at all times and for all purposes. The first president of the newly organized Congregation Baith Israel Anshei Emes was Harris Copland, father of composer Aaron Copland. The marriage of these two religious institutions, one with good facilities, the other with a growing membership, proved fruitful. Baith Israel's bold "if you acquire it, they will come" attitude had been proved correct.

In December 1908 the Sisterhood was organized as a charitable organization to benefit the community as well as the Congregation, and it subsequently became a charter member of the National Women's League. This was the first of many successful efforts made by Congregation members to serve the larger Jewish community and to participate in the formation of national organizations. Members raised thousands of dollars for Keren Hayesod, the Jewish National Fund, and the United Palestine Appeal. They supported the formation of the Brooklyn Federation of Jewish Charities, the Brooklyn Jewish Council, and the Brooklyn Heights branch of B'nai B'rith. Member Mrs. Charles Rosenthal was a founder and a president of the Brooklyn Jewish Home and Hospital for the Aged. Pincus Weinberg, a Congregation president, moved to Flatbush and founded the East Midwood Jewish Center. When Congregation vice-president Samuel Brown moved to Bay Ridge, he helped organize the Bay Ridge Jewish Center. Two trustees, Messrs. Wiersch and Werner, moved to Harlem and founded the Hebrew Tabernacle. Three members were among the founders of the "Ra'ananna" colony in Israel, which grew into a flourishing town. Today, Congregation members lead monthly Shabbat services at the

Cobble Hill Nursing Home, help to staff a neighborhood homeless women's shelter, and serve on a Social Action Committee that supports a variety of extra-congregational causes.

In 1913, under the leadership of Rabbi Goldfarb, the Congregation became a charter member of the Conservative movement's congregational arm, the United Synagogue of America. A Congregation president, Louis Moss, served for many years as president of that umbrella organization.

By the time of the Congregation's sixtieth anniversary in 1916, ten stained glass windows had been fitted into the east and west walls, electric lighting had been installed, a new pulpit had been built, and large bronze menorahs had been added to flank the reader's lectern. The Congregation employed a paid staff of six: Rabbi Goldfarb, a secretary, a sexton, a Torah reader, a superintendent, and a choirmaster. Dues were twelve dollars per year, payable in four installments, and Sunday school tuition was two cents per session. The Congregation held a grand bazaar to celebrate its sixtieth anniversary.

After World War I the Congregation continued to grow. Its seventy-second year, in 1928, was notable as the year in which a magnificently executed renovation of the sanctuary was started. Bronze memorial tablets were installed at the rear of the sanctuary and an illuminated stained glass window was built over the ark. The sanctuary was repainted. The work was designed and overseen by member Julius I. Kahn, a master painter and general contractor. He designed the repainting in a trompe l'oeil manner, a popular late-nineteenth-century technique. The sanctuary walls were painted to look like Jerusalem limestone, its columns were made to look like marble, and an exquisite gold-leaf border in a scroll and vine design was painted in an arch high over the ark. This was not the first nor was it the last act of service Julius Kahn performed on the synagogue's behalf.

Julius Kahn's family belonged to Talmud Torah Anshei Emes. After amalgamation, his father, Adolph Kahn, became a Congregation trustee. The family lived next door to the synagogue and operated a general contracting business on the same premises. Julius was the oldest child and became the head of the concern. By 1916 Mr. Kahn was secretary of the Sixtieth Anniversary Grand Bazaar Committee. Down through the years Julius Kahn always eschewed the position of president, but he served in all other capacities, including Sunday school chairman, Dinner-Dance

and Journal Committee chairman, Cemetery Committee chairman, and Building Committee chairman. He retired from business in 1960 and for the next twenty-five years of his life he volunteered four hours a day, four days a week of his time to constant and devoted synagogue service as treasurer and as much more.

These were hard times for the synagogue as the postwar flight to suburbia drained away all new members. Julius Kahn assisted the presidents of that era, brothers Jacob and Oscar Hertz, in keeping the synagogue alive. He organized the synagogue's finances, keeping strict account of every penny, nickel, and dime. He supervised daily maintenance and repair. He made all arrangements for each holiday, conducted the fund-raising drives, and composed and edited the annual journals. Most of all he kept watch for new members, and in the 1960s, as urban gentrification began, he graciously received and welcomed into the Congregation the young people who began to appear. It was his example, wise counsel, and fond training that inspired them and gave them the know-how to regenerate the Congregation.

Upon conclusion of Mr. Kahn's 1928 beautification achievements, impressive sanctuary rededication ceremonies were held. The scrolls were carried in a procession and replaced in the ark by Julius Kahn and Philip Lille (father-in-law of future president Jacob Hertz), and the perpetual lamp was rekindled.

Despite the Great Depression, a diamond jubilee was celebrated in March 1931 with a bazaar, banquet, and ball. Congratulatory messages were received from President Herbert Hoover, Governor Franklin D. Roosevelt, Lieutenant Governor Herbert Lehman, Mayor Jimmy Walker, Felix Warburg, and others. Nevertheless, in this period of ruined fortunes and general despair, membership declined and many activities were curtailed.

Then came the horror of World War II and the Holocaust, and the attention of the members was devoted to the war effort and the support of international Jewish relief causes. Their contribution to the worldwide effort reached fulfillment after the war in the founding of the state of Israel.

Sometime during the middle of World War II new life, hope, and spirit came to the Congregation by virtue of the membership of Herman Belth. He perceived that, in his own words, "Brooklyn's oldest Synagogue deserves to be saved for posterity as a holy shrine and as a living monument to the pioneering spirit of the founders of this great community which, in the course of a century, has grown to be the largest Jewish Community in the world."

Mr. Belth was a man of culture, deep religious conviction, and means. He gave generously to the Congregation, inspired its continuation, and secured its rehabilitation. In the late 1940s and early 1950s he raised over $40,000, half through his own generosity and the generosity of his personal friends, toward physical rehabilitation of the synagogue. At this time the exterior blue-veined white stone-faced brick walls were finished in brownstone-type stuccoed slabs, and the structure was fortified. Scaffolding was erected in the sanctuary and, except for the front wall, it was entirely repainted. Herman Belth's efforts were crowned on January 11, 1953, when another rededication ceremony was held. Mr. Belth unveiled a bronze honor roll tablet bearing the names of all those whose generosity made the newest renovation possible.

No one, however, not even Herman Belth, could stem the postwar exodus of Jews from the community and the consequent decline in membership. During these years people were determined to realize the American dream of owning their own home in the suburbs developing around the "inner city." In the 1950s membership declined; the marvelous choir, which had been inspired by Rabbi Goldfarb's great musical talent, was abolished; the Sunday school and Talmud Torah were discontinued; and the paid staff of the Congregation was cut back.

In the entire history of the Congregation only one family continued as members through three generations and over eighty years, enduring the synagogue's bad times and enjoying its good ones. This was the Goldman family. The first generation were the brothers Harry and Louis Goldman, who, like many of the Congregation's members, owned a retail establishment in the area. One of Louis's sons, Sol Goldman, befriended the Kahn family and, as he waited for his Hebrew school class to begin, would do his homework in their house next to the synagogue. In time, Sol Goldman founded one of New York City's largest and most prominent real estate concerns, with major holdings in all types of commercial and residential properties. Despite the important position he attained, whenever Julius Kahn called, Sol Goldman answered. After he died in 1987, his daughter, Amy Goldman, assumed membership and kept the family's relationship with the synagogue alive. As recently as 1996 and 1998, The Sol Goldman Charitable Foundation and the Goldman family made major contributions to the synagogue.

The historical downturn of the 1950s was endured by the Congregation, and it reached another landmark in its own history, its first centennial in 1956. The first one hundred years were celebrated by three separate events: a devotional convocation in tribute to leaders of the bench and bar who had made outstanding contributions to organized Jewish life in Brooklyn; a moving anniversary service honoring the centennial and the fiftieth anniversary of Rabbi Goldfarb's spiritual leadership; and a joyous jubilee dinner at the Waldorf-Astoria. The participation of bench and bar was a stroke of genius masterminded by Jack and Oscar Hertz. They were attorneys who reached out to members of the Brooklyn bar for support. This gave the declining Congregation a circle of outside supporters to sustain it until it could be rejuvenated.

Better times came with the gentrification of the inner city, a brand-new phenomenon that started in Brooklyn Heights and Cobble Hill. New members such as attorneys Arthur Lichtman and Paul Fink and businessman Steven Cohen, who purchased brownstones in the area, typified the new life-giving trend.

In 1965 newlyweds Seth and Judy Greenwald attended services at Baith Israel, then conducted by Rabbi Berger, who had taken over the pulpit on a part-time basis upon the retirement of Rabbi Goldfarb. They were the first new faces to be seen in the Congregation in many years and were so warmly welcomed by Julius Kahn and the other members that they became committed to the Congregation forthwith and to such an extent that each served terms as Congregation president.

The enthusiasm generated by Israel's success in its six-day war of 1967 attracted more new members, who were drawn to the Israel Bond Drive in which the Congregation participated. Rabbi Berger was succeeded by Henry Michaelman, grandson of Rabbi Goldfarb, who gathered more new members into the fold.

By 1970, with the accession of Rabbi Elliott Rosen to the pulpit, a core of new members including the Lichtmans, Drukers, Badners, Greenwalds, Cohens, Finks, Schneiders, Rubensteins, Leemans, Huttenbachs, and Horowitzes founded the Young Couples' Club with the wholehearted support of the longtime members.

In a flurry of fervor and activity and with the encouragement of the Young Couples' Club, the establishment of a nursery school was undertaken by Arthur Lichtman and Isaac Druker; it served the community from 1971 through 1975. Arnold Badner organized the Prozdor, and once more the Congregation could offer children a Jewish education. The Belth Room, a small chapel area, was constructed in 1975 with the generous aid of Herman and Florence Belth, and the community room was renovated in 1978.

Once again the synagogue rang with sounds of life at Purim carnivals, Sukkot dinners, Passover seders, street fairs, holiday celebrations, and country shabbatot. New members Arthur Lichtman and Isaac Druker became successive presidents, supported by a rejuvenated membership, eager and willing to assume the responsibilities of running the Congregation. The Scheindlin, Wasserman, and Friedman families joined, bringing to the Congregation broad and deep Jewish knowledge. Each Rosh Hashana new faces appeared in the sanctuary and then joined the roster of members. Robert Weinstein joined and undertook to lead morning prayers in a strong and beautiful voice, to organize the services, and to provide for the ritual and financial needs of the synagogue, serving in many capacities including president and treasurer. Upon the initiative of Raymond P. (Ray) Scheindlin, a group of members revived the choir and named it the DeRossi Singers, in honor of the Renaissance composer whose beautiful liturgical music the choir performed.

In 1979 Ray Scheindlin, a well-liked and respected member, and a rabbi and professor at the Jewish Theological Seminary, graciously assented to become the Congregation's part-time spiritual leader. His academic brilliance appealed to the college-educated and professionally trained membership. He gave illuminating sermons, which attracted still more members and won the enduring loyalty and attendance of the entire membership. Eventually, under Ray Scheindlin's charismatic leadership, the Congregation grew too large, and Rabbi Scheindlin announced that the Congregation was ready, once again, for the services of a full-time rabbi.

During Rabbi Scheindlin's tenure one of the boldest and most beneficial decisions ever made in the Congregation's history was adopted. During the early 1970s the women's movement had liberated the energies of female constituents. It had the blessings of the Sisterhood, led by President Sally Solomon. In Rabbi Rosen's tenure, women were called to the Torah. Several, among them Paula Scharf, Miryam Wasserman, and Ellen Friedman, read Haftorah. Evelyn Rubenstein organized many successful street fairs. Judy Greenwald took turns with Isaac Druker and Ben Zalman in organizing the anniversary dinner-dances and publishing the dinner-dance journals. Miryam

Wasserman served as Prozdor principal. Rachel Epstein edited The Scroll and Geraldine Gross prepared the press releases and newspaper articles about the synagogue and its members. The impact of the Congregation's women reached a zenith in 1980 with the election of Nancy Fink, a Brooklyn Law School professor, as president. To this position she brought considerable energy, intelligence, and administrative skill.

In 1982 President Fink called a full membership meeting to consider whether women should be accorded full ritual participation. There were three questions to be answered: may a woman serve as sheliah tzibbur, may a woman blow shofar on Rosh Hashana, and may daughters of Kohanim duchen (recite the blessing of the priests over the congregation). Rabbi Scheindlin addressed the meeting and carefully instructed the Congregation about the halakic principles involved. He explained that the principle underlying the first two issues was one of agency: may a congregation's men deputize a woman to perform time-bound rituals that they are obliged to perform but she is not? Historically women were not required to carry out time-bound rituals whereas men were obliged to perform them. While the Rabbinic answer to this question is no, Ray Scheindlin observed that the rabbis had based the exemption of women from time-bound rituals not upon scripture but upon certain social conventions that no longer obtained. This explanation indicated to the Congregation that when the reason for a rule ceases, the rule may cease. If the social conventions no longer existed, women should not be exempt from time-bound obligations, in which case they could legitimately be authorized to serve as sheliah tzibbur.

A different principle was involved with respect to duchening. Ray Scheindlin made it clear that a woman is not of priestly status but that duchening did not involve any exclusively priestly practices. This indicated to the Congregation that daughters of Kohanim could duchen without violating any halakic principle.

"The rest is history." The Congregation's consensus was to accord full equality to women, and the Board so resolved. Since then two women followed in Nancy Fink's steps. Judith R. Greenwald and Ellen A. Bowin served as Congregation presidents, and women have participated fully in all aspects of Congregation life.

The Congregation's decision to adopt entirely egalitarian ritual practices was a natural decision for it to make, but it was a bold decision. It was a natural decision because the Sisterhood had played an active role in the Congregation from its earliest days until the early 1970s, and from then on women and men had shared in the operation of the Congregation. This sharing meant the sharing of real work, for after the Great Depression the Congregation's paid staff, exclusive of Hebrew school staff, had never numbered more than three, only one of whom was ever full-time. It also was a natural decision because it was an extension of the modern social practices of the Congregation. The membership was mainly composed of families in which both husband and wife were employed in full-time professional positions and did not divide the labor of family life. Instead, they shared child-rearing and other responsibilities of the home. Sharing equally in religious ritual and synagogue responsibility fit the pattern of their lives and the reality that the Congregation probably could not function unless it could call upon the participation of both and not merely one extremely busy member.

This egalitarian decision was a bold decision, nevertheless, because it did not please everyone. Some members left the Congregation. Yet, given the difficult lives led by members and the enormous claims on their time, it is apparent that had this decision not been made, this largely participatory, volunteer-run Congregation would not have had sufficient strength to carry out its ambitious educational, social, and ritual programs.

The decision to be fully egalitarian led to the next bold decision: to ask a woman, Rabbi Debra Cantor, to accept the position of rabbi. This displeased a few more members, and they defected to play a major role in the development of a new neighborhood Orthodox minyan into a viable and vibrant Orthodox congregation. Yet these bold moves, like previous bold moves, proved fruitful once again. They had the positive effect of bringing into being a new Orthodox congregation in the area. Once again, Congregation Baith Israel Anshei Emes was a "mother" congregation, seeding new congregations with its own members. They also enabled the Congregation to draw upon an enlarged pool of members who could read Torah and lead in ritual obligations. For a participatory congregation, strength in numbers is vital. They also attracted scores of young couples for whom egalitarianism was a reality and a commitment. They also served to motivate the next generation. Today, after their bar/bat mitzvahs, young men and women read Torah and serve the Congregation at services shoulder to shoulder with their elders. In the summer of year 2000, two young women of the Congregation, Alice Phillips and Liba Rubenstein, went to Israel for summer study on Bronfman grants, a prestigious nationwide award made annually to only twenty-six students. The statistical fact that two young women from one small congregation won such an award in a nationwide competition is a telling sign that Baith Israel Anshei Emes's bold egalitarian decisions have been correct on all counts.

Today the Congregation is a vibrant, active organization, planning to celebrate its one hundred and fiftieth anniversary in 2006 in expanded, fully restored, and fully rehabilitated premises. In the words of Rabbi Goldfarb, written in the "Centennial Journal" twenty-five years ago: "May we never fail nor falter in the support of God's house. May it always stand for the principles on which it was founded—the principles of traditional Judaism, as handed down to us by Moses and expounded by our sages."

The Early Years of the Hebrew Educational Society of Brooklyn

DANIEL SOYER

In discussions of Jewish immigrant adjustment to American life, the Lower East Side usually takes center stage. The dense and vibrant neighborhood of Brownsville, Brooklyn, generally attracts far less attention than its storied Manhattan counterpart. Yet many of the dramas that played themselves out on the East Side also animated Brownsville. For example, Brooklyn was also scene to the kind of strained relationship between so-called Uptown Jews (wealthy, Americanized Jews mainly of central European origin) and Downtown Jews (poor eastern European immigrants) that has become almost legendary in Manhattan. The difference was that in turn-of-the-twentieth-century Brooklyn the wealthy philanthropists lived in downtown brownstones, while the immigrants settled in the newly developed neighborhood of Brownsville.

In 1899, those prosperous Brownstone Jews founded the Hebrew Educational Society of Brooklyn (HES) to serve as a community center for the immigrant masses of Brownsville. Like the neighborhood itself, the HES is often overshadowed by its illustrious counterpart on the Lower East Side—the Educational Alliance. But the HES was a remarkable institution in its own right, with a vast array of activities. Since it was established by the wealthy elite to Americanize the newcomers, its early history illustrates well how each group struggled to influence their relationship. By the 1920s, eastern European Jews and their children had assumed leadership of the organization.

The HES came into being barely a dozen years after the first Jews had settled in what was then a sleepy farming village on the edge of Brooklyn. The pioneers had fled the Lower East Side in search of low rents and a more healthful country environment. Jewish real estate developers immediately recognized the area's potential and encouraged its development. Several New York garment manufacturers and contractors soon decided to join the exodus, bringing along not only their families but their workers and workshops as well. The neighborhood grew up around the clothing factories, and by the early 1890s Brownsville had a Jewish population of about four thousand.[1]

Brownsville's most spectacular growth came in the first two decades of the twentieth century. With improved transportation links to Manhattan, many more garment workers and others could live in Brownsville and commute to their jobs in "New York." The opening of the Williamsburg Bridge in 1903, the Manhattan Bridge in 1909, and the first direct subway line between the two boroughs contributed to the neighborhood's advance. In 1910, one journalist noted that what had been swampy wasteland a decade earlier now contained "rows miles long of four and five story modern pressed brick tenement houses."[2] Brownsville's boom continued into the 1920s. By that time, some quarter million Jews called the neighborhood home and made up 80 percent of its population.

At its height, Jewish Brownsville harbored a vibrant and diverse community, with a full complement of institutions and organizations. Known in Orthodox circles as the "Jerusalem of America," the neighborhood boasted dozens of synagogues (the most prominent of which was Oheb Shalom, founded in 1889), the Stone Avenue Talmud Torah, and the Rabbi Chaim Berlin Yeshiva. Radicals met at the Labor Lyceum. The Socialist Party briefly dominated local politics, but by 1920 the Democratic Party had returned to power under the colorful leadership of the homegrown, Yiddish-accented Hymie Shorenstein. The Jews of Brownsville also built a number of charitable institutions, the largest of which was Beth El Hospital.

Despite its lively atmosphere, Brownsville remained a poor and troubled neighborhood. In the early years, the area lacked adequate sewers and pavement, leading outside observers to comment on the "miasmatic mudholes" that served as streets and the "squalor" in which the people kept house. Conditions improved, but the residents continued to be among the poorest Jews of the city. As its most famous native chronicler, Alfred Kazin wrote that Brownsville was "notoriously a place that measured all success by our skill in getting away from it."[3]

In 1898, a group of prominent New York and Brooklyn Jews associated with the Baron de Hirsch Fund (named for the European Jewish nobleman and philanthropist) decided that their poor co-religionists in Brownsville needed an institution similar to Manhattan's Educational Alliance. The Fund's leaders used the Alliance as a model and opened a small center on one floor of a private house. There they ran a vacation school for children, English classes for adults, clubs for young people, and a lecture program for all.[4]

The following year, department store magnate Abraham Abraham (of Abraham and Straus) helped to transform this small operation into a full-fledged community center under the sponsorship of Brooklyn's own Jewish elite. The founders of the Hebrew Educational Society were mainly prominent merchants and professionals. They made up a close-knit group, sharing membership in the same clubs, congregations, and, in some cases, families.

Their favorite synagogues included Temple Israel and two Congregations Beth Elohim (one of which later merged with Temple Israel to form Union Temple, the other of which was also known as the Garfield Temple). Their favorite club was the Unity Club.

At the turn of the century, this small circle of well-established American Jews felt anxious. First, they feared that the influx of uncouth eastern Europeans would undermine their own hard-won respectability. Second, the Brooklynites nervously compared themselves with the much larger and wealthier community in Manhattan. Sometimes the Brownstoners urged one another to bear the troublesome responsibility of Brownsville independently, just as the Manhattan Uptowners took care of the Lower East Side. At other times they demanded assistance from the Manhattanites. After all, had not most of the Brownsville poor come from the East Side?

Not surprisingly, the elite founders of the Hebrew Educational Society thought that the new institution's main task should be to Americanize and uplift Brownsville's immigrants. The HES therefore put most of its early emphasis on instruction of the newcomers in English and citizenship. But it could also do anything that would impart to its clients something of middle-class Anglo-American culture.

Brownsville's benefactors may have seen the community as "densely ignorant," but this was not really the case. In fact, while some eastern European Jews "made much fun" of the new Hebrew Educational Society, others cooperated with it eagerly. Upwardly mobile students, professionals, and businessmen greeted the new organization with particular enthusiasm. A group of local doctors and lawyers were among the first to take advantage of the facilities by forming a chess club. These Brownsville residents hoped that the Society would help improve living conditions within the community as well as the neighborhood's image. As one announced, "The time has come when nobody has to be ashamed anymore that he lives in Brownsville, and the Irish car conductor will soon also have to give up his arrogance when he comes through Brownsville."[5]

The Hebrew Educational Society ran an impressive range of programs. Activities included children's and youth clubs, English and citizenship classes, religious instruction and worship, a gymnasium, a variety of manual-training and vocational courses, a kindergarten, recreation rooms, a children's garden, a summer roof garden, a milk station and baby clinic, a library, a branch of the Penny

Provident Bank, a music school, a citizenship bureau, community theaters in English and Yiddish, a study room, dances, and holiday celebrations. All the activities were designed to uplift their participants by teaching them valuable Americanizing lessons in thrift, manners, and citizenship. Despite the condescending intentions behind many of the programs, Brownsville participants responded favorably. At the same time, the local clientele began to influence the nature of the programs.

CLASSES AND LECTURES

Classes and lectures in English language, civics, American history, and current events furthered the Society's aim of Americanizing the immigrants. The founders hoped that teaching the Brownsville residents civic responsibility would dampen the neighborhood's dangerous enthusiasm for such radical doctrines as socialism and anarchism. But what really went on in the classrooms? This is hard to say, but it may have been very different from what HES leaders intended. After all, at least three of the Society's English teachers—Abraham Shiplacoff, William Feigenbaum, and Barnett Wolf—later represented Brownsville as Socialists in the state and city legislatures.

CLUBS

Dozens of clubs drew hundreds of young people to the HES each week. Like every other aspect of the Society's work, the clubs had a definite socializing mission. Their volunteer leaders attempted to "instill gradually and unobtrusively into [their] members, right thinking and right feeling."[6] Some club activities reflected the patriotic leanings of the Society's leaders—an entertainment given by the Young Hildegards, for example, included a "pantomime" of "My Country 'Tis of Thee." But the members themselves also helped to decide what the clubs would do, so other activities reflected the Zionist and socialist inclinations of Brownsville's eastern European population.

RELIGIOUS EDUCATION

The elite founders and sponsors of the Hebrew Educational Society were nearly all Reform Jews. Their supporters in the neighborhood favored a modernized form of traditional Judaism. The latter very much wanted the Society to offer religious instruction to children to counteract the pernicious effects of Brownsville's many so-called kheyders—tiny, ill-equipped, unsanitary, private Hebrew schools taught by unqualified, old-fashioned European teachers.

The HES leadership certainly agreed that the kheyders had a demoralizing effect on the local children, but they dragged their feet when it came to opening a school, partly because they realized that they and their neighborhood supporters would not see eye-to-eye on the school's curriculum. In the end, the HES reached a compromise: It established two separate religious schools—a weekday afternoon "Hebrew school" with a traditional curriculum, and a Reform-oriented "Sabbath school."

The Hebrew school, opened in March 1901, provided its pupils with a basic Jewish education. It met three afternoons a week, for two hours each session, and offered instruction in Hebrew, the Bible, and the prayer book. It saw itself as "progressive," by which it meant that it taught Hebrew not by the traditional rote translation method, but as one would teach any other modern language. In addition, the language of instruction was English, not Yiddish, as in the despised kheyders. The Hebrew school had a paid staff consisting entirely of men, at least partly drawn from the Jewish Theological Seminary, the flagship of the emerging Conservative movement in Judaism.

The Sabbath school, taught by female volunteers, took a very different approach. It opened in 1902, with the modest purpose of "keeping the small children off the streets when not in school." Its aims soon expanded to include the teaching of ethics, Jewish history, and Jewish ceremonies. The Sabbath school promoted Reform Judaism: Its weekly assembly for worship services offered English-language hymns, Bible readings, prayers, and blessings. The Sabbath school also fully expressed the Hebrew Educational Society's Americanizing mission. All school exercises featured enthusiastic declarations of patriotism, including the singing of "America." Holiday celebrations included similar mixtures of Jewish lore and American patriotism.

MOTHERS' MEETINGS

The Women's Auxiliary of the HES sponsored regular "mothers' meetings" as part of its mission to "uplift the race" through its services to Brownsville's women and children. Programs generally included a Yiddish lecture by a doctor, rabbi, or social worker, a musical program, and refreshments, often served by members of one of the girls' clubs. The gatherings were lively, and mothers asked questions of the speakers and commented freely on the talks. Lecture topics included "Why We Should Be Thankful," "The Moral Training of Children," "Hygiene and Care of the Child at Home," "What Is Culture?" "Education of the Jewish Child in America," "Proper Amusements and Recreation for Children," and "Care of the Child."

It is hard to say how the mothers themselves responded to these efforts at uplift, since no such testimonies survive. But hundreds attended the meetings. Perhaps the ladies of the auxiliary were mistaken in their belief that these mothers constituted a backward element in need of special supervision. It seems, after all, that the mothers were as eager as their benefactors to hear the advice of experts on modern methods of child-rearing. As Margaret Sanger understood when she established her famous birth-control clinic in Brownsville, many Jewish women in the neighborhood held advanced views on issues concerning the family.

YIDDISH

Many members of the American Jewish elite viewed Yiddish, the everyday language of eastern European Jewry, as a badge of backwardness, separatism, and Jewish national feeling—all things that they wanted to root out among the new immigrants. HES founders had contempt for Yiddish and urged the newcomers to forget the language in favor of English. Yet the HES never excluded Yiddish from its activities, viewing it as a necessary medium through which to reach the surrounding community. Despite the views of its founders, the Society even gradually became an active center of Yiddish culture. Speeches, lectures, and performances in Yiddish took place regularly at the Society, drawing large crowds.

By the 1920s, with Brownsville in its heyday as a thriving Jewish neighborhood, the HES began to promote Jewish culture over its traditional aim of Americanization. By that time eastern European Jews and their children had themselves moved into leadership roles in the Society. They put more emphasis on traditional religious education and worship, allying the HES with the Conservative and Modern Orthodox trends in American Judaism. They supported Zionism, collecting money for Zionist causes and helping to welcome Zionist leader Chaim Weizmann during his visit to New York in 1921. They also adopted a more appreciative attitude toward Yiddish, establishing classes in the language for children and adults.

The changes in policy at the HES had much to do with the changing leadership. Lithuanian-born Alter Landesman, a rabbi trained at the Jewish Theological Seminary, became executive director in 1922. By 1930, many members of the board of trustees were from eastern Europe, or were children of immigrants. The leading congregation for HES directors was now the Brooklyn Jewish Center, an elite Conservative synagogue founded in Crown Heights in 1918. The change continued into the 1940s, as Brownsville natives took over direction of the Society for the first time.

By then Jewish Brownsville had entered terminal decline. The Jewish movement out of the neighborhood, which had begun as early as the 1930s, accelerated in the 1950s and, especially, the 1960s as Jews fled an influx of African-Americans. By 1968, only five thousand Jews remained in the neighborhood, most of them elderly. The Hebrew Educational Society of Brooklyn pulled up stakes too in 1965, following much of its constituency south to Canarsie, where it continued to serve many of the same people as a community center.

NOTES

Thanks to Marc Arje and the Hebrew Educational Society of Brooklyn for allowing me access to the Society's early records. Thanks also to Jocelyn Cohen and Nikolai Borodulin for their research assistance, and to Fordham University for the faculty research grant that made it possible to hire them.

1. On the history of Brownsville, see Alter Landesman, *Brownsville: The Birth, Development and Passing of a Jewish Community in New York*, 2nd ed. (New York: Bloch, 1971); Gerald Sorin, *The Nurturing Neighborhood: The Brownsville Boys' Club and Jewish Community in Urban America, 1940–1990* (New York: New York University Press, 1990); Max Halpert, "The Jews of Brownsville, 1880–1925: Demographic, Economic, Socio-Cultural Study" (D.H.L. Dissertation, Yeshiva University, 1958); Deborah Dash Moore, *At Home in America: Second Generation New York Jews* (New York: Columbia University Press, 1981); Beth Wenger, *New York Jews and the Great Depression: Uncertain Promise* (New Haven: Yale University Press, 1996), 84–87. Contemporary newspapers such as the *Bronzvil un Ist Nyu York progres*, the *Brukliner naye tsyatung/Brooklyn New Journal*, the *Idishe gazeten*, the *Jewish Daily Forward*, and the *Brooklyn Daily Eagle* also provide much material. On Brownsville's early years see also the series of articles by B. Botvinik that ran in the *Forward* in January 1930.

2. "Brownsville an Example of Rise of Values in Brooklyn Realty," *New York Herald*, undated clipping, A. J. Virginia Scrapbook. New York Public Library Jewish Division.

3. On miasmatic mudholes see "Some Phases of Life in Brooklyn's Ghetto," *Brooklyn Daily Eagle*, July 2, 1999, p. 8. For Kazin, see Alfred Kazin, *A Walker in the City* (New York: Harcourt, Brace, 1951), 12.

4. On the history of the Hebrew Educational Society see Landesman, *Brownsville*, 170–200, as well as the annual reports of the Society, and other records held by the Society itself.

5. "Bronzvil," *Idishe gazeten*, May 4 and November 30, 1900, p. 18.

6. Hebrew Educational Society, *Annual Report* (1910), 9.

Syrian Jewish Life

MARK KLIGMAN &

WALTER ZENNER

The Bat Yam Market on Kings Highway delights the senses, its smell of Middle Eastern spices filling the air. Middle Eastern dry goods wrapped in clear plastic show their native color. In the back of the store several open barrels are filled with olives in marinade. Music fills the market with popular Arabic, Israeli, and American songs. The Bat Yam Market, like the community it serves, is at the nexus of Arabic, Jewish, and American culture.

Syrian Jews immigrated to America over one hundred years ago and continue to thrive in several neighborhoods within Brooklyn. The Syrian-Jewish population is located in Bensonhurst, Flatbush, and Gravesend. Originally situated on the Lower East Side of Manhattan, Syrian Jews first moved to Williamsburg and Bensonhurst after World War I. Between the wars, Bensonhurst was the central neighborhood for Syrian Jews. After that, members of the community began moving to Flatbush and Gravesend, which subsequently surpassed Bensonhurst as the primary home of Syrian Jews. It is estimated that over twenty thousand Jews from Syria, or of Syrian descent, live in Brooklyn.

Today most of the community resides along Ocean Parkway from Avenue I to Avenue Z. While some own renovated dwellings from the 1940s, others have purchased newer homes on Bedford Avenue. As the community has grown over the years, its geographic base has expanded. Kings Highway is the primary shopping center for the community. While maintaining insular familial ties and religious practices to varying degrees, it retains many elements of Middle Eastern culture.

In the spring of 1992, President Assad of Syria lifted travel restrictions for Jews living in Syria. This resulted in a surge of immigration into the community—over 3,500 in the mid 1990s, primarily from Damascus. Before this, immigrants had mostly come from Aleppo in northern Syria.

Forty organizations serve this community, including synagogues, schools, bikur cholim (providing assistance for the sick, elderly, and immigrants), senior living facilities, and two community centers. Fifteen Brooklyn synagogues serve this population. Thirteen follow the customs of Aleppo and two of Damascus. Many Syrian Jews maintain summer homes in New Jersey.

SYNAGOGUES, RABBIS, AND RELIGIOUS SCHOOLS

We all need religion, if not for ourselves, maybe for our children.
— *Max A. Haddad (see Sutton 1988, 369)*

After the first wave of Syrian Jews arrived from Aleppo, the first synagogue was established in 1911 on the Lower East Side. Prior to this, services were held in people's homes or their businesses. As Syrian Jews crossed the bridge to Brooklyn following World War I, a synagogue was established in Williamsburg in 1919. Syrian Jews remained isolated even while living in close proximity to religious Ashkenazic Jews (Sutton 1979, 34). In Bensonhurst, the Magen David Congregation was established in 1921. Still in existence, the Magen David Congregation housed a school at Sixty-seventh Street and Twentieth Avenue that educated many prominent Syrian leaders.

As Syrian Jews migrated to Flatbush in the 1940s, several synagogues opened along Ocean Parkway. The largest Syrian synagogue in Flatbush is Congregation Shaare Zion, located between Avenues T and U. Across the street and one block north is the Sephardic Community Center and the Ahi Ezer Congregation, the synagogue of Damascus immigrants. Congregation B'nai Yosef is close by on Avenue P, and Congregation Beth Torah lies between Avenues J and K. The Kol Israel Congregation, located on Bedford Avenue and Avenue K, marks the expansion of the congregation in the 1980s (see fig. 1). Like most Syrian and Middle Eastern synagogues, the men's section is on the bottom floor and the women's section is located in an upper balcony (see fig. 2; the men pictured here are celebrating the use of a new *sefer* Torah).

Syrian Jews in America continue to respect their rabbis a great deal, as they did in Aleppo. This respect establishes rabbis as leaders within the community and influences religious observance and the religious organization of the community. A senior rabbi has much autonomy in decision-making for his congregation. However, major issues that affect the community (kashrut [religious dietary laws], marriage laws, and educational goals of the schools) are decided by an organized religious court, the Sephardic Rabbinical Council, which is led by Chief Rabbi Saul Kassin. His father, Rabbi Jacob Kassin (1900–94, see fig. 3), guided the growth of the community for over fifty years.

Since all Syrian synagogues are Orthodox-affiliated, members of the community take great pride in their "religious orthodoxy . . . different from the more mainstream

Fig. 1. *Exterior of front door, Kol Israel Congregation, located at Bedford Avenue and Avenue K. Photo courtesy of the Sephardic Heritage Center at the Sephardic Community Center, Brooklyn.*

Reform and Conservative wings of American Jewry" (Zenner 1983, 181).[1] As Allan Ashear reflects on his religious upbring in the 1950s and 1960s:

In my home here [in Brooklyn], although my father was quite religious he wasn't very demanding, he gave us considerable latitude. Of course he required and we went along with it, Sabbath and holiday observance, no lights turned on, no travel during Saturdays. We respected the religious order, while he lived; while we lived at home. When we lived away—I lived in the city on my own for a time, we didn't observe the same rules. He knew how we behaved, he knew what we were doing, but he didn't make an issue of it. The only thing that aroused him, made him angry, was fanaticism, ultra-orthodoxy—he couldn't take that. Being very religious wasn't the only important thing for my father; also important was for us to be happy, to fulfill

Fig. 2. Torah dedication at Kol Israel Congregation, 1990s. Photo courtesy of the Sephardic Heritage Center at the Sephardic Community Center, Brooklyn.

Fig. 3. Rabbi Jacob Kassin with two of his great-great-grandchildren. Photo courtesy of the Sephardic Heritage Center at the Sephardic Community Center, Brooklyn.

ourselves to our capacity. He taught us through his example; most importantly, that things were "relative," not absolute." (Allan Joseph Ashear, see Sutton 1988: 380–81)

A more devout religious current appeared in the 1980s. Ultra-Orthodox Syrian rabbis, many from Israel, have tried to move the "normative" community religious practices to a stricter level. Some embrace a renewed religious conviction, but older members of the community desire moderation. The present chief rabbi of the community, Rabbi Saul Kassin, seeks to maintain a balance in favor of a middle-of-the-road approach to unify the community (Yellin 1995, 17).[2]

Today Syrian children attend one of several Jewish day schools including the Magen David Yeshivah (Bensonhurst) and the Yeshivah of Flatbush. These schools enroll 1,800 from nursery to twelfth grade.

LIFE CYCLES AND HOLIDAYS

Community life is vital, prosperous. We must be doing something right!
Joseph Isaac Shalom (see Sutton 1988, 374)

Celebrations of life cycle events and holidays help to build communal ties. These events provide the opportunity for a gathering of family and friends. From lavish weddings to Shabbat meals, life cycle events and holidays perpetuate Jewish Syrian customs, engender a deeper connection to Judaism, and foster closer familial and social ties.

For example, the night before a *brit milah* a party is held to protect the newborn. At this party, called *Shad-il-az*, cele-

brants read a portion of the *Zohar*, sing *pizmonim* (paraliturgical songs), and serve delicacies. The *brit milah* itself includes a unique Syrian custom, *seneet Eliyahu ha-nabi* (tray of Elijah the prophet; see fig. 4):[3]

Guests place contributions on the tray, its tiers filled with flowers, candles and coins. They light a candle and take out a coin to keep for good luck.

At the conclusion of the Brit Milah, family members bid on the contents of the tray with the highest bidder donating all monies to charity. Some people retain the money on the tray as Mamon shel berakh (blessed money) to be used to start a new business, to make a down payment on a home or for another special purchase, with the belief that this money will bring blessing to the endeavor. (*Celebrations* 1991, 15)

Often a single woman holds the plate. During the ceremony the baby boy receives a name. For the birth of a girl a naming ceremony takes place during the Torah service and a celebratory kiddush is held in the synagogue. This is known as a *sebet*. Syrian Jews, like other Sephardim, name a first son and daughter for living paternal grandparents. The second son and daughter are named for maternal grandparents. Such naming customs strengthen family ties and encourage children to appreciate their ancestry (Dobrinsky 1986, 3; *Celebrations* 1991, 14).

A *pidyon haben* (redemption of the firstborn) ceremony occurs thirty-one days after the birth of the first son in the presence of a kohen and invited guests. According to Syrian custom, the mother of the baby, wearing her wedding dress and veil, brings the baby on a pillow covered in white (see fig. 5). The ceremony consists of declarations made by the father and the kohen whereby silver coins are given to the kohen to redeem the child. The father makes a blessing in fulfilling a commandment, and the kohen states the child is redeemed and then blesses the child. A festive meal follows with the singing of *pizmonim*.

Syrian Jews in the community celebrate a bar mitzvah in two parts. First, on a Monday, Thursday, or Rosh Hodesh—days the Torah is read—the bar mitzvah boy wears his *talit* (prayer garment with fringes) and *tefillin* (phylacteries) for the first time. Members of the family and rabbis take turns winding the strap around the boy's arm. Second, on Shabbat, the boy is called to the Torah. Afterward family and friends celebrate a *sebet*, a festive meal, and the singing of *pizmonim* (*Celebrations* 1991, 16). While the prevailing Jewish practice is to undergo the bar mitzvah ceremony shortly after the thirteenth birthday, some Syrians follow the custom of having a boy twelve years and six months of age perform the ritual. A celebratory meal with music and dancing may be held after the Sabbath or on the following day.

The joyous celebration of marriage is also marked by special Syrian customs. Until the 1950s, a *shadkhan* (matchmaker) facilitated the meeting of bride and groom, and

Fig. 5. Mother, in wedding dress and veil, bringing in her son at a pidyon haben (redemption of a baby boy), 1965. Photo courtesy of the Sephardic Heritage Center at the Sephardic Community Center, Brooklyn.

many in the community remember arranged marriages. Among contemporary Syrian Jews the dating period is typically short, since the intention of dating is to lead to marriage. The predominance of in-group marriages reflects the insularity of the community, although it is not uncommon for Syrian men to marry Ashkenazic women born in America.[4] Several prenuptial parties may be celebrated, including a "coming over party," for the families to meet and rejoice after the announcement of the engagement. A *swehnie*, an often lavish party for women given by the groom's parents, celebrates the bride's immersion in a *mikveh* (ritual bath):

> A very beautiful pre-marital Sephardic tradition is the Swanee [*sic*], plural for the Arabic word Seniyeh (plate or tray). The groom sends his bride trays filled with gifts, including flowers, perfumes, candles, sweets, and money to enhance the ritual of family purity. Today, Swanee tables are often arranged with great creativity and artistic flare by the groom's family, incorporating all of the symbolic items, as well as other special gifts. In turn, the bride's family prepares a table for the young man, displaying religious articles, books and other personal gifts. (*Celebrations* 1991, 18)

Many comment that the purpose of the lavish *swehnie* celebration is to highlight the importance of the laws and customs of family purity, which are followed by many in the Syrian community (Dobrinsky 1986, 41–42). The chief rabbi of the Syrian community is available to provide a blessing to the bride and groom; he may even officiate at

Fig. 4. Two women holding the seneet Eliyahu ha-nabi (tray of Elijah the prophet), 1970s. Photo courtesy of the Sephardic Heritage Center at the Sephardic Community Center, Brooklyn.

Fig. 6. Bride and groom at their swehnie, a party given by the groom's family after the bride immerses in the mikvah (ritual bath) prior to the wedding, 1988. Photo courtesy of the Sephardic Heritage Center at the Sephardic Community Center, Brooklyn.

the wedding ceremony. Many weddings are extravagant, with elegant apparel and sumptuous cuisine (see fig. 6).

Holidays throughout the year are times of celebration and rejoicing. Holiday meals are usually the time when traditional Syrian and Middle Eastern foods are eaten such as *kubbe*, baked goods, and the fine dessert delicacies.

A unique Syrian custom is associated with the holiday of Hanukkah (see fig. 7). The typical Jewish custom is to light the number of candles that correspond to the day of the holiday with an additional candle, the *shamash*, used to light the others. Some Syrian Jews light a second *shamash*. The lighting of this second candle reflects the history of the community. While Jews have lived in Syria for nearly three thousand years, a significant number, estimated to be several hundred, were expelled from Spain and came to Syria in the fifteenth century. Initially, the Jews in Aleppo and Damascus were divided between these refugees and the indigenous community (Zenner 1965, 32). When these new immigrants were accepted by the community in the sixteenth century, it was made offi-

cial on *erev hanukkah* (the day of the first night of the holiday). The lighting of a second *shamash* commemorates the thanksgiving of the Spanish Jews resettled into the community (Dobrinsky 1986, 369). This custom continues to this day.

For all these life cycle celebrations special melodies are sung. *Pizmonim*, paraliturgical songs combining well-known Arabic melodies with newly written Hebrew texts, are a repertoire unique to the Brooklyn Syrian community. Some *pizmonim* sung today were written by nineteenth-century Aleppo rabbis. Others were written by Aleppo-born rabbis like Moses Ashear (1877–1942), who moved to Brooklyn. Performance of the repertoire remains the mainstay of Syrian celebrations.[5]

OCCUPATIONS

In the early twentieth century, many Syrian immigrants were employed as "Oriental Jobbers" (Sutton 1979, 11–12), individuals who sold dry goods and garments supplied by more established immigrants. As merchants, they fol-

Fig. 7. Children lighting Hanukkah candles, 1980. In the middle window note the use of two shamash candles. The use of a second shamash commemorates the acceptance of Spanish Jews, who immigrated to Syria in the fifteenth century and were accepted into the community on Hanukkah in the sixteenth century. Photo courtesy of the Sephardic Heritage Center at the Sephardic Community Center, Brooklyn.

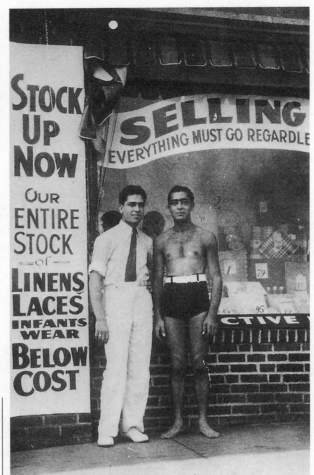

Fig. 8. Textile shop owners on the Lower East Side, 1940s. Photo courtesy of the Sephardic Heritage Center at the Sephardic Community Center, Brooklyn.

lowed the occupations they had practiced in Aleppo. Others worked at garment factories and as pastry bakers. The main goals of early immigrants were to establish stable lines of work and to send money to support their families in Syria.

After 1910, some immigrants developed their own businesses in the retail and wholesale clothing industry. They sent money to family members in Syria, who in turn immigrated to the United States. A network of Syrian Jewish business and family connections established in this period still thrives today (Zenner 1965, 352; Chira 1994, 67–69). Many Syrian businessmen have had retail clothing and linen or lace stores in New York City, including the Lower East Side (see figs. 8 and 9). Syrian Jews specialized in linen (particularly household linens), lace, and infant wear. They sold these products in Brooklyn, first as peddlers and later as shopkeepers. They also opened shops in tourist areas well beyond New York, such as in Estes Park, Colorado, and resorts in Maine.

Some Syrians developed businesses in manufacturing, importing, and the selling of electronics that are still operated by their descendants (Zenner 1982). Syrian Jews founded and owned Crazy Eddie and Nobody Beats the Wiz (Zenner 2000, 145–47). Bargain discount or closeout stores were also common Syrian businesses in Brooklyn and Manhattan. Only in the past twenty years have more

Syrians chosen professional careers, such as in accounting, law, and medicine. Some of these professionals have remained in the community; others left.

FOOD AND LEISURE

Food remains an important tie to the past for Syrian Jews in Brooklyn. The actual everyday cuisine has been considerably influenced by modern American and American Jewish styles of cooking. Thus *Deal Delights*, a cookbook prepared by the Sisterhood of Deal in 1980, includes recipes for *hamentashn*, an Ashkenazi pastry for the holiday of Purim, as well as other dishes shared by Americans. A recent article in a food magazine featured the cooking of Lisa Antebi, a Syrian Jewish professional living in Manhattan. She still prepares Syrian foods, including stuffed grape leaves and dishes made with bulgur wheat. However, some dishes that typified Aleppan cooking in the past, particularly *kubbe*, a

Fig. 9. Linen and lace store, 1949. Photo courtesy of the Sephardic Heritage Center at the Sephardic Community Center, Brooklyn.

dumpling made with either bulgur or rice, have declined in importance and are underrepresented in recent cookbooks (Hellman 1997).[6] Some traditional dishes are now as likely to be purchased in the specialty food stores on Kings Highway in Brooklyn as cooked at home, and they are more likely to be eaten only on special occasions.

At the Bat Yam Market, the back corner freezer is stocked with Middle Eastern foods. Filo dough meat-filled cigars, *kibbe*, and *lachminjan* are placed on a white styrofoam board hand-wrapped in cellophane. A small label on the front describes only the contents of the package; preparation directions are not provided. At the front of the store a women places dozens of frozen packages on the counter, inquiring in English, with a few Arabic and Hebrew words interspersed, how to prepare these Middle Eastern foods. The clerk answers in English, with a noticeable Middle Eastern accent. The woman listens intensely and asks for recommendations on desserts. What celebration lies ahead for her and her family? She, like other Syrian Jews, is not living in the past but integrating life today with her traditions.

NOTES

1. Elazar notes that the Syrian community is the most religious of the Sephardic communities in America (1989, 171).

2. Sutton describes normative religious practice as "middle-of-the-road Orthodoxy" (1988, 98).

3. The prophet Elijah, called "The Angel of the Covenant" (Mal. 3:1), is said to be present at every circumcision. A common custom in Ashkenazic and Sephardic ceremonies is the *kisse shel Eliyyahu*, the chair of Elijah. This chair, often ornately decorated, is left empty, signifying the presence of Elijah. The Syrian custom is not to have a decorated chair; rather a *parokhet* (embroidered cloth) with the name of Elijah is placed on a chair (Dobrinsky 1986, 5).

4. Sutton estimates that two-thirds of Syrian Jews living in Brooklyn marry other Syrians (1979, 55, 226). Others marry different Sephardim, Israelis, or Ashkenazim. A few have married non-Jews; Syrian men have married Italian women living nearby in Brooklyn (see the comments of Max A. Haddad, Sutton 1988, 370).

5. For a recent study focusing on the interconnection of the singing of *pizmonim* and Syrian life see Shelemay 1998. The repertoire of the *pizmonim*, as well as the *bakkashot*—originally composed paraliturgical poetry and songs sung before Shabbat prayers—are the source for melodies sung in the synagogue; see Kligman 1997.

6. Also see Claudia Roden, a food writer of Turkish and Syrian Sephardic origin (1996): on her background, pp. 1–15; on Aleppan cooking in general, pp. 564–69; on *kubbe*, pp. 412–18.

REFERENCES

Celebrations: The Sephardic Life Cycle. 1991. Brooklyn: Sephardic Community Center.

Chira, Robert. 1994. *From Aleppo to America: The Story of Two Families.* New York: Rivercross Publishing.

Dobrinsky, Herbert. 1986. *Treasury of Sephardic Laws and Customs: The Ritual Practices of Syrian, Moroccan, Judeo-Spanish and Spanish and Portuguese Jews of North America.* Hoboken and New York: Ktav Publishing House and Yeshiva University Press.

Elazar, Daniel J. 1989. *The Other Jews: The Sephardim Today.* New York: Basic Books.

Hellman, Peter. 1997. "Aleppo on the Hudson." *Saveur,* no. 23: 88–97.

Kligman, Mark. 1997. "Modes of Prayer: Arabic Maqamat in the Sabbath Morning Liturgical Music of the Syrian Jews in Brooklyn." Dissertation, New York University.

Roden, Claudia. 1996. *A Book of Jewish Food: An Odyssey from Samarkand to New York.* New York: Knopf.

Shelemay, Kay Kaufman. 1998. *"Let Jasmine Rain Down": Song and Remembrance among Syrian Jews.* Chicago Studies in Ethnomusicology, ed. Philip V. Bohlman and Bruno Nettl. Chicago and London: The University of Chicago Press.

Sutton, Joseph A. D. 1979. *Magic Carpet: Aleppo in Flatbush, the Story of a Unique Ethnic Jewish Community.* New York: Thayer-Jacoby.

———.1988. *Aleppo Chronicles: The Story of the Unique Sephardeem of the Ancient Near-East in Their Own Words.* New York: Thayer-Jacoby.

Wertheimer, Jack. 1989. "Trends in American Judaism." *American Jewish Yearbook* 89: 63–162.

Yellin, Deena. 1995. "A Legacy Continues." *The Jewish Week,* 16–17.

Zenner Walter. 1965. "Syrian Jewish Identification in Israel." Dissertation, Columbia University.

———.1982. "Arabic-Speaking Immigrants in North America As Middle Man Minorities." *Ethnic and Racial Studies* 5: 457–77.

———. 1983. "Syrian Jews in New York Twenty Years Ago." In *Fields of Offerings: Studies in Honor of Raphael Patai,* ed. Victor D. Sanua, 173–93. London and Toronto: Associated University Presses.

———. 2000. *A Global Community: The Jews from Aleppo, Syria.* Detroit: Wayne State University Press.

Tastes of Home in Three Brooklyn Groceries

ILANA GOLDBERG

INTRODUCTION

Kings Highway, the main commercial strip that runs through the Syrian Jewish neighborhood of Midwood in Brooklyn, is lined by a variety of kosher eateries, bakeries, and grocery stores catering to a diverse clientele. I visited Kings Highway for the first time in the fall of 1997 with the intent of finding an Israeli grocery store (Hebrew: *makolet*) to feature in a short video I was producing at New York University's Department of Anthropology.[1] I was operating on a hunch: At the site of a corner grocery, I would find tangible signs of how Israeli expatriates in New York preserved their attachment to Israel. My research had begun in Manhattan, but my informants soon pointed me to the Brooklyn neighborhoods, where many Israelis of Middle Eastern origin had settled since the mid-1970s. On Kings Highway, they promised, I could find a typical Israeli *makolet*. As I ambled down the street, searching for visual cues, I noted that the storefront notices and the names of the stores not only described their merchandise or bills of fare but also signaled, in subtle ways, the social and ethnic identities, and the tastes, of both proprietors and clientele. A fast-food joint for pizza and falafel was playfully named Kosher Hut, invoking the minority status and difference of the Jewish community in relation to mainstream America, represented by a nonkosher chain like Pizza Hut. Next door was a small catering business named Se'uda—the word for "meal" in a quasireligious register of Hebrew. In distinction from the neighboring fast-food joint, this storefront seemed to address an Orthodox clientele, offering more festive fare, suitable for the Sabbath meal (Hebrew: *se'udat shabbat*).

Several blocks west of Kosher Hut, I found what I had been looking for: two adjacent grocery stores, with the words Holon and Bat Yam printed vividly on bright yellow and blue awnings. Surrounding the names was an array of other significant designations and symbols: "Middle Eastern Groceries," "Glatt Kosher," and a Star of David. These words and symbols worked together to qualify one another and to produce a finely nuanced definition, broadcast simultaneously to different publics. To Israelis the names of the stores were sufficient as identifiers: Holon and Bat Yam are working class towns just south of Tel Aviv. The Star of David transformed the typical connotation of "Middle Eastern"—not Arab or Muslim, in this case, but Jewish. The "Glatt Kosher" sign indicated that the products were acceptable to Ultra-Orthodox (Ashkenazi) customers, while yet another sign alerted the Sephardi public that the proprietors adhered to the tradition of "Bet Yosef" *shekhita* (ritual slaughtering). More subtly still, the term "Middle Eastern" conferred a very particular meaning about the Israeli character of the store: Israeli-ness, at least in respect to food, is decidedly Middle Eastern, hence "Oriental" or "Sephardi," and not Ashkenazi.

The storefront windows of both establishments were plastered over with advertisements for imported Israeli food products, snack foods, milk products, and baby foods. There were posters advertising upcoming performances by visiting Israeli artists, and even political bumper stickers, such as "Stop Oslo" or "The people are with the Golan." Both stores offered a similar inventory of locally produced and imported foods, as well as Middle Eastern specialty items: dried fruits and grains, pickles and olives, and a variety of savory pastries and baked sweets. The Holon grocery had a deli counter, complete with *shawarma* rotisserie (usually grilled turkey or lamb) and an Israeli salad bar. Indoors, customers lingered at the deli counter and at the checkout, reading the Israeli paper and gossiping. The atmosphere was very informal, and to me unmistakably familiar, as customers freely tasted food, helped themselves from behind the service counters, fed samples to their small children, or asked to have their purchases put down on credit. However, on subsequent visits, as I interviewed customers on videotape, I began to identify other ethnic components that had been layered over by the Israeli facade. The stores are in fact a polyglot environment where one hears a mélange of languages spoken: Egyptian, Syrian, and Lebanese dialects of Arabic; French; and of course ubiquitous sounds of English and Hebrew. The stores are also patronized by non-Jewish residents: Italian-Americans, Russian immigrants, sometimes even Arabic-speaking Muslims. One of the Mexican employees I met had become conversant in Hebrew and Arabic after seven years working in the store. The view that emerged, and which I sketch below, is of these stores as multicultural social spaces, which serve an important practical, social, and cultural role for the immigrants in the neighborhood. The grocery stores, in turn, provide a window onto the complexities of multicultural social existence in the surrounding communities at large. My analysis draws on different types of impressions: visual, textual, and verbal. Working from the assumption that deep cultural meanings and values can be encoded in mundane vehicles such as food, and in everyday forms such as storefronts, my reading of the grocery stores begins by looking extrinsi-

cally at the aesthetic organization of the sites. At the next level, the interpretation is informed by statements that customers, owners, and workers shared with me about the significance of the stores, the social makeup of the neighborhood, and their feelings about the food they buy.

SETTON, HOLON, AND BAT YAM

The Jewish population around Kings Highway is composed of diverse strata, both in socioeconomic and historical terms. The most established and veteran component of the neighborhood is the Syrian Jewish community, most of whom immigrated to the United States before midcentury. Members of this community refer to themselves as Syrian, but since the neighborhood has drawn immigrants from other countries of origin in the Middle East, as well as Israeli "Oriental" Jews, residents now often use the more general rubric "Sephardi" to characterize the community. On one visit, I encountered a group of young men who were distributing the latest edition of the *Sephardic Yellow Pages*, listing local Jewish businesses. The Bat Yam grocery is owned by a Lebanese Jewish family who immigrated to Israel in 1968, resided in the town of Bat Yam for a few years, and then settled in the United States. Holon was founded by an Egyptian Jewish couple who migrated directly to America in 1973, while other family members moved to Israel. Holon and Bat Yam, with their almost exclusively Hebrew storefronts, stand in contrast to an older grocery store, named Setton, about a block and a half away. Setton, a Syrian grocery where the old-timers tend to shop, is a neighborhood landmark, which existed well before the influx of Israeli immigrants. The rectangular sheets of lime green and hot pink posted on its exterior window are printed entirely in English—"Pistachio Nuts," "Orlando grape leaves," "Turkish coffee"—as though it has resisted being absorbed or colored by the Israeli character imposed on the other storefronts. Seen as a cluster, the three stores, with their divergent aesthetics, reflect the social diversity and the history of the neighborhood.

The present owner of the Holon grocery explained that originally their store had borne the family's last name. At one point a relative visiting from Israel suggested they change the name to Holon, his town of residence. In Israeli speech the pair Holon–Bat Yam form a kind of composite toponym when referring to the area south of Tel Aviv. These two towns are prototypical of a working-class locality. In the parlance of Tel Avivians, the two names are sometimes compacted into a portmanteau word to refer to the crowds that come in on weekends to nightspots in Tel Aviv. Hulbatim are Israel's equivalents of the "bridge and tunnel" crowds of New York. On first sight, the pair of names on the adjacent storefronts strikes the knowing observer as a sort of visual gag—one that perhaps also celebrates a working-class sensibility in the midst of the wealthy Syrian community. Moreover, the names Holon and Bat Yam do more that just reinscribe the Israeli towns on a Brooklyn thoroughfare; they also map the social relations pertaining between Holon–Bat Yam and Tel Aviv onto the Manhattan-Brooklyn axis.

The owners of Holon and Bat Yam are not Israeli, nor are they members of the old established Syrian community; they are relatively recent newcomers to the United States, with strong ties to Israel. It seems that as their Brooklyn neighborhood has changed and absorbed more Israelis, their stores have readily taken on a dense Israeli symbolic presence, which pervades the shops thoroughly. The Middle Eastern Jews of this neighborhood, even those who never lived in Israel, have had their identity inflected by the experience of Israeli nationality, in marked distinction from the older stratum of American-Syrian Jews. The fact that the owners of the Holon grocery renamed the store after an Israeli town may be interpreted as a moment signaling this shift.

"TO LIVE IN AMERICA AND FEEL AT HOME"

It seems a truism to say that immigrants relocated in a new country desire contact with home, and preserve their connection and attachment through consumption of imported foods. But the grocery stores seemed to serve other purposes as well. As I listened to customers talk about their food preferences, I derived a sense of how some of the discontinuities, disruptions, and disparities that are a result of immigration may be articulated through the everyday activities of food shopping and preparation. In this regard, the underlying meanings assigned to the opposition between America and the Middle East (including Israel) are seminal.

One of the recurring tropes I heard in the grocery stores was that Middle Eastern food is healthier and more nutritious than American food. This was especially evident in conversations with mothers who spoke about their children's diet. One of the most popular products in demand at the stores is Bamba, an Israeli snack food for babies. Bamba crisps are peanut butter puffs with a relatively low sugar content. "I prefer to give them Bamba—it's healthier, and not like the sweetness of all the candy they

have here," said one mother. Similarly, "traditional" foods for adults were seen as healthier. The owner of Holon explained, "It's health food, the way people used to eat, going back in time: grains and beans. . . ." She went on to reminisce about her childhood in Egypt, and how much simpler it was to make a living back then. "A person had only to sell or deal with one thing. There were men on the street corners who prepared one tray of *basboussa* [a flat almond-flavored semolina cake—I.G.] every morning and sold it to pedestrians on their way to work as breakfast. Then they went home and were at leisure for the rest of the day. But here in America you have to sell many different things and work all day." Paradoxically, others characterized Americans as "lazy." A high school student on his lunch break grabbed a bag of precut packaged salad and tossed it between his hands: "In Israel you have to work hard, but people here are *lazy*. Here you just buy—toss—make a salad." An American-born woman who presented herself as "half and half: Italian and Arabian [sic]" confessed, "I should learn how to make Middle Eastern food, but I don't really know how to make it. . . . My mother rolls the grape leaves and the stuffed squash, and prepares the hummus . . . but I just buy it." After she left, one of the cashiers cast a meaningful look at the door and said, "Some people are *lazy*—they buy the food prepared."

This sort of denunciation was not reserved only for American food practices but was also directed toward the Ashkenazim. A cashier at the Holon grocery volunteered: "Most of the customers here are Sephardi. . . . I happen to be Ashkenazi, and unfortunately you can feel the difference." I asked what she meant, and she proceeded to quote typical derisive remarks she had overheard from customers: "Ashkenazim don't know how to clean, they don't know how to cook . . . what kind of home do they keep?" To which she retorted, "What kind of home could it be already? Like any other home! I could ask the same question about them!"

In residents' popular conception of the opposition between America and the Middle East, Ashkenazim are partially equated with America. They appear to share some of the negative values associated with America (laziness, inferior food), while Sephardim bear the positive qualities of "home," which include cleanliness, superior food, and adequate care and investment of time in food preparation.

Perhaps one of the most important symbolic and sensory vehicles that concretizes the opposition between America (or Ashkenazim) and the Middle East is *spice*, or spiciness. An American-born child of a Yemenite-Israeli mother said of her eating preferences, "My mom likes practically everything that's spicy." The cashiers at Holon noted that customers would often ask questions about how to use certain spices. An Egyptian (Muslim) cook who works for an Israeli restaurant described her recipe for Yemeni soup: ". . . flanken meat, tomato paste, and every spicy [sic] I put inside, a small onion, a little Chinese parsley, potato . . . that's it." At the phrase "every spicy" she was transported for a moment, as if overcome with awe and reverence for the spices. A high school student insisted on putting skhuq (a hot Yemenite condiment) on his (American) turkey sandwich, citing a domestic proverb: "Bli skhuq ein ta'am la-okhel" (Without skhuq, food has no taste). "Having taste" marks the positive end of the polarity between Ashkenazim and Sephardim.

This sense of pride in Middle Eastern food is consistent with the historical process of the formation of an Israeli national cuisine, which came to be primarily Middle Eastern in its derivations. For Israeli expatriates in this Brooklyn neighborhood, the continuation of food practices from home is not simply an unreflective fact but is actively pursued. Cashiers at Holon say that they are constantly solicited for advice about the preparation of classic Middle Eastern grains such as bulghur wheat, wheat berries, and couscous. The neighborhood bookstore sells a large number of Hebrew cookbooks featuring predominantly Middle Eastern cuisine. Propped up next to them in the display is a small decorative plaque with a verse entitled "Blessing for the Home."

While nostalgia for the home country is palpable in this Diaspora setting, optimism about life in America is not thereby diminished. An Israeli high school student earnestly tried to explain to me why he was going to stay in America: "Here . . . it's the future." His friend jokingly added, "Believe me—they've got everything here." As they guided me around the shelves these students would point out American analogues to Israeli products, expressing both an appreciation of American foods and lively excitement about the availability of the Israeli products. Surveying the shelves, one student said, "There's Yoohoo here . . . and Choco—where is the Choco from Israel?" Pointing to a package of ramen noodles, he addresses the camera: "Remember mana khama from Israel—new in Israel—here it's already old." Lifting a bottle of Tabasco sauce, he translates: "This is like your shkuq, to put on grilled meats—it's amazingly tasty," and a friend interjects "like

barbecue sauce!" The pride in the Israeli imports is still marked by an acknowledgment of America's lead in terms of invention and innovation: "Here it's already old."

The theme of America's plenty came up again when I investigated the provenance of a popular food item called Krembo. All three grocery stores carry Krembo, an Israeli confection consisting of a chocolate-coated mound of white sugary fluff set on a round tea biscuit. The boxes of Krembo on display at different strategic locations in the stores—at the checkout, on top of the deli counter, or on the shelves—virtually jumped into view when I first entered the stores. Krembo has been produced for about seventy years, dating all the way back to pre-1948 Palestine. It has the status of a pop-cultural/national icon, much as Oreo cookies have for Americans. Like Oreos, Krembos are a children's favorite. But the grocery owners pointed out that in America it is mostly adults who buy Krembos regularly, consuming them as a comfort food in a ritual of nostalgia to remember their youth in Israel. This was viewed by one of my interlocutors as compensation for times during childhood in Israel when "plenty did not prevail." As children, being allowed to buy even one Krembo was considered a huge treat. Now in America people could indulge as much as they pleased. In fact, because of the demand for this item, an Israeli entrepreneur had begun to manufacture Krembo locally in a small factory in Williamsburg. Despite the symbolic appreciation of homemade, healthy Middle Eastern foods voiced by many customers, and their disdainful characterization of American food as junk or as excessively sweet, the overly sweet Krembo was embraced enthusiastically. This suggested to me that in the opposition between America and the Middle East, Israel may be interpreted as a mediating term. While Israeli foods are for the most part perceived as intrinsically Middle Eastern, some elements of Israel's food repertoire are not. The Krembo, a naturalized icon of Israeli identity, is in fact originally a European product and is industrially mass-produced.

These observations imply that, for the Sephardi Jews in this community, the fierce attachment to Middle Eastern and Israeli foods serves not only to collapse the distance between adulthood and childhood, or between America and their home countries, but also to mediate the contradictions between the idealized values associated with both places. The Middle Eastern countries left behind decades ago represent a past life of simplicity, leisure, and sometimes scarcity, where due investment in preparation of healthy, tasty food contributed to the well-being of the home. America's abundance and technological development, while holding more promise for the future, are compromised by the degradation of some of the values associated with home-keeping. Symbolically, Israel's "modernity," embodied in the imported packaged foods, bridges the cultural difference between the "Middle East" and "America," while its "Oriental-ness" ameliorates the negative impact of the values associated with a less domestic, faster-paced life in America.

Residents' investment of time and effort in continuing food practices from home, or learning them afresh, ensures the preservation of the value of a real sense of home. This conscious effort is evident not only in regard to the imports of Israeli food products and in the quotidian tasks of food shopping and preparation; it also cuts across other important domains of socialization. At the Israeli bookstore Sifrutake, the local broker of Israeli culture, I found an explicit articulation of the same message deduced from residents' attitudes to food: a T-shirt for sale emblazoned with the store's logo and a Hebrew slogan: "likhyot be-amerika u-lehargish ba-bayit"—To Live in America and Feel at Home.

NOTE

1. Ilana Goldberg, *Makolet: A Middle Eastern Grocery in Brooklyn*, 24 mins. VHS (English and Hebrew with subtitles), distributed by Filmmakers' Library, New York.

Brooklyn as Refuge
Yaffa Eliach's *Hasidic Tales of the Holocaust*

ALAN ROSEN

An immigrant's story is always connected to a sense of place. For a person assumes an identity as an immigrant in the movement from one place to another. One land is exchanged for another, one home for another. In the case of the refugee—the involuntary immigrant—the personal link to a particular place is perhaps even more complex, for the refugee takes flight when the home becomes inhospitable. In flight and at risk, the refugee leaves a homeland that has been transformed into a place of peril. Only later, from a secure distance, can the violated bonds of affection to the homeland be healed.

For the Hasidim who fled Europe and came to America, the sense of violation of European home was clearly extreme. On the one hand, the eastern European milieu in which they for centuries had lived gave birth to and nurtured their religious movement. Indeed, often the towns from which the names of the individual Hasidic groups were derived were even imbued with a kind of holy stature. America, on the other hand, although a place of greater physical safety, had an ambiguous reputation: liberal modes of life were frequently viewed as going against the grain of Hasidic piety.

America nonetheless offered oases of religious life to Hasidic Jews. Brooklyn became one such oasis. New York City in general had attracted Hasidim since the late nineteenth century. A few decades later, Brooklyn became the home to several smaller courts of Hasidim, enfolded within the borough's burgeoning Jewish life. These initial Hasidic footholds were sufficient to lure wartime and, in even greater numbers, postwar refugees, among whom were leaders of important Hasidic dynasties. These leaders and their followers—including the rebbes of Lubavitch, Satmar, and Bobov—in turn transformed Jewish life in Brooklyn, creating large and vibrant Hasidic communities in Crown Heights, Williamsburg, and Boro Park.

Since the 1960s, researchers have attempted to decipher the life of Brooklyn's Hasidim, trying to give an intimate portrait of a seemingly alien group or assessing cultural patterns of tradition and modernity. *Hasidic Tales of the Holocaust* is of a different order. Rather than having us gaze at Hasidic Brooklyn, it lets us listen quietly at the door.

Herself a child survivor of the Holocaust, pioneering scholar in Holocaust studies, and professor at Brooklyn College, Yaffa Eliach has frequently linked her work to Brooklyn. In 1974, Eliach founded the Center for Holocaust Documentation and Research in Brooklyn, the earliest institution of its kind. Housed at the Yeshiva of Flatbush, the

Center provided a library and educational programs, spearheaded interviews with liberators of concentration camps, and drew on the special population of the borough to assemble a singular collection of interviews with religious survivors. It is these interviews that form the basis for *Hasidic Tales of the Holocaust*.

According to Eliach, *Hasidic Tales of the Holocaust* (1982) is the first collection of Hasidic tales to be published in a hundred years. Eliach collected the eighty-nine tales from 1974 to 1981, translated, edited, and worked them into a "unified form." Virtually all the tales are set in Poland and Russia. Yet it is Brooklyn that inspires Eliach. Brooklyn functions here as a civilizing presence, as counterpoint to the terrors of Europe. Brooklyn is the safe haven from which the stories can be told. Here memory can confront trauma yet also relinquish it, returning the teller to a life of pleasure, success, learning, devotion, and celebration. And while it is true that Brooklyn remains generally on the margin of the tales, it occasionally becomes central. Whether on the margin or at the center, Eliach's view of Brooklyn, haven for pious survivors from eastern Europe, also has striking implications for representation of the Holocaust, countering as it does the general vision of a malevolent America.

After publishing *Hasidic Tales* in 1982, Eliach continued to teach at Brooklyn College and to direct the Center for Holocaust Documentation and Research, while also playing a pivotal role in the choreography of the Holocaust Museum in Washington. She supplied the photographs of her home shtetl, Eishyshok (the Lithuanian town of Eisisky) that make up the museum's Tower of Memory. In recent years, Eliach has taken the elegy of a vanished town another step by publishing a massive book that chronicles the thousand-year history of Eishyshok. Indeed, Brooklyn and Eishyshok form two poles of Eliach's life and work, the thriving life in the one sustaining her elegy to the extinguished life in the other.

Eliach takes pains to articulate her debt to Brooklyn. She notes, for instance, that Brooklyn has the highest proportion of Holocaust survivors in the world. Yet the contribution of Brooklyn is not only in numbers but also in access. Eliach enters the world of Hasidic survivors because of her Hasidic students at Brooklyn College. Brooklyn is thus singular in that it nurtures such a hybrid institution, where members of a traditional culture (Hasidic Jewry) attend a modern institution. "Perhaps," says Eliach, "only at Brooklyn College, can one find college students from such

a background." Brooklyn's elastic infrastructure enables the Eliach project to take shape.

Brooklyn also nourished tales: "More and more, the Hasidic community and its tales, the legends that grow in Brooklyn, have become part of my life." Like a garden, Brooklyn lets the tales that form the collection "grow," that is, emerge out of Brooklyn, nourished by it. Eliach's use of an organic metaphor shows how much of Brooklyn is in the tales. And as Eliach richly figures it in this metaphor, it is Brooklyn's nurturing role for the stories that allows her—someone who is not a Hasidic Jew and hence an outsider—to make the tales "grow" in her book. Seen in this way, both the book and Brooklyn provide the figurative soil in which the tales can "grow," spreading beyond the Hasidic community into the world at large.

The subject matter of the tales, concerned exclusively with the Holocaust, locates them in Europe: occasionally in ghettos, frequently in concentration camps, sometimes in the trains or forests that demonically linked one to the other. Yet Brooklyn gently intrudes, sometimes with a phrase, occasionally with more. After describing the remarkable lighting of a Hanukkah menorah coming on the heels of a "selection" in Bergen Belsen, for example, Eliach concludes with "some years later, the Rabbi of Bluzhov, now residing in Brooklyn, New York, received regards from Mr. Zamietchklowski," one of those in attendance at the lighting. Mr. Z's message also said that "the answer that he [the Rabbi] had given him that dark Hanukkah night in Bergen Belsen had stayed with him ever since, and was a constant source of inspiration during hard and troubled times." Reference to Brooklyn brings the story into the present, into a time and place that is both distinct from the ravages of the Holocaust and yet linked by memory to it. In effect, a conversation begun in the camp continues in Brooklyn—a Brooklyn alert to the consequences of what took place in the camps.

In another instance, the Rabbi of Bluzhov, the protagonist and source of many of the tales, has ended an emotional postwar meeting in London "and boarded the plane. That evening I prayed Maariv, the evening prayer, here at my beit midrash on 58th Street in Brooklyn. " The return to Brooklyn to "my beit midrash" conveys strongly the sense of a home, a place where the rich vitality of religious life now receives full expression. Brooklyn is the place of refuge, the secure zone where Hasidim can live a life of devotion in full flower. Moreover, it is also the site where the tales steeped in violence and deprivation can be told. The telling itself, the reflection back on a time of relentless trauma, signals that Brooklyn lies at the other end of the spectrum, a place from which the horror of Europe can be gauged.

This perception of America as a haven departs from an important strand of American Holocaust literature. Those writings paint America as equivalent to Europe in pathologies, showing Jews in America vulnerable to violent, and at times lethal, assault. In Philip Roth's "Eli the Fanatic" (1959), for example, the protagonist at first oppresses survivor refugees trying to move into his neighborhood. Eventually he comes to identify with them only to be himself drugged and institutionalized—a kind of American version of a concentration camp. In Saul Bellow's *Mr. Sammler's Planet* (1970), New York City in the 1960s epitomizes America's assault on civilized values, an assault that echoes the frenzy of prewar Europe. Ultimately, the protagonist, a Polish-Jewish survivor, is himself attacked in his apartment building. Finally, Cynthia Ozick's "Rosa" (1977) provides a culminating fantasy of equivalence, where the most brutal forces of Europe—Hitler and Stalin—are outdone by the arbitrary but pervasive violence of America. "Just look," says Simon Persky, as he reads his Yiddish newspaper:

Just look, first he has Hitler, then he has Stalin, he's in a camp in Siberia. Next thing he gets away to Sweden, then he comes to New York and he peddles. He's a peddler, by now he's got a wife, he's got kids, so he opens a little store. . . . And they come in early in the morning, he didn't even hang out his shopping bags yet, robbers, muggers, and they choke him, they finish him off. From Siberia, he lives for this day. (17–18)

This account sees America as sequentially complicit, as it were, with the worst evils of totalitarian Europe. In contrast, *Hasidic Tales* steers away from any analogue between the two continents. Representing America, Brooklyn is hospitable, dynamic, benign, conducive. Having absorbed the refugee survivors en masse, Brooklyn keeps the evils of Europe contained within the legends that it grows.

This is not however always an easy task, as the two tales in Brooklyn attest. Both feature survivors living in Brooklyn in the 1970s and show that what is taken for granted by the normal citizen is precious to the survivor. The tale "To Marry a Baker" takes place, despite its title, not at a wedding but at a bar mitzvah. Eliach begins by emphasizing the Brooklyn setting, which plays a vital role in the story.

Despite the New World setting, all but one of the main characters in the tale are Holocaust survivors. Full of life and joy, the survivors here nevertheless bear the physical and emotional weight of those events, and, in the midst of celebrations, recount stories about that period:

Next to me [Eliach] sat a vivacious blond with a sense of humor who introduced herself as Tula Friedman. . . . When the music interfered with our conversation, she asked me to raise my voice since her hearing was impaired in one ear. "A souvenir from an Auschwitz beating," she explained to me while pointing to her ear. (206)

Tula then "recalled the event, blow by blow . . . describing various episodes related to that beating and its aftermath." It is surely an abrupt move from Brooklyn celebration to Auschwitz beating. But within the tale, the shift seems almost natural, an effortless flow between one reality and another, the Brooklyn festivity cushioning, if not dissipating, the pain from the past. It is as if the Brooklyn celebration allows an ironic distance from which such stories can be told.

The motif of the marriage surfaces in the second part of the tale, connected to bread—its abundance or deprivation. "There was especially one recurring dream that one day I would marry a baker and in our house there would always be an abundance of bread." Tula never does literally marry a baker. But "the abundance of bread" at the Brooklyn bar mitzvah celebration clearly fulfills her dream. In this sense, the tale envisions a symbolic "marriage" of Tula to Brooklyn itself, that is, to the source of an ongoing abundance of what is vital to life.

But the waiter moves to a different drummer than the survivors:

A waiter came to the table with a basket of assorted breads. Tula closed her eyes and inhaled the aroma of freshly baked bread as one inhales the sweet smells of a bouquet of freshly cut flowers. She passed the basket to me without taking any.

When none of the survivors at the table choose to eat from the basket, it becomes clear that Tula's restraint is also a souvenir from Auschwitz. The waiter however does not catch on:

The bread on the table was still untouched. The waiter came again to the table. "Ladies, I see that you are not hungry today." "Not today," replied Tula, "and not ever again."

Tula's aphoristic response—"not ever again"—shows that the survivors' decision is not a fleeting impulse but an enduring condition. The waiter, not connected to the survivors' world, continues one last time to go through the motions:

> The waiter was about to remove the bread. "Leave it on the table," said another woman. "There is nothing more reassuring in this world than having a basket of freshly baked bread on the table in front of you."

Brooklyn cannot restore appetites that were suppressed in Auschwitz. But it can provide a "basket of freshly baked bread," a symbol of abundance which confirms that the Brooklyn the survivors now inhabit is light-years away from the world they left behind.

A much darker tale than the first, "The Road to Mother" is also set in postwar Brooklyn. Mrs. Gross, an Auschwitz survivor, runs a successful Brooklyn grocery, at which Eliach shops on Mother's Day. Mrs. Gross tells Eliach of her dream of trying unsuccessfully to reach her own mother. She eventually dreams that she reaches her, but the dream is associated with the stillborn birth of her child. Finally, Mrs. Gross recounts the last moments of seeing her mother at Auschwitz and receiving the news of her murder. As the tale shifts back to present-day Brooklyn, one hears that, for Mrs. Gross, Mother's Day is impossible. For Eliach, in contrast, the tale of brutal loss and haunting presence has the opposite effect, making her appreciate the mother that she is.

Again, as in "To Marry a Baker," a repeated dream is pivotal. But in this story it is horribly corrosive. Once Mrs. Gross begins her monologue, it takes over, leaving Brooklyn behind and entering fully the dreamworld that is the legacy of Auschwitz.

The story turns around a terrible irony: the yearning for her deceased mother is intense, and the reader longs as Mrs. Gross does to consummate the journey on the "road to mother." She finally reaches her mother: "There was no end to my joy as we hugged and kissed each other." But the association between reaching her mother and losing her child seems tantamount to arriving at a zone of death, a place that infects whatever touches it with the evil of the death camp.

The tone of the dream reminds Mrs. Gross of her arrival in Auschwitz, and she concludes with what is clearly the most brutal scene, the moment she learns of her mother's murder:

> That night, my first at Auschwitz, I asked the Czech stubhova [barracks supervisor] about my mother. The healthy-looking stubhova grabbed me by the hand, pulled me to the door of the barracks, and pointed to the chimneys: "There is your mother." (208–209)

Only now, having reached a point of no return—the place and time where mothers were not celebrated but annihilated—can the story come back to the Brooklyn store and to the Mother's Day meeting between Eliach and Mrs. Gross. "For some, it is Mother's Day today. For others, it will never be."

Time does not heal these wounds, but only intensifies suffering. But if time fails to achieve its end, place—Brooklyn—offers at least a tolerable zone, an arena where one can be "successful," busy, useful, more or less at home. To be sure, as Eliach's rendering of the story shows, Brooklyn cannot hope to compensate for such violation; once Mrs. Gross begins to count her losses, her story takes over, making Auschwitz more tangible than the Brooklyn where she now is. But Brooklyn doggedly returns at the tale's end, refusing, as it were, to let Auschwitz have the final say.

Notes on the Celebration of Purim in Williamsburg

JACK KUGELMASS

Just before setting out for Brooklyn I receive some pointers from an Orthodox secretary at my office in Manhattan on where to see costumed children delivering *shalekhmones* (the fruits and candies that religious Jews exchange on the day of Purim). She suggests I wear a yarmulke ". . . to fit in better." When I pull one out of my pocket and place it on my head, she begins to giggle. How strange I must appear to her, masquerading as an observant Jew. How strange, too, that having long ago abandoned her disdain for non-Orthodox men, she has now become my co-conspirator, teaching me how to infiltrate her world. Only later do I learn that as a non-Hasid and a daughter of Polish Jews, she too is an outsider in Williamsburg. I learn this only through a conversation I have with her about television. She wants to know what I watch and then reveals she has one at home, too: "I keep it in the bedroom. This way if a neighbor comes by, they don't need to know I have one. I wouldn't say no. But I don't need to advertise it also." "What do you watch?" I ask. "*Dynasty* I like. And I like *The Newlywed Game.*"

I head out to Williamsburg, the home of the seemingly reclusive Hungarian Hasidim. With me is an Israeli who has come to America to make a film on Yiddish for the BBC. We emerge from the elevated train and, seeing the many bearded Jews surrounded by a cityscape of shop signs in Yiddish and Hebrew, my Israeli friend comments jokingly: "There are only Jews in America!" We spot some children in costume and begin to take photographs. Someone advises us to head to Lee Avenue. We do so and see scores of Hasidic children in costume: bears, witches, humpbacks, trolls, Arabs, Ronald Reagan, policemen, old Jewish men with canes and lengthy beards or bent-over women, Torah scrolls, Disney characters. Perhaps, on this day, we will not be conspicuous in this forest of long black coats, with their foliage of fur-trimmed hats. We follow the crowds along Lee Avenue, photographing as we go. Some people move away from the camera. Here and there someone warns us not to take pictures: "It's not permitted." A few pose. Others ask why we are shooting: "For somebody or just for yourself?" "For myself," I reply. "Good. *A gut Purim* to you." Many opinions even here, in this Ultra-Orthodox community.

I continue photographing. A young Hasid in costume, holding a large wad of dollar bills, approaches and asks for money. The proceeds, I later learn, are for charitable work here and in Israel. He is very aggressive in his approach,

Hasidim celebrating Purim in Orthodox Brooklyn in 1985. Photo by Jack Kugelmass.

the result of a deeply rooted Jewish belief that since the giving of alms saves one from death, charity is a gift of sorts from the recipient to the donor. The costumes are apparently closely linked to soliciting alms. Jews believe that the highest form of charity is when neither the giver nor the recipient know one another; the masks promote anonymity. But charity on Purim has a special meaning. Haman, the ancient persecutor of Persian Jews, offered the king a large sum of money for the privilege of killing the Jews. The giving of charity is an inversion of that act, a transformation of a profane cause into a holy deed. Later in the evening I will visit the Satmar *besmedresh* (study hall) to witness the rebbe *firn a tish* (conduct a ritual meal). Even the much-cherished voice of a rebbe cannot silence these solicitors, armed to the teeth with zeal, displaying ever growing wads of bills. Not all who beg do so in the name of others. Outside the Satmar *besmedresh* sits a beggar. Today he is king: all who enter or leave are obliged to greet his outstretched hand with money. Him I avoid, but the young boys with their wads of bills are relentless. I give the one who hounds me two quarters. He pockets the money and stares at the camera: "What kind is it?" "A Minolta." "How much does it cost?" Something deep within causes me to flaunt an extravagance, a gentile's pleasure: "Six hundred." "Six hundred?" The astonishment in his voice betrays the fact that the revelation has had the intended effect. "So it's a professional?" "Yes." "I have a Canon Program. It's good?" "Yes. It's

good." "Where did you buy this, at 47th St.?" "No." "Why not?" "They don't sell it there." The question sounded like an accusation. I guess his thoughts: What kind of Jew buys retail? A real Jew purchases cameras and electronic products from 47th St. Photo, the Hasidic discount emporium located in the heart of the Hasidic-dominated diamond exchange in midtown Manhattan. Perhaps he thinks I am so deracinated that I lack even this bit of knowledge. And I wonder about him and the community. Why does he have a camera? And such costumes among people who shun television—do the children know anything about the cartoon characters they masquerade? I photograph a husband and wife walking with a large fruit basket for *shalekhmones*. Trailing a few feet behind them is their little girl, clad head to toe in a witch costume. An odd family.

Later I notice a Hasidic family out for a stroll. The woman pushing a baby stroller, as all Hasidic women seem to do, greets others, while the man is busy videotaping the children in costume. A non-Hasidic Orthodox young man approaches. "Are you here for a magazine or just for yourself?" "Just for myself." "That's good. I suppose you came to take pictures of the burning?" "What burning?" "Burning the Israeli flag! Every year Satmar burns the Israeli flag. I took about ten pictures, just to document it." The man proudly waves his Instamatic camera in my face, as if I could verify somehow that inside it he has captured a still-flickering flame of heresy in Jewish

Hasidim celebrating Purim in Orthodox Brooklyn in 1985. Photo by Jack Kugelmass.

cultural history, anti-Zionism. A Skverer Hasid I meet later whose apartment is decorated with Israeli "folk art" depicting Jerusalem and the Western Wall would not consider a Satmar for a son-in-law because he has trouble with anyone who would look down on him. "They make a religion out of anti-Zionism." He explains that the protest, although done by extremists, has its merits: "Should a state insist that corpses be defiled with autopsies? Should it allow missionaries to build a campus on Mount Scopus?" I respond with diplomatic silence. The Hasid insists the protest is against the policies of the state, not against its existence. I, however, see it differently: this is a public demonstration. Satmar's protest is probably aimed directly at American Jewish "false gods," the so-called civil religion implicitly guiding American Jewish beliefs and behavior. The sociologist Jonathan Woocher (1985) argues that there are seven elements to that civil religion: among them are charity, mutual aid, a sense that there is an ever present threat to group survival, the Holocaust, and the centrality of the state of Israel. I, the anthropologist, absorbed in the harmless masquerade of children, missed the serious spectacle of adult men burning a flag in protest. Had I spoken to someone sooner, I too could have documented it. The camera, I realize, sets a barrier between me and this community. Only dialogue will give me entry into their world. Fortunately I am running out of film. And fortunately too, as the folklorist Barbara Kirshenblatt-Gimblett has noted, the "spontaneous" dem-

onstration is an annual event at 3:00 P.M. on the day of Purim. This too I will see another year.

My new acquaintance has no more time for conversation. His ride comes for him, and he is on his way back to Boro Park. "If you come tonight to Boro Park, perhaps I will see you," he shouts as the car drives off. Later that night I and a photographer friend stand by the side of an access road to the Brooklyn Queens Expressway and hitch a ride. This is a common way of commuting between the two neighborhoods. We are picked up by a Hasid wearing a plastic fireman's helmet. When we reach Boro Park it is nearly 1:00 A.M. The Hasid drives his other passengers to their destinations. Then, using a bullhorn, he announces to an inebriated pedestrian that he is looking for the Bobov *besmedresh*. The startled pedestrian, it turns out, is the Hasid's brother. He wobbles into the van and slumps into the front passenger seat. The Hasid looks at us and says with a mixture of sarcasm and apology, "Don't mind him. He's a little under the influence." "It's Purim," I respond. "It's OK to be stoned." "Oh, I wouldn't call him stoned. He's more like pebbled." Purim is one of the few times each year when drunkenness is prescribed, and the more zealous Hasidim assume the task with such vigor that in a short time they are quite unable to carry themselves and move about only if they are supported by their friends. Those without such aid often fall, and every once in a while unlucky individuals are brought to hospitals to repair broken bones.

Hasidim celebrating Purim in
Orthodox Brooklyn in 1985.
Photo by Jack Kugelmass.

Boro Park is the turf of the non-Hungarian Hasidic groups, and many Ultra-Orthodox non-Hasidim. It is a thriving neighborhood. With its strip of kosher pizza parlors, dairy restaurants, and discount electronic equipment emporia it is less charming and more worldly than Williamsburg. (There are smaller electronic shops in Williamsburg—local places that cater to natives rather than strangers. The only pizza in Williamsburg is served in a drab falafel joint. Watching a Hasid twirling dough in the air may be the only redeeming feature of dining out in the area.) What Boro Park lacks in physical charm is more than made up for by the annual Purim plays performed inside the study houses of the Hasidic courts of Munkacz and Bobov. The former boasts a huge new building with a Jerusalem stonelike interior; the latter is held in a drab fifties-style building, its grand new headquarters still under construction (the many failings of the contractor have already made their way into the play). The performance begins well after midnight, only after the completion of the *tish*, the ritual meal over which the rebbe presides, and continues until the early hours of the morning. By then I will have tired of the event, the pushing for a place to stand, the craning of the neck to see above the fur-trimmed hats, and the terrible feeling that my academic Yiddish will not suffice, that I can have only a peek at a culture's innermost presentation of itself.

In Williamsburg I continue along Lee Avenue, alone now, having lost my Israeli friend. Here and there I see young Hasidic men in costumes less elaborate than the children's: a police baton and matching hat, a Mexican bandanna, a straw hat. One or two look inebriated. A few Hasidim carry ghetto blasters blaring pop renditions of Hasidic and religious music. The same music can be heard emanating from the projects, occupied in this area by Jews more than by blacks and Puerto Ricans. I learn later from a Puerto Rican director of a non-Jewish YMCA about the formula the respective communities have worked out with the city for distributing available public housing. There is room for compromise: Hasidim prefer to live on lower-level floors because they will not ride in elevators on *shabes*; Puerto Ricans believe Hasidim are better able to wield political clout than they are, so having them in the building guarantees better maintenance.

The loud music contributes to the sense of cultural reversal. Now Puerto Rican neighbors are accosted by loud strange-sounding music. Couples accompanied by children are out for a stroll, with prepackaged parcels of *shalekhmones* wrapped in bright yellow, orange, or green cellophane. I follow them as they head away from the main avenue onto the side streets. Here the beautiful old brownstones, the once fashionable homes of a nineteenth-century gentry, are being transformed into dwellings more suited to Jewish life. Balconies are being added to the facades, making space to construct the outdoor makeshift abodes for the annual Sukkot festival. They are strangely asymmetrical, since, to open toward the sky, they cannot

Hasidim celebrating Purim in Orthodox Brooklyn in 1985. Photo by Jack Kugelmass.

be stacked one upon the other. But now other changes are for style and comfort, and they reflect, too, the impact of the outside world.

Each Hasidic neighborhood has its own social ecology. Williamsburg is home to Puerto Ricans as well as Hasidim. Crown Heights, the Lubavitcher's turf, is home to a large West Indian community. Boro Park is entirely occupied by Jews, but it borders on a middle-class Italian neighborhood. The transformation of simple brick or clapboard structures into gaudy flat stone facades looks to me like a design conspiracy of southern Italian contractors and Jewish homeowners. In Williamsburg, the changes reflect the encroachment of suburban design on an ancient city neighborhood; Satmar has relocated part of its community to Monsey; Skver to New Square; Pupa to Ossining. Old narrow windows with classical finials are being replaced by wide picture windows. As it turns dark, I can see inside the homes, each with a long table covered with a white lace tablecloth, itself covered with clear plastic. Two lit candles are perched on top of tall silver candlesticks. A challah and bottles of kosher wine and Slivovitz are on the table. Although most Jews treat Purim as a minor holiday, Purim is a major festival for Hasidim and they celebrate it accordingly, with ritual garb, festive meal, and a rebbe's *tish*. I, a secular Jew, envy them. I would like to enter one of those homes and wash my hands in preparation for the Purim *sude* [feast].

I return to Lee Avenue, where I see my old friend Joel Cahen busily snapping photographs. Joel and I were graduate students together: he, a Dutchman, and I, a Canadian, had both come to New York to study the language and culture of eastern European Jewry. Later, Joel moved back to Amsterdam, where he codirected the Jewish Historical Museum. He is in New York this week on official business (New York, after all, was once called New Amsterdam, and the Jewish connection with the city's European namesake is kept alive in archives and cemetery tombstones), and he had agreed to look for me in Williamsburg. We continue together. The sun has gone down, and I am now freezing and famished; I insist on entering a bakery in search of warmth and food. The store is everything a kosher bakery should be: it is dark, with antiquated wood and metal shelving, and a pungent smell of fresh pastry wafts through the room. I point to some Danish and in Yiddish ask for two. The old, hunched-over baker mumbles something and then, in a stiff cranelike movement that betrays the countless times he has done the same task today, scoops them up with a piece of waxed paper. He begins hunting for a bag, but I tell him there is no need. Once outside the store we devour the Danish as we walk. Another year I went to the same bakery with a friend. We ordered coffee, and the owner's son put each container into a medium-size white paper bag. Once outside, I tossed the bag into a garbage bin, but my friend examined it carefully while she sipped her coffee, then held it up to my face so I could read the blue print that read "FOR MOTION SICKNESS,

Hasidim celebrating Purim in Orthodox Brooklyn in 1985. Photo by Jack Kugelmass.

CAPITOL AIRLINES." This rather unaesthetic juxtaposition made me think of a nearby store: one side had counters of freshly slaughtered meat, the other side had shelves of luggage. It looks like a joke performed. A degree of sensual coarseness finds its way into undainty Jewish renditions of Polish pierogi and Chinese egg rolls. But baking is another matter, and simple Jewish breads and pastries offer welcome relief from an otherwise ordinary cuisine.

Kosher baked goods often do not contain dairy products; they then can be served together with meat without violating religious proscriptions. The chocolate filling of the pastry Joel and I eat is rich and dark, conforming to both the laws of *kashres* and contemporary tastes. Taking great pleasure in the bittersweet chocolate flavor, I am oblivious now to my surroundings, and I am taken completely by surprise when we are suddenly accosted by a hefty Hasid, unsteady on his feet, accompanied by two children. The man is in his late thirties. He is stout, with a full brown beard streaked with gray. His mouth seems to foam as Yiddish sentences splatter off his lips. "Have you made the blessings for the holiday?" "Yes, we have," I lie. Apparently shared ethnicity permits this invasion of each other's turf. I ease my conscience by reminding myself that such small deceptions for the sake of Jewish ethnography are hardly my own invention. When the Yiddish playwright and folklorist Sh. Ansky conducted his ethnographic expedition to

the small Jewish towns in the Ukraine shortly before World War I, lying became a prime way of eliciting data from otherwise difficult informants, particularly the elderly women who provided charms and incantations to people in need (Rekhtman 1958). Besides, Joel and I are both wearing yarmulkes. To admit to not making the blessings would betray the masquerade. I pray that the Hasid does not probe. Apparently God is listening, because the Hasid accepts what I tell him at face value. "Good," the Hasid responds. "Our rebbe, Rabbi Teitleboim, has explained the importance of Jews reciting the blessings. That's how to bring the Messiah. Not Peres or Begin you should believe in. They're just like the Amelikites. You must believe in God and recite the blessings. When the Messiah comes then we'll all be in the land of Israel."

As the man talks the two children tug at his sleeve. They are in a hurry to go somewhere. The father is in no hurry to leave. He has a message he wants to relate to us. "Where do you live?" he asks. "Amsterdam," my friend answers first. "Amsterdam? Do you know rabbi so and so?" "Yes." An instant bond. "And you, too, are from Amsterdam?" "No, no. I live in New York. " "New York? What part of New York?" "Manhattan. The Village." "Manhattan?" But this time there is no connection. Manhattan is a remote island, much farther from this Hasidic enclave in Brooklyn than faraway Amsterdam is. One day a cartoonist will draw

a map of the world as seen through Hasidic eyes. Manhattan will be reduced to a small sliver labeled "47th St.," the heart of the Hasidic-dominated diamond exchange. Brooklyn will loom large, only slightly smaller than Jerusalem. Between them will be Paris and London (very small by comparison with the more illustrious American and Israeli cities), then Antwerp. Here and there a city will appear because within it resides a great rabbi.

Fortunately, the *skhus* (merit) of a great rabbi of Amsterdam Jewry seems to apply to me too. Friends of the Hasid stop to greet him. He introduces both Joel and me as "Jews from Amsterdam." "Where is everyone off to?" I ask, watching scores of people heading down Lee Avenue. "Home." "Are they off to a *sude*?" "Yes, to a *sude*." "Could we see one?" "You want to see a *sude*? Of course! Come with me I'll take you to a *sude*." The Hasid grabs us both by the arm and pulls us in the direction he was headed. "Come, I will take you to my father-in-law's." The Hasid has called my bluff. I would like to see a *sude*, not take part in one. I look at Joel, hoping that he will intervene and invent some excuse, a previous engagement perhaps. Joel does no such thing. He, after all, is here to experience American Jewry. This will be an event, a souvenir to take back with him to Amsterdam, to heighten the meaning of the snapshots he is taking. Together they will form a collection, a private museum on contemporary Judaism. After all, he is a curator, and assembling dioramas of oddities is his stock-in-trade. But for me, the anthropologist, there is a great sense of

risk here. I feel less secure about the nature of the enterprise because anthropology does not lend itself to casual encounters. Besides, I am worried that my ruse will be exposed, that the Hasid will see who I am behind the yarmulke mask. But the Hasid insists we go with him. And so I go, to please him and to please Joel, and much to my surprise, to please myself too.

We turn off Lee Avenue, then head down a side street, entering the first apartment building we come to. I tell the Hasid that we can stay only for a few minutes. "Maybe just for a kiddush," I suggest. "As long as you like. As long as you like." The Hasid is breathing heavily, panting as he climbs the flights of stairs in this old five-story walk-up. "No one's going to keep you here. Maybe you think I'm a little strange because I am drunk. So I want to apologize. Today is Purim and we are supposed to get drunk. I've had maybe a liter and a half of wine. But now it's wearing off and I'm not so drunk anymore." At the end of a dark corridor there is a tan-colored door smeared with shellac for a wood-grain look. He pushes open the unlocked door, marches us down a hallway covered in badly frayed linoleum, and announces to the women preparing food in the kitchen and to his father-in-law seated at the dining table that he has brought guests for dinner. The old man cuts a striking image, ensconced in a seat at the head of the table. He smiles approvingly and with such benevolence that, with his flowing white beard and ruddy complexion, he's a dead ringer for Santa Claus. The illusion is shattered the moment the old man speaks his Hungarian Yiddish. I do not understand the question he asks. The son-in-law explains: "He wants to know if you want to wash your hands." I understand that he is referring to ritual, not hygiene. I say yes, and we head to the kitchen, where one of the children fills a silver two-handled container with water and leaves it in the sink. I pour the water over the fingers of each hand three times. I refill the container and leave it in the sink for Joel. He repeats the ceremony. The boy points to a roll of paper towels hanging from a wall, then he escorts us back to the dining room. The father recites the blessings over challah, cuts it, dips it into salt, then bites off a piece. We are instructed to do the same, and although I have seen and performed this very simple ceremony many times before, I am uncomfortably aware now that there are details that I am not sure of. Must the challah be dipped in the salt, or may the salt be sprinkled on the challah? Can I ask questions now or must I be silent until all the men have performed the ritual? I dip without asking questions. I resent my ignorance, less because it impedes my work than because it demands constant vigilance. I cannot hide behind a mask of knowing. That too has its advantages. I must accept my lot as inferior to my host. I am to be his apprentice. We sit down and the food is brought out, the father served first, the guests second, and the family next. The women do not sit at the table. They serve, then eat separately in a second room adjacent to the dining room. My initial fear that we have usurped their places recedes as I realize that besides the ritually prescribed separation of men and women, logistics alone make the two rooms necessary. Even without us, the house is overflowing with people. My Hasidic friend has nine children, not unusual in this community, and we are joined shortly by his brother-in-law with the same number of children. I am curious to know more about these people, and I ask if I might pose some questions. My Hasid friend explains that Passover is the holiday when questions are asked, but I can ask now, too; he is referring to the questions the youngest child asks at the seder. And he is referring, too, to the fact that Purim and Passover are closely linked, both temporally and thematically. Both signal the special relationship between God and Israel, that peculiar combination of nationhood and religion that characterizes Judaism. More ignorant than the children of the household, I am now the youngest. I accept the demotion in age because through it I can dispense entirely with the masquerade and become a harmless ignoramus rather than a dangerous skeptic.[1] This meal will be a seder for me. The questions go only one way. The Hasid has little interest in me and the world I live in. "Were you born here?" I ask. "No. In Rumania. Then I lived in Israel for twenty years. I came here four years ago." "You live in Williamsburg?" "No. In Monroe. We have a Satmar community there." "What kind of work do you do?" "I correct manuscripts of holy books that are being published." "A proofreader?" "No. Not a proofreader. I have to check the original to make sure there are no mistakes in the manuscript, and I check the typeset copy to see that it, too, is accurate. I also write for our newspaper, *Der Yid*." I tell him that we have something in common, that I, too, do some journalism. He gives no response, an indication that he sees no connection between his sacred work and the profane work I do. But that realization comes to me much later. On this night I am caught within the magic spell of the encounter, and I take the lack of response as a positive response. The attempt to establish a common bond between us is unnecessary; I tell myself it is already evident by the invitation to join the family for the *sude*, and by the gracious way we are being treated. Our hosts insist that we pour ourselves soda, or wine, that we cut off pieces of challah, and they offer us additional helpings. More food is out of the question. Both Joel and I are big eaters, but even our prodigious appetites are appeased by what we are given: an hors-d'oeuvre of dense, salty gefilte fish, chicken soup with thin noodles, and meat kreplakh, an entrée of boiled chicken, roast beef, stuffed cabbage, and a spicy stuffed derma side dish, followed by a dessert of stewed fruit.

The stuffed cabbage and kreplakh are traditional Purim dishes but my hosts are unable to explain why: "Why? Cabbage is the season." What does this mean? I repeat the question but make no further progress. Later, another Hasid will explain the meaning: Purim has none of the restrictions that normally accompany a Jewish holy day. One can work, cook, and travel. Yet it is a significant holiday for Hasidim, its importance hidden, and therefore it is proper to eat foods that likewise hide their inner selves. Tonight, despite my questions, I cannot turn the occasion into an ethnographic interview. What for me is an entry into an exotic world is for my host a chance to fulfill the mitzvah of hospitality to a sojourner. So I must accept the fact and be grateful for it, and be grateful, too, for their otherness, for it is that which draws me to them.

Between courses my Hasid prods his children into joining him in singing Hasidic songs. They sing loudly: their voices are meant to reach the ears of neighboring families and perhaps with luck or just force of will of God, too. The melody is simple and the voices pounce upon it like swimmers to a wave. Now they ride with it and a harmony emerges. Then they fall back into the ebb and it seems as if their voices are about to be swept out to sea. Content to listen and accept my lot as their Purim mitzvah, I think: here we are, Jews from Canada, from Holland, from Hungary, from Rumania and Israel, celebrating together in America the holiday of Purim. We are as different from each other as night is from day and yet I, the non-Jewish Jew, feel perfectly entitled to sit here with them. I try without success to make the encounter serve my own purpose. They, Jews from a faraway time, enveloped within a world very much of their own fabrication, feel entitled to use me, too, for their own ends, to have me say the holiday blessings and work with them to bring on the Messiah. How odd it seems that this ethnographic encounter should join together Judaism's disparate segments. And yet through the encounter the parameters of the whole are defined not as a unified thing, for that American Jewry cannot be (nor could any ethnic group be that in modern society), but rather at certain moments such as these, as an emerging dialogue of the parts. Like all ethnicity within contemporary society, Jewishness is a turning inward, an alternate system of meaning in which "power" and "wealth" are constructed fictively through a system quite different from that used by the normative majority. But Judaism is also a text. And all of us bring to it our separate social universes through which we interpret the text's meaning.[2] What unites us is the commitment to dialogue, the belief that we are entitled to infringe upon each other's autonomy as if one could, indeed, as if one were compelled to define through argument what is a Jew: the observant Jew feels he has a mission to reach out to a fellow Jew and bring him into the fold, his way of bringing on the Messiah; the secular Jew seeks the "quintessential" Jew in the Hasid, turning to him, in part perhaps in much the same way that American Jews turn to the rabbis to be the exemplary Jews, the guarantors that Judaism will continue to exist despite the assimilation of the many. And there is in part, too, a quality here of going back in time, a turning inward on a temporal dimension, to an older, that is, an authentic Judaism. Anthropology may never entirely shed its sense that the subject of its study is separated from the field's practitioners through time, that one is more "primitive" than the other (Fabian 1983). Nor are we who study Jews less time-bound in our formulations. Indeed, herein lies the great dilemma of Jewish eth-

nography: the problematic nature of encountering the Other cannot be transcended, no matter how close the observer feels himself to be to the subject of study. As James Clifford (1986) suggests, ethnography has an allegorical quality to it. We are looking for a more authentic self, and who more so than those who would study their own? But if making subjects into historical relics is our way of making sense out of otherness, they, that is, our subjects, are not bound by such formulations, even when we have subjugated them politically. So they respond to us not as relics but as equals or as our betters, determined to define in ways that suit them the nature of our interaction, the point to our dialogue, sometimes even as co-writers of the ethnographic text so that they might tell their story to a broader world. The Hasid who has read Lis Harris's *Holy Days* welcomes my visits: perhaps he thinks I can explain his group to outsiders much the way Lis Harris did the Lubavitcher.

Strangely, it is through the dimension of time that the Hasid, too, sees himself bound to the secular Jew: if one seeks to reclaim the past, the other seeks to alter the future; when all Jews obey the commandments, the Messiah will appear. Argument between us is possible because of a deeply rooted belief on both our parts that even though we do not share a common present we share a common history, and in our separate ways we believe that we will share a common destiny. And there is another bond here. Judaism is a combination of blood and custom. But if custom involves problematical issues, given the great multiplicity of Judaisms in modern times, blood is less problematical. The Hasid has his own way of looking at this. When I tell a Skverer Hasid that my father's father came to Montreal from a small town in Galicia, he demands to know its name. I tell him that it's not a well-known place, that he's probably never heard of it. "How do you know?" he asks. "Horodenka," I respond expecting only a blank look. "Horodenka?" he responds animatedly. "You've heard of it?" I ask surprised. "Of course! I can even show you where it is on the map." Horodenka, he explains, figures prominently in Hasidic rabbinic genealogy. "It is possible that your grandfather was a Skverer Hasid." I am a soul finding its way back to its long-never-forgotten home. So I am accepted for an essential rather than existential me. The latter me he, too, sees as a relic soon destined for the junk pile of social history. By his reckoning, secular Judaism is crumbling. A poor bulwark against the tide of assimilation, it will be replaced by his way of being Jewish, just as my way once replaced his. We are like fortune-tellers, gazing at the future.

So dialogue between us is fraught with tension. There are expectations that cannot be met, attempts to categorize experience that are not right. But the problem of dialogue has much to do with the matter of agenda. I do not wish to become the Jew that he would have me be;[3] he insists I engage him in debate, to express my opinion, so that he might use the opportunity to explain his world and undermine mine. Yet when two Satmar students arrive at the door to solicit alms on Purim, there is no debate. He invites them in, offers them wine, which they take, and pastry, which they do not. They offer in return a *dvar toyre* (homily). When they have finished he offers one of his own, and when he is finished, they leave. Only then do I realize that he is more comfortable with me than he is with them. I ask him what they said, explaining that between the ghetto blaster blaring Hasidic music and their use of *loshn koydesh* (Hebrew-Aramaic, the language of holiness), I picked up maybe 5 percent of the *dvar toyre*. "That's pretty good," he responds, "I picked up maybe one percent."

A friend who introduced me to the Skverer Hasid is asked by the man why he is a vegetarian. "Is it for moral reasons or because you don't like the taste of meat?" "What's the difference?" I ask. "Well," the Hasid explains, "if it's for moral reasons then you are guilty of arrogance." "Why?" "Because there are four levels of things on earth. Things like stones, for example, which have no life. Things like grass, which are alive but have no consciousness. Animals such as cows, which have a limited consciousness. And man. Each is higher than the other. When it consumes the lower form, it also raises it beyond what it would achieve on its own. So when a man eats the flesh of a cow and derives from it the strength to perform a mitzvah, the cow benefits from the mitzvah, too. So if you refuse to eat meat for supposedly moral reasons, you're actually denying the cow the benefits it would attain. But if you abstain because you don't like the taste, that you're entitled to do."

Mythopoesis, I think to myself. I like the metaphorical imprint, but I am wary, nonetheless. Am I the cow that must be consumed? Is there no way for us to be together without one of us consuming the other? And then I think that this is not our dilemma alone; it occurs whenever cultures are in contact, no less so when ethnographer and informant meet. But there is here another level of meaning, because the interaction and its significance does not emerge from a tabula rasa; it encapsulates rather the his-

tory of Jewry and attempts to assert control over it. Indeed, those attempts are the driving force behind the emergence of ideologically based Jewish subcultures. Because they are revivalistic, they are expansionist; their legitimacy derives in large measure from the number of their adherents, from the extent of the larger group they embrace. So they attempt a cultural hegemony: their Judaism is the real Judaism; mine is not, although my soul is. Can I resist them?

The singing is seductive. Joel adds his voice to the others, humming when the words are not familiar. I am still hesitant to join in. Instead, I look around the room at these faces, the adults with their beards and cloaks, the children still displaying through greasepaint mustaches the fading traces of Purim. But I am entranced by a still-powerful sense of illusion: now I see in them not the strangeness of a separate existence but the almost familiar world of my own Galician ancestors, the grandparents on Esplanade Street at the foot of Mount Royal, whom I once feared because of their oldness, their otherness. How strange it seems that a one-day field trip should send me on such a long journey backward and rob me of a hard-won distance from the past. And yet I feel drawn to these Hasidim, not so much because of any real sense that through them I could reclaim a forgotten past, but rather out of admiration for their valor, for their suspension of disbelief. And then I think that I, too, must suspend disbelief—not so that I might become them—but because what exists between us is indeed meaningful, because the discomfort and the challenges have a purpose, because what we create in coming together represents a dialogue of cultures, a kind of bridge between two worlds, so that whatever the future holds in store, at the very least there remains through the work of this profession a trace of an old, vibrant, and cacophonous universe.[4]

NOTES

Research for this essay was made possible by a grant from the Wenner-Gren Foundation for Anthropological Research, Inc. It first appeared in an expanded version in Jack Kugelmass, *Between Two Worlds: Notes on Purim Among New York Jews* (Ithaca, N.Y.: Cornell University Press, 1985).

1. Charles Liebman (1974), the sociologist of religion, has identified a distinct pattern of ritual behavior and belief—a folk religion—among the nonelite, that is, those outside the rabbinate and Orthodox circles. Perhaps its most striking feature is the emergence of "kosher-style" food, which for many takes the place of food that actually meets the laws of *kashres*. When the Jewish hero of a recent Woody Allen film decides to convert to Catholicism, among the icons of his new identity are Wonder Bread and Hellman's mayonnaise. Marshall Sklare (Sklare and Green-

blum 1979), another observer of American Judaism, suggests that the religion of American Jews has moved significantly away from Judaism's traditional stress on sacramentalism. Indeed, most Jews believe that being a good Jew inheres in what you believe rather than in what you do and, in this sense, the religion and their way of celebrating Jewish holy days closely resemble the religion of moralism practiced by the majority's Christian culture.

2. For further elaboration of the concept of skeptic versus ignoramus see Janet Belcove-Shalin (1988).

3. For a discussion of this point in regard to the human sciences in general see Todorov (1984, 17).

4. For a discussion of Bakhtin's notion of constitutive duality as a source of enrichment in the human sciences, see Todorov (1984, 108–9).

REFERENCES

Belcove-Shalin, Janet. 1988. "Becoming More of an Eskimo: Fieldwork among the Hasidim of Boro Park." In *Between Two Worlds: Ethnographic Essays on American Jews*, ed. Jack Kugelmass, pp. 77–102. Ithaca, N.Y.: Cornell University Press.

Clifford, James. 1986. "On Ethnographic Allegory." In *Writing Culture: The Poetics and Politics of Ethnography*, ed. James Clifford and George Marcus. Berkeley: University of California Press.

Fabian, Johannes. 1983. *Time and the Other: How Anthropology Makes Its Object*. New York: Columbia University Press.

Harris, Lis. 1985. *Holy Days*. New York: Summit Books.

Liebman, Charles. 1974. "The Religion of American Jews." In *The Jew in American Society*, ed. Marshall Sklare. New York: Behrman House.

Rekhtman, Avrom. 1958. *Yidishe etnografye un folklor*. Buenos Aires: Yivo.

Sklare, Marshall, and J. Greenblum. 1979. *Jewish Identity on the Suburban Frontier*. Chicago: University of Chicago Press.

Todorov, Tzvetan. 1984. *Mikhail Bakhtin: The Dialogical Principle*. Minneapolis: University of Minnesota Press.

Woocher, Jonathan. 1985. "Sacred Survival." *Judaism* 34, 2:151–62.

Holy Rolling
Making Sense of Baking Matzo

EVE JOCHNOWITZ

For fully six months of every year, sixty or so men and women work full-time in a small bakery in Brooklyn to make a product that will be valuable for eight days. The fragile matzos made here will be consumed at Passover seders worldwide, and the performance of matzo-making in the factory will be followed with great interest by visitors who come every week to take part in the Hassidic Discovery Welcome Center tours of Lubavitcher Crown Heights, directed by Rabbi Beryl Epstein (Epstein, n.d.).

As stringent as the everyday practices of observant Jews appear to the casual observer, they are several orders of magnitude removed from the full-fledged hysteria that accompanies the preparation for the Passover holiday. Rabbi Epstein comments, "We are commanded not to become too overwrought in carrying out mitzvahs, but for Passover, you can go crazy."

Kashres, or the Jewish dietary laws, are the laws that most fully sculpt the aesthetics of the everyday life of observant Jews. Every bite of food at any time of day recarves the law into the very body of the diner. The cryptic and complicated prohibitions of Leviticus regarding animal food have been expanded by centuries of rabbinic commentary to apply to almost any food one might encounter. Any food that has been handled, processed, or packaged must be subject to strict rabbinic supervision, and even raw fruits and vegetables, theoretically the kosherest foods there could be, must also be meticulously examined for bugs and dirt.

A vast literature exists of commentary expounding the actual practice of observing the laws of *kashres*. Every detail that can be thought up related to the preparation and handling of food is discussed not just in sacred texts written by Talmudic scholars but in the introductions to cookbooks that will be used by the women who cook the food themselves. No amount of rabbinic supervision can make food kosher if the cook who handles it is the least bit ignorant or careless. In the Jewish home, it is the housewife who is the ultimate *mashgiakh*.

In a matzo bakery, the *masgiakh* guards against *hametz*. The narrowest definition of *hametz* is grain that has been in contact with moisture for more than eighteen minutes. More broadly, *hametz* refers to any grain product at all except matzo itself, any oils or derivatives from any grain product, including the starches and glues in many paper plates, any leavening agent, any food or utensil that has come into contact with any of the above. Another category of food avoided during Passover is food that is not specifically permitted for Passover—a potentially huge class of foods. Bananas may have become unkosher in St. Louis in the last century because a new rabbi, just over from Europe, who had never seen a banana asked, "For eight days you can't live without this?"

Banning bananas, to be sure, is an extreme case, but it is not without parallels in contemporary Passover literature. *The Spice and Spirit of Kosher-Passover Cooking* (Lubavitch Women's Organization 1981) states, "It is the custom not to use any garlic, fresh or ground," and "It is the custom in many communities not to use spices." If you can find a community that forbids a particular ingredient during Passover, it is considered safest and most inclusive to follow along—when in doubt, throw it out. Since the holiday is only eight days long, no prohibition is all that cumbersome.

The holiday is preceded by a thorough search of the home and any other property where *hametz* might possibly have been left. Once the cleaning of the house is complete, and every part of the house has been searched for *hametz*, a ritual search is performed by all members of the household on the evening before the first night of Passover. The search party finds a small amount of *hametz* that has been left out for just this purpose and burns it the following morning after reading a declaration that any *hametz* that has not been destroyed is nullified (Fredman 1981).

These restrictions might give the impression that Passover is a time of hardship or deprivation analogous to Lent, Ramadan, or any period of fasting and penitence, but nothing could be further from the truth. Passover is a joyful and very auspicious holiday when the inconveniences of being deprived of everyday foods are more than offset by the excitement and anticipation associated with Passover foods, and by far the most important, relevant, polysemous, and even delicious of these is matzo.

MATZO

After the preparations for Pesach are complete, and the house cleaned of all *chometz*, we are ready to usher in the Yom Tov of Pesach, with its many special laws and customs. Of all the laws of Pesach it is the *mitzva* to eat matzo which truly encompasses the teachings of Pesach, reflecting both the history of the holiday and our own personal involvement in the Yom Tov.
(Lubavitch Women's Organization 1981)

The foods that are called Jewish foods are almost always the regional foods from areas where Jews have settled in large numbers. These Jewish foods may be different from the local non-Jewish food, but they bear more resemblance to non-Jewish foods of their own region than to Jewish foods from far away. Most of Jewish cuisine could in no way be inferred from the laws of *kashres*. The exception is matzo, which varies little from region to region since the laws of matzo manufacture are so very specific.

It is in the baking of *shmura* (guarded) matzo that all the aesthetics associated with Passover are most perfectly performed: the care and meticulousness, the seriousness and purity, the speed and urgency, the love and devotion, and most of all the intention. It is intention that supplies the difference between behavior and action (Fredman 1981).

Matzo-baking is a natural subject for an educational tour, because it has a beginning, a middle, and an end, and it is a great show. Documentary makers and museum curators choose matzo-baking to appear again and again whenever Jews are being displayed, because it subsumes so many Jewish issues—*kashres*, the yearly cycle, ritual, and intention. Even the planners of the 1939 New York World's Fair wanted to include a working matzo bakery as one of the food demonstrations to be exhibited in the World of Tomorrow.

I had the good fortune to visit several matzo bakeries and a matzo importer and the remarkable good luck to work one day in the Lubavitcher matzo bakery while writing this paper.

MAKING MATZO

The D&T Matzo Bakery on Albany Avenue in Crown Heights is surely the most famous and accessible *shmura* matzo bakery in the world. The greatest source of exposure for the bakery is the guided tour of Lubavitcher landmarks in Crown Heights every Sunday by Rabbi Beryl Epstein, director of the Hassidic Discovery Welcome Center. The tour is somewhat flexible, but for the half of the year when matzo is baked, the tour never skips the matzo bakery, the undisputed highlight of the tour.

The tour group enters through an unmarked doorway on Albany Avenue and passes through a narrow wrapping and office area where packages of finished matzo are put together and sold to locals, tourists, and shoppers who have traveled to New York just to buy this very matzo. The first person visible upon entrance to the factory proper is the kneader. This medium-size man is built like Popeye with disproportionately large forearms from kneading all day. The kneader stands between two isolation booths, one for flour and one for water. The wheat from which matzo flour is made must be fully dry and ripe, and the water is drawn from a well the day before and kept still overnight. The reason for this is that freshly drawn water is too wild for the very sober purpose of matzo-baking. The inside and outside walls of the flour and water booths are covered with brown wrapping paper, and this same paper covers every horizontal surface in the entire bakery. When an eighteen-minute cycle begins, first the man in the flour booth opens a little speakeasy-type window in his booth and drops a measured portion of whole wheat flour into the freshly polished stainless steel bowl of the kneader. The flour dispensed is about twelve cups, or three pounds. When the flour man closes his little door, the man in the water booth can slide open his little speakeasy door and pour a premeasured quantity of water onto the flour. Immediately the kneader pronounces "L'shem matzo mitzva" (in the name of the mitzvah of matzo) and kneads the dough into a ball. When no scraps of dough are left sticking to the sides of the bowl, the big dough ball is hustled into the next room, where there is a long table of women with rolling pins. A new dough ball is started as soon as the bowl is empty.

Action at the rolling table is directed by a coxswain who stands at the center of the table, making sure every roller has a piece of dough, or *teygele*, to work on. The women use wooden dowels they call sticks to roll the dough into disks one thirty-second of an inch thick. This is even harder than it seems because the ice-cold dough is stiff and very sticky. When a disk of dough is thin enough, the roller calls out "Matzo!" and a runner comes to take the matzo to the docking table, trading a stick with matzo for a freshly cleaned stick. The roller can also flip the matzo onto the runner's stick or, if she is close enough, can just reach over and roll the matzo off her stick onto the docking table. The women work as fast as they possibly can, snapping *teygelekh* out of the air, shouting "I need stick! STICK!" when they have to wait more than five seconds to start rolling again, and whapping their sticks loudly on the table if a new *teygele* does not come flying over immediately.

At the docking table a cylinder with hundreds of rows of tines is run twice over every sheet of matzo. The docker sweeps over the matzo so fast that the disks of dough fly a few inches into the air. A second docker catches the matzo in midair and lays it on one of the long sticks to be carried into the oven room. This is practical as well as showy—by now the matzo is so very thin it is difficult to pick up with the fingertips.

When a long stick has six or so matzos, a runner carries it into the oven room and the baker unrolls the matzos onto the floor of the oven, which is heated to twelve hundred degrees. Fifteen seconds later the matzo is fully baked. The trip from raw flour and cold water to fully baked matzo takes not the eighteen minutes permitted by law, but only about three minutes. Six complete dough cycles can be started and finished in one eighteen-minute cycle.

At the end of eighteen minutes a buzzer sounds near the kneading station. It is the kneader who sets the pace for all the workers. The kneader stops, washes his hands, and changes his apron. He thoroughly cleans and polishes his bowl. Fresh brown paper is unrolled onto all the surfaces of the station. The rollers have now finished the last of their dough as well. They wash their hands and change their aprons while fresh paper is rolled onto the rolling table. The dockers also wash, change aprons, and repaper their table. They also clean out the docking cylinder with an elaborate spinning brush. All the rolling pins are sanded by machine. The medium and long sticks are sanded by hand. The baker takes the last matzos out of the oven and throws in a few extra logs. By the time the wave of purification has reached the end of the bakery a new cycle has already started up at the beginning, so that there is no point at which all production shuts down. The *mashgiakh* examines in turn the hands of all the workers before they return to work; there is an entirely new bakery to work in, and the wave of purification has rolled through the whole bakery in about one minute.

The tourists burst into enthusiastic applause and edge their way back to the corridor in front of the bakery to buy their matzo.

The *podraden* or matzo factories of Poland described by Beatrice Weinreich were places of hard work and antic good times. The women workers would frequently sing during their eighteen-hour workday except when a supervisor approached. A child dispensed well water that had been drawn the previous evening and kept still overnight. Customers could come in to watch their matzo being baked, or they could join the regular workers to bake the matzo they would take home (Weinreich 1960).

FIELD REPORT

At 7:30 in the morning I stand outside the locked Matzo bakery on Albany Avenue. No one is in sight, and I really wonder if business will begin on time. Soon dozens of Russian women pour out of the grocery store next-door. Apparently, that is where they wait for the owner. I huddle close with the women and introduce myself to the rabbi who runs the bakery. I take cues from the other women and go downstairs to hang up my coat. A narrow flight of stairs behind the docking station leads to a low-ceiling basement with tables and coatracks. Back upstairs, we put on our plastic aprons. All the woman workers are cheerfully humming, talking, and joking in Russian. One of them, Rosa, is clearly the center of attention, telling jokes that make the others roar with laughter.

The *mashgiakh* examines our hands after we wash them thoroughly, and Rabbi Dubrowsky gives each of us the ritual ablution. I tore several pieces of dough during the day and dropped my rolling pin several times (this was the most embarrassing thing), but I am proud to say that I did not flunk handwashing once!

The other workers are all in by eight—the men who work the flour and water stations; the man who kneads the dough; Borya, the coxswain of the rolling table, who brings over the dough and sees that every roller always has a *teygele*, or ball of dough; the men who work the docking station; David, who sands the poles on which the matzo dough is transported, and who puts on the best show for the frequent tour groups, cutting up like a character from vaudeville; and Reuven, who works the oven station. Reuven, as Rabbi Epstein will inform every tourist and reporter who comes to the bakery, risked his life for the sake of baking matzo in the old Soviet Union. In addition to the workers are the *mashgiakhs* who will supervise every step of the baking. Today there is also a group of Yeshiva students coming in to work. They have paid for the time to work in the bakery so that they can buy matzo they have personally supervised.

At eight, production begins. A pile of wooden dowels of one-and-a-quarter-inch gauge and eighteen inches long is dropped on the long, central rolling table. Each roller takes a stick, as the pins are called. The women test the sticks and try to pick out a good one, but there is no way I can distinguish one stick from another, and I grab the one nearest to hand. The women point to a spot at the table where I should stand, on the left side of the table toward the far side of the room as one enters, so that I am facing the wall rather than the room. Women on the right side of the table have boxes to sit on during our short breaks and get to make eye contact with the tour groups. They seem to be the most skilled and senior rollers. Rosa is on the right side. Borya takes his position at the center of the table on the left side, and Dubrowsky stands at the head of the table with his back to the entrance. He has a notebook with many columns. I guess he is keeping track of who makes how many matzos. He does not speak at all. This, in fact, is the first time I have noticed he is there after four tours. My first piece of dough is in front of me—time to start rolling.

The wholewheat dough used to make matzo is very stiff. The first step is to knead the *teygele* into a round seamless ball so that it can be evenly rolled. I cannot get this right at first, and someone else gives me a neat little disk of dough to work with. I drop my stick on the floor almost immediately and almost bend over to pick it up. Another no-no. Nisan, who gets matzos from the rolling table to the docking table, gives me a new stick. I drop this one too. There is a bar that runs parallel to the table about two inches away from it so that we do not belly up directly to the table, and this is where my sticks are falling. I roll a piece of dough into a boomerang shape. It is just thirty seconds before I drop my third pin on the floor. I roll a piece of dough into a passable circle and one of the ladies finishes it. I drop my fourth pin. It is time to wash our hands for the next eighteen-minute cycle. Barukh Hashem!

Rosa indicates that I should stand by her during the next cycle. I stand opposite Rosa and directly to the right of Borya. Rosa tells me I am doing very well for a first-timer and shows me how to make a circle without letting the dough stick to the brown paper on the table. I do not drop a single stick during this cycle or the next. The workers at the table speak and joke in Russian as they work. They work very hard and remarkably fast, but everyone is having a good time, some of it at my expense, I suspect, but I have no reason to complain about that. The matzo makers are not only putting up with my presence but also being very kind and helpful. They deserve a few laughs.

I am getting much better, although I still cannot finish a matzo. A finished matzo is about a thirty-second of an inch thick, almost as thin as paper. For the next cycle I go back to the far end of the table. I drop another stick but continue to improve. At ten we go downstairs for our break. I have a cup of hot water with two heaping spoons of sugar and two dunks of the communal tea bag. Normally, there are tea bags to go around; they just happen to have run out today. I think the break lasts about fifteen or twenty minutes. I feel great when we go back upstairs. I can't wait to make more matzo. "We are all speaking only Russian here," Rabbi Dubrowsky says to me before we begin again. I cannot tell from his tone whether he is apologizing that I cannot understand or complaining that I cannot make myself understood. The kneader, the man who reminds me of Popeye, actually spends his breaks smoking a straight corncob pipe.

At irregular intervals Rosa shouts "Ale Tsuzamen" (All together), and we all say "L'shem matzo mitzva." Sometimes we do this more than once in a cycle, and I think there are some cycles when we do not say it. There are other signals that I cannot understand. Rabbi Dubrowsky has a bell that he sometimes rings, and Borya does many different birdlike whistles. I cannot tell what is indicated by the birdcalls or bells, and no one can explain when I ask.

I am thrilled when I finally finish my first complete matzo. Sonya, who is working at the very end of the table directly to my left, asks me how many children I have, if I have been married, for how long, and what went wrong. Sonya then speaks loudly in Russian to the table at large for several minutes, giving them what must be a highly elaborated version of my story. By the end of the cycle, they have come up with a solution.

During the next handwashing break, Sonya tells me, "I have boyfriend for you. I know him six years. Good man. He was also married (here she makes some very emphatic hand gestures, which I think indicate his troubles). Very good man. This man." She points at the person the matzo ladies have selected for me. I feel terribly ungracious to decline the match. How can I deprive Sonya of the chance to do this mitzvah?

For the lunch break, Rosa says to buy instant soup across the street. There is an urn of hot water downstairs to mix with it. I try to sneak out because Rosa has already told me she will get money from Dubrowsky for my lunch, and I think I can avoid taking it. Rosa has anticipated this and is waiting for me. She takes me in hand to the grocery store and we get the soup.

After lunch some of the women do a bit of cleaning up. When we begin working again, I can feel for the first time that my hands hurt and I am very tired. At least the Yeshiva students are gone. The ladies are curious about Craig, my research partner, who comes in before the tour and again at the end. I hardly notice the tours at all. How many cycles until the day is over? One more. I am the last roller left at the table, but I get the final matzo out on time.

MAKING SENSE?

Before I leave I thank the impassive Rabbi Dubrowsky effusively and indicate that I want to buy some matzo. He asks me to wait so that he can give me some made this day. My cup runneth over, but there is more to come. "This is Rabbi Tennenbaum, my partner." I nod my head up and down with my hands clasped firmly behind my back. The biggest gap between this culture and mine just might be the absence of the handshake. Other women from our class have also displaced the handshake onto other parts of their bodies, either nodding their heads or bouncing on their heels. I speak briefly to Rabbi Tennenbaum, whom I have not seen until now. While I am waiting, many matzo buyers come in and out. None are Hasidic, and some might not even be particularly religious. For them this matzo might be the whole ball game. While they may have abandoned traditional Jewish practices in their own daily lives, many Jews continue to cherish the memory of these performances (Mintz 1992).

The overwhelmingly Jewish crowds who show up every Sunday for Rabbi Epstein's tours of Crown Heights have a mixture of romance and revulsion for the Hasidim they are visiting. They want to make some connection with their Jewish lives, but are at a real loss as to how to do this. Anything that would involve learning the Hebrew language, as almost all ceremonies would, is really out of the question. But anyone can eat matzo, which is after all quite possibly the most important mitzvah of the most important holiday of the year. The same tourists who are made edgy and ill at ease by the ritual requirements of Hasidism are satisfied and comforted by the matzo.

There are striking similarities between the *shmura* matzo bakeries in Brooklyn today and the procedures described by Beatrice Weinreich of matzo-baking in Poland nearly a century ago, down to the detail of the illicit singing (Orthodox men are forbidden to hear the voices of women singing). The tours also fulfill one vestigial function that was also required in the Old Country. They bring in non-Jews to witness every step of matzo manufacture. Bakeries in Europe right up until the eve of the Second World War all employed at least one non-Jewish baker, who could be called upon to testify, if necessary, that no blood was used in the baking of matzo.

It may be absurd to suggest that there is any danger of Blood Libel in the Brooklyn of 1994, but it is no more absurd than the unspeakable and unmotivated crimes that have been committed against Lubavitchers in recent years. In this light, the task of the matzo bakers is of profound importance. While preparing the most essential food of the year, they are also showing the world their very basic decency. The bakers who make matzo are protecting their community from murder as well as from *hametz*.

NOTES
Enthusiastic thanks to my research partner Craig Rosa.

REFERENCE LIST
Epstein, Beryl. n.d. "Hassidic Discovery Welcome Center." World Wide Web page. Available at www.jewishtours.com.

Fredman, Ruth Gruber. 1981. *The Passover Seder: Afikoman in Exile.* Philadelphia: University of Pennsylvania Press.
Lubavitch Women's Organization. 1981. *The Spice and Spirit of Kosher-Passover Cooking.* New York: Lubavitch Women's Organization.
Mintz, Jerome R. 1992. *Hasidic People: A Place in the New World.* Cambridge, Mass.: Harvard University Press.
Weinreich, Beatrice S. 1960. "The Americanization of Passover." In *Studies in Biblical and Jewish Folklore,* ed. Raphael Patai, Francis Lee Utley, and Dov Noy. Bloomington: Indiana University Press.

New Synagogues
Rabbi Ellen Lippmann Talks about Congregation Kolot Chayeinu

LAURA MASS

The answering machine for Congregation Kolot Chayeinu/ Voices of Our Lives, in Park Slope, beeps and the recorded message begins: "Hello. You've reached the progressive Jewish congregation in Brooklyn whose members eat and pray together, study and schmooze together, and look forward to having you join us." The voice on the other end of the line is mellifluous, filled with a warmth and serenity that invites you in almost as much as the casual tone of the message itself. It is the voice of Rabbi Ellen Lippmann— founder, rabbi, and virtual personification of this relatively new addition to Brooklyn's evergrowing and increasingly diverse Jewish community.

Seven years ago, before the establishment of Kolot Chayeinu, Rabbi Lippmann was working as the East Coast representative for Mazon: A Jewish Response to Hunger, an organization that provides grants to organizations fighting hunger. As part of her job, she frequently spoke at synagogues, oftentimes attending their services. What she was struck by, more than anything else, was how uninspiring many of these gatherings were. "It was often a deadening experience," remembers Lippmann, "with the prayer leaders seeming detached from the words they were speaking and the people half-asleep." Asleep, that is, until the service was over and the reception began. "The transformation was incredible," she recalls. "You put a piece of cake and a cup of coffee in someone's hand, and all of a sudden they come to life."

Thus Lippmann was struck with the simple, obvious, and yet profoundly powerful connection between Jews and food. It is a connection, she says, that extends beyond the universal role of food as an icebreaker. "Food is a specifically integral part of the Jewish religion," Lippmann explains. "Our most commonly observed holiday, Passover, is one in which we sit around together and eat. There is also an early Jewish notion of food as a metaphor—that by taking something in, it becomes a part of you." From this concept, an idea emerged. Why not switch the conventional order, eat first, and allow the warmth and camaraderie that is generated from a collective meal act as the catalyst for enlivening the service?

The idea came at an auspicious time, not only in Brooklyn's Jewish community, but also in Lippmann's own life. "I had been having a lot of conversations with people here who were frustrated that they hadn't found a congregation they felt comfortable with," says Lippmann. Among the many complaints she heard was what people perceived as an overemphasis on money. "Not only are many of the congregations in Brooklyn very expensive to join," Lippmann explains, "but they frequently ask people for additional contributions as soon as they walk in the door. Kolot Chayeinu also has to raise funds, obviously, but it is not the first thing we ask. We try to wait weeks or even months before approaching people about membership."

On a personal level, Lippmann was also ripe for a change. Growing up in Arlington, Virginia, she had always been extremely active in her Jewish community. Both of her parents were major leaders in their Reform synagogue and Lippmann herself had spent many summers at Reform camps. Although her interest and involvement in Judaism waned during college, the year she graduated—1972—was a watershed for both her and the Reform movement in America. It was the year that Sally Priesand was ordained as the first woman rabbi. The event had an enormous impact on Lippmann, who began entertaining the idea of becoming a rabbi.

At twenty-one, Lippmann was nervous about spending five more years in school, so she convinced herself that it wasn't the right time for her to go to rabbinical school. And when the idea reemerged every five years, she continued to convince herself. She was successful until the third time the idea of becoming a rabbi came up, in 1985. "I was working in the fiercely passionate environment of adult literacy education at the time. I recognized that I wanted to be involved in something where I could feel the same passion I saw around me there, but knew that work wasn't where I would find it. I was thirty-five years old; I figured that if I was ever going to rabbinical school, I'd better go then." Lippmann enrolled at Hebrew Union College and was ordained as a rabbi in 1991.

After several years with Mazon, finding, or in her case, founding, a congregation, was the next logical step. Unclear of any definite goal, Lippmann called an informal meeting of approximately ten people to talk about creating a new congregation, one specifically formed around the idea of eating together as part and parcel of the community. The first several meetings were "each one bring one," and soon the original ten people had become forty. It was not long before the first Shabbat potluck dinner was held in someone's home and the evening overflowed with spirit. Rabbi Lippmann led the Shabbat service as members of community provided music and storytelling and everyone feasted on home-cooked vegetarian dishes.

Kolot Chayeinu has since grown into a congregation of more than one hundred members. The progressive approach to Judaism established by Lippmann attracts a down-to-earth, politically liberal crowd in which there is a high degree of acceptance for various life choices. For the most part the members are not wealthy. They are artists and musicians, teachers and social workers, AIDS activists, and people involved in theater. There are numerous interfaith and interracial couples, and approximately one-third of the congregation is gay and lesbian.

In order to manage the array of people and family structures that make up Kolot Chayeinu, the congregation has had to make certain policy decisions. The only type of membership available, for example, is an individual one. The reason for this, as Lippmann explains, is that many single people in the community were tired of being discriminated against by being asked to pay more than would one member of a couple. Additionally, says Lippmann, "by offering only individual memberships, we are recognizing the reality that, even within a family, there are often different levels of desired involvement. This allows one member of a couple, for instance, to join the congregation when the other has no interest in doing so."

The unusually high level of acceptance within the congregation does not preclude the establishment of certain boundaries. Non-Jewish members, for instance, have thus far not been permitted to serve on the board. "I ultimately believe that Jews should be running a Jewish community," explains Lippmann of her position on this issue. "Still, it is a constant struggle to determine when 'community' is the most important word and when 'Jewish' is the most important word."

As the membership base of Kolot Chayeinu has expanded, so has the range of its programming. Operating out of both people's homes and space rented in the Church of Gethsemane on Eighth Avenue, the congregation now runs services for every major Jewish holiday. Although the once-a-month Shabbat dinners continue to be the mainstay of the congregation, they are now followed up by weekly Saturday morning services, monthly Kabbalat Shabbat services on Friday evenings, and a recently initiated monthly Tot-Shabbat for children. Every new program is an opportunity for this still-young community to grow and evolve. Participants of the new Siddur project, for example, meet regularly to study and discuss Jewish prayer. "Beyond using prayer study as a means of exploring ourselves," explains Lippmann, "our possible long-term goal is to write our own prayer book and, by doing so, help further define who we are as a congregation."

Although food is not the focal point of every new activity, Kolot Chayeinu attempts to incorporate eating into the programs whenever possible. On Saturday morning, congregants are welcomed with a glorious spread of bagels and coffee; Rabbi Lippmann frequently notes, "the service begins when we say the motzi [prayer thanking God for bread] and eat." Lippmann has actually observed a difference in the level of enthusiasm during programs that do not involve eating. Referring to the Kabbalat Shabbat service, Rabbi Lippmann observes, "it is a beautiful service that focuses on music, but we have missed that special feeling of people coming together with food that just doesn't happen without it."

The continued expansion of Kolot Chayeinu is both necessary and inevitable. The congregation is already part of the Brownstone Brooklyn Jewish Coalition, the UJA-funded organization that attempts to bring together the seven non-Orthodox congregations of the Brownstone District. They have also collaborated independently with several of the member congregations to celebrate certain holidays.

As they continue to grow, the congregation eventually hopes to acquire a space that they can call their own. For now, however, the members of the congregation seem perfectly content renting their modest space from a church. "We all wrestle with wanting the congregation to grow and not wanting it to lose its cozy intimate atmosphere," says Lippmann. Yet the intimacy that exists in a community such as Kolot Chayeinu is not the type that is diminished simply by incorporating more people into a larger room. It is an intimacy that exists because the members of the congregation feel a powerful connection to what they are a part of. And while this connection may initially have been sparked by the satisfaction of a good meal, it is perpetuated by something more. Like Lippmann herself, who emanates warmth and compassion and makes people feel completely at ease, there is a high level of comfort generated from the welcoming informal environment of Kolot Chayeinu. It is this comfort that draws people in and makes them want to stay. "For a lot of people who haven't been involved in Jewish life, this congregation is helping to bring them in," says Lippmann. "The most important thing we do, therefore, is to provide people with the opportunity to learn." That and a good bagel on a Shabbat morning.

Living in Brooklyn

Coming of Age in Brooklyn's Neighborhoods

Bar mitzvah boy Hirsh Boyarsky with parents, Rose and Louis, Brooklyn, N.Y., 1960.
Courtesy of the Museum of Jewish Heritage. Gift of Rose Boyarsky.

Waves upon the Sand
Jewish Immigrant Life in Brighton Beach

ANNELISE ORLECK

Photographs by Elizabeth Cooke

On a narrow strip of land at the outer edge of Brooklyn sits a tiny bustling neighborhood that has been a mecca for eastern European Jewish immigrants for most of the twentieth century. Crowded, colorful, noisy Brighton Beach sits at the center of a skinny little peninsula that runs from Jamaica Bay to the mouth of the Hudson, containing on one end the "Brooklyn Tudor" and faux Mission-style homes of Manhattan Beach, with its well-heeled synagogues and private security patrols, and on the other the eerie amusement park povertyscape of Coney Island, dotted with rusting roller coaster skeletons and shadowed by massive public housing projects. Across a narrow waterway bob the fishing boats of Sheepshead Bay, advertising daily dawn departures, and behind them street after street of row houses and apartment blocks stretching halfway through Brooklyn. These are all areas with long histories of Jewish settlement. Still Brighton Beach, more than any of its larger neighbors, retains the taste and feel of an immigrant ghetto, its streets redolent with the smells of frying onions, overripe fruit, hot piroshki, and oiled metal, an acrid scent that drifts down from the elevated tracks that tower overhead.

A wooden boardwalk stretches expansively between the car-clogged streets and the wide sandy beach, but there is nothing pastoral about this overcrowded slice of working-class Jewish immigrant life. Grimy art-deco apartment buildings line the side streets, each fronted whenever the weather permits by lines of elderly Soviet immigrants, who pass the hours in folding beach chairs scrutinizing passersby and catching up on local gossip in a stage-whispered mix of Russian, Yiddish, and English. The weather almost always seems conducive to these wizened sentries who are not at all afraid of cold or wind. They simply pull their fur hats down over hard-of-hearing ears, or tie their gold and paisley headcloths tighter.

The neighborhood's main artery, Brighton Beach Avenue, is a gaudy strip of "international food" stores, overflowing fruit and vegetable stands, European clothing "emporia," and Russian-style nightclubs with darkened glass exteriors and lots of chrome. Street vendors sell everything from cheap luggage to powdered antelope horns. These and other magic elixirs in little zip-lock bags are guaranteed to cure a host of ills their purveyors swear the doctors at nearby Coney Island Hospital have no idea how to treat. Above it all hovers the elevated subway track, cutting the street below into stripes of light and darkness. And every few minutes another train pulls in or out, the deafening roar causing rhythmic pauses in conversation and in commerce. Screeching sudden halts between stations send shivers down the bent spines of the slow-moving pedestrians below.

At first glance, Brighton Beach can feel as old-fashioned as sepia-toned photographs of the mythical Lower East Side: live carp still swim in fish store windows, pickles are sold from barrels, women in headscarves squeeze melons with long-practiced fingers, and music in minor keys drifts from narrow dark doorways. There are ways that this community feels much the same as it has since World War I, its large elderly population reinforcing the sense of stopped time that many visitors feel when first stepping down into the bantering, haggling stream of people that always fills the Avenue. But if Brighton evokes long-gone Jewish times and places, it is also very much a late-twentieth-century Jewish immigrant enclave: bass-heavy dance music pulses from boom boxes set up behind toppling street vendors' displays. Young electronic engineers, Website designers, and stock analysts visit their parents here, dressed in cashmere and soft leather, driving Lexus SUVs and BMWs. And, hidden inside the cavernous art-deco apartment buildings, Jewish and non-Jewish Russian émigré crime bosses plan and direct complex diamond-smuggling and money-laundering schemes involving three or four countries and sometimes as many continents. These latter day *gory*—thieves—have made as much of a mark on late-twentieth-century Brighton as the legendary Jewish gangsters of the 1920s left on Brownsville and East New York. Still, like immigrant criminal entrepreneurs in neighborhoods across New York, they represent just a tiny fraction of the honest and hardworking fifty thousand who live here, and it is upon their fellow émigrés that they prey most often.

Portal for the massive exodus that has brought half a million Jews from the Soviet Union to the United States since 1967, Brighton has been sensationalized in newspapers, on television news, and in recent cinema as "Little Odessa," the label reflecting the Ukrainian origins of a majority of Brighton residents. World famous now, Brighton Beach has become both a thriving ethnic enclave and a symbol—the place that Soviet immigrants measure themselves against as a marker of their success or failure in America. Though it is still the cultural heart of the immigration, the place where middle-aged Soviet émigrés from across the metropolitan area come to shop, where families celebrate rites of passage in gaudy restaurant/nightclubs

—more than a few breathe a loud sigh of relief when they drive away. Only the poor, the ill-educated, the old stay in Brighton—you will hear many Soviet immigrants say—only the *proste*, the common. We are not like them. Brighton Beach has been reinvented by these émigrés from Moscow, Petersburg, Minsk, and Kharkov, sharpened by their insecurities about finding a place for themselves in this culture, softened by their nostalgia for all things Russian. It is a process not so different from that which made an earlier generation of Jewish immigrants run as fast as they could from the hated slums of the Lower East Side and then construct memoirs that grew ever more golden the farther away they moved from that first taste of America.

As closely associated as it is with the recent Soviet emigration, Brighton has Yiddish roots that lie not far beneath its current Russian surface. There are remnants still of the first and second waves of eastern European Jewry to settle this bit of urban Atlantic seashore. Hundreds of Holocaust survivors still live in Brighton, as they have since the late 1940s when their community numbered in the thousands. And a tiny fragment of an even older immigrant population survives here as well—a few hundred very elderly Jewish émigrés who came to the United States sometime after World War I. Attracted to the subsidized Warbasse apartment houses opened on the edge of Brighton by the Amalgamated Clothing Workers' Union in 1967, tens of thousands of Jewish retirees from the garment trades flooded the neighborhood in the late 1960s, leaving behind longtime residences in decaying inner city neighborhoods. Until recently, they represented the second largest concentration of senior citizens in the United States. Only Miami Beach had more.

I grew up in Brighton during the 1960s and early 1970s, when the influence of that first wave of elderly eastern European immigrants was still dominant. It was a time when three Yiddish daily newspapers did a brisk business on the newsstands. Commercial rents were so low that you could take your pick of charity secondhand clothing stores. Locally known as "schlock shops," they were run by various women's charities (synagogue sisterhoods, Hadassah, or ORT) and piled high with a dusty array of prewar treasures: red silk bathrobes with tasseled belts and slim-hipped dresses made of beaded purple velvet. Street conversations ranged from Yiddish literature to the roller-coaster fortunes of the Mets. The Communists were still battling the Socialists. Everyone knew that "the International" meant the International Ladies' Garment Workers' Union. And

[top] *Kosher food store.* © Elizabeth Cooke. [bottom] *Matzo people.* © Elizabeth Cooke.

Help Israel. © *Elizabeth Cooke.*

old Zionist ladies, without a trace of embarrassment, served drinks on plastic coasters emblazoned with technicolor action shots of Israeli women in military fatigues.

Restless as any teenager, I walked the Avenue daily and nightly, hoping to find something different and exciting to do. I came to know every deli, bakery, tailor shop, and shlock shop intimately. I paced and bicycled the Boardwalk through summer nights alive with balalaikas and Yiddish show tunes, and winter days when only the burliest white-haired bare-chested polar bears dared plunge into the snowy sea. As distant from my youthful experience as these flamboyant and fragile elderly all around me were, I enjoyed their bravado. And, as I grew older and a bit more aware, I could feel the poignancy of what was happening to Brighton in the 1970s: this Yiddish-speaking world was poised on the edge of the void. I knew that many of those aged émigrés who valiantly braved biting sea winds year-round to "take some air" on the Boardwalk would not still be there a few years hence. A generation—carriers of a tradition of secular *Yiddishkayt*, radical politics, cheese blintzes, and cold beet borscht—was slipping away. It was impossible not to notice as empty spaces opened on the benches, and suddenly darkened storefronts gaped on the Avenue.

During the five years that I was away at college between 1975 and 1980, the neighborhood was indeed transformed by the arrival of nearly forty thousand Soviet Jewish émigrés. For a while, the elderly longtime residents coexisted uneasily with the Soviet newcomers, clashing on matters of religion, politics, manners, and style. These refugees from Tsarist Cossacks and Nazi storm troopers decried the Soviet émigrés' failure to go to synagogue, their gruff demeanor and agressive behavior, and what seemed to them garish "un-Jewish" dress and jewelry. Twenty years later, few traces of the old Brighton survive. The elderly immigrants from Poland, Czechoslovakia, Rumania, and Germany have mostly died or moved to Florida. Cyrillic-lettered broadsheets have elbowed aside the Socialist and Anarchist Yiddish tabloids that used to fill the newsstands beneath the subway stairs. And Russian has almost competely replaced Yiddish as the neighborhood's language of commerce and camaraderie, making the ultrareligious in Borough Park and Williamsburg the only Jews in Brooklyn still using the *mamaloshn* (mother tongue) for their daily conversations.

Bare-chested polar bears. © Elizabeth Cooke.

Sometime during the past twenty years, Brighton ceased to be my home and became a subject about which I write and lecture. This essay mixes my own recollections with residents' reflections and yellowing newsclips—many of which, having never been microfilmed, are growing brittle in file boxes at the Brooklyn Public Library and the Brooklyn Historical Society. It is an account of one hundred years of Jewish life in Brighton Beach, but it is history seen through the unevenly refracting lens of assorted personal memories. Like so many who have written about the Lower East Side, like any author remembering a childhood home, I have found that I have had to stay two steps ahead of my own nostalgia in writing this. I've also had to read beneath the romantic glaze or the decades-long conflicts that tinge the reminiscences woven together here. As a neighborhood of immigrants, Brighton has long been animated by the creative tension between memory and fact, ghosts and bricks. For as long as there have been Jews in Brighton, there has been a fractious and contested Jewish community life: radical and old-fashioned, devoutly religious and slathered, half-naked with suntan oil, and always ready for a good argument.

"ALL THE JOYS OF A SAIL WITHOUT MOTION": BRIGHTON BEACH AS JEWISH SUMMER RESORT

Brighton Beach was first developed as a resort in the late 1870s by a German-American railroad magnate named William Engemann who sought to create a respectable family-oriented counterpart to the lurid working-class attractions that had given neighboring Coney Island the nickname of "Sodom by the Sea." Aware of the large numbers of young Jewish immigrants flocking to Coney Island, Engemann pointedly excluded Jews from his squeaky-clean Brighton Beach Hotel. But the neighborhood around the sand-dune beach soon sprouted boardinghouses and bungalow colonies that drew Jewish immigrant families from across the city. Engemann himself sped that change when he built the Brighton Rapid Transit elevated train line that brought riders all the way from the inner city for only a nickel. The BRT enabled Jewish families to summer at the sea together. Unlike the Catskill bungalow colonies, where working family members could come only on weekends, a summer rental in Brighton enabled fathers and other workers to commute daily to the garment shops of

Williamsburg and Lower Manhattan with time for an ocean dip at dawn or at dusk.

By the early years of the new century, Brighton had plenty that appealed as well to the working sons and daughters of the immigrants. A horse-racing track, Reisenweber's restaurant/dance hall, and the Yiddish Repertory Summer Theater, the nation's first Yiddish summer stock company, all drew young men and women with a little extra in their pockets, a few dollars not dutifully handed over to their mothers, saved just for this kind of spree. Jewish vaudevillian Georgie Jessel recalls those years when he headlined at the New Brighton Theater, after which he and fellow vaudeville greats would blow their paychecks on the horses and then forget their losses over drinks on the seafront balcony of Reisenwebers. Across the street, the stars of the Yiddish theater on summer break from Second Avenue rubbed shoulders with fearsome Jewish gangsters in the bar of the Rickadonna Hotel, buying drinks for the house, and trading stories of dimming glory and the times they almost hit big.

A three-mile wooden boardwalk built by local hoteliers early in the century also attracted happy refugees from overheated inner city neighborhoods. Developer Joseph P. Day, who had bought Engemann out in 1914, took this as a personal affront. Hoping to make all of Brighton into his own private resort, Day had hired armed guards to stop anyone besides hotel guests from walking on the beach unless they paid a steep admission fee. Court battles for beach access raged for years, until populist Brooklyn Borough president Abraham Riegelmann took an ax one hot day in 1919 to the wooden fence that Day had erected to keep "strangers" off "his" beach. Almost twenty years later, master builder Robert Moses bought the beach and boardwalk for the city of New York and renamed the seaside walkway "the Riegelmann Boardwalk." Countless people have walked, roller-skated, and bicycled past Riegelmann's plaque since that time, without a pause or a backward glance. History does not long remember even the most flamboyant of borough presidents.

On the grounds of the old Brighton Beach Hotel, Day opened The Brighton Beach Baths, his attempt at an urban Jewish equivalent to the country club. Boasting three saltwater pools and live big-band performances by Benny Goodman and lesser lights, "the Baths" would become the only vestige of Brighton's resort days to survive almost to the end of the new century. Lockers, rented quite inexpensively for a ten-month season, became much-coveted shelters by the sea to which Jewish families from sweltering Brooklyn and Bronx apartments could flee in the days before air-conditioning. During the 1930s the Baths became known for grooming a generation of Jewish handball champions who competed successfully against players from across the country. Handball, Walter Bernard remembers, was a Depression-era favorite because it required only a hard rubber ball and a callused hand. "We called it 'the poor man's tennis' because you didn't need racquets or expensive tennis clothes." The World War II battlefield death of Jack Garber, Brighton's national champion, quieted the neighborhood enthusiasm for handball. By the 1960s the cement courts at the Baths had becoming more often a site for senior aerobics and ballroom dancing in bathing suits.

Generations of New York Jews have their own sandy memories of the Baths. In the 1930s, my mother shared a locker with my great-aunt Bessie, who stored warmed pots of *tsholent* swathed in towels in her locker. Bessie cheerfully lugged her Sabbath stew of meat and beans all the way from the Bronx on the subway. She dished it out to family and friends on the beach—sandy, hungry, and without money to buy the "hot knishes" hawked from steaming paper shopping bags by enterprising young neighborhood boys. Half a century later, my mother returned to the Baths, bought a locker, and stepped gingerly from the cocoon of early widowhood. In her flowered bathing suit and silver dancing shoes, she waltzed smooth-stepping white-haired bachelors around the cement dance floor cum handball court. Her entry into the world of over-sixty dating was not without its rough spots, but in the end the Baths worked its magic and she moved a few crucial steps toward healing. More than a few widows and widowers found their solace there as the Baths became a much-needed recreation center for local senior citizens. Joseph P. Day got his final revenge in 1990 when his heirs won the right, after a decades-long battle with neighborhood residents, to build a block of twenty-story condominium buildings on the site of the Baths.

At the dawn of the twenty-first century the lot remained empty but for billboards advertising million-dollar apartments. Reclad but still recognizable, only the old octagonal wooden snackbar still stood amid bits of smashed handball court and rusted swimming pool pipes. One gray, moody day I listened to the the wind off the ocean whine through the huge empty lot and whip against the rubble with a rhythmic clicking. It sounded for a moment like a

[top] *The rabbi's dresser.* © Elizabeth Cooke. [bottom] *Man in slatted light from the subway.* © Elizabeth Cooke.

clarinet line and the shuffle of leather-soled dancing shoes. In a few years, even those ghosts will be gone.

In the years after World War I, Brighton actually looked more like a remote village than a Brooklyn neighborhood, its unpaved, sandy thoroughfares and winding alleyways lined with miniature wood and tarpaper homes. On larger streets framing the warren of bungalows were rickety two- and three-story wooden boardinghouses whose rooms had once been rented to summering families. By the 1920s these efficiencies were mostly rented as year-round homes to single immigrant men and women newly arrived in New York. And Brighton Beach Avenue had begun to look as it would for half a century to come: small tailor's shops, kosher butchers and bakers, glaziers, shoemakers, "home cooking" stands lined the seafront strip. The Boardwalk, splintered by years of storms and hardly suited for strolling, had also become a European-feeling marketplace lined with stalls selling what Sadie Reiss described to me as "old-fashioned things, food and clothing like you could get on the East Side." (A flood in 1932 and a hurricane later in the decade destroyed the Boardwalk businesses.)

Reiss moved to Brighton with her parents in 1920. They had fled from Byelorussia when she was three years old to escape the anti-Jewish rampages that followed the Russian Revolution of 1905. "The bungalows were all filled with Jewish people from Europe," she remembered of her first years in Brighton. Most commuted to garment shops in Williamsburg and Lower Manhattan but the five-cent trip often felt like an epic journey. "The El was here then but it was very shaky. The wind was so strong blowing off the beach I was afraid I'd fall off. There was nothing between the Boardwalk and the Avenue. So when the wind blew, the whole platform used to shake from side to side."

Walter Bernard recalled that in the early 1920s Brighton residents still felt as though they lived in a seafront outpost. Many supplemented their incomes or earned a living outright catering to summer visitors. "When people first started living here all year round they would build lockers in their backyards and then send a kid to stand by the subway shouting: 'Hey, Get your lockers here! Ten cents for the whole day.' People from Manhattan came for a day at the beach and had no place to change. So they used these lockers to change in and the people who lived in the bun-

galows made some money. It gave them a little extra. I used to peddle on the beach to make a living. The cops always chased me. So I would run into the ocean and the cop with his heavy woolen suit would stand on the shore screaming and waving his stick. Sometimes I would find a little old lady and ask: 'Hey lady can I hide my ice cream under your chair?' Then the cop would come and grab me and in five minutes he'd be surrounded by a group of Jewish women screaming at him: 'Why don't you leave the boy alone? He's just trying to make a living. Go and catch a real crook instead.' And the cop would get all embarrassed and let me go."

Brighton's frontier feel was sharpened by the lack of a synagogue in the early years. Reiss recalled that until 1923 adults would pray and the children study in tents in a muddy, puddly lot. For much of the rest of the 1920s, a shack heated by a wood stove served as the neighborhood's only synagogue. Selling old clothes, baked goods, and hand-sewing, immigrant women, most of whom had come from southwestern Russia in the years before and after World War I, raised money for Brighton's first synagogue: the Hebrew Alliance of Brighton by the Sea Inc. Completed in 1928, the sanctuary was modeled after a fifteenth-century Florentine synagogue with white clouds painted on a heavenly blue dome that rose above the Torah ark. A stained glass rose window high on the facade let rainbow fragments of light onto the walls during Sabbath and holiday services.

A few blocks away, a smaller congregation had set up housekeeping in a rambling green wooden, three-story building, once the summer home of a wealthy racetrack denizen. The haunted-looking Victorian structure was transformed by a group of Jewish refugees who had fled the violent anti-Semitic rampages sweeping post–World War I Poland. They opened the Beth Ha Midrash Ha Gadol synagogue on the ground floor of the building. In an apartment above the sanctuary lived the devout Polish couple who founded the synagogue in 1927, Rabbi Samuel Horowitz and his rebbetzin, Rivke. They taught, led prayers, married congregants, visited the sick, and buried the dead for more than half a century, even after they were nearly killed by smoke inhalation during the fall of 1980, when anti-Semitic vandals set a fire in the wooden ark that held the Torah scrolls. I first met the rebbetzin the day after the fire. Her hands blackened with soot, she was scrubbing the synagogue's fire-damaged memorial name plaques, donated by family members in memory of loved

Dancers at the baths. © Elizabeth Cooke.

ones who had died, many in Nazi death camps. By the early 1990s, Beth Ha Midrash Ha Gadol had become largely a congregation of Hasidic and Modern Orthodox. When the change began, the rebbetzin mourned a loss of humour and ease. "A simple balcony was enough for us, for the women to pray. Then they had to put up a folding door so we can't even see the men. It seems too much, really."

The Hebrew Alliance has also survived the passing of decades, even opening Brighton's only functioning mikveh (ritual bath). Still, time has left its marks. Aged, poor, and dwindling, the congregation was kept from disappearing entirely in the 1980s only by the evangelical fervor of its longtime rabbi, David Hollander, whose fiery preaching and fluent Russian enabled him to reach out to Soviet émigrés with some success. The signature stained glass window was broken by vandals. It can never be replaced, Sadie Reiss explains, because the Czech artist who made it died in the Holocaust, and the secrets of his craft died with him. The congregation has neither interest nor money enough to comission a living artist to rebuild. Once touted as a symbol of an immigrant Jewish community's robust

growth and hopes for permanence, the Hebrew Alliance of Brighton by the Sea Incorporated now sports a cracked facade. And traces of unreadable graffitti, only partly washed off, twine along the lower face, obscuring the Hebrew letters on the 1928 cornerstone.

When that cornerstone was laid, Brighton was in the throes of a real estate boom. Jewish immigrants from the Lower East Side, Brownsville, and Williamsburg poured into the neighborhood, fueling construction of a dozen synagogues in Brighton between the late 1920s and the start of World War II. A lucky few of them were able to get relatives out of eastern Europe in the years after the United States closed its doors in 1921. From the pogroms in Poland to the humiliations of the Nuremberg laws, these new arrivals brought harrowing tales and assured Brooklyn relatives that they were lucky to be safe on this side of the Atlantic. In 1937, Dr. Maxwell Ross dedicated the newest of Brighton's synagogues with this reflection, as news of Hitler's increasingly frightening anti-Jewish policies filtered into Brighton: "Brighton Beach, not Europe or Palestine, is the real promised land for Jews . . . where we may

Rebbetzin Rivke in her kitchen. © Elizabeth Cooke.

practice the religion of our forefathers without interference from narrow minded bigots or maniacs."

Still, most of the Jewish immigrants who moved to Brighton during the 1920s and 1930s were fleeing not persecution in Europe but overcrowded and unsanitary conditions on the Lower East Side, Williamsburg, and Brownsville. The *Brooklyn Daily Eagle* opined in 1925 that "the advantages of Brighton Beach as a health resort have long been well known. Almost every physical ailment is benefited by the fresh ocean air, freedom from dust, smoke and pollen. Abundant ozone is especially beneficial in the case of neurotics." If Brighton's similarities to the Lower East Side drew some newly arrived immigrants, it was its differences from inner city ghettos that attracted an influx of first thousands and then tens of thousands of Jewish families who had been in the United States for some time. Walter Bernard's immigrant parents brought him to Brighton in 1923 to relieve his sinus infections. "They told my mother if you go near the water and sniff it up then the sinuses will be cleared." But, says Bernard, their decision to settle in Brighton was, like that of many other young Jewish families, an attempt at social mobility. "Brighton was

really the coming place at that time," Bernard remembers. "Young people came here like today they go to Long Island or Connecticut to start a new way of life."

Brighton's growing cachet as a hot neighborhood for upwardly mobile Jewish families sparked a real estate boom that transformed the face of the neighborhood, making it seem for a brief time the height of 1920s modernity and, ever after, as if it were caught in an art-deco time warp. The years from 1921 to 1929 saw the construction of thirty apartment buildings, quite large for the time, six stories high, serviced by modern elevators and with ten or more apartments on a floor. They were fanciful buildings advertising "a year-round resort lifestyle." The very first, the Miramar, boasted three tennis courts, eight handball courts, a children's playground, miniature golf, and ocean views. The Shelburne apartments—where the old Rickadonna used to be—offered glamour in the place of family amenities: a grand entrance with fountains, a rooftop solarium for private sunbathing, and "Hollywood style" bathrooms with circular lavendar-tile showers. As so many times in the history of the city when a neighborhood suddenly appeared "hot," lots, homes, and buildings were demolished, constructed, bought, and sold with feverish speed. Brighton land values literally tripled during the summer of 1925 and continued to rise through the decade. Then they fell just as fast when the 1929 crash and the sky-rocketing unemployment rates that followed brought a new Jewish influx into Brighton. Worn and wearied by the sudden decline in fortunes, jobless and homeless Jewish families began to show up at the doors of loved ones they hoped would take them in. By 1932, those new six- and seven room apartments, the bungalows, the old boarding-houses were all jammed to the rafters as three and four generations moved in together. City authorities declared Brighton officially an overcrowded slum. Its brief moment as a "coming" community came quickly to an end.

"WE REALLY BELIEVED THE REVOLUTION WAS COMING": THE RED DEPRESSION YEARS

Shirley Kupferstein, a pink-faced stout woman with a white Prince Valiant haircut, was one of the thousands who moved to Brighton with her husband and children early in the Depression to pool scant resources with ex-tended family. (I met Shirley at the Shorefront Y Senior Center in 1981. She told this story, her voice edged with biting irony, while wryly observing a modern dance class for senior citizens—eight women and one man—taking place in one corner of the multipurpose room where we spoke.) Throughout the Depression years her family of eight crowded together in a small two-story bungalow. "We took the upstairs, his parents lived the down. We had three rooms and for that we paid thirty-three dollars a month. Believe me that was expensive for that time. It was right after the stock market crashed and we didn't have jobs and we didn't have money. Nobody else did either. There was no Medicare then. No food stamps. My parents lived with us. It was very nice. We all starved together. My mother and father died painful deaths during the Depres-sion. And we didn't have money to take them to the doc-tors or to buy them painkillers. That's what it was like being a senior citizen then. Now with drugs and shots they keep us alive, dancing at seventy-five, much to Uncle Sam's regrets. He'd like us all to kick at sixty, so he wouldn't have to pay our social security. I am going to live to one hundred just for spite."

The overcrowding, the desperation of the time, and the concentration of Jewish immigrant trade unionists in one small neighborhood made Brighton a center of radical ac-tivism during the Depression. "I think it was because so many people came here from Russia," Walter Bernard speculates. "Well, they thought they were headed for the *goldene medineh* [the golden land], but as soon as they got off the boat somebody stuck a proverbial pin in their balloon. It wasn't all peaches and cream here." Jack Friedman, a Russian émigré who moved to Brighton in 1929, felt that it was "like the suburbs of Paris. Red was all that you could see." Shoe-workers organizer Sidney Jonas, an impish blue-eyed firecracker, elaborates: "The Communist Party had a tremendous influence in Brighton in those days. Some people were reading the *Freiheit* [the CP's Yiddish daily.] Others were reading the *Daily Worker* [the official CPUSA publication]. When somebody wanted to Ameri-canize himself he read the *Daily Worker* because it was in English. . . . It was a time when you heard on the Board-walk only Communist songs. Revolutionary songs in En-glish, in Yiddish, in Russian. We really believed that the revolution was coming."

The Communist Party attracted not only committed po-litical activists like Jonas and Friedman. According to Shir-ley Kupferstein, virtually everyone she knew in Brighton at least flirted with the Party in those years. "My husband got a job driving cab and he took me to all the Communist ral-lies. There were lots of Communists here then. Sure. Who doesn't want to be a Communist when they're hungry? Now that their bellies are full, there is no more Communist movement here. You know what I say? Let them *fress* [gorge] until they burst. That's what America is all about."

The Communist Party was far from the only political in-fluence on Brighton in that era. By the early Depression years, Brighton was as highly politicized as any commu-nity in the United States. Along the fifteen blocks that Brighton Beach Avenue ran, one could find headquarters for the Communist, Socialist, Mizrachi, Labor Zionist, Democratic, and Republican Parties. Both garment workers' unions and the shoemakers' unions had active neighborhood associations. All these groups organized rallies at the crossroads of the community, where the ele-vated subway tracks turned from Brighton Beach Avenue north toward Manhattan. The Workmen's Circle, a Yid-dish Socialist benevolent association, sponsored dances, concerts, and literary readings. And the children of these various movements trotted off every day at three or four to afternoon schools where they were taught Yiddish and He-brew, Jewish history and culture—colored and flavored to instill the values of Zionism, Communism, Socialism, or

Jewish religious orthodoxy. Whatever their parents' ideological slant, these youngsters approached their afternoon studies with about as much enthusiasm as immigrant children throughout the century whose parents have insisted that they receive cultural or religious instruction on top of their regular schooling.

Meanwhile, the adults battled loudly on the Boardwalk, on streetcorners where competing soapbox-speakers sometimes shouted each other down, and in local delis and dairy restaurants. "There were," Friedman remembers, "very serious differences between the various political groups in Brighton." Sara Levy, a devout Labor Zionist, summed up her distaste for her Communist neighbors less diplomatically. "To me they were—I don't know if you'll understand this—*a treyf posl*. They were Jews who had become not-Jews. It was obnoxious. They praised Stalin so much, in the meantime he was busy killing Jews. I grew up in Russia. I was there when so many fine young Jews helped to make the Revolution to make things better for the peasants and downtrodden people. Then as soon as the Revolution was won, Stalin killed them all. I was not surprised, because I was a Zionist in my mother's stomach. I dreamed my whole life to make a Jewish homeland."

The arguments would continue for decades to come, making fiercely argued political disputation perhaps the favorite communal pastime in Brighton Beach. But during the Depression, Friedman recalls, "we put aside our differences and worked as one on the serious problems of our day. . . . We had leaders here who were raised in the sweatshops, and they knew how to organize. They came from Russia in a time of revolution and they did not take crisis lying down." Food and shelter were the paramount concerns of the day; it was a time when millions of Americans faced hunger and homelessness. And, since those were the workplace issues of wives and mothers, it was middle-aged women who did the lion's share of the organizing and who were the street soldiers in what they were soon calling "the war against the high cost of living."

One of the most famous leaders in the Depression-era housewives' movement was Clara Lemlich Shavelson, a longtime garment union activist whose fiery speech at Cooper Union in the fall of 1909 set off the largest women's strike to that time—popularly known as the Uprising of the Thirty Thousand. (Most of them were barely out of their teens and recently immigrated from Russia and Poland.) By the 1930s, Shavelson was in her midforties, the mother of three children and cofounder of a city-wide Communist-affiliated housewives' union. The Brighton Beach branch was named the Emma Lazarus Tenant's Council, for the Jewish socialist poet whose words are enshrined at the base of the Statue of Liberty. Brighton women in the council planned a series of consumer strikes against the high cost of milk, bread, and kosher meat that spread from Brighton Beach and Coney Island to involve thousands of housewives in Jewish and African-American neighborhoods across the city. During one citywide strike in 1935, Shavelson led neighborhood councils of mostly Jewish housewives across the city as they shut down four thousand butcher shops, picketed the wholesale meat market on Forty-second Street, and visited Secretary of Agriculture Henry Wallace in pursuit of lower meat prices. When they did not receive satisfaction, they called on fellow housewives across the nation to strike, which they did in August of that year—winning front-page headlines from Brooklyn to Los Angeles. Housewives' consumer organizing continued into the early 1950s, with Brighton Beach, home of Clara Shavelson orating from her stepladder under the El, always at the center of the agitation.

After hunger, the most vexing issue of the time was shelter. Poor and working-class families across the country faced the threat of eviction for failure to pay the rent. In Brighton Beach, families' attempts to stave off homelessness by moving in together and sharing costs brought down the wrath not only of landlords but of city officials. Housing inspectors levied exorbitant fines wherever they found too many people occupying too small a space. When frightened tenants called the Emma Lazarus Council, they were usually visited by a militant and self-assured woman neighbor who casually tore up the summons and announced that there was nothing to worry about. Friedman recalls that the Emma Lazarus Council vowed that there would be no evictions in Brighton. "Every time the landlords would put the furniture out onto the street, the women from the Emma Lazarus Council would come and move the furniture back into the apartment. There were many evictions then all over America. But not here, because we did not allow it to happen." When the City Council threatened to cut off relief payments to everyone in Brighton if the practice of "taking in" family members was not stopped, women of the Emma Lazarus Council collected signatures, picketed, and lobbied City Hall, warning that such a move would take food from the mouths of hungry children. The city soon backed off, but

Sidney Jonas's kitchen, 1980: reading the United Auto Worker. *© Elizabeth Cooke.*

the women simply turned to different struggles. Angry Brighton housewives took to the streets often, into the 1950s. They protested school overcrowding and lack of parental control over curriculum development. Shavelson and the others also loudly denounced state anti-Communist investigating committees that threatened to fire any Brighton schoolteacher unwilling to take a loyalty oath.

Sand and sea remained both resource and release, from the worst years of the Depression and the war to the years of Red-baiting and loyalty trials that followed. Rae Appel recalls that, after successful actions of the Emma Lazarus Council, she and her friends "got together on the beach . . . and we'd go swimming and sunning and discussing. Someone would bring out a thermos of coffee. Someone would bring sandwiches. . . . It was delicious . . . since all of us were very much involved in the same work . . . to sit together and talk." It was so pleasant, Appel admits, that feelings of guilt often pierced the golden glow of the beach and Boardwalk in the evenings. "There were times we felt like we were committing a sin, bathing when there were so many things to be done."

"I HAVE LIVED THIS THROUGH": SURVIVORS OF THE HOLOCAUST MAKE NEW LIVES IN BRIGHTON

The Second World War destroyed the last of Brighton's feeling of newness and innocence. Hundreds of Brighton's young men, the neighborhood's first American-born generation, served in the European and Pacific theaters, many of them taking part in the amphibious landings that cost so many lives. The death toll among Brighton sons was extraordinarily high. Nearly one in two were killed during the war. Even before the war's end, before local residents were able to get accurate reports about the fate of European family members, Brighton was a community in mourning. The loss of so many young men, and the wear and tear from overcrowding during the Depression, contributed to a feeling that, in the words of one longtime resident, "Brighton would never be young again."

Most of the young men who did return to Brighton after the war found little to keep them there. The poverty and overcrowding of the Depression years had worn the housing stock down and created a shortage of available housing that made it exceedingly difficult for returning soldiers to

Sam Glantz with the Yizkor book from his town, in the office of the 4th St. shul. © Elizabeth Cooke.

find homes of their own. Those who were married began to look toward suburban Long Island and New Jersey. A small but steady exodus continued through the 1960s until few American-born families could be found in the old neighborhood.

Between 1948 and 1958, however, the neighborhood saw yet another influx from Europe. Unable or unwilling to return to the places where they were raised, survivors of Nazi death camps and wartime partisan brigades received exit visas and left the displaced persons (DP) camps where they had lived since war's end to come to New York City. Before they could immigrate, the U.S. Bureau of Immigration and Naturalization Services (INS) required affidavits from American citizens promising that these refugees would not become dependent on public aid. Several thousands such affidavits were signed by the people of Brighton Beach.

Unlike the first wave of immigrants to settle in Brighton, most of whom were from small towns and villages in Russia's old pale of Jewish settlement, these survivors of the Holocaust came mostly from the large industrial towns and cities of Poland—from Vilna, Lodz, Kraków, and espe-

cially Warsaw—the capital of eastern European Jewish life between the wars. Smaller numbers came from Czechoslovakia, Hungary, Rumania and Germany, from big cities like Berlin, and from the small, isolated villages of the Carpathian Mountains.

The first survivors to arrive in Brighton were those who had some connection to people already living there. From the DP camps they had written to family, friends, or acquaintances in Brighton who sent affidavits to U.S. authorities promising that the newcomers would be cared for. Once this first group was settled, the New York Association for New Americans (NYANA), an immigrant aid society founded by New York Jewish philanthropists to aid in the resettlement of European Jewish war refugees, decided that Brighton would provide a safe and supportive environment in which to settle survivors who had no family in the United States. By the end of the 1950s, Brighton was home to one of the largest survivor communities in the country. One of them, Polish partisan Nathan Minsky, would say of Brighton on the fortieth anniversary of the liberation of Auschwitz in 1985, "Brighton became a home when we

Elsie in her dancing clothes at the Brighton Beach Baths. © Elizabeth Cooke.

had no other. It gave refuge to thousands of survivors. It was a place where our souls could rest, and a place where we could build new lives."

Nathan's wife, Rose Minsky, a survivor of the 1943 Warsaw ghetto uprising, remembers her arrival in Brighton quite differently. "People asked me silly questions," she said, still angry decades later. "One uncle I had, my mother's brother, he asked me: 'Was it really true what the papers are saying?' Ha! How could any paper tell half of it. 'I'm very surprised that you can ask such a question like that when your own sister died in the gas chamber.' I had to tell it to him like that. People thought the whole thing was an exaggeration."

Auschwitz survivor Samuel Glantz, president of the "4th St. shul" as it is popularly known in Brighton, was stunned at his first encounter with New York Jews. "I first came to this country in 1948," he recalled. "I had about a hundred and fifty regards from people dead and living to families they had here. So, since I didn't know the English language at all, I would go up to someone on the street and show him the address I had. One man understood who I

was. He said, 'Do you speak Jewish?' I said, 'Of course.' So he said, 'I'm gonna ask you a question and if you'll give me the answer, I'll take you where you want to go.' And he asked me, 'How come six million died and you lived?' I told him, 'I am all the time asking myself this question. I have no answer. I have no explanation.'"

Rose Bokser, another survivor of the Warsaw ghetto, arrived in Brighton in 1952 with her husband, David. They had met and were married in the DP camp where she became pregnant. Though she had a young baby, her husband was quite ill by the time they emigrated, and so she had to be the family's sole support in New York. "We moved to Brighton Beach, where we lived in a garage. They charged us plenty for that garage. Whatever we got, we gave our landlords. We had no money, no furniture, no nothing. . . . I went from place to place before I got a job, looking for work. Nobody wanted to give." Others who arrived in Brighton during the late 1940s and the 1950s describe similar experiences. Troubled by this, Auschwitz survivor Max Brandwein opened Brand's Knish Parlor and Dairy Restaurant on Brighton Beach

Avenue and hired a staff of cooks and servers made up almost entirely of other survivors. For forty-five years, until the restaurant closed in the mid-1990s, these women cooked and fed, comforted and lambasted the elderly customers who streamed past them all day—some sweet and sad, others spoiling for a fight.

Shadows of the Holocaust were everywhere in Brighton during the 1960s and early 1970s. Brandwein's daughter Margie sat next to me in the seventh grade. Several of my schoolmates were the children of survivors. I learned about the Holocaust from them not as a vast historical evil but as a deeply personal horror that tore the darkness with screaming nightmares and strained the loving relations between children and parents, that left empty spaces at the family table on holidays, and crammed linoleum kitchen counters with *yarzeit* candles flickering through the nights in remembrance of too many dead. But my earliest encounter with the legacies of the Holocaust came as a very young child, when I asked why there were numbers tattooed on the thick, well-muscled arms of the women who ladled creamed spinach, potato pirogen, and kasha *varnishkes* from behind the steamy glass counters at Brand's.

Several thousand survivors left their mark on Brighton and surrounding neighborhoods in a variety of ways. Through Brand's and other retail businesses on Brighton Beach Avenue, they both transformed and reinforced the neighborhood's immigrant feel. By the early 1950s, many of the shopkeepers who'd opened up for business as far back as the 1920s had died or were ready to retire. Survivors opened a range of businesses on the Avenue, many simply taking over long-thriving concerns: tailors', glaziers', bakers' shops. Others opened more modern businesses: clothing stores, bookstores, household goods. Like the first wave immigrants before them, a majority of Brighton survivors worked for a time at least in the city's garment shops, though the industry was fading after World War II, as manufacturers fled the strongly unionized northern cities for nonunion centers in the South and Midwest. Still the union provided a home for some survivors who came with no family, and no friends. Mottl Grzenda, a Polish émigré who survived the war living in tunnels in the forest, recalls that the Amalgamated Clothing Workers' Union "became my family, like now the seniors in Brighton are. And many of the seniors are also from the union. This became my life in America, the union and now the senior center. They are the only family I have left." A smaller number of survivors entered the white-collar professions. And a few, physically and emotionally disabled by their experience of the camps, remained permanently unable to work.

I met Elsie on the dance floor at the Brighton Beach Baths during the early 1980s. Born and raised in Berlin during the century's first decades, she was married and a young mother when the war broke out. Neither her husband nor her daughter survived. Scarred by her memories, crippled with guilt about not being able to save her child, Elsie lived on disability payments and on the reparations paid by the German government to survivors living outside the Eastern Bloc countries. To keep from remembering, and to feel a sense of joy that she believed was her personal victory over the Nazis, Elsie danced wherever and whenever she could: at the Roseland Ballroom, weddings, bar mitzvahs, and finally at the Baths, daily and well into her eighties. She also walked on the Boardwalk in all but the most brutal cold. "The ocean I need to breathe. It calms me when I feel panic. To feel the sea in my lungs I know I'm alive."

THE FADED 1960S AND 1970S: "THE DEATH-DEFYING LEAP OVER A PAPER BAG BLINDFOLDED"

By the time I was old enough to make sense of what was around me, Brighton had become a place whose character was defined by the elderly, tens of thousands of Jewish seniors who lived between Ocean Parkway and Manhattan Beach. The opening of the Amalgamated Clothing Workers' Union Warbasse apartment houses in 1967 brought thousands more Jewish union retirees, mostly immigrants, into the community. And yet, even with so many new arrivals the neighborhood had begun to feel faded and tired by the early 1970s. It was an eccentric place too, on the edge psychologically as it was physically. The aura of fragility and psychic displacement that inevitably surrounded this community filled with so many who were elderly, who were immigrant, who were survivors of unthinkable tortures was intensified in the late 1970s by the arrival of a new group of urban refugees.

Facing bankruptcy, the city of New York made all sorts of deep cuts in services in those years, including one that had a profound impact on Brighton. Nonviolent mental patients in city hospitals and care centers were released and sent to halfway houses or to apartments under the supervision of social workers. Sent forth with just an address and a subway token, some never made it to their appointed destinations. Instead they rode the D train to the end of the line in Brighton and wandered down the subway stairs onto the Avenue. During the early 1980s Brighton was filled with shadows, people who spoke only to each other as they huddled together for warmth on the rock jetties or curled up beneath ratty coats and newspapers under the Boardwalk. More recognizable were a group of well-known Jewish "crazies" or *mishegoyim*—white-haired Queen Esther swathed in turbans and headscarves, who shouted her miseries at passersby; bespectacled Hymie, who murmured lovingly at his baby carriage full of socks as he shuffled endlessly up and down the Avenue; the Actor in his long gray overcoat, who orated passages from Yiddish translations of Shakespeare wandering among the tables at the Brighton Dairy Restaurant.

Most dazzling of these new street people was Disco Freddy, a wiry man in his sixties with close-cropped steel-gray hair, a deep tan, and a gleaming set of white teeth. Wearing mirrored sunglasses, a maroon neck scarf, and army surplus pants, Freddy performed several times daily on the Boardwalk in the early 1980s. Waving his arms like a windmill, he would begin rapid-fire banter with an audience primed for his mixture of reverent and mocking allusions to Yiddish culture, alternating golden memories of his "Yiddishe mameh's" Rosh Hashana dinners with crude jokes about Sabbath sex. He had once been a street person in midtown Manhattan, he once told me, but the audience missed most of his jokes. In Brighton all the Boardwalk was his stage. Hundreds, maybe thousands, saw his act over the years.

"I'm sixty-one years of age, Disco Freddy, coming to you from Brownsville and Disco WKTU. I'm a boy of the streets. East New York is not a pretty place and Freddy's not pretty. For sixty years I've lived in the gutter. My name is *meshugena*. . . ." Freddy's audience always bantered back. "Jump already," someone would say, usually an elderly man wearing a cotton beach hat, waving a fat cigar. "Jump already. We haven't got all day." The taunting would begin: "So you want it, eh," Freddy would say. "The death-defying leap over the paper bag blindfolded? You'll get it all right. But first a word from our sponsor." And then Freddy would pull a suitably frail woman from the audience for some impromptu ballroom on the boards. In 1984 Disco Freddy ran a presidential campaign from the Boardwalk, as the standard-bearer for the Schnorrer Party. "Reaganomics wants to starve you. Reaganomics wants to take the food

out of the little children's mouths. But I stand up for you people. I shame him. It's easy. Ever see one of those old movies of his? Come on. I'm a better actor than he is!" And then came the jump. Drumrolling with his tongue, Freddy would set down a crumpled paper bag, don his blindfold, press skinny arms tightly against his sides, and daintily skip over the bag. A performed leap of faith, resonant metaphor for an audience of elderly immigrants hanging onto a neighborhood that was slipping away from them.

FROM BRIGHTON BEACH TO LITTLE ODESSA: PORTAL FOR A NEW IMMIGRATION

In 1975, before large numbers of Soviet Jewish immigrants began to arrive in Brighton, the neighborhood had begun to take on the unmistakable air of decline: rising crime rates; dark, gated storefronts; echoing, empty hallways with apartments that stayed vacant for too long. Then a transformation of grand proportions began to take place. The first Soviet Jews were settled in Brighton in the mid-1970s by NYANA caseworkers who hoped, since most of those already living in Brighton were also eastern European Jews, many of them born in Russia, that the settlement process would proceed smoothly. The neighborhood quickly became a mecca for Russian and Ukrainian immigrants. Within a decade Brighton Beach had begun to fade away, and in its place grew Little Odessa—the most famous "Russian" neighborhood in America. When I returned home from college in 1980, I felt that I had to study Russian to make my way around its suddenly unfamiliar streets.

I found my way into this community of suspicious newcomers with the help of two new friends: my Russian teacher Tamara, a highly cultivated woman from an assimilated Petersburg family who spoke French and English as fluently as Russian; and the writer/director Alexander Sirotin, who was literally raised backstage at the old Moscow Yiddish theater. Because they came to trust me, other "Russians" were willing to speak to me. They provided not only linguistic translation but, just as important, cultural insight.

For, just as the Holocaust survivors found an ambivalent reception when they arrived in Brighton during the 1950s, relations between Soviet newcomers and Brighton old-timers had quickly become strained. Each group developed quick and strong impressions of the other as they interacted on Brighton streets, in the hallways of apartment buildings, in senior centers, shops, and synagogues. Old and newly arrived Jewish immigrants in Brighton

Alexander Sirotin, in the studio of Radio Liberty. © Elizabeth Cooke.

adopted a charged and awkward intimacy like estranged cousins bound to one another by bloodlines in the distant past, related but uncomfortable. They had high expectations because each had nurtured idealized images of the other during the long struggle to "free Soviet Jewry." And so there were inevitable disappointments, turf wars, and misunderstandings.

The issue of Jewish identity among the Soviet Jews was perhaps the greatest bone of contention in the early years of the immigration, and remains an issue to this day. In the 1970s, observant Jews throughout Brooklyn reached out to the newcomers, hoping to school them in the fundamentals of a religious practice that Jews in the Soviet Union had been prevented from observing for half a century. Brooklyn synagogues and yeshivas launched outreach programs to attract and teach the new immigrants. They leafleted apartment buildings with invitations to attend special Russian-language holiday services. Of the eleven synagogues in Brighton, only five were able to attract Soviet immigrants to join, and these were almost all people over sixty.

With such a lukewarm response, tempers flared among older Brighton residents. Many felt that the Soviets were pushy and unfriendly, unwilling to return greetings or wait their turn on line. With less justification, they also railed against the generous federal and private subsidies that the newcomers received, perhaps forgetting that they too had been aided by Jewish charitable groups when they arrived decades earlier. Their resentment was openly expressed. You could hear it on the streets, on the Boardwalk, in synagogues, in stores. "Why did we fight to bring them here? Why did they want to come here? They're not even Jews. They don't want to be Jews."

Some strongly Jewish-identified members of the immigrant community tried to mediate. Alexander Sirotin formed the Jewish Union of Russian Immigrants to sponsor activities with a Jewish theme among the new arrivals. Through the 1980s he was host of *Gorizont* (Horizon), a Russian-language radio show on the Lubavitch Hasidic radio network. The message of Sirotin and other Jewish-identified leaders in Brighton was: Let the Soviet immigrants nourish their Jewish identities in their own ways, in their own time. As examples, Sirotin pointed to an émigré Yiddish theater troupe and to gatherings of senior citizens at which Yiddish songs and poems were sung and recited by recent Soviet immigrants. "American Jews try to teach the Russian immigrant about Jewishness using a strange language, and then wonder why he does not understand," Sirotin noted. He saw Soviet émigrés as akin to concentration camp survivors, when it came to their Jewish identity. "We are not starving physically but we are starving for Jewishness," Sirotin wrote in 1981. "You can't shove food down a starving man's throat. It is the same with these Jews. They must be fed *Yiddishkayt* [Jewishness] with a teaspoon."

In truth, like American-born Jews and earlier waves of eastern European immigrants, Soviet Jewish émigrés embraced a wide range of Jewish identities. Among the new immigrants were some who were very religious and others who identified strongly with Yiddish language and culture but not with religion. Some began attending synagogue and studying Hebrew in the 1960s and 1970s as an act of resistance. Others, schooled in a communist society, saw religion as a vestige of premodern superstition and so rejected it out of hand. Some identified themselves as both Russian and Jewish; others claimed Russian language and culture as their own. All knew that they were Jews. Living in the Soviet Union, where they were forced to carry internal passports with the letter J emblazoned on them, where appearing Jewish, bearing a Jewish name, revealing a Jewish ancestor might lead to all sorts of petty as well as serious harassment, all of these émigrés were keenly and always aware that they were Jews. Indeed, they had all paid a terrible price in the blood of family and friends for the crime of being Jewish.

Having survived decades of murder, torture, and imprisonment at the hands of Cossacks, Nazis, and Stalinists, Soviet Jewish immigrants were outraged that those who had lived comfortably in the United States for much of this time would dare to tell them that they were not Jews.

Surveys of Soviet immigrants in the United States show that a large majority strongly identify as Jews, far more strongly than do most American Jews. More than one-third enroll their children in Jewish afternoon or Sunday schools. Like American-born Jewish families, the vast majority celebrate the more popular and less religious holidays like Passover and Chanukah with family gatherings and ritual meals at home. A staggering number of adult men have had themselves circumcised since their arrival in the United States, more than ten thousand in New York City alone. But Soviet émigrés balk at what they see as coercive pressures by religious Jews. Despite offers of scholarships and tuition remission, a great many Soviet émigré families withdrew their children from Brooklyn yeshivas when school authorities demanded that uncircumcised immigrant boys submit to the operation.

After decades of repression, finding comfortable ways to express Jewishness has taken time for Soviet Jewish immigrants. Brighton storekeepers who at first offended the sensibilities of observant Jews by staying open on the Jewish High Holy Days—Rosh Hashana and Yom Kippur—soon began to close their businesses on Jewish holidays and post signs wishing their customers *mazl* (luck) and *shalom* (peace). Hearing the language again on the streets of Brighton after half a century, many elderly and middle-aged Soviet immigrants revived the Yiddish of their youth. The *mamaloshn* (mother tongue) peppers the Russian repartee in crowded groceries, bakeries, and butcher shops. "Many years ago I used to hear my grandparents speak," one store owner explained. "But I forgot it all until I moved here. Suddenly it came pouring back."

The refreshing of distant memories has not always been easy or comforting for Soviet émigrés. Like many Vietnamese, Cambodian, Salvadoran, and Haitian immigrants now living in New York, elderly Soviet Jews are a highly traumatized population. They have lived through Stalin's purges, the Nazi occupation during which one of every two Soviet Jews was murdered, and the "black years of Soviet Jewry" after World War II, when most of the Soviet Union's Jewish artists, intellectuals, and physicians were either executed or sentenced to hard labor in the gulag. Almost all have lost loved ones to violent deaths. Many feel crippling guilt at having survived—and at leaving family graves behind. The symptoms of posttraumatic stress disorder are common among them. Bits of random memories surface suddenly in the conversations of the aged immigrants who line benches in the asphalt parks that dot Brighton. Flashbacks and nightmares can easily bleed through the thin tissue separating a happy present from a more troubled past.

These traumatic memories sometimes make it difficult for elderly émigrés to meet their needs in a new and strange place. Sophie Spector, who worked for many years at the Shorefront Y and Senior Center in Brighton teaching English and helping elderly Soviet Jews to adjust, found that simply calling for an ambulance could evoke memories of the era in Soviet history when political dissidents were whisked off to hospitals and never heard from again. If a police car arrived before the ambulance, as is often the case in New York City, the elderly immigrant panicked. An uncomprehending medic, arriving moments later, would then try to push the terrified old man or woman into the vehicle. Far too often, Spector recalled, a simple ambulance call escalated into a hostile encounter between police, medics, and a crowd of immigrants.

Many émigrés find the health care system in New York cold and impersonal compared to the small neighborhood clinics in the Soviet Union where they received a great deal of personal attention. They grow frustrated and angry at not being able to find physicians near their homes who will accept Medicaid and when they do, at waits of up to four hours. Having received substandard medical care at understaffed and overcrowded Soviet hospitals, some view Western medicine as a whole with suspicion, turning instead to herbal remedies. Brighton pharmacies now carry a bewildering array of dried herbs in hand-labeled bags. The emergency room staff at Coney Island Hospital, the major public health facility in southern Brooklyn, keep a Russian-language herbal remedy book so that they can figure out what patients may have taken.

Such confusions notwithstanding, most elderly Soviet émigrés have found Brighton Beach to be a place where they can begin to heal from the traumas of the past. Brighton's tradition of public communal mourning has helped them to voice openly long-suppressed pain at the loss of loved ones. Soviet immigrants have flocked to long-established Brighton commemorations of the Holocaust. Alongside Brighton's concentration camp survivors they pray and mourn, read poetry, sing Yiddish partisans' songs, light memorial candles, and say Kaddish (the Jewish prayer for the dead.) For Soviet immigrants over the age of seventy, a vital part of the adjustment to Brighton has been a recognition that they are not only refugees of authoritarian communism but also Holocaust survivors.

For nearly half a century, the Soviet regime repressed facts about the Nazi occupation and destroyed sources. Through all this time, Soviet Jewish survivors of World War II carried their memories with them as the only documentation of the murder of 1.5 million of their friends, family, and loved ones. Once in Brighton, they began to tell and to record their own family stories, marking the losses not in millions but in memories of individual loved ones—mothers, husbands, fathers, wives, children, friends.

As part of their recognition of themselves as a community of survivors, Soviet émigrés added to Brighton's communal calendar of mourning a day of remembrance for the tens of thousands of Jews shot to death by the Nazis in the forest of Babi Yar, near Kiev, in 1941. And a few blocks from the Y, they erected a sign marking Babi Yar Triangle, a tiny park of tarred ground, wooden benches, and a few stone tables with inlaid chessboards over which old men in berets bend low in concentration. A public marker of the kind that one could not find in Kiev, it represents freedom to mourn, freedom finally to name the dead aloud without fear of reprisal, freedom to cry in public, or even to laugh and remember the good times. As their grandchildren play around them, say Soviet émigrés, they have finally begun to heal. And they have slowly come to feel at home in Brooklyn.

The food stores and restaurants that line Brighton Beach Avenue have served not only as means to a livelihood for hundreds of new émigrés but also as daily gathering places where a sense of group identity is forged and reinforced. Brighton Beach hums with the business of buying and selling. From the beginning of the Soviet Jewish immigration, small businesses were a major source of income for new arrivals—both those who already had some experience with retail sales in the former Soviet Union and professionals who felt they needed some new way of making a living in the United States. Partly this was an idealized vision of American capitalism. To own a business was to have no boss, no restrictions on where one could settle, and no limitations on what one could earn. It was also a recognition that, with limited English, it might be difficult to find other work. Many new arrivals believed that they could create thriving businesses in a Russian immigrant neighborhood without becoming fluent in English. Brighton Beach Avenue is testament to their success.

The first of Soviet immigrant-owned stores to appear on the Avenue were groceries: clean, bright, and modern, they stood in stark contrast to the old-fashioned corner stores of an earlier generation. These new stores occupied a special place in the life of each immigrant family, for they offered daily reminders of the difference between the former Soviet Union and the land where the family now lived. Every day in Brighton was testimony to the miracle of abundance at the core of so many dreams of America. In Moscow, Leningrad, or Minsk, keeping a family fed meant standing in one line after another for hours each day just to purchase the essentials, bribing truckers, farmers, and grocery workers and scouring the city for the latest black-market shipments. In Brighton immigrants could choose between at least a dozen groceries offering Polish, Hungarian, German, Russian, and American meats, cheeses, juices, chocolates. Bakeries, butcher shops, fish stores, and fruit stands compete with the groceries and with each other to create increasingly eye-catching displays of delectables. These stores became informal community centers as a largely elderly clientele exchanged news and congratulations or offered condolences and remembered the dead. These stores play a somewhat different role for immigrants who live in other parts of the city or the country. Like suburban Jews who come to shop and eat out on the Lower East Side, upwardly mobile Soviet Jewish immigrants now come to Brighton to assuage pangs of nostalgia, to bask in the smells, the Russian banter, the fashions that are evocative of home.

Brighton's Russian restaurants and nightclubs also draw émigré families from across the New York area. The names, the food, and the decor reflect the geographic diversity of those who have come to New York since the fall of the Soviet Union. Ukrainian food, not surprisingly, is the most commonly served cuisine, along with traditional Ashkenazi (northern European) Jewish specialties and an odd amalgam known as Odessan-style Continental. But Georgian dining is also popular, as are restaurants serving Uzbek and other Central Asian cuisines. Meat, cheese, and potato-filled dumplings are variously called *pirogi* (Ukrainian), *pelmeni* (Central Asian), and *vareniki* (Russian), but they can be found almost everywhere. So can *shashlyk* (shish kebab, made with lamb, chicken, or sturgeon and served on a swordlike skewer), and chicken Kiev (fried with butter and mushrooms at the center). Regional specialties include Odessan shrimp in garlic sauce, *lavash* (crusty round Georgian bread eaten hot and sliced like a pie), *chakokhokbili* (a Caucasian chicken stew with tomatoes) and *baklazhan* (eggplant) with pomegranate or walnut sauce. Whatever the restaurateurs' region of origin,

Grandparents and grandchildren at a Brighton birthday party. © Elizabeth Cooke.

groaning banquet tables are the norm, covered with *zakuski* (appetizers), flowers, and elaborate place settings. Plates of smoked fish, pickled vegetables, and cold vegetable salads greet arriving guests, with bottles of vodka, water, wine, and soda rising like islands in the sea of food.

Brighton restaurants vary greatly in size and grandeur. But they all share an extravagant taste in interior design that makes even the smallest eatery feel more like a stage set than a dining room. From the red walls of the Primorski restaurant, with its small colored lights and stained glass sailing ships, to the marble bathrooms, crystal chandeliers, chrome and black enamel banquettes, and strobe-lighted dance floors of the big nightclubs, these restaurants are soaked with fantasy. Blonde Russian torch singers in skintight low-cut spandex, a perfect Stevie Wonder impersonator at the Primorski, big bands with congas and horns, even full-scale floor shows like the pistol-packing dance number at the Rasputin, complete with dancers in fedoras and double-breasted pinstripes, suggest a sense of irony and a capacity for self-parody in the owners and patrons of these clubs. The fantasy, the irony, the food, the music, and the vodka all work together to create moments of shared emotional release that build in-

timacy and group feeling. They also make for great parties.

These restaurants have their roots in Soviet Jewish culture, where from the 1930s to the 1980s it was not only difficult but dangerous for Jews to gather in groups. With the KGB on the steps of many synagogues, and gatherings in private homes subject to sudden police raids, restaurants were among the only places where Jews could gather in a relaxed atmosphere. "The spirit of Soviet Jewry really came to life in restaurants," says Alexander Sirotin. "There, ordinary workers, by day forced to comply with Soviet officials, to submit to constant harassment, could finally become people of character, of unique identity. This was the only place where they could remove all masks to reveal openly a Jewish face. In the absence of other possibilities, the restaurant became the center of life for many Jews in Soviet cities. This custom was carried here."

In the Soviet Union, these communal spaces were hidden from prying eyes of unfriendly officials. That custom, too, was carried here. For many years, Russian restaurants in Brighton hid their fabulous interiors with blank fronts, heavy curtains, and blackened street-facing windows. This camouflage, which reflected both a lingering distrust of strangers and a desire to discourage casual browsing by

Russian gift shop, Brighton Beach Avenue. © Elizabeth Cooke.

outsiders, was meant to mark the restaurants as off-limits to tourists. The lavishly decorated National removed a large plateglass window and replaced it with a metal wall, broken only by a windowless wooden door. The owners of Sadko, a two-floor black and silver discotheque built on the site of an abandoned pizzeria, were even more intent on hiding. For years, the club owners preserved the pizzeria storefront as it was on the day that it closed, complete with white formica counter and pizza ovens. Over the faded sign for Mama Mia Pizzeria, small black letters advertised Sadko. There was no indication that a chic, expensive club lay within those walls. Yet each weekend, dark cars and limousines pulled up at the side entrance to the former pizzeria, where a signless wooden door admitted those in the know. Sometime during the mid-1980s, the owners erected a more elaborate nautical facade, but the porthole windows were placed high above the street. Some habits die hard.

Twenty-five years after the immigration began, these restaurants have become more relaxed, more open to outsiders. The *Village Voice*, the *New York Times*, and other city newspapers regularly review the restaurants in Brighton. Even the infamous Rasputin, reputed gathering ground for the local Russian mob, attracts curious non-Russian customers. Outsiders may still be greeted with stares, as if they have crashed someone else's family gathering. But both restaurateurs and patrons have grown accustomed to the odd "American" family joining in the Saturday night festivities. Tourism in New York's ethnic enclaves is, after all, a time-honored part of American pluralism.

So, too, is the tendency of some immigrants to assimilate to the American way of crime. Since the 1970s, the "Odessa mob" has made the name of Brighton Beach infamous among law enforcement agents from New York to Moscow. This small group of primarily Ukrainian Jewish gangsters learned their trade in the wide-open port city of Odessa. Released from prison, they were granted exit visas in time to accompany the tens of thousands of honest citizens departing for Israel and the United States. They slipped into this country unnoticed by the FBI or local law enforcement. Some were non-Jews who used the identification papers and visas of deceased Jews.

Reading the New Russian Word on the Brighton Beach Boardwalk. © Elizabeth Cooke.

Typical of these early gangster immigrants was Evsei Agron, a short Josef Stalin look-alike who listed his occupation as jeweler when he arived at Kennedy Airport in 1975. He neglected to mention the seven years he had served in a Soviet prison camp for murder or the gambling and prostitution rings he had been running in West Germany. Agron became the first boss of a Brighton-based Soviet mob operation profiting from extortion, prostitution, and drug sales. A far more sophisticated organized crime syndicate was established in the late 1970s by Odessan black marketeer Marat Balagula, who masterminded multimillion-dollar gasoline frauds and created a crime network that stretched from Brighton to San Francisco. Though Balagula was convicted of fraud in 1994, his organization continues to run a network of corporations that invest illegally obtained cash in oil refineries, tankers, gas stations, and truck stops.

Brighton was a good spot for Russian mobsters for a variety of reasons. It was just a short drive from Kennedy Airport, air link to fellow gang members in Europe and the former Soviet Union. Its teeming streets gave perfect cover; it was easy to hide among the tens of thousands of Soviet immigrants already living in Brighton. During the 1970s there were still plenty of vacant apartments, some of which were bought up in large blocks by gang bosses and rented to street soldiers as needed. One immigrant who moved to Brighton in the early 1980s recalled that there were entire buildings in one part of the neighborhood— huge art deco edifices with turrets, mosaics, and long dark hallways—that belonged to criminal families. Everyone knew where they were and steered clear of those blocks.

Like most criminals, the Russian mob preyed first on their own. Evsei Agron ran protection rackets in Brighton that, by 1980, averaged fifty thousand dollars per week, extorted from local émigré shopkeepers with threats of violence. Loan sharks lent money at astronomical interest rates to naive aspiring entrepreneurs, new immigrants wary of official paperwork. Car theft rings began to prowl the streets as well, sometimes recruiting children under the age of sixteen—who could not be sentenced to long prison terms—to commit the actual crime. The transformation of this neighborhood, which had always been one of the least violent in New York, came as a shock to longtime Brighton residents. The early 1980s were a particularly violent period. A mob boss was shot to death in his car in front of the Odessa restaurant late one night. A well-known former journalist was gunned down in a jewelry store. And one Yom Kippur (the Day of Atonement), a man was shot to death at close range on the Boardwalk. Stunned elderly Jews, first and second wave immigrants dressed in Holy Day attire, gathered around the scene of the crime. One angry voice could be heard above the crowd: "There is something very sick happening in this neighborhood. They shoot each other on the holiest day of the year. These cannot be Jews."

Since the collapse of the Soviet Union in 1991, many Soviet émigrés most active in the New York underworld are in fact not Jewish. The most powerful competitor to Balagula is a *gory* (crime boss) named Vyacheslav Ivankov who moved to Brighton in 1992, masquerading as an ordinary Jewish immigrant. Sent by a consortium of crime syndicates that believed the U.S. market was too profitable to be left to Jewish gangsters alone, Ivankov established bases for more than two hundred Russian crime families in U.S. cities. In 1995 Ivankov was arrested in Brighton for extorting $3.5 million from two Soviet émigré investment bankers whom he had kidnapped at gunpoint in the bar at the New York Hilton.

The reputation of Soviet Jewish immigrants, particularly those who live in Brighton, has suffered as a result of adverse publicity generated by these criminals. By the mid-1990s, new Soviet émigrés shuddered angrily when asked if they lived or wanted to live in Brighton. "I am not like the people there," one woman said vehemently. "I work. Everyone in my family works. We are not like *that*." The 1994 film *Little Odessa* by Tim Roth exemplified the media stereotyping that makes Russian émigrés leery of association with Brighton Beach. In this grim portrayal, Brighton is populated almost exclusively by leather-jacketed, gun-toting thugs. Though most Russian émigrés reject that depiction, they fear that it still reflects badly upon them and are quick to distance themselves from the neighborhood. What they don't talk about are the ways that Brighton continues to serve as an emotional and cultural home base for Soviet Jews across the New York area—a place to shop, to visit relatives, and to celebrate birthdays, weddings, and anniversaries at Russian restaurants. It is the symbolic portal through which many, if not most, Soviet

immigrants pass, but like most immigrant ghettos, it has become a revolving door.

COMING HOME

These days, when I'm in Brighton, I usually spend an hour at Mary's Unisex Hairstyles—a tiny beauty shop run by two glamorous, edgy sisters from Baku who watch a cross section of all that Brighton is pass through their black Naugahyde barber chairs. Fast Central Asian music blares from a small boom box as Mary and Esther do their rapid razor cuts, perms, dye jobs—pausing to purchase slinky shirts or leather bags from some traveling street salesman, or to make a point in heated Russian conversation. They like to line up my family in generations—my eighty-three-year-old mother, myself, my little daughter for excellent short haircuts that do not require much daily rearranging. We fit easily into the mix made up mostly of young and old Russian and Urkainian émigrés, men and women wearing everything from floral prints to black leather. These are seasoned with a sprinkling of elderly longtime Brightonites still sporting red or blonde curls well into their eighties, always ready for some banter about what things cost these days or how long they have to wait. Here and there: a sweet drag queen with a faint Brooklyn Jewish accent who needs a perfectly executed cut and dye for his European tour; a newly arrived Mexican immigrant family; crew cut and tattooed gang boys; wanderers off the D train. Nothing fazes Esther and Mary. Everyone is welcome. Everyone is treated with the same easy professionalism: fast cuts, fast talk, low prices. Esther doesn't have much time or inclination to follow the news from Russia or Azerbaijan very closely anymore. Brooklyn is home, she says. Everyone is here (or in Israel.)

Like other Jewish immigrants before them, the newest residents of Brighton/Little Odessa have become Brooklynites—fast-talking, unflappable, quietly amused by the variety of human life that passes each day along the Avenue. Street vendors hawk their wares in Russian, Yiddish, and English. Eagle-eyed women shoppers browse the vegetable stands. The very old and the disabled zip through the crowds in motorized shopping carts. Above, the trains come and the trains go. And the beach, newly replenished with sand sucked by giant hoses from the ocean floor, faces back to Europe as if waiting for the next wave.

The New Wave from Russia

LOUIS MENASHE

I offer Social Sciences 121, the "History of the Soviet Union," every spring at Polytechnic, a small, predominantly engineering university in downtown Brooklyn. During the 1970s, the period of détente, students were curious about the Soviet Union, and SS 121 always had a large enrollment. So many students signed up for the course, in fact, that I developed a little ice-breaking routine. "This class is too big," I would announce. "I'm afraid I'll have to limit the course to only those who can read and write Russian. Will all who do so, please stand." No one stood. Just a little joke, I reassured the class.

I did it again in the spring of 1980. Only this time a lanky young man with reddish-brown curly hair stood up—a little cockily, I thought. At that moment I realized two things: first, I would have to abandon that routine; second, the Russians were coming.

It was Leonid who stood up. I remember him vividly, as I do scores of Igors, Mischas, and Irinas who have turned up in my classes since then. These students are part of the "Third Emigration"—recent arrivals from the Soviet Union now living in Brooklyn's Brighton Beach ("Little Odessa by the Sea"), near Ocean Parkway ("Russian Parkway"), and in other parts of New York ("Moscow on the Hudson").

Like other generations of immigrants and children of immigrants before them and in our own day, they look to the engineering degree as a sure ticket to a comfortable corner of the American dream. En route to that degree, by a strange twist of academic fate, they are offered courses on the history and politics of the homeland they have just left behind.

Those Igors, Irinas, and I—we are sharers in that perplexing thing, the Soviet experience: I through professional immersion in the study of the Soviet Union; they through the living of it. By Soviet standards, they represent relatively upscale social backgrounds: They come from the large urban centers of European Russia, and their parents belonged to the intelligentsia—engineers, educators—or worked in the white-collar sector. They are, by self-definition, and by Soviet ethnic criteria, Jewish, not Russian. Ironically, in the United States, they tend to be viewed as Russians, not Jews.

My dialogues with them spill out of the classroom, into the elevators, the corridors, into my office. I get to know them personally; I learn that though they are victims and critics of Soviet society, they are—more than they care to admit—its representatives and beneficiaries as well. Their educational background, if tendentious, is solid. They are keen on political and social analysis and have a taste for culture; they are uncommonly well read.

Although they bare their wrath at the Soviet system, they show no small amount of respect for its power, and pride in its achievements. Interestingly, their anti-Soviet discourse is tinged with the kind of dogma and polemical edge that we associate with the official Soviet style. They enjoy America, but criticize it from a Soviet perspective: too much crime, too much looseness, too much materialism, too much competitiveness, not enough friendliness, too little culture. They are, to use a term from the excellent, literate Marxist they speak, contradictions.

It is intersession, January 1985. I run into Valery Berman in the elevator.

"Hello, Professor," he greets me warmly.

"Hello, Val. Kak dela?" (How are things?)

"Wonderful. What can be bad? Reagan was elected!"

Yes, if I were to poll the Russian caucus, Reagan would win in a landslide here, too. Reagan is strong, they tell me; he knows how to stand up to Moscow.

Val is spoiling for an ad hoc discussion. He is big and burly, with high color in his cheeks and a languid, faintly aristocratic air about him. There is something else, a way of looking at me that I notice among others in the Russian caucus, a look of condescension and gentle indulgence. It is as if our roles are reversed, and I am their student. "You mean well, Professor," the look seems to say, "and you know a lot about Russian history. But you are very naive about the Soviet Union. We know what it's really about."

I mutter some insincere congratulations to Val on Reagan's victory and leave him in the elevator. Val is one of a troika that collars me after class, twice a week, for quick hallway seminars. The troika wants to "correct" things I say in my lectures. Roman Litvak, a troika regular, has made it his mission to prove to me that the world is in mortal danger from the Soviet threat. Roman is a streetwise math major from Ukraine, with a command of colloquial English. He is short, but he could knock over a tree trunk with his shoulder, and has the temperament to match. He is always ready for ideological combat, and he sees everything through political lenses. A great deal of the official Soviet view of the world has rubbed off on Roman. He, too, sees the globe as a vast arena in which the forces of capitalism and communism are locked in daily, permanent battle. Class interests govern the behavior of political leaders everywhere. Nothing is ever accidental—in politics, economics, or culture. Governments manipulate and lie to their people. That's the way it is.

Soviet social science education has done its job well, even, as in Roman's case, before the university level. Most of my Soviet students have been through high school; many attended what are known in the Soviet Union as "higher technical institutes," and a handful began university studies before their departure. In their school transcripts, I see courses such as "Marxist Ethics" and "History of the Communist Party of the Soviet Union" sandwiched between "Technology of Construction Materials" and "Thermodynamics and Heat Transfer." These students are familiar with the language and concepts of Marxism-Leninism. No, not just familiar with them; they accept them as naturally as they quote Pushkin.

The "Glossary of Marxist Terms" I distribute at the start of every course in Soviet history draws condescending smiles from the Russian caucus. It takes some effort for an American student to define and use the term "bourgeoisie," not to mention spell it properly. For the Russian students, bourgeoisie, proletariat, capitalism, intelligentsia, the state, imperialism are all components of their normal analytic language. Of course, they also know the send-ups that go with the Soviet terms. One of the Russians volunteers a better definition of socialism for my glossary: "Socialism," he tells the class, "means a shortage of sand in the desert."

The Russian students may complain of the Soviet political climate, but their resentments over shortages and the inequitable distribution system are stronger. If only there were a little more meat, they seem to say, we wouldn't mind the political shortcomings. Meat is a recurrent image, a measure of things. When I describe my Moscow and Leningrad visits to the class after a trip during Easter recess, American students are fascinated by my experiences in the Evil Empire. I tell of the warmth of Soviet citizens, of their concern over Reagan's foreign policy, of the many improvements I noticed compared to a previous trip.

"Did you see any meat in the stores, Professor?" Sergei Poliakoff cuts in; he is obviously annoyed with my benign account.

"Well, apart from plentiful meat at hotels and restaurants, I saw some meat at a small supermarket I used to browse in near my hotel in Leningrad...."

"If you had gone to other cities," retorts Sergei, "you wouldn't have seen any meat at all. And what you saw in

Leningrad was what we call soup meat, not good for eating alone."

Someone (not a Russian) asks: "Were you allowed to go anywhere?"—a question I hear often from Americans.

"My visa specified Moscow and Leningrad," I explain. "In those cities, I went wherever I pleased and no one followed me, if that's what you mean." This brings guffaws from the Russians, all twelve of them, about a third of the whole class. "I know, I know, you think I was tailed by the KGB."

"Of course you were, Professor!" says the caucus in unison.

Among them is Dina Yershova. Before I left for Moscow, Dina had warned me against acting like a "*spasibo*–big shot." (*Spasibo* is Russian for "thank you.") "Russians get suspicious when foreigners know the language," she explained. Now, after my trip, she and the caucus are insisting I was watched continuously inside the Soviet Union. "Look," I appeal to their reason, "the USSR doesn't want to scare Western tourists; it wants their hard currency and it wants them to come back. Besides, do you think the KGB has the resources to keep tabs on the hundreds of thousands of Western tourists who visit every year?" Of course! The caucus holds firm.

That smug, dogmatic certainty of theirs, hard as birch wood—where does it come from? Is it their youth and naivete? Or am I the naive one? They are, after all, Jewish emigrants, many of whom know refuseniks or have them in the family. Brushes with the KGB and other Soviet bureaucracies are among their youthful experiences. It is understandable that they hold these attitudes. Oddly, however, it is not fear or even hatred that they express, but a species of Soviet pride. "The prevailing faith" in the USSR "encourages a belief that the Soviet people are better, smarter, more altruistic, self-sacrificing than, and generally morally superior to, other peoples," observe Polly Howells and Mikhail Galperin, two psychotherapists working in Brighton Beach (Galperin is himself an emigrant). Some of the émigrés, they continue, "will tell you that the light bulb was invented by a man named Yablochkov, the radio by Alexei Popov, and the steam engine by two serf brothers from the Ural Mountains. Lenin is often quoted as saying the Russian language is the richest, most powerful tongue in the world.

So why shouldn't the KGB be the most powerful security organization in the world?

After seeing the film *Moscow on the Hudson*, I am eager to discuss it with my Russians, anticipating their approval of Paul Mazursky's satire, particularly its gloomy Moscow sequences. Not so. They are indignant. They may criticize the motherland, but they seem to resent images of Soviet backwardness that prevail in the United States. "Why do all Americans think we have no refrigerators in the Soviet Union?" they have often complained to me. Even Sergei Poliakoff is annoyed by Mazursky's film. "Really, Professor. . . . Muscovites standing in line at night, waiting for toilet paper. . . ." "But don't Russians suffer from endless queuing for basic commodities?" I reply. "Right!" shouts Roman. "I remember waiting for toilet paper once." "That's because you come from Ukraine," retorts Sergei, the proud Muscovite.

Others argue Roman down; they can't recall queuing for toilet paper. "Americans think Russians are robots," adds Yevgeny from Kiev. "No Russian would stand in line the way they stood in the film. Russians are too, too . . . lively to be robots." It is true. In my classroom, activity and a general buzzing emanate from wherever the Russian caucus is sitting. I ask for silence. The buzzing continues. I finally shout, "Zamolchite!" (Quiet!). They laugh. There is a moment's silence. The buzzing resumes.

When it comes to Russian history before 1917, my Russians have as hard a time sorting out the reigns of the various Ivans and Alexanders as do my other students. Interest develops with the Soviet period. A residual respect for Lenin is surprisingly common. Many of my Russians exempt Lenin from the great sins that followed him. But their respect is tempered by criticism, ranging from the thoughtful to the abusive. Sergei Poliakoff attacks Leninism at its ideological root—the utopian vision of a communist future. American students always ridicule the idea of a harmonious, classless society with colossal wealth available to all. "People are too selfish for that," they say. Sergei offers a sophisticated gloss on that common critique. "If there were absolute material abundance," he comments, his blue eyes smiling, "this would lead to degeneration. No one would want to work in such a society."

Alyosha, by contrast, is cruder in his deflations. Alyosha is pudgy and wears a perpetual melancholic hangdog look. His ultimate source of authority is the impersonal, oracular "It is well known."

"Professor, you did not mention that Lenin was a German spy," Alyosha corrects me after a discussion of

Lenin's return to Petrograd from exile in 1917. I will not entertain this hoary red herring. "Who taught you that, Alyosha?" I kid him. "Solzhenitsyn?" "No," he replies, unblinking. "It is well known."

Our discussion of the Lenin cult in the young Soviet state carries us to the mausoleum in Red Square, the national shrine. "His so-called body is made of wax," Alyosha tells the class mournfully. "Also, Professor, you said Lenin died of stroke. Impossible." "Impossible, Alyosha? What's your diagnosis?"

"Lenin died of syphilis. It is well known."

FIFTEEN YEARS LATER: THE NEWER WAVE

After leaving Polytechnic, those Mischas and Irinas disappeared from my view, and I have often wondered how they fared these last fifteen years. (I wonder as well: Do they ever think of me, and our exchanges?) Except for a couple of contacts, they have not been in touch. I saw Roman, the most colorful of the "troika," recently; he came by to pick up some documents at Polytechnic and we ran into each other. He promised to call, but didn't. He looked chipper and prosperous, and his two-color calling card showed he was in business, which didn't surprise me. Making it in America wasn't through the doctoral degree in mathematics he once pursued. Just after the collapse of the USSR in 1991, I was delighted to get a phone call from Nadia, now a medical student in Florida. She remembers my telling her class once that if ever monuments of Lenin came down, as they already were before the end, it would signal the finale of the Soviet Union. "How right you were!" she told me breathlessly. (I wonder: Did she ever get her medical degree?) And what did all the others think, how did they all react when the erstwhile motherland they loved and hated disappeared into the history books?

There are new Mischas and Irinas now. If the older group was part of the "Third Wave" of emigration, the current cohort is part of a New Tidal Wave. The Third Wave ebbed during the chilly Reagan years, when Moscow blocked emigration. But Gorbachev's glasnost and perestroika (and better relations with Washington) opened the sluice gates again, and they remained wider than ever in the post-Soviet Yeltsin years. Formerly, the Russians merely enriched my classes; now they fill them wall to wall. Of the thirty-two students registered for the course "Stalin and Stalinism" I'm now teaching, all but five are from the former USSR. (If it weren't for those five, the class could be conducted in Russian.) Another novelty: They now come from all parts of the Russian land, not just Moscow and Leningrad. Identifying their birthplaces is a lesson in Russian geography and history: Kursk, site of the greatest tank battle of World War II; Ulyanovsk on the Volga, where Lenin was born, and bearing his real family name; Irkutsk, deep in Siberia. And from the non-Russian former Soviet republics, they come not just from the capitals—from Kherson, not just Kiev (Ukraine); Tiraspol, not just Kishenev (Moldova); Gomel, not just Minsk (Belarus).

They certainly got around, those Soviet Jewish families.

The new students are still overwhelmingly Jewish, but like their secularized predecessors, not particularly observant. And they still come largely from respectable social and professional backgrounds, children of engineers and school administrators and laboratory heads. Another constant: they have settled in Brooklyn. Brighton Beach and Bensonhurst have replaced Samara and Tula in their lives. Soviet anti-Semitism and the lure of a better material life brought their predecessors to our shores. Those are constants as well for the new arrivals, but from changed circumstances. If post-Soviet Russia has seen the revival of Jewish religious expression and culture, it has also witnessed the flourishing of a rabid Russian nationalism with ugly anti-Jewish components. Students have told me they weren't especially bothered by anti-Semitism, but their parents were worried for them, and for what a possibly uglier future might bring. In the old days, the malfunctioning Soviet economy meant long lines and chronic shortages; the post-Soviet economy has eliminated the lines and shortages, but is in arrears on wages and pensions, and fiscal crises are endemic. Old and new, the result is little faith in the future (no "perspective," as the Russians say), so why not emigrate?

The new arrivals are just as voluble, frisky, engaging as their predecessors; they have a presence. But since there are so many more of them, they are also much more disruptive in classes. In lounges and hallways, Russian is still their preferred tongue. They were born into late Soviet culture, and raised in the dramatically changed environment of the Gorbachev years and after. So while they remember Pioneers and Lenin Portraits and Red Holidays, they have none of that subliminal Soviet patriotism I detected in my old students. They are still well prepared for studies at Polytechnic—earlier, electrical engineering was the preferred major, now it's computer science—and you can spot all the many Russian names on the Dean's Lists, but their preparation in Marxism and "History of the Communist Party of the Soviet Union" is not what it used to be. Generally, they are politically indifferent. We don't have those animated, sometimes heated political encounters of old. But I have changed too. This is another story, but suffice it to reveal that I no longer rush to defend the USSR and Soviet socialism as I once did, so what's to argue about?

Roman would be pleased.

NOTE
This chapter originally appeared in the *New York Times Magazine*, May 5, 1985.

A Williamsburg Childhood in the 1930s and 1940s

RENATA SINGER

Childhood can be another country, left long ago but held safe inside us. Norman Kruger is back there on a cold, dark winter night, on Rodney Street, in Williamsburg.

"I'm out on the streets just when it turns dark in a stinging frost. A vendor comes by calling out *hayse* knishes. And for a nickel, in a little piece of brown paper, the hot onion and potato flavor, at a time when everything is so cold and your fingers are frozen, even through mittens. It was magical."

In his cozy kitchen, sipping the hot strong coffee he's brewed, I see the small boy's glittering eyes across the table from me and almost reach out for some delicious knish. Instead I bite into the fresh sesame bagel that the hospitable Norman Kruger bought and schmeared for me with cottage cheese. The mirage of thirties Williamsburg is made real by his skills as an actor, and because it has stayed bright in him.

Born in the Williamsburg Maternity Hospital in 1931, Norman Kruger, with a good head of hair and abundant energy, does not look his age. Williamsburg was his home until he left for Israel on the day before his eighteenth birthday. His career began in the fifth grade at PS 16 after he wrote a play about the war effort and overheard his teacher remark approvingly, "a leibedik stik sroire." Soon he was writing more plays as well as being the school artist. Despite his mother's concern that he would starve in a garret, he attended Music and Art High School. Combining acting, in Yiddish and English, with teaching, he has taught for many years in the Theatre Department at the College of Staten Island and shows no sign of retiring.

Norman's Williamsburg was so Jewish that the few non-Jews stood out as not belonging. "A girl called Irene told me that when it rained, God and Jesus were crying because the Jews didn't see the light. You felt the Sabbath. And a lot of people who didn't observe it completely, like my mother, were very much intimidated by it. She wouldn't do anything on the outside. On the inside you could play the radio. My father wouldn't smoke in the street on *shabbes.*"

The Yeshiva Torah Vodaath was an important institution in the neighborhood. Norman recalls it as right-wing Orthodox but Misnadgish, like the largest synagogue in Williamsburg, the Brisker, rather than Hasidic. "Misnadgish means opponents, opponents of the Hassidim," he says in teacher mode, "but before they were opponents of the Hassidim they were simply Orthodox Jews. More people went to those synagogues. The Satmar Hassidim from

Hungary came to Williamsburg during and after the war in large numbers and became the dominant group. The Satmar Hassidim, as opposed to the Lubavitcher, are anti-Israel and discourage Jews from going there."

Sprinkled all over Williamsburg were *steiblech*, mini shuls. Next door to Norman's home was a one-family three-story building that was *steibel* and home for the Dollmer rebbe. Although he never davened there Norman remembers him well. "The Dollmer rebbe was tall, broad-shouldered, very brawny. He looked more like a stevedore or teamster but he wore the capote and the *streimel*. In the morning he would go out of his back door and call to a kid in our apartment house, 'Meyer, kim davenen.'" The rebbe's deep heavy Polish-accented Yiddish comes out of Norman, and it's almost as if he's grown in bulk; only the beard and Hassidic outfit is needed to bring the rebbe back. "Boy!" he calls thickly and imperiously to the small Norman, "Buy three cigarettes," and gives him a nickel from which Norman can keep the penny change.

For Norman, his apartment building encapsulated the sense of closely knit community that was his Williamsburg. "I knew all the neighbors in our six-floor walk-up with its telephone in the lobby. We had no phone in the house until 1944. The janitor lived on the ground floor, and he, or anybody, would pick up the phone and shout up and people would come running down. People wouldn't make as many calls as today. It was quite an event."

He pauses, mentally moving through the building from basement to top floor to check, before saying, "By and large the population was Jewish but the whole range. From a Jewish Communist who lived underneath us to Hassidim, Orthodox. It didn't mean they embraced each other, but they were all influenced by each other to some degree." One by one the neighbors return to him, including Stanley Kowalski, the janitor, "just like in *Streetcar*," and the Sicilian families on the upper floors. "Distant relations of my father from Poland even moved in. The matriarch of the family was already eighty-five years old but a very energetic woman wearing a *sheitl*. She had one son who was a bookie and into the limousine service, and he was either shot or died in an unusual way. Another two daughters were close to us, always playing cards with my family. The doors were open; not only distant relatives but neighbors would walk in and out, sometimes without knocking."

In his teenage years Norman and his friends hung about the corner candy store, where the owner was hos-

pitable even to boys who didn't buy much. "You'd get such an assortment of people—that was what was so amazing and rich about Williamsburg." Norman spreads his hands in a gesture telling me he'd love to tell me about them all if only there was time. Without "naming names" he tells of the Jewish ex-boxer who "would hold forth and instruct younger boys about how he could satisfy women. He'd arrange to meet these women pushing babies' carriages and would kiss and fondle them in the street just so the kids should know he wasn't bullshitting. And every story finished the same way." Norman moves into a harsh gravelly James Cagney voice. "She gotta husband but her husband can't satisfy 'er, I can satisfy 'er." Smiling at what he's not going to tell me, Norman says, "and we were characters too."

His parents arrived in the States in the 1920s, his mother from Odessa and his father from the Polish shtetl of Shrensk. Of course, they met in Williamsburg when his mother needed a fur collar for her coat and was recommended a furrier, his father. Norman was already a raconteur in kindergarten, eagerly retelling the other kids the stories his mother read to him about "Jack and the Beanstalk and the hooj castle." Her Russian accent changes back into his own American when he says, "I heard the teachers refer to me as the refugee boy because of the accent."

Listening to his parents and Yiddish radio started him on Yiddish. Soon he was learning Yiddish and Hebrew at the Williamsburg Folkshul and then in the schools of the Labor-Zionist Farband. Eventually he attended the Jewish Teachers' Seminary on the Upper East Side. With a father who "was such a big Russophile that he was bordering on being a fellow traveler," the Republican *Daily News* was taboo in their house. His father read the *New York Post* and then *PM* and *Freiheit*, the Yiddish-Communist paper.

He describes the family religion as "observant and aware of Williamsburg." Although his father was "at most an agnostic," he loved to go to synagogue and went whenever he didn't need to work on *shabbes*. "But it was just to go there and to listen and to participate. He would leave the synagogue and buy a newspaper." His maternal grandparents were more observant. His grandmother "had her own religion . . . to stay in shape she would fast Mondays and Thursdays, the days of the weekday Torah readings." One morning when he came to walk his grandmother to shul, she hadn't completed her coif. Demonstrating, Norman pushes his hair back from his forehead. The foyer was dark and "all of a sudden I saw her turn the light on on shabbes. She winked at me, fixed her hair, and we went out." He laughs at the memory of his vain grandmother taking his arm and strutting off to shul. "I wasn't concerned with these mixed signals. I liked them."

"I relish all the different ingredients but I can't stick with an Orthodox discipline, because at the heart of it I can't believe." Echoing the concern of many deeply Jewish secularists, Norman says, "Yet I believe in preserving Judaism, and it's getting sadder and sadder. I'm worried about how much less I gave my son than my father gave me and what he is going to give his children."

Williamsburg was not a suburb of wealthy people. Norman's father was among the strugglers, at one time being a street peddler. "He went into business as a furrier three times and failed every time," says Norman. By the time Norman was seven the worst of the Depression was over. He doesn't remember going hungry but did go with his mother when she "hocked her diamond engagement ring a number of times. They were that close to the edge, but they never really fell off." His parents were haunted by the fear of dispossession, and this has affected Norman. "As a result I thought I must always have something to back me up. With the theater I never cut loose where I let go of a job." It wasn't until his mother's sister and her new husband moved in with them during the war that the family moved to a four-room apartment and had a living room for the first time. Before that family life centered in the small kitchen.

Even poor people could afford to escape to the movies. In 1942 Norman took his five-year-old brother to see Nelson Eddy in *Balalaika*. "Nelson Eddy's a Cossack." Norman settles himself into the plush seat of the luxurious Commodore. "He's holding up a silver cup and there are candles lit. He sings a song, and as soon as he drinks my brother yells out, 'What a goy! Without kiddush!' And everyone's laughing in the packed movie house. So everybody had the same frame of reference there." Although

there were many movie theaters in Williamsburg, Norman's most vivid memories center around The Dump. His eyes go glassy and his tongue passes over his bottom lip. "I'm very hungry, three features without food, in the middle of a cowboy movie with lots of singing, and they're barbecuing beef and hot dogs—a thing I couldn't relate to—it only went on in the movies. And who comes in but my grandmother. She came in on a pass with food from the delicatessen. So here I am eating real frankfurters with sauerkraut and watching the barbecue. What gratification. A wonderful moment, blending reality and the movies." The Dump was aptly named, with cats wandering through and "maybe even a dog once in a while." Once part of the potato knish Norman was eating fell on the floor. "Afterwards two people come in and one guy sits down right next to me and says, 'I bet I stepped in shit again.' He probably had his shoe in the knish. Those were the expectations."

In the darkening kitchen the Williamsburg icons glow warmly: Peter Luger's Steak House, the dome of the Williamsburg Savings Bank, and, brightest of all, the Williamsburg Public Library. For Norman it was his magical Emerald City, with people dimly seen upstairs through the frosted green glass floor. "It's almost an oval. You don't see buildings like that in Williamsburg. I don't know anything comparable. Built during the Depression with civic pride, energy, and optimism. A belief that government does something and should do something."

Norman identifies strongly with "a time when within one family you would find people who were Orthodox and people who were very strongly influenced by the Haskala, the scholar and the boxer, secularists, and Communists— all under one roof." Jewish life in Williamsburg was vibrant, the various strands of Judaism living in "peaceful coexistence" in the one neighborhood. An immigrant culture, still alien enough in America to be bound by a Jewishness that included all persuasions and nonbelievers. On the streets the Hassids didn't hassle, and the atheists didn't openly break the Sabbath.

Sephardic in Williamsburg

LOUIS MENASHE

To begin with, my names were different, first and second. There I was, a Loooey—among Yusse, Heshy, Melvin, and Sheldon (and the occasional John and Frankie). The Anglo-Saxon Looiss is the way my schoolteachers pronounced it (and I was too shy to correct them), but my Francophile mother intended I be a *Louis*, in the French manner, just as my brother, whose birth certificate had him as Mordochai, became a *Robert*. But in my neighborhood, *Louis* became Loooey (just as *Robert* became Bobby). And there among Steinfeld, Rosenberg, Zipris, and Osofsky, I was *Menashe*. This resulted in frequent and tiresome jibes associating me with a certain, as I later learned, Yiddish actor. For example, on being introduced to someone's father I would get the inevitable: "So you're related to Menasha Skulnick (Ha, ha, ha)." It may have been a given name among the Ashkenazim, but among us, it was always a family name. But if we were Jewish, how is it, my friends' parents wanted to know, the Menashes don't know Yiddish? This later led to problems when I was courting my Ashkenazic wife-to-be. He speaks Spanish?—what is he, Puerto Rican or something? my future mother-in-law wanted to know. (It's something that still, I think, puzzles her after many years of marriage to her daughter.)

I'm Sephardic, and we spoke Ladino at home. (And as Sephardim from the venerated Salonica, "The Mother of Israel," we spoke only to God.) Ladino is the language of the Jews of Spain who kept the tongue alive through five centuries of exile after their expulsion in 1492, who spoke it in settlements from the eastern Mediterranean to Williamsburg, Brooklyn, where I was born and raised. Williamsburg wasn't then the "enclave of cool," and Brooklyn's "wildest nabe," as *Time Out New York* recently described the ensemble of bars, restaurants, galleries, antique shops, and bookstores that have now made Williamsburg a hip rival to Manhattan's bohemias. It was far from hip back then, populated by working-class families of Irish, Slavic, and Italian descent, many of whom found jobs in the big plants nearby—Pfizer Pharmaceuticals, the Schaeffer Brewery, and the Domino Sugar factory. We knew that part of Williamsburg as the Northside (north of Grand Street), and ventured there for Police Athletic League ball games in McCarren Park, or for our first experiences of a pizzeria (and thereafter repeatedly to catch a glimpse of the owner's raven-haired daughter who served the incomparable pizza). Otherwise, the Northside was vaguely menacing territory, close to the even more menacing Greenpoint. Our zone was the Southside, with its

Bertha and Louis Menashe, ca. 1946. Courtesy of the Menashe family.

Bertha Menashe (far left), Louis Menashe (lower left), and friends, ca. 1940. Courtesy of the Menashe family.

tenements housing predominantly working-class and lower-middle-class Ashkenazic Jews of eastern European immigrant origins.

In that zone, I was something of an outsider. Being Sephardic became a source of great pride, even arrogance, as I matured, yet as a boy I was sensitive about it; it made me different from my friends, and from the community. I don't want to exaggerate. I was hardly alienated or lonely; I had lots of friends, I was a decent stickball hitter, and did well academically. But I often tore up the invitations for school visits addressed to my parents because I was ashamed of their *Spanish* accents. As for my friends, I didn't speak their mother tongue, I didn't eat their foods, I didn't celebrate the holidays in their way, or go to their synagogues—thanks to my agnostic father, I didn't go to synagogue at all. Their parents drank schnapps (whatever that was); mine drank raki, the bathtub kind, poured from unmarked gallons delivered to my father periodically by one of his buddy distillers. They said Gesundheit! we said Vivas y Crescas! They said Mazel-tov! we said Mash'allah!

(something picked up from our Arab neighbors in old Spain; or was it from the Turks?). At their weddings, musicians affected the klezmer, *freilich* style, and played "Tumbalalaika"; at ours, the band was obligated to play "Miserlou"—"Ai, muy amargo, es muy amargo, el sufrir!" sang all the adults. They exclaimed Oy! we intoned Ai! At home, my mother sang the beautiful Sephardic *romanzas* that originated in fifteenth-century Spain, or earlier. At informal musical soirees, someone would strum the exotic oud, accompanying the mournful sounding Turkish songs, or the jollier Greek ones. Oh, how my parents loved Eartha Kitt singing "Ishka Dara." Or Andy Russell crooning "Besame Mucho." To my parents' delight, these were big hits, part of American pop culture, but sung in their language(s). It was for them, you might say, validating.

So Williamsburg—America!—brought Sephardim and Ashkenazim together, and yes, we were all Jewish, but a certain cultural distancing kept us apart; a demarcating tribalism operated, on both sides. There were even two different words for Jew in our lingo: They were *Judeos*; we were

Djidios. "Your kind," my mother would say to my friends, without malice, but drawing the lines in the sand. Less charitably, though she didn't mean it in the way others might use the phrase, she would speak of "los yiddishin fithyendo" (roughly, the reeking Yiddishers) an allusion to the garlic and onions and gefilte fish in their kitchens. As to their language, it was all guttural *ukhti-mukhti* to her.

But what was abrasive to her was what I didn't have, and consequently desired. Not that I wanted to speak Yiddish—I was happy enough that the fluent Ladino my brother and I spoke made my father proud—but I envied Irwin Goldman when he showed me his first primer in Hebrew and sounded out the alephs and beths. I associated Hebrew with Yiddish, even though *La Vara* (The Law), which arrived regularly in our mailbox for my father to read, was a Ladino publication printed in Hebrew typography. My mother, a superb cook in the Levantine fashion, used to prepare her own sauce for our pasta dishes, but when Irwin Goldmanís mother served us spaghetti with ketchup, I was convinced our cuisine was embarrassingly provincial by comparison. I outraged my mother when I asked for spaghetti in Mrs. Goldman's style at home. Adio!—ketchup?! she shouted. And why couldn't I have salami sandwiches like my friends? (My non-Jewish friend John enjoyed the even more tempting ham in his sandwiches.) At the Osofskys' I tasted my first kreplach, mmmm.... My family never ate out, as did my friends with their parents. Arthur Gilman introduced me to Chinese food, a must on Sunday afternoons, at the Jade Garden on Broadway. Old Brooklynites will remember the racist term we used naturally in those days for dining at a Chinese restaurant. Our idea of Chinese food meant little more than wonton soup, spare ribs, and egg roll. My mother would make a face when I described the dishes. But my crowning discovery, thanks to Irwin Goldman, was the ineffable pastrami at the original Jack's Pastrami King on Roebling and South Second, a block away from my house. Saturday afternoons were devoted to the movies at one of the several theaters on Broadway, under the El. There we sat gladly through marathon cinema sessions that included two features, several Looney Tunes, the Movietone newsreels, "coming attractions," and what we called "chapters," the short serials with cliff-hanger endings. Our appetites were then ready for the ample delights of Pastrami King. Anyone lucky enough to have eaten there knows it dished out the most succulent pastrami, always sliced by hand, in North America, possibly the world. Jack smoked it in cedar, not the customary hickory, and flavored it with fresh garlic, not garlic salt. Press, the harried waiter, would ignore us kids—our tips weren't so good—but the long hungry wait was worth it.

Later, a culinary breakthrough developed, reversing earlier attitudes, and with good reason: I, my friends, and my brothers' friends, older, more discerning, came to appreciate my mother's ways in the kitchen. They couldn't get enough of her Sephardic fare, derived from mainly Graeco-Turkish traditions; they flocked regularly to my apartment to savor her *fijon y arroz* (beans and rice), a Salonica specialty on Fridays; her Greek salads; her *keftes de puero* (meatballs laced with leek); and her triumphal baked specialties—*toupishti*, a sweet honey-and-walnut cake, or *bourequitas*, glazed, crescent-shaped pastry filled with, depending on the occasion, cheese, spinach, eggplant, pumpkin, or walnuts (*bourequitas*: note the Hispanic suffix for the Turkish word). That my friends came to dine with us and hang out at our Roebling Street apartment pleased my father immensely. Not only did he take this as proof of the superiority of "our" kitchen over "theirs," but—he was overprotective, my dad—it kept us off what he saw as the mean streets of the neighborhood.

Those streets weren't particularly mean, not by modern inner city standards. Their boundaries for me and my friends in our younger years were the two neighborhood schools and their schoolyards, Junior High School 50 and, not many blocks away to the east, PS 19. The JHS 50 schoolyard, on Roebling and South Third Streets, was diagonally across from my building on Roebling, and my mother aborted many a softball or stickball game for me when she called out the window to get home. Another embarrassment: My parents didn't relate to sports; my mother was indulgent but uncomprehending, while my father was positively scornful. My grandmother, "Nona," a born wit, was playful about the rabid Brooklyn Dodger fans my brother and I were. She spoke no English and mocked us with her wordplay. "Dodger" sounded to her like our *dodgeh*, Ladino for twelve, and when we were glued to our radio listening to Red Barber, she would announce, with great oratorical flourish, "Ah, los Dodgehs y los Tredgehs!"—literally, the Twelves and the Thirteens!

That my parents had no love of sports was another sign for me of their insularity; here too, I saw my friends' families as more worldly, more integrated into the mores of the land, more *American*. How odd. My mother, educated in French schools, polylingual, culturally sophisticated in ways none of my friends' parents could match—my mother I saw as somehow backward. The Yiddish-accented, singsong English of Mrs. Steinfeld was, I thought, an English superior to my mother's. There was something else about the Ashkenazim, rather more difficult to put my finger on, but I felt it, we all felt it: They were more with it; they were go-getters, more adept at handling the competitive impulses of American life than we were, it seemed. Like my father and his circle, they too were shop-keepers or cutters and pressers in the garment industry "uptown." And my father could bargain down their haber-dashers with virtuoso skill when we went on special shopping trips across the river to the Lower East Side. A later insight told me that talent of his perhaps originated in his culture, the ancient ritualistic haggling of Mediterranean bazaars. Yet when he practiced it for my new pants, I may have found it amusing, but it was also another source of embarrassment. Would Melvin's father have done that? Melvin's parents owned a brownstone near PS 19. We played Ping-Pong in his finished basement. Now that was something. Melvin also owned a bicycle, a Columbia two-wheeler, something my father forbade out of fear for my safety. Yet another sign of what I saw as that humiliating, old-fashioned, somehow *European* disposition I had to suffer. (I learned to ride on the sneak; my brother never did learn.) And what about Gilda Goldman, Irwin's older sister? Gilda would take us to the movies, holding money from me in advance to cover admission and candy. After several of these outings, I noticed she habitually used my money for her candy, not leaving me any remainder. Now that was an impressive piece of commerce on her part. Would any of our Sephardic big sisters do that? I reasoned not. Brava, Gilda, that's the Ashkenazic way, I felt. They knew how to pull things off; we were so old-world. I wasn't (and am not) making a moral judgment. It's just that I perceived a difference of posture, an attitudinal difference in their style from mine, and I associated that with the group ethos of our respective tribes.

On learning I was Sephardic my future father-in-law commented, Oh, your people are so clannish. I resented the statement, but he had a point. Our world was richly communal, but circumscribed. Visiting each other *por un café* (for coffee, Turkish of course), or gathering for all-night sessions of poker and pinochle (*spinaka* they called it) was what our families did. All the time. And I had to go, forfeiting some schoolyard basketball or a good movie. Often I woke up in someone else's bed. I would fall asleep

while my parents played cards or just gabbed, endlessly. They wouldn't wake me, and left me where I was for the night. In our Williamsburg Sephardic enclave we visited the Mevorahs or the Benrubis or the Matalons. But there were also frequent excursions to other families in other like enclaves—the Bejas in New Lots, the Confinos in Flatbush, or across the river to the Varsanos on the Lower East Side, where there were still some Sephardim. They may have started out there, like other Jewish immigrants coming to our shores, but when I was growing up, most had moved out to Brooklyn and The Bronx, a common passage resulting naturally from their improved financial situation. Visiting the Lower East Side made me uncomfortable. The teeming streets, the pushcarts, the tiny apartments—the Varsanoses' bathroom was, ugh, in the tenement hallway. Williamsburg was upscale, expansive by comparison. But we visited real grandeur when the D train, to which we transferred at Delancy Street in Manhattan, took us to see Aunt Lily, my mother's sister, on the Grand Concourse in the Bronx. These visits are all treasured memories now, and I know now they enveloped me in a warmth I have rarely experienced since. It was like paying visits to a familiar extended family, with or without blood ties, that dwelled in villages scattered among alien (non-Sephardic) territories. At the time, though, it all felt so old-fashioned to me; all things considered I would rather have been in Melvin Zipris's finished basement.

Knowing Spanish had its advantages. The new immigrants to Williamsburg in the 1940s and 1950s came from Puerto Rico; later they would displace us entirely. I knew a few at JHS 50 (I had a crush on Alicia); I met others on the ball field. In one of those encounters we've all experienced in whatever Brooklyn neighborhood, with whatever other ethnics, I bumped into a group of Puerto Rican teens I didn't know when I crossed the park on South Fourth Street one evening. It was as if we all knew the choreography, and were about to rehearse the dance: They surrounded me, and their body language spoke hostility. I brought out the mother tongue: Que pasa, amigos? No me conocen? Vivo aquí, a Roebling Street. (What's up, friends? Don't you recognize me? I live here, on Roebling Street.) Laughter and friendly handshakes all around. Whew. Surely they hadn't taken me for Puerto Rican, and I've often wondered, Did they think I was from some other Hispanic land, or were they just impressed that this gringo knew Spanish?

On another occasion my "Spanish" identity led to a different kind of encounter. Frankie Santanello, who lived upstairs from me, was for a time a close friend, even though he gave me my first lesson in the primeval hate. After school one afternoon in front of the grocery at the corner of South Third Street, he suddenly knocked me to the ground, informing me solemnly that we Jews killed Christ. Frankie was, in the inflection of the neighborhood, "Catlick," and he attended the Roman Catholic Church of St. Mary's of the Angels adjoining our building on Roebling Street. The incident left me in tears, but it didn't hurt enough to overcome my envy of Frankie for what he told me of the recreational activities at St. Mary's. During Easter, for example, he dressed as a bunny. Such fun! Frankie suggested I come and see for myself, and so I did. He introduced me to Vinnie the sacristan as "Loooey, he's Spanish." Welcome, said Vinnie, and he promptly swept me into a rehearsal for the Sunday services the boys and girls were going through. I was instantly an altar boy marching down the central aisle swinging these silver things, and I did well enough to please Vinnie. So well that there was a knock at the door very early Sunday morning. My father answered, and I could hear the exchange from my bedroom. A girl's voice questioned my father, "Where's Loooey? He has to come to Mass." What? asked my father edgily, probably not understanding. "He has to come to church for Mass," she elaborated. Now he understood. "Get the hell out of here," I heard him growl, and he slammed the door on poor Cathy or Elizabeth. I had some explaining to do. My father may have been agnostic, but ecumenical he was not. Nona, bless her, came to my defense on the grounds that it didn't hurt to learn what the interior of a church looked like. After all, she had sent her four daughters to one of the best schools in Salonica, a Catholic school run by the Sisters of St. Vincent de Paul!

Brownsville and Irving Levine
The Making of a Jewish Liberal Activist

GERALD SORIN

For at least two decades beginning in the mid-1950s, Irving M. Levine was a ubiquitous and supremely effective activist in the transcontinental battle for civil rights, social justice, and urban reform. Consistently interested in racial integration from his youth, Levine was equally committed to combating anti-Semitism in all its forms. He also, earlier than most, recognized and worked to relieve the grievances of lower-middle-class ethnic Americans. The breadth of his social concerns was remarkable; Levine insisted tirelessly that although there often would be conflict between them, the rights of Jews, blacks, and "white ethnics" were largely inseparable. As an adult he channeled his militancy through a variety of organizations and institutions, including the New York City Human Rights Commission, the Indiana and Ohio Conferences on Civil Rights Legislation, and especially the American Jewish Committee (AJC), where he served first as director of education and urban planning and later as director of national affairs and director of the Institute for American Pluralism, which he created.

It is my contention that the liberal values and vision that Irving M. Levine brought to his work were directly influenced by his youthful experiences in 1930s and 1940s Brownsville, a predominantly Jewish working-class neighborhood in Brooklyn, New York, with a small proportion of non-Jews, including an increasing number of blacks, and by his participation in and eventual leadership of the Brownsville Boys Club (BBC).

The BBC was established in 1940 when the Board of Education of New York City ruled that boys over fourteen could no longer use after-school centers. Dozens of Jewish boys of Brownsville, who were members of street-corner teams and clubs, had been using the facilities of PS 184 for basketball competition. In response to the Board of Education decision, the clubs, under the leadership of sixteen-year-old Jacob "Doc" Baroff, joined together in a rudimentary organization and won their way back into the gym and schoolyard of PS 184. The leaders of the temporary confederation of clubs, having gained a direct sense of the power of community organizing, decided to keep the association in operation. They raised funds and solicited materials and equipment from merchants and philanthropists, as well as from other institutions, and the BBC went on to become a prime source of recreation, education, and entertainment, and a powerful force for social welfare in Brownsville. The organization and all its programs were run until 1947 entirely by boys, including, eventually, Irving Levine, who joined at the age of eleven in 1941 and served in various positions including president during the war years, and as athletic director from 1947 to 1950.[1]

The Brownsville of the 1930s and 1940s that produced the boys who produced the club was a poor neighborhood with a reputation as a spawning ground for criminals like those of the Murder, Inc. crime syndicate, but it was also a vibrant immigrant Jewish community, brimming with vitality. In 1925, Brownsville had a Jewish population of 95 percent, the highest concentration of Jews in New York City. By 1940, when the BBC was formed, Jews still made up close to 80 percent of the community, providing significant ethnic homogeneity and security.[2] As late as 1949, a writer for the *Brooklyn Eagle* described Brownsville as a "close-knit neighborhood," parts of it resembling the Lower East Side of Manhattan.[3] On Jewish holidays the public schools were virtually empty, stores were closed, and the streets were deserted, except for the sidewalks in front of Brownsville's eighty-three synagogues, which were jammed with Jews.

Jewish ethnicity meant more than the mere concentration of people nominally Jewish. Although the mothers and fathers of the boys could be described as Orthodox Jews in only 20 percent of the cases, 44 percent had at least one parent who was moderately observant, and an additional 54 percent of the boys, including Irving Levine, had mothers and fathers who lived demonstrably Jewish lives.[4] Irving's parents attended synagogue often, and in their home, which was kept "strictly kosher," the Sabbath was observed, as were all the Holy Days and festivals.

Fathers and mothers, grandparents, and other relatives, including the Orthodox cousins and uncles of Irving Levine, one of whom served as president and another as treasurer of the Bet Yisrael synagogue in Brownsville for some thirty years, taught Jewish identity and ethics by exhortation and by example. And virtually all the boys received some degree of formal Jewish education in one of dozens of Hebrew and Yiddish schools punctuating the eighty square blocks that made up Brownsville. Irving attended Hebrew day school for several years, and later Talmud Torah, until he, like the vast majority of other Brownsville Jewish boys, became a bar mitzvah.

Ethnically cohesive neighborhood life, visible Jewish religious and social institutions like *shuln* and *landsmanshaftn*, as well as Jewish shops and the Yiddish language of the street, home, and business allowed Jews to develop a sense of Jewish identity whether or not they belonged to formal organizations or went to shul regularly. And Irving M. Levine, who stayed associated with Jewish institutions and causes throughout his life, was no exception to this powerful influence of what Alfred Kazin calls the "secret treasure of family and Jewish togetherness."[5]

The boys who made and sustained the BBC, who produced from street-corner teams and clubs a successful self-help and community welfare organization, had not only this "secret treasure" but also models of mutual aid in the dozens of philanthropic organizations that punctuated Brownsville's streets—like the Hebrew Day Nursery, the Hebrew Orphanage, and the Hebrew Free Loan Society on Hopkinson Avenue.[6] The parents of the boys were active in these institutions, in unions, and in progressive social and political organizations. Fifty percent of the Brownsville boys, including Irving Levine, had parents who belonged to *landsmanshaftn*, and the youngsters understood, at the time, the *shaftn* mutual aid character of these societies. Furthermore, most Brownsville *shuln* to which the parents of the boys belonged were organized as *khevrot* or mutual aid societies.

In addition, 45 percent of the boys reported that their parents were members of such progressive organizations as the Workmen's Circle, the International Workers' Order, or labor unions, all of which had local branches in the neighborhood. Dozens made statements that reflected the Jewish commandment of *tsedaka*, or charity in its broadest sense of righteousness and social justice, and *tikn olam*, the obligation to repair or improve the world. Similar numbers, including Levine, remembered the radical street speakers and talked about an atmosphere "permeated with a socialist orientation."

Of course, the majority of Jews in Brownsville were not Socialists, and the "regular" political parties had local offices in the neighborhood, too. But liberal Democratic politics was for all practical purposes the rule.[7] Progressive politics, *yiddishkayt*, and Jewish communal consciousness provided the context and foundation within which Irving Levine and the Brownsville Boys grew up. These forces helped Levine and other boys from Depression-impoverished working-class families to avoid serious social deviance and moved them to create the BBC. In turn, building the club and sustaining it strengthened interdependence; and the successful use of the club in winning benefits reinforced the boys' self-esteem and gave them a broad and abiding sense of the possible. The boys, raised in a politically progressive Jewish community, in a context of Jewish ethical teaching and behavior, and surrounded by institutions for mutual aid, went on to become achieving as well as socially concerned adults. A very significant proportion continued to lead lives informed by the traditions of *tsedaka* and communal responsibility, and fully 25 percent, including Irving Levine, committed themselves to the helping professions, especially schoolteaching and social work.[8]

Even as youngsters the boys manifested a growing interest in social questions including racial justice, which was becoming an increasingly important issue as Brownsville's black population increased. The number of blacks in Brownsville doubled between 1940 and 1950, and by 1957, thirty-eight thousand blacks made up 22 percent of Brownsville's overall population.[9]

Younger, poorer, more recently uprooted, and victims of historic oppression and deprivation, blacks in Brownsville were disproportionately the perpetrators and victims of vandalism and violence.[10] Some of the Brownsville Boys thought that recreation, the "excitement and adventure of athletic competition," as one of them put it, would redirect the energies of poor and minority youth along less brutal lines. But many of the boys also knew that recreation alone, although valuable, was no substitute for fundamental improvements in social conditions. Several, particularly Irving Levine, who remembers himself in the 1940s as "a politically aware kid," and Jacob Deutch, Norman Goroff, and Lenny Dryansky—Socialist sons of Socialist fathers—knew, for example, that "better paying jobs were also essential." And all knew too that decent shelter was critical.[11] Having been exposed as "kids" to more than a decade of highly visible public lobbying for state and federal funds to improve housing in Brownsville by the Brownsville Neighborhood Council, and by Milton Goell and other reformers, Levine and Baroff and many of the other boys were well aware of the housing issue and were supportive of reform.[12]

As early as 1946 the boys of the BBC publicly dedicated themselves to campaigning for housing projects, health centers, and high schools to improve the social conditions of Brownsville. Throughout the following year the club newsletter dealt with a variety of social justice issues, including inadequate shelter and racial discrimination. Reflecting the idea that reform was more important than mere recreation, Norman Goroff said in 1947 that the goal of the club was "not to keep the boys off the streets, but to make the streets attractive and safe."[13]

For many of the boys, recreation—especially sports, which provided the joy of competition and accomplishment—was a vehicle for different groups to get "to know one another" and to have "a common bond." These last two concerns took on acute importance in the face of Brownsville's growing black population.

In Alfred Kazin's 1920s Brownsville, "Negroes were the shvartse, the blacks. We did not think about them. They were people three and four blocks away you passed coming home from the subway. I never heard a word about them until the Depression, when some of the younger ones began to do private painting jobs below the union wage scales, and when still another block of the earliest wooden shacks on Livonia Avenue near the subway's power station filled up with Negroes. Then some strange, embarrassed resentment would come out in the talk around the supper table. They were moving nearer and nearer. They were invading our neighborhood."[14]

Undoubtedly some of the 1940s Brownsville Boys were also resentful of what could have been perceived as an even larger "invasion" in their era. Milton Kirschner remembers only too well being beaten unconscious by blacks when he was eight years old. And one small group of boys, led by "Shimmy," chased and beat blacks whenever they saw them on their block.[15] The main thrust of interracial relations, however, was acceptance and, even, integration. As early as March 1943, at the club's original Children's Library meeting room, "the Negro question was brought up" on more than one Friday night by Irving Levine and others, and at least one invited speaker that year, representing the Society for the Prevention of Crime, asked the boys to continue to "promote interracial relations." In September 1943, Norman Goroff responded by encouraging club members to attend a Negro Freedom Rally at the Premiere Palace, and over the next three years the issue of racial cooperation appeared several times on the agenda of BBC meetings.[16]

By 1947, when professional social workers, philanthropists, and politicians were sought out by the boys in return for their fund-raising potential, the Reverend Bosie S. Dent, a black man, joined the Brownsville Board of Directors, and a black program director, Vincent Tibbs, was hired to work out of the BBC's new Christopher Avenue storefront. In April 1948, in conference with the Brownsville Neighborhood Council, Irving Levine, Jack Leavitt, and a number of other BBC boys agreed that "the speed with which the Brownsville Houses were being inhabited

. . . posed the need for a welcome by the community," as well as exercises in "interracial understanding" at "the housing project, which was nearly 45 percent Negro."[17]

A small number of boys, particularly Irving ("Hooker" for his basketball hook shot) Levine, continued throughout to take an intense interest in racial integration. The child of Jewish immigrants, a Lithuanian pocketmaker and a Polish homemaker, who were "the poorest of [his] relatives," Levine "identified strongly with the Brownsville Neighborhood Council and its policies" of progressive social action and vigorous pursuit of interracial cooperation. And early on, in 1946, Irving, at the age of sixteen, initiated a freewheeling discussion about active recruitment of blacks for clubs and teams.[18]

The recruitment of blacks worked, but only to a point. As most of the teams and clubs were street-corner teams and clubs, and as Brownsville's streets were virtually segregated, many of the teams were also racially defined. There were at least three all-black BBC teams by 1947: the Cobras, the Saints, and the Nobles. And at least two other clubs, the Rams and the Spartans, included blacks. In addition, several black players were on the BBC All-Star Softball Team, the boxing and track teams, and the "one-weight" teams (e.g., all 110-pounders, all 120-pounders) in a variety of sports.[19] The general pattern, then, with a few exceptions, was that individual clubs were segregated as a consequence of residential patterns but that intramural competition and BBC "varsity teams" were forces for integration, as were the general meetings to which all the confederated clubs sent representatives—"proof," read the Brownsville Boys Club newsletter, that "the boys of Brownsville can work and play together in perfect harmony."[20]

Irving M. Levine "said he identified with black kids on a number of levels." We "thought of them as strong physical types, and some of us even believed, in the immediate aftermath of the Holocaust, that if we were black, we would have killed the Nazis instead of them killing us." Earlier, in junior high school, Irving had won a civics medal for an essay he wrote on civil rights. He had been stimulated by American Jewish Committee and American Jewish Congress materials on the subject and was "proud and delighted" when he discovered how much Jews were tied to the movement for racial justice.

Hooker got to know blacks more directly when in 1946 and 1947 he took fifteen children, many of them black, to the Stone movie theater every Monday afternoon, and when increasing numbers of even younger blacks began spending a good part of the day at the storefront. There, at age sixteen, Irving was running the game room. "There were so many children, for so many hours, it was almost like day care," he recalled.[21] He became more and more aware of racial injustice and increasingly committed to integration and racial equality as he worked with these black youngsters. "I crossed the street one day," Irving recalled, "to pick up George Alexis, one of the black kids I was working with, and when I went into his building for the first time, it struck me that I work with these kids but had never been in their homes. I was struck because of an overwhelming sense of difference and distance. The cramped quarters, the cooking odors, the unemployed adult males—I was in fact repelled by the virtual smell of abject poverty. And this was just across the street from us. We knew we were poor too, but there seemed to me to be a qualitative difference in our poverties. I knew, for example, that ultimately I was employable. A cousin or an uncle could get me a job in the garment center or at least in a grocery store. Blacks did not seem to have this particular ethnic economic network. This was an epiphany for me—'crossing the street.'"[22]

Beginning in 1947, Hooker Levine ran all the BBC league competitions as athletic director. "Some of us," he said, "became even more aggressive in recruiting blacks, as black basketball became prominent. Speed, one-handed shooting, and the more open style promoted blacks in the game. And we wanted our teams to win. This desire reinforced a trend already established in a number of us by our social welfare ideology and our progressive, even 'left,' politics."[23] And that "trend" was in turn reinforced as blacks and Jews played on the same teams and traveled together. At the Madison Square Boys Club and the Flatbush Boys Club, neither of which were in Jewish neighborhoods, the integrated BBC basketball teams were subjected to blatant racist and anti-Semitic jeers and taunts. "This did not happen," Irving remembers, "at the Williamsburg Y," which was predominantly Jewish. For Levine, these "events" confirmed at least two things: his pride in being Jewish, especially being part of a "tribe" that appeared to be more progressive, or at least more tolerant, than many non-Jewish groups; and his sense that anti-Semitism and racism were linked under the same yoke of irrational bigotry. These episodes made Levine and several others even more anxious to integrate BBC teams. And besides, as more than one BBC boy said, "we finally were winning!"[24]

There were others who had similar, even if not as intense, experiences. Camp Clearpool, run by the Madison Square Boys Club, served mainly Irish and Italian boys. The Brownsville Boys Club, with Doc Baroff as counselor, brought Jews—and in the early 1940s, two blacks—for two-week vacations. Herb Grosswirth recalled, sadly, "It was at Camp Clearpool that I ran into anti-Semitism for the first time. We were called 'Baroff's Bagel Boys.' We took the two black kids into our bunk because no one else wanted them. They were called the 'Burnt Bagels.' However, we showed the Gentiles what the Brownsville Bagel Boys could do; we finished first or second in every event."[25] Not only was integration, in the minds of these boys, the "right thing" to do; it also appeared to produce positive results.

It is important to remember that in the 1940s, activist integration was a radical position. "Separate but equal" was the legal order of the day; separate and unequal was the reality, North and South. Even the United States government had fought the Second World War with segregated troops, and it was not until the summer of 1948 that Harry S Truman issued an executive order barring separation of the races in the armed forces. One understands in such a context why the boys, according to Irving Levine, "were not only proud to be the first Jewish-led boys club, but also the first boys club to integrate."[26]

Irving Levine, though not altogether typical of the Brownsville Boys in his attitudes and particularly in his rigorous commitment to racial integration and racial justice, did represent the values and actions of a half dozen or so other leaders of the club, including Norman Adelman, Norman Goroff, and Lenny Dryansky, all of whom shared or came very close to sharing Irving's militancy. Perhaps even more important in understanding the cultural environment within which Levine worked is the fact that the vast majority of Jewish boys in the BBC remember interaction with blacks as either a neutral experience or as explicitly positive. A few said, along with Eddie Eshkenazi, that "my best friends [not some of my best friends] were African Americans. They ate in my house and I ate in theirs." But several had stories like the one Martin Karduna tells: "We had a very nice member of our club [who was black], Glenford Taylor. . . . I had him in my house many times and he got along with everyone in my family. Even my old grandfather who called him a schvartze liked Glen. I had other black classmates in JHS 109." And Irving Kunis spoke for many when he wrote: "my block had Blacks, never any problems.

I also attended JHS 66, a school in which whites were the minority. Again no problems. The issue of 'integration' never came up among my friends or classmates. We lived together, most of us poor. Race never was an issue. We accepted each other."[27]

Perhaps faded memory has smoothed over some of the rough spots, but the number and consistency of the stories lend credibility. Moreover, several African Americans remember the black-Jewish relationship in much the same way. James Grant, during the late 1940s, was the first black to play basketball for Thomas Jefferson High School, where the vast majority of BBC boys were educated. He was recruited by Mac Hodesblatt—a Jew—and felt "very comfortable" with his teammates, all of whom were Jewish. Grant "was accepted by them as an equal" and was welcome in their homes and at their dinner tables.[28] James Johnson, an African American and one of the founders of the Brownsville Old-Timers Day Basketball Tournament, remembered when the area was predominantly Jewish, in the days when Max Zaslofsky, a BBC alumnus who led the National Basketball Association in scoring in 1947, ran on the Brownsville courts. "We were all together then because there wasn't enough of us to be a threat. We played in Nanny Goat Park [in the heart of BBC territory]. We were welcome in people's homes. It was beautiful."[29]

It was not all beautiful. Several blacks recall, with some bitterness still, that they were alienated at Thomas Jefferson High School, where an occasional teacher or guidance counselor was "condescending." Tommy Hemans, director of the New York City Public School Athletic League, was counseled out of accepting a basketball scholarship to Harvard University despite a science and math average better than 90 percent. Solly Walker chose to go to Boys' High School because of Jefferson's "reputation" in regard to blacks, and Chicky Smith had similarly negative feelings. These feelings, however, were in each case directed at no more than a handful of Jefferson staff members and not at the students, who were perceived as much more tolerant and occasionally even as friends.[30] At Thomas Jefferson High School then, and at the BBC at least until the mid-1950s, relationships between blacks and Jews were generally peaceful and often friendly. And it was in this world of positive social flux that Irving M. Levine lived and worked as a teenager and young adult.

As a college student Irving continued as a volunteer to direct athletics at the BBC, but he grew increasingly disenchanted with sports as a primary vehicle for changing social consciousness, and by 1950 he became a part-time paid social worker for the Brownsville Boys Club. Along with a number of other professionals, whom Levine describes as having been "the best of the 1940s . . . left," Irving brought a much broader orientation and a set of social work methodologies to the BBC.

The new group of professionals included several, like Baroff, Levine, and Lenny Dryansky, who were former members and officers of the Brownsville Boys Club in its preprofessional era. They were encouraged by major figures in social welfare, as well as by militant unionists and social activists including radical community organizer Saul Alinsky. Reinforced, Irving Levine and the Brownsville Boys Club professionals and the volunteer staff continued through 1954 to do creative social work and community organizing in the face of the increasing difficulties of changing demographics and economic decline in Brownsville.[31]

Levine left Brooklyn in 1955 to join Norman Adelman as a part-time director of youth activities for the Jewish Community Center in Milwaukee and to study for a master's degree in social work at the University of Wisconsin. Here Irving met several men and women "with political savvy who were involved in civil rights activism and in the anti-McCarthy movement." It was not long before he gave up his job at the Jewish Community Center for the more exciting work of the racial justice crusade. Even this, however, was not enough for Irving, who knew that the "real work, the real civil rights militancy," was in New York City. And by 1957 he was back in New York as assistant director of the Brooklyn office of the American Jewish Congress, which was heavily involved in racial justice issues, and soon thereafter with the Commission on Intergroup Relations (COIR), a division of the City Human Rights Commission.

As COIR's field representative for the borough of Queens, Irving Levine was very quickly thrust into race relations. In Springfield Gardens, a predominantly Jewish section with a small number of black home owners, real estate agents attempted to promote panic selling. But white owners struggled to fight back, and COIR sent in Levine, who aided the fledgling self-help movement in becoming a powerful force against blockbusting. When confronted with the implication that his actions might prevent some blacks from becoming home owners, Irving Levine said: "We're concerned with minority groups getting out of the ghettos. But we're also concerned about new ghettos being created."[32]

The emphasis here on the needs of the Jewish community, as well as on the long-term needs of blacks, is reflective of the balance of particularism and universalism—the pluralism—that continued to characterize Levine's ideology and approach throughout his career. His pluralism did not remain limited to Jews and blacks; it eventually included those people who would come to be known as "white ethnics"—the Poles, the Germans, the Irish, the Italians, and the Slavs.

Having witnessed the ferocity of white resistance to integration, especially when it meant mixing people across class as well as racial lines, as in the Queens neighborhoods of Ridgewood and Glendale, Levine said: "We began to realize that you simply couldn't work one-sidedly for progress for blacks without addressing the concerns of working-class and lower-middle-class white people who felt left behind." Indeed, he came to believe that the "social revolution" would be blocked for blacks if whites failed to understand it and were not part of it.[33]

Levine's interest in, and regard for, the real and felt needs of the white ethnics in no way diminished his commitment to civil rights for blacks. From the end of 1959 to early 1961 in Indiana, Irving served simultaneously as the executive director of the Indiana Jewish Community Relations Council, codirector of the Civil Rights Coalition, and executive secretary of the Indiana Conference on Civil Rights Legislation, which he organized and which became the primary group lobbying the Indiana State Legislature on civil rights.[34]

During the course of these accomplishments, Levine worked with many Jewish agencies and "came to see the American Jewish Committee as a 'class act.'" When the committee announced an opening for its area director in Ohio in 1961, Irving jumped at the chance. In Ohio from 1961 to 1964, Levine "remained primarily engaged in the vast work [of] safeguarding . . . the rights of Jews everywhere." But he served simultaneously as codirector of the Ohio Conference for Civil Rights Legislation. Levine's leadership was critical to the passage of a major fair housing bill in 1962, which had failed in two previous legislatures. He was also involved in the school desegregation crisis in Cleveland in 1963 and 1964.[35]

Levine's militant activism, however, continued to be grounded in the recognition that even though "segregation was an unmitigated disaster for blacks, one that we wanted to dismantle, indeed to smash, we did not know how to implement or define integration." His experience taught him about the need carefully to prepare people, black and white, for any integration plan, and he advocated, among other things, the building of new schools in "border areas" to avoid the coercion of busing and the sense of "invasion" of neighborhood. He talked too about an intensified movement for "quality education" in already racially mixed areas and about open and adequate housing and employment opportunities as longer-range vehicles for a less engineered, more durable integration."[36]

Levine brought these ideas and his continuing commitment to liberalism and racial justice back, once again, to New York City when he became director of community relations for the New York chapter of the AJC in late 1964. Between 1964 and 1970 in the face of nationwide urban riots by blacks on the one side and the potential for massive repression on the other, Levine was instrumental in developing the American Jewish Committee's "urban strategy."

In several cross-country tours of the major cities of the United States, in an almost uncountable number of speeches, papers, and memos, Irving Levine called for a completely new environment to save the cities and for Jews to become a major force in "the big city renaissance." His proposals often reflected his Brownsville experience, particularly when he urged Jews to use "their special leverage and knowledge in the field of housing . . . , ethnic self-help development . . . , and social science . . . in the remaking of [the] cities." Connecting the issues of shelter, economic change, and education, Levine envisioned a "package" that contained "something for everyone": job training, tax benefits, and new social security programs for the poor and for the young working and lower-middle classes; "subsidized home ownership," as well as massive low- and moderate-cost public housing development "available to anyone regardless of race or color"; and educational parks.[37]

Serving also as chair of the Citywide Commission on Educational Parks, Irving Levine continued to defend the "park" as an answer to the need for quality integrated education. And his vision of a central educational resource for the whole community, young and old, black and white, with a variety of learning and teaching modes and technologies, rooftop planetariums, and art and music centers, bore a striking resemblance to the vision and actuality of the Brownsville Boys Club in its new building in 1954.

Once again carrying on in the tradition of the BBC, which had worked so effectively out of a storefront for so many years, Levine said, "We are advocating storefront police stations, storefront welfare and job counseling offices,

storefront everything."[38] Day camps, retreats, sports, and innumerable storefront services, including a place and a voice for nonviolent militants, constituted a blueprint for an AJC urban action program and a short-term presummer strategy.

But Levine warned that it was neither right nor safe to work for the advancement of only the most depressed minorities. It was necessary to have programs that spoke to the frustrations of all American "minorities," including white ethnics, who he said "are potentially, if not already, an antiprogress bloc cut off from the true benefits of the affluent society." American liberals, Levine argued, "must convince actual or potential backlash groups that alliances and cooperation can yield constructive results for themselves as well as blacks." He insisted that the new strategy would not mean "capitulating to a regressive ideology or slowing down on black demands." But, he went on, we must have a "new pluralism" in the nation, which will be responsive to certain needs, material and emotional, of "white ethnics."[39]

Just as Irving Levine's commitment to racial justice was partly a product of his having been raised in progressive Jewish Brownsville, so his concern for the needs of the white working and lower-middle classes was partly a product of a strong Jewish identity. His closeness to the Jewish community and to his family allowed Levine to see that it was an insensitive oversimplification to use the term "bigot" or "racist" to describe those upset by, or reacting to, the black movement. When he came back to New York in 1964 after more than five years "in the Shaker Heights of the world, working as a civil rightsnik," Irving moved into Flatbush. "I had almost forgotten my own roots. . . . My own motivations were more pro-black than pro–my own family." But back in Brooklyn, Levine also began to see the emergence of Jewish uncertainty and disaffection in regard to the black school movement. "If Jews who are the most liberal of New Yorkers are reacting this way," Irving realized, "then something more than racism was at work here. [It was] legitimate group self-interest in conflict."[40] His realization was reinforced during the 1968 New York school crisis that pitted schoolteachers, administrators, and teachers' union leaders, a significant disproportion of whom were Jewish, against the Ocean Hill–Brownsville experimental district governing board, a disproportionate number of whom were black. In the aftermath of the crisis, which was marked by vicious accusations and verbal assaults, Levine said, "We must recover from our shock at having at least for the time being passed out of the brotherhood–intergroup relations–dialogue stage of racial progress and into a more difficult era of group conflict, group interest, and group identity. We must utilize whatever is positive about this new era by creatively meeting demands for power by emerging ethnic groups, without destroying either the fabric of our society or the lives and fortunes of those who have only recently 'made it.'"[41]

Aware of the dangers to Jewish rights and power, and to American individualism lurking in various interpretations of the new pluralism, Levine and several of his colleagues nevertheless continued to use the concept of ethnicity and to promote group associations. It was still believed that group associations represented "a solid ground on which to stand, a reassuring base from which to go forth, a comforting home to which to return in a despairing and alienating society." At the same time, these associations, it was argued, must not become a "battlefield from which to undermine the larger society."[42]

To the degree that the new pluralism helped to make diversity acceptable it did fortify a major democratic tenet. But it is unlikely that the initial emphasis on difference reassured a people confused and divided by such things as the Vietnam War, poverty, prejudice, urban violence, police repression, and the excesses of the counterculture. Unlike the "old pluralists" like Horace Kallen, the social philosopher who had coined and defined the term "cultural pluralism" some fifty years earlier, there never was among the new pluralists a systematic, intense effort to demonstrate how the persistence of ethnic differences could be compatible with a sense of national wholeness.[43] Nor did the speeches, news releases, pamphlets, conferences, and literature produced by the ethnic revivalists add up to an emphasis on the crucial point—perhaps the most important point of all—that the nation's various ethnic groups had many things in common as Americans.

Later, in 1982, Levine himself virtually admitted this failure when he said of his directorship of the Institute for American Pluralism and Group Identity: "We are making a return to what I call the intergroup relations movement. After a couple of decades of ethnic and racial assertion, we're trying to put it all together in a new framework of coalition."[44] David Roth, the midwest director of the institute, agreed: We are "trying to find some common ground between the different groups," he said, "all of whom are asserting something. . . . Society [in 1983] needs some glue."[45] After years of reflection and introspection, Levine

recently admitted that more attention ought to have been paid to commonalities, to those things all ethnic groups shared as Americans, or as Americans in the making, and that somewhat less attention ought to have been paid to ethnic differences: "My critics within the progressive community were more tuned in than I was to the dangers of dealing so openly with ethnic group identity, self-esteem, and self-actualization. I was right in pointing up the lack of frankness about the continuing influence of ethnic culture on values and behavior, and about the objective need for the articulation of group identities and group interests; however, I may have underestimated the risk of this becoming narrow and overpoliticized."[46]

But the original force that drove Irving Levine and other creators of the new pluralism derived primarily from the urgently perceived need to unplug the white backlash and to rescue the progressive coalition of labor, minorities, and liberals from dissolution, and Levine continues to think in these terms. He said in 1989 that although the preservation of distinct groups is vital to the enrichment of society, a state of polarization develops when they fail to interact positively, or at all, as in current race relations and in relations between blacks and Jews, leading to an impasse in the pursuit of the just society.[47]

Putting the progressive coalition back together in the long run, and promoting positive intergroup relations in the shorter term, remained the goals of the boy from Brownsville well into the 1990s. A product of a predominantly Jewish cultural milieu that fostered the universal ideals of mutual aid, communal responsibility, and social justice, as well as the particular sense of Jewish peoplehood, Irving M. Levine combined in his life and work a loyalty to his own group at the same time that he, along with a significant number of other "Brownsville Boys," pursued justice for all groups.

NOTES

A longer version of this chapter originally appeared as "From the Brownsville Boys Club to the Institute for American Pluralism," in *An Inventory of Promises: Essays on the American Jewish History*, ed. Gurock and Raphael (New York: Carlson, 1995).

1. For the full story of the Brownsville Boys Club and the boys who built it, see Gerald Sorin, *The Nurturing Neighborhood: The Brownsville Boys Club and Jewish Community in Urban America, 1940–1990* (New York: New York University Press, 1990).

2. Morris Horowitz and L. J. Kaplan, *The Jewish Population of the New York Area, 1900–1975* (New York: Federation of Philanthropies, 1959), p. 49; Nettie P. McGill and Ellen N. Mathews, *The Youth of New York* (New York: Macmillan, 1940), appendix, table 3.

3. *Brooklyn Eagle*, March 30, 1949.

4. Percentages were derived from interviews with nearly 100 BBC alumni and from returned questionnaires from an additional 150.

5. Alfred Kazin, "My New York," *The New York Times Book Review*, August 26, 1986, pp. 29–30.

6. Alter Landesman, "A Neighborhood Survey of Brownsville," typescript, 1927, pp. 5–9, 12; Jewish Division, New York Public Library; Landesman, *Brownsville: The Birth, Development, and Passing of a Jewish Community in New York* (New York: Bloch Publishers, 1971), pp. 50–56, 323–24; Reuben Fink and Bernard Richards, eds., *Jewish Community Directory of Greater New York: A Guide to Central Organizations and Institutions* (New York: Jewish Information Bureau, 1947).

7. Rae Glauber, *All Neighborhoods Change: A Survey of Brownsville, Brooklyn, USA* (New York: n.p., 1963), pp. 29–30; Landesman, *Brownsville*, pp. 116–19; Irving Howe, *World of Our Fathers* (New York: Columbia University Press, 1981).

8. The BBC youngsters, like so many college-educated second-generation Jews, were culturally predisposed in the direction of teaching and social work. Nathan Glazer, *The Social Bases of American Communism* (New York: Harcourt, 1961), pp. 143–68.

9. Community Council of Greater New York, Bureau of Community Statistical Services, *Brooklyn Communities: Population Characteristics and New Social Resources*, vol .1 (New York: Community Council, 1959), pp. xii, xvi, 164–65; Ron Miller et al., "The Fourth Largest City in America—a Sociological Survey of Brooklyn," in Rita S. Miller, ed., *Brooklyn, USA* (Brooklyn: Brooklyn College Press, 1978), pp. 3–44.

10. Community Council, *Brooklyn Communities*, pp. xxxviii, 168–170; *Brooklyn Eagle*, November 20, 1954.

11. Author's interviews with Irving Levine, October 8, 1986; Jack Deutch, October 19, 1986; Leonard Dryansky, August 11, 1988; and Norman Goroff, July 23, 1987; "BBC News," no. 6 (July 1947).

12. Milton Goell, *Brownsville Must Have Public Housing* (Brooklyn: Brooklyn Community for Better Housing and the Brownsville Neighborhood Council, 1940). Goell was a lawyer, poet, and social reformer in Brownsville and neighboring Easing, New York, from the early 1930s to the early 1950s. He was a key figure in the Brownsville Neighborhood Council and had occasional direct contact with the Brownsville Boys Club.

13. "Sixth Anniversary Meeting," flyer, March 22, 1946; Norman Goroff, "The Brownsville Boys Club," typescript, 1947, pp. 5–8; "Minutes," BBC weekly meeting, March 1946.

14. Alfred Kazin, *A Walker in the City* (New York: Harcourt, 1951), p. 141.

15. Milton Kirschner, letter to author, June 14, 1993; author's interviews with Kronenberg, January 13, 1987; and Irwin Millman, September 21, 1993.

16. "Minutes," BBC weekly meetings, March 1943 to December 1946.

17. "BBC News," 7, no. 6 (July 1947); David Suher, *The Brownsville Neighborhood Council* (New York School of Social Work, 1948), pp. 46–65.

18. Irving Levine interviews, October 8, 1986; April 11, 1988.

19. Irwin Millman interview; Irving Levine interview, September 7, 1993.

20. "BBC News," 7, no. 9 (September 1947).

21. Irving Levine interviews, October 8, 1986; April 11, 1988.

22. Irving Levine interviews, September 7, 1993.

23. Irving Levine interviews, October 8, 1986; April 11, 1988.

24. Irving Levine interview, September 7, 1993; Herb Grosswirth, letter to author, February 1, 1987; William Brief, letter to author, May 30, 1993.

25. Herb Grosswirth, letter to author.

26. Irving Levine interview, October 8, 1986.

27. Eddie Eshkenazi, letter to author, June 15, 1993; Martin Karduna, letter to author, July 18, 1993; Irving Kunis, letter to author, September 11, 1993; and letters of William Maltz, Arthur Spetter, Lester Brezenoff, David Behar, Solomon Behar, Herman Thaler, and Eli Matsil.

28. Author's interview with James Grant, September 9, 1993.

29. *The New York Times*, August 8, 1993.

30. Author's interviews with Thomas Hemans, February 1, 1994; Irving Millman; and James Grant.

31. Irving Levine interviews, October 8, 1986; August 11, 1988. For changes in the neighborhood see Sorin, *Nurturing Neighborhood*, pp. 95–119, 159–88.

32. *The New York Times*, November 22, 1958; see also Albert J. Morrow, *Changing Patterns of Prejudice* (Philadelphia: Chilton Company, 1962), pp. 99–111.

33. Irving Levine interview, April 11, 1988

34. Irving Levine interview, September 7, 1993. Arnold Aronson of the National Community Relations Advisory Council (NCRAC), the primary liaison organization for the American Jewish community, urged Levine to take the Indiana job, insisting that Indianapolis was an "incubator city" for a national position. Levine did want to return to the "Jewish field," but not, as he put it, to "the home of the American Legion." A good interview, however, and a doubled salary, along with Aronson's persuasiveness about future possibilities, enticed Levine "reluctantly" to leave New York.

35. American Jewish Committee, Cleveland chapter, "Memorandum," August 3, 1964; Irving Levine, letter to Ed Lukas, May 14, 1963.

36. Irving Levine, "Jews and Their Responsibilities in Civil Rights," lecture, May 31, 1965, East Flatbush YM-YWHA; *Miami Beach News*, May 1, 1966.

37. *Louisville Courier Journal*, January 14, 1968; AJC file, "Speaking Engagements," Irving Levine.

38. *San Francisco Examiner*, March 14, 1968; Levine, "A Proposal for Community Organization."

39. These views were expressed in several nationwide tours to stimulate AJC chapters, and Jews generally, to become a major force in the "urban strategy." They appeared in more than a dozen newspapers between 1966 and 1968. See also Irving Levine, "A Strategy for White Ethnic America," in Jack Rothman, ed., *Issues in Race and Ethnic Relations* (Itasca, Ill.: F. E. Peacock, 1977), pp. 272–74.

40. Quoted in Kevin Lahart, "Ethnics '71: What Happens When the Melting Pot Fire Goes Out? *Newsday*, June 5, 1971.

41. *Cincinnati Post and Times-Star*, January 11, 1968.

42. Philip E. Hoffman, "Reflections on the Future: Address by the President of the American Jewish Committee to the Committee's Annual Dinner," May 4, 1972, pp. 12–13.

43. Horace Kallen, "Democracy vs. the Melting Pot," *The Nation*, February 18 and 25, 1915; Horace Kallen, *Culture and Democracy* (New York: Arno, 1970); Moses Rischin, "The Jews and Pluralism: Toward an American Freedom Symphony," in *Jewish Life in America*, ed. Gladys Rosen (New York: KTAV, 1978).

44. *The New York Times*, December 26, 1982.

45. *Cleveland Jewish News*, October 28, 1983.

46. Irving Levine interview, September 7, 1993; February 3, 1994.

47. *Pittsburgh Post Gazette*, November 18, 1989.

Nice Jewish Girls
Growing Up in Brownsville, 1930s–1950s

CAROLE BELL FORD

*As a girl, I couldn't go beyond being exactly as
my parents expected me to be.*
—Raye Roder Cohen

I was born in Brownsville, in the midst of the Great Depression. The tracks of the elevated subway, the "IRT El," ran right beside the windows of our second-story flat, above Abramowitz's grocery store, on the corner of Livonia Avenue and Barrett Street. It was diagonally across from a nondescript corner candy store, Midnight Rose's, which harbored one of the major crime syndicates of the Depression and wartime eras: Murder, Inc.

I moved away from Brownsville in 1958 and hadn't returned until, more than thirty years later, I became involved in an oral history project and found myself in the old neighborhood once again: figuratively but sometimes literally, as I interviewed women who, like myself, had grown up and come of age there. I was interested in the women's stories since Brownsville, the Jewish working-class—and desperately working to achieve middle class—community in which we came of age was dominated by a culture in which women played a traditional, separate, and, critics say, unequal role to the men: a role transported from the shtetlach, the small towns and villages of eastern Europe. None of the more than forty women I interviewed live in Brownsville today, but I often chose to drive through the old neighborhood on the way to appointments in other parts of Brooklyn, Queens, and Long Island. I wanted to see, once again, the streets where we had been raised to be nice Jewish girls, learning to become good wives and mothers. Indeed, most of the women, even today, refer to each other as "the girls."[1]

Ashkenazim, the first generation of Jews in America who migrated from eastern Europe—Poland, Russia, Lithuania, Latvia, Bulgaria, Romania, the Austro-Hungarian Empire—and their second- and third-generation descendants, were the predominant inhabitants of Brownsville, although there was also a small Sephardic presence in the community. In their new homeland they continued to follow old-world cultural, if not religious, traditions. The signs and symbols of Jewish life were visible everywhere, from the most trivial to the profound.

Almost every Brownsville home had its mezuzah in the doorway, the miniature replica of a scroll that identified a Jewish home. There was always a *pushke*, a collection box sitting on the kitchen table, with its distinctive blue Star of David, for the United Jewish Appeal or the Jewish National Fund. Most of our mothers "kept kosher"; whether we accepted the rules or not, we all knew them. Even those of us who were not observant got dressed up on Saturday. We didn't think about observing the Sabbath; it was part of our lives.

Everyone celebrated the Jewish holidays; the minor ones, such as Purim, were our Jewish history lessons. As non-Jews got special outfits for Easter, Rosh Hashanah (the Jewish New Year) and Pesach (Passover) were when we got our new clothes—and promptly dirtied them when we "played nuts" in the street, a traditional children's game, similar to marbles. The Passover seder was celebrated in most households, although it was changing from the solemn commemoration of the story of the Exodus to a more raucous family gathering. Even Thanksgiving, the most American of holidays, had a Jewish *tam* (flavor), since the obligatory turkey was invariably preceded by typically Jewish starters of chopped liver and stuffed derma and ended with fruit compote instead of pumpkin pie. Chanukah was not yet competing with Christmas.[2] It was celebrated modestly. I remember receiving Chanukah gelt, usually fifty cents but sometimes a silver dollar, from my father. "Here's a shekel," he would say (long before the state of Israel reappropriated the biblical term for its currency). What we absorbed while engaging in these and many other simple acts was a deep, visceral, internal realization of our Jewishness.

Although, by the 1940s and 1950s, families had begun to disperse (what an editor of the Jewish weekly newspaper, *The Forward*, termed "the re-diasporization" of American Jews,)[3] most of our aunts, uncles, cousins lived only a short walk away. It was common for more than one generation to share a two-family home; many grandparents lived "upstairs." Some extended families all lived in the same apartment building.

When I lived in Brownsville, cultural programs could be heard over radio station WEVD. Mostly in Yiddish, programs ranged from Seymour Rechzeit and the Barry sisters singing folk and popular tunes to Moishe Oysher's cantorial and operatic arias. On Sunday mornings our parents listened to Art Raymond's Sunday morning Jewish news. And there was the popular, if somber, *Tsores bei layte* (People's Troubles).

Even the schoolteachers in Brownsville public schools were predominantly Jewish. There had been a growing presence of Jewish teachers in the city schools since the early part of the century. In 1916, with their understanding of the labor movement, Jewish teachers helped create the first teachers' union in the city, and by 1924 a Jewish teachers' organization was formed. By the 1940s, twelve thousand Jewish teachers had been placed in schools in Jewish neighborhoods as, with its reductionist thinking,

the Board of Education "saw them as more effective in socializing" Jewish children.[4] In looking over the names of the teachers who signed my autograph album when I graduated from PS 156, I found three names that I couldn't identify as Jewish. One was the school nurse; in those days, Jewish girls did not become nurses.

Sadly, Brownsville has become one of the most destitute communities in New York City, perhaps rivaled only by the South Bronx for its problems. It was never affluent, but how very different it was when it was the almost totally Jewish neighborhood of Brunzvil, as my parents called it, in their Ukrainian-Jewish-accented English.

From the start, in the late nineteenth century, when it took its name from the farmer Charles Brown, it was a poor, working-class community. Yet, it was a suburban haven from the Lower East Side of Manhattan, where immigrants from eastern and southern Europe settled when they first came to America. Soon, the East River Bridge and improvements in transportation from Manhattan, such as the expansion of the BMT and IRT subways and elevated lines into Brooklyn, made commuting possible.

Brownsville began where Crown Heights ended, reaching down from the Eastern Parkway, its northern border, and stretching eastward toward the "New Lots" area, which retained its name from an earlier time. Brownsville's eastern boundary was demarcated by the BMT train tracks at Junius Street, on the other side of which was East New York. Its other borders merged into the more affluent neighboring community of East Flatbush, where the poet Richard Fein was raised. He wrote:

> Eastern Parkway implicitly meant that it wound into the dens of Brownsville and toward Jews even poorer than my parents, a lower social class my family feared falling back into without so much as saying so, intuitively recognizing those minute class divisions that could be measured by social dividers called avenues. Below Utica Avenue, the Parkway squirmed off in the distance toward the din of Pitkin Avenue, a brassy notch above the hustle of Orchard Street.[5]

Until it came to an end in the 1960s, Brownsville was an authentic, living, Jewish community. It was a place the historian Deborah Dash Moore called "a world of its own."[6] Although it was in the midst of irreversible change from the community it had been earlier in its history, it was still 80 percent Jewish. And, it was "provincial," as one of the women said: "Everything was in a small nucleus. I was taught in Brownsville, met a boy from Brownsville. When I got married and my husband was offered a fellowship at Duke University, how could I leave my mother? I couldn't have a baby without my mother nearby."[7]

A broad range of social, political, educational, and religious experience was represented in each of the Jewish communities in New York. Each had its distinctive character: Williamsburg was more Orthodox, the East Bronx was more radical, Borough Park was more Zionist. The Upper West Side was called the "gilded ghetto" because it was where the more prosperous immigrants, primarily from Germany, had settled during an earlier migration. But Brownsville, unlike the other Jewish neighborhoods, had, "an egalitarianism in tone and manner." Within its boundaries it was possible to find the "entire spectrum of Jewish political and cultural associations."[8] And it had a secular character.

In spite of the fact that most of our mothers kept kosher homes and our fathers went to shul, the synagogue, on occasional Saturdays and on the High Holy Days, for the most part Brownsville was a secular Jewish community. "There are six hundred and thirteen mitzvoth in all," I was told with great patience. "The more of them you observe, the more religious you are."[9] But, in the 1940s and 1950s, when I and many of "the girls" were growing up, being Jewish did not require religious observance. Brownsville's synagogues "regularly attracted a mere eight percent of the neighborhood's adult Jewish males."[10]

Because many immigrants lived in Brownsville, Jewishness was rooted in the culture: in the customs, language, literature, shared history, and values. In the early days, Yiddish was the common language, the mame-loshen (mother tongue). It already dominated the streets of the neighborhood before the turn of the century, and even as late as the midtwentieth century, with Yiddish spoken in the homes, Yiddish daily and weekly newspapers, signs and menus in Yiddish, Jewish shopkeepers, Jewish delicatessens, restaurants, and bakeries selling Jewish dishes, it was possible to live in Brownsville without ever having learned a word of English. Nowadays, although many Yiddish words and Yiddishisms are part of New Yorkese, and some survive as part of the American lexicon, it can only be heard as a spoken language among the Orthodox.[11]

Along with the language and customs, the immigrants brought the values of the Old Country to the New World, the naya velt. They became deeply embedded in the culture of Brownsville: values such as an abiding belief in educa-

tion, which would bring not only wisdom but yikhes, or status; takhlis, a belief that one's activities must be goal-directed and lead to some positive final result; tsedakah and gemuluth hasadim, charity and the obligation to help the less fortunate. These values were interwoven with the tradition of social consciousness, based upon the principle of tikn olam, the repair or improvement of the world. They were expressed, reinforced, and carried out in landsmanshaftn, fraternal and mutual benefit societies, and in other community organizations. Charitable organizations were particularly important to the "sisterhoods" or "women's auxiliaries" of these organizations. The women brought the old-world custom of gehen kleiben, house to house collections, to the neighborhood.

But the primary job of the women was to raise their children in a Jewish home, a home in which Jewish values were perpetuated, in which Yidishkeit, and the Yidishe yerushe, the Jewish culture, were preserved. It was a home that, whatever other form it may have taken, was child-centered, and one in which the highest value was family.

Boys and girls growing up in the crowded community of Brownsville—by the 1940s it had grown to a quarter of a million people—felt safe there. One reason surely was that if, in the absence of a working parent, there was no one of the extended family about, a neighbor was apt to tell you to go indoors if it was getting late, make sure you had an after-school snack, or scold you if you were misbehaving. "We had to behave ourselves," one of the women told me. "People were watching."[12]

There was a sense of cohesion in the community that had a great deal to do with its ethnic homogeneity. Because everyone shared the values of the community, they could be involved with the rearing of the children and, more important, had tacit permission to be involved. My father told a story of someone who stopped him in the street when he was a young man to chastise him for smoking on shabes (the Sabbath). He didn't know the man's name; he referred to him as feter, literally uncle but also a term of respect. My father never questioned the man's authority (and never again smoked on shabes)!

Brownsville typified a kehillat, a Hebrew word meaning the community where each is responsible for all and all are responsible for each, closely knit and intimate. Every street, so densely packed, seemed like a neighborhood in itself. "Like a little city," one of the women remembered, "because of the big apartment buildings."[13] Each street had its grocer, its candy store, its pharmacist who took care of little bruises and scrapes—got things out of children's eyes. Everyone's address was fixed by identifying cross streets. "Everybody said two streets, no one just said where they lived. The avenue was very long, so you always said the corner."[14] They named three streets if they were asked, "Where are you between?": Powell Street between Blake and Dumont Avenues, Rockaway Avenue between Sutter and Pitkin, Saratoga between Livonia and Riverdale.

The Brownsville women share their deep fondness for the old neighborhood when they meet at special events: a grandchild's wedding or bar mitzvah, a bat mitzvah (the rite of passage for girls, signaling full participation in the religion, which is now accepted by all but the Orthodox). Some have periodic or annual gatherings of friends' clubs. Some meet more formally, at reunions of the alumni associations of Brownsville organizations, or of their junior and senior high schools. There, they love to "tell and retell the stories . . . share, and share again, the memories of their childhood and teenage years in the neighborhood."[15]

Most of the women remember their childhood in Brownsville as carefree. "We lived in the streets."[16] The girls came home from school, did their homework (on the roof if it was warm), and, with their skate keys on a soiled string around their necks, went out to play. They roller-skated, played with "jacks," jumped rope singly or in groups—some turning the ropes, which almost always were shortened clothesline. They played other, typically "girls'" street games such as "potsy," which I didn't learn, until I was an adult, was a sidewalk version of the ubiquitous hopscotch. Sometimes they ran around the block playing ring-a-levio with the boys. Fifty cents was enough for admission to Loew's grand movie palace on Pitkin Avenue, a special treat. Some girls took music lessons after school, usually at the Hebrew Educational Society on Hopkinson Avenue. They had few playthings but found active ways to amuse themselves. "We had to, we didn't have TV to entertain us, mostly we made our own times. When we were teenagers, we socialized on the block."[17]

Sometimes, rarely, the girls sat on the porches of the few private, usually two-family homes, but you were more likely to find them sitting on the front "stoops" of their apartment buildings (a New York word taken from the Dutch, meaning steps). It was long before portable radios boomed from the midst of a group of teens, and in any case radios were for the evenings. "We didn't go out at night on weekdays."[18]

It wasn't uncommon for snacks to be sent down to the youngster in the street from an upstairs window, via a paper bag tied to a length of string, and it was a favorite way to send change down for a quick trip to the corner grocery. The grocery was also one of the meeting places. "We would sit on the milk boxes."[19] Sometimes, in the afternoons, the girls went for malteds, for walks to look in the bridal shop windows, and, if they could afford to, stopped at a deli to buy a hot dog, fries, and a Coke, each for a nickel. "Everything took place in groups, groups of girls, groups of boys. We were always together and hanging around a candy store."[20] For some, "Nanny Goat Park was the central point; right after school we ran to the park."[21] Few of the girls participated in organized after-school sports activities, although some did play handball and even basketball in the park. There were almost no girls' teams. In the schools, they were the cheerleaders.

On weekends, free from school, they might "hang around" Lincoln Terrace Park and sometimes, from there, dare to cross the boundary of the neighborhood into Crown Heights to skate at the Eastern Parkway Roller Rink or to walk almost the entire length of Eastern Parkway to the Botanical Gardens, the Brooklyn Museum, or the huge Brooklyn Public Library on Grand Army Plaza.

If, by the 1950s, Brownsville had lost its shtetl quality, it was still very Jewish. There were still fresh carp swimming in tanks for gefilte fish. The aromas of the *shabes* meal still permeated the air on Friday nights. If shopkeepers sold nonkosher items they were kept out of sight. While many families did not strictly observe kashruth, they would never bring *treyf*, nonkosher food, into their homes. They ate it out, however, sometimes at the neighborhood Chinese restaurants. Ours was on Saratoga and Livonia Avenues, one flight up, almost touching the El, with its enticing sign, "High Class Chinese Food." My mother would meet me there for an occasional supper when my father worked late. She would have the egg drop soup and chicken chow mein, but would draw the line at the truly forbidden fruit: pork, bacon, shellfish, and especially ham. "It's pink!" she would say, as if that were explanation enough.

By far the most popular eateries were the kosher delicatessens, a Jewish-American invention. There was a deli on every block because, said the manager of Grabstein's, "a hot dog and a pastrami sandwich and a knish was a way of life." With their "salami sandwiches and pickles wrapped in coarse white paper," the delis were "the culinary hearts, if not the heartburn, of working-class and immigrant Jewish neighborhoods."[22]

(Left to right) Carole Bell with friends Elaine and Judy, ca. 1948. Photo courtesy of Carole Ford.

Like all poor neighborhoods, Brownsville had its fair share of social problems: delinquency, street crime, gambling, pimps and prostitution, even some alcoholism, contrary to Jewish myth. It had higher health risks, higher infant and maternal mortality, higher rates of sexually transmitted diseases, more tuberculosis and diphtheria.[23] But today's face-to-face crimes, muggings, rape, were infrequent. People felt physically safe in Brownsville. Within what Moore called the "sheltering neighborhood," they were able to acquire the "psychological attitude of a majority."[24] They developed an "unselfconscious Jewishness" that made it possible for them to live comfortably in the neighborhood even though they were a small minority in the vast city.[25]

In urban neighborhoods that were more multicultural or in Jewish communities in other, smaller cities such as Pittsburgh, where my mother's family settled, or even on the Lower East Side with its mix of Jews, Italians, Irish, and other ethnic groups, it was impossible not to be conscious of your ethnicity. But in Brownsville, "we were all

the same," one of the women said. Growing up there, it was possible to think everyone was Jewish. They were not outsiders; the rest of America was made up of "the others," *der anderers*—the goyim—often to be ridiculed and often feared but usually just avoided. Brownsville was so insular—an ethnic pocket that encouraged negative, chauvinistic, and ethnocentric attitudes.

In spite of the fact that the vast majority were not observant, in the 1940s and 1950s, there was still a shul on almost every Brownsville street. Almost the entire population of the neighborhood filled the synagogues when Kol Nidre was chanted on Yom Kippur, the most solemn Holy Day of the year. We couldn't read, or play, or listen to music, or eat! "Pitkin's stores were all dark," wrote Alter Landesman.[26] Since it was forbidden to do anything else, my friends and I used to dress up and parade around the neighborhood. We would stop at the shul to see a parent, or grandparent who was ensconced there for the entire day. We visited the women in the balconies, or sitting behind the *mehitzah*, the formal partition that separated the women's from the men's section. My aunt, Tante Hudel, always examined my tongue for a white coating, to check whether I was fasting.

Boys and girls who weren't required to remain inside could be seen playing together on the sidewalk. To the despair and frustration of the elders, they ran in and out of the building, chasing each other up and down the fire escapes. Our early religious experiences were full of messages about many things: continuity, reverence (and lack of reverence), family—and certainly gender.

Our shul was the Congregation Ezrath Achim, on Newport Avenue and Bristol Street. Although it was a long walk from our apartment and there were many other orthodox synagogues along the way, it was our family shul; the entire mishpokhe, our extended family, could be found there on the holidays. I was told that my grandmother (Chaya Sore, my father's mother) had worshipped there and, when she died, was honored in a way that was rare for women: her funeral procession passed in front of the shul and stopped there for a moment, long enough for the doors to be opened. It was a token of respect for this charitable woman who epitomized the Jewish guiding principle of tsedakah, or righteousness: she was the eishit chayil, the "woman of valor," revered because she "stretcheth her hand out to the poor."

My father's customary seat was on the ground floor of the synagogue, the more modest part of the shul, which had a small square corner of the room set aside for the women. When I was very little I was still allowed to sit with my father (he always was in the same place). As I got older, my mother told me not to "bother him," to stay with the women behind the partition, the mehitzah. I couldn't see my father in his well-worn talis, his black and white prayer shawl and new yarmulke (a souvenir skullcap from the most recent bar mitzvah or wedding), but I knew he could participate in all of the important rituals and honors: carrying the Torah, being called to the dais "for an aliye" (to read from the Torah), opening the ark. The women were "excused" from these practices as they were excused from the minyan (the quorum of ten required for communal prayer). The women sat out of sight; they prayed behind the mehitzah. They were dressed in their holiday finery but didn't wear special garments; they wore ordinary hats. Messages about the differences between boys and girls, men and women, were unspoken, but clear nevertheless. As Susannah Heschel wrote, in Jewish culture, women's role and their identity begin with and are "entangled with the theological positions that legitimate them."[27]

Based upon the biblical injunction "and you shall teach your children," women were entrusted with raising their children as Jews; they were honored as the carriers of tradition. "What could be more important than family," one of the women asked, "more important than raising your children, passing on Yidishkeit?"[28] Like her, the Brownsville girls saw themselves growing into an important role, rooted in tradition. And like their mothers before them, they did not see that they had a choice: that they could do more than limit themselves to a supporting role—enabling their husbands to study and work, transmitting Yidishkeit to their children, helping their children go forward in the world and rise to an even higher station in life than they expected to achieve. Because women were, still are, praised and even honored for performing the traditional, secondary, supporting role well, the girls made decisions that ensured that they would continue the tradition:

> As a girl, I couldn't go beyond being exactly as my parents expected me to be, which was to marry Jewish, teach my children to carry on the traditions, and conduct myself in a reasonably Jewish manner. It's as if there was no other way; you never pondered about it, you never questioned why or thought any differently than the way they expected of you.[29]

Of course, the problem was not in doing these important jobs well but in "the exclusion of all else."[30]

In his study of the Brownsville Boys' Club, Jewish historian Gerald Sorin claims that, in spite of its poverty, Brownsville was a "nurturing neighborhood." The culture of the Jewish immigrants, in combination with the American environment, provided Brownsville boys with a strong and stable foundation upon which they built successful lives. The Brownsville women believe that they too were nurtured, socialized to be successful, but within the limitations of their traditional feminine role, the role of the baleboste, the homemaker, in its broadest sense, the good Jewish wife and mother.

But because, in Brownsville, the deeper cultural values were also transmitted to them, they were able, eventually, to overcome the limitations set by the traditional society. Like other Jewish-Americans, they were given to "ignoring, retaining, modifying, adapting, inventing, reappropriating, and reconstructing tradition."[31] The women may not have been able to articulate the values of the immigrant culture but had taken them in, internalized them, and had applied these values to themselves. They gave new meaning to *takhles*, the expectation to lead a goal-directed, meaningful life and to shun idleness. It meant more than homemaking. *Tikn olam*, the repair or improvement of the world, meant social work. *Tsedakah* meant responsibility for the welfare of the community, but not only through charity—through other types of service. Unlike the boys, who were pushed to succeed by these values, the girls had to struggle against being limited to, as one of the women put it, "marriage, home, children, family." And, in redefining their role, they became less traditionally yet more fully Jews.

Brownsville, however, was insulated, not isolated, from the mainstream. Even when it most resembled a ghetto, the outside world came into the community: through radio, film, and after the 1950s television. The newspapers that were carried by the commuters on the New Lots line of the IRT subway were not only the Jewish *Daily Forward* and *Tag* but the *Daily News* and the *Star*, later the *New York Post*. Brownsville men and women worked in "the city," in multiethnic Manhattan; barriers broke down as they entered the workforce. The process of shifting from Jews in America to Jewish-Americans had begun for them.

And, at the same time, the Jews left Brownsville.

More than 175,000 Jews lived there in the 1930s and 1940s. In the late 1960s, after a "wholesale exodus," fewer than 5,000 were still there, mostly the elderly who found it difficult to break their ties with the community.[32] Their children were born into a world unlike the one they knew: a world in which the Jewish culture itself was eroding as the dominant American culture first touched and then washed over it, even as solid rock is eroded by the constant friction of the sea.

Young Jewish-Americans today, many fourth and even fifth generations on American soil, are thoroughly enculturated. They may have become bar or bat mitzvah but, unless they are part of an observant community, it is more often their last traditional act than the beginning of their adult observance. They may be intellectually outraged and bewildered by the Holocaust, but to them, it's history. Israel, connected somehow to that history, seems always to have existed. Do they think about the contradictions inherent in that society? Those who grew up in observant families have experienced a kosher home and have observed the dietary laws. Others dismiss dietary restrictions as archaic practices. Most young Jews can't possibly imagine the preparation for the Sabbath. They have no sense of the massive work that went into the cleaning and cooking and "changing over" for the Passover holidays: stocking dozens and dozens of eggs for the flourless sponge cakes, the matzo meal bagels, the other ritual Passover foods. They don't know the old dances—or songs, and how could they understand them? They have rarely heard Yiddish spoken, perhaps a few words by their grandparents. They may recognize some Hebrew from the Torah reading at their bar or bat mitzvah but have no knowledge or affection for the Yiddish language. Although when young Jews marry non-Jews they hope their children will absorb the best of both cultures and be enriched by the diversity, they have been given little of the Jewish culture to pass on to their children.

On the other hand, so many positive changes have occurred in American society since those Brownsville days. Young Jewish men faced quotas in engineering, medical, law schools. Today Jews are prominent in these and other, newer professions. Women still have to contend with the sexism that conspires to keep them in traditional roles and careers, but the Brownsville women are witnessing their daughters having both family and careers, not either-or. Unlike the Brownsville women themselves, who did clerical work or, if they completed college, became schoolteachers, few of their daughters are in feminized occupations. In fact, a relatively large percentage of their daughters, not only their sons, have become attorneys as law, along with medicine, is losing its male domination. It's a far cry from the days when being a doctor wasn't, as the one Brownsville woman who became a nurse said, "a girl thing." All the grandchildren of the Brownsville women are encouraged to go to college, to pursue careers, to do anything they can or wish to do.

The other morning I saw a footrace of four- and five-year-olds that had been organized by a local temple. The children, behind the starting point, were eager and ready to give it their best; it was very, very dear. But it was also very important, if not for the reasons that it was planned. It was important because there was no distinction between girls and boys. The girls weren't standing on the sidelines, watching and cheering the boys on; they too were competing. It was a powerful representation of change. For some, however, the price for such change is too high and is frightening. They think it may be American Judaism itself.

There are still Jewish communities in New York City in which the religiously observant live: Borough Park, Crown Heights, and Williamsburg in Brooklyn—and in suburbs such as Kiryat Joel. There are other communities where the

Jewish population dominates and which, I suppose, can be thought of as secular Jewish communities. They can be found on Long Island and in parts of New Jersey; some are new self-imposed ghettos, "gated communities." But there is little in these places that distinguishes them from non-Jewish communities. To be a secular Jew today means that you must actively seek out educational and cultural activities offered through Jewish organizations such as the New York Jewish Historical Society, the 92nd Street YM-YWHA, the National Council of Jewish Women, the Workman's Circle. Communities such as Brownsville no longer exist—communities in which *Yidishkeit* was simply a way of life.

NOTES

1. Thus, the title of my book, *The Girls: Jewish Women of Brownsville, Brooklyn, 1940–95* (New York: SUNY Press, 2000).

2. See Jenna Weissnman Joselit, *The Wonders of America: Reinventing Jewish Culture, 1880–1950* (New York: Hill and Wang, 1995), 229–43.

3. Jonathan Rosen, "A Dead Language, Yiddish Lives," *The New York Times Magazine*, 7 July 1996, 26.

4. Gerald Sorin, *The Nurturing Neighborhood: The Brownsville Boys Club and Jewish Community in Urban America, 1940–1990* (New York: New York University Press, 1990), 98–99.

5. Richard Fein, *The Dance of Leah: Discovering Yiddish in America* (Cranberry, N.J.: Associated University Presses, 1986), 92.

6. Deborah Dash Moore, *At Home in America: Second Generation New York Jews* (New York: Columbia University Press, 1981), 62.

7. Interview with Isabel Herman Cohen, 4/25/91.

8. Moore, *At Home*, 70.

9. Interview with Lorraine Zakow Nelson, 10/13/94.

10. Moore, *At Home*, 127.

11. Deborah Sontag, "Oy Gevalt! New Yawkese, an Endangered Dialect?" *The New York Times*, 14 February 1993, sec. 1, p. 1+. See also Herman Galvin and Stan Tamarkin, *The Yiddish Dictionary Sourcebook*

(Hoboken, N.J.: Ktav Publishing House, 1986), and "Campuses See Revival of Interest in Yiddish as Field of Study," *Chronicle of Higher Education*, vol. XLII, no. 4, 22 September 1995, A18. They quote the famous Yiddishist and Nobel laureate Isaac Bashevis Singer, who said, however, that "from Yiddish you have not yet heard the last word."

12. Interview with Vea Finkelstein Larkin, 4/6/92.

13. Interview with Katie Tepper Stavans, 2/24/91.

14. Interview with Shirley Hershenson Donowitz, 2/24/91.

15. Sorin, *Nurturing Neighborhood*, 1.

16. Interview with Frances (Fagye) Rosenthal Lubin, 3/27/91.

17. Interview with Minette Zharnest Cutler, 3/28/92.

18. Interview with Sydelle Koran Schlossberg, 2/25/91.

19. Interview with Rae Margolis Mirsky, 1/26/91.

20. Interview with Minette Cutler.

21. Interview with Sydelle Schlossberg.

22. Joseph Berger, "As Delis Dwindle, Traditions Lose Bite," *New York Times*, 15 May 1996, sec. B p. 1+ According to this article, the number of "authentic kosher delicatessens" in New York City and the suburbs has declined to thirty-five; their decline has followed that of Jewish communities in the city. Since 1950 the Jewish population in New York has decreased from over two million to one million.

23. Sorin, *Nurturing Neighborhood*, 20.

24. Moore, *At Home*, 62.

25. Ibid., 3.

26. Alter F. Landesman, *Brownsville: The Birth, Development and Passing of a Jewish Community in New York* (New York: Bloch Publishing Company, 1971), 12. Landesman not only was executive director of an important community organization, the Hebrew Educational Society; he also helped initiate the Brownsville Neighborhood Health and Welfare Council and represented Brownsville on twenty or more civic organizations.

27. Susannah Heschel, *On Being a Jewish Feminist: A Reader* (New York: Schocken Books, 1983), xxii.

28. Interview with Sarah Barbanel Lieberman, 8/19/91.

29. Interview with Raye Roder Cohen, 2/23/91.

30. Adrienne Baker, *The Jewish Woman in Contemporary Society: Transitions and Traditions* (New York: New York University Press, 1993), 135.

31. Joselit, *Wonders*, 4.

32. Landesman, *Brownsville*, 371.

My Mother's Borough Park

MICHAEL TAUB

On most early Friday afternoons Amnon's Kosher Pizza on Thirteenth Avenue in Boro Park is so crowded that most people finish their meals standing up. The popular eating place is in the heart of this largely Hasidic community, a restaurant famous for its falafel, knishes and, of course, pizza. Making her way through the throng of noisy yeshiva students is my mother. After a long walk on the Avenue, as Thirteenth Avenue is affectionately known by the locals, she needs a rest and a taste of Rose's delicious potato knishes. My mother has lived in Boro Park for the last twenty-five years. She knows every store and street vendor on the Avenue. She can tell you who sells the plumpest tomatoes for the lowest price, the freshest cheese Danish, the fluffiest challa, the juiciest prime cut around.

She can also tell you how much things have changed. Twenty years ago, Boro Park was a quiet neighborhood where Hasidim and secular Jews lived side by side in relative peace. While some Ultra-Orthodox families opted for the greener lawns of Rockland County, thousands from nearby communities in Flatbush, Kings Highway, and Eastern Parkway migrated here. Soon enough, new homes sprung up, old buildings got a face-lift, and real estate prices went though the roof. Another change occurred in the 1990s when Russians began arriving as well. Although most of these new immigrants are ignorant in matters of religious customs and rituals, the Hasidim seem to tolerate them because of what they suffered under Communism. I imagine that in the eyes of these strict observers of tradition Russian Jews are like Holocaust survivors, remnants of what could have been another national disaster had not radical changes swept Eastern Europe and the Soviet Union a decade ago.

In the midst of this rather strange human mix—Hasidim and recent Russian immigrants—one finds a sprinkle of old-timers like my mother. These are Yiddish-speaking traditional Jews, Holocaust survivors, who would rather live in a self-imposed ghetto than move to sunny Florida or an old-age home in Riverdale or Westchester. True, at least twice a year even these rugged Boro Parkers join the legions of other American retirees at play: during the months of January and February when they head to Miami Beach, and in July–August when they travel north to the "mountains," the Catskill Mountains, of course. Other than that you will find them on the Avenue, playing cards at someone's house, swimming at the Y, or in shul on Saturdays and most religious holidays. Although outwardly they look religious—yarmulkas, modest dress, kosher food, no travel on *Shabbes*—in the privacy of their homes they are fairly lax.

With curtains drawn and sound lowered, they watch television, listen to music, and talk on the phone, all forbidden activities during *Shabbes* and most holidays.

I think the strongest bond that keeps them together all these years is the fact that they are all Holocaust survivors. No matter how scattered they are, survivors always find each other. They recognize each other even if they never met before. Something in the look, the speech, or the demeanor tells them right away that the other person is one of them.

For my mother the thing that has sustained her for so long is a handful of neighbors who, like her, went through the hell of Auschwitz and other concentration camps. Miraculously, Berta, a woman who lives in her building, was in her barrack for a short while. In watching my mother I sometimes marvel at how even fifty years of life in freedom could not completely wipe away certain fears and paranoias. An official letter, a summons for jury duty, even statements from insurance companies are an immediate cause for alarm. No matter how many times you remind them that money is best kept in the bank, they feel more comfortable if some of it stays hidden in the house. And, if you leave the house to go somewhere, be it a short trip to Manhattan or a flight to Chicago, you must take food with you because you never know what's awaiting you on the road. . . .

Like most ethnic neighborhoods, Boro Park, especially Thirteenth Avenue, is one giant food court. There are a variety of kosher restaurants, everything from the basic sandwich deli to four-course establishments, eastern European cooking to Yemenite cooking. Like many of the stores in Boro Park, these restaurants too live off the thousands of tourists flocking the area on Sundays and on the eve of major Jewish holidays. On busy days when streets are jammed with double- and triple-parked cars, and the air is filled with the piercing sounds of honking horns, my mother and other locals prefer to get out and visit friends and family in other parts of the city. If you are coming into Boro Park on those days, make sure you start looking for parking at least ten blocks from the main shopping areas, and do not forget to sharpen your elbows, because Boro Park consumers do not believe in lines. And, if by some miracle you do find a metered space, make sure you feed it properly because, unlike the rest of New York City, the meters here are off on Saturdays, not Sundays.

Having lived in Israel for a while, I am familiar with the *shuk*-like, chaotic atmosphere of shopping or negotiating in Boro Park. But after thirty years away from the craziness of the Middle East one loses the edge, that aggressiveness

necessary to survive in these types of urban jungles. My mother, who has lived in Boro Park a quarter century, is as sharp as the day she left Tel Aviv in 1969 for a new life in *di goldene medine*. Whether she is buying a fresh *shabbes chala* at "Straus Bakery" or making a deposit at the corner bank, my mother, even at seventy-five, somehow manages to get it done in less time than it would take an average Manhattan shopper to purchase a slice of Norwegian lox at Zabar's on a slow Tuesday morning.

Life in Boro Park has a rhythm of its own. Most of it is dictated by the arrival of the Sabbath or the holidays. While relatively quiet during the week, on weekends the neighborhood fills up with visitors, shoppers, and family guests. The week before such major holidays as Rosh Hashana, Yom Kippur, Sukkos, Pesach, or Shavuos is marked by intense activity: street vendors selling everything from ritual objects to radios, parents buying clothes for their children, families awaiting the arrival of someone from Cleveland, Israel, or Europe.

On the holiday proper all the hustle and bustle comes to a halt. Except for a few stores on the edges of the neighborhood, everything is closed. Hasidim in their long coats and fur hats are seen rushing to shul. No matter what time it is, before prayer they are always running. After prayers, however, the pace slows down considerably; here and there you see couples pushing strollers, small groups gathering at street corners to discuss the day's pressing issues. The holiday lull is punctured only by an occasional passing car, drawing angry looks from observant shulgoers on the sidewalks. With nightfall and the conclusion of the Sabbath or holiday comes the din of thousands of engines starting up and restaurants like Amnon's Kosher Pizza opening their doors to hungry night crowds.

You will probably not find my mother in these crowds; if she is not playing rummy (a form of card game), she is most likely at the Y with her friends watching a Yiddish movie. Thus ends another week in Boro Park, perhaps the busiest Jewish neighborhood in the world. For my mother, a Romanian-Israeli Holocaust survivor, this corner of Brooklyn has been the only place she has ever felt at home in America. Despite the many trappings of modern life—televisions, telephones, subways—this place reminds her of another home, far away in northern Romania, where she lived happily until the storms came and took her to Auschwitz. Much as I would want her to be living closer to me, I realize that for her Boro Park is the only place she can ever be happy in exile.

A Hasidic Woman in Borough Park

RENATA SINGER

Rivke Braitman stands out immediately. She's the only woman sitting alone in the café off Thirteenth Avenue, her corner table for two heaped in papers and well-worn books. Kibitzing groups of women feeding toddlers and bouncing babies fill most of the tables. These other women wear broad-shouldered suits in navy blue or gray with knee-covering skirts, matching pumps, and impractical handheld leather bags. Their jewelry is real, their lipstick and foundation discreet. Rivke wears no jewelry or makeup, and her wig is short and fair compared with their smooth and straight, shoulder-touching chestnut *sheitels*. Her bold black and white patterned shirt also marks her out from her more staid Hasidic sisters, a bright spot among the sober women and the men in black *streimels* and distinctive dark garb.

"The food here is good." She is encouraging me to eat, shiny white teeth in a too-thin face. And Rivke's right, though it looks unappetizing. The café is utilitarian rather than stylish, rather like the rest of Borough Park, where aesthetics is not a primary consideration.

"I know that you are meant to be interviewing me, but I have so many questions." Curiosity sparks her blue eyes as she probes my lineage, needing to connect our Jewishness. She succeeds. We are both the children of eastern European Holocaust survivors, and my grandfather had the honor of studying with the Amshenov rebbe. Both her parents come from very religious families. On her father's side they belong to the Hasidic sect called Bobov, named after a town near Cracow in Poland. "The Bobov rebbe today has become the most important Hasidic group in Borough Park," she says. "When my father came there was almost nobody left, only about six boys."

The Orthodox community has subtle variations. A few streets away, in neighboring Flatbush, there are very few Bobov and comparatively few Hasidim. Most religious Jews in Flatbush have a TV, and most women go to college. "It's more liberal than Borough Park," sighs Rivke, who sees her community as having grown in numbers and economic security whilst becoming more rigid and right-wing. "Oy. What shall I tell you? After the war it was common to have three or four children. Today that's a very small family. Today the average in Borough Park is eight." As she talks, her voice is full of longing to return to the "modern" Hasidism of her postwar youth.

"The Jewish sociology has changed radically in the religious world. When I was growing up my father didn't have a beard, he didn't wear a *streimel*. My mother would not cover every bit of her hair. I went to the movies. My father never went but my mother went. That was common. I grew up totally within this community, which had a specific flavor during those years. A certain liberalism was taken for granted. I would routinely go to the library with a black girl, and that was considered absolutely fine. Nobody blinked an eye. At high school I had a black teacher, and he would drive my friend and me home every day. And that was also considered absolutely normal."

As a young girl Rivke was given a lot of independence, for example, at ten, traveling uptown to shop for her own winter coat, and reading anything she liked. In contrast, she says that today "either children don't go to the public library or if they do then all the books are scrutinized." There was less fear and a lot of trust but also, she thinks, that generation of parents was preoccupied with establishing themselves in a new country.

One aspect of modern religious life that has greatly improved is the education of girls, to the benefit of Rivke's small daughter. The girls' yeshivas Rivke attended were "very badly run, particularly the Hebrew Department." Rivke had intended to go to high school at Beis Yakov Esther Shoenfeld, in the Lower East Side, but a friend she made at summer camp convinced her that she would burn in hell. "And we both went to the more conservative neighborhood Beis Yakov for a year. And we both decided we'd rather burn in hell and switched schools. I was so ecstatic to be in a school where there was a real gym, there was a real library; the school I had gone to was like a funeral home in comparison." One significant difference in these two girls' religious schools, both aimed at educating mothers and wives, was that Esther Schoenfeld encouraged and supported their students in getting to college whereas from Beis Yakov very few went on to further education.

Today, according to Rivke, the girls' elementary school in Borough Park is one of the biggest in the world with about twenty-five hundred girls. She attended Brooklyn College, but now there are many more options available. For example at the many campuses of Touro College, started by Bernard Lander to encourage the religious Jewish community to go to college, classes are held on separate nights for men and for women—there is no interaction. "It's a big change with even women from Williamsburg—ultra religious—attending college." Rivke cites the example of Skver, "an Ultra-Ultra-Orthodox enclave, named after a little town in the Ukraine where their rebbe came from.

There's no radio, nothing else of course. Women with ten to fifteen children needed education because they wanted to get jobs in government programs like Early Childhood centers and make some money." She leans across the table, eyes alight, as she outlines her dream to improve the lives of women in the Hasidic community, to provide a center "where they could have day care and do something for themselves at the same time. There's so many tens of thousands of Jewish women and Jewish children, and there's no place for them."

And there's no place for Rivke either. Pale skin flushed, this daring woman moves on to talk about herself. Her pain, unhappiness, depression. "I've always been aware of being an outsider to everything. I didn't feel I had a community to fall back on. That was part of it—not belonging. Also there's such an emphasis on modesty and taboo—you don't touch a man's finger until you're married. It seems to outwardly work for most women, but for me it was too shrouded in all these secret layers. At seventeen my parents started talking about marriage, and I said no way. I felt I had to know myself better, and marriage felt like this horrible box where you gave up your identity and it was all negative. I felt very stuck. And I was very lonely." Pausing only to take a breath and a sip of coffee, she says, "What was most missing in my life was a woman role model. A mentor, someone to really talk to."

At seventeen, a friend persuaded her to try therapy. "I was basically in therapy for twenty years of my life." Though uncommon when Rivke first tried it, there is now acceptance of the practical value of therapy in her community, which today includes a number of Hasidic psychologists. Rivke, looking back, says, "It was very hard on me that my therapists were not religious. Very, very difficult. They were very conflicted about religion." In therapy Rivke achieved understanding. "I need to live on a certain level, and if I don't I get depressed. I need an intense activity that uses all my emotions and thoughts." She also experienced something "intense and so satisfying emotionally and intellectually." What the men in her family could look for in their religion, Rivke found in therapy.

Unhappy, in conflict with her family, and alienated from her community, Rivke moved to an apartment in Manhattan. "I was too lonely and I wasn't geared—I mean no one else I knew had their own apartment." She spent many summers in Jerusalem and remembers the predominant emotion of her twenties and early thirties as loneliness.

Married in her late thirties, Rivke's experience makes

A poster on Coney Island Avenue promotes Jewish women as wives and mothers. The speaker, a rabbi's wife from Israel, is viewed as an authority on these matters. Photo courtesy of Seán Galvin.

her sympathetic to the growing problem of singles in the religious community. The principal of a very religious girls' school told Rivke he has three thousand names of girls over the age of thirty, his graduates for the last ten years. Religious women are becoming "modernized." And marriage is no longer an economic necessity for them. "Women want to be in love and women want to be enchanted, and it's not easy." Rivke's advice is that the ideal is the enemy of the good. "If you're waiting for that fairytale thing to happen, it's not going to happen."

Being married and having a child has given her a securer place in her community. "Outwardly I'm protected. Once you have children, as the woman you enter a whole different realm because you're creating little Jews, and that's the core of Judaism—family life." But the fact that she married late and has only one child still puts her "in a different boat than most women in this community, and"—she waves her hand with its bitten-down nails at me for emphasis—"I need to create with my mind as well."

"But I'm very much a product of this culture." Rivke laughs at what she calls her "prudery" in summarizing a John Cheever short story to her literature class instead of reading it with them. "It went into great detail about the straps of the bra, and you could see the shade of the suntan. And it wasn't just that I knew the parents would not have been happy. I'll turn red and purple at an off-color joke. I don't want to change. There's something that would make you cry at the purity of these girls in today's day and age." And she is convinced that within observant Judaism there is genuine respect for women and their role. "Women's position is critical. It's in the home, it's more private, and who says what's public should be more valued? That's a Western concept. I do think that in Judaism what's inner is just as valuable, maybe of more value."

Nevertheless, Rivke is torn between the comfort and warmth of belonging and the knowledge that what she craves is not available to her in Judaism. "I was teaching ancient literature in a well-known university. A black student, an older lady, came up to me after class and said, 'I know what you should be.' And I asked, 'What should I be?' She said, 'You should be a rabbi!' That's when I realized what I wanted to be. I hadn't allowed myself to think it. For a woman, for me. My calling is to be a rabbi. I'm just in the wrong religion for it."

Hearing the beautiful sound of singing from the shuls in Borough Park on *Shabbat* fills her with spiritual longing. Her husband and brothers go, but she can't join in. "I can hear them moan. I can hear them daven. It is so beautiful and so full of life and activity, and I feel why I can't have this?"

Shutting down the yearning with action she stands up, gathers up all the books and papers, and stuffs them into an already bulging shoulder bag. "You must see Eichler's Judaica Emporium," she says. It's a beautiful day as we stroll down Thirteenth Avenue. With five Yiddish-language newspapers in the stationery shop and kosher everything shops and cafés, I understand why many people live a completely full life without ever going out of Borough Park. Rivke admits she doesn't leave for weeks at a time. This is Rivke's shtetl, where every few steps we bump into a relative and are greeted with "sholem Aleichem" or "a Git tog" rather than "have a nice day."

Crown Heights in the 1950s

MARK NAISON

I grew up in a red brick apartment building at the intersection of Lefferts and Kingston Avenues in the Crown Heights section of Brooklyn. Today, Crown Heights is a national symbol of Black-Jewish tensions, with Afro-Caribbeans and Hasidic Jews living in uneasy proximity. When I was growing up in the 1950s, it was a peaceful neighborhood populated largely by second- and third-generation Jews and Italians, with a sprinkling of Irish and African-American families. The absence of racial and religious conflict was not accidental. Cherishing the opportunity to retreat into private life after years of war and economic hardship, Crown Heights residents seemed determined to shield their children from the weight of history. Anxious to have their children grow up American in a society opening its doors to minorities, my parents' generation worked hard to hide the scars that had been inflicted by the Depression, the Holocaust, and the terrors of the Jim Crow South. Through a communal code of silence joined in by religious leaders and the mass media, the people of Crown Heights tried to erase tragedy from their daily experience and give their children a feeling that the world was fundamentally benign, a place of adventure and opportunity where no accomplishments were out of reach.

Nevertheless, the social geography of Crown Heights was strongly influenced by immigrant traditions and ethnic differences. Most of the Jews in the area lived in six-story elevator apartment buildings built in the 1920s; there were four at the intersection of Lefferts and Kingston, one on each corner, and ten more within a three-block radius. Most of the Italians lived in a five-block-square area of wooden and brick one-family homes that everybody called "Pigtown." Located one block south and west of my corner, Pigtown had its own Italian-language parish, which ran annual street festivals, and backyards that contained vegetable gardens and chicken coops. Directly to the south of my apartment house was PS 91, a huge red brick public school with a concrete schoolyard containing several basketball courts, and rows of three-story walk-ups where Italians and Jews lived together. There was also a vest-pocket park directly adjoining my apartment building that contained a playground, handball courts, a full-court basketball area suitable for competitive games, a large softball and football field, and several rows of benches. Six blocks to the south was the Kings County Hospital complex, the largest concentration of hospital buildings in New York City. Six blocks to the west stood Ebbets Field, the fabled home of the Brooklyn Dodgers.

Neighborhood life was highly ritualized, giving Crown Heights a village-like atmosphere. On weekdays, men went off to work, some by car, some by subway, while women walked their children to school, conversed with one another from apartment windows, and dried their clothes on clotheslines that hung from or between apartments or stood in backyards. On weekends, the men sat in folding chairs on street corners or stood outside the candy stores talking with the local bookie, while the women sat on benches by the park, the grandmothers in one section, the women with baby carriages in another. There were still street peddlers, a roving knife sharpener, a ragpicker in a horse-drawn wagon who yelled "any old clothes," and numerous vacant lots, where children could chase one another, play ball, and even roast potatoes and marshmallows over a fire. Several small stores within a block or our apartment met most family needs. We had a grocery store, a cleaner, two candy stores, a hair salon called Blonds and Dolls, and a Jewish appetizer store that sold pickles, nuts, smoked fish, and a Middle Eastern delicacy called halvah.

Although the neighborhood contained a sizable number of elderly people who spoke only Yiddish and Italian, the largest group in the community were American-born married couples who were educated through high school and spoke English at home and at work. Crown Heights in the 1950s was filled with young children, most of whom had been born during World War II or immediately after. Most of the men and women in these families had been poor during the Depression and cherished the modest prosperity they were experiencing. Although two-bedroom apartments were the largest anyone lived in, they seemed spacious, if not luxurious, to people who had been doubling up with relatives for most of their adult lives. Cars and television sets, once rare in this neighborhood but virtually universal possessions by the mid-1950s, had become important centers of family life. People gathered in groups on weekday evenings to watch their favorite shows and took excursions throughout the city on weekends to visit their relatives.

But despite new technologies, the vitality of street life remained the neighborhood's defining characteristic. While adults sat or stood in groups to gossip, gamble, or talk politics, kids used every available piece of space for games and contests. The lives of children, like those of adults, were rigidly divided by gender. While boys played cowboys and Indians in the alleys, used sidewalks for boxball and box baseball, and played stickball, football, and punchball in the street, girls played with dolls in their apartments and jumped rope and played hopskotch on sidewalks under the watchful eye of their mothers. If you were a boy, every nook and cranny of the neighborhood was a zone of adventure and competition, a place where kids fought, tested each other, and made friends and enemies; but girls were prohibited from activities that involved physical aggressiveness or the risk of getting dirty. In all my years in Crown Heights, I never saw a girl play basketball or stickball, throw a football or hit a baseball, roast potatoes in a vacant lot, or join in games of ring-a-levio and johnny on a pony. Girls also missed the teasing and fighting that accompanied these activities, but I doubt this compensated for the experience of spatial confinement and physical constriction. My childhood world of ball fields, streets, and alleys, of war games and frontier fantasies, of nicknames and insults and neighborhood legends, had an invisible sign attached to it that said Girls Keep Out.

Racial boundaries in the Crown Heights, at least on the surface, were far less obvious. In the 1950s there were only a sprinkling of black families in the fifteen blocks between Eastern Parkway and Kings County Hospital, and most of them seemed solidly working-class. None of my neighbors appeared to fear the black people in our midst or worry about their children's behavior. The poor and troubled families in the neighborhood, the ones everyone kept away from or felt sorry for, were all white. Whereas Crown Heights today is a community where Black-Jewish divisions permeate every aspect of life, from schooling to shopping to patterns of sociability, in the early 1950s working-class and lower-middle-class Jews seemed to express little overt hostility toward Crown Heights's small black population. Unlike the Hasidim of today, whose fundamentalist outlook and religious mysticism tend to sharply curtain contact with people who aren't Jewish, the Jews whom I grew up among were secular, politically liberal, and—at least until large numbers of blacks started entering their neighborhood in the early 1960s—reluctant to express racial hostility in front of their children. In my entire childhood, I never heard a neighbor or a member of my family use the word "nigger," either as a racial insult or as the punch line of a racial joke. Feelings about African-Americans, whether positive or negative, were masked behind the very ambiguous term *schvartze* (Yiddish for black), which could be either a term of description or a racial epithet. As a child, it was difficult to know which meaning was being employed, because adults invariably reverted to Yiddish when talking about African-Americans. Their racial prejudices, whether subliminal or explicit, were not something proudly passed on from parents to children, as they were in the American South. Adults seemed embarrassed, even ashamed to talk about racial issues. While their affect in racial discourse suggested discomfort with African-Americans, they employed a race-neutral language in family settings to shield their children from prejudice.

The children I grew up among were even less prone to make race a public issue. There were two black kids in the pack of thirty-odd boys I hung out with, Franny and Franklin, and they were included in every one of our activities, from running in the alleys to playing handball and basketball and football. At least in my presence, I never heard anybody insult them with a racial slur or exclude them from an activity because of their racial background. I had very little exposure to overt racial and religious prejudice in my childhood years. The biggest division in our neighborhood, between Italians and Jews, was not tinged with great hostility. Jewish kids from Lequerville (the term we used to describe our section of Crown Heights) played with Italian kids from Pigtown as much as we fought with them, and neither group referred to the other as "kikes" or "guineas."

The neighborhood also had little, if any, violent crime. When I go back to Crown Heights today and see rows of police cars parked in front of the World Lubovitch Headquarters on Eastern Parkway, I shake my head in amazement. Until I was ten or eleven years old, the only policemen I saw were traffic cops. Our neighborhood had a muted presence of organized crime—my friend Barry's father was the local bookie—but almost no burglaries, muggings, car thefts, or assaults, much less rapes or murders. There were also no graffiti. Other than chalk-inscribed boxes for stickball games, apartment and schoolyard walls were completely unmarked. Adolescents, like everyone else, played and socialized under the careful, and sometimes suffocating, scrutiny of a host of informal block watchers, from housewives looking out of apartment windows to grandfathers congregating in front of candy stores to grandmothers sitting on benches in the vest-pocket park. Because Crown Heights was filled with extended families and people (mostly women) who were not in the paid labor force, there was no need for volunteer security patrols or a heavy police presence. The neighborhood was safe and secure at all times of day and night, a feature that my parents, who had grown up in much poorer

and more dangerous areas, appreciated greatly. In the mid-1950s Crown Heights had few very poor people and only a handful of rich ones, and the rough equality of condition undoubtedly inhibited social tensions.

However, one manifestation of social inequality did stand out in this generally harmonious atmosphere: the employment of African-American and Afro-Caribbean women as domestic workers. Almost every Jewish family in our neighborhood, even those where wives were not employed, had African-American women come in to clean their apartments or help care for children. Jewish women referred to these workers as their "girls," even though the women they employed were often older than they were. Every morning, they arrived in a group on the Kingston Avenue bus from Bedford-Stuyvestant, and left by the same route early in the evening. The educational and cultural level of these workers, as of the people who employed them, varied greatly. The person my mother employed, "Adler," had no trace of servility or deference. A well-spoken woman with a light brown complexion and straight hair, Adler carried herself more like a schoolteacher than a maid and sat down with my mother for coffee like a family friend. My mother, an ardent trade unionist who had worked at numerous blue-collar and clerical jobs before becoming a teacher, insisted that I treat Adler with politeness and respect. But Adler's presence raised some disturbing questions. Why was someone so capable and intelligent cleaning our house? Why wasn't she doing what my mother was doing? Racial barriers in New York's economy, which kept African-Americans from getting jobs as secretaries, sales clerks, and bank tellers, had created a pool of black women workers with few alternatives to domestic labor. By drawing upon this labor force, lower-middle-class Jewish families simultaneously improved their standard of living and acquired a morally damaging complicity with racial discrimination.

CHILDHOOD IDIOSYNCRASIES

The racial issues in my neighborhood, overt and covert, did not have much impact on my early childhood. The big problem I faced was a dissonance between the values of my parents and those of most families in my neighborhood. My parents were schoolteachers, Jewish intellectuals who revered education and wanted me to become a professor or scientist. They took me to zoos and museums and concerts, gave me piano lessons, provided me with electric trains, chemistry sets, and books on dinosaurs, animals, and outer space. For their own enjoyment, they stocked our apartment with books, records, and musical instruments, and filled our walls with inexpensive reproductions of paintings they saw in museums. My parents regarded themselves as members of an intellectual elite condemned to bringing culture and civilization to unappreciative New York public school students. My achievements were to provide proof that their talents had not gone to waste.

When I describe this family background, many people say "a typical Jewish household," assuming that Jews are more cerebral, intellectual, and culturally literate than most other Americans. But in the early 1950s the Jews of my section of Crown Heights did not fit that stereotype. Most of my neighbors were tough earthy people who were more influenced by American popular culture than Jewish traditions. Although their occupations were rather varied—they did skilled factory work, ran small businesses, drove taxis, supervised work crews in transportation companies, did clerical work in city agencies—they had the cynical air of people who had to fight their way out of poverty by means both fair and foul. Their cultural tastes were hardly high-brow. They spent much more time watching television than reading, and were more inclined to go to the racetrack than a museum. Gambling and card playing were omnipresent. Women played mah-jongg and canasta, while the men played pinochle, casino, and gin rummy, and bet on ball games and the horses. Little attention was given to religion. Most people went to synagogue only on the High Holy Days and sent their kids to Hebrew school so they could go through the ritual of a bar mitzvah, not so they could become religious Jews. Child-rearing was approached rather casually. Children were expected to do well in school but also to be well-rounded individuals who could dance, play cards, compete in sports, and, if they were girls, dress up and look pretty. Ideas, whether political or religious, were not taken very seriously. People were judged by their physical appearance, the clothes they wore, the cars they drove, and the food they served at weddings, bar mitzvahs, and family parties.

Eating seemed to be the neighborhood's favorite pastime, the activity where social ties were cemented and the burdens of a painful history set aside. Wherever they went, children my age were deluged with food, from homemade potato latkes and matzo ball soup prepared by grandparents, to chow mein and egg foo yong ordered at Chinese restaurants, to deli sandwiches made of roast beef, corned beef, tongue, and chopped liver, to Sunday breakfasts combining bagels, cream cheese, and platters of smoked fish with onion and salami omelettes. Among the secular Jews of Crown Heights, the size and health of their children was more important than their children's aptitude for learning or knowledge of Jewish tradition. Most of the children and adolescents in the neighborhood were big and strong, reaching their parents' height and weight by the time they were twelve or thirteen years old, and possessed a physical self-confidence rarely seen in the shtetls of eastern Europe or the crowded immigrant slums in which their grandparents had once lived.

Unfortunately for me, my parents were determined to uphold the banner of Jewish intellectualism in this earthy, materialistic community no matter how much it isolated us. Although their combined income as schoolteachers was no more than that of our neighbors, they regarded themselves as intellectual royalty in a sea of philistines, and decided use me, their only child, as the vehicle to display their superiority. I was taught to read by the time I was three, forced to perform at piano recitals and to enter science fairs, and paraded in front of neighbors and relatives to show off my knowledge of science, politics, and current events. While exposure to books and museums awakened my intellectual curiosity, being shown off as an embodiment of exemplary child-rearing exposed me to incessant teasing. Since my parents deluged me with information, in large part to make other kids and families feel envious of my intelligence, I became the target of considerable hostility. My peers mocked me for having early curfews, for having to leave the streets to go to lessons and recitals, for getting high scores on standardized tests, and for being praised by teachers for winning science fairs and spelling bees.

Two things saved me from complete social ostracism. First, my parents both worked full-time and didn't have the time or energy to supervise my weekday afternoons and weekend mornings. During those times, I could run relatively unsupervised with the pack of neighborhood boys. Second, I was strong, reasonably athletic, and given valuable fighting skills by my father, who had been victimized as a child on the streets of Brownsville, Brooklyn's toughest and poorest Jewish neighborhood. Only 5 feet, 4½ inches tall, with a receding hairline, glasses, and shoulders slightly hunched from adolescent rickets, my father taught me three wrestling holds—a hammerlock, a headlock, and a full nelson—and bought me my first pair of boxing gloves at age three. He also stocked the house with sports equipment and played catch with me whenever he could, even though he was horribly uncoordinated. By the time I was eight, I had become competent in most ball sports and could use my wrestling holds to fling tormentors to the ground and sit on them until they "gave up." These skills won me some respect in a community where physical prowess was regarded by local Jews as a symbol of transcendence of the group's reputation for weakness and vulnerability.

The tension between my parents' standards and neighborhood mores made my quest for social acceptance a daily struggle. Every once in a while, my parents seemed to display an uncanny ability to let their ambitions and fears transcend the boundaries of common sense. It was bad enough that I couldn't drink out of other kids' soda bottles, share their candy, or go with them to the movies and the bowling alley; I was also saddled with the burden of skipping a grade while I was still in elementary school. While I was attending third grade at PS 91, the public school one block from my house, my parents became so excited at my score on a citywide reading test that they marched me into the principal's office and insisted I be accelerated on the spot. The next day, the principal placed me in a fourth-grade class, where the students looked at me as though I were a quiz-show geek suddenly dropped into their presence. Very quickly, they assigned me the nickname "Eggy" (for Egghead) and warned me not to raise my hand too often when the teacher asked a question.

What followed next could have made an episode of *Dead End Kids*. Two tough Italian boys in my new class, Anthony and Charley, approached me and asked me to pay them five cents a week in protection money. If I gave them this money, they would make sure that nobody in the school would beat me up. If I didn't, they would beat me up. Intimidated by my new surroundings, I went along with their scheme and discovered it had a surprising wrinkle. At the end of each month, Anthony and Charley would take the five or six kids under their protection to the local Italian candy store in Pigtown, where they would buy each of them a "mush," a local delicacy that consisted of sauerkraut and mustard on Italian bread. Someone, probably the mafiosi they had observed in Pigtown, had taught them that a good criminal displays benevolence and community spirit. In an era when organized-crime families controlled much of New York's waterfront, trucking industry, restaurant business, and construction trades, Charley and Anthony were being given valuable training.

Several months and many nickels later, I decided to rebel. When Anthony asked me for his weekly stipend, I solemnly told him I no longer needed protection. Determined to teach me a lesson, Anthony started raining punches on my head and discovered, at about the same time I did, that I had an extremely high pain tolerance. When his barrage ended, I shook my head, grabbed him in a headlock, and squeezed him until he said "I give up." As he got up, I worried that I might have to fight every Italian kid at PS 91, but Anthony had a more creative way of saving face. He put his arm around me, congratulated me on my victory, and invited me to play on a neighborhood football team his father was coaching.

Being part of the Pigtown junior football team was a gratifying experience, something that to this day makes me sentimental about Brooklyn Italian culture. Anthony's father was a good-natured man who loved to watch boys tackle each other and made extremely creative use of the word "fuck," employing it as a noun, a verb, and an adjective. There were no uniforms and no opponents; practices consisted of brutal intersquad scrimmages where, in our coaches' words, we would try to "run the fuckin' ball down their fuckin' throats." In the clashing of bodies and the dirt-encrusted pileups that ensued with every exchange of the football, I found a blessed anonymity. To Anthony's father, I wasn't a future scientist, scholar, or inventor, I was just a thickbodied kid who enjoyed hitting anything that moved and never complained when he got cut or got dirty.

Unfortunately, my parents took a very dim view of this experience. It was bad enough that I had to associate with the children of crude and uncultured Jews, but to play a brutal and violent sport in the company of a "lower class of people"—namely working-class Italians—was not what they had in mind for their son. To protect me from injury, and from the implied threat to my upward mobility, they prohibited me from playing tackle football. I decided to disobey them. Pretending to play punchball or hide-and-seek in the alleys, I snuck off to join the football game and hoped I could disappear in the pileups. However, my parents, who had a view of every field and schoolyard from their bedroom window, and who enlisted my grandmother to watch me with binoculars whenever they weren't around, quickly found me out. One rainy Sunday morning, as I was smashing through the line to make a tackle, I looked up and saw an extraordinary sight—my father, all five-foot-four of him, running in my direction in his teaching uniform, a sport jacket, slacks, and a bow tie. When he reached me, he slapped my face, grabbed me by the back of my shirt, and dragged me off the field in front of the thirty-odd players and spectators, all the while screaming "You brat, you ingrate, how can you do this to us!" Anthony's father, a heavyset longshoreman who ran practices in work-shirts and boots, looked on in silence and evident sympathy, stunned by my father's appearance as much as by his behavior. By the next day, every kid in my class had heard about what had happened, but my father's action was so bizarre that no one even had the heart to tease me about it.

But this incident took its toll. No words could convey the rage I felt at my parents for humiliating me in front of the entire neighborhood. In moments of vulnerability, I now felt a white-hot anger that quickly turned to physical aggression. Throughout the rest of my elementary school years, my relations with my parents became volatile, marked by screaming tantrums, slammed doors, and thrown objects, and punishments that ranged from with-holding television privileges to slapping my face and washing my mouth out with soap—their antidote for a "fresh mouth." Even my friends became wary of provoking me, fearful that a good-natured comment about my piano lessons or science fair projects could draw a barrage of punches to the head or midsection.

A CHILD OF POPULAR CULTURE

Fortunately, I was able gradually to find more construc-tive outlets for my anger. Although I was prone to resort to temper tantrums to keep my parents at bay, I also learned to subvert my parents' goals without resorting to direct confrontation. My father may have ended my promising football career, but he could not force me to embrace the life of the scholar and aesthete that had helped guide him through his own difficult childhood. Prohibiting me from playing tackle football did not transform me into a concert pianist or inventor; rather it drove me to channel my en-ergy into baseball, stickball, basketball, and punchball, and devote huge amounts of time to watching and reading about college and professional sports. Increasingly, I shut my parents out and retreated into a world of my own, ruled by the symbols of an American popular culture that they held in contempt. Sports became the hallmark of my per-sonal identity, the one thing I did well that my parents couldn't claim credit for. Every weekend morning, I would get up at seven to shoot baskets in the schoolyard, pitch tennis balls at a rectangular box drawn on an apartment building, or throw a Spalding rubber ball (spaldeen)

against a handball court and catch it with my glove. On weekday evenings, I would go to the night center at PS 91 and play basketball, nok hockey, or Ping-Pong. The end-less repetition of solitary practice offered valuable mo-ments of calmness, which, even more than games, offered an escape from the tension I experienced trying to cope with my parents' rules and expectations. Standing alone in the schoolyard while everyone else slept, shooting hun-dreds of layups, hook shots, and one-handers, feeling my heart pounding and the sweat running down my back, I found an order and predictability that escaped me in per-sonal relationships.

I also became fanatically absorbed in the activities of New York's professional sports teams, which in Crown Heights aroused the same kind of passions that religion and politics had once inspired in New York's Jewish neigh-borhoods. In my entire childhood, I never saw anyone hold a street rally, pass out a leaflet, or recruit people for a dem-onstration, but I overheard hundreds if not thousands of conversations about baseball, basketball, football, and the horses. The men on my block, most of whom were union members and some of whom had once been Socialists, were at their most animated when talking about sports and transmitted these enthusiasms to their male children. In my section of Crown Heights, located less than a mile from Ebbets Field, knowing Jackie Robinson's batting average, Duke Snider's home run total, and Willie Mays's latest box score served as passwords to enter the informal fraternity of male street life. Becoming fluent in this discourse be-came a personal mission, especially since I knew it held no interest for my parents. I studied the daily sports pages, memorized the box scores of local teams, and watched every baseball, basketball, and football game that was shown on television. I could sing the jingles of the beer companies and razor blade manufactures who sponsored these events, imitate the announcers, and reel off the final scores of every game I watched. I had finally found a useful application of the study skills my parents had taught me.

I had an important ally in this mission of subversion, my Uncle Mac, who lived directly below us with his wife and two sons. Mac, who was my mother's younger brother, knew my parents disapproved of his values and lifestyle. A tall, handsome man who worked as a dispatcher for a coal delivery, Mac was a knowledgeable sports fan and an invet-erate gambler. Offended by my parents' condescension to-ward him, he extended a permanent invitation for me to join him for evening and weekend television watching in his apartment, knowing full well that my parents much preferred that I spend my time reading or practicing the piano. Mac made this space a zone of male camaraderie. With the television turned to baseball, basketball, and football games, Mac would hold forth on the strategy of the games and the characteristics of the players, periodically punctuating his comments with cries of "Esther, bring me a so-dah," directed at my beleaguered, long-suffering aunt. At the time, I felt privileged to be in Mac's living room, although he offered an ugly example of the role sports could play in enforcing female subordination. I worshiped my two cousins, Harvey and Stephen, who were among the best athletes in the neighborhood, and I loved being able to sit back and enjoy the action without feeling any pressure to display my intellect.

Ironically, the Jewish working-class culture of Crown Heights—at least when it came to sports—seemed far more flexible in dealing with racial boundaries than with gender divisions. In Mac's apartment, I encountered an environment where women were treated like servants but race was regarded as irrelevant, as least in the artificial world of professional sports. In the mid-1950s, African-American athletes were beginning to appear in every major venue of televised sports, from Friday night fights to high school basketball and football, but the media rarely employed a language of racial difference. Announcers and sportswriters didn't refer to the race of players and almost never discussed the problems black athletes encountered with teammates, opponents, coaches, fans, and hotels and restaurants. My Uncle Mac and his friends seemed comfortable with this "color-blind" approach. In my hundreds of hours of watching television with my Uncle Mac or listening to him talk sports on the corner, I never heard him, or anyone else, refer disparagingly to the race of a player, or indeed comment on it at all. Whether this was a particularly Jewish phenomenon or characteristic of all Brooklyn ethnic groups in the 1950s is difficult to say. As a group, Jews of my parents' generation did not see the emergence of black athletes in professional sports as a threat, and may have viewed it as something that would benefit Jews and other minorities. They were an important part of the cohort of Brooklyn fans who had embraced Jackie Robinson when he broke into the major leagues in 1947. At least in my neighborhood, they tried to do nothing to undermine the media's depiction of sports as a place where fair play and ability ruled and race and religion were irrelevant.

Because of this confluence of media images and neigh-borhood attitudes, my friends and I grew up viewing black and white athletes playing ball together as natural and normal. We were passionately involved with the careers of star black athletes, especially baseball and basketball players. We practiced stealing home like Jackie Robinson. We made basket catches like Willie Mays. We took hook shots like Ray Felix, the tall (and not particularly outstanding) center of the New York Knicks. But we did the same for white players we admired, and we didn't see a player's color as a plus or minus in our endless comparisons and evaluations. In arguments about who was the better center fielder, Duke Snider of the Dodgers, Mickey Mantle of the Yankees, or Willie Mays of the Giants, I heard kids refer to the players' batting stance, power, running ability, grace, fielding prowess, and ability to perform under pressure, but never to a player's color. We had no sense that the black athletes we saw on television were pioneers, that they were challenging a centuries-old legacy of exclusion and contempt. Rather we saw them as individual ballplayers with distinctive ways of performing the techniques their sport required, people we admired or despised for "nonracial" reasons.

Our relative racial innocence was remarkable, especially in comparison with the attitudes of kids growing up in Brooklyn today. To my son Eric and his friends, who are streetwise teenagers of diverse racial backgrounds, racial problems and issues are part of what make sports interesting. They refer to the race of players and coaches, and the racial composition of teams, with little embarrassment. They joke about racial stereotypes and are knowledgeable about the history of discrimination in sports. Their ease with racial discourse stands in sharp contrast to my childhood peer group. In Crown Heights in the 1950s, white kids didn't refer to the race of athletes they admired. We had black athletic heroes without seeing their "blackness" as socially significant. Yet our attachment to black athletes, even in this "color-blind" form, had important social consequences. The activities we loved the most, that touched the deepest chord in our emotions, evoked visual images of blacks and whites working together. When race relations became polarized in the 1960s, these images may have conditioned us to respond more positively than our parents to African-American activism and changes in the racial composition of Brooklyn schools and neighborhoods.

The same mixture of openness and tunnel vision marked our response to another racially hybrid cultural phenomenon that entered our lives in the 1950s, rock and roll. When I was in fifth grade, the "rock and roll craze" swept through my peer group, awakening our preadolescent sexuality and turning us into passionate consumers of popular music. The eleven- and twelve-year-old boys I spent time with suddenly began to listen to music radio, buy cheap phonographs with plastic converters suitable for playing 45-rpm records, and invite female classmates to rock and roll parties to dance to the latest hits and retreat to the closet for kissing games. This change was sparked by a shift in the format of mass-market radio stations. After years of anesthetizing the public with songs like "How Much Is That Doggy in the Window," disc jockeys began to promote records that had hard-driving rhythms and seductive harmonies, many of them performed by African-American artists, and to market them to adolescents as a sign of generational rebellion. The people behind rock and roll shrewdly promoted the music with images of young people—most of them white—screaming in the aisles at rock and roll shows, doing flamboyant and acrobatic dance steps, and singing on street corners while snapping their fingers to the beat. My friends and I responded to these images by trying to learn the latest dance steps, by playing the music at dances and parties, and by spending our money on records, phonographs, transistor radios. It also brought us together with girls in our neighborhood, whom, prior to this time, we treated as though they were a different species. They responded to the music as passionately as we did, and became far more adept in learning the new dance steps. If we wouldn't dance with them at our parties, they would dance with one another.

Because rock and roll crossed gender lines, its role in exposing white kids to African-American cultural influences may have been even greater than sports. Through clever marketing, a group of Jewish kids in Crown Heights were persuaded to adopt African-American music as the centerpiece of their generational identity, something that sharply distinguished them from their parents and teachers. I vividly remember the first rock and roll record that was played at our parties, Frankie Lymon and the Teenagers' "Why Do Fools Fall in Love," a masterpiece of harmonic singing that had an irresistible opening passage. We were fascinated by this record, which was representative of a genre—rhythm and blues—that had been popular in black urban neighborhoods for years. We not only danced to it; we sang along with it over and over until we had mastered its central elements—a bass line establishing rhythm, choruses in three-part harmony, and lead

singing that used falsetto to reach higher octaves. But we never thought of ourselves as "white" people imitating "black" music. "Why Do Fools Fall in Love" was not promoted as the product of an African-American musical tradition but as part of a *nonracial* phenomenon that brought black and white performers together and appealed to people on the basis of their age. The rock and roll show, whether on the airwaves or live, was an exercise in musical eclecticism, throwing together the country harmonies of the Everly Brothers, the barrelhouse piano of Fats Domino, the rockabilly and blues of Elvis Presley, the gospel-influenced shouting of Little Richard, the electrifying guitar riffs of Chuck Berry, with rhythm and blues artists like the Platters and the Drifters. But even though the earliest rock and roll stars were African-Americans and southern whites, third-generation immigrant kids like us adopted the music as our own, producing not only a loyal consumer market but a host of talented artists. By the late 1950s, Italian and Jewish teenagers from the Northeast like Dion and the Belmonts, Bobby Darin, Frankie Avalon, and Neil Sedaka had become rock and roll idols, and street corner singing groups were popping up all over New York. Like the sports teams we followed religiously, rock and roll drew us away from our immigrant past and made America seem like a magical and inviting place, open to people of every background who possessed the requisite talent. For our generation, part of becoming American was becoming culturally "black."

By the time I entered junior high school, my energies and my fantasy life had become totally absorbed in this racially hybrid popular culture, widening the already substantial gap between me and my parents. While my parents kept driving me toward academic excellence, I seized upon sports and rock and roll as my vehicles for social acceptance among boys and girls in my neighborhood and my new school. At Winthrop Junior High School, a five-story white brick building about a mile from my home, I found myself, along with about a hundred classmates, in an accelerated track that completed three years of school in two. Knowing that I was going to enter high school at age thirteen, I put ferocious effort into making myself as inconspicuous as possible in the world outside the classroom. I studied sports figures and rock and roll stars with the same passion that my parents had approached science and history, determined to win acceptance from older, more confident youngsters who appeared to float through life without the academic pressures I encountered.

Winthrop Junior High proved to be a comfortable place for me, an all-Jewish enclave in a neighborhood about to undergo rapid racial change. Located on Remsen Avenue and Winthrop Street on the border of East Flatbush, in a neighborhood that is now predominantly Afro-Caribbean, it had about a thousand students, no more than twenty of whom were black. (When my son went to play basketball there with his junior high school team in 1994, one of his teammates said, "Your dad must have been the last white person to attend this school!") Most of its students were lower-middle-class Jews who lived in newly built two-family houses or six-story apartment buildings built in the 1920s. Drawing on a larger and more prosperous neighborhood than PS 91, it had only a handful of really tough kids, most of whom hung out by a nearby luncheonette showing off their black leather jackets. The majority of students at Winthrop were clean-cut, ambitious, and academically serious; getting good grades there did not subject you to ridicule. Sports at Winthrop were omnipresent and highly respected. The morning began with handball or stickball games played against the concrete wall of the schoolyard. These were followed by games of johnny on a pony, often involving fifty boys at a time. When school started, the most popular game was basketball, which would be played in every gym class. This was an all-male activity, and it was highly competitive. The baskets in each gym class were organized by ability, and the goal of each player was to get acknowledged by the local superstars, who selected the kids who played on the top court. To make myself valuable to them, I spent hours alone in the schoolyard practicing, trying to compensate for my lack of foot speed with shooting skill and strength.

My efforts to gain popularity with girls were equally energetic, though far more confused. Because I had no sisters or female cousins, and because the culture of my neighborhood was rigidly sex-segregated, I found it difficult to talk to girls I was interested in romantically. The things I cared about most—why the Dodgers had left Brooklyn and whether Mickey Mantle was better than Willie Mays—were not things I could talk about to most girls I knew. I had two brilliant classmates, Linda Calvert and Miriam Halpern, to whom I talked about math problems and history tests, but they made no attempt, in their dress, mannerisms, or conversation, to show they were interested in boys. In this setting, rock and roll became the outlet for my romantic longings and the antidote to my social awkwardness. I learned the words of every new rock and roll song and practiced singing the bass lines and lead voices in the hope that I would be invited to join a group, thereby making me popular even if I was tongue-tied in conversation. I also learned the three dances that were in vogue in the late 1950s, the lindy hop, the fox-trot, and the cha-cha, and took advantage of my one opportunity to practice them in mixed company, the bar mitzvah circuit. During my junior high school years, I went to at least ten bar mitzvahs, most of which ended with large parties at catering halls that utterly overshadowed their religious services. There, amidst trays of caviar and cold cuts, chopped liver sculptures, and dinners that began with Jewish appetizers and ended with baked Alaska, teenagers joined in wild celebrations of Jewish-American materialism that often ended with drunken men dancing on tables and women in low-cut dresses performing burlesque routines. The bands at these events, in between Frank Sinatra songs and Jewish staples like "Hava Nagilah," played rock and roll for the younger crowd, and with the help of screwdrivers and manhattans stolen from the bar, I found the courage to ask girls to dance. The louder and faster the music was, the happier I felt. I was much more comfortable moving to the beat than talking. Slow dances were more difficult, but I found a solution to this problem by singing along with the music, a ritual that my partners often joined in gratefully.

By the time I graduated junior high school in 1959, I was starting to feel optimistic about the future. With a lot of hard work, I had learned to insulate myself from my parents' demands and construct an alternative identity drawn from popular culture and the folkways of my Brooklyn neighborhood. My parents were still capable of embarrassing me with emotional outbursts—such as screaming at me for coming in third in my junior high school graduating class instead of first—but I could forget about them by plunging into sports and music, and I now had a large group of friends to join me in these endeavors. Like most people in Winthrop, I was looking forward to high school. Through years of practice, I had made myself a strong all-around athlete and looked forward to playing on a high school team. I had become skilled in tennis during summer vacations and expected to compete in that sport on the varsity level if I wasn't good enough to make it in basketball. The prospect of success and acceptance in the things America valued beckoned to me, unimpeded by the doubts and insecurities that plagued my parents' generation, or by the financial pressures they faced. To me, high school evoked images of ball games and dances, of athletes in letter sweaters flanked by cute-looking cheerleaders, of academic triumphs and a vibrant social life. I never dreamed it would bring violence, class conflict, and racial tension.

But the age of innocence was ending in Crown Heights. The opening of a new high school in our neighborhood, George W. Wingate, coupled with a rapid southward expansion of Brooklyn's black population, was bringing a rapid end to the "color-blind" era in the history of our community. The Wingate student body included several hundred African-Americans who took the bus in from Bedford-Stuyvestant, and their arrival triggered waves of anxiety among Jews and Italians who had previously lived in harmony with their small number of black neighbors. For residents of Crown Heights, young and old alike, "race" would become a central preoccupation, something they talked about, and acted on, in a highly conscious way. My insular, homogenous world was about to open up.

NOTE

Mark Naison, "Crown Heights in the 1950s," is excerpted and published here by permission of Temple University Press. Forthcoming from Temple University Press in 2002. © Temple University. All rights reserved.

Cruising Eastern Parkway in Search of Yiddishkayt

MIRIAM GOTTDANK ISAACS

The Brooklyn of my parents was all Jewish, all recent immigrants. When we first moved to Brooklyn from Montreal in the 1960s, my father would only consider neighborhoods were he could find greenhorn Jews like us, who spoke Yiddish and understood their world. So we always lived in Jewish enclaves. Also, in looking for a place to live, proximity to a relative was important. From an ad in the *Forverts*, my father made contact with a Mr. Futerman, in Brighton Beach, who had a room for us to let. We were poor, my father working as an upholsterer for minimum wage. His boss, Hy Dworkin, was a *makher* who regularly went into bankruptcy after putting all his money into his wife's name. He then stiffed the workers, and a few months later he reopened and rehired them, offering his version of vacation benefits. Brighton Beach was attractive because our Uncle Charlie, the only one who had ever helped when we were refugees in Germany, lived in Coney Island. Attractive too was the beach, edged with a boardwalk where one could sit and discuss the Yiddish paper. The air was rich with the smell of good knishes from the nearby stands. In the summer, at Bay 3, we Jewish kids met, splashed in the waves, finding coolness in the hot urban summers. Brighton Beach is now reincarnated again as an immigrant community housing many Jews, this time from Russia. It is known as "Little Odessa," and Russian is the lingua franca. Restaurants and specialty food stores line the avenue, while at nearby Kingsboro Community College, with many faculty members steeped in *Yiddishkeit*, a new generation of immigrant students have an entrée into America.

It was not to Brighton Beach we moved but Crown Heights, close to my mother's Tante Lilly. This neighborhood and the adjacent Flatbush have many fine, six-storied apartment houses with regal British names. In them in the sixties lived many Jews of many backgrounds (even then Crown Heights was the world headquarters of the Lubavitch Hasidim, but their scope was much more modest at the time). My Tante Lilly lived in one of these regal buildings. She was the family matriarch and came from my mother's town in Maramoresh Sighet, somewhere between Transylvania and the Ukraine. Tante Lilly had, in another era, assimilated to Hungarian-Viennese culture and was whispered to have married and divorced a goy. She was cultivated, with tidy, coiffed blue-white hair, manicured nails, and aspirations to elegance. Her claim to fame was that she did Zsa Zsa Gabor's hair at a Fifth Avenue Salon and then she subwayed home to Brookyn. Mostly her twinkling dark eyes gave her Jewishness away. Our Hungarian cousins gathered at her place on Montgomerey Avenue, where she and my mother played gin rummy. She even had a cigar-smoking, cheek-pinching lover named Moe. In front of her apartment building, just two blocks away from Brooklyn's Mafia headquarters on President Street, women in pastel mesh scarves lined lawn chairs along the pathway to talk and watch people go by. Later these rows of chairs relocated to Florida.

Sitting and talking while watching people go by was an important aspect of Jewish life, perhaps a recreation of the shtetl in that one had to find out who was going where and with whom. My parents sat along Eastern Parkway evenings and weekends with the "grine" to talk politics, to give one another eytses, to simply be together. At one end of the Parkway was where the rich, Americanized Jews lived, near the Brooklyn Museum and the library at Grand Army Plaza. These Jews were alien to us, ate different foods like pastrami and chow mein, and spoke only English. At the other end of the Parkway lived the frum Jews, the Chabad "rebbe" and his followers, with whom we also had no business. In the sixties it seemed there were mostly older frum Jews, immigrants, with beards and dusty black coats. But there were also frum boys in white shirts and yarmulkes and girls in long dresses.

While my parents sat in their spot near Nostrand Avenue, I, a restless teenager, drifted from one end of Eastern Parkway to the other. At the Grand Army Plaza end I could gather up high culture, but it was at the frum side I hung out with friends. Many of the Chabad kids I met were from other countries. My troubled friend Linda, ironically, was the one to introduce me to the frum kids. She was having it on with handsome Gabor, from Romania, who also wore black and white but seemed not so observant. While these two spent their hours "making out," I got to know many of the others, among them a girl who had been shipped off to school from Mexico and who complained bitterly that the rebbes had taken away all her cosmetics. I even had my first date there, Andre, who played the piano like an angel to the delight of his parents and who took me to a Juilliard master's class with Leonard Bernstein. Andre pulled off his yarmulke as soon as we got on the subway. But my strongest memories of Eastern Parkway are of the drunken Hasidim, only the men, dancing in circles on the streets at Simchas Torah, grabbing people to pull into their moving rings.

A generation and a half later, Chabad has been transformed and has changed Crown Heights. Where there had once been Jews of many sorts there is now a large and homogenous Hasidic enclave. A mixed Jewish area had narrowed, deepened, and evolved. There is diversity again but of a different sort. Economically the area has sprouted businesses not visible before, Jewish tree-cutting services among them. There are more bookstores with an ever wider array of Hasidic publications. One can also hear Hasidim speaking many languages, including Arabic. Youths from across the world are coming to study Judaism in Brooklyn and export it again. What a strange journey it has been for Hasidism, from the rural world of my parents' Carpathian Mountains to urban Brooklyn. Yet, in strange ways the Ukraine and the largely black Brooklyn neighborhood shared traits. In both cases Hasidim thrived in a multiethnic environment where there would be no danger of assimilation.

Hasidim, back in the sixties and even more so now, are separated into distinct neighborhoods and sects. There is now a chain of enclaves, in Brooklyn and beyond. In another corner of Brooklyn is the Satmar-dominated Williamsburg, only a bridge away from the old Jewish Lower East Side of Manhattan. That was a frum center even in the sixties but now is considerably larger and even more entrenched with schools, shops, even newspapers. When I took a bus from downtown Brooklyn to Williamburg I noticed that at the edge of the neighborhood was a yeshiva, and the youths of the yeshiva, standing outside and very visible to the people on the bus, were a sight to behold, in part because of their distinctive traditional clothing but also because these were guys built like football players. No more the skinny scared yeshiva students from Poland but an American breed, unafraid and not inclined to cower. The other sizable Hasidic enclave is Boro Park, once, like Crown Heights, a very mixed Jewish area and now mainly Hasidic, housing the Bobov and other Hasidic sects.

What draws me to the Hasidim, and especially Williamsburg, is the fact that my mother came from an Orthodox family from the same region as the Satmar Hasidim. And for this reason so much is familiar to me about them. The familiarity derives from the look of the wigs the older women wear, the dialect of Yiddish, the mix of Yiddish and Hungarian among the older women, the foods, and even the customs. As a girl I never felt drawn to them, for that was what I had at home. But now I must go there to find that part of myself, a lost child looking for family. But the younger Satmar women are quite different from their mothers, wigs notwithstanding. Their wigs are nicer, their clothing is more tailored, their Yiddish no longer mixed with Hungarian but with English. Still, much is unchanged. As I read the Yiddish publications the same expressions are still there. Now they put out their own newspapers, and I read them. I inhale the good pickles and cakes, drink in the atmosphere feeling assured that our culture has a future as well as a sorrowful past. My youthful memories are almost entirely of old religious Jews, but now there are many more young than old. There has occurred a kind of generational inversion, for I have known old and young Hasidim but almost none my own age.

My world of Brooklyn was of a different kind, but still very Jewish. Having survived Lefferts Junior High and Erasmus Hall High School, Brooklyn College offered another dimension. Brooklyn College, for those who wanted it, offered as good an education as one could get to those prepared to deal with the crowds and lines. A friend once said that Brooklyn was the Athens of our time, and it seems to be the case. It was a place to waken the mind, sharpen the wits. I have no doubt that Jews in Brooklyn contributed greatly to this intellectual climate of social consciousness that led to civil rights and antiwar activism. We were intellectually like hungry puppies, and the interaction of many cultures made the process fun. I had a communist social studies teacher who taught us the dangers of capitalism, a devoutly Irish Catholic history teacher who gloried in the process of transubstantiation. The intellectual climate was intense, in the many programs designed to stimulate and motivate us, in the political movements awakening us to a world out there, in the museums, theaters, and concert halls where we were treated to the best at affordable prices, and, most of all, in the free public higher education at the City University.

In Brooklyn I never felt myself a minority, for everyone there was a minority. My classmates were from everywhere, Greeks, Italians, Haitians, but mainly Jews. Many of my teachers were Jews. "I Heard It through the Grapevine" came blasting through our apartment walls. We walked in Japanese botanic gardens; little plaster madonnas adorned the Italian lawns. It was the combination of being secure in being with many of your own while in a climate surrounded by and open to others that the experience of Brooklyn was enriching. So our statue of the Brookyn Athena should be holding a pizza, reading the *Forvetz*, wearing a dashiki. Then it will be *Haymish*.

Growing Up in Interwar Bensonhurst

PAUL S. GREEN

I was born in the Lower Bronx in 1917. Shortly thereafter, my family moved to the Lower East Side. During this time, my father worked in sweatshops in the garment district. When I was three or four, he got a raise and we moved out of the crowded downtown neighborhood to what was then almost a suburb, the Bensonhurst section of Brooklyn. This was several elevated stations away from the famous sand beaches of Coney Island, where hundreds of thousands of New Yorkers would fill every inch of space to escape the stifling heat of midsummer and get a chance to dip into the refreshing waters of the bay.

The twin four-story apartment buildings where we lived—a pleasant change from Manhattan's crumbling tenements and teeming streets—were separated from Gravesend Bay by a vest-pocket beach and surrounded by a broad green lawn. After our previous homes, it was almost idyllic, and we reveled in suburban life.

The sand beach has long since disappeared to make way for the roaring cement ribbons of Belt Parkway that encircle the city. The two buildings, much shabbier than when we lived there but still well maintained, are dwarfed by high-rises on surrounding streets, but enough single-family homes remain to make it still a pleasant place to live and bring up children. However, in recent years tensions have arisen at the other end of Bensonhurst between Italians and blacks.

In those far-off days, life was pleasant for a child. It was there I began kindergarten and then went on to grade school. I attended Public School 128, a massive old-fashioned four-story structure a dozen short streets away. I had a memorable first day of school when my mother escorted me and showed me that by leaving at the end of the day from the same doorway that we had entered in the morning, and walking straight ahead with only one right turn, I could reach home by myself. Automobile traffic was very light in those days, and traffic guards were very helpful in crossing streets.

Our little beach became my favorite spot. It was a great place for day-dreaming, one of my favorite diversions. I looked out across the spacious harbor, fascinated by the sight of mighty transatlantic steamships bringing their hundreds of passengers in and out of the great city. I frequently fantasized about the moment when I would walk up the gangplank on my own way to strange lands thousands of miles over the horizon. Little did I imagine that I would sail on my first overseas voyage from these very waters en route to a war-torn world barely two decades later.

On the beach at Coney Island, ca. 1920s. Photo courtesy of Paul Green.

We lived at the apartment along the shore for some years and then moved to a succession of apartments in other parts of Bensonhurst. As my father's income dwindled, our first move was to a less desirable neighborhood farther up Bay Parkway, the broad street that cuts through the main artery to other parts of the borough. This was on Eighty-fifth Street, with Eighty-sixth Street another major road intersecting Bay Parkway. There streetcars, replaced eventually by busses, made their noisy passage underneath the elevated structure that carried the West End subway line from Coney Island, going underground before reaching Manhattan's Forty-second Street, the "Gay White Way," on a forty-five-minute lurching and grinding odyssey between light and darkness. We lived on the top floor of a narrow four-story building, in three small rooms.

A snapshot of those times remains in my memory. I am playing marbles with my playmates, flipping them between thumb and forefinger along the curb, winning or losing according to a ritual I no longer remember. Although I am usually a loser, on this particular day my luck

has turned. Dozens of marbles (we called them "immies") that I have won are weighing down my pocket. It is getting late and I know my mother wants me home, but the other kids won't let me leave with all their marbles. As I keep on winning, my mother leans out of our fourth-story window and calls loudly for me to come up. I tell her that I can't because the others insist that I have to continue playing. She is exasperated and urges me to hurry upstairs. The losers won't let me go and I keep flipping my marbles impatiently. Finally they give up and let me leave. I bounce up the stairs triumphantly, holding fast to the marbles I have accumulated.

From there we moved from one to another set of rooms on nearby streets. Landlords then required tenants to pay extra for having their apartments painted. Tenants often moved at that point because in another apartment the landlord would pay for painting before they moved in. We sometimes did that because money was scarce. Most of these places were dingy walk-ups, with very little space and hardly any sunlight. Only once can I remember living in fairly spacious rooms on the ground floor of what was called an attached house, made up of four separate apartments.

For my father working at his trade, the hazards were more than just long hours and low pay. The operators of the shops were continually under pressure to produce as much as possible in the shortest time, and they pressured the workers to work at high speed. That led to many injuries. A moment of carelessness, taking your eyes off the sewing machine for an instant, could bring serious accidents. In one such moment my father ran the needle deep into the thumb of his right hand, leading to a long-running injury and a considerable amount of recurring pain. He had it treated by doctors but it did not completely heal for years. When it did, it left a large, ugly scar, continuing to pain him for long periods of time.

Moving to Brooklyn, though pleasant for us, meant that he had a longer distance to travel to the mid-Manhattan garment district on the swaying subway, jammed during rush hours and in the summer stifling hot.

To secure better wages and working conditions, agitation began in the shops for a union. My father, with his background in Warsaw, was always a strong supporter of unions, and he took an active part in speaking up for the idea of a union in his shop. The embroiderers' local of the International Ladies' Garment Workers Union was organized at a meeting in our apartment by a small group of activists. My father was too bookish to push himself forward into a position of leadership, but all his life was a faithful union member.

The union was able to secure somewhat better conditions, but life was never easy. We had few luxuries, but we never lacked for enough to eat. Though his work took most of his waking life, he never talked about it to my brother or to me. A long time later we realized that he had never taken either of us downtown to see any of the shops in which he had worked. To him it was a job, a way to enable his family to survive, and it allowed him to live the life of the mind to which he was so passionately devoted.

He read everything he could lay his hands on, mostly in Yiddish, and as he grew more familiar with it, in English too. He read newspapers and magazines on the subway going to and from work. I still remember the sight of him walking rapidly down the steep subway steps and along the street, his eyes on the newspaper he stole glances at as he hurried home.

In the early 1920s embroidery flourished; scarcely a dress appeared without a trace of it. A fellow worker, Malerman, persuaded my father to take a chance and become partners with him in opening their own shop. He helped my father to borrow the small amounts of money required. This venture turned out to be disastrous. My father had absolutely no head for business. The simplest transactions were beyond him. The truth was that he just wasn't interested in business. More important, with the coming of a new freedom for women as the 1920s advanced, women's clothing styles changed abruptly. They became simpler and less ornate. The use of embroidery was drastically curtailed, and completely eliminated from many lines.

The shop closed and Malerman vanished when the time came to pay off the accumulated bills. My father insisted he had to settle all outstanding debts, which he did slowly over a period of years, leaving us just barely managing to survive. That was how the great financial depression of the 1930s hit us personally before it did the rest of the country.

Of course my father had to go back to working in the shops, but work was scarce for everybody because times were so bad. Employers called on him during "the season," a period of a limited number of weeks when all the embroidery required for many months could be shoehorned into a month or two of steady activity, but during the rest of the year only a day or two a week was required, if that much, for him to be called now and again.

We could not get along like that, and he had to try other ways to earn extra money. At one time he sold insurance that our friends bought just to help us out, but they soon had more than enough, and anyway the premiums they paid were very small and didn't amount to much. My father was a gentle man, not gifted in persuading others to part with their money.

Under these circumstances my parents felt desperate in those difficult times and began considering what some of their friends were being forced to do—finding a small retail business of some kind. Others occasionally had to leave the city to seek opportunities elsewhere. A popular venture was to operate a chicken farm in the "wilds" of New Jersey, but wisely my parents rejected that course.

Trying to borrow money, my mother took me along with her to visit her cousins and an elderly aunt in Rochester and Buffalo in upstate New York. I was too young to know what she was doing, but I think she was also scouting for prospects of setting up a business there. But her relatives had no money to spare. Finally they decided that the most practical idea was a retail store of some kind, a small one requiring a minimum investment and no experience.

Producing that first "poem" on the beach years earlier seemed a natural outcome of my development as a child. The written word was all around me. My father's face was usually buried in a book or newspaper or magazine, as was my mother's when she had the time to spare. Printed publications in various languages were all over our tiny apartments. My parents managed to find the money to buy me the *Book of Knowledge*, a twenty-volume compendium of literature, history, and science for children. I devoured it from cover to cover.

After my name appeared in the Yiddish newspaper above my contribution, there was no stopping me. I was continually scribbling some awkward, rhyming lines on subjects mostly concerned with either nature or politics. My Yiddish offerings were usually mailed to one Yiddish daily newspaper. Wider vistas opened up with the English press. I began to contribute to the children's columns of several New York dailies, especially the *Brooklyn Eagle*, then a major metropolitan daily. Once I was paid two dollars, and another time a small picture appeared alongside my verse. Eagerly I read and reread my clippings.

Then I discovered books. They included what we called "the pulps," formula-type series such as those featuring a detective called Nick Carter, the Rover Boys, and the like. My father disdained such a low literary level, and he expressed his disapproval as the cheap volumes piled up at home. One day he'd had enough and he insisted that I carry all those trashy books downstairs and give them away to passing children. Tearfully, I did so. Subsequently my taste improved. One rainy day I started a thick edition of *Les Misérables* after breakfast and finished it by evening. I couldn't put it down.

Besides elementary school, my brother and I also attended Yiddish school, which was different from the experience of many other Jewish youngsters. Most Jewish kids went to "*cheder*," or Hebrew school, where they learned in Hebrew the rituals of the bar mitzvah, a ceremony for Jewish males on reaching the age of thirteen. Most of them usually lost interest in formal religious practices immediately afterward, except for holiday celebrations, and promptly forgot the bits of Hebrew they had painfully memorized.

My parents were part of a very small group of left-wing Jews who believed so fervently in passing on to their children their nonreligious Yiddish beliefs that they organized a school system of their own and ran it themselves. It was an offshoot of a larger Yiddish school system called the Arbeiter Ring (Workmen's Circle) based on the membership of the big, then mostly Jewish, men's and women's garment industry unions.

The Arbeiter Ring was solidly liberal and mildly socialist, but it was not left-wing enough for my parents' group and so they set up what they called the Sholom Aleichem Folk Institute. It was named for the great Yiddish writer and humorist who is often called the Yiddish Mark Twain. (It has been said that Mark Twain, in a humble moment, referred to himself as the English Sholom Aleichem.) They rented space in Jewish neighborhoods in various parts of New York—and several other large cities—in whatever modest, low-rent spaces were available at low cost, sometimes subsidized by a sympathetic real estate firm or small business.

We youngsters would come home after our classes were over at elementary school, refresh ourselves with a glass of milk and a cookie, and go off to attend our "shul" for several more hours, or perhaps on Saturday mornings. The school I attended was several streets away in a sturdy low brick building. Classes were held on all aspects of Jewish life—history, reading, writing, literature, and so on. Religion was taught as a historical subject. Classes were conducted in Yiddish—Hebrew was not taught.

After five years I graduated with a diploma that attests in Yiddish that I completed the courses offered in Sholom Aleichem Folk School Number 16 and had earned the right to attend the Sholom Aleichem High School. It was signed by the president, Dr. Sh. Elsberg, and secretary, Israel Nocks, of the Sholom Aleichem Folk Institute, and dated June 1930. My brother attended the Yiddish high school for several years, but I did not.

As a child, I was always aware that because of my parents' beliefs, I was a different kind of Jew than the other kids I played with on the street, but it never bothered me. I accepted my parents' values. I was convinced that our attitude to Judaism was the proper one for us, though it differed so greatly from that of the much more numerous traditionalists. The fact that it was a tiny minority view was consistent with my nonconformist attitude to life generally.

Neither my brother nor I were bar mitzvahed. When he reached thirteen, my parents held a big birthday party for him, completely lacking in religious overtones of any kind. By the time I was thirteen, they could no longer afford a party like that, and the milestone was not observed in my case. During my youth I never attended a synagogue or temple service. One irony was that while I prided myself on being knowledgeable about many things removed from daily life, I knew very little about the actual content of religious Judaism. It wasn't until I was an adult that I participated in a synagogue service, a Passover seder, a bar mitzvah, or even a Jewish wedding.

On Yom Kippur, instead of fasting as did most of our neighbors, even those who stayed away from religious services on that Holy Day, my parents and their friends feasted at a banquet. Yet their very act of defiance seems to me to be paying tribute to the key role of that occasion in traditional Jewish life. It would have been much more significant simply to ignore the occasion, but it had too strong a hold on them to permit that. Two thousand years of Jewish life, forged in blood and suffering, cannot be shaken off that easily. They could not ignore that day, so they observed it in their rebellious fashion.

Though we always needed money, we never thought of ourselves as poor. My parents' friends all helped each other with the scarce funds they had, passing loans around when required and paying back when they could. Just about all our friends—with a few exceptions—had as little as we did. Those few usually managed to gain more through fortunate real estate transactions.

It never bothered me that others might be better off than we were. Certainly it never occurred to me to judge them on that basis. As far as I was concerned, we always had enough clothes, a decent place to live though not quite all we might have liked, enough food on the table. Certainly we never went hungry. There were no luxuries, but I never missed them.

Much as in other Jewish families, my brother and I were pampered by our parents. They fussed over us, always protecting us from imaginary dangers. It was not possible for them to help us with our schoolwork, but they watched our progress very carefully and were very proud when we did well.

My mother was very short, just below five feet. Her early photos show her as quite attractive. In adult life she had a tendency to stoutness. She knew nothing of nutritional matters, was not a good cook, and served what we consider today all the wrong foods, heavy in calories and cholesterol. It was the food of central Europe, Jewish and non-Jewish, and that was how she was brought up.

My father was medium height, a bit taller than my brother, which was unusual. He looked like a Jewish intellectual, often wore Russian-style shirts, had long, wavy brown hair. He lost practically all his hair in his thirties, though he retained a few wisps that he carefully combed to try, unsuccessfully, to cover at least the front part of his scalp.

There was a generation gap between my parents and me, especially because of their European upbringing, but that did not prevent us from discussing cultural, political, social, and literary developments. Our talks did not extend to aspects of American life that they were not aware of or did not understand. I was never apologetic of the way they lived, their background, or what they stood for.

I loved them both very much. As I grew up, I realized what made them different, but I never judged them or blamed them and I understood that it was economic deprivation that was responsible for most of our problems. I felt very close to them, but I could not communicate with them on personal matters, for example, sex or girls. They never brought the subject up with us, and we never referred to it.

It was just the way they were, and I did not think of them as old-fashioned. I was very proud of them for the sacrifices they had made to reach this country and for their courage in facing their difficulties.

In that environment, it was easy for me to develop an early interest in politics. To them, in their milieu, concern with political matters was as natural as eating. Jewish radicalism was divided into many splinter groups, usually determined by views on the Soviet Union, ranging from acceptance to bitter antagonism. But even those who looked favorably on theoretical Marxism had no accurate idea of what was really happening in Russia. It was in the nature of my parents to shun violence; they were gentle people. In arguing with others about differences of opinion, they were much like the Talmudists of old who debated the fine points of religious belief. It was ideas and ideals that attracted them, in very abstract terms.

Consistency was not a virtue in their political orientation. In spite of their theoretical radicalism, they were with few exceptions enthusiastic supporters of Franklin Roosevelt. To them, FDR could do no wrong. He was the one who brought the country out of the depths of the Depression and who fashioned the international coalition that defeated the monster, Hitler. They never lost faith in FDR and wept bitterly when he died.

Outside of their work to earn their daily bread, their lives revolved around the Sholom Aleichem movement. To them, it was more significant than just a group of schools, though that was very important in bringing up their children. It was a cause that meant much more to them than anything else they did. The parents had to run the school themselves, and my mother and father took a leading part in those efforts. Above all, this meant continual attempts to find money, always in short supply, to meet the ever present expenses.

Culturally, it kept them busy as well. Several evenings a week there was some sort of affair at the school of interest to the parents. It might be a lecture about the latest political development, a musical offering with local or visiting talent, occasionally a traveling actor or performer, a dramatic presentation, a banquet honoring an active member on a birthday or anniversary. All these occasions were used as a vehicle to raise a few dollars to be spent for the school.

Parents served on committees to find new teachers, supervise carrying out necessary chores around the building, be available for recurring crises—there was always something that needed to be done.

Always my father pursued his Yiddish interests. He read avidly the publications of YIVO, the Yiddish Cultural Institute, which issued a stream of magazines, books, and pamphlets on every conceivable subject. As he became more comfortable with English, he began devouring those publications as well.

At that time there were four major Yiddish newspapers serving New York City. On the right was the *Jewish Morning Journal*, which spoke for the traditional, usually Orthodox, religious audience. In the center was the mildly socialistic *Jewish Daily Forward*, founded by the famed editor Abraham Cahan around the turn of the century. It was an indispensable resource for the immigrants flooding into the area. Then came *The Jewish Day*, a lively left-liberal paper that my father enjoyed for its independent views. On the far left was *The Freiheit*, which was a spokesman for the Communist movement and an apologist for the Soviet Union. My father habitually looked at one or the other, or all, of the latter three papers; he was not interested in the *Morning Journal*.

My mother read widely too, when she could find the time. My father picked up English faster than she did, but they both retained their Yiddish accents and made minor errors in their speaking, especially in the use of idiomatic phrases. They wrote English with some difficulty. In their daily English conversations, they frequently used Yiddish expressions, but they understood completely what was said to them.

My father was passionate about music. We had an old scratchy Victrola that went with us from one apartment to the next. We had to wind it by hand, but from it emerged what was to us the wondrous, if brutally distorted, sound of those early recordings. I can still hear the incomparable voice of Enrico Caruso, the great Metropolitan Opera tenor and a special favorite of my father, as he sang the well-known "Prologue" to *Pagliacci*. Youngsters who are brought up today on the superb fidelity of sound recordings may well wonder how people of my father's generation could bear the tinny sound of the platters as they wound around under the worn needles that had to be replaced frequently. When the Victrola was silent, my father would find classical music on the crystal radio sets then coming into use. Their sound had to compete with the noise of static that kept floating through the air. . . .

My parents were enthusiastic playgoers in the Yiddish theater of their day. In those years it flourished, attracting large, enthusiastic audiences. They particularly enjoyed the classics in translation: Shakespeare, Strindberg, Dos-

toyevsky, all the great ones. Several Yiddish theaters were located in downtown Manhattan, along Second Avenue on Lower Broadway. After the show many in the audience crowded into the Cafe Royale, a European-style coffeehouse and restaurant that was known as the Yiddish Sardi's. The foremost Yiddish acting troupe was built around its star, Maurice Schwartz, who played the lead in all the great dramas. My parents didn't care for the crude Yiddish musicals of the period that featured skimpily dressed young, or heavily made-up older, women posturing and simpering on stage.

My father and mother often differed on cultural tastes. They once attended a performance of *The Merchant of Venice*, which was my mother's first exposure to that classic tragedy. Maurice Schwartz had been widely praised for his portrayal of Shylock, and my father was lavish in his compliments. But my mother was puzzled. "Shakespeare is such a great playwright? Maybe the words sound like poetry. But he must be an anti-Semite," she exclaimed indignantly. "Who else but an anti-Semite would make a Jew want to cut off a pound of flesh? How could he make Shylock such a monster? This you call such a wonderful drama?" And they argued on and on. She could not be convinced that such a biased portrait of a Jew could be acceptable as great literature.

My father had no patience with the soap operas based on Jewish themes that had mass audiences on the radio. One of the most popular featured Molly Goldberg, a typical Jewish yenta (busybody) with a heart of gold who managed to get involved in situations requiring her to solve common family dilemmas. To my father, they were trash. My mother agreed with him in theory. But when she was alone at home, she would sometimes tune in to the program. If we caught her listening, she wouldn't admit that she liked it. "But what else is there to listen to?" she would say defensively.

Though my parents and their friends lived out their lives on the edge of poverty, they were not at all filled with gloom. They knew how to enjoy themselves when they got together, which they did at every opportunity. Whether squeezed into a cramped apartment, or the meeting room of the Yiddish school, or around a cafeteria table sipping coffee, they were always very animated. They sparked each other to a great degree.

When they assembled for a "banquet," as they called any sumptuous group dinner, the men began with a drink of potent liquor called schnapps, though never more than a shot glass. I never saw anyone even slightly tipsy, downing just enough to produce a lively glow. The women served many courses of heavy food, accompanied by wine, and they ate heartily of the heaping dishes.

Those were convivial evenings as the heavy meals launched them into a series of jolly Yiddish songs. Those with good voices took the lead. Hymie Siegel, a short, rotund, balding man, had a strong lyric tenor. He would step forward, close his eyes, throw his head back, and burst out into a popular melody—a nostalgic tune about times past, a lament about a lost love, or a lively tribute to one among them who was being singled out for a birthday, anniversary, or special accomplishment. His wife, Sarah, buxom and a head taller, beamed at his side.

> Lummir alle in aynem, in aynem,
> [name of honoree] mikabbel punem zein.
> (repeat)
> Lummir alle in aynem,
> Lummir alle in aynem,
> Lustig un fray ay-aylich zei-ei-ei-ein.
> (repeat)
>
> (Let us all together, let us all together,
> Congratulate [name of honoree].
> Let us all together, let us all together,
> Be cheerful and happy!)

This little ditty was a great favorite, and they bellowed it out on every possible occasion, reaching a crescendo and ending on a crashing note. It contained two of their goals in life—to be together as often as possible, and to be "cheerful and happy" as much as they could considering the daily problems they faced.

Another frequent performer was my father. He was usually called upon, and his contribution was to read a long extract from a literary work, a short story, a poem, that related to the occasion. His friends always told me that he could move his listeners to tears with his recital.

More so in their younger years, the men, and a few of the women, would often play a card game called pinochle. Most of them were addicted to smoking, and the room was often filled with thick smoke as they played. As a child, I would stand beside my father and watch the game. He preferred a slightly more expensive cigarette called Murads, featuring Egyptian tobacco. As they got older, the card games petered out, and their smoking, at least for most, came to an end.

They loved in the warmer weather to visit the "country," as they called any place outside the confines of the city. Back in Poland, the countryside had been less attractive. My mother remembered being taken as a child to visit a farm outside Warsaw. The primitive conditions encountered there, the filth and garbage and animal waste everywhere, had been so appalling that she was horrified. The experience left her with a lifelong aversion to dairy products, having seen the cows wallowing in the mud and defecating underfoot. For years she would not eat dairy foods, a distaste she took a long time to overcome. As an adult she was left with a prejudice against butter, which she would not taste for the rest of her life.

In America, the "country" was different. Families would fill their cars—those who could afford cars, which did not include us—with friends and take off on short vacations. Usually the drives out of the city were pleasant in the sunny weather, but in those days the roads were often rough and narrow. I remember one trip in a packed car when the driver lost control in avoiding a truck and slipped off to the side. The car flipped over on its roof and came to a stop against a tree. Miraculously, no one was hurt, merely terrified, but there was no damage to the car. Turned right side up, we just continued on our way.

That was the heyday of the Borscht Circuit, named after the popular Russian beet soup and referring to favorite resorts in the Catskill Mountains outside New York City. Families with money to spare patronized the big, splashy hotels where they relaxed in easy chairs on spacious porches, and ate huge amounts of food served just about all day long, in between interminable card games.

My parents' group preferred two types of vacations. One was to stay at a *koch-alleyn*—modestly priced single rooms where the women could "cook alone" preparing meals for their own families, in kitchens shared with other guests. More popular were summer camps, some only for adults but many for children where parents could come to visit and stay over on weekends in separate quarters.

My brother went to a camp called Boiberik, a name with comic allusions to a story by Sholom Aleichem. This was a very Yiddish place with all types of activities centered around a beautiful lake and featuring many different sports facilities. Parents could keep busy apart from the children, with evening attractions—lectures and concerts—offered after the children went to bed.

These camps had political affiliations related to the group that set them up and ran them. Boiberik was mildly socialist. Two others leaned more to the left, militantly union-oriented. As a child I attended Kinderland (Children's Land), while my parents sometimes went to Nitgedaiget—a colloquial expression meaning a place without worries, which was for adults. I looked forward to the two weeks my parents would send me to camp, coming back reluctantly to the hot, sweaty city and its fiery pavements. I remember once on returning to our cramped, dark apartment, I locked myself in the bathroom and cried. The cost was small—twenty-five dollars a week—but after several years they couldn't afford even that. . . .

Returning to my parents' financial problems in those early years, my father's seasonal work in embroidery grew less and less frequent, and his efforts to earn additional income were unproductive. Something had to be done. We were running out of money. It became a matter of urgency to go into a small business. They finally decided that the most practical choice was to buy a candy store.

With a few exceptions in large cities, candy stores don't exist anymore. At one time they could be found everywhere, especially in ethnic and working-class neighborhoods of urban areas. A candy store was a small shop that sold a variety of products based around a soda fountain dispensing soft drinks and ice cream products. Other items for sale included newspapers and magazines, cigarettes and other tobacco products, small toys and dolls, greeting cards and stationery, and of course, candy—in boxes at a dollar a pound, candy bars for a nickel or a dime, and loose candies down to a single penny—and a few other odd items. Some candy stores offered a selection of simple sandwiches. It was considered "a penny business" because so many sales were made in pennies.

During the 1920s and 1930s we owned one candy store that we eventually sold to buy another. The first was located in a mixed Jewish and Italian neighborhood in Brooklyn, on a corner not far from New Utrecht High School, which my brother attended. In the street along the outside wall was a newsstand where the newspapers were laid out—there were a dozen or so New York papers in those days, some in the morning and some evening—topped by a wooden rack in which magazines were displayed.

Inside the door was a small soda fountain with four fixed stools. Glass-doored shelves built into the walls held many varieties of tobacco products, mostly different brands of cigarettes, with Camels and Lucky Strikes selling briskly at two packs for a quarter. Glassed display cases in front of the shelves held many brands of candy bars, dishes holding loose candies, and other popular products. A large display case in the rear held larger items such as toys and dolls. In the center between the shelves and display cases were three small tables and wooden chairs.

Our customers included mostly immigrants—divided roughly between Jews and Italians—and their American-born children. Most of the Italians were from Sicily and southern Italy, the Jews mainly from eastern Europe. Both peoples were very much alike temperamentally, given to voluble conversations accompanied by graphic body language, especially the use of hand movements. There was a wide generation gap in the families, with parents often frustrated at failure to pass along their values to their children, generating frequent culture clashes between them. Fathers were mostly workers, mothers usually remained at home, daughters often joined their brothers in the workaday world until they married.

Usually it was my father who opened the store at 6:00 A.M. He untied the bundles of morning newspapers and arranged them on the newsstand ready for the commuters as they hurried to the New Utrecht station of the BMT subway line. (That stood for Brooklyn-Manhattan Transit.) My mother came out to the store later in the morning after my brother and I had had breakfast and had left for school.

After my brother graduated from high school, he started in college but soon dropped out. After that, he worked full-time in the store. I would usually help out after school, evenings, and weekends, especially to give the others a chance to have meals at the apartment or to rest. The store was open from six in the morning to midnight, seven days a week. We locked our doors only three days during the entire year—the Jewish holidays of Passover in the spring and, in the fall, Rosh Hashonah and Yom Kippur.

We sold this store after several years, hoping to find one in a better neighborhood that would provide a somewhat larger income. The second store we kept for a longer period, right up to the war. . . .

. . . It served a somewhat more affluent, almost completely Jewish neighborhood about a mile away from the first one. It was located on Bay Parkway, a major road bisecting Bensonhurst, halfway between Eighty-fifth and Eighty-sixth Streets. The elevated subway ran along Eighty-sixth Street, a busy shopping street with many small stores located for a considerable distance below the subway tracks. The Bay Parkway station was on the corner of Eighty-sixth Street, only yards away from the store, with a long flight of rickety stairs leading up to the subway platform. The trains squeaked and rattled and groaned overhead all day and into the night, making their run between the broad sand beaches and carnival atmosphere of Coney Island and the teeming entertainment and commercial center of Times Square. Directly across the Parkway was an identical line of stores as on our side, with another candy store in almost exactly the same spot, and another flight of stairs leading to the station.

Beyond Eighty-fifth Street, leading away from the station, private homes and a few small apartment houses stretched for many blocks. Across Eighty-sixth Street, on the other side of the station, were more private homes and apartments for only about three long blocks, ending abruptly at the small sand beach beyond Cropsey Avenue, with the apartment where we had first lived on moving to Brooklyn, on the shores of the bay extending into the waters of New York Harbor. In this section lived many Italians who took care of their little homes in much the same meticulous way as their parents had done back in Italy. Unlike the Jewish families on our side, they had the ability to fix up their homes in imaginative ways that recalled the Old Country. Among the many honest and hardworking homeowners were scattered a handful of Mafia figures involved in the "rackets" who lived quietly with their wives and children. They did not mix with neighbors, Italian or Jewish. The few occasions we realized they were there was when gunfire erupted between contending gangsters, providing big headlines for the newspapers.

We lived in a small dark apartment on the ground floor of a worn building around the corner from the block of stores of which we were a part. One of our windows looked out on a narrow open space within a few yards of the rear barred window of our store. Sunlight never reached any of our rooms no matter how bright the day was. The interior of the store, though a bit larger than the earlier one, had almost the same layout, except for our installation of a removable window on the counter open to the street where passersby could stop and drink their sodas without entering the store. Another innovation was a small lending library of popular books renting at three cents a day.

Our modest income permitted us to survive, but at the price of a very difficult and confined existence, bearing down hardest on my parents. It meant spending most of the eighteen daily hours our doors were open inside the tiny perimeter of the store. Profits were counted literally in pennies. About once a week we piled thousands of pennies on one of the tables and several of us would carefully count out individual piles of fifty pennies and slip them into wrappers for deposit in the bank. We also had to wrap nickels and dimes.

We always had to be careful of spoilage, damage, or neglect of any of our items, which would mean losses we could not afford, no matter how small. We always looked for ways to earn a bit more wherever we could. Until the city outlawed their use, we had a slot machine that brought some extra income. These machines were owned by businessmen who installed them in stores in various neighborhoods hoping to entice nickels from the residents. Storekeepers like us were given a certain percentage of the take. In a store like ours, the total proceeds added up to relatively small amounts.

It distressed us to see customers throw nickel after nickel into the machine if we were aware that they could not afford it. We knew they could never come out ahead if they kept playing, because the longer they played, the more they would lose. It was exactly the way the slot machines and gaming tables of Las Vegas operated, though on the tiniest scale.

Of course, to some customers it didn't matter if they lost some nickels; they just wanted to have a little fun. But some of our players were barely making enough to live on and needed every nickel they earned. We were aware that the machine was "fixed"—it contained a mechanism that could be set to pay out a lower percentage of nickels than were put in. Sometimes a player who was unemployed developed gambling fever and wouldn't quit even when we begged him to. We would even phone a worried wife who would hurry in and drag her husband away. Only nickels were involved, but tossing in one nickel after another for an hour or two added up to a total they couldn't afford to lose.

We tried if we could to squeeze out a few extra coins for ourselves. The machine was often out of order and we had to put in nickels to see if it was working, or provide nickels to give a player a few extra pulls to make up for those that had not worked. For that purpose, the man who serviced the machine gave us a handful of metal slugs that worked like nickels. When dealing with a player we knew, we gave him a few slugs for his nickels, then threw in a few extra ones. He got a few free plays out of it, and we got a few extra nickels. That was "Las Vegas" gambling, Bensonhurst style.

It made up in some degree for money that we lost. We were forced to give credit, though we preferred not to. A customer would ask for a pack of cigarettes, search in his pockets, say he had left his money at home, and rush out promising to bring it the next time. After a while we had a long list of people who ran up sizable bills and didn't pay. It used to infuriate us when we noticed a debtor cross the street to patronize our competitor because he didn't want to pay his bill to us. In that way we not only lost the amount of the debt, but we lost the customer who owed it. Conversely, if a debtor continued to patronize us, we had to provide more credit for fear he would stop coming in. We would argue among ourselves about the proper time to cut someone off when his debt was on the increase.

Little kids would come in, with or without a parent, and stand at the penny candy case for quite a while, unable to make up their minds how to spend the single penny they were grasping. When you finally handed them their choice, they would often change their minds and switch to something else. Parents sat at the soda fountain drinking "for two cents plain" our smallest glass of fizzy soda without any flavoring, or a big ice cream soda with real whipped cream for a dime. Boys with nothing to do hung around for hours, gabbing with friends or standing at the magazine rack reading their favorite publication.

Newspapers and magazines were my direct responsibility. I handled the bundles of the latest issues tossed from delivery trucks. I replaced the unsold issues, which I bundled up again ready to return to the distributor. I was familiar with every magazine that we carried and its location on the rack, as well as with the titles of articles inside. When a specific request was made to my mother or father, they would turn to me.

Every Sunday morning two of us—usually me and either my brother or father—arrived after dawn to put together the various sections of the very thick New York Times and pile them on a wheeled wooden wagon and prepare to deliver them to a list of purchasers who had paid for them in advance. We took turns pushing the wagon up Bay Parkway, in every kind of weather, dropping the papers on porches and front stoops of homes and trooping inside big apartment houses, up flights of stairs, to leave them outside doors. Every week the list of paper orders had changes that we were expected to remember or we'd get an angry phone call—"Where's my paper? It's paid for!" Back I'd go with the delivery.

The four of us hated the store. We called it *schklaferei* (slavery). And it was, especially for my parents. My brother would go off at quiet times of the day to see a friend. My parents would shoo me out when a friend of mine showed up to suggest taking a walk. But they had to stay hour after boring hour, week in and week out, year after year after year.

NOTE

This chapter is excerpted from Paul S. Green, *From the Streets of Brooklyn to the Wars of Europe, 1917–1945* (San Francisco, Calif.: Council Oaks Books, 1999), pp. 37–82. It is reprinted here with the permission of the author and Council Oaks Books.

The Brooklyn-American Dream

LORI ROBINSON

My family's journey to Brooklyn began in a Russian shtetl. A hasty escape from pogroms led the family to the Lower East Side, where my grandmother Bertha was born. They eventually moved to a less crowded Bronx apartment, and afterward to a private house in Brooklyn. Each move was a rung up on the ladder of the "American dream"—more space, a better neighborhood, and eventually, homogeneous middle-class prosperity.

Throughout, Bertha and her sisters lived dual lives. They were "all-American girls" who ate apple pie and swooned at the sight of Errol Flynn. They were also nice Jewish girls who memorized the *sh'ma* and kept kosher both in and out of the house. They had no conflict between fitting in and retaining their Jewish identity. When I asked my grandmother how she knew she was Jewish, her response was, "What do you mean, how did we know we were Jewish?! We were Jewish! We just knew!"

Bertha lived her childhood in the Bronx during the Depression. As a child, Grandma was a bit of a scamp. She, her older sister Pauline, and the younger twins Simmie and Mullie created homemade contraptions made of a stick, some rope, and a wad of gum that fished coins out of subway gratings to pay for their penny candy habit. Once, she was dispatched to get the candy and, after dropping a piece down the subway grating, finagled an extra free piece by saying she never got one in the first place.

Bertha didn't have much of a formal Jewish education. As a very young child, she attended Yiddish school for a short time. When the school moved, her parents ended her enrollment, as the new location was too far. My grandmother was disappointed but had no further Jewish education. This nonchalance about Jewish learning (and Judaism as a whole) is as much a family tradition as buying prepared mix to make potato latkes at Hanukkah time.

Although neither of Bertha's parents went to shul very often, they bought tickets for High Holiday services (although there were several years when they didn't go to services because tickets were not affordable), and the family always bought new clothes or dressed their best. The girls weren't allowed during the holidays to play hopscotch (much to Grandma's chagrin). They spoke only Yiddish at home. They also ate Jewish foods like challah, knadle soup, chopped liver, and hamantaschen. ("Yes, she [my mother] made hamantaschen. I remember, they were filled with prune and poppy seeds, and they were *delicious!*").

In fact, what little Jewish observances my family had often revolved (and continue to revolve) around Jewish food items—gefilte fish, stuffed cabbage, macaroons—these are my family's sacred objects. Bertha's mother kept a strict kosher house, with separate sets of dishes for dairy and meat. My cousin remembers that even in her elder years, Great-grandma would kosher every chicken with salt.

The family moved to the Bensonhurst section of Brooklyn when Bertha was a young woman. The move was motivated by an overly ardent admirer of Pauline's who would sit on the stairway to the family's apartment, dissuading suitors from visiting her. The family was concerned about her marriage prospects; thus they packed their belongings for a "safer" borough. They also moved from a three-room apartment to a private house with a backyard.

Bertha's family were working-class immigrants. Once she and Pauline grew older, they went to a free vocational training school to study teaching, while also working at live chicken markets (Bertha in Manhattan, Pauline in Bensonhurst). Grandma remembers freezing in the icy, sub-zero office that was a magnet for the winds whipping around the corner of Amsterdam Avenue. On Saturday nights a *shochet* would prepare and kill that week's kosher chicken supply, and on Thursday nights Bertha would bring one home to her family.

Like the family devotion to Jewish food, there is also one to Jewish egalitarian ideals—my grandmother had (and continues to have) no use for pretensions. Once she was dispatched from the market to deliver a chicken to a wealthy woman's house. When she arrived, the maid who answered the door chastised her for not using the service elevator. My grandmother thanked the maid for her "advice" and proceeded to go back down in the regular elevator, just like she came in.

While living in Bensonhurst, Pauline met Al, a nice Jewish boy. She wasn't too keen on him, so when he asked her to join him on a cruise that was the biggest party of the year in his men's club, she insisted that he find a date for Bertha, presuming that no one would want a blind date at the year's best party.

Al pleaded with his friend Willie (who was also Jewish—both grew up in Williamsburg, Brooklyn), who agreed to take Bertha on the cruise, sight unseen. The girls were expected to pack a lunch. Great-aunt Rae thought this was absurd, so when they were deciding what to pack, Rae grumbled, "They're too cheap to buy you lunch? Give them cheese sandwiches!" Lunch choice decided, the girls made cheese sandwiches and packed them for the next day.

The day of the cruise, Willie and Bertha were getting along well when lunchtime arrived. My grandmother and Pauline handed a sandwich each to Al and Willie. Willie (famous for a quick temper) took one look and bellowed, "Cheese! I hate cheese!" Midriver, not much else was available. Willie appealed to everyone on the boat and finally made do with whatever scraps he could collect. Nonetheless, he was not very happy.

Despite an awful first date, my grandmother's beauty and charm won Willie's heart. They continued to date. Pauline was swayed as well, finally surmounting Al's nervousness. In 1937, Pauline and Al married at the site of a relative's summer camp. Bertha and Willie followed one year later in 1938 and were married by a rabbi in a formal ceremony at a Brooklyn wedding hall. Both couples had kosher weddings (not a cheese sandwich in sight), and both pairs started their lives in Bensonhurst, Bertha and Willie living in an apartment upstairs from her mother, and Pauline and Al in a house nearby.

In Brooklyn in the 1940s, being Jewish was far from an anomaly. Appetizing stores that sold everything from knishes to whitefish salad, and Chinese restaurants with Sunday night crowds, were ubiquitous. My grandmother, Pauline, Al, and Willie didn't think twice about being Jewish, not only because of their surroundings but also because Judaism rarely dictated the rules of their lives.

Their Shabbat was a very loose translation. "Saturday you used to sleep late," according to my grandmother. They never went to shul. She and Willie both worked during the week, Bertha as a schoolteacher and my grandfather as a CPA and lawyer. On weekends they relaxed and socialized. "We did the same things young kids do today—you know, go to the movies, things like that."

Then came the next generation. In 1941, baby Carole was born to Pauline and Al, and in 1942, twins Nancy and Neil were born to Bertha and Willie. There was a *briss* for Neil. It wasn't long before Willie left to serve in the Army. When Bertha pushed the twins in their stroller, each time they saw a uniformed man they pointed and squealed "Daddy!" since the most recent picture of Willie showed him in uniform. The stroller sat them side by side, and they often squeaked "Daddy!" at the same time, pointing in opposite directions.

Eventually Willie returned from service, and he and Bertha moved to Flatbush while Pauline and Al stayed in Bensonhurst. Pauline and Al occasionally went to Friday night services, as she liked to listen to the cantor. Despite a lack

(Top row, left to right) Bertha, Pauline, Sylvia (Simmie). (Bottom row, left to right) Neil, Nancy, Carole. Coney Island, 1950. Photo courtesy of Lori Robinson.

of religious life, both couples' social lives centered around a core group of Jewish friends.

Both couples socialized through the Mr. & Mrs. Club of Temple Emmanuel of Boro Park (which was Al and Pauline's main social connection). The club sponsored concord weekends, holiday events, and a New Year's Eve gala, held at the temple (in 1952, a $12.50 ticket included cocktails, food, music, and entertainment). Pauline was also very active in the temple's musical programs, singing soprano in the Mr. & Mrs. Club Choral Society and musically directing *Fahrblunget*—a Yiddish version of an operetta including Gilbert and Sullivan songs (in which Al played a starring role). They probably went to temple more through the guise of the club and its activities than they did to worship.

Bertha and Willie eventually followed the exodus to Florida, where my grandmother resides today. Pauline died in Brooklyn and Al left soon after, and now there are no longer any family members living in Brooklyn. In a way, my family's story is not so very different from that of other ethnic groups—it could easily be the personal history of an Italian or Irish family, with a few details changed. Yet, there was something special about the close-knit Jewish community in Brooklyn in the forties and fifties that made it a remarkable time, and place, to be a Jew.

From Brownsville to Park Slope

An Interview with Simon Dinnerstein

ILANA ABRAMOVITCH

If there were such a thing as a typical Brooklyn Jewish visual artist, Simon Dinnerstein would not be it. He has never painted portraits of the Brooklyn Dodgers, he is not known to capture impressions of Hassidim, and there are no references to the Brooklyn Bridge in his work. On the other hand, Dinnerstein is very much an artist, very much of Brooklyn, and he is, in an interesting way, Jewish. A thoughtful speaker, he often slows down in midsentence as he ponders the weight of an important conversational detail.

Certain angles of Brooklyn life, its surprisingly radiant light, are captured in Dinnerstein's world. Traveling far away brought Brooklyn closer to his artist's vision, sharpening his interest in what fascinated him about Brooklyn life near at hand. Views from his windows and of his studio, Brooklyn's strong personalities, and his own family have become his subjects. Since childhood he has been gazing out the window with prolonged attention at the dreamily revealing side of life.

Dinnerstein revels in ambivalence: he is suspicious of harmony and wants his work to be the kind that causes viewers to pull close, to then draw back; to see the inside and the outside. His paintings could be called realist, in their closely observed views of identifiable objects. But this realism is one that reveals the inner world of the person or the thing. The inwardness is often depicted in the play of light that radiates from the object and renders it mysterious.

Simon Dinnerstein greeted me in his Park Slope brownstone, where he lives, teaches, and paints. The kitchen, where we sat and spoke for hours, is a whirling play of wood textures. The graininess speaks to Dinnerstein's art, devoted to finely detailed textures and to patient craftsmanship. Striking examples of Dinnerstein's work line the walls, flanked by art postcards from Italy. A Brooklyn resident for most of his life, Dinnerstein won fellowships to study abroad, in Germany and in Italy. There he painted some of his strongest works, much of it pointing back to his family life.

What makes someone into an artist? An essentially mysterious process, it happens perhaps when inborn talent meets the necessary catalysts. For Dinnerstein, growing up as a red-diaper baby in his Brownsville family in the 1940s and 1950s set the reaction in motion. The senior Dinnerstein was a union activist and a card-carrying member of the American Communist party, paid up in full when he died in 1975.

Simon Dinnerstein, Garfield Place, 1970, charcoal, 30″ × 59″. From the collection of Audrey-Stier Adams, Scarsdale, N.Y. Courtesy of ACA Galleries, New York.

Simon pauses and looks up quizzically as he reveals this quiet, yet extraordinary, tidbit. Who was still a Communist believer in 1975? His father was a committed Communist down to the end—way beyond the era of mass movements in the 1930s and 1940s, when dreams of a new society blinded so many idealists to the brutality of the Soviet system. To his son, the father's single-minded absorption could seem rhetorical, leading to family scenes of anger and frustration. Simon's art absorbed his father's concern with the hidden treasures in the ordinary and the marginal. Yet young Simon was influenced not so much by his father's large vision as by the incongruity between public ideals and the private person. How do general solutions to social injustices mesh with the struggles on the domestic front?

The Dinnersteins' marriage was not a happy one, the dogmatic idealist father intimidating his tiny fragile wife. She was the one who felt art and music deeply. Something about this ambivalence, the disparity between people's insides and outsides, remained with Simon. It provides a key to his art.

Surprisingly, Dinnerstein sees himself as quintessentially Jewish. But he was brought up in an atheist family where, like author Vivian Gornick, he knew he was a member of the working class before he knew he was Jewish. He did not have a bar mitzvah, had never been inside a temple. Why quintessentially Jewish? He explains: His Jewishness is in the quest to understand, to live with the riches of learning, rather than with material goods. It provides a double vision. Simon received a secular Jewish sense of social justice from his father. From his mother, he received a creative dreaminess that pervades his paintings, as well as his personal style. Each parent provided Simon with something transcendent, something that goes beyond the here and now. It fortified him to remain unconcerned about fashions in the art world, just as his parents were oblivious to displays of wealth. Simon: "It frees you up to follow something that you feel."

Dinnerstein's childhood is obliquely referenced in his paintings, for example in the image of two boys looking out the window in the family choreography in *A Dream Play*. As they look out from their dark background, we look in at them and with them gaze toward the light. Growing up, Simon spent much time and continues to spend time looking out windows. "In Brownsville you are surrounded by human beings in boxes. Looking out and looking in." A surprisingly large number of his paintings feature windows, or the light reflected from a nearby offstage window (Simon's favorite film, and the title of a self-portrait, is Alfred Hitchcock's *Rear Window*). But *A Dream Play* is about much more than looking at the mysteries of others' lives. It is a wide tableau vivant of Dinnerstein family life, past and present. Simon, the artist with his crayons, is in the left corner, while his wife, Renée, and daughter, Simone, flank the right. Living and dead relatives mingle and nurture each other. The title comes from August Strindberg's *A Dream Play*, whose introductory note suggests, "Anything can happen; everything is possible and probable. Time and space do not exist. . . . The characters . . . evaporate, crystallize, scatter and converge. But a single consciousness holds sway over them all-that of a dreamer. . . ."

The sensitive dreamy boy growing up in Brownsville was exposed to the full racket of New York life, including the el. An aunt's house was only half a block from the elevated train. Every fifteen minutes the house shook. After about forty-five minutes, you did not notice it anymore, but it stayed within your psyche. The train, its roaring appearances and disappearances, its tunnels that swallow up and deliver metal beasts and their human cargo—these fearsome constants in a Brooklyn child's fantasy life make

their way into his adult paintings. *A Dream Play* shows a line of brownstones in the background that is as full of repetition as a string of subway cars. A detail from *Night* shows a child in a paper-bag Halloween costume frightened by the images he and his classmates conjured when they made their masks. Here the child's anxieties are symbolized by the train, the tunnel, the bats, his flying fears.

Dinnerstein and his wife Renée moved to Park Slope in 1965 and have lived there ever since. Park Slope provided a setting for the artist not so different from his native Brownsville. The Slope was run down then, and the brownstones had not been renovated. Yet, here too he could look out the window and be nurtured by views of people's lives. In the meantime, his developing career brought many awards and teaching opportunities in colleges, such as the New School for Social Research and New York City Technical College in downtown Brooklyn.

Dinnerstein's social consciousness, activated by his father and by his own experiences in the 1960s, is currently alert to what has happened to the Slope. When he first moved in, it was a place for artists and young people. All his neighbors were from Brooklyn. "In the last ten years, it's rare to find someone from Brooklyn. In the last three years it's beyond rare. It's now not possible to live here

Simon Dinnerstein, A Dream Play, 1986, Conte crayon, colored pencil, pastel. 38¼″ × 82½″. *From the artist's collection. Courtesy of ACA Galleries, New York.*

cheaply. Artists would not move here now. . . . And it used to be more politically engaged. We noticed the flyers posted recently in the neighborhood, and none of the signs were political. Instead it was all for care of the body, health, that kind of thing."

Dinnerstein expressed pride in having an exhibit at Gallery 1199 in the Martin Luther King, Jr., Labor Center in 1985. It was the same organization in which his father had struggled for greater African-American representation in leadership positions. Simon dedicated his exhibition to his father's memory as a "man who followed his deep convictions." In recognizing that his complex and troubling father was also a radiant muse, Simon is grappling in personal terms with the Wittgenstein quote he placed in his most famous early painting, The Fulbright Triptych (1971–74): "And to the question which of our worlds will then be the world, there is no answer. For the answer would have to be given in a language, and a language must be rooted in some collection of forms of life, and every particular form of life could be other than it is."

From Flatbush to SoHo
An Interview with Ivan Karp

ILANA ABRAMOVITCH

What does a sophisticated SoHo art dealer with two honorary doctorates have in common with a cigar-smoking Brooklyn booster who never graduated from high school? They are, in fact, one and the same in the person of Ivan Karp, novelist, lecturer, and adventurous tastemaker. Always in the vanguard.

Karp is a fixture on the New York art scene, a gallery owner and dealer who has discovered and promoted some of the most important names in the contemporary art world. He was an early promoter of artists later to become art stars, including Andy Warhol, Claes Oldenburg, Jim Dine, Roy Lichtenstein, and Cy Twombly. Karp is a man with a keen eye and an instinct for creative adventure in the arts.

Karp clearly loves what he does. He greets me at OK Harris, his grand gallery on West Broadway in SoHo, ebullient, laughing, smoking a cigar, and in charge. He talks warmly and flowingly about his Brooklyn childhood—he is a compelling raconteur, elegant, and generous with telling details. He remembers the street fights but also his mother's cleansing prayers after sneaking out to eat non-kosher Chinese food.

Born in the Bronx, Karp moved with his family to Flatbush when he was five years old. Like many Brooklyn Jews in the 1930s, his family usually lived in a six-story apartment building. It was a period of many vacancies in the real estate market. As an enticement, landlords were offering new tenants three months' free rent. This was the Depression, and for the struggling Karp family, three months' free rent was an offer they could not refuse: they moved frequently in those days. Barely making ends meet, they nonetheless maintained certain priorities: "You must have culture!" was the family's cri de coeur.

Ivan's mother, a rabbi's daughter, taught her child of his family's cultured old-world origins. Family lore had it that fully 25 percent of the male population were violinists in the family's hometown of Kovno, Lithuania. This claim provided the family with a bulwark of pride. Mrs. Karp lived this cultivation with an expansive sensibility—but always with modesty. Her potato latkes, Karp insists with grave conviction, were the greatest in the world.

Ivan's paternal family had less exalted origins. They came from Białystok, where his grandfather was a baker. No less devoted to the arts, Ivan's father "read all the great books." He worked as a manager at a Brownsville men's hat store, laboring twelve hours a day, in total dedication to the salvation of his family. A devoted union worker, the elder Karp believed in the working man's rights. He always saved just enough money for the family to spend the summer in little hotels in the Catskills. Father would come up on weekends and would experience life's profound pleasures: cold seltzer, a pillow on the porch, pinochle in the lounge.

Culture provided elevation of the spirit in the Karp family home. The *New York Post* in its liberal days offered series of reproductions of artistic masterpieces: paintings by artists such as Van Gogh, Gauguin, Sargent, Winslow Homer, and Thomas Hart Benton. The Karp family took advantage of such offerings and rehung the prints in each of their successive apartments. Fine art and architecture were a wonderment to young Ivan from an early age. Later on, the abstract art of the 1940s—Pollock, Kline, Rothko—was a revelation. He was fascinated. Ivan began to discover that he was more sensitive to sights, scenes, and spectacles than many of his friends. It took him many years to figure out what to do about this.

Classical music was central to the Karp household. You simply had to listen. His father would take Ivan to synagogue on Friday night, then to a band concert, something like Rossini overtures, on Sunday afternoon, often at the Brooklyn Museum. On his way to the rest room alone one day, Ivan, age seven, discovered, looking at the Coptic tapestries, that he was in fact in an art museum (he thought it was a concert hall). He started looking at the art as he had begun to listen to music. Thus began a lifelong dedication to art and to the Brooklyn Museum. (Now a "Founder" of the Brooklyn Museum of Art, Karp has donated a sculpture garden of decorative devices of New York City architecture.)

By twelve, Ivan "knew all recorded classical music." He was less attracted to religious studies. He went to synagogue on Church Avenue and Ocean Parkway—but found it a big burden. Hebrew school and private lessons he despised. Trying to elude his Jewish education, he was gracious enough to agree to go through with his bar mitzvah. Jewishness, nonetheless, was for Ivan and his cohorts a profound source of pride, a kind of anchor or refuge.

As an art dealer, Karp has an extraordinary eye, based on years of discernment in viewing. He also demonstrates a keen memory of the senses, recalling pungent details of life in Flatbush when he was growing up. The neighborhood was 95 percent Jewish, 5 percent Italian, with a few Irish. Italian homes were similar to Jewish homes in emotional valence and in the centrality of food. The main difference, aside from pictures of the Virgin Mary, was that Italians drank wine rather than the Jewish elixir, Pepsi. Coke, it seems, was considered "goyish."

The Karps served typical heavy, Jewish, central European food. Meals were enormous ceremonial events. A good traditional cook, Ivan's mother did not rest on her laurels but scoured women's magazines to improve her cuisine. Each day of the week was planned out and predictable. Tuesday was for macaroni; Wednesday, lamb chops; Thursday, potato latkes; Friday, chicken. On Sunday, the family bought exactly three slices of lox. Food rituals were critical to daily life. The whole block ate the same food. Karp still remembers the vapors of pickles, of butter in kegs, the Białystok kuchel. The iceman came by two or three times a week. The milkman delivered milk in bottles, with cream on the top. "You had to buy Ebinger's baked goods. Their store left an impression: it was very clean; there was something 'goyish' about this."

Jewish holidays brought a special atmosphere. New clothes for Passover, going to synagogue. Even if the services drove Ivan crazy, something in the whole ceremony felt purifying. Boys had their own rituals, too. They would leave the shul to play games outside. Everybody had a handkerchief. You would tie a knot in your handkerchief and hit the other boys on the head with it. On Yom Kippur you fasted: it was considered very strenuous to get through a whole day without food. But you had a big meal at sundown beforehand and another one the next sundown. "Nonetheless, it was a very serious day. You could not hit a kid with the knots on that day."

Like most of Brooklyn, Ivan was a fanatical Dodgers fan. "It was the pulse of your day. The lifeblood of Brooklyn, of our mood. If they won, you felt great. If they lost, you were in a foul mood. Ebbets Field and Prospect Park—they were like saying home. The park provided the critical adventure of my life. It was like the Congo."

Growing up then, being Jewish meant you were chosen for culture and the elevated things of life. But it seems not to have meant pretensions to the Karp circle. Family life was insular, with many interconnections. The lower middle class felt a sense of entitlement to the use of high-culture institutions, seeking out free concerts, museums, and libraries and feeling ownership of such institutions.

How Karp moved from the life of playing ring-a-levio in the street to visiting vanguard artists' studios involves many other tales of quitting high school to enlist in the army, traveling in Europe, and wandering aimlessly for about ten years. But to make a long story short, Karp went from being the first art critic of the *Village Voice* in 1955 to joining the year-old Leo Castelli gallery in 1959 (which had Jasper Johns and Robert Rauschenberg in their first show). His willingness to look at all kinds of art brought him out as an early champion of the pop art movement of the 1960s. With his fierce independence and passionate openness, Karp started his own large gallery in the fresh new district of SoHo in 1969. SoHo then had cheap rents, no name, and a lot of artists' studios. Karp has been at his SoHo gallery since then with the philosophical principle "to exhibit the broadest spectrum of the most adventuresome art being offered."

Karp named the gallery OK Harris. Why? "For myself, I decided a gallery should bear the name of a person, because then you can blame everything you do on that person. 'I am only the caretaker, the manager, the director, but basically the final decisions are made by Mr. Harris.' So I used the name because it had a kind of presence, a fast-talking, energetic, lively, Mississippi gambler type of character. We have a portrait in my office of a bearded man and it says Oscar Klondike Harris, 1789–1969. We still blame things on him."

You could say that Ivan Karp has traveled a long way from Flatbush to his current life in SoHo, but that would not be telling the whole story. First of all, Karp and family make regular excursions to Brooklyn on Sunday evenings, in between football and baseball seasons, to different Italian restaurants in the neighborhoods. Karp visits artist studios in Greenpoint and Williamsburg. But perhaps, even more important than these current visits, Karp keeps alive in his sophisticated SoHo art-world life the spirit that he inhaled from his family in Flatbush: the passion for the high arts, the joy of popular culture, the eagerness of pursuit, and the expansive showmanship of his parents' generation. Furthermore, Karp's wife, Marilynn, herself an artist, learned to make the finest potato latkes from his mother.

Living in Brooklyn

Cultural Influences and Community Life

Jews living in Brooklyn.
Photograph by Martha Cooper, courtesy of Peter Arnold, Inc., 1181 Broadway, New York, N.Y.

Mazel Tov!
Klezmer Music and Simchas in Brooklyn, 1910 to the Present

PETER SOKOLOW

When Jews from eastern Europe began settling in Brooklyn more than a hundred years ago, they were quick to adapt their new environment to their specific needs. Synagogues (mostly small Orthodox *shtiblach*), kosher butchers, grocery stores and pushcart vendors, seltzer men (my grandfather was one, working with a horse and wagon), "high cash clothes," and so forth, rapidly appeared in the neighborhoods of Williamsburg and Brownsville, the first areas in Brooklyn with large concentrations of immigrant Jews. An ancillary need soon arose—proper facilities and music for Jewish weddings and other social functions. What is presently called klezmer music developed in all countries of eastern Europe over a period of a few hundred years. The initial demand of the Brooklyn Jewish community was for very traditional music and food that adhered to kosher dietary laws. An industry arose which continues, with certain modifications, to this day.

The first catering establishments of any consequence appeared in Williamsburg and northern Bedford-Stuyvesant (just south of Williamsburg, where Jews started to move in about 1910). Two of these were the Regina Mansion, at 601 Willoughby Avenue (between Tompkins and Throop Avenues, R. Herscovici, caterer), and the Knapp Mansion, at 554 Bedford Avenue (at Ross Street, Maurice Goldschmid, caterer). A whole cavalcade of Mansions, Manors, Terraces, Palaces, and Chateaus would soon follow, expanding into other neighborhoods as Jews moved there. As one entered any given Palace, the ambience was basically the same: a carpeted or marble lobby floor, crystal chandeliers, mirrored ballrooms with polished wooden floors. Menus were invariably similar, consisting of grapefruit or citrus fruit cup, chicken soup with noodles, matzo ball, or both, and half a roast chicken ("top" or "bottom"—light meat or dark) or roast beef, which cost more than chicken and appeared less frequently. Dessert usually meant fruit compote and/or strudel. Some caterers would substitute baked apple for the citrus appetizer, and some served whitefish or gefilte fish instead of, or in addition to, the fruit. The "smorgasbord" or hors d'oeuvres served before the meal at today's parties came later, becoming common after the Second World War.

When I entered the world of simchas as a musician in the late 1950s, the waiters were what I would describe as Local 2 Altitchkes—men in their sixties and seventies with angry faces, shuffling gaits, and shaking hands. Soup was served from individual metal cups and poured into the soup bowls by these veterans; many the customer who ended up with a lapful of soup! Local 2 was the Brooklyn local of the Waiters' Union, which lost its iron grip on the Jewish catering business in the mid-1960s. Dozens of Brooklyn catering halls specialized in Jewish parties between the 1920s and the mid-1960s throughout Brooklyn. In addition, several large synagogues, built between 1919 and 1950, had deluxe facilities for catering and were considered the finest that Brooklyn had to offer.

In the early years, most Jewish functions were planned by, and for, immigrants. This meant that the music required was essentially old-world in content and style, and was supplied by musicians from the community. These players were called klezmorim, the plural of klezmer, which is simply the Yiddish word for musician(s). This implies that the style played had a pronounced Yiddish accent and was a folk/dance musical form. In America, there was also a strong Yiddish musical theater movement, exemplified by the theaters on Second Avenue, in Manhattan's Lower East Side. Actually, Brooklyn had some major Yiddish theaters as well: the Hopkinson and the Rolland in Brownsville, and the Lyric in Williamsburg, which was owned for two years (1909 and 1910) by my great-uncle; my grandma Luba was the ticket seller in the box office! American klezmorim had to know the dances—freylekhs, bulgars, shers, etc.—and the tunes from the Yiddish theater as well. Some of the most important early klezmer performers lived in Brooklyn. There was Berish Katz, a talented trumpeter, violinist, and composer. Max Peters, a trumpeter and early bandleader, had a reputation as a showman. The king of klezmer clarinet, in Brooklyn and anywhere else, was the great Dave Tarras (1897–1989), who lived in Brooklyn from his arrival in America in 1923 until his death. Tarras was a formidable player, with a classic tone, virtuoso technique, and fluent music-reading ability, a rarity in early klezmer. He was also a rather forbidding personality in a band—he scared the daylights out of me when I first worked with him in 1959, when I was all of nineteen. He was a demanding leader and taught by method and example. Later, I had the good fortune to be his last regular keyboard accompanist, and we cemented a wonderful relationship based on mutual respect.

The business of providing music for parties saw its first flowering around 1920. Before that, the business was very casual. By 1920, bandleaders began to appear who were most adept at selling bands; usually, their musicianship was inferior to their skill at marketing. One of these was a barber and, supposedly, a clarinetist named Nathan Ri-

tholtz, whose business office was his barbershop. Ritholtz was a notorious "underscaler": he paid salaries far below the current standard and usually used low-grade and/or apprentice players in his bands. Another of that ilk was violinist Sam Ash, who sold bands and opened up his first music store on Saratoga Avenue in Brownsville. His sons Jerry and Paul, and his grandsons, have made Sam Ash Music into a merchandising empire, with megastores all over the country. Some others of that group were Max Ellison, Ben Sherman, and Abe Gubenko. Aside from weddings, music was needed at annual banquets for unions, professional organizations, and landsmanshaftn, societies of immigrants from given towns. Clarinetists Max Epstein and Sid Beckerman have told me stories about playing for such immigrant groups. The successful klezmer was the one who could play the right dance tunes at just the right tempi—each group had specific repertoire and dances they preferred. Bands were often hired by local businessmen for store and market openings, and by synagogues for the donation of new Torah scrolls. For these events, the bands played in the street. The ubiquitous bar and bat mitzvah parties of today didn't really come into existence on a large scale until after the Second World War, when they appeared with a vengeance.

The generation that followed the immigrants, known as "first-generation Americans," were bilingual and bicultural. The mores and culture of the old world were essentially supplanted by American popular culture; it was "hip," or "hep," to be Yankee, and decidedly undesirable to be a "greenhorn." The musicians who inherited the business from the European-born klezmorim were, in general, better trained on their instruments; many could play classical music well. Moreover, they were required to learn a complete repertoire of American dance music, including Broadway show tunes, Latin American music (rhumba, tango, cha-cha, merengue), swing, Dixieland, Viennese and French waltzes, and so forth, in addition to the traditional klezmer and Yiddish theater music. Many of this generation came from musical families. Immigrant trumpeter and house painter Yossl Musiker produced three who became first-class professionals: pianist Beverly, klezmer and swing superstar Sam (Dave Tarras's son-in-law, who was featured on clarinet and sax by Dave and by Gene Krupa), and master sax-clarinet-flutist Ray, probably the best klezmer clarinetist of the present time. The Musikers lived on Willoughby Avenue. From Ashford Street in East New York came the four Epstein brothers: Max (clarinet, sax, violin), Isidore, called "Chizik" or "Chi" (sax and clarinet), Willie (trumpet), and Julie (drums). Max was the most traditional player of his generation; he and Sam Musiker were the only ones considered peers by the Europeans. All the Epsteins established good reputations in Jewish and American music. A film called *A Tickle in the Heart*, including the author, who worked as "the fifth Epstein brother," was released and has made them, myself, and Brooklyn reedmen Ray Musiker and Paul Pincus featured concert artists in Europe and America.

Other musical families from Brooklyn are the Gubenkos, Kutchers, Beckermans, and Levinskys. The Gubenkos, sons of bandleader Abe, are percussionists: drummer Sol and vibraharpist Julius, who, under the name Terry Gibbs, is an internationally famous jazz star. The Kutchers, drummer Joe, trumpeter Harry, saxophonist Sydelle, trombonist Sam, and Harry's son Marvin, a fine drummer, were at the top of their field and much in demand. The Beckermans stem from two European-born brothers, clarinetist Shloimke and saxophonist Harry. Shloimke's son Sid lives in Brooklyn and is well known as a master klezmer. Harry's sons Benny (violin and sax) and Sam, a highly regarded accordionist-pianist who recorded with Dave Tarras, worked and lived in Brooklyn. The Levinsky brothers—trumpeters Frank and Lou, who used the name Levinn, and trombonist Jack, who called himself Levitt—had deserved reputations as well schooled musicians. Jack's son Marty, a clarinetist and bandleader, was the only leader to feature traditional klezmer music in the 1960s and early 1970s. Marty's son David is an outstanding young trombonist who is equally adept at jazz and klezmer. Two cousins of the Levinskys worthy of mention are reed players Howie Leess and Danny Rubinstein, sons of two Levinsky sisters. Leess is an outstanding harmony player on the saxophone; his early teacher was Shloimke Beckerman!

After the Second World War, the music business (and the borough of Brooklyn) underwent cataclysmic change. Klezmer music, the music of the immigrants, was disappearing as the older generation died off; it also served as a reminder of the society destroyed in the Holocaust. The new Jewish music of choice was Israeli—lively new music from a brand-new Jewish state, a rebirth, as it were. Concurrently, assimilated Jewish-Americans began to abandon the old homeland, Brooklyn, for the green, sterile suburbs, allowing new groups to move into former Jewish neighborhoods. It was at this juncture that the D.P. (displaced persons) camps of Europe finally closed, allowing Holo-

Henry Sapoznik (banjo), Peter Sokolow (keyboard), Sid Beckerman (clarinet), 1986. Photo courtesy of Peter Sokolow.

caust survivors to seek new homes in Israel and America. Most of those who came were members of Hasidic and other Orthodox groups, and most of them settled in Brooklyn. Bandleader Max Goldberg tells of being approached by the caterer at the Gold Manor in Williamsburg about the possibility of supplying music for Hasidic weddings to be held there. Realizing that his musicians were not capable of performing the specific repertoire required at such parties, Goldberg had to refuse, advising the caterer to find someone from the Orthodox community. That bandleader turned out to be Joe King, a pianist and accordionist who promptly put together a nucleus of klezmer-trained first-generation American musicians, including reed players Chizik Epstein, Harry "Rudy" Tepel, and Howie Leess. King soon found that he had all the work he could handle; much of the work took place on weeknights. Eventually, Tepel and Epstein formed competing orchestras (I worked for both), and more competition came from the community itself—violinist Yidl Terner had a band, and a popular group was formed by two brothers from the Hasidic dynasty of Stolin, Lazer (clarinet), and Mayer (sax) Klitnick, with an accordionist from the Satmar community named Yomtov Ehrlich (I kid you not!). The musical quality of the Klitnick-Ehrlich band was nonexistent until trumpeter Willie Epstein was brought in as contractor (the person who hires the musicians). Before long, the top Hasidic band was the Epstein Brothers Orchestra. A typical phone conversation with a prospective client, according to Willie: "I vant all de brudders. Ve need ten moosickers, so I vant ten brudders!" (You may remember that there are only four, or five with myself included.)

Perry Voultsos and his orchestra, early 1930s. Partial personnel of Voultsos band: Perry Voultsos (leader), Manny Cohen (trumpet), Izzy Drutin (trombone), Max Epstein (clarinet, violin, sax), Isidore (Chizik) Epstein (tenor sax), Beverly Misuker Cohen (piano), Murray Kalevsky (drums). Photo courtesy of Peter Sokolow.

The very nature of the Hasidic wedding demanded major modifications in setup. Men and women were separated by a room divider called a *mechitza*, or they were in two separate adjacent rooms. The latter setup often required the use of two bands, booked by the same leader, one for the men and a smaller unit for the ladies. The ladies' band could play the Israeli folk dances taught in girls' yeshivas at the time, while the men's band could only play Hasidic *nigunim* (songs); in early years, each sect (Satmar, Lubavitch, Bobov, Klausenberg, Stolin, etc.) wanted only their own *nigunim* played. Fortunately, this liberalized as time passed.

The timing of Hasidic weddings is a thing unto itself. First comes the *kabolas ponim* separately for bride (women only) and groom (men only). In the women's section, cold cuts and Hungarian-style hot dishes are served. The band is

set up, playing entrance music for the bride as she is led in by the two mothers. The men review the wedding contract (*tenoyim* and *kesuba*), the mothers are brought in to break a plate to signify acceptance of the contract, and the groom is led into the bride's room to cover her face with a veil (*bedeck'n*), accompanied by a lively *nigun*. The ceremony follows—no long processions or speeches. The groom is led in by the fathers, blessings, the bride and mothers, more blessings. The contract is read, followed by seven benedictions, called *sheva brochos*, the groom breaks a glass with his heel, everyone yells Mazel Tov! (good luck), and the band plays the *nigun* used for the *bedeck'n* as a recessional. The bride and groom, who have been fasting, go into a private room to break their fast; some say that the marriage is consummated at this time. When bride and groom enter the ballroom(s) where dinner is served, frenzied dancing breaks out. These dance sets can last for an hour or more, which makes playing Hasidic weddings, especially night after night in the busy season, something akin to digging ditches! After the meal, the women enter the men's space for *bentching* (grace after meal) and a repeat of the seven benedictions said at the ceremony. A *badkhen*, who makes up rhymes and tells stories, all in Yiddish, now conducts the *mitzvoh tantz*, in which various male relatives "dance" with the bride, who sits still holding one end of a *gart'l* (the ropelike band tied around the waist of the long coat worn on holidays, *shabbos*, and Simchas by Hasidic men) while the relative holds the other end and does a little dance. Sometimes the band accompanies the *mitzvoh tantz*; more often, a small contingent, or just a keyboard, is left, or the musicians are sent home and the male guests sing the *nigunim*. At the weddings of children or grandchildren of important rebbes, and I have played several, a huge hall is rented for the thousands of guests. In Brooklyn, the Hotel St. George, in Brooklyn Heights, was the standard venue because of its cavernous ballroom. These mammoth Simchas can last for twelve or thirteen hours, including five hours of *mitzvoh tantz*!

The enormous demand for Hasidic wedding music grew exponentially, as each family had from six to thirteen(!) children. Demand for housing also grew alarmingly, as the Hasidim expanded out of their original Williamsburg base into Crown Heights (center of the Lubavitch community), Boro Park (today probably the most populous Orthodox community in the world), Midwood, Bensonhurst, and such non-Brooklyn areas as Monsey (Rockland County), Kiryas Yoel (Monroe, in Orange County) and New Square, a town in Rockland named, indirectly, for the Hungarian town of Skvar—hence the group name, the Skvarer Hasidim. As it happened, there weren't enough catering halls to handle all of the new business. At first, old catering places brought in *glatt kosher* Hasidic caterers. Later, catering rooms were added to yeshiva buildings, and former factories, garages, supermarkets, and even a bowling alley have been converted into Simcha Palaces! The original Williamsburg halls, the Gold Manor and the Grand Paradise, have long been abandoned.

As the Jewish population of Brooklyn has become increasingly Orthodox, trends in the Simcha business have followed changing tastes in that world. The first "young" Orthodox bands, made up of yeshiva graduates mixed with veterans, appeared in the mid-1960s. Bands such as the Mark Three, Minzer-Cord, the Messengers, Josh Gold-

berg, the Chosen Ones, and Neginah began to cut into the veteran leaders' territory by going directly to prospective brides and grooms, rather than by booking through the parents, who seemed just as happy to leave that decision to the kids. A nonmusician, law student Yitzchok Gross, built a musical empire out of Neginah using a superb sense of salesmanship. Starting with the musical Lamm brothers' trumpeter Yisroel, clarinetist Michoel, and saxman Yitzchok ("Pitz"), Gross built an organization based on the principle used in the rock world, that the young like to be entertained by their peers. When Gross handed over the running of the business to singer-keyboardist Shelly Lang, he ensured the survival of Neginah as the General Motors of Orthodox music purveyors. This continues to the present, despite the defection of several key people from the organization to form competing groups.

Two events that changed the course of Orthodox music were the arrival of Israeli rock-oriented players in the late 1970s and the ukase issued by the powerful Satmar rebbe ordering his followers to "cut down on the spiraling cost of weddings" through the elimination of bands in favor of the "vun men bend," an electronic keyboard player with rhythm synthesizer, in the mid 1980s. The appearance of the Piamentas (guitarist Yosi and flutist Avi) and saxophonist Yoel Kokel brought a real hard-rock sound into Jewish music; in one fell swoop, the klezmer influence disappeared. Jewish bands at weddings are playing a new Jewish pop-rock at seismic volume levels, forcing the players to use earplugs and microphones. The clarinet has virtually disappeared from the lineup, replaced by a keening alto sax; every band now has to have a string-bending, effects-laden, mind-blowing electric guitar. As far as the "vun men bend" is concerned, he is usually a self-taught member of the Hasidic community who comes in with a large sound system and, sometimes, two or three keyboards. All these young men are electronically sophisticated and know about all the latest programs—and—they can play as loudly as any band! Oddly, the very latest development in this situation is the advent of the "two-piece vun men bend" or the "three-piece vun men bend," achieved by adding one or two horn players, thereby circumventing the Satmar rebbe's edict! For the musicians, the net result is the elimination of midweek Hasidic work, leaving only Sundays and a paltry few weekdays except in the June rush, in which so many couples want to get married that all available catering halls are quickly booked up for the Sundays and many have to settle for weekdays.

Max Kletter Orchestra, ca. 1953. Saxes (left to right): Max Epstein, Paul Pincus, Ray Musiker; trumpet: Willie Epstein; trombone: Sam Kutcher; piano: Al Hausman; bass: Charlie Galazan; drums: Lou Weissman; guitar: Tommy Lucas; vocal: Bunny Fisher; leader: Max Kletter. Photo courtesy of Peter Sokolow.

At this juncture of my musical career, I find myself more an interested observer of events in the rapidly changing Brooklyn Jewish music scene than an active participant. I was fortunate enough to have taken part in much of the history of the scene, and my historian's instinct led me to learn as much as I could about events that preceded my career from those who came on the scene before I did. I started playing music professionally in late 1956 as a student clarinet and saxophone player; I took my first clarinet lesson in the spring of 1954, and started sax in mid-1955! Gifted with absolute pitch (I can tell the pitch of a note without having to have it played on an instrument) and a natural harmonic sense, I was able to play any song I knew immediately, without having to read the melody off a sheet, and in almost any

key. My first love was jazz, and I began to improvise jazz choruses almost as soon as I knew the musical scales. My first job was a teenage dance at the Boro Park YM-YWHA, with a four-piece "kid" band, three hours for five dollars! At about that time, I had also started to teach myself the rudiments of jazz piano. My father was a piano teacher who had done some work with bands in the 1920s. He played a full, old-time oompah or "stride" style. We had a beautiful old Steinway grand (which, happily, is now mine), and I received some lessons from him at age ten and eleven. I got little out of those lessons—my father was a pedantic, uninspiring teacher who actually taught me far more as I listened to his powerful playing, and to his 78-rpm records of bands, small groups, and piano soloists. I first heard "Fats"

Waller on one of my father's records at age seventeen (1957); I found myself spending as much time at the piano as with my reed instruments.

My entry into the world of the Brooklyn klezmer came in the summer of 1958, when I was hired for a summer job in a Catskill hotel by a later edition of the infamous Nathan Ritholtz, a trumpeter (he was awful!), bassist (he never got past page one of book one), and vocalist (don't ask!!!) named Ralph Kahn, né Cohen, and his partner in crime, accordionist-pianist Harry Berman, whose lack of harmonic sense was legendary. The music may have been awful, but they taught me the Jewish music business—repertoire, dance tempos, and the value of entertainment in a musical presentation. More important, they introduced me, directly or indirectly, to virtually all of the first-generation Jewish-American musicians, and some of the immigrant pioneers as well. I became a "talented kid"; trombonist Boris Malina, a famous Russian-American loudmouth, called me "der naier Genius" (the new genius). One of Berman's cohorts was sax-clarinet man Rudy Tepel, at the time an important leader of Hasidic bands. Harry gave Rudy American jobs, and Rudy used Harry in his Hasidic groups. We played Hasidic tunes for non-Orthodox Jewish parties, and Rudy soon gave me my first Hasidic work; this would enable me to make a full-time career in professional music about ten years later.

I left Ralph and Harry in 1962 to work for leaders who would pay me union-scale wages for my work—they usually paid eight to fifteen dollars under scale per job, when the scale was twenty-eight dollars for a four-hour job and seven dollars per hour overtime. I managed to work for most of the Brooklyn leaders booking Jewish-American work in those years: Walter Werbel, Herb Sherry (the biggest at the time), Max Goldberg, Jack Tyler, Teddy Werbel (Walter's cousin), and others. In 1966, I became part of a dynamic young party band, the Esquires, led by Brooklynites Norm Robbins and Arty Quentzel and featuring many of the best young players of my generation. Concur-

rently, I did a considerable amount of Orthodox work with the Mark III, the first successful young band in that field, led by Bronxite Sy Kushner (accordion) and Brooklynite Benjy Hulkower (drums). Through them, I met many of the most important players in that end of the business. I joined the Epstein Brothers organization in late 1969; shortly thereafter, I left my "day gig" as music teacher in an East New York elementary school for a full-time career as a commercial musician.

I bought my first electronic keyboard, a Farfisa compact organ, in early 1971, and began playing it on Epstein Brothers Hasidic jobs. This made me the fifth Epstein brother: the four of them and me. I phased out the reed instruments gradually, doing my last job on them in 1976. I found myself in the curious position of rebuilding the considerable reputation I had as a reed player on keyboard and piano; I'm extremely proud to say that I did it quite smoothly. Through the following years, I have played in virtually every Hasidic band of the time, in "society" bands (Lester Lanin, etc.), in "name" Dixieland bands, and have participated actively in the revival of good old-time klezmer music, through the good offices of Henry Sapoznik, banjoist, ethnomusicologist, and Brooklyn native, as I am—I've lived in Brooklyn (Crown Heights and Marine Park) for fifty-eight of my fifty-nine years. My position in the klezmer world is that of "the youngest old guy"—I have introduced the younger performers to the veterans, personally and musically. Interestingly, I find myself playing the music of my youth with many of the same players, for international audiences, who receive us royally, at prestigious concert venues! If someone had told me in my Kahn/Berman days that I would be recreating the freylekhs of old Brooklyn catering halls in Zurich and Amsterdam, not to mention Vienna and Berlin, I'd have been laughing hysterically, and yet—"dos Redl dreht zakh" (what goes around, comes around). We didn't know it then, but there was quite a bit of artistry in that old-time music, and it reached its peak in Brooklyn.

Klezmer Revived
Dave Tarras Plays Again

WALTER ZEV FELDMAN

This was the final sound check before the crowd would come pouring in. The turnout for this concert of "Jewish klezmer music," featuring The Dave Tarras Orchestra on November 19, 1978, was much higher than anyone had expected. Over one thousand elderly Jewish people were forming a line outside, and several hundred more had to be turned away. The hall where the concert was being held, now rented by a Spanish *landsmanschaft* and called the Casa Galicia, was familiar to many of the people as Webster Hall, where klezmer bands led by such stars as Naftule Brandwein and the young Dave Tarras had played for their frequent dance parties back in the 1920s when they were all young, and newly arrived from their poor and pogrom-ridden homelands in Russia, Ukraine, Poland, and Romania. New York became the great urban concentration of Jews. My Bessarabian father had told me, "we never danced so much at home as we danced in America." Eventually most of them found a place for themselves somewhere in the growing American middle class, many at its lower end, a few toward the top. Their children usually entered the professions and business, but the music to which their parents or grandparents had danced as young immigrants was no longer a major part of their lives. Several families I knew still owned a few old 78-rpm discs; more owned the newer long-playing records on which they could hear the clarinet, trumpet, and saxophone playing the klezmer dances that had been popular in the New York of forty or fifty years ago—the freylakhs, the sher, the zhok, and especially the bulgar.

An hour before the doors opened a tall, slightly overweight but solidly built man in his late seventies began to step slowly and carefully across the wires that crisscrossed the semi-lit stage. His stride expressed both confidence and caution, great willpower tempered by a precise knowledge of his current physical limitations. When he reached the center of the stage the lights revealed a handsome, almost boyishly fleshy face, with remnants of reddish-blond hair still not entirely white, while his blue eyes shone behind thick eyeglasses. While the lights were being adjusted he went over an old tune on the clarinet. Standing in the wings I watched his fingers fly up and down the keys. I recognized an old bulgar which was the first recording that Tarras had made in this country. This scene was to be repeated at each concert he would give during the following two years. Prior to each one he invariably warmed up his fingers with the same bulgar, which, however, he never performed on stage. By now his repertoire consisted exclu-

Dave Tarras on clarinet. Courtesy of the Center for Traditional Music and Dance. Photo by Jack Mitchell.

sively of the old Yiddish theater songs that were more familiar to this audience than the dance tunes of their distant youth. I felt the poignancy in Tarras's persistent, indeed unshakable habit of checking the clarinet and loosening his fingers with the same tune that had helped to bring him recognition and success as a young immigrant klezmer.

Before Tarras went out on stage his students, Andy Statman and I, played a few very old klezmer tunes from Europe, most of them not part of the American klezmer repertoire in living memory. Our instrumentation was also exotic—I accompanied the familiar clarinet with the eastern European hammer dulcimer, called in Yiddish a *cimbal* (*tsimbl*), the diminutive ancestor of the large Hungarian concert *czymbalom*. Andy's tone on the clarinet was sweet and remarkably mature. The audience reacted enthusiastically even to this exotic material. When Tarras emerged he and his accompanists gave them something of the faded post-klezmer repertoire of twenty years ago, but with a warm and subtle style that retained much of the appeal of his music since the 1920s. Perhaps only his improvised *doina* suggested something of his earlier klezmer repertoire. The audience, my mother included, was literally entranced. By the end of the program pandemonium was breaking loose. During one of the encores a middle-aged man wearing a yarmulke leapt up from his seat and danced spontaneously; the entire audience was seized with something approaching frenzy. I thought of the Golden Calf, and how we ought to have prepared one to place in the cen-

ter of the dance floor. Soon the floor was cleared of chairs, and many people danced whatever they could. Tarras played a few of the klezmer tunes still in his active repertoire; I led a line of the bulgar. I leaned back and allowed my shoulders to bounce lightly as my father had while dancing. When I stopped dancing I observed that the audience was more diverse than I had initially thought—a variety of American-born Jewish types were there dancing, in addition to the immigrants in their seventies and eighties. If the "klezmer revival" had a beginning I would give this date in November 1978 when "Dave Tarras played again."

Dave Tarras was no one's "discovery." He had been a dominant force in American klezmer music for forty years; his American recordings had been known in eastern Europe prior to the Holocaust and were widely imitated by the native klezmorim of Mandate Palestine. The influence of his style and repertoire spread also through his performances and recordings with Yiddish theater singers. All of us who have heard those little clarinet sighs and glottal catches behind a throaty Yiddish singer have imbibed Tarras's conception of Jewish music. During the 1950s and 1960s I heard his recordings on WEVD, and I bought several of his 78-rpm and LP recordings.

In those days (end of the 1960s) Yiddish dance music had no status among young Jewish intellectuals and artists, even among those who were involved in folklore and folkdance. For the intellectuals all folklore was "primitive," but an exception was made for popular "protest" songs and their Anglo-American or Afro-American antecedents, or sometimes for the fiddle and banjo music of the Appalachian Mountains, which was part of a socialist avant-garde. For the "folkies" Yiddish dance music did not really exist; it was a potpourri of the various styles of northeastern and southeastern Europe. This attitude had developed after World War II—before then the folkdance movement had included a number of Jewish dances like the sher and *beroygez tants*. When I innocently showed an LP recording of Tarras to one of my folkdance colleagues, who had done fieldwork in several Balkan countries, I could elicit no interest. Around the same time I showed the same LP to an elderly Romanian woman friend. She leapt on the recording, and asked to borrow it. The following week she brought it back, saying that she and her son had felt like dancing to these "Jewish sîrbas." I was beginning to get the impression that it was only for American Jews that Jewish music was indistinguishable, something like a whistle of too high a frequency to be heard by human ears.

At that time even the word *klezmer* was unknown, surviving only among American Yiddish speakers as an opprobrious term for an illiterate musician. From age twenty-two I had traveled the road to klezmer music together with my friend Andy Statman. I had met Andy through friends from high school, and some of them from my Bronx neighborhood, with whom he had played ol' timey and bluegrass mandolin. Andy was introduced to me after one of their concerts. He had come up and asked me to get together in order to learn about musics of the Near East. We had spent a year playing little duets of mandolin and Persian *santur*/dulcimer, drawing on a repertoire ranging from Armenian to Greek and Macedonian dance tunes. Occasionally when playing for a Greek audience Andy and I performed a couple of Jewish freylakhs we had learned from old 78-rpm recordings he had found in Brooklyn.

After one year with me and the Greeks Andy came to a decision—he would learn Jewish music, klezmer music. The Greek, Bessarabian, and Armenian musicians with whom Andy was currently studying all knew and played a few Jewish tunes, which they had learned from klezmer musicians in Europe or America, but these tunes were peripheral to their larger repertoires. He asked me whether I knew of anyone who specialized in klezmer music. Without having to do much thinking I remembered the name of Dave Tarras, which appeared on so many old and fairly recent recordings, and whom my parents had heard only a few years earlier. Andy took it from there by consulting the handbook of the local musicians' union. Tarras's name appeared among the clarinetists, with an address and telephone number in Brooklyn. Andy telephoned Tarras, and he turned out to be receptive to his interests and willing to give him lessons. At that time Andy's only wind instrument was the alto saxophone, on which he and I had played some Macedonian *zurla* dance tunes. Tarras quickly convinced him he could not play proper klezmer music on that instrument. Andy took up the clarinet and quickly learned the new fingering. This also enabled him to pursue his interest in Greek clarinet music with the old Epirote musician Perikles Halkias. After six months of lessons Tarras sold Andy one of his old clarinets, and playing this vintage but still bright-sounding instrument added to his enthusiasm for klezmer music. From time to time I would ask Andy for his impressions of Tarras, and his most characteristic reply was that Tarras was "like an old watchmaker," precise and cautious in all his dealings.

After a year of study Andy's work suffered a setback when Tarras's wife suddenly died. Theirs had been a very long and happy marriage. The two of them had fled through the Ukraine together, and come to America as immigrants. Tarras was disconsolate, and for several months he was unable to teach. He moved out of his house he had shared with his wife, tearing up some of his sheet music and throwing out some of his 78-rpm recordings. Even before the death of his wife, I had felt that it was important that I not meet Tarras until Andy had established a firm relationship, which would be based on his study of the clarinet. I was confident that Tarras would recognize Andy's extraordinary talent, and he did.

For most of 1975 I was traveling through the West, and on to Europe and Turkey. I kept up with Andy's studies through his occasional letters. At one point he was working simultaneously with Tarras, Halkias, and two Caucasian fiddlers, Zevulun Avshalomov and Antranik Aroustamian. When I returned to the States I purchased a Greek *santuri* which I tuned like a *cimbal*, the klezmer dulcimer. I was ready to learn the tunes Andy had studied with Tarras. My spacious new apartment at 110th Street and Broadway resounded with a few Tarras favorites, such as the "Bessarabian sîrba," or the "Hebrew dance," as well as older freylakhs and zhoks. Two years after he had started to take lessons Andy and I decided that it was time for me to meet Dave Tarras.

Tarras had remarried recently, to Adele, the owner of the country club that had cleverly used his name as bait to lure my parents. He had moved into her Coney Island apartment in which she had been living alone since the death of her first husband.

At first glance the apartment we entered and the elderly couple who greeted us were so unexceptional I almost felt that we must have come to the wrong place. Looking around I could have been visiting one of my father's *landsleit* in the Bronx of thirty years ago. Every visible object might have been chosen by a Feldman family decorator. The only somewhat unusual point was the extreme cleanliness and order that was evident in every corner of the living room. Adele was a very short woman with faded blonde hair, large thick eyeglasses, and a meek, pleasant smile. I recognized Dave Tarras's face from one of his LP record jackets, but I was not prepared for his height and the intimidating forcefulness of his movements. Tarras was standing as Adele opened the door. His posture and expression as he greeted us told me that he viewed Andy as a special person in his life, and that I might partake of some of that specialness. Tarras spoke English about as well or as badly as my father had done. His intonation was similar—a broad southern Yiddish accent that few in America would recognize as Jewish. They were of about the same height, but Tarras had blond hair and blue eyes instead of my father's black curls and dark eyes. Tarras's speech was slow and deliberate, due partly to his discomfort with English grammar but also to his habit of carefully weighing every word.

Andy made the introductions, and Tarras offered me a seat on the couch while Adele rushed to serve tea and cookies. I was then a graduate student, and I had some trouble explaining what I was supposed to be writing about. Andy told them that I played the *cimbal* and then Tarras mentioned his late friend Josef Moscovici, who had been an outstanding performer of Romanian and Jewish music on the large concert *czymbalom*. He asked me about my parents, and when I answered that my father, who had died seven years earlier, had been a Bessarabian from Yedinits he warmed up visibly, praising the country, its music, and its wine. He had even spent some weeks or months in Yedinits. Tarras described it as "a lively Jewish town."

This introduction opened the way for my weekly or biweekly visits to Tarras's apartment over the next two years. I also made frequent visits to the home of his accompanist, the accordionist Sam Beckerman. I became used to carrying my *cimbal*, wrapped in its woolen and canvas cases, on the IND subway line from Manhattan to Brooklyn. On some occassions I brought my tape recorder as well. Meanwhile Ethel Raim and I had written a grant proposal to the National Endowment for the Arts, requesting a year's funding for a new project in what we called "Jewish instrumental folkmusic," as *klezmer* was still an obscure term of the Yiddish lexicon. The concert of November 1978 was one result of this project, which had been funded through the organization she and Martin Koenig directed, then called the Balkan Arts Association, later Ethnic Folk Arts, and currently, the Center for Traditional Music and Dance. In a short time Tarras shifted his perspective on life from that of a successful but now retired musician to that of an active performer and authority on a music that was gradually coming back into demand—that obscure object of desire to be known henceforth as klezmer music.

The public reception of Tarras's first and of subsequent concerts was surprisingly strong. Shortly after the first concert Nat Hentoff published an article in *Jewish Living* titled "King Klezmer and His Dynasty," describing Tarras as "a stately, broad-shouldered man, [who] played with that total authority which requires no extraneous dramatics." And Hentoff also recognized a link between Tarras and us, his students: "Dave Tarras' musical lineage spans three generations, and he needn't look far for an heir." Two years later, after a second concert Harold Steinblatt's lengthy review article in *Jewish World* was titled "Klezmer Music Is Alive and Well and Playing in New York."

The next stage of our NEA klezmer project involved bringing Tarras and his group to the senior centers of the Jewish Association for Services for the Aged (JASA) located in Brooklyn. These were always festive events, during which the incredulous residents seemed to be greeting a part of their past, miraculously returned to life. The director of the Williamsburg Center wrote to us: "As the director of the Center, I was overwhelmed with joy to see my people sing and dance and clap with such enthusiasm. . . . It was a cold snowy day outside, but in our center it was 'fraylach' and warm." For these people the resonance of Tarras's music and personality was immediate—they had heard him long ago, and they required no mediation to discover his significance. But what surprised me was the broader recognition of the value of Tarras's music, even among Jews who might have heard him only on records or on the radio, and only in their childhood.

Tarras himself was no longer playing his own repertoire. He left that to Andy and me. Our first solo concerts were not only received enthusiastically; some of them were stampedes. At one concert held on the Upper East Side I rushed out before the performance to be sure that my elderly Romanian woman friend—now totally blind—would not be hurt by the crowds. The tones of Andy's clarinet seemed to awaken some distant memory, some dream of childlike happiness that this music had once symbolized in the Jewish collective memory in America.

The year following the first concert Andy and I prepared our album, to be titled *Jewish Klezmer Music*. Only one piece on the album—the "Ternovka Sher"—came directly from Tarras, but most had been in his repertoire at one time. We conducted our final rehearsals for the recording in Tarras's living room in Brooklyn. We were pleased that he had no criticism to make of our version of "Ternovka Sher." And for me the best moment came when we played him our "freylakhs fun der khupe." When I switched from doubling the melody to playing a strong rhythm on the lower strings of the *cimbal*, Tarras lay back in his easy chair and let out a groan of delight. That was his highest praise.

New Jewish Music in the Orthodox Community

MARK KLIGMAN

In the 1960s some musicians in the Orthodox community wished to change the kind of music Orthodox Jews listened to. A significant challenge arose: the post–World War II generation of Orthodox Jews—many of whose parents were new to America after the war—maintained an observant Jewish life but wanted to satisfy the desire to be modern. A question arises: how to create a contemporary music acceptable to the Orthodox community.

That postwar Orthodox musicians succeeded in creating such a music is proved by the proliferation of Orthodox musicians who currently make a living as writers and performers. In fact there are more Orthodox recordings and they are more popular than Reform, Conservative, or klezmer recordings.

The Orthodox music industry, based predominantly in Brooklyn, includes performers, songwriters, arrangers, and distributors. This industry has grown significantly over the past twenty-five years, in large part due to the popularity of the music among the growing Jewish religious community. Orthodox Jews eschew popular American music in favor of music with Jewish content. The Bible and liturgy are not the only sources of the texts for new Orthodox music. In the 1970s, Orthodox musicians developed a genre of English songs that deliver a powerful message of faith and devotion. This new music satisfies a need for religiously appropriate entertainment. For Orthodox Jews who avoid TV, film, and theater, religiously sensitive music is an important means of entertainment.

THE RECORDING OF HASSIDIC MUSIC

In the late 1950s and early 1960s, the Orthodox began recording other than cantorial music. Ben Zion Shenker, born in 1925 and raised in Williamsburg, performed as a youth with some of the great cantors but later, influenced by his friendship with Modzitzer Rebbe Shaul Taub, began recording Modzitz melodies. Shenker composed 450 original pieces, some of which, such as "Mizmor Le-David" (Psalm 23) and "Aisheds Chayil" (A Woman of Valor, Proverbs 31:10–21), continue to be sung in Orthodox homes and on the Sabbath. In the early 1960s, Duvid Werdyger, a cantor, also recorded Hassidic melodies. His recordings through the 1970s featured the music of Gerrer, Melitzer, Skulener, Bobover, Boyaner, and Rodomsker dynasties (Werdyger 1993, 308–14). Recordings of the music of the Lubavitch Skulener and Munkacs dynasties followed.

INNOVATIONS OF SHLOMO CARLEBACH

Jewish musical artists of today credit Shlomo Carlebach (1925–94) as the father of contemporary popular Orthodox music. Carlebach combined the participatory nature of folk music, the energy of newly created music from Israel, and the religious fervor of the Hassidic *niggun* (melody) in his songs and in performances. Carlebach drew from the European tradition and combined it with a contemporary style and Jewish message. He laid the foundation for a new form of Jewish music.

Carlebach set out to create a music that would educate and inspire Jews to renew their Jewish identity and discover the beauty of living a Jewish life. In his prolific career he recorded over twenty-five albums. Some estimate that he wrote close to a thousand melodies, and singers have recorded his songs on hundreds of recordings (Brandwine 1997, 37).[1] Known throughout the Jewish world, Carlebach established Jewish music as a new creative entity. He

Songwriter Yossi Green. Photo courtesy of Seán Galvin and used with permission of Yossi Green.

created new vistas for Jewish music by writing for nonliturgical contexts and performing in intimate settings such as a *kumsitz* (religious gatherings) or public places like nightclubs or concerts.

CONTEMPORARY POPULAR ORTHODOX MUSIC SINCE THE LATE 1960S

New Jewish music in the 1960s and 1970s liberated itself from eastern European modes, styles, and aesthetics. Songwriter Yossi Green, co-owner of a Brooklyn medical supply company, has written over 320 songs for the most successful Orthodox performers. Green describes his music with a refreshing lack of sentimentality:

Klezmer music is more of a caricature of what Jewish music used to be . . . . And that really has nothing to do with where Jewish music is today. That's my opinion; I'm at the center of this music and have been writing for years. . . . New Hassidic music [his name for new Orthodox music] has definitely replaced klezmer. If

"New Recordings of Shlomo Carlebach." Courtesy and used by permission of Sameach Music Inc.

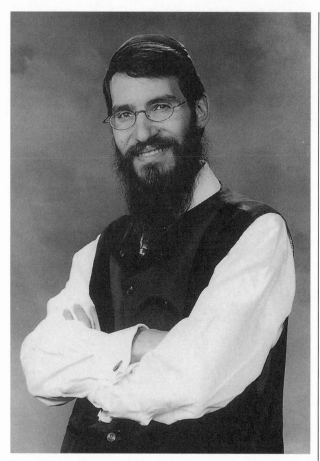

Singer Avraham Fried. Photo by Barry Studios, courtesy and used with permission of Avraham Fried.

klezmer was the downtrodden, stepped-on poor little shtetl Jew's music, then this is the music of today for the young, wealthier, more educated, forward-thinking Jewish mind. . . . Klezmer is totally Jewish when ours is influenced by Elton John. You listen to "Tanyeh" or "Didoh Bei"[2] and you'll tell me how beautiful these songs are. It is fresh, it is new. It is the young Jewish person saying, "I'm here, it's the nineties, I'm proud of my Judaism, I'm learning a lot but I'm also having fun—it's allowed and it's okay, my kids are having fun, we're relaxing and enjoying ourselves, we're Jewish and we're proud of it." (Interview, 1 July 1998)

This new spirit necessitated a new musical style. Singer Avraham Fried believes there is no market for contemporary recordings of hazzanut: instead people want good dance songs and ballads (interview with Avraham Fried, 6 July 1998).

The most influential groups to follow Carlebach are The Rabbi's Sons, Mark III, Ruach, and Simchatone. The

Rabbi's Sons recorded their first album in 1967 and three others thereafter. Kol Solonika, led by Baruch Chait, formerly part of The Rabbi's Sons, incorporated a similar folk sound but added a Greek style with the bouzouki, a stringed instrument. Kol Solonika's first recording, Kol Solonika: The New Greek Hassidic Sound (1972), was followed by five other recordings. At the same time a number of boys' choirs were popular, such as Pirchei and London Pirchei, now known as the London school of Jewish song.

In the 1970s, Jewish music was again transformed. American popular music was increasingly entwined with the drug culture, as manifest in their song lyrics and discordant sounds. Orthodox Jewish artists, however, maintained a strong religious message in their music. Abie Rotenberg, the composer for D'veykus, wrote songs with liturgical texts that were easy to sing. Their melodious tunes can be heard at Orthodox weddings, in the synagogue, and as zemirot sung at home.

The Diaspora Yeshiva Band was also influential in the late 1970s and the early 1980s. Their music provided a gateway for other ba'alei teshuva as well as those raised as

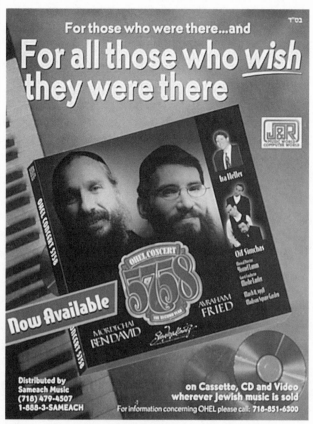

"Recording of Ohel Concert 5758 (1988)." Courtesy and used by permission of Sameach Music Inc.

Orthodox Jews, to experience a truly contemporary Jewish-American music. Their melodies were often complex, and the arrangements included virtuosic instrumental playing. The current generation of Orthodox musicians vividly remember the Diaspora Yeshiva Band and the impact it had on music in the community.

Mordechai Ben David had the most significant impact on music in the Orthodox community in the 1970s and 1980s. The son of Duvid Werdyger (hence the use of the father's name, Mordechai the son of Duvid or David), Mordechai often sang in his father's concerts and recordings. With twenty-five recordings to date, Mordechai Ben David is one of the most successful solo performers. His first solo recording in 1974, *Hineni* (I am here), which is the response given by forefathers Abraham, Isaac, and Jacob when God called upon them, had two important innovations: it included a song with an English text, and the arrangements used a full professional orchestra.

Where Carlebach was a link between folk music and Jewish music, Ben David appropriated American popular musical styles and adapted a secular idiom to fit a Jewish message. Some members of the community recall rabbinical objections to these songs; some rabbis felt the music was too secular and would cause Jews to leave the community. But for the musicians—and their predominantly Orthodox listeners—these songs in English offered inspiring religious messages in an accessible musical style. Most of

Ben David's songs are in Hebrew, which also appeals to his primarily right-wing Orthodox audience.

Avraham Fried, who began singing in the early 1980s, is among the most popular musicians of the last decade. Encouraged to sing at home, at the *Shabbes* table, he recorded his first English-language song in 1981. Titled "No Jew Will Be Left Behind," and written by Yossi Green, the song says that when the Messiah comes all Jews will go to Israel and no one will be left behind. Fried, a Lubavitcher Hassid living in Crown Heights, incorporates the message of the Messiah and redemption in many of his songs: "The Time Is Now" (1982), "We Are Ready" (1988), "Goodbye Golus" (1989), "On Giants' Shoulders" (1993), "Don't Hide from Me" (1995).[3] Fried sees the English songs as "a chance to say how I'm feeling at that moment, in my own words, not based on a verse or taken out of psalms" (interview, 6 July 1998).

In the mid 1980s Orthodox popular music took some surprising turns. In January of 1988 a concert at Lincoln Center's Avery Fisher Music Hall featured Moredechai Ben David, Avraham Fried, and Yoel Sharabi. This marked the first time a concert of Orthodox popular music was performed in a venue outside of Brooklyn or Queens.[4] Since 1988 Orthodox musicians have performed at Carnegie Hall, Radio City Music Hall, the Paramount Theater of Madison Square Garden, Nassau Coliseum, Westbury Music Fair, and most recently the Metropolitan

Opera House. Outside of New York, in performances throughout America as well as Europe and Israel, concerts are held at synagogues, schools, or other locations in the community large enough to hold an audience of several hundred people. Performers play between thirty and fifty concerts a year. Producer Sheya Mendlowitz states: "There are masses out there that are interested now and it is growing. The younger generation is into Jewish music. The market is growing. I don't even think we've touched the tip of the iceberg yet" (interview, 22 July 1998).

While a generation of Orthodox Jews grew up with the music of Mordechai Ben David and Avraham Fried, their children are listening to Shloime Dachs, Sandy Shmuely, Mendy Wald, Yisroel Williger, and Yehuda. Children's music is also popular, with multiple recordings of stories and songs with Jewish messages and themes: Uncle Moishy, Country Yossi, 613 Torah Avenue, Mitzvah Tree, Rabbi Shmuel Kunda, and Torah Tots.

CONCLUSION

To the outsider, contemporary music in the Orthodox community is simply a replacement for American popular music. Insiders experience this music differently: it serves as a vehicle for texts focusing on religious-oriented ideas, and for Judaic values. The goal of the creators, performers, songwriters, and producers is to elevate the listener. Yet at the same time, the new Orthodox music is a serious business enterprise. Marketing and promoting records matter. Indeed the music is everywhere in the community. It is sold in book and gift stores—such as Eichler's and Mostly Music in Borough Park, Eichler's on Coney Island Avenue in Flatbush, and electronic stores in these neighborhoods. It can be heard at pizza shops, bakeries, and markets. New Orthodox music has become synonymous with the community (Kligman 1994).

Contemporary Orthodox music reflects the growth and creativity of the American Orthodox community in the final three decades of the twentieth century. The generation that created modern Orthodox music over the past twenty-five years has also developed a viable Orthodox music industry. Some have commented that the improved production quality of the music and the sum total of experiences of producers, arrangers, and performers has created music "as good as anything else you hear on the radio" (interview with Avraham Fried, 6 July 1998). According to Jewish radio host Nacum Segal (interview, 29 July 1998) it has become "cool to listen to Jewish music."

Perhaps an unexpected hurdle for Orthodox artists arises from the greater exposure of their music to non-Orthodox Jews. Through radio stations, national retail selling venues, and Websites, artists, producers, and distributors sell more recordings. Some wonder whether Jewish music has become too commercial, and worry that it no longer serves its spiritual role in the Jewish community (Sears 1997). Balancing commercial success with a Jewish message is the challenge and future of Orthodox Jewish musicians.

NOTES

1. Others estimate that he wrote five thousand melodies with only a relatively small number of melodies put onto his recordings; see Schreiber 1989,30.

2. These two songs are among the most popular songs composed by Yossi Green and performed by Avraham Fried. "Tanya" (We learned) appears on *Avraham Fried: We Are Ready!* (1988); the text is taken from Babylonian Talmud Tractate Brachot, page 7a. "Didoh Bei" (If you have knowledge) appears on *Avraham Fried: Chazak!* (Be strong) (1997); the text is taken from Babylonian Talmud Tractate Nedarim, page 41a.

3. The first three songs come from recordings of the same name; the last two are from *Shtar Hatnoim* (wedding engagement document) (1993) and *Brocha V'Hatzlocha* (Blessing and good luck) (1995).

4. This does not mark the first time "Jewish" music concerts have appeared in similar venues. There have been many performances of cantorial and Yiddish music in a variety of settings in New York City concert halls and other cities in the United States.

REFERENCES

Ben-David, Calev. 1955. "Music with a Soul." *The Jerusalem Report*, 42–43.

Brandwein, M. 1997. *Reb Shlomele: The Life and World of Shlomo Carlebach.* Trans. Gabriel A. Sivan. Efrat, Israel: M. H. Brandwein.

Kligman, Mark. 1994. "The Media and the Message: The Recorded Music of Orthodox Jews in Brooklyn, NY." In *Jewish Folklore and Ethnology Review: Special Issue on Media*, ed. Jeffrey Shandler,. vol.16, no.1, 9–11.

——. 1996. "On the Creators and Consumers of Orthodox Popular Music in Brooklyn, New York." *YIVO Annual* 23, 259–93.

——. 2001. "Contemporary Jewish Music in America." *American Jewish Yearbook*, forthcoming.

Miller, Rochelle Maruch. 1995. "Benzion Shenker: An Exclusive Interview with the Master of Jewish Music." *Country Yossi Family Magazine*, 50–51.

Schreiber, Gitta. 1989. "Shlomo Carlebach: An Exclusive Interview." *Country Yossi Family Magazine* 2, no. 4, 30.

Sears, Dovid. 1997. "Who Took the 'Jewish' out of Jewish Music?" *The Jewish Observer* XXIX, no. 10, 12–16.

Werdyger, Duvid. 1993. *Songs of Hope, the Holocaust Diaries.* As told to Avraham Yaakov Finkel. New York, London, Jerusalem: CIS Publishers.

Bad Jews
Jewish Criminals from Brooklyn

ROBERT A. ROCKAWAY

In addition to Jewish artists, writers, and scientists, Brooklyn spawned some of the most violent and vicious Jewish criminals in the annals of American crime.

At the turn of the century, perhaps the most notorious Jewish denizen of the New York underworld was Brooklyn-born Monk Eastman. Herbert Ausbury, a contemporary chronicler of New York's early criminal gangs, called Monk "the prince of gangsters" and "as brave a thug as ever shot an enemy in the back or blackjacked a voter at the polls."

Monk, whose real name was Edward Osterman, was born in Williamsburg in 1873, the son of a respectable Jewish restaurant owner.

Monk began life with a bullet-shaped head and a bull neck. During his turbulent career, he acquired a broken nose, cauliflower ears, heavily veined jowls, and a face pocked with battle scars. His ferocious appearance belied the fact that he stood only five feet and five inches tall and never weighed more than 150 pounds.

Before his twenty-first birthday, Eastman's father opened a pet store for him, but Monk abandoned it for the crime-ridden streets of Lower Manhattan. Nevertheless, Monk retained his love for animals, especially cats and pigeons, all his life. He was said to have owned more than a hundred cats and five hundred pigeons at one time. "I like de kits and boids," he would say, "and I'll beat up any guy dat gets gay wit' a kit or a boid in my neck of de woods."

His love for animals didn't extend to people. At his peak, Eastman bossed a Jewish street gang and could field as many as 1,200 gangsters on short notice. After a series of wars with other gangs, Eastman and his men took over much of the crime on the Lower East Side. They engaged in robberies, burglaries, assault, muggings, and murder for pay. Eastman also seized control of many of the houses of prostitution and gambling dens, and street walkers and hoodlums had to pay him for the privilege of operating on his turf. He and his mob derived additional income from delivering votes to the local Democratic Party political machine, Tammany Hall, and from a variety of protection rackets. And Monk was one of the first underworld figures to furnish strong-arm men to warring unions and employers.

Eastman patrolled his domain armed with a huge club, a blackjack in his hip pocket, and brass knuckles on each hand. In an emergency he could expertly wield a beer bottle and a piece of lead pipe. Monk was also a skillful boxer and street fighter. As powerful as he became, Eastman could not resist doing violence himself. He would lead members of his gang on raids and personally carried out some of the blackjacking commissions. "I like to beat up a guy once in a while," he said. "It keeps me hand in."

In all fairness, it should be mentioned that Monk never struck a woman with his club, no matter how much she annoyed him. When it became necessary to discipline a lady, he simply blackened her eye with his fist. "I only gave her a little poke," he would exclaim. "Just enough to put a shanty on her glimmer. But I always takes off me nucks first."

In 1904, Eastman's life in crime finally caught up with him. He received a ten-year prison sentence for robbery and shooting a Pinkerton detective. By the time he left jail conditions had changed and his power was gone. Bereft of his gang, Monk became a sneak thief, burglar, dope peddler, and a sometime bodyguard and collector for the gambling czar Arnold Rothstein.

In December 1920, at age forty-seven, Eastman was shot and killed by a corrupt Prohibition agent with whom he was running a small bootlegging and dope-smuggling operation. During the Prohibition era (1919–33), Brooklyn served as home to a number of fierce Jewish gangs. The more prominent among them included those of the Shapiro brothers (Irving, Meyer, and William) and the Amberg brothers (Joseph, Louis, and Hyman).

Louis Amberg was nicknamed "Pretty" because of his ugliness. He was so ugly that the Ringling Brothers circus offered him a job, asking him to appear as the "Missing Link." Rather than being insulted, Louis was flattered and often bragged about the offer.

Little else was funny about him. By the time he was twenty he was the terror of Brownsville. He and his older brother Joe ran a loan-sharking business that charged 20 percent interest a week. People who borrowed money from the Ambergs were told at the very outset that if they did not pay on time they would be killed. No one was late.

During Prohibition, Louis and his brothers controlled bootlegging in Brownsville and successfully defended their business from inroads by other gangsters. Dutch Schultz, the "Beer Baron of the Bronx," once told Amberg that he was thinking of becoming his partner in Brooklyn. "Arthur," Pretty said, "why don't you put a gun in your mouth and see how many times you can pull the trigger."

Pretty was good friends with Legs Diamond, but he even warned him about coming into Brownsville. "We're pals, Jack," said Amberg. "But if you ever set foot in Brownsville, I'll kill you and your girlfriend and your missus and your whole damn family."

Pretty managed to protect his interests from other gangsters until the early 1930s, when he engaged in a series of intramural wars. Louis and his brothers lost and his end was anything but pretty. In 1935, he was found trussed up in a burning car near the Brooklyn Navy Yard. He had been hacked to death.

Perhaps the most infamous cohort of Brooklyn Jewish criminals consisted of a loosely allied group of professional killers whom police reporter Harry Feeny dubbed Murder, Inc.

The history of organized crime in America is filled with myths. One of the more enduring is that sometime in the early 1930s Jewish and Italian mobsters in New York met and established a National Crime Syndicate to divide up the rackets across the United States in an orderly and businesslike fashion. This syndicate supposedly created an enforcement arm of Italian and Jewish gangsters to maintain order. Primary members of this unit were Brooklyn-based Jewish thugs such as Abe "Kid Twist" Reles, Harry "Pittsburgh Phil" Strauss, Abraham "Pretty" Levine, Martin "Buggsy" Goldstein, Charlie "The Bug" Workman, Mendy Weiss, Albert "Tick Tock" Tannebaum, and Irving "Knadles" Nitzberg.

Fact or fiction, what we do know for certain is that these men were part of criminal syndicates that, working separately or in loose alliances, engaged in all manner of illicit enterprises, including bootlegging, gambling, narcotics, extortion, and murder. Their expertise in killing made them useful to various mob bosses who wished to eliminate rivals, and at one time or another they were employed by Louis "Lepke" Buchalter, Charles "Lucky" Luciano, and Albert Anastasia.

Because of the gang's activities and notoriety, Brooklyn acquired the reputation of being a wild and dangerous place. After crime boss Lepke Buchalter's 1940 conviction for extortion, newspapermen asked him about the Brooklyn murder mob. Feigning a look of innocence, Lepke replied, "Why, I haven't been in Brownsville in twelve years. I'd be afraid to walk the streets there. Anyone that does is crazy."

The Jewish members of this gang hung out in a tacky candy store located under the elevated subway tracks at the corner of Saratoga and Livonia Streets in Brownsville. Owned by a woman named Rose, who kept the place open twenty-four hours a day, the store became known as "Midnight Rose's." Allegedly the two main topics of conversation in the store were how many runs the Brooklyn Dodgers would lose by that day, and murder. Wags claimed that more individual murders were planned in the store than at any other spot on earth.

Because of their ruthless efficiency at killing, a number of these men attained somewhat mythical status in the underworld. Perhaps the most famous professional killer in American gangster history was Harry "Pittsburgh Phil" Strauss. Phil killed more than one hundred (some said over three hundred) men from the late 1920s to 1940, making him the most prolific killer New York, and perhaps syndicated crime, has ever produced.

The Brooklyn-born Phil was so good that when an out-of-town mob needed someone eliminated, they almost always asked for him. Phil packed his valise with a shirt, a change of socks and underwear, a gun, a knife, a length of rope to tie or strangle his victims, and an ice pick. He then hopped a train or plane to his destination, pulled the job, and caught the next connection back to New York. Often Phil didn't know the name of the person he had killed, and he usually didn't care enough to find out.

The autopsy report on one George Rudnick shows the kind of work Phil was capable of. According to the medical examiner, "There were sixty-three stab wounds on the body. On the neck, I counted thirteen stab wounds between the jaw and collarbone. On the right chest, there were fifty separate circular wounds. . . . His face was intensely cyanic, or blue. The tongue protruded. . . . When the heart was laid open, the entire wall was found to be penetrated by stab wounds."

In 1941, Phil was executed in the electric chair of Sing Sing Prison for murder. He had been put on death row by his erstwhile pal and fellow killer-for-hire Abe Reles. Reles became one of the most famous stool pigeons in criminal history, furnishing prosecutors with the particulars of eighty-five New York murders and hundreds more nationwide. Not only did he put his friends Pittsburgh Phil and Buggsy Goldstein in the electric chair, but he provided Brooklyn assistant district attorney Burton Turkus with insight into the workings of the Brooklyn-based gang of murderers for hire.

An incredulous Turkus finally asked Reles how he brought himself to take human life so casually. "Did your conscience ever bother you?" asked Turkus. "Didn't you feel anything?"

"How did you feel when you tried your first law case?" countered Reles.

"I was rather nervous," Turkus admitted.

"And how about your second case?" asked Reles.

"It wasn't so bad, but I was still a little nervous," said Turkus.

"And after that?" asked Reles.

"Oh, after that, I was alright. I was used to it," answered Turkus.

"You answered your own question," said Reles. "It's the same with murder. I got used to it."

Reles's testimony made Lucky Luciano, Frank Costello, Albert Anatasia, Bugsy Siegel, and other top organized crime figures extremely worried. Reles knew too much about their business, and no one knew where this would end. "If he keeps on goin'," Costello told Luciano, "they're gonna get everybody for murder." Reles had to be stopped.

The police put Reles under protective custody on the sixth floor of the Half Moon Hotel on Coney Island, with two policemen and three plainclothes detectives guarding him around the clock. On the morning of November 12, 1941, his fully dressed body was found on the ground more than twenty feet from the wall of the building. Two knotted bedsheets lay near by.

Theories on how it happened abounded. The police said Reles fell while trying to escape. Others speculated that Reles became conscience-stricken over his past misdeeds and fearful of his future, and committed suicide. Neither these nor other theories explain how the 160-pound Reles landed twenty feet from the wall. He could only have done so if he had wings.

Lots of people had wanted Reles dead. Even his closest pals wanted to see him in a coffin. In 1961, Lucky Luciano told his biographer that it had cost upward of fifty thousand dollars to get rid of Reles. "The whole bunch of cops was on the take," he said. "Reles was sleepin' and one of the cops give him a tap with a billy and knocked him out. Then they picked him up and heaved him out of the window. For Chrissake, he landed so far from the wall he couldn't've done that even if he had jumped."

No one was ever prosecuted for Reles's death, and the entire underworld heaved a collective sigh of relief. Reles has gone down in underworld history as "the canary who could sing but couldn't fly."

With the demise of Reles and the incarceration or execution of those he had implicated in murder, an unsavory episode in the history of Brooklyn Jewry came to an end.

A Brooklyn Accent
Borough Park in the 1940s

GEORGE JOCHNOWITZ

On a spring day in 1989, my younger daughter, Miriam, and I boarded a train in Baoding, Hebei Province, China, where we were living and teaching. I was looking for empty seats when I heard a voice call to me in English: "There a' some seats here."

"What part of Brooklyn did you grow up in?" I asked, but I already knew the answer. He had to be from Borough Park, or perhaps Bensonhurst. It turned out that he was from Twelfth Avenue, just as I was, and had gone to P S 131, my alma mater.

I don't know what tipped me off. He hadn't said the word that generally separates Borough Park and Bensonhurst speakers from other New Yorkers: *ran*. Most Americans rhyme *man* and *ran*. Those of us who grew up in Borough Park in the 1940s, however, rhyme *man* with the noun *can*, as in "*a tin can.*" *Ran*, on the other hand, rhymes with the verb *can*, as in "*yes I can.*"

William Labov, in his pioneering book *The Social Stratification of New York City English*, writes the noun *can* phonetically as [kehn]. The [eh] sound is found in the words *bad* and *bared*, which were homonyms for me and for most residents of New York City when I was a child. The r in *bared* was only pronounced when one was on one's best behavior, or when trying to make a distinction that was not clear in context, for example, "*The big bad wolf bared his teeth.*"

New York City English is an r-less dialect. So are Boston English, New Orleans English, London English, and others. R-lessness doesn't mean that there are no rs; it means that r is dropped before a consonant or at the end of a group of words. Thus, *roar* and *raw* sound the same. Labov spelled them [roh]. The initial r is always pronounced. So is the final r if the next word begins with a vowel—even if there is no final r. A *raw egg* sounds like a *roar egg*.

The r is replaced with a centering glide, a brief schwa sound, which Labov wrote as [h]. Nobody would confuse the words *hot* and *heart*. The former is [hat] and the latter [haht]. Once this distinction exists, it can be used elsewhere. Americans generally don't distinguish intervocalic *d* from intervocalic *t*, which makes *betting* and *bedding* sound the same. New Yorkers can utilize their centering glide to make *otter* different from *odder*. The latter word sounds the same as *ardor*.

As for the [eh] vowel, it is found in *madder* but not *matter*, *halve* but not *have*, *rarely* but not *rally*, *Mary* but not *marry* (both of which are different from *merry*, of course).

Let's get back to *ran*. I, a native of Borough Park, rhymed "I can" with "I ran." I never did a survey of New

York speakers to determine how widespread this pronunciation was at the time I grew up. It is too late to do so; the pronunciation I am talking about is no longer characteristic of my old neighborhood. As I suggested above, the only other New York City neighborhood that agreed with Borough Park was adjacent Bensonhurst, according to my own observations. I have, rarely, encountered individual New Yorkers from different areas in the city who pronounced *ran* as I do. Nevertheless, my personal experience leads me to believe that "I ran" rhyming with "I can" was a feature of Borough Park and Bensonhurst in the 1940s.

Another characteristic of the Borough Park accent I remember is that the names *Molly* and *Polly* don't rhyme. The former has a long stressed vowel, [mahli]; the latter has a short stressed vowel, [pali]. *Molly* rhymes with *dolly*, which has to have a long vowel, since the one-syllable word *doll* has to be [dahl]; the sequence [al] simply doesn't occur in words of one syllable. The common noun *dolly* is *doll* plus the suffix *-y*. It doesn't sound like the first name of Dolly Madison, which sounds like *Polly*, both the proper name and the word meaning "parrot," as in "Polly wants a cracker." As far as I know, people from other parts of the city rhyme *Molly* with *Polly*.

There is no such thing as a Brooklyn accent. There are lots of New York City accents, some of which are Brooklyn accents. The many accents in Brooklyn, as in all five boroughs, vary with neighborhood, age, ethnicity, educational level, and so on. When I was young, people from Brownsville, East New York, and Williamsburg made no distinction between *poor* and *pour*, and sometimes pronounced *hear* and *hair* as homonyms. Little did I know that they were the vanguard. Young people all over New York have lost these distinctions. The New York accent has not become uniform, however. There will always be variety.

One aspect of this variety is ethnic. In the 1940s, Borough Park was Jewish and Italian. My own parents were immigrants; most of my friends and classmates were either the children or grandchildren of immigrants. Nevertheless, one heard surprisingly little Yiddish or Italian on the streets. Words for Jewish holidays were usually Yiddish, but we said "matzo balls" rather than *kneydlakh*, despite the fact that this type of food was specifically linked to the celebration of Passover. *Yente* is an example of a Yiddish word that had made it into Borough Park English. The only Italian I learned on the street was [duzibats] (standard Italian *tu sei pazzo*, meaning "you're crazy") and [fangul] (standard Italian *fa in culo*, which I will translate as "up yours").

My generation did not say [woyk]. All of New York City, at one time, used a diphthong sounding something like the French word for eye, *oeil*, in words like *turn*. Before the letter l, the distinction between the vowels of *oil* and *earl* was lost. By 1940, however, this was old-fashioned and highly stigmatized. The only people who did it were immigrants who could not pronounce an American r. Once in a while, one heard hypercorrection: "terlet" instead of "toilet," but only rarely. I find it odd that people still think of Brooklyn as a place where one says "Toidy-toid Street. For one thing, the pronunciation of *th* as *t* is related to class and educational level, not geography; it is heard in many parts of America. For another thing, [woyk] was already on its way out fifty years ago.

Borough Park today looks similar to the way it looked in the 1940s, but its population is somewhat different. It is an Orthodox Jewish neighborhood. Much more Yiddish is heard; most of its Jewish children do not attend public schools. The Italian population is smaller. In neighboring Bensonhurst, a new Italian population has introduced Italian—standard Italian—into the area. People who speak like me may be found anywhere, even in China, but Borough Park speech has evolved into something new.

REFERENCE
Labov, William. 1966. *The Social Stratification of English in New York City.* Washington, D.C.: Center for Applied Linguistics.

Seltzer Man

ZACHARY LEVIN

"S-s-s-s-h-h-h-t. I love that sound," says the second-generation seltzer man Barry Walpow. He's at the Seaview Diner in Canarsie, simulating the joyful noise of seltzer squirting from a glass siphon bottle, before heading off to make an end-of-the-day delivery in Williamsburg. The tall fifty-one-year-old, wearing a battered black baseball hat and glasses as thick as the bottoms of the seltzer bottles he shoulders all day, is one of the last survivors in his trade. The sound brings him back to his father's time, when seltzer bottlers were scattered all over Brooklyn and the Lower East Side, and the term "two cents plain" (a glass of naked seltzer) was a part of the vernacular of the city.

Walpow purchases his seltzer at Gomberg Seltzer Works in Canarsie. Established in 1953 by Mo Gomberg and now run by his grandson Kenny, the company creates its bubbly offering with a Barnett and Foster Siphon Machine, built in London in 1910.

"Good seltzer should hurt," says Kenny of the mixture of tap water and carbon-dioxide gas (no salts or minerals added). "The term we use is 'bite.' When you swallow it, you feel the bubbles in your throat and it's like painful."

At Gomberg Seltzer Works, New York tap water is first triple-filtered, making it conceivably the purest water anywhere, and then cooled, which facilitates carbonation. Once in the carbonator, the water is beaten with a series of rotating paddles so vigorously that its molecules bind together. The bottles are filled in an upside-down position at seventy pounds per square inch; a machine depresses the lever on the siphon, forcing seltzer to rush upward through the nozzle.

Gomberg does not claim his product is superior to the numerous store-bought seltzers that have taken over the market, nor does he deny it. Instead he grabs a newly filled seltzer bottle from the sputtering machine. It's a special one: old, dark-green, hand-blown in Czechoslovakia, seamless, with half-inch sides and a bottom almost an inch thick—antique dealers have been known to pay as much as forty dollars for a classic bottle. He raises the bottle high above his head and sprays a stream directly into his mouth, as if to ask, How can a twenty-two-ounce plastic bottle possibly compare?

Walter Backerman of Queens, a third-generation seltzer man and a factotum for all things seltzer-related, puts it more explicitly: "Look, when you open store-bought, there's pressure leaking out—it's flat by the time you hit the bottom. With seltzer squirted out of a siphon, the valve is only open long enough to let it out—no excess gas escapes." He pauses. "Besides, you think the flimsy bottles they use can handle serious pressure?" (*Pressure* is a major word when you're talking to a seltzer man.)

Backerman goes on to expound on the finer points of his trade, but he keeps returning to the main theme: "Don't ever underestimate the power of nostalgia." For seltzer men and for others who relish drinking seltzer the old-fashioned way, it's about connecting with your roots.

In the 1920s in New York, soda water gradually became known as seltzer—two different names for the same product. The word *seltzer* originates from the German *Selterser Wasser*, meaning mineral water from Nieder Selters, Prussia. Immigrants from eastern Europe brought the word from their homeland, and it stuck.

There has always been a strong association between seltzer and Jews, who were often the purveyors of seltzer. Once explanation for its popularity among Jews is that it complements the rich foods found in kosher diets. This may be a polite way of saying that it makes you belch. In the old days, seltzer was called "*Belchwasser*" or "Jewish champagne." But the ethnic makeup of customers ran across the board: Polish, Irish, and especially Italian.

Back when everybody drank the stuff, Barry Walpow's father, Sam, delivered seltzer with a horse-drawn wagon before graduating to a truck with a hand-cranked engine. Sam, the son of Jewish immigrants from Russia, was like any other young man in Brooklyn at that time, hungry to get ahead and willing to work as hard as it took.

"My father was a workaholic," Walpow says, taking in the old, peeling walls of the Seaview Diner. "He never took a day off, even on the holiest holidays." Then, one Yom Kippur morning, when Sam went to spin the hand crank on his truck, it kicked back and broke his arm. He saw it as an Act of God. From then on, he rested on Jewish holidays.

"In summer, as a kid, I used to ride shotgun while my father drove his route," Walpow remembers. "I learned all there was to know about seltzer from him. We covered every corner of Brooklyn—everybody was buying then." The elder Walpow even provided seltzer to a family in Flatbush with a little girl named Barbra Streisand.

The demise of the local seltzer industry occurred in the 1970s, when soft drink companies began to produce and market seltzer and club soda (carbonated water with sul-

fates), and designer mineral water became popular. Walpow doesn't quite buy it. "You wanna know what killed seltzer?" he says, poking at his rice pudding. "When the wives started working. No one was home to receive the order. The seltzer men couldn't leave their valuable product out in the open. Not that I got anything against women's lib," he adds carefully, "but it spelled the end for us."

The waitress places a glass of water in front of Walpow. He holds it up, examining it in the afternoon light, as if looking for bubbles that aren't there. "Now, I think everything's like fast food." He frowns, putting the glass down and pushing it aside. "Things have become less personalized."

Walpow has a loyal network of customers who rely on his product and appreciate what he's doing. Ke Wilde, a painter living in Williamsburg, says he's been getting his seltzer from Walpow for ten years. "Barry's such a nice guy and a classic character, you want to support him," says Wilde. "I got a daughter who is a little less than two, and now she calls for seltzer at every meal. She wants you to squirt it into her cup. She likes the whole experience."

Walpow rises up from the booth slowly. As he walks over to the cashier, his right shoulder slopes down, from several decades of schlepping seltzer crates. He heads outside toward his van, a decaying brown Econoline with the company name, Lots of Seltzer, Inc., printed on its flank. He climbs inside for his Canarsie-to-Williamsburg run.

Walpow parks at the corner of 79 Berry Street, in front of Oznot's Dish, a restaurant with a bohemian feel to it. The seltzer man and Oznot's seem an odd pairing at first, but inside the hip restaurant Walpow's bottles line a mosaic-tiled wall, exuding a retro-cool. He looks around at some of the chic, young patrons who are drinking his product like old-timers.

"One thing I know for sure," Walpow says with a smile. "You can't beat a little spritz of seltzer on a hot summer day."

Brooklyn Bridge, February 1999

NOTES

This chapter was first published as "Keeping the Seltzer Bottles Spritzing" in *Brooklyn Bridge*. It is reprinted with the permission of *Brooklyn Bridge*.

Candy Stores and Egg Creams

JILLIAN GOULD

How is it that certain foods disappear, and where do they go? Some dishes, like the Jewish delicacies *tschav* or *petcha*,[1] are true memory foods; they exist mostly in the mind's eye, seldom spoken about, rarely re-created. Other foods have a dual existence; they exist both in the present and in the past. These foods, such as a charlotte russe or an egg cream, can be found and prepared today, but for many people, to ingest these foods is to consume nostalgia.

Many New Yorkers, particularly Jews who grew up in Brooklyn between the 1920s and the 1950s, feel a strong connection to the egg cream; not only is it an important foodway into their childhood, but also the candy store itself—where egg creams were invented and served—was an important social center in countless Brooklyn neighborhoods. For many of these people, drinking egg creams, or even just hearing about them, initiates a storytelling pattern in which the narrative structure brings them back to a certain time in the past, as well as to a specific place: the candy store.

In an introductory letter for *The Brooklyn Cookbook*, Brooklyn borough president Howard Golden asks, "Where would we be without such Brooklyn originals as the egg cream?"[2] Golden may claim the egg cream as a Brooklyn original, but there is no evidence to back the statement up; in fact, theories of who invented the egg cream, where and when, and how it got its name are the subject of many great New York debates. And though it is less likely that egg creams were invented in Brooklyn, and more probable that they arrived with the influx of Jewish people from the Lower East Side to certain Brooklyn neighborhoods in the 1920s, 1930s, and 1940s, Brooklynites nevertheless feel a fierce pride toward the near mythic drink.

Most people agree that the ingredients of an egg cream contain milk, chocolate syrup, and seltzer—but proportions, order of ingredients, even the brand of chocolate syrup—are often points of contention. There are even regional variations in the preparation of the drink: in the Bronx, the seltzer goes in after the syrup, giving the drink a brownish head. A Brooklyn egg cream is always white on top. One woman recalls the egg cream of her youth, growing up in the 1940s. "I can see it in front of me," she says. "The top is frothy and white, like a whipped meringue. The bottom is chocolate." She opens her eyes and smiles. While there are no arguments about the ingredients of an egg cream, we are left to wonder how the egg cream got its name—for this is a drink that contains neither eggs nor cream.

There are some dissenters. Daniel Bell insists not only that his Uncle Hymie invented the egg cream but also that the drink originally contained both eggs and cream. In "The Original Egg Cream—Its Birth, Death and Transfiguration, or: The Creaming of Uncle Hymie," Bell declares: "I happen to know that the egg cream was invented 40 years ago by my Uncle Hymie. It did have egg and it did have cream. And when I was ten years old, I worked behind his soda counter serving egg creams."[3]

As this story goes, Uncle Hymie invented the egg cream at his candy store on Second Avenue and Eighth Street. His main item—like most candy store owners—was the chocolate soda, which was simply syrup and seltzer. While Uncle Hymie prepared his homemade chocolate syrup, he would sip a chocolate soda with a scoop of chocolate ice cream. As the ice cream melted, the drink became too rich, and Hymie would add extra seltzer to dilute it. This was the first variation of the egg cream: a chocolate cream soda made with syrup, seltzer, and melted chocolate ice cream. Prepared in large batches, however, the beverage would not hold together. Thereupon Uncle Hymie was inspired by the egg malted, in which the raw egg thickened the malted. Bell affirms: "And thus the egg cream was born. The chocolate cream soda sign went down, and in its place rose the new one: Hymie's Egg Cream—syrup and cream held together by real egg, plus seltzer. It was an instant success."[4]

Competitors, including another Hymie, whom Bell calls "the false Hymie," began to advertise their own egg creams. When the Depression hit, customers and store owners could no longer afford egg creams. Bell relays, "The false Hymie had found that he could dispense with the egg and the cream and, by putting in some milk and reversing the spigot of the seltzer machine, concentrate the pressure in a narrow, powerful carbonated stream so as to fizz up the liquid into a frothy drink which, to the unwary and the innocent, tasted something like the original egg cream." Of course, Uncle Hymie wanted nothing to do with this adulterated version of his creation, so he stopped selling egg creams. Ironically, if Bell is right, the false Hymie is the true inventor of the egg cream as we know it today. For it is his drink that continues to be consumed, and not the drink of the "real" Uncle Hymie. Or maybe we are all drinking false egg creams.

Another tale of invention comes from Stanley Auster. He is the grandson of the late Louis Auster, the candy store maven who, like Uncle Hymie, also invented the egg cream. According to Auster: "It all started because [his grandfather] wasn't happy with the soda he was selling. He was fooling around and he started mixing water and cocoa and sugar and so on, and somehow or other, eureka, he hit on something which seemed to be just perfect for him." He continues: "The name egg cream was really a misnomer. People thought there was cream in it, and they would like to think there was egg in it because egg meant something that was really good and expensive. There was never any egg, and there was never any cream. There were milk products, but not cream, although it looked and tasted creamy, because we also made a delicious chocolate syrup, which was the base drink."[5] Stanley Auster tells this story from his own personal experience. He worked in one of his grandfather's five candy stores on the Lower East Side in the 1930s and 1940s.

While Auster explains how the drink was created, he does not give an explanation for the origin of the name. In this way, a third component to the story comes in. How the following story originated is unclear, although certain versions of it blend into Auster's telling. It goes something like this: a Yiddish actor, some say it was Boris Thomashevsky, had a delicious drink in Paris called un chocolat et crème. When the actor returned to New York, he went to his local candy store (some say it was Auster's) with the recipe, and the proprietor reproduced the drink. With his Yiddish accent, however, the chocolat et crème became the chocolate egg cream. A slight variation on the story reveals that the candy store owner (again, it could have been Auster) had already concocted the drink soon to be known as the egg cream. The Yiddish actor returned from Paris, tasted the drink, and told the counterman about the chocolat et crème that tasted nowhere as good as the nameless New York drink. As result, the latter became known as the egg cream.

While most people agree that the egg cream has a history that is specific to New York, they are less likely to acknowledge that the drink has a Jewish history. Mysteriously, the Jewish roots of the egg cream get lost in its New York origins. When does this slippage occur, when something ethnic becomes closely identified with a city? Think of bagels, pickles, and the knishes that are sold on every corner at hot-dog carts. Even the soft pretzels that are sold on New York streets are said to be descended from bagel dough. Like the Jewish immigrants who invented the egg cream, the drink itself has gone through a process of assimilation.

At the turn of the century, hundreds of thousands of immigrant Jews from eastern Europe made their first homes in America on New York's Lower East Side. Of course, living conditions were far from easy, and as soon as Jews were able to move away from the neighborhood, they did. They moved up—to the Bronx, Queens, uptown Manhattan; and of course, many moved to Brooklyn. As new Jewish neighborhoods flourished, so did the cultural amenities: synagogues, kosher butcher shops, grocery stores, and candy stores were abundant. While candy store owners—unlike kosher butchers—were not exclusively Jewish, a majority of them were. Moreover, it was common for Jewish immigrants to open small businesses, because minimal capital investments were needed. While many of these businesses were hit during the Depression, candy stores were thriving. One reason these shops survived is that they were not merely about a commodity. Rather, they were as much about the pivotal role they played within the community.

If today most people consider candy stores to be nowhere other than places to buy candy, sixty years ago they were an important element in the social fabric of many neighborhoods. These establishments were gathering places, meeting spaces, centers of the community. The store was the local communication center, offering telephone service, the newsstand, and a meeting place for the local kibitzers. What happened around the store crystallized what was happening in the neighborhood at large. Every block had at least one candy store, and often the store represented the customers who frequented it. Some catered more to students, others to adults. In this way, there is no typical candy store, because each was unique, depending on the clientele.

A woman in her midsixties is happy to tell me her candy store memories as she sips an egg cream. She is a regular egg cream customer at the Lexington Candy Shop and Luncheonette on the Upper East Side—a couple of times a week, and almost every day in the summer. I ask her if she knows of other candy stores/luncheonettes in the city that still serve egg creams. She does not know, but points to a middle-aged man ordering an ice cream. "I bet he'll know," she says. I ask him about egg creams. His face lights up. "Egg creams, I haven't had one of those since I was a kid." I ask him where he grew up. "Brooklyn," he replies. He begins to tell the story of the "candy store ritual" of his childhood. He says: "My father was a kosher cop—a kosher cop! Every Friday night after dinner, he'd send me to the candy store to pick up the evening paper. My friends and I would

hang around outside the store, and we'd always get an egg cream. Somehow, my father always found out, and I'd get in trouble for drinking milk after our meat dinner."

The man did not have to drink an egg cream in order to set off the narrative; rather, the very mention of the drink was enough to spark childhood memories. Furthermore, his story reveals once again the significance of place to the memory. The "candy store ritual" he describes is not unique. In fact, most of the male collaborators I interviewed over the age of fifty shared similar memories, including hanging out at the candy store and around the store—playing stickball, buying the evening paper for their parents, and drinking egg creams. The egg cream does not simply evoke temporal memories of "when we were young"; it also prompts spatial memories of the neighborhood candy store.

Often parents who grew up drinking egg creams in Brooklyn candy stores in the 1940s and 1950s want their children to share in their cultural experience, and egg creams are their surrogates. Most of the young people I interviewed had their first egg creams at home, prepared by their parents. Sipping the drink today brings about memories of childhood and home. For their parents, on the other hand, egg creams are condensed memories of a time and place that was the candy store, not home. The parents reproduce this lost past by way of the egg cream.

People from the younger generation have a dual, or shared, memory experience—that is, they have both their own personal memories of egg creams and their parents' memories, by egg cream proxy. Consider the college-age woman who is drinking an egg cream at Gem Spa in the East Village. I ask her when she had her first egg cream. She can't remember if it was at home or at Eisenberg's Sandwich Shop, a place as famous for its egg creams as for its tuna sandwiches. In any case, her narrative recalls both her own as well as her mother's childhood experiences drinking egg creams. "My parents used to take my sister and I out for egg creams when we were kids. Our mom grew up in Brooklyn. She always talked about the egg creams she had when she was a kid. She loved egg creams." When I ask why she likes egg creams, she responds: "I don't know—I've always had them. It's very New York. My friends from college [in New Hampshire] don't even know what an egg cream is. They wouldn't like it. It's weird—no eggs and no cream!"

It is clear from this exchange that egg creams evoke two sets of memories for the woman. One set is based on her mother's memories of the drink—"She always went to Schrafft's." Here the woman shares her mother's memory, one she will never know from experience; yet she is still able to feel nostalgic for the time when her mother was a little girl. The other set is grounded in her own recollections of drinking egg creams as a kid.

Another collaborator, Brooklynite Naomi Berkowitz, is a seventeen-year-old high school senior who grew up drinking egg creams at home in Marine Park. For Naomi, egg creams were as much a staple in her home as orange juice. She never considered egg creams unique until she realized that most of her classmates did not know what egg creams were. Naomi recalls having chocolate milk at friends' houses and wondering why they didn't put seltzer in their egg cream. Her reaction illustrates a different kind of egg cream memory: one of the past, though not attached to any romantic notions of that past. Naomi was aware that her parents drank egg creams when they were young, "but they drank Coke and milkshakes too," she explains. And though she heard all about candy stores, her egg creams were not wrapped up in nostalgia.

Oddly enough, not one of the collaborators discussed the taste of an egg cream. Appearance, method, and ingredients, yes. But the actual taste of an egg cream, no. The desire for the egg cream, then, is not for the "thing itself"; rather, it is for what it has come to represent: childhood, home, the "good old days." The egg cream is an intermediary of past-present. Can today's nontraditional flavored egg creams evoke the past as well? When I asked people what they thought about variations on the chocolate egg cream, such as cherry-, lime-, mango-, or tamarind-flavored drinks, most were quick to say that the unusual flavors could not possibly be egg creams. One gentleman, however, was able to keep his past egg creams separate from the present. "Of course I like a chocolate egg cream," he said. "But who's to say any of the other flavors aren't egg creams as well? An egg cream is an egg cream is an egg cream." But for those who use the drink as foodway into the past, an egg cream is not just an egg cream.

The introduction of new flavors raises some important issues. For example, mango and tamarind egg creams would not likely be found at the Lexington Luncheonette, Katz's Deli, or theme restaurants such as the Comfort Diner or the Brooklyn Diner—places that serve nostalgia on a plate. The customers who frequent those establishments are not looking for something new. They go to taste the "classics." Mango and tamarind egg creams are served, however, at Ray's Candy Store on Avenue A and Seventh Street. The flavors, which are popular in the Caribbean and Latin America, appeal to Caribbean-American and Latino residents in the neighborhood. Here is a new egg cream, for a new community. Could this be the Egg Cream Diaspora?

At the beginning of the essay I asked, How is it that certain foods disappear—and where do they go? Why is the egg cream a drink that is closely associated with nostalgia, while other drinks from the soda fountain days, such as malteds, milkshakes, or even flavored soda have become a part of the present? It seems the egg cream nearly vanished along with the "disappearance" of candy stores and the spread of bottled soft drinks. Willy Goldstein, a forty-something Brooklynite, muses on the staying power of the egg cream: "It contains all the basic elements of life," he says. "Milk, chocolate, and seltzer—what else is there?"

Today egg creams are taking on a new popularity. They are popping up in trendy restaurants, and intermixing with popular drinks of today, such as the "egg cream cappuccino" served at the Comfort Diner. Most intriguing, perhaps, is the latest attempt to mass-market nostalgia: a bottled drink called the Big Brooklyn Egg Cream Soda. If it takes off, who knows what might happen next? It could be the beginning of a new generation of egg cream drinkers.

NOTES

1. *Tschav* is a sour soup made from creamed sorrel. *Petcha* is calf's-foot jelly.

2. Lyn Stallworth and Rod Kennedy, Jr., *The Brooklyn Cookbook* (New York: Knopf, 1994).

3. Daniel Bell, "The Original Egg Cream," *New York* (March 8, 1971), 32–34.

4. Jeff Kisseloff, *You Must Remember This: An Oral History of Manhattan from the 1890s to World War II* (San Diego: Schocken, 1989), 60.

5. Kisseloff, *You Must Remember*, 61.

Street Games in Brooklyn

LAURA GREENBERG

The world has only four seasons, but on the streets of Brooklyn there were many more. They came and went like the weather, with no known cause. There was baseball card season, marble season, jacks, yo-yo, hopscotch, and handball season.

Sometimes we played pack, a poor kid's version of horseshoes. Packs were the heels of men's shoes, and we aimed them at designated sidewalk cracks. Whoever landed closest won. We never thought it odd or mysterious that men's shoe heels were suddenly strewn about our Canarsie neighborhood.

During territory season, all of us apartment-house kids crouched around a small plot of dirt in the alley behind the garbage cans. Taking turns, we each aimed a pocketknife into the earth. My friend Gloria clutched the knife handle with a tight fist, but she didn't have accurate aim. I threw like the boys did, holding the blade between my thumb and index finger, aiming with one eye closed, straight into the dirt. When the shiny metal of the blade sliced the hard-packed earth, the marbleized handle vibrated. The winner landed the knife so that without lifting it from the ground he could carve out the largest piece of territory. Looking back, it seems owning that small yet grand piece of earth for the few seconds before the dirt was smoothed over for the next round was more than enough compensation for our tiny apartments. The ground was smoothed over many times but my grains of earth knew who they were, and whenever I won a round of territory, the shape of my plot appeared in my drawings at PS 233 the next day.

World War II had ended five years earlier and war games were popular. The name of one game, "Babies in the air, Bulls rush" reminded me of my grandmother's stories of the Russian pogroms where Cossacks threw babies in the air and caught them on their bayonets. We played in the gutter of East Ninety-fifth Street between two facing driveways. There were two teams, the Enemies and the Allies. At the cry of "Babies in the air!" or "Bulls rush!" everyone ran to the opposite driveway while trying to avoid any contact with someone from the opposing team. Arguments erupted:

> "I tagged you, you're out!"
> "No, you didn't touch me."
> "Yes, I did."
> "Did not."
> "Did so."
> "Not."

These arguments were never resolved. Whoever lasted longer won. Running across the street without checking for cars provided our game with the thrill of real danger.

Sometimes we chalked scelly courts on the sidewalk in front of our four-story red brick apartment house. We divided a sidewalk cement square into zones of different value. Then, while we crouched on our hands and knees, we shot bottle caps into the different zones by pressing the nail of the index finger against the thumb and then flicking it against the edge of the upturned bottle cap, scraping our fingers against the sidewalk as we did so.

Sometimes we attached our heavy metal skates to the bottoms of our shoes with a skate key, buckled the leather ankle strap, and roller-skated in the gutter. We followed the paths of our chalked lines until a car came. Then we zoomed into the fender of a parked car and held on while we waited for it to pass.

We played sidewalk games on the corner of East Ninety-fifth Street and Avenue A. Our favorites were "Red light, Green light" and giant steps, both involving locomotion in spite of obstacles, perhaps our interpretation of life. The thrill of "Red light, Green light" was in being quick enough: to stop running in time when the person who was "it" called "Red light," and to dash fast enough during "Green light" to reach the front of the pack before the light changed. Giant steps also involved motion control, and just as in real life, if you followed the rules correctly you might get a chance to make them yourself. "It" called on you and told you how many and what kind of steps you could make to approach the goal, which is where "it" stood. If you remembered to ask "May I?" "it" granted you permission to proceed. You took either giant steps, baby steps, or umbrella steps (twirl steps with one finger extended to touch the top of your head). The first person to reach the area near "it" tried to tag "it" before anyone else and hopefully became "it" for the next round.

We didn't have a handball court, so we played against the brick wall of our apartment house. If the ball bounced at an angle off a windowsill or screen, it was called a Hindu and was a do-over.

I MAKE a shimeLecha in the
OLD man's BACK and
SOMEbody sticks it IN.

We all recited the heavily accented chant as we stood around the person who was "it." She hid her eyes in the crook of her elbow leaned against a street light, while one

Left to right: Harold Serebrenick, Gloria Rosenberg, Kalman Rubenstein, David Klieb; Michael Rosenberg (small boy in front, brother of Gloria Rosenberg); Laura Greenberg. Photo courtesy of Laura Greenberg.

of us slowly and rhythmically traced a circle on her back as we chanted. On the word IN, one of us poked a finger into the center of "its" back, the center of the traced circle. "It" turned around and leveled her eyes at each of us as we all held our index finger in our mouth and jumped up and down and hollered, as if nursing a sore finger. "It" had to guess which one of us had poked her. If she was correct, she had the honor of maintaining her status and getting poked again. If she was wrong, the person who poked her became "it" and the game continued.

A grandchild of a Russian immigrant, I had heard stories of Cossacks and pogroms. Were my friends and I, two generations and half a world away, dramatizing what the soldiers did to our ancestors with their bayonets?

Our long summer afternoons were punctuated by the sounds of the ice cream truck bells. It was either the Good Humor Man or Bungalow Bill. Good Humor had better ice cream but Bungalow Bill had a better truck, with a sloped shingled roof and a chimney, just like a bungalow house. When I heard the bells I ran to the part of my apartment house that was under my kitchen window and hollered "Ma!" as loudly as I could. When she stuck her head out the window I yelled, "Money for ice cream!" Her head disappeared for a minute, then she threw down either a nickel and a dime, a dime and five pennies, a nickel and ten pennies, or even fifteen pennies. The money was wrapped in a torn-off piece of a brown paper grocery bag that sometimes opened on impact, sending me scrambling to collect the change before the truck pulled away. Fifteen cents bought a pop, or a cone, or almost anything.

David Lieb lived down the hall in my apartment building. His mother, Lucy, was a terrific gossip and stared at you through magnifying eyeglasses, pushed you gently on the shoulder with an open hand, and shouted "Go 'way!" in a singsong voice whenever you told her anything. David's apartment was light and airy, with no curtains, and linoleum in every room, even the living room. This made me wonder if they were really Jewish. On rainy summer days we went to David's apartment because everybody in his family was at work. We gathered in the living room, where we had kissing contests. While one couple kissed, the rest of us shouted "One Mississippi, two Mississippi," and so on. Gloria and I, the only girls, didn't get to do much counting. David and I were the champs, although his lips were hard and cold as the linoleum. We figured out a way to keep our lips touching yet leave one corner open so we could breathe.

On rainy Saturdays when we couldn't play outside, my mother packed two salami sandwiches on rye in a wrinkled brown paper bag, and I met my friends at the Waldorf Theater on Church Avenue for a day at the movies. Starting with the first show at ten in the morning, we watched *Movietone News*, cartoons, and the double feature. Then we watched it all over again. One feature was always a Western, filled with the sound of cowboys' ricocheting bullets. The sound had two parts: the report of the gun and then that lovely zing when the bullet bounced off something instead of hitting its target. If the bullet bounced off metal the echo had a clear ring to it, but rocks gave it a more dusty resonance. When we imitated the sound of gunshots with our ker-pows, the ushers sometimes tried to quiet us with their flashlight beams. If they flashed the pale beam on the screen we booed, but they mostly left us alone because no one was in the theater except us noisy kids. Leaving the dark theater in the late afternoon felt like arriving back in Brooklyn from very far away. The time and space of the day had gone by without me, and I enjoyed the foreign feeling in the familiar streets.

Poultry in Motion
The Jewish Atonement Ritual of Kapores

AVIVA WEINTRAUB

Immediately following Rosh Hashanah, the Jewish New Year, are the Ten Days of Repentance (*aseres y'may t'shuva*), a period that serves as a window of opportunity for intensive atonement, culminating in the holy day of fasting and prayer, Yom Kippur. One available vehicle for repentance is the ritual known as *shlogn kapores*, and while kapores is not widely practiced, it is quite common in Hasidic communities in Brooklyn.

Kapores (in Yiddish; *kapparot* in Hebrew) literally means atonements. The kapores ritual involves revolving a chicken around one's head while reciting passages from Psalms and declaring, "This fowl is my substitute, this is my surrogate, this is my atonement." Some texts add, "May it be designated for death, and I for life." Or a variant, ". . . this cock (or hen) shall meet death, but I shall find a long and pleasant life of peace." After the ceremony, the fowl is slaughtered and customarily donated to charity or eaten by the family.

From Rosh Hashanah through the day before Yom Kippur, throughout Crown Heights, Borough Park, and Williamsburg, "ad hoc" kapores centers are set up. Photocopied signs go up around the neighborhoods, and the *Jewish Press* carries many ads listing these centers, which spring up on empty lots, in alleys between stores, and on sidewalks. Bright red and yellow plastic crates of live chickens are stacked on the ground. The sound—and the stench—are recognizable from quite a distance. Copies of the prayers are handed out or tacked to makeshift walls. It is customary for men and boys to use roosters, while women and girls use hens. Many groups of families came to *shlog kapores*. Sometimes the men hold the chickens for their wives and daughters; boys are encouraged to hold the chickens themselves. A woman who is pregnant uses two chickens: one for herself and one for her unborn child. After the prayers are said, the chicken is handed back to an attendant who takes it to be ritually slaughtered, often by an on-site *shoykhet* (slaughterer) in an enclosed area nearby.

In these Brooklyn kapores centers, the charity aspect of donating the chickens is emphasized. Many centers offer to donate the chickens directly to Tomche Shabbos of Boro Park and Flatbush, a charitable organization that delivers food for *shabbos* (Sabbath) meals to the needy, or to other institutions.

Though the ritual is meant to be a solemn, even awe-inspiring one, there tends to be an air of festivity around the kapores centers. Several factors contribute to this. Hasidim favor large, often extended, families, members

ב"ה

KAPAROT

THIS YEAR, G-D WILLING,
KAPAROT AND SHECHITA
WILL BE CONVENIENTLY LOCATED
ON THE CORNER OF
AVENUE M AND
CONEY ISLAND AVENUE

SHECHITA PERFORMED
BY THE FAMOUS SHOCHET
RABBI YEHUDAH BEN SHIMON
WHO HAS OVER 20 YEARS EXPERIENCE
AND IS WELL KNOWN IN AMERICA AND ISRAEL

ALL CHICKENS WILL BE GIVEN TO CHARITY

HOURS		
TUESDAY 12AM TO 10PM	WEDNESDAY 11AM TO 10PM	THURSDAY 10AM TO 12PM
FRIDAY 8AM TO 3PM	SATURDAY 9PM TO 1AM	SUNDAY 8AM TO 2PM

PRICE: $10

Advertising chickens for the Ten Days of Repentance. From "Jewish Rituals" series. © Michael Macioce, used by permission of the photographer.

of which usually go to *shlog kapores* together. A group activity such as this can take on the air of an outing. While some children are intimidated by the squawking of the chickens, some (mostly boys) seem eager to play with the animals.

Since the kapores centers are by and large outdoors, in public space, a street fair atmosphere of sorts prevails, and provides an opportunity to see friends and neighbors. While neither as playful nor as prevalent as the revels during Purim, kapores stamps a distinct Jewish presence in this period between Rosh Hashanah and Yom Kippur.[1] And though kapores as a custom may be marginal, it is quite visible when performed on the sidewalk.[2] Many families go from the kapores centers to nearby Judaica

shops for the annual purchase of the *lulav* and *esrog*, ritual flora to be used in the coming weeks during the holiday of Sukkot. Since the buying of these items is a mitzvah, there is added incentive to purchase them during the Ten Days of Repentance.

Within Jewish communities, *shlogn kapores*, particularly with live chickens, is associated with Hasidim, who in New York are concentrated in several Brooklyn neighborhoods. This article primarily examines kapores as it is practiced in the Borough Park region of Brooklyn by several Hasidic groups including Bobover, Skver, Vishnitz, and others. Kapores centers can also be found in other Brooklyn neighborhoods including Flatbush, Williamsburg, and Crown Heights.

While many American Jews practiced kapores with chickens through the 1930s, as customs that were considered "old-world" began to be left behind, money was commonly used in this ceremony instead of live chickens. Among Hasidim, too, a shift from chickens to money also occurred as money was seen as a perfectly legitimate alternative.

Using live chickens for kapores is currently very popular in Borough Park. Dr. Philip Kipust, director of the Borough Park Historical Society, suggests that this might reflect a general increase in commitment to religious practice in the Jewish community in this area. As Hasidic Jews look for ways to do the best and most pious possible mitzvahs, doing kapores with live chickens offers an opportunity for greater and more direct participation in this act. He also points to the dramatic nature of using a live bird, and the added level of feeling that a participant may experience.

Since most people *shlog kapores* in the street, there is also a feeling of community participation. Though it is difficult to say which came first ("the chicken and the egg," forgive the pun), the proliferation of kapores centers has made it easier than ever to *shlog* with a live chicken. Through the 1960s and 1970s, those wishing to use a live chicken would purchase one from a local butcher. The ceremony would take place in or near the butcher shop, and if the family wanted to take the bird home to cook, the butcher would oblige. In the past ten years or so, the practice of kapores has become institutionalized, some would even say commercialized, as different centers compete with one another for business.

It is somewhat ironic that today it is the younger generation that practices kapores using the method of the "Old

Practicing shlogn kapores. From "Jewish Rituals" series. © Michael Macioce, used by permission of the photographer.

Country," while the older members of the same community may use money for their *kapores* ritual. It is possible that some younger Jews are drawn to using chickens for nostalgic reasons, a desire to be closer to the Judaism of their grandparents' time. For many, however, this is simply part of a larger general shift to a more conservative, more fundamental observance of Jewish law. It is part of a package of many religious practices, including for instance the tendency of older Hasidim to refrain from geting drunk on Purim, while younger Hasidic Jews do (in observance of an edict), and the tendency of the younger generation to wear tzitzis on the outside of their clothing, as visible evidence of their piety.

Many of the Ultra-Orthodox Jews living in Brooklyn are *baaley tshuva*, Jews who have gone through a repentance experience and have become Orthodox though they may have been raised in entirely secular Jewish homes. For these Jews, using a chicken for kapores may be seen as providing a more "authentic," hence more spiritual Jewish experience, though there is probably an equal level of observance of this custom among *baaley tshuva* and those in the same neighborhoods who are "*frum* [observant] from birth."

MARKETING THE CHICKENS

The *Jewish Press*, a weekly newspaper that mainly serves Orthodox and Ultra-Orthodox communities, carries many ads for kapores. Hand-drawn chickens frame the invitation, "Come shlog kaporos" (*shlogn* in Yiddish literally means to beat; here it functions to say, come do kapores). Beneath it is written, "All chickens and proceeds are donated to *Tzedoka* (charity for the poor)." The ad for the Kapores Center of Boro Park–Flatbush proclaims: "Live Chickens For *Kapores*. You can pick up your Koshered Chicken the next day or you can donate it to *Tomche Shabbos* of B.P. and Flatbush or to whichever *Mosed* [institution] you prefer. Remember we are the only *kapores* center with a *shochet* [ritual slaughterer] on premises every day. Make sure you come to a place where there are no doubts about where your chicken is going!"

The majority of text in the newspaper ads is in English. A Yiddish phrase of good wishes for the New Year is sometimes appended. Yiddish or Hebrew words appear in English transliteration, when a Jewish concept is refered to, as in *mosed* and *shochet* above. This written "code-switching" mirrors speech patterns in this community, in

Practicing shlogn kapores. From "Jewish Rituals" series. © Michael Macioce, used by permission of the photographer.

which English is liberally peppered with Yiddish words and phrases.

This is taken a step further in advertisements whose intended audience is even more circumscribed. A photocopied sign that was taped to a telephone pole in Borough Park is almost exclusively in Yiddish. While the prices and address of the kapores center are provided (albeit misspelled) in English, the Yiddish text contains reassurances that each individual gets his/her own "fresh" chicken, that is, a chicken that has not already been used by someone else for their kapores.

Despite its controversial standing, the practice of the kapores ceremony continued over the centuries among Jews around the world. It is important to understand that kapores is classified as a *minhag* (custom) and not a religious commandment. Many Jews who practice kapores at all today swing coins about their heads and then give the money directly to charity, eliding the direct contact with and subsequent slaughter of the chicken.[3]

Whereas many Jewish rituals such as the seder, *tashlikh*,

and *bris* have been adopted and reinvented by Jewish feminists and other Jewish subcultures, kapores has yet to engage these groups.[4] Perhaps a return to the earlier, vegetarian version (beans in a basket) would allow for renewed interest in the practice of *shlogn kapores*.

Kapores has always been a marginal custom, tolerated if not forbidden by the Jewish establishment, encouraged only by mystics. Today it is practiced (with chickens) mostly among Hasidim and *ba'alei t'shuva*, notably in many neighborhoods of Brooklyn. Located somewhere between street fair and religious duty, the appearance of brightly colored crates of chickens is among the local signifiers of the coming of the Jewish New Year.

NOTES

1. Cf. Barbara Kirshenblatt-Gimblett, "Performance of Precepts/Precepts of Performance: Hasidic Celebrations of Purim in Brooklyn," in *By Means of Performance: Intercultural Studies of Theatre and Ritual*, ed. Richard Schechner and Willa Appel (Cambridge: Cambridge University Press, 1990), 109–17.

2. Given the multiethnic makeup of a neighborhood like Crown

Practicing shlogn kapores. From "Jewish Rituals" series. © Michael Macioce, used by permission of the photographer.

Heights and recent, well-publicized incidents of racial confrontations and violence in the streets, this is not an insignificant event. In 1994, the West Indian–American Day Parade, which is always held on Labor Day, coincided with Rosh Hashanah. An article in *The New York Times* of 2 September quoted a police chief as saying, "The trick . . . is to insure that members of the Hasidic Lubavitch movement can prepare for Rosh ha-Shanah while floral-bedecked floats, steel bands and costumed celebrants parade down Eastern Parkway, and then to make sure revelers are off the streets by sundown so Jewish worshipers can go to synagogue." Ownership of the streets in Crown Heights is constantly being contested and negotiated.

3. In households that substitute money for a live animal, coins that add up to a total of eighteen (the numerical value of the word *Chai*, which means life, in Hebrew) are usually used. Eighteen and multiples thereof are popular denominations to give to charity, and carry a symbolic reference to wishes for a long life.

4. Aviva Weintraub, "'We Don't Dis Tradition': A Passover Performance of Jewish Identities," paper delivered at Jewish Folklore: The Challenge of Traditional Identities, a conference at UCLA at the Armand Hammer Museum, 9 February 1997.

Suits and Souls
Trying to Tell a Jew When You See One in Crown Heights

HENRY GOLDSCHMIDT

One of the first things visitors to Crown Heights often notice, just walking down Eastern Parkway, Kingston Avenue, or any other busy block, are the gazes and glances that follow them down the street. The streets of Crown Heights are shot through with lines of sight, as the Afro-Caribbean immigrants, African-Americans, and Hasidic Jews who live in the neighborhood check each other out. Contrary to the sensational media image of black-Jewish conflict during the violence of August 1991, Crown Heights is generally a peaceful neighborhood, where some 170,000 blacks, 12,000 Jews, and others live together as intimate strangers, sharing the streets at a respectful distance. But it is undoubtedly a nervous neighborhood, where blacks and Jews look at each other from across a racialized divide—wondering about each other's lives, trying to make sense of their neighbors' actions, and looking for clues to the identities of strangers. But these "identities" are not always easy to see. How, for example, do Crown Heights residents know when they are looking at a Jew? What clues do they look for? What catches their eyes?

I often posed these question to Lubavitch Hasidim from Crown Heights as they did the kind of outreach work that Lubavitchers are known for worldwide: asking passersby in Manhattan if they are Jewish, and encouraging them in Orthodox observance and Lubavitch beliefs. How, I wondered, do they decide whom to stop and ask: "Excuse me, are you Jewish?" One yeshiva student tried to explain: "It's just something up here," he said, gesturing toward his face: "It's just a look." Then he held a hand up by his forehead, stretched out his fingers like beams of light, and said: "It's the *neshoma* [the Jewish soul]. . . . It just shines out."

In the luminous world of Hasidic thought, the soul of a Jew is fundamentally different from that of a non-Jew. Its spiritual roots lie in a wholly different realm of godliness, in a higher realm that reveals a greater degree of God's pure light. This "Godly Soul" sets Jews apart from non-Jews, ties them directly to their God and His Torah, and exudes a spiritual radiance that makes every Jew, quite literally, "a light unto the nations" (Isaiah 42:6). And a young yeshiva student claimed to apply this mystical vision of Jewish identity to the hustle and bustle of New York street life, picking Jews out of a crowd, regardless of what they may look like—be they secular or Orthodox, male or female, Ashkenazic or Sephardic, black or white—by a visible quality of their souls. In practice, of course, things are not quite so simple. But this vision of a luminous Jewish soul says a great deal about the beliefs of Lubavitchers in Crown Heights—about the clarity Lubavitchers imagine, and struggle to produce, at the heart of Jewish identity.

TWO JEWS, TWO SCENES, ONE SEEN

Jewish visibility has sometimes been an urgent, practical concern for Jews in Crown Heights. On August 19, 1991, the first night of the Crown Heights riots, it was a matter of life and death. The riots began after a car in the motorcade of the Lubavitcher rebbe—the spiritual leader of Lubavitch Hasidism—struck two black children, Gavin and Angela Cato, killing Gavin instantly. Some three hours after the accident, shouts pierced the summer night at the corner of President Street and Brooklyn Avenue. By the pallid glow of a streetlight, refracted through humid night air, an African-American man named Charles Price saw an Orthodox Jew named Yankel Rosenbaum, and called out to a crowd of ten to twenty rioters: "There's one! Get him!" "There's a Jew! Get the Jew!" The crowd surrounded Rosenbaum and started beating him; a sixteen-year-old boy named Lemrick Nelson stabbed him four times. Rosenbaum died of his wounds later that night. The deaths of Gavin Cato and Yankel Rosenbaum sparked the Crown Heights riots—three days of violence that a government report called "the most widespread racial unrest to occur in New York City in more than twenty years" (Girgenti 1993,132).[1]

Without diminishing the tragedy of these deaths, I want to step back a bit and ask a question that may seem a bit obtuse. When Charles Price first saw Yankel Rosenbaum, how did he know that Rosenbaum was a Jew? Even in the absence of a Jewish soul "shin[ing] out," the answer seems quite simple; as the attorney who prosecuted Price and Nelson in 1997 noted in her opening statement to the court: "Yankel Rosenbaum was an Orthodox Jew, and he was readily identifiable as Jewish by his beard and yarmulke." Like most Jewish men in Crown Heights, he bore a number of highly specific visual signs: a full beard and light skin; a black yarmulke, light blue button-down shirt, and black pants, with the fringes, or tzitzis, of his tallis katan hanging out over his belt. This was not exactly the "typical" dress of a Lubavitch Hasid—and Rosenbaum was not a Lubavitcher—but it was pretty close. It was the visual image that Charles Price had in mind when he went to "Get the Jew."

The significance, and the specificity, of this "Jewish" image will become clearer if we compare the murder of Yankel Rosenbaum to another act of violence against an Orthodox Jew in Crown Heights. On May 29, 1988, on a lazy Sunday afternoon, children were playing on the sidewalk of President Street between Utica and Schenectady Avenues, and an eight-year-old black girl snatched a ball away from a Hasidic toddler. As happens sometimes in Crown Heights, violence escalated from this innocent exchange. The toddler's father shoved the young black girl to the ground, and the young girl's teenage cousin came to her aid, confronting the Hasidic man. He then shoved and punched this teenage girl, knocking out one of her teeth. But the Hasid didn't and couldn't know—or could he? and if not, why not?—that the teenage girl he'd punched out was an African-American Orthodox Jew, an honor student at a high school affiliated with Yeshiva University.

Ten years later, I discussed this incident with an older sister of the girl who was punched, showing her an article about the assault in the *New York Amsterdam News* (Browne 1988). She spoke of it passionately, describing how her sister ran upstairs to their apartment, bleeding from her mouth and carrying her tooth, and how their father held her back as she tried to run downstairs to avenge her sister. Finally, she told me how the Hasid who had punched her sister apologized, profusely and repeatedly, once the whole thing was sorted out: "I'm so sorry!" he cried to her and her family: "I didn't know she was Jewish! I'm so sorry! I didn't know!"[2]

Already then, the simple clarity of "It just shines out" has dissolved, or fractured, into a jarring disjuncture between "There's one! Get him!" and "I'm so sorry! I didn't know!" One Jew was attacked on the streets of Crown Heights because his Jewishness was clearly visible, while another was attacked because hers was not. What are we to make of this difference and the deeper tensions in Jewish identity and visibility that it points to? According to a widely shared, commonsense view of Jews and identity, both Charles Price and the Hasidic father were simply responding the empirical facts of Jewishness in Crown Heights: light skin, a beard, and a yarmulke usually indicate a Jew, while dark skin, nappy hair, and casual clothes usually do not. But these typical images cannot be taken as straightforward facts. There is no necessary or essential reason why a white man with a beard and a yarmulke should "look Jewish," while a black girl in casual clothes should not.[3] And yet, as I will show, there are many historical, social, and cultural reasons why this is the case in today's Crown Heights. In the rest of this essay I will examine the views of race and gender that make the Jewishness of Hasidic men visible in Crown Heights, while relegating the Jewishness of black Jews and Hasidic women to relative invisibility. I will begin with a short look at a long coat.

LONG BLACK COATS: VISIONS OF JEWS IN CROWN HEIGHTS

Perhaps more than any other item of their social life and material culture, the black suits, black hats, and black coats worn by many Hasidic men have become a visual icon of the Hasidic communities of Brooklyn. In Crown Heights, Williamsburg, and Borough Park, black coats mark the presence of Hasidic Jews. In the very first line of *Holy Days*, her popular account of Hasidic life in Crown Heights, Lis Harris uses the well-worn image of a well-worn coat to capture the "strange spectacle" of Hasidic men celebrating Simchas Torah in front of the Lubavitcher rebbe's shul at 770 Eastern Parkway:

> In the small hours of a cold fall morning, when most of Brooklyn was asleep, some five thousand bearded, dark-hatted men, wearing nearly identical dark suits and coats, danced around a decrepit synagogue, arms clasped. (Harris 1985, 9)

Like many other secular New Yorkers, Harris projects preconceived images of Hasidic life onto the ready-made screen of a long black coat: "they" all look alike, and so different from "us," like someone's great-grandfather, from another time, escaped from a sepia-toned photograph. Let me be clear: Brooklyn's Hasidim are not survivals from another time; in their own ways, they are very much a part of twenty-first-century American society. But, in fact, they do dress differently from other Americans. In certain ways, they tend to look alike. There are diverse customs and styles of dress in the various Hasidic communities, but there is a certain Hasidic "look."

The Lubavitch Hasidim of Crown Heights have never dressed in the elaborate garb that characterizes many Hasidim in Williamsburg and Borough Park. Even in the nineteenth century, Lubavitchers dressed a bit less distinctively than other Hasidim and a bit more like the surrounding Gentile communities. Lubavitch men do not wear the stockings, knickers, and slippers that certain other Hasidim wear (in the fashion of eighteenth-century Polish nobles, according to some scholars [Rubens 1967, 125–32]). Very few Lubavitch men wear the long peyos, or side-locks, that are typical of other Hasidim—and fascinating to so

Lag b'Omer celebration in Crown Heights. Photo © Miriam Rubinoff, used by permission.

many secular observers. Even on Shabbos and holidays they do not wear streimels, the lavish round fur hats favored by most other Hasidim. Indeed, Lubavitchers are often criticized by other Hasidim for being too "liberal" and "modern" in their dress—and much else. But there is still a Lubavitch look, to which many Lubavitch men conform, or aspire. Following their rebbe (who continues to set the tone in dress and much else in Crown Heights, even after his death in 1994), most Lubavitch men wear relatively simple black fedoras on top of their black velvet yarmulkes; some make a point of denting the crowns of their fedoras just so, so that they fold in a triangle rather than a straight line—just like the rebbe's. They wear simple black suits in all weather, usually single-breasted and always buttoned with the right side over the left—as the right side represents God's kind mercy, while the left represents God's strict judgment, and one always wants mercy to win out over judgment. Most wear plain white dress shirts under their suits, usually with stiff buttonless collars, and rarely with ties. The fringes, or tzitzis, of their tallis katan (fringed undergarments) are usually worn hanging out over their black slacks. Like other Hasidim, many Lubavitch men wear their beards long and unkempt, not trimmed in any way. Yet despite his full beard and strict observance of rabbinic law and Hasidic custom, the "typical" Lubavitch man looks more like an American businessman of the 1950s than a Polish nobleman of the 1750s.

And of course, Lubavitch men often depart from this typical norm. Many younger men wear fashionably cut suits, sometimes in gray or muted colors. In the summer, while on vacation, some are even rumored to wear shorts — though the rebbe himself found this a bit scandalous (Dalfin, ed. 1998, 9). Some men trim their beards, and a few go clean-shaven (removing their beards with depilatories or electric razors, so as not to break the unequivocal law against shaving). Some wear darkly colored fedoras, or other hats; and a few wear no head covering beyond their yarmulke. A neighbor of mine when I lived in Crown Heights had a huge black cowboy hat, which he wore to see the country music star Garth Brooks play in Central Park, and joked that he would one day wear to shul—much to his wife's chagrin. As in all communities, religious and secular, there are substantial variations on many social norms in the Lubavitch community, including norms of dress.

But these variations on the typical Lubavitch look are usually limited to private or profane spheres of everyday social life. In general, the more an individual Hasid is acting as a part of the community—in public, ritual settings—the more he or she is expected to look the part. Nearly all Lubavitch men, regardless of how they dress during the week, have special clothes set aside for Shabbos and holidays—a newer black suit, a nicer black hat, and a clean white shirt. So in Crown Heights synagogues, one sees an ocean of men in more or less identical black hats and coats, a Hasidic community performing an image of solidarity and uniformity that does not hold in quite the same way during the rest of the week. This image sets Hasidim apart from other Jews—or at least it seems to, by drawing a line in the shifting sands of Jewish identity, and imposing a simple visual opposition on community boundaries that are actually far more complex.

These Hasidic styles reflect a long history of struggle and debate over Jewish dress and identity. In medieval Europe—as in contemporary Brooklyn—there were some strictly observant Jews who chose to set themselves apart by wearing distinctive clothing, while other Jews wore clothes similar to those of their Gentile neighbors (for examples see Rubens 1967, 91–124). But contemporary Brooklyn is not medieval Europe, and the cultural politics of distinctive Jewish dress are substantially different in these different contexts. Medieval Christian rulers often decreed that Jews and Muslims must wear distinctive clothes, or brightly colored badges, to prevent them from passing unnoticed into European Christian societies. American society, however, has encouraged Jewish assimilation to mainstream norms of dress—and most everything else. European Jews arriving in the United States in the nineteenth and twentieth centuries faced pressure from Jewish and Gentile authorities—and their own desires—to conform to American norms and fashions (for examples see Schreier 1994).

The process of Jewish assimilation to American society was hardly as simple or inevitable as images of the American "melting pot" would have us believe. But nevertheless, by 1940, when the previous Lubavitcher rebbe arrived in New York City fleeing the Holocaust, and brought his community to Crown Heights, the vast majority of New York's Jews had adapted American norms in many ways. Crown Heights at this time was, by and large, home to a Jewish immigrant elite. Despite substantial diversity in social class and religious observance, the neighborhood was known for its middle-class "alrightniks"—Jews who were financially well off and culturally assimilated. In his memoir of life in nearby Brownsville, Alfred Kazin quipped that these Crown Heights Jews, "were . . . Gentiles to me as they went out into the wide and tree-lined Eastern Parkway" (Kazin 1951, 9). In this milieu, the handful of Hasidim living in Crown Heights stuck out like a proverbial sore thumb. The art historian Linda Nochlin, who grew up in Crown Heights in the 1930s and 1940s, later recalled the uncanny image a group of Hasidim at prayer presented to her assimilated eyes; she described "seeing Them crowded together, like black beetles, bowing and mumbling, little men wearing odd, identifiable garments, so different from my . . . grandfather's white linen summer suit and jaunty straw boater" (Nochlin 1996, xvii). Already, by the 1930s, the black coats of Hasidic men in Crown Heights were an object of secular curiosities and fantasies—fantasies that sometimes cast "Them" as "black beetles" whose very humanity seemed in doubt.[4]

By 1950, when Menachem Mendel Schneerson became the Lubavitcher rebbe (following the death of his father-in-law, the previous rebbe), Crown Heights was far more Jewish than it had been in the 1930s. Many of the Irish and Italians who had shared the neighborhood with Jews moved out after World War II; they were replaced by secular Jews moving up in the world from other neighborhoods, and by a few thousand Hasidim—Lubavitchers and others—who arrived in Crown Heights as Holocaust refugees. These Hasidim settled in Crown Heights because it was a predominantly Jewish neighborhood, but the black coats of Hasidic men distinguished them from their secular Jewish neighbors and marked them as exotic or disturbing interlopers. In this new context, the new Lubavitcher rebbe—who, it was rumored, had refused to wear a long black coat when he was a student at the Sorbonne in the 1930s (Weiner 1957, 238)—often pointed out that according to the Talmudic sages, the ancient Israelites had only merited redemption from Egypt for their refusal to change their names, language, and dress. And thus, the rebbe argued, distinctive Jewish clothes must remain a part of the community—and redemption—he would build in Crown Heights.

But the Hasidim were not the only new arrivals to Crown Heights in the 1940s and 1950s. The local African-American and Afro-Caribbean population increased fourfold between 1940 and 1957, by which point blacks made up some 25 percent of the neighborhood. These newcomers were hardly the first blacks to live in Crown Heights—indeed, the area was known as Crow Hill in the 1800s, a derogatory reference to the African-Americans ("crows") living in Weeksville and other communities—but they were the first to move, in large numbers, to what had since become a predominantly Jewish neighborhood. This was just the beginning of the dramatic demographic shift in Brooklyn and other American cities that created the "black inner city" and its "white suburbs." By 1970, the population of Crown Heights was about 70 percent black, and included a growing number of Afro-Caribbean immigrants. Most Jews left Crown Heights, and the rest of North Brooklyn, for South Brooklyn or the suburbs. The Lubavitchers were the only significant Jewish community to stay in Crown Heights—at the insistence of their rebbe, who declared his opposition to Jews leaving the neighborhood in a dramatic public address in the spring of 1969. Similar demographic trends continued through the 1970s and 1980s, and by 1990 the Lubavitch commu-nity of Crown Heights made up about 6 to 8 percent of an overwhelmingly black and predominantly Afro-Caribbean neighborhood.[5]

Thus, for the most part, today's Lubavitch Hasidim can be distinguished from their non-Jewish neighbors by skin color, hair texture, and the other bodily features that Americans use to make distinctions by "race." Although there are a number of black Orthodox Jews living in Crown Heights, as well as Sephardic Lubavitchers who may not seem "white" by current American racial standards, the Lubavitch Hasidim can generally be distinguished from their neighbors as "white" is from "black."[6] Yet even in this racially polarized context, Crown Heights Hasidim continue to be identified by their distinctive Jewish customs—including the distinctive dress of Hasidic men. As was the case in the 1930s, long black coats help define the differences between Hasidim and other Crown Heights residents. The symbolism attributed to them structures both positive and negative feelings toward the Hasidic community.

For example, as tensions between blacks and Hasidim developed in the late 1970s, some African-American leaders used images of black coats to paint a malevolent picture of the Lubavitch community. One of the first major Crown Heights conflicts broke out in June of 1978, following the beating by Hasidim of a sixteen-year-old black boy, whom some Hasidim alleged had accosted or assaulted an elderly Hasid (see Mintz 1992, 146–47). In demonstrations that summer, many black activists accused the neighborhood crime patrols organized by Hasidim since the 1960s of anti-black vigilante attacks. The activist pastor Reverend Herbert Daughtry cofounded the "Black Citizen's Patrol" and predicted—or perhaps threatened—gang violence between these black and Hasidic patrols. According to the *New York Post* (June 20, 1978) Daughtry told a crowd of black demonstrators on Eastern Parkway: "We will get the Jews and the people in the long black coats." Though Daughtry vehemently denies this provocative wording (Daughtry 1997, 37–45), he clearly saw the Hasidic community as a threat to black Crown Heights residents and imagined that threat wearing "long black coats." But as the conflict continued, Hasidim found ways to turn this popular image to their advantage. In the 1979 trial of two Hasidic men charged in the assault that sparked the conflicts of 1978, the suspects sat in the court gallery, surrounded by other Lubavitch men—all wearing black suits and full beards. Witnesses were thus hard-pressed to identify the accused, who were eventually acquitted on all counts (see Mintz 1992, 152). But Hasidim had claimed from the start that the suspects were innocent passersby, arrested by police who couldn't tell one Hasid from another. Either way, their black clothes and beards shaped their relationship with the legal system and their role in Crown Heights racial politics.

In sum, the distinctive features of Hasidic men's dress make the Jewishness of these men visually obvious to Jewish and non-Jewish observers alike. Moreover, many observers mistake this typical—or stereotypical—image for a simple, empirical fact. Bearded men in black coats thus tend to stand in for a Jewish community that is, in fact, far more diverse. This is why Yankel Rosenbaum was so clearly visible as a Jew on the first night of the Crown Heights riots. Though Rosenbaum was not a Lubavitcher, he looked close enough. The rioters easily understood Charles Price's command: "There's one! Get him!" Indeed, the violence in Crown Heights in August of 1991 was often structured by the criteria of Jewish visibility I have sketched. For example, a day after Rosenbaum's murder, a Lubavitcher named Isaac Bitton was attacked and severely beaten by a group of rioters. Bitton's black coat and beard made him an object of violence despite the fact that he was a Moroccan Sephardic Jew with "olive" skin, who had long identified and associated with black Jews, and had sometimes faced prejudice from white Lubavitchers. Fortunately for Bitton, however, he was able to flee Crown Heights the next day, hiding in the backseat of a car driven by a neighbor—an African-American Orthodox Jew who does not dress like a Hasid and was not recognized as a Jew by the rioters.

Finally, the power of these images of the "typical" Crown Heights Jew was eerily confirmed in the murder of Anthony Graziosi on September 5, 1991, about two weeks after the riots. Graziosi—a sixty-seven-year old Italian-American salesman from Queens—had stopped his car at a red light in north Crown Heights when he was attacked by four black men, and shot to death. The only man tried for the murder was acquitted in 1992, so the identity and intent of Graziosi's killers may never be clear. But his family's attorneys claimed that Anthony Graziosi was killed because he looked like a Hasidic Jew—he had a full beard and was wearing a black suit. Even in the absence of a Jewish soul, a black suit "just shines out."

COLORED KIPPAHS AND MODEST SKIRTS: EVIDENCE OF JEWS NOT SEEN

As I have argued, not all Jews are equally visible as Jews—at least not in the eyes of all observers. The same popular images that led a group of black men to mistake an Italian-American from Queens for a Jew from Crown Heights also lead many observers to overlook the Jewishness of Crown Heights residents who are in fact Jews. For example, the Hasid who punched a black Orthodox girl in 1988 would surely have known he was facing a fellow Jew if he had been arguing with a bearded White man in a black suit, but the Jewishness of a black girl in casual clothes was not quite as clear to him.

There has never been a very large number of black Jews in Crown Heights, but there has been a small community since at least the early 1970s.[7] Their numbers have fluctuated from about twenty families in the late 1970s to a half dozen or so families today. For a few years in the 1970s an African-American rabbi named Avraham Coleman led a predominantly black synagogue and yeshiva on Crown Street, and published a magazine that proclaimed itself "The Voice of America's Black Jews" (Edelstein 1977; Silver and Szonyi 1978). But despite their long-standing presence in the community, these black Jews remain invisible to most Lubavitch Hasidim, and to the broader world. On the streets of Crown Heights they are met with startled looks, double takes, sly glances, and brazen stares. Brief interactions like this may seem trivial, but a number of black Jews in the neighborhood described to me the profound effects of their neighbors' failure to recognize them as Jews—the anger that wells up when Hasidim turn their heads to stare or seem not to hear a neighborly greeting of "Good Shabbos" on a Saturday morning.

This misrecognition is rooted in basic assumptions about Jewish whiteness and tied to further assumptions about Jewish clothing and appearance. Black Jews in Crown Heights are not seen as Jews, in part because most do not wear distinctly "Jewish" clothes. Though there is one family of black Lubavitchers (see Simmons 1992), most black Orthodox Jews in the neighborhood identify as modern Orthodox and/or Sephardic, and dress accordingly. The men wear plain business suits, slacks, or jeans. The women too may wear slacks or jeans—which are forbidden to Hasidic women by their community's understanding of modesty—or they may wear dresses and skirts that do not fit typical Hasidic styles. Some black Orthodox men wear full beards, and some do not. Most wear their tzitzis (fringes) tucked inside their pants, and many wear brightly colored and intricately patterned yarmulkes based on Sephardic styles. These distinctive yarmulkes are usually meant as statements of Sephardic identity but are often confused with the "African" style cuffees worn by some Black Muslims and black nationalists. One black Jew in Crown Heights told me he is frequently mistaken for a Muslim: "Because of this particular type of kippah, not the little small one or the little beanie . . . [most people] don't say: 'Oh! Are you Jewish?' Now some people do, but [most say]: 'You've got to be Muslim.'" He says, with dignity and patience, that he has learned to overlook these misconceptions. But he worries about his teenage sons, who want to wear mainstream fashions. He says it's not enough for them to wear baseball caps that cover their heads (as do many modern Orthodox teenage boys); as black Jews living in Crown Heights, he tells them: "You even have to look more like a Jew—because of your color."

Some black Jews in Crown Heights have done just this and taken steps to increase their visibility. For example, though he was not Hasidic, Avraham Coleman (the rabbi of the black synagogue and yeshiva mentioned above) felt a close personal bond with the Satmar rebbe, and dressed for Shabbos like a Satmar Hasid, wearing a wide fur streimel and a coat brocaded with richly colored velvet—a far more "traditional" Hasidic style than the black fedoras and coats of his Lubavitch neighbors (Silver and Szonyi 1978). But despite such efforts, the majority of black Jews in Crown Heights remain invisible, as Jews, to their Hasidic neighbors and the broader Jewish world. A white Hasid once told me of a time he stopped to talk with a black Jewish acquaintance of his—a clean-shaven guy, wearing a business suit and a small kippah—on a street corner in Crown Heights. During their chat, a young Lubavitch boy stopped in his tracks and stared at them, until finally the black Jew turned and asked him: "What's the matter? You never seen a black Jew before? What's the matter? Here I am! See, I'm Jewish!"

This invisibility is shared, in some ways, by Jewish women—even Hasidic women. Of course, Hasidic women rarely face incredulous stares from their male counterparts and are never mistaken for Muslims. But in some contexts, in the eyes of some observers, Hasidic women are just as hard to see as black Jews.

Hasidic women certainly do wear distinctive styles of dress, as regulated by the standards of tznius, or modesty, that are codified in Orthodox law and elaborated in Hasidic custom. The laws of tznius require women to show humility in the eyes of God, and to shield their bodies from the eyes of men, so Hasidic women and girls tend to dress quite conservatively—wearing long skirts or dresses, dark stockings that cover whatever part of their legs might otherwise show, and loose tops with long sleeves and high necks. Married women tend to follow these standards more strictly than single women and girls, and as with Hasidic men's fashions there is a broad range of more or less acceptable tznius styles. Indeed, some young Lubavitch women follow secular fashion closely, looking for just the right balance between tznius and SoHo; and a few wear clothes that follow the letter of tznius law while flouting Hasidic custom in a public display of sexuality. But all girls above the age of four or five are concerned to dress tzniusdik and reprimanded when they fail to do so. Finally, the laws of tznius require married women to cover their hair, which is thought to incite improper sexual thoughts and desires in men. So married Lubavitch women tend to cut their hair short—two inches or less—and cover it with a wig in public.

The tzniusdik styles of Lubavitch women are often noticed, scrutinized, and discussed by Lubavitchers and other Hasidim. Indeed, Hasidim often read the smallest details of tznius—the seam of a stocking, or the slit of skirt—as signs of a woman's religious observance, and marks of distinction among the various Hasidic communities.[8] But the wigs and modest skirts of Hasidic women have rarely been seen as signs of Jewish identity—as marks of Jewishness, per se—by the secular Jews and non-Jews with whom the Lubavitch community has shared Crown Heights. The factors contributing to this symbolic invisibility are themselves hard to see. The appearance of Hasidic women does seem less distinctive than that of Hasidic men. A business suit with a tailored knee-length skirt, a sweater over an ankle-length denim skirt, or a long-sleeved sun dress—these are all tzniusdik styles that mark their wearers as Hasidim only to practiced and careful eyes. And a woman's wig can look much like her natural hair, in any color or style. Hasidic women can thus blend in, or "pass," far better than Hasidic men. But visual distinctions between Jews and non-Jews have always rested largely on fantasies of Jewish difference, and never simply on "objective" facts of appearance. Jews have often been marked as Jews by far less than long

A day at Coney Island. Photo © Miriam Rubinoff, used by permission.

skirts and wigs, so we cannot explain the relative invisibility of Hasidic women—as Jews—simply by the facts of their appearance.[9]

But regardless of its root causes, the invisibility of Hasidic women's Jewishness often has significant effects on their relationships with non-Jews. For example, one Lubavitch woman—a prominent behind-the-scenes community activist, businesswoman, and grandmother in her fifties or sixties—told me of an incident on the second day of the Crown Heights riots that helped spark her political involvement. She had spent the first day of the riots hiding in her house, unable to sleep for fear of the violence outside, but the next day:

> I was walking in [Manhattan] after I had an appointment, and I was carrying an attaché case—I will never forget this. Two blacks, delivery guys, right off Fifth Avenue, . . . I heard these two guys saying: "Hey man, did you hear about what happened in [Crown Heights] last night? . . . You heard what they did to that guy? Hey man, he deserved it." And I was just livid . . . and I reacted in the worst possible way that you can. I actually stopped dead in my tracks, I turned around, and I eyed them as though—y'know, if looks could kill they would die. . . . So they saw me—it was very obvious— and one of them said, . . . "She must be a Jew" and "She must be one of them" or something like that. I guess my anger was really written on my face.

In Manhattan, then, a Hasidic woman dressed for a business meeting, "carrying an attaché case," may be entirely invisible as a Jew. In this case, two black men could not tell a Lubavitch woman was "one of them" until she "eyed them as though—y'know, if looks could kill they would die." Only at this point was her Jewishness, and her anger, "written on [her] face." This brief interaction was a transformative experience for my Hasidic acquaintance, pushing her from fear to activism. And the experience was predicated, in an important sense, on her invisibility as a Jewish woman. The gendered nature of her experience is clear when compared with her husband's experiences of anti-semitism. He told me he often hears comments like "Heil Hitler" from black children on the subway, and it shocked him at first because when he was growing up—as a secular Jew in a small town—he never heard such things. His wife then explained:

There's reasons for that. Number one, when he was in a small town he didn't look like he was particularly Jewish. And when he was here, he was noticeably Jewish. In other words, the Orthodox Jew brings out this red flag and somehow [non-Jews] feel they have to, . . . We're singled out!

Yes, I agreed, as we kept chatting—but singled out in ways that are different for women and men. In the eyes of most non-Jews, the Jewishness of Hasidic women simply does not "shine out" like that of Hasidic men.

IDENTITY AND VISIBILITY

A black man says of an angry Hasidic woman: "She must be one of them"; a black Jew says to a dumbfounded Hasidic boy: "See, I'm Jewish!"; a thug calls to a gang: "There's one! Get him!"; a Hasid apologizes to a family: "I'm so sorry! I didn't know!" And in the midst of all this confusion, a yeshiva student claims: "It's the *neshoma*, . . . It just shines out." These visions of Jewish identity in Crown Heights each take shape within a complex social history and cannot be reduced to a set of taken-for-granted facts about Jews. We can sometimes tell a Jew when we see one, but this visual clarity is not due to the spiritual light of the Jewish soul, the distinctive features of the Jewish body, or even the traditional cut of Jewish clothes. Rather, our visions of Jewish identity are effects of Jewish history in all its immense complexity—the history of black coats and hats, colored kippahs and modest skirts, migration and assimilation, race and riots.

Of course, there is far more to *being* a Jew than just *looking* like one in public. The popular images I have discussed here do not determine the truth of Jewishness in Crown Heights. Anthony Graziosi, for example, did not become a Jew simply because he looked just like one to his killers. Black Jews and Hasidic women are no less Jewish than Hasidic men, simply because they are less obviously so in the eyes of some observers. My goal here is certainly not to cast doubt on their Jewishness; quite the contrary, I hope this essay shows that there are many Jews in Crown Heights, and elsewhere, who don't "look Jewish" according to our images of a "typical" Jew. And yet, these images do shape what it means to be a Jew in Crown Heights, not just what it means to look like one. They were a matter of life and death in the murder of Yankel Rosenbaum. They are a matter of insult and alienation in the daily slights faced by black Jews in Crown Heights and elsewhere.

Being a Jew on the inside cannot be reduced to looking like one on the outside; yet the "inside" and "outside" of Jewish identity are inextricable in everyday life. According to one young Lubavitcher, the Jewish soul "just shines out" like a beacon in a complex social world. But on the streets of Crown Heights, the dappled rays of the social world shine back in. In Brooklyn, as elsewhere, Jewish identities are defined in this kaleidoscopic play of light.

NOTES

1. Unfortunately, I cannot offer a full account of the Crown Heights riots in this brief essay. The factual details of the riots are extremely complex, and hotly contested. For more information and multiple perspectives see Girgenti 1993; Smith 1993; Rieder 1995. My account of Charles Price's words is drawn from testimony at the 1997 federal trial in which Charles Price and Lemrick Nelson were convicted of violating Yankel Rosenbaum's civil rights, and sentenced to long prison terms for the equivalent of second-degree murder. Nelson had been acquitted of the stabbing by a New York State criminal court in 1992 but was retried on federal charges. As of the summer of 2000, their convictions are still under appeal.

2. Though my goal here is not to offer an ethical analysis or critique, it is important to note that the sister of the victim in this attack recounted these words with contempt—horrified by the Hasid's implication that it would have been acceptable for him to attack her sister if she hadn't been Jewish. It is also important to note that this sort of disregard for non-Jews is not shared by most Hasidim in Crown Heights.

3. This basic premise of my argument draws on a number of recent analyses of Jewish identity and visibility. See, for example, Gilman 1991; Kleeblatt, ed. 1996; Segal 1999.

4. I should note that Nochlin presents this disturbing image of the Hasidim in a spirit of self-criticism, to explore the discomfort many secular American Jews feel at Jews who look "too Jewish."

5. The statistics in this paragraph are drawn from Community Council of Greater New York 1959; Department of City Planning 1973, 1988, 1992.

6. Most scholars since the midtwentieth century have argued that "race" has no absolutely validity as a biological concept. In recent years, many have explored the cultural and political roots of racialized identities and communities. See, for instance, Gregory and Sanjek, eds. 1994; Lubiano, ed. 1998.

7. For reasons of space, I am referring only to African-American and Afro-Caribbean people who are considered Jews by Orthodox halachic standards. There are also communities of "black Israelites" or "Hebrew Israelites" in and around Crown Heights who claim Jewish identities and practice Jewish rituals outside of Orthodox or mainstream Judaism.

8. The anthropologist Ayala Fader has discussed the telling details of *tzniusdik* style that Bobovers in Boro Park use to make distinctions among various Hasidim and between Jews and non-Jews (see Fader 2000, chapter 3).

9. Indeed, Jewish women are often singled out for styles of dress that seem less distinctive than the *tzniusdik* fashions of Hasidic women. For example, the misogynist myth of the "Jewish American Princess" points to the supposedly extravagant clothes of Jewish women as signs of American Jewish identity (see Prell 1996).

REFERENCES CITED

Browne, J. Zamgba. 1988. "Are Police Afraid to Arrest Hasidic Jews in Brooklyn?" *New York Amsterdam News*, June 11, p. 3.

Community Council of Greater New York. 1959. *Brooklyn Communities*. New York: The Community Council of Greater New York.

Dalfin, Chaim, ed. 1998. *The Rebbe's Advice, Book 2*. New York: Mendelsohn Press.

Daughtry, Herbert. 1997. *No Monopoly on Suffering: Blacks and Jews in Crown Heights (and Elsewhere)*. Trenton, N.J.: Africa World Press.

Department of City Planning. 1973. *Community Planning Handbook: Brooklyn Community District 8*. New York: Department of City Planning.

———. 1988. *Caribbean Immigrants in New York City: A Demographic Summary*. New York: Department of City Planning.

———. 1992. *Demographic Profiles: A Portrait of New York City's Community Districts*. New York: Department of City Planning.

Edelstein, Andy. 1977. "Black Rabbi Leads Integrated Synagogue, Strictly Halachic." *The Jewish Week–American Examiner*, December 25, p. 16.

Ellison, Ralph. 1947. *The Invisible Man*. New York: Random House.

Fader, Ayala. 2000. *The Morality of Difference: Self, Language and Community among Hasidim in Boro Park*. Ph. D. dissertation in anthropology, New York University.

Gilman, Sander. 1991. *The Jew's Body*. New York: Routledge.

Girgenti, Richard. 1993. *A Report to the Governor on the Disturbances in Crown Heights*. 2 vols. Albany, N.Y.: New York State Division of Criminal Justice Services.

Gregory, Steven, and Roger Sanjek (eds.). 1994. *Race*. New Brunswick, N.J.: Rutgers University Press.

Harris, Lis. 1985. *Holy Days: The World of a Hasidic Family*. New York: Summit Books.

Kazin, Alfred. 1951. *A Walker in the City*. New York: Harcourt Brace.

Kleeblatt, Norman, ed. 1996. *Too Jewish? Challenging Traditional Identities*. New York and New Brunswick, N.J.: The Jewish Museum and Rutgers University Press.

Lubiano, Wahneema, ed. 1998. *The House That Race Built*. New York: Vintage Books.

Mintz, Jerome R. 1992. *Hasidic People: A Place in the New World*. Cambridge: Harvard University Press.

Nochlin, Linda. 1996. "Forward: The Couturier and the Hasid." In *Too Jewish? Challenging Traditional Identities*, ed. Norman Kleeblatt, pp. xvii–xx. New York and New Brunswick, N.J. : The Jewish Museum and Rutgers University Press.

Prell, Riv-Ellen. 1996. "Why Jewish Princesses Don't Sweat: Desire and Consumption in Postwar American Jewish Culture." In *Too Jewish? Challenging Traditional Identities*, ed. Norman Kleeblatt, pp. 74–92. New York and New Brunswick, N.J. The Jewish Museum and Rutgers University Press.

Rieder, Jonathan. 1995. "Reflections on Crown Heights: Interpretive Dilemmas and Black-Jewish Conflict." In *Antisemitism in America Today*, ed. Jerome Chanes, pp. 348–84. New York: Birch Lane Press.

Rubens, Alfred. 1967. *A History of Jewish Costume*. London: Vallentine, Mitchell & Company.

Schreier, Barbara. 1994. *Becoming American Women: Clothing and the Jewish Immigrant Experience, 1880–1920*. Chicago: Chicago Historical Society.

Segal, Daniel. 1999. "Can You Tell a Jew When You See One? or, Thoughts on Meeting Barbra/Barbie at the Museum." *Judaism*, vol. 48, no. 2, pp. 234–41.

Silver, Marc and David Szonyi. 1978. "Black Jews: Struggling for Acceptance." *Baltimore Jewish Times*, August 18, pp. 36–37.

Simmons, Curtis. 1992. "Man of Faith and Color." *New York Daily News*, November 29, p. 18.

Smith, Anna Deavere. 1993. *Fires in the Mirror: Crown Heights, Brooklyn and Other Identities*. New York: Anchor Books.

Weiner, Herbert. 1957. "The Lubovitcher Movement." *Commentary*, vol. 23, nos. 3–4, pp. 231–41, 316–27.

Living In Brooklyn

Jewish Institutions and Interethnic Life

Grillwork from window of Young Israel of Flatbush. Photo by Seán Galvin.

Brooklyn Yiddish Radio, 1925–46

HENRY SAPOZNIK

You could hear it in the kitchens of Brownsville, the restaurants of Flatbush, and the sweatshops in East New York. It was Yiddish radio, which provided, from its inception in the mid-1920s, some of the most dynamic and homespun programs in broadcasting history. Although Yiddish radio met the needs of millions of listeners, the tumultuous competition for frequencies in an overpacked broadcasting area would, by the mid-1940s, spell the end of this once vibrant medium.

RADIO COMES TO BROOKLYN

Late in 1925, the Flatbush Radio Labs in downtown Brooklyn applied for a license to augment their production of radios with the production of actual radio programs. The station, WFRL, named for their parent company, changed its call letters to WLTH to reflect its new broadcast home, the swanky Leverich Towers Hotel at Clark and Willow Streets in Brooklyn Heights. Soon after, WBBC (the Brooklyn Broadcasting Company) emerged, as did a host of other Brooklyn-based radio stations. The land rush for Brooklyn radio was on.

Unfortunately, there were just not enough frequencies to house them all. Forced to share inadequate and weak frequencies, fledgling radio stations were hobbled with clumsy and unenforceable time-share agreements. Newly expanding broadcasters began hopping frequencies—grabbing willy-nilly the best dial transmissions available. The result was a chaotic crush of programs ramming into one another, much like Coney Island bumper cars.

This traffic congestion on the dial forced the U.S. government in 1928 to enact a time-share arrangement among the contentious Brooklyn stations. Rival stations were crowded together onto 1400 kilocycles, one of the least desirable dial positions. Indeed, the government's mandated schedule seemed designed to give station owners ulcers and their listeners whiplash. For example, on Sundays, WBBC aired from 9:00 to 10:30 A.M., returned from 6:00 to 7:00 P.M., and made a final appearance from 9:00 to 10:00 P.M. During the week, WBBC got morning hours on Tuesdays, Thursdays, and Saturdays from 9:00 until 11:30. Its weekday P.M. arrangement was a crazy quilt of late afternoon and early evening hours alternating every other day with early afternoons and late evenings.

Other stations fared no better. And if this weren't enough, as Brooklyn stations battled tooth and nail over pip-squeak allocations of well under 500 watts, WABC, the jewel in the crown of the new Manhattan-based CBS network, was saturating the airwaves with broadcasts of 50,000 watts.

THE RISE OF YIDDISH RADIO

Despite (or because of) such problems, programming for the little Brooklyn stations was always a catch-as-catch-can affair. In the halcyon days of radio, when the shows were neighborhood productions—everything from kids hefting unwieldy accordions to showerstall sopranos—stations aired it all. But as competitive markets for listeners developed, Brooklyn stations began to "narrowcast" and consolidate their local listener base. Most often targeted were Brooklyn's ethnic communities—Greeks, Italians, Irish, and Germans. The increasing population of Jews, however, provided an especially desirable audience. By the early 1930s, many low-power Kings County stations offered a variety of Yiddish programs to appeal to this group of listeners.

WLTH led the way. President and general manager Sam Gellard realized that to attract the hundreds of thousands of potential Yiddish listeners living in Brooklyn, he'd have to air the best Yiddish talent. Gellard scoured the Yiddish theaters for performers and personalities who fit the bill. He snagged the young theater composer/pianist Sholom Secunda to host a children's talent show called *Feter Sholom un zayn Klaynvarg* (Uncle Sholom and His Little Guys). This popular show featured children singing, declaiming, strumming mandolins, and generally making their parents proud.

When the Jewish daily *Forverts*, a leftist newspaper based in the Lower East Side, assumed control of the faltering socialist station WEVD in 1932, they stole Secunda from WLTH. Shortly after, WEVD also lured the great Yiddish linguist/dramatist Nahum Stutchkoff away from WLTH. Stutchkoff was replaced by a little-noticed WLTH staffer, the eccentric and unique Yiddish radio personality Victor Packer (1900–1958). Born in Białystok, Packer early forged a taste for Yiddish theater in his hometown and soon hit the road with a multilingual avant-garde theater troupe. He arrived in the United States in the early 1920s and joined WLTH a decade later. Given the station's dwindling pool of talent and limited financial resources, Packer was directed to make much with little, which he did extraordinarily well. In the late 1930s he pioneered "man on the street" interviews (*Shtimes Fin der Gas*, Voices from the Street), schlepping a huge ungainly acetate cutting ma-

chine to centers of Brooklyn Jewish life to ask questions of everyday Yiddish speakers.

In December 1940, Packer dramatized, directed, and starred in a serial called *Spies* based on a book by Yiddish author Moshe Duchovne. An old-fashioned World War I-era potboiler about double identities, forbidden love, and international intrigue, it started out as a fully staged radio play with orchestral accompaniment and a live studio audience. Within a month, it was clear that even with the sponsorship of Joe and Paul's clothiers, WLTH could not maintain the series, so Packer junked the actors, musicians, and audience and simply read the book aloud.

Packer also created game shows (*Frages Af der Luft* /Questions in the Air), an early example of a disc jockey show (*The Music Store*), musical comedy programs including one with Yiddish theater star Aaron Lebedeff (*The Sante Cheese Program*) and another featuring two treacly twin sisters (*Reyzele un Sheyndele: di Freylekhe Tzviling*) sponsored by Kirsch Double Fruit Beverages. But it was as a writer and performer of Dadaist Yiddish poetry that Packer would make his most unique contribution to radio. In a series of original surreal sound poems, Packer read about subways, trains, Coney Island, and sports, and even included an overheated translation of Rudyard Kipling's "Boots." Twenty years ahead of the better-known hip poetry of Lord Buckley, Packer established a unique place for himself in the avant-garde of avant-garde performance.

WLTH also featured the ongoing comic serial *Der Brownsviller Zeyde* (The Brownsville Grandpa) starring Yiddish theater star Boruch Lumet and his five-year-old son "Sidnele," who went on to become famed TV and Hollywood director, Sidney Lumet. WLTH also aired one of a phalanx of singing women cantors, Freyedele Oysher as "Freydele di Khazente" (Freydele the Lady Cantor).

WBBC, as interested as WLTH in showcasing Yiddish talent, promoted its Yiddish-speaking commercial manager Arnold Jaffe to Yiddish programming manager. Despite a thick speech impediment that made him nearly incomprehensible, Jaffe developed a formidable cadre of Yiddish performers. He signed the lively Yiddish theater couple Moyshe Oysher (brother of Freydele) and his wife Florence Weiss to appear on the triweekly *Stanton Street Clothiers* program, where they hawked garments from the Lower East Side haberdashery consortium. He also signed cantor Leybele Waldman, the famed "Radio Cantor," to star in a weekly request program.

Other stations had their own rosters. Over at tiny

WCNW in Brownsville, a weekly talent show called *The Parkway Theater Program* featured "the well known actress and star" Madame Bertha Hart. A genial Yiddish-speaking Margaret Dumont, Madame Hart offered her mike to a wide swatch of local Brooklyn talent. The hostess's regular exaltations of "wonderful" and "magnificent" following every guest performance (regardless of quality) underscored the show's local feel. After her guests performed, Madame Hart reminded listeners that they were for hire and repeated their addresses and phone numbers numerous times.

The *Parkway Theater Program* that aired November 11, 1936, demonstrated (unintentionally!) that most performers and audiences were recent immigrants. Programming on this date was to celebrate the eighteenth anniversary of the armistice that ended World War I. After using a bit of Kabbalistic ciphering to cite the eighteenth anniversary in relation to its Hebrew equivalent of "Life" and peace, Madame Hart exhorted her guests to sing the "Star-Spangled Banner." After the first few bars, however, it became clear that although everyone knew the melody, nobody knew the words.

WCNW also featured live broadcasts from the stage of the Parkway Theater of the works of Jacob Jacobs (the lyricist of the crossover hit "Bay Mir Bistu Sheyn"). These broadcasts, surviving today on deteriorating sixteen-inch aluminum discs, are the only known live examples of Yiddish theater in its prime.

The variety and quality of these local shows were ably chronicled by the first publication to take an interest in Yiddish radio: the English-language weekly *Brooklyn Jewish Examiner*. The paper offered its readers program listings, highlights of upcoming shows of Jewish interest, and features on Jewish radio personalities. Most important, it ran a regular radio column by "Dial Settings" (aka Sam Brown), a fierce and vinegary critic who vividly documented the relationship between the Jewish community of Brooklyn and radio broadcasters and advertisers. Despite its acidic critic, the *Examiner* soon had its own show on WLTH. Aired on Sundays in mid-1931, The *Examiner* program featured noted rabbis from across the borough repeating the sermons they'd offered their congregations the previous day. The *Examiner* program later moved to WBBC and then to WFOX.

During its heyday in the 1930s, fans of Yiddish programs could tune in to hear their native language on fifteen-minute programs any day of the week. Mondays nights at 9:30, WLTH would air *Songs of Israel*, sponsored by Horowitz-Margareten matzos. Listeners were encouraged to write in to receive their free bilingual Yiddish/English *Songs of Israel* songbook. WCNW aired *Jewish Science Talk* on Wednesdays at 12:30, sponsored by Max Bernstein, a furrier at 507 Nostrand Avenue. A weekly address by the Jewish communal leader Gustave Hartman followed. Thursday mornings, WFOX offered the Hebrew-language *Ivriah Program*, while at the same time WBBC aired *Tales from the Talmud* in Yiddish and English. That same evening Jewish listeners could tune in to WLTH's *Jewish Musicalia*, which broadcast operettas like *Kol Nidre* and *Ben Ami*. The remainder of the week was filled with more programs reflecting every aspect of the communal, religious, and cultural life of Brooklyn's growing Jewish population.

Both WCNW and WBBC broadcast klezmer music, a favorite with its Yiddish-speaking audience. Sometimes different stations shared musicians, thereby cutting costs. As klezmer clarinetist Max Epstein describes it:

> I used to play five times a week and that started right after Labor Day until June 30. You played in one studio but you had two or three different stations coming in. One would go off the air; this one would go on the air. They used the same transmitters, see? So I played on almost all of them—WARD, WBBC, WCGU, WCNW, all of them. It made no difference to me because I didn't have to go anywhere. I just stayed in the same studio in the downtown section of Brooklyn and that was it.

"BUT FIRST A WORD FROM OUR SPONSOR"

Programming was paid for part and parcel by advertising. Indeed, this was Dial Settings's pet peeve: "We listened the other night to three Jewish programs emanating from a Brooklyn station out Brownsville way. . . . Out of the 33 minutes allotted, 22 were devoted to advertising" (September 19, 1933). Despite the potential negative effects of so much advertising, Jewish programming could survive only by reaching out to middle-class shopkeepers or Jewish specialty producers of kosher foods. By charging local businessmen for advertising time, radio stations allowed these vendors to become bite-size patrons of the arts, low-rent de' Medici who brought culture to the masses and customers to their shops. Indeed, a promotional brochure published by WLTH in the 1930s shows a map of Brooklyn overlaid with concentric circles emanating from a transmitting tower. Proudly claiming that it had access to what advertisers wanted—the ears and pocketbooks of Jewish listeners—WLTH was especially successful in both underwriting its costs and marketing itself to its audience through its use of the Jewish business community.

THE BEGINNING OF THE END

In April 1933, Brooklyn station WCGU was taken over by one of the most colorful—and controversial—personalities in the history of Brooklyn radio: "Rabbi" Aaron Kronenberg. Kronenberg, who claimed to be a rabbi, appointed himself station director and changed the call letters to WARD, a political sop to the Fifth Ward in Brooklyn, where the station was located. In short order, Kronenberg would show himself to be one of the canniest of the radio moguls. He entered the frequency fray with a robust enthusiasm that turned up the heat among the warring stations.

In 1934, the *Brooklyn Daily Eagle*'s new owner, Colonel M. Preston Goodfellow, decided to apply for a broadcast license for his paper. On the one hand, given the *Eagle*'s solid reputation and the fact that newspaper ownership of radio stations was as old as commercial broadcasting itself, the *Eagle* was a perfect and logical choice to be the sponsor of a powerful new radio station. On the other hand, the paper—a conservative bastion of the old-line Protestant stock—had never taken any interest in Brooklyn's ethnic communities. Why should its new radio station? This worried segments of the Jewish radio community. When the *Eagle* entered the fray for frequencies and airtime, all the smaller stations banded together to resist paper's initiative.

In March of 1934 WLTH, WVFW, and WARD organized as Broadcasters of Brooklyn, Inc., uniting under a common banner to resist the perceived hegemony of the *Eagle*. The Broadcasters of Brooklyn arrangement was especially difficult for Gellard's WLTH to maintain, since the station was housed in the *Eagle* building and often broadcast for the paper. Packing up, Gellard moved WLTH to its auxiliary Manhattan studios at 105 Second Avenue, in effect transferring the first radio station founded in Brooklyn to the City. Despite its new address, WLTH continued to sign on and off with its old motto, The Voice of Brooklyn. It took WLTH four years to come up with a new slogan: The Radio Theater of the Air.

THE END OF BROOKLYN RADIO

Meanwhile, Broadcasters of Brooklyn was involved in nonstop hearings concerning their broadcast competency. In a complicated bit of scheduling, the Federal Radio Commission (FRC) merged two different hearings: the Brooklyn *Eagle*'s license request and the license renewal of Broadcasters of Brooklyn. What linked them were charges leveled against Aaron Kronenberg's WARD.

On December 12, 1934, the Regional Labor Board of New York Compliance Bureau brought Aaron Kronenberg up on charges of sweatshop conditions filed by the International Brotherhood of Electrical Workers. Two fired former "disgruntled" employees claimed that Kronenberg ran a sweatshop whose "only difference to the better known clothing factories was that the needles we were using weren't sewing machine needles, but phonograph needles." In addition, Kronenberg was accused by advertisers of fraudulent charges, and even with attempting to bribe an FRC inspector. On November 15, 1935, as a result of these hearings, the FRC ordered the Broadcasters of Brooklyn off the air, ostensibly to make room for the new Brooklyn *Eagle* station (WBDE). More behind-the-scenes wrangling killed WBDE, which never aired. And the Broadcasters of Brooklyn continued time-share scuffling among themselves.

When the dust finally settled, "Dial Settings" was optimistic that, "as a result of protests by Jewish radio audiences, small broadcast stations will be saved from extinction and from being swallowed up by larger networks. As bad as Jewish programs are we would not like to see them disappear. After all, they do offer some diversion to the older Jews . . . it gives one satisfaction to observe the expression on their faces as they crowd around a radio when a Yiddish program is on."

But community-based Jewish radio was living on borrowed time. In an effort to rationalize the chaos of the Brooklyn airwaves, the FCC announced in January 1941 that WBBC, WLTH, WVFW, and WARD would merge into a new station, WBYN which would become the full-time 500-watt occupant of a new frequency, 1430 kilocycles. But even this wouldn't last. By 1946, WBYN was sold to the *Newark News* and transformed into WNJR.

The tumultuous era of Brooklyn Jewish radio was off the air.

Jewish Commitment and Continuity in Interwar Brooklyn

JEFFREY S. GUROCK

During the decades that bridged the two world wars, American Judaism was in a state of crisis and decline. Disinterest in synagogue life was rampant among the masses of second-generation eastern European Jews—who then constituted the largest single segment of this country's Jews—as they were increasingly disinclined to identify formally with their people's religious past. As such, they were approximating, in their religious values, the level of disengagement that earlier groups of this country's Jews had reached some generations earlier.

Socological studies showed how profoundly disaffected so many American Jewish young people of the time were with religious life. For example, surveys of Jewish college students from upstate New York to New England to Chicago to as far west as North Dakota indicated that only a negligible proportion felt that synagogue attendance was essential to their lives or to their identities as Jews. While sure to feel that Judaism's "code of ethics" spoke to them, most of "our young men and women," the surveyors found, "observe few of our customs." And, everywhere the younger generation was shown to be less interested than their elders in the "preservation of existing religious organizations."[1]

The tenuous hold traditional folk religion had maintained over their immigrant parents in inner-city hubs was now broken as those born here resettled in communities situated on the outskirts of the city. There, they continued their efforts to advance in America at the expense of nonadherence to the demands and requirements of Jewish law. If, typically, synagogues downtown were half-filled on the Sabbath morning because Jews were out working—or maybe because they were tired from having attended the Yiddish theater Friday night—houses of worship in the new neighborhoods were almost completely empty on the holy day due to the Jews' affinity for American work and recreational patterns.[2] Interestingly enough, the problem of disinterest afflicted all Jewish religious expressions, and almost to an equal degree. So admitted Rabbi Henry P. Mendes, president of the Orthodox Union, as he surveyed an unhappy national scene. "It is perfectly true," he wrote, "that Sabbath desecration is painfully noticeable in the Middle-West, the West and the South, where Reform Judaism is so powerful. But it is also true of the East, where Orthodox Judaism has its strongholds."[3]

The High Holidays were the only time where synagogues of all ritual stripes were full. Then, a combination of nostalgia, awe over these Days of Judgment, and the desire to be among, and to be seen by, their fellow Jews brought families near to the shul. Such a pattern of attendance and observance obtained in "Easttown," an unnamed city situated some sixty miles from New York City. There, in 1931–32, a sociologist observed a "Jewish community" where "religion played a relatively small part in the life of the Jewish family as compared with the aspects of making a living, marrying and educating one's children."[4] Another on-the-scene reporter, in Stamford, Connecticut, found that even those who attended the Orthodox synagogue on the Sabbath and holidays "as a rule" keep their stores "open on these days and everyday activities are carried on as usual, although some of the more strict absent themselves . . . leaving them in the hands of their children or hired help. . . . only three times a year [did] the synagogue fill all its pews."[5]

Arguably, what kept interwar communities from complete disintegration had much to do with the residential propinquity of Jews to one another in their urban neighborhoods. Simply if dramatically put, while 1920s–1930s Jews at home on the Bronx's Grand Concourse might never set foot in their local synagogues or open a siddur after mastering enough Hebrew to recite by rote a bar mitzvah portion, they could still spend their lives among Jews. Residential anti-Semitism played a part in keeping Jews together as did, for that matter, the evident desire of other urban ethnic groups to live in their own largely homogeneous groupings. Not incidentally, given these social circumstances, even the most religiously apathetic Jewish youngster usually ended up marrying a fellow Jew who had also grown up in that predominantly Jewish neighborhood.

The Jews of interwar Brooklyn contributed their share to this national pattern of religious decline. For example, memoirists who grew up in Brownsville have recalled that while there were "eighty-three synagogues . . . and dozens of Hebrew and Yiddish schools" in a "less than two square mile" section of their neighborhood, few boys "continued their Jewish education or frequented synagogues past the age of thirteen." A 1940 neighborhood survey confirmed these recollections. It revealed that "only about nine percent of adult males in Brownsville attended synagogue with any regularity." Seemingly, while the High Holidays witnessed closed stores and empty public schools in this predominantly Jewish enclave, more people stood outside the synagogue than prayed within. Or as one early Brooklyn chronicler put it, while "the pious Jew every Rosh Hashonah . . . chants . . . 'penitence, prayer and charity can

avert the evil decrees,' . . . the Jew today, for the most part, considers his communal obligations from the point of view of charity and experiences no pangs of conscience when he ignores every other obligation of Judaism."[6]

Yet, these same streets, which were so mean to Judaism, were also home to a committed core of second-generation Jews whose outlooks stood in sharp contrast to those prevalent national patterns. These were youngsters whose lives revolved around Jewish schools, clubs, synagogues, and other forms of religious institutional life. A variegated group, this committed cohort included, first, an American yeshiva community that, in a new ecological setting, continued to uphold, and actually intensified, commitment to older Jewish ways on American soil. Indeed, to the extent that this country possessed, during interwar days, groups of Jews fired with an interest in a staunchly separatistic Jewish educational system, intent on keeping pupils away from the lures of American culture, Brooklyn was the national hub and home.

Williamsburg's Mesivta Torah Vodaath was the foremost and most comprehensive of some five Brooklyn-based schools for boys and young men that placed a high premium on the transmission of traditional Torah and Talmud learning and evinced only marginal interest in modern Jewish disciplines, including the study of Hebrew, while discouraging students, as much as possible, from actively pursuing secular studies beyond the high school years prescribed by state law.[7] Nowhere else in this country, not even on the Lower East Side, were there so many young Jews studying more of the Torah and less of the secular in such a way. By contrast, the Bronx, which also possessed the demographic potential to support comparable institutions, had not a single school with such an orientation.[8] As a pillar of separatistic education, Torah Vodaath's reputation was such that it attracted to its less than bucolic Williamsburg setting not only local youngsters—including some graduates of Brooklyn-based elementary yeshivas who gravitated to the Mesivta—but students from outside the New York area as well. Of course, in places like Scranton and McKeesport, Pennsylvania, the numbers of the most observant and committed were almost never sufficient to support their own separatistic initiatives.[9]

Williamsburg, the oldest of Brooklyn's Jewish communities, also was home beginning in the late 1930s to a modest distaff counterpart to Torah Vodaath, America's incipient Bais Yaacov schools. While Bais Yaacov constituted, in its own way, the transplantation of a modern vision of

Jewish education to American shores—its mother movement born some twenty years earlier in Poland was revolutionary in its provision of comprehensive schooling for girls and young women—its mission was to socialize its disciples and devotees apart from America. The first Bais Yaacov school in America, a fledgling elementary school with 35 students, was established in Williamsburg in 1937. Over the next seven years, two other branches were established in East New York and Brownsville, and enrollment rose boroughwide to approximately 160 students. A Boro Park branch would open in 1946. And after World War II, it became a national school system. While not all of these Yeshiva men and women remained forever within their schools' well-defined ideological fold, religious observance was a given within their community as their schools and shuls complemented each other.[10]

But interwar Brooklyn's committed core was broader and deeper than just this yeshiva community. Concomitantly, this borough's neighborhoods also were America's first and foremost home to a second generation of religious-cultural Zionists, a locus for the children of America's first Mizrachi men and women. Indeed, to the extent that the dreams and ideas of religious Zionist thinkers from Rabbi I. J. Reines to Rabbi Meir Berlin resonated at all among interwar American Jews, it was at Brooklyn schools like the all-girl Shulamith School, the boys' Hebrew Institute of Borough Park (also known as Yeshivath Etz Chaim, Yeshiva of Borough Park), and the Crown Heights Yeshiva, which began as an all-boys school but soon thereafter established classes for girls, and the always coeducational Yeshivah of Flatbush, that their hopes for an ongoing, Hebrew-speaking, nationalist and modern Orthodox constituency could largely be found.[11]

Actually, Brooklyn got an all-important head start[12] in establishing a religious Zionist presence in its borough when it became home, in the late nineteenth century, to a series of so-called Jewish national schools. A decade before there even was a formal Mizrachi—the first faltering attempts at forming an American branch date from 1903—Williamsburg saw the creation of the Shaarey Zion School, which ambitiously attempted to build an elementary day school for boys "where Hebrew in all classes is taught as a living language . . . so that children six or seven years old speak Hebrew wonderfully." Older boys were offered an after (public) school program and there were separate classes for girls, who imbibed a modern curriculum consisting of Hebrew language and literature along with

Bible, Talmud commentaries, "and other subjects, taught according to the best methods, mostly original." General neighborhood apathy coupled with some parents' undermining of the school's mission doomed this incipient modern-day school effort. Still, Shaarey Zion persevered with its afternoon programs through the World War I.[13]

In 1906, Williamsburg acquired a second comparable school when The National Hebrew School was organized. Possibly drawing upon Shaarey Zion's sad experiences, this school's leader, Ephraim Kaplan, initially limited his "Ivrith b'Ivrith" natural method curriculum to girls only because, reportedly, "it was easier to get parents to permit the teaching of these modern fads to girls . . . and because the nationalist movement made the education of women an essential part of its program." In time, as the school progressed and the movement created a second branch in Williamsburg and a third in Brownsville, classes were also initiated for boys even if, as late as World War I, girls overwhelmingly predominated.[14]

In 1914, Rabbi Meir Berlin arrived in the United States with the goal of according greater vibrancy and visibility to a movement dedicated to "educating people in the way of the Torah, in observance of the Mitzvoth, in the knowledge of the Hebrew language . . . and in the love of the land of Israel." Toward that end, he endeavored to establish a comprehensive teacher-training program to raise students who would ultimately man (the school was for boys only) a series of Mizrachi schools. And in fact, as early as May 1917, a Mizrachi Teachers Institute (TI) was established with a handful of students on Orchard Street in Manhattan. But Berlin's initial forays were not crowned with immediate success. Finances were a constant problem. Arguably, moneyed communal leaders were patently unconvinced that the city needed two modern Talmud Torah systems. And people like Orthodox philanthropist Harry Fischel and other wealthy Orthodox Union lay leaders had already cast their lot, some years earlier, with the New York Kehillah's Bureau of Jewish Education schools, which also utilized the Ivrith b'Ivrith system, had its own Zionist orientation, and was a growing presence on the communal scene. Berlin pressed his more specific and ideological approach to Jewish education, with just minimal success, against the more popular community-based Talmud Torah system that then dominated the scene.[15]

It remained for the aforementioned pocket of Mizrachi support in Brooklyn to give Berlin's ideas their largest measure of support as local religious Zionists ambitiously linked his ideas to a new form of Jewish education, the modern Orthodox day school. Without noting and crediting the Shaarey Zedek adumbration, an educational program evolved that granted youngsters diversified Jewish learning and a general studies curriculum to approximate and rival the neighborhood's public schools. Such was the pedadogic approach of Max Kufeld, first English principal of Brooklyn's Etz Chayim, established in 1917 in the new Jewish community of Boro Park. Characterizing his day school as a "Jewish Public School . . . in contradistinction to Jewish Parochial Schools (emphasis his) which to the average Jewish mind savors of sectarianism" or separatism, Kufeld and his lay board promised to raise "our sons to be good Americans . . . [and] good and loyal and enlightened Jews." Accordingly, the secular department was "modeled after the public schools." Meanwhile, as "the first Hebraic all-day school—a modernized version of the old yeshiva" and as "the first yeshiva to introduce Hebrew as the sole language of instruction in the religious studies department," Etz Chayim boys were schooled in "an elementary knowledge of Torah . . . the Prophets, Mishnah, Talmud, Jewish History and Hebrew Literature." Essentially, Etz Chayim was a primary school version of Berlin's Teachers Institute program sometimes taught by TI men daylighting in Brooklyn.[16]

Remarkably, for three years, from 1918 until 1921, Etz Chayim had a companion Mizrachi school in none other than Williamsburg's own Torah Vodaath. This aforementioned school, destined to be the paradigmatic interwar "Jewish Parochial School," began in 1918 under the Mizrachi rabbis Wolf Gold and Eliyahu Mordecai Finkelstein with a mission of effecting a viable mixture of general studies, the most traditional of Jewish learning, and a variegated Hebrew curriculum. One student who attended during this early period has recalled ruefully that "the teachers were strongly Zionist . . . the principal at the time . . . was definitely a maskil, very learned in Hebrew matters. . . . They were, one might say, quite modern for that particular time . . . had the Yeshivah remained under that direction, it would have become quite a different institution from what it later became." With the arrival of Rabbi Shraga Feivel Mendlowitz in the early 1920s, Torah Vodaath departed forever from its nascent Mizrachi way of life. In time, this yeshiva would become a local stronghold for the Agudath Israel as, in the 1930s, that anti-Zionist group began to make its social and religious impact on the Williamsburg community.[17]

Flag-raising ceremony (circa 1929). Photo courtesy of the Kufeld family.

Though the Religious Zionists lost out in that Williamsburg school, their presence and ideas continued to be strongly felt in that neighborhood and in the Boro Park of the 1920s and spread, by decade's end, to neighboring Flatbush and Crown Heights. The Flatbush and Crown Heights yeshivas and the Shulamith School, all of which opened in 1928–29, emulated Etz Chaim's philosophy and drew their religious studies faculty from the erstwhile TI which was now formally linked with Manhattan's yeshiva rabbi Isaac Elchanan.[18] And although all were spiritual disciples of the Shaarey Zion School and Ephraim Kaplan's philosophy on how to educate young women, they did differ on when and how they would accord girls the benefit of religious Zionist day school education.[19]

As previously suggested, this string of schools, paralleled nowhere else in America, attracted a cadre of committed Jews whose outlooks differed both from American Jewry's rank and file as well as from their own borough's

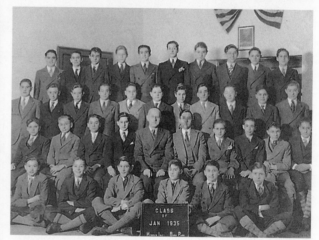

[top] Group of boys in front of school (circa 1929). Photo courtesy of the Kufeld family.

[left] Portrait of Max Kufeld, z'l (circa 1935). Photo courtesy of the Kufeld family.

[above] Class portrait (circa 1935). Photo courtesy of the Kufeld family.

Purim scene (circa 1931). Photo courtesy of the Kufeld family.

noticeable yeshiva community. Unlike the masses of second-generation youngsters, those who attended the "Jewish Public Schools" came from families anxious to have their children avoid—at least for the first tender eight years of their formal education—the assimilatory pressures of America's public schools. So trained and socialized, when they moved on as teenagers to Thomas Jefferson or Abraham Lincoln or Tilden, James Madison, or Boys High Schools, they were the students who, very often, elected to study Hebrew, introduced in 1930 as a Regents-approved foreign language, and were the leaders in the Hebrew Culture Club, which conducted a wide range of intraborough and intracity Zionist and Hebraic activities. In each instance, they expressed a staunch ethnic pride in a highly secular American setting. Additionally, these erstwhile day school youths also had the opportunity to continue their Jewish education in afternoon classes that Etz Chayim and the Flatbush and Crown Heights yeshivas conducted.[20]

At the same time, while all these day school students were uncommonly Jewish, not all of them possessed the full set of very traditional religious values that were characteristic of the highly punctilious yeshiva community. Indeed, some of these children came from homes that were defiant in their deviance and whose parents objected to their children—boys to be sure—being "forced to wear a *Tallis Koton*." (I have been told that "for some time there were *zizith* inspections which stirred sharp dissension" and that "parents who objected could opt their children out by means of a letter.") Many of these families would have been happier had these "Orthodox in character" schools provided their youngsters mostly with a "nationalist Hebraic education," uncoupled from "strict religious observances." Still, even the most secularized of Brooklyn's so-called cultural Hebraists who supported, and challenged, day school education to "engender in [students] a love for their people and its cultural heritage and a strong attachment to the Zionist way of life" truly possessed a higher level of Jewish religious consciousness than the overwhelming majority of Jews of their time.[21]

These "Jewish Public School" children and their families were closely related, in their own right, to the final identifiable part of this variegated community of committed interwar Jews: the student stars of Brooklyn's own Talmud Torah system. Like other boroughs and other cities, Kings County's Jewish supplementary schools were the places where most young people, even those who came from observant Orthodox homes, received their Jewish education. These were the schools that our Brownsville memoirist skipped out on, or otherwise avoided, as best he could. To be sure, many students perceived the long week of up to fifteen hours of Jewish studies at schools like Brownsville's Stone Avenue, Tiffereth Israel of East New York, or the New Lots Talmud Torah as a burden that they were happy to dispense with after bar mitzvah age. Others, boys and girls both, showed their disinterest through high absenteeism or "dropping out" earlier in their "training." Generally, as one observer pointed out, "when attendance at the Hebrew School ceases to be a novelty, the children realize their sacrifice in terms of time and play. Then the exodus begins." Or, as another interwar expert of Jewish education reported, "The average Jewish child probably does not receive more than two or three years of elementary instruction throughout all the years of childhood and youth."[22]

Still, notwithstanding these melancholy realities, there was a coterie of involved students, maybe those who were encouraged or monitored closely by their parents, who made the most of the best of the supplementary system. One such star pupil has recalled that in her East New York communal school, out of a class of "twenty-five to thirty" youngsters, there was a small but "critical mass" of "bright, interested [students] who went along with the teacher." The Hebraist instructors paid scant "attention to the rest," the soon to be drop-outs, and focused on the elite, equipping them, not incidentally, with Hebraic and Judaic skills "comparable to what youngsters were getting at the Yeshivah of Flatbush."[23]

As high schoolers, the educational opportunities available to them in Brooklyn centered around the Marshaliah Hebrew High School system, which ran weekday classes in Brooklyn as well as other boroughs and a Sunday program in Manhattan. These schools were conducted with a strong Zionist cultural spirit, mixed formal training with informal

social activities, and endeavored always to create a sense of enduring community among their students. Brooklyn's special teenagers could also travel to Manhattan to attend the secondary school—the so-called Preparatory—program of the Jewish Theological Seminary of America (JTSA) or the somewhat more intensely Zionist Herzliah Teachers Institute to capstone their years of high school Jewish training. It was here, in these ideologically related educational institutions, that the best Talmud Torah boys and girls frequently met up, in their classes, with their closest of counterparts, the graduates of their borough's elementary day schools who were there continuing their own Jewish education. Occasionally, their classmates also included renegades or drop-outs from Torah Vodaath and other Brooklyn yeshivas who either did not subscribe to their erstwhile schools' anti-Zionism and unbending religious values and/or simply had had enough of their institutions' studied separatism.[24]

To be sure, these secondary schools were not the only places where committed core members, who shared what one Brooklyn youngster called "general convictions," found each other, much to the dismay of Torah Vodaath and other like-minded yeshiva officials. On the Sabbath and holidays, Brooklyn's fourteen Young Israel synagogues were renowned central meeting places for committed Jews who often went to different schools during the week. There they met and discussed the compelling issues of contemporary Jewish life. Young Israels were also meccas for meeting members of the opposite sex at lectures, socials, and parties, all within the parameters of synagogue life. Other local synagogues established their own separate youth congregations that attracted this variegated group of youngsters possessed of strong nationalist and religious feelings.[25]

One Torah Vodaath student who has asserted that the "Young Israel of Brooklyn was, for me the principal influence during my period of growing up," has recalled how all-inclusive his core institution was in the early 1930s. Among his peers as a high schooler were boys and girls attending Herzliah—his own brother earned there a Hebrew teacher's certificate, after studying at Torah Vodaath. This same brother affiliated, for a while, with the radical Zionist ha-Shomer ha-Tzair, while a third brother bounced back and forth in membership between the religious ha-Shomer ha-Dati (the Mizrachi youth movement) and radical ha-Shomer ha-Tzair. Still others in his circle frequented the Teachers Institute of the seminary (JTSATI). Indeed, he remembered that "one who attended classes at the Seminary and attended services at the Young Israel did not find it incompatible at all." And while some officials at Torah Vodaath, "particularly those connected with the Agudah, began to frown upon association with the Young Israel" and students were "discouraged from going there," determined dissenters did what they pleased. Our memoirist was vice president of the Young Israel of Brooklyn in the 1930s.[26]

At Brooklyn boroughwide Young Israel conclaves, this independent, erstwhile yeshiva *bochur* from Williamsburg may well have met up with Boro Park teenagers like the one who spent his school days attending public high schools where he took Hebrew-language courses and participated in the Hebrew Culture Club before studying in Marshaliah classes in his local community. For this youngster too, Young Israel gatherings were the defining moments of his week, as activities there, often held in conjunction with ha-Shomer ha-Dati, reportedly inspired him to someday "work in Palestine for and under the Mizrachi ideals."[27]

In fact, lives and careers of commitment to Jewish education would ultimately characterize many within this unusually committed cohort of interwar Jews. Those trained first and nurtured within Brooklyn's shuls, schools, and clubs were destined to constitute an identifiable leadership cadre spanning Jewish religious expressions of several stripes for subsequent generations. For some, the educational career path out of Brooklyn led from the borough's day schools to the great Manhattan Yeshiva on the road to the American Orthodox rabbinate or to careers in Jewish education. Some began their trek as high schoolers, crossing the Williamsburg Bridge to attend the Talmudical Academy so long as it was ensconced on the Lower East Side. With the removal of the school to Washington Heights in 1929, the travel became more arduous, but some boys made that trek. (It was more than a one-hour ride from Brownsville to Upper Manhattan on the New Lots IRT Seventh Avenue Line.) Larger numbers returned to the dual-curriculum educational system as collegiates, enrolling in Yeshiva College in the 1930s. Some were enamored with the Teachers Institute, that capstone school for Mizrachi, Etz Chayim-style training. Others fit in better with the more traditional yeshiva program. Joining them on Amsterdam Avenue were some of the best young men of Brooklyn's Talmud Torahs, public school Hebrew Culture Clubs, Zionist organizations, and the like, the prime constituency for the TI. As of 1935, in the midst

of Yeshiva College's first decade, four out of ten students enrolled in the then still small college came from the streets and schools of Brooklyn. These numbers also included another brand of renegades from the borough's aforementioned yeshiva community that looked askance at their young men attending the more modern Orthodox school. Notwithstanding these defectors, the incipient Brooklyn yeshiva community more than held its own in keeping its charges in the fold. Its Mesivta graduates played a discernible role, as we will note presently, in bridging generations in their own distinctive American yeshiva world.[28]

Meanwhile, the JTSA was also a beneficiary of, and a final training ground for, some of this elite of Brooklyn youngsters. For some local men who ended up in rabbinical school on Morningside Heights, their educational peregrinations took them from Brooklyn's elementary-level yeshivas to the Talmudical Academy and on to Yeshiva College before shifting over to JTSA. Others came by way of Torah Vodaath's Mesivta program and attendance at secular college prior to enrollment at the seminary. Our Williamsburg memoirist, who was so involved with the Young Israel, has recalled that "we had a fair number from the Williamsburg group who studied for the rabbinate at the Jewish Theological Seminary." In fact, he would have liked to have been one of them too. In 1934, and after graduating Brooklyn College, Harold C. Wilkenfeld ascended Morningside Heights but was turned back due to poor grades. Wilkenfeld got over this early disappointment and would go on to a distinguished career as an tax attorney, once serving (between 1954 and 1959) as adviser on tax law to the Israeli Ministry of Finance.[29]

The variegated group that, in the 1930s, did gain admission to JTSA also included men trained in Brooklyn day schools, Talmud Torahs, and Marshaliah in their precollege days. At one high point in the 1930s (1930–34), this borough's sons constituted one quarter of the men graduated as rabbis from a school that ostensibly recruited its students nationally. These numbers included some foreign-born students—first-generation Jews—who resided in Brooklyn as their first American homes. They moved quickly through local yeshivas and then studied at the Manhattan yeshiva before gravitating to the seminary.[30] Meanwhile, the local Talmud Torahs were the starting point for most of the Brooklyn men and women who chose to train for careers in Jewish education at JTSATI. And here in this school, which attracted mostly local students, Brooklyn's sons and daughters predominated, even more than in the rabbinical school.[31]

East New York's Sylvia Cutler Ettenberg's road to Morningside Heights (JTSATI, 1937) was typical and is illustrative of her generation of Brooklyn Talmud Torah stars. Born into a Hebraic and observant family, she attended Tifereth Israel's community school conscientiously and religiously from ages six to fifteen. As a teenager, she frequently spent her entire Sabbath day at her congregation's Young Israel–like youth services in the company of like-minded boys and girls, "some of whom went on to the Seminary and the Yeshiva." While a student at Thomas Jefferson High School, she participated actively in the school's Hebrew Club. She did not enroll in Jefferson's Hebrew course because she was too far advanced in her knowledge of Hebrew to benefit from this course. However, she was once called upon to teach the class when the instructor, herself a woman graduate of the JTSATI, took ill. Her proud moment of standing in for her role model confirmed her desire to attend the seminary after she graduated high school.

When she arrived on Morningside Heights among fellow students from Tifereth Israel, Stone Avenue, and Avenue N Talmud Torahs, she met up with a young man, a graduate of the Stone Avenue school and Marshaliah, whom Ettenberg recalls "did not have as strong a Hebrew background as I did." But Moshe Davis did very well in his JTSATI studies and later moved on to the rabbinical school for his ordination training. Sylvia did not have that career option. But later in life, they joined forces in both the administration of the JTSATI and in the founding of Ramah Camps among a myriad of other youth-related activities that advanced Conservative Judaism.[32]

But beyond providing significant man and woman power, multidenominationally, to mid-twentieth-century American Judaism, Brooklyn's committed community bequeathed a noteworthy historical legacy to postwar American Orthodoxy. That minority of Jews who practiced, with lesser or greater punctiliousness, what their faith preached, adumbrated patterns of social and religious behavior that reached well beyond the interwar Brooklyn experience. Indeed, in some cases, Brooklyn day school or yeshiva alumni were the actual progenitors of suburban Orthodox communities as these Jews too took their places within the "crabgrass frontier." For example, as of the early 1960s, Far Rockaway, New York, had earned for itself the proud reputation as a "Torah Suburb by the Sea," even if it was legally still in Queens. That community boasted of being home to some four to five thousand "observant Jews . . . in the 35–45 age range . . . part and parcel of the American milieu [who] migrated to Far Rockaway from such nurturing grounds of American Jewish Orthodoxy . . . as Brooklyn's Williamsburg and Boro Park." One booster of this community described it as "a community adjacent to a major metropolis, whose residents earn their livelihoods in the city—and who, being imbued with the spirit of Torah, cheerfully and zestfully relish the pure joy of Torah living. They are American-born, most of them, educated in American yeshivoth; they study Torah constantly and use it as the guide to complete, "shlaimusdik" [complete] Jewish living."[33]

Meanwhile, even as Brooklyn lost some of its earliest schools and as many of its committed, second- and third-generation Jews removed to new city neighborhoods or to suburbia, the borough, its remaining long-standing Jewish schools, and those yeshivas that would be created there would be invigorated and influenced by new Jewish religious and ethnic incursions. During and after World War II, Williamsburg and Borough Park, particularly, would become first-settlement neighborhoods to refugees and survivors who brought to this country and to these neighborhoods new and heightened levels of commitment to the most traditional of forms of Jewish religious life. In time, their values and attitudes would flow out of Brooklyn and impact upon the wider American Jewish community.[34]

NOTES

1. Nathan Goldberg, "Religious and Social Attitudes of Jewish Youth in the U.S.A.," *Jewish Review* 1 (1943): 146–49.

2. See Goldberg, p. 148, and Nettle Pauline McGill, "Some Characteristics of Jewish Youth in New York City," *Jewish Social Service Quarterly* 14 (1938): 266.

3. Henry Pereira Mendes, "Orthodox Judaism (the Present)," *Jewish Forum* (hereinafter JF) (January 1920): 35.

4. Langer, "The Jewish Community of Easttown, 1931–1932" (unpublished abstract of thesis written at the Graduate School for Jewish Social Work, New York, 1932, files at the American Jewish Historical Society).

5. Samuel Koenig, "The Socioeconomic Structure of an American Jewish Community," in Isacque Graeber and Stuart Henderson Britt, eds., *Jews in a Gentile World: The Problem of Anti-Semitism* (New York: Macmillan, 1942), pp. 227, 229.

6. Gerald Sorin, *The Nurturing Neighborhood: The Brownsville Boys Club and Jewish Community in Urban America, 1940–1990* (New York and London: New York University Press, 1990), pp. 15–16; Samuel P. Abelow, *History of Brooklyn Jewry* (Brooklyn: Scheba Publishing Co., 1937), p. 334.

7. On the curriculum at Torah Vodaath, which used Yiddish as its

primary language of instruction, see George Kranzler, *Williamsburg: A Jewish Community in Transition* (Brooklyn: Feldheim, 1961), p. 142; Zvi Scharfstein, *History of Jewish Education in Modern Times* (New York: Ogen Press, 1946), p. 81; Sidney Lieberman, "A Historical Survey of the Yeshiva High School Curriculum of New York" (unpublished Ph.D. diss., Yeshiva University, 1959), p. 81. See also William Helmreich, *The World of the Yeshiva: An Intimate Portrait of Orthodox Jewry* (New York: Free Press, 1982), p. 26. Helmreich suggests somewhat differently from these sources that under Rabbi Shraga Feivel Mendlowitz "Hebrew grammar, Jewish history and philosophy" were part of that school's curriculum. But, clearly its Hebrew curriculum was not much akin to the "Ivrith b'Ivrith" curriculum to be discussed below. Torah Vodaath is here described as the most comprehensive by virtue of its having a program in the interwar period from elementary through advanced Mesivta. The other four yeshivas, though seemingly sharing its orientation, were not as comprehensive. Yeshiva Rabbi Chaim Berlin did not begin its high school program until 1935. Yeshivas Toras Chaim of East New York and Ohel Moshe of Bensonhurst were solely elementary schools. And Chofetz Chaim, an offshoot of Torah Vodaath, was an advanced Torah school. On the orientation of Chaim Berlin, which began as early as 1912, see Meir Kimmel, "The History of Yeshivat Rabbi Chaim Berlin," *Sheviley Hahinuch* (fall 1948): 51–54, and Alter F. Landesman, *Brownsville: The Birth, Development and Passing of a Jewish Community in New York* (New York: Bloch, 1969), pp. 234–35. See also Abelow, p. 139, who notes the existence of Ohel Moshe in Bensonhurst and also points out that some schools that were actually Talmud Torahs bore the name of yeshiva. He notes, for example, the Yeshiva Reines and the Yeshiva of Bensonhurst. See pp. 129–30.

8. As of 1930, Manhattan had some 300,000 Jews, 261,000 of whom still lived downtown. Brooklyn was the largest Jewish borough, with 850,000 Jews, while the Bronx had some 600,000 Jews. See Deborah Dash Moore, *At Home in America: Second Generation New York Jews* (New York: Columbia University Press, 1981), pp. 23, 66. Also, as of 1933, over 1,350 boys were studying in Torah Vodaath-style elementary schools in Brooklyn (Chaim Berlin, Torah Vodaath, Ohel Moshe, and Toras Chaim) as opposed to 881 in Manhattan (Rabbi Jacob Joseph, Mesivta Tifereth Yerushalayim, and Solomon Kluger). See Jacob I. Hartstein, "Jewish Community Elementary Parochial Schools" (unpublished ts., circa 1934, Yeshiva University Archives), table 1, p. 14. All counted, the Mesivta, including its so-called Parochial Jewish High School (which until 1936 extended its general training only as far as the sophomore year, leaving students, if they chose, to study by night at Eastern District or New Lots evening schools) could boast, by 1940, of some 1,000 students at a time when nationally only 7,700 students availed themselves of any sort of Orthodox yeshiva education. See Alvin Irwin Schiff, *The Jewish Day School in America* (New York: JEC Press, 1966), pp. 39, 69.

9. Kranzler, p. 142. See also the interview with Harold C. Wilkenfeld conducted by Evelyn L. Greenberg, November 29, 1973, for the Oral History Program at the University of Maryland, p. 16.

10. Zevi H. Harris, "Trends in Jewish Education for Girls in New York City" (unpublished Ph.D. diss., Yeshiva University, 1956), pp. 94, 134–37, statistics derived from Harris's survey of school records and reports.

11. Hartstein, table 1, p. 14. Or, to put it statistically, by 1933 of the some 1,500 elementary school youngsters receiving an all-day religious Zionist education in New York, 1,060 or 70 percent dwelled in Brooklyn. The remaining 30 percent were Bronx boys who attended the Yeshiva Rabbi Israel Salanter. For the record, Manhattan, which had its share of old-line yeshivas, would acquire an enduring Mizrachi-style day school only in 1937 when Ramaz opened its doors to a handful of students. On

Ramaz's founding see Jeffrey S. Gurock, "The Ramaz Version of American Orthodoxy, in Gurock, ed., *Ramaz: School, Community, Scholarship and Orthodoxy* (Hoboken, N.J.: KTAV, 1989), p. 40.

12. Although the statistics quoted on yeshivas and day schools and the statistics to be quoted later on the popularity of Young Israel synagogues clearly evidence that Brooklyn widely outdistanced the Bronx and uptown Manhattan Jewish areas as a second-generation community possessed of a religious tenor, the question remains as to why Brooklyn emerged predominant in that way. Historian Deborah Moore has pointed out that during the interwar period different neighborhoods in varying boroughs had different personae. Thus, she notes, in line with what we have indicated, Williamsburg was synonymous with Orthodoxy, Boro Park with Zionism, and Pelham Parkway and elsewhere in the Bronx with radicalism. She suggests that some neighborhoods, like those in the Bronx, developed their character due to the ideological orientation of those who built apartments there. Thus, the Bronx's cooperative apartments contributed to their left-of-center orientation, not to mention ILGWU activity there. Word-of-mouth information about neighborhoods also helped the process of neighborhood selection. Such explanations don't truly transfer well to the Brooklyn story. There were no Orthodox or Zionist builders as such, and word-of-mouth communication is not easily verifiable. However, it may be suggested that the earliness of a religious Zionist presence in the Brooklyn neighborhoods may have given it a character that attracted those of similar disposition later on. See Moore, pp. 64, 74.

13. Alexander Dushkin, *Jewish Education in New York City* (New York: Bureau of Jewish Education, 1918), pp. 81–84. See, on American Mizrachi's early history, Yosef Salmon, "Mizrachi Movement in America: A Belated but Sturdy Offshoot," *American Jewish Archives* (fall–winter, 1996): 165–66.

14. *Jewish Communal Register* (New York: Kehillah [Jewish Community of New York], 1917), pp. 373, 374, 378.

15. See Jeffrey S. Gurock, *The Men and Women of Yeshiva: Orthodoxy, Higher Education and American Judaism* (New York: Columbia University Press, 1988), pp. 77–79.

16. Max Kufeld, "The Hebrew Institute of Boro Park," JF (April, 1924):268–69; Moses I. Shulman, "The Yeshivath Etz Hayim-Hebrew Institute of Boro Park, "*Jewish Education* (hereinafter JE (Fall 1948): 47; Noah Nardi, "A Survey of Jewish Day Schools in America," JE (September 1944), 22–23; idem. "The Growth of Jewish Day Schools in America," JE (November 1948): 24–25.

17. Wilkenfeld, pp. 3–4; Lieberman, pp. 80–81; Helmreich, p. 26 ff. Alexander Gross and Joseph Kaminetsky, "Shraga Feivel Mendlowitz," in Leo Jung, ed., *Men of Spirit* (New York: Feldheim, 1964), pp. 557–63.

18. On the qualifications of teachers who taught in these schools, including their Mizrachi and Yeshiva TI connections, see Hartstein, p. 44.

19. On the founding of these three Brooklyn yeshivas and their basic orientation see Lieberman, p. 163; Harris, p. 61; Schiff, pp. 42, 75; Abelow, pp. 125, 138; Samuel M. Segal, "Jewish Elementary Day Schools in New York City through 1948" (unpublished Ph.D. diss., New York University, 1952), pp. 77, 461. On these schools' affinity for Mizrachi-style, Hebraic education see Schiff, p. 75, and Harris, pp. 102, 131. Another commonality between schools was that, for many years, Kufeld was the English studies principal of Etz Chaim, Shulamith, and Flatbush all at the same time. See *Yeshiva of Flatbush Golden Jubilee Commemorative Volume, 1927–1977* (Brooklyn: Yeshivah of Flatbush, 1977), p. 31. See that volume, p. 29, on the relatedness of Flatbush to the earlier Jewish National Schools. See also Harris, who notes importantly that one of the most important figures of the Mizrachi and Yeshiva TI, Rabbi S. K.

Mirsky, was an early leader of Shulamith. See Harris, p. 131 and Gurock, *The Men*, pp. 195–96. It is not clear when, precisely, the Crown Heights Yeshiva admitted girls. Segal claims that it was "the first co-educational all-day school," while Harris argues that "it was originally limited to boys before it subsequently admitted girls." However, he does not date that change. See Segal, p. 77; Harris, p. 61.

20. Boys High School students, during the 1930s, could even take a two-semester Survey of Jewish History course as part of their regular academic program. See Judah Lapson, "A Decade of Hebrew in the High Schools of New York," JE (April 1941): 34–45. For examples of students who attended Brooklyn's early string of day schools through eigth grade and then attended public high schools where they studied Hebrew and were active in the Jewish organizations see Gurock, *The Men*, pp. 103–6. Etz Chayim students did have the option of the two yeshiva high schools in New York, Torah Vodaath in their vicinity and the Manhattan Talmudic Academy, whose orientation was closer to Etz Chayim than the Williamsburg alternative. Of course, students choosing the Manhattan school had a very long commute.

21. Nardi, "A Survey," pp. 21–22; idem, "The Growth," pp. 24–25; Lloyd P. Gartner to Jeffrey S. Gurock, September 3, 1998.

22. Azriel L. Eisenberg, "A Study of 4473 Pupils Who Left Hebrew School in 1932–1933," JE (April–June 1935): 93; Isaac B. Berkson, "Jewish Education: Achievements and Needs," in Oscar I. Janowsky, ed., *The American Jew: A Composite Portrait* (New York: Harper and Bros., 1942), pp. 77–78.

23. Interview with Sylvia Cutler Ettenburg conducted by Mychal Springer, July 12, 1989, tape on file at the Ratner Center, Jewish Theological Seminary of America.

24. Nathan H. Winter, *Jewish Education in a Pluralist Society: Samson Benderly and Jewish Education in the United States* (New York: New York University Press, 1966), pp. 112–18, 131–37; Isidor Margolis, *Jewish Teacher Training Schools in the United States* (New York: National Council for Torah Education, 1964), pp. 88–91, 242–53.

25. Gurock, *The Men*, p. 118; Ettenberg interview, July 12, 1989.

26. Wilkenfeld, pp. 9–10, 16, 18, 21–22, 28, 36–37. The Agudath Israel began to make an impact on the Brooklyn community only late in the interwar period. See Kranzler pp. 167–68. His account fits chronologically with Wilkenfeld's recollections.

27. Gurock, *The Men*, p. 118. On the relatedness of Mizrachi and Young Israel ideals and activities see Kranzler, pp. 165, 169 and Jenna Weisman Joselit, *New York's Jewish Jews: the Orthodox Community in the Interwar Years* (Bloomington: Indiana University Press, 1990), pp. 17–18.

28. See Gurock, *The Men*, pp. 114–16, 271–73, for statistics on the Brooklyn-based cohorts that attended Yeshiva College and for memoirs of students from the incipient yeshiva world who defected to the more modern college and seminary.

29. Wilkenfeld, pp. 1, 37.

30. For information on the backgrounds of Brooklyn-born and -based students who aspired to attend, like Harold C. Wilkenfeld, and in fact attended JTSA see "Reports of the Committee on Admissions" contained in *Faculty Minutes, 1929–1938* (Library of the Jewish Theological Seminary). For an analysis of Brooklyn-born (and other) defectors from Yeshiva to the Seminary see Gurock, "Yeshiva Students at the Jewish Theological Seminary," in Jack Wertheimer, ed. *Tradition Renewed: A History of the Jewish Theological Seminary of America* (New York: Jewish Theological Seminary, 1997), pp. 492–98.

31. In a typical academic year, 1931–32, some 54 students enrolled in the JTSATI; 29 (53%) hailed from Brooklyn. Fourteen came from Manhattan and 8 from the Bronx. *Jewish Theological Seminary Registers* (1930–1934).

32. Interview with Sylvia Ettinberg conducted by Mychal Springer, July 12, 1989. Gurock phone conversation with Ettinberg, July 9, 1998. On Ettinberg and Davis's later professional relationship, see Nadell, p. 346.

33. Michael Kaufman, "Far Rockaway—Torah Suburb by the Sea," *Jewish Life* (August 1960): 20.

34. For the transformation of the committed communities of Brooklyn under the impact of immediate pre- and post–World War II migrations, including the impact these changes made on the nature of Jewish education, see Kranzler, pp. 132–83 and passim, and Egon Mayer, *From Suburb to Shtetl: The Jews of Boro Park* (Philadelphia: Temple University Press, 1979), especially pp. 110–20.

"A Home Though Away from Home"
Brooklyn Jews and Interwar Children's Summer Camps

LESLIE PARIS

At an evening campfire in the summer of 1924, Schroon Lake camper Maurice Broder gave a speech about a place he knew well: the borough of Brooklyn. During the school year, the young teenager lived on Sterling Place near Prospect Park. And contentedly so, for as he told the other campers gathered together that night, Brooklyn was the best city in the whole country in which to live. His appraisal was, however, somewhat controversial; some of the campers at this elite camp for Jewish boys responded to his speech with hoots of derision, while others, no doubt Brooklyn boys, cheered him on.[1] The Brooklyn of which Broder spoke was a real entity: not exactly a city since its incorporation into Greater New York in 1898, but a thriving metropolis nonetheless, with a diverse Jewish constituency. It was also a changing symbolic space. No longer at the outer limit of a Manhattan-centric world, it was a point of departure in its own right, a center of Jewish camping patronage, and a home against which other experiences, such as summer camp, might be measured.[2] Brooklyn Jews' choice of camps was much like their choice of neighborhood: a reflection of class status, aspirations and opportunities, communal networks, and religious and political beliefs.

This is a study of two thriving groups: camps serving Jews, and Jewish Brooklyn itself. In the late nineteenth century, the first summer camps had served elite Protestant boys. But by the interwar years, the industry had grown to become far more diverse. Widely disparate groups shared the belief that rural spaces were healthier and safer for children than cities and proposed that camps were especially suited to teach children the arts of social acculturation and good citizenship. And Brooklyn Jews sent their children to camps in particularly large numbers. Schroon Lake Camp, located near the southeastern edge of the Adirondack Park, dated from a time when the Jewish community of New York was based almost exclusively in Manhattan. In 1906, Rabbi Isaac Moses, of the Reformed Central Synagogue, started the camp for his own son Eugene and eleven other boys from the Lexington Avenue congregation.[3] His "uptown" German Jewish clientele was, at the turn of the twentieth century, well established and relatively affluent, as compared with the more recent immigrants from eastern Europe who lived primarily on the Lower East Side. But by the early 1920s, at which time Eugene Moses had assumed the camp's directorship, the camp had grown to include the children of successful, acculturated immigrants. And of ninety-nine campers, twenty-three came from the borough of Brooklyn.[4]

The shift in the camp's clientele mirrored the changing landscape of New York Jewish life. Well before the immigration restrictions of the early 1920s, the Jewish population of the Lower East Side, once the center of first-generation immigrant life, had begun to decline.[5] As individual families achieved a measure of economic success, they relocated, settling new Jewish neighborhoods in a process that historian Deborah Dash Moore has described as "concentrated dispersal." The rise of Brownsville, by 1923 the leading area of Jewish concentration in New York City, exemplified the first wave of immigration to the borough from Manhattan.[6] By the 1920s, second-generation Jews registered their improving status both by moving to Brooklyn and by leaving behind Brownsville and other working-class neighborhoods for more desirable settings, including Flatbush, Borough Park, Canarsie, Bensonhurst, Bath Beach, Sheepshead Bay, Coney Island, Manhattan Beach, and Crown Heights. Smaller Jewish communities grew in Midwood-Marine Park, Greenpoint, and Bedford-Stuyvesant.[7] Brooklyn had become the most significant site of Jewish out-migration from Manhattan, especially for the rising middle class. During the Depression years, economic opportunities—and geographical mobility—lessened.[8] Still, in 1940, nowhere in the world were more Jews living in one place.[9]

The Jewish families moving into the borough juggled twin imperatives: the maintenance of ethnic community and acculturation into American life. The majority distanced themselves from the traditions of the immigrant generation, including regular synagogue attendance and strict observance of ritual laws.[10] Yet this same cohort remained attached to the world of their parents. As Moore argues, they "remained Jews and brought their children up as Jews."[11] Through their neighborhoods, social clubs, political affiliations, and summer camps, they expressed an ethnic identity that transcended religious observance. In fact, their children were more likely to become campers than were most of their gentile peers. A 1928–29 survey of 3,192 local children (most between the ages of twelve to sixteen) showed that approximately 25 percent of boys and 16.5 percent of girls had attended a camp within the past two years. Jewish boys had among the highest rates of camp attendance, 30 percent, of any group of boys.[12] Jewish girls were more likely than Protestant or Catholic girls to attend camps: 22.2 percent of them did by the age of sixteen.[13] As Brooklynite and local writer Samuel Abelow noted in his 1937 *History of Brooklyn Jewry*, "Many children are sent to summer camps. The popularity . . . is increasing from year to year."[14]

Why did the borough's Jews find camping so compelling? For one, historian Andrew Heinze notes, New York Jews were avid proponents of summer vacations. The immigrant generation saw the ability to retreat from the heat and noise of New York City summers, however briefly, as a symbolic measure of success in the New World. Wealthier Jews affirmed their own class status and respectability through the ability to pursue such leisure, even in the face of Christian-owned resorts' anti-Semitic restrictions. In the early twentieth century, the expanding network of vacation resorts for all classes, produced and consumed by Jews, became a pivotal site for the articulation of a Jewish American identity.[15] In summer camps more particularly, Jewish parents saw the opportunity for social improvement, a model of Jewish physicality (an implicit rejoinder to the idea that Jews lacked athletic prowess), and an escape from the threat of citywide summer health epidemics. Like piano lessons and Chanukah presents, camps provided American Jewish parents with a tangible means to demonstrate their parental affection and to celebrate their children's potential and their own improving place in American life.[16] And at a time when restrictive entrance policies marked the most prestigious colleges, camps offered a safe staging ground for Jewish-American success; the Schroon Lake Camp boys had their own honor society, Beta Rho, and played in a baseball league with teams named for Harvard, Yale, Princeton, and Notre Dame.[17] As historian Jenna Weissman Joselit suggests, specifically Jewish summer camps melded the imperatives of assimilation and ethnic persistence.[18] Judaism, camps proclaimed, was entirely compatible with a summer of achievement and fun.

To some degree, the creation of specifically Jewish camps reflected the exclusionary realities of many Christian camps. Yet Jewish camps also represented a kind of privilege: the ability to stay within ethnic networks and to create Jewish culture (in a variety of forms, from kosher food to Yiddish to Zionism) in new places, while participating in activities deemed desirable by a broader spectrum of Americans. In neighborhoods of extensive Jewish in-migration, children of several religions and ethnic groups shared local resources, including public schools and after-school clubs.[19] Camps, on the other hand, could be more exclusively bounded. The majority of private camps, for example, served either Christian or Jewish children, but not both. Young Brooklyn Jews were more likely than their Christian peers to have attended such camps, a reflection of the value accorded camping, the buying power of the rising Jewish middle and upper classes, and the enduring efforts of the interwar Jewish community to create independent social networks.[20]

Many private camp owners, advertising in the *Brooklyn Jewish Chronicle* or the *Brooklyn Examiner*, highlighted their camps' social or religious exclusivity. In 1924, the Crown Heights–based owners of Camp Hoh-Wah-Tah pledged to accept "75 girls of cultured Jewish families," including "prominent Brooklyn families," while in 1936, Camp Machanaim advertised as "The American Camp with Jewish Spirit" and "The Recognized Camp of Kashruth."[21] The Jewish camps around Schroon Lake served fairly acculturated families.[22] Yet these campers also participated in a Jewish world, one that included the parents who came to visit and the hundreds of other Jewish children attending area camps. While downplaying traditional religious practices, such camps allowed their clientele the comfort and pleasure of ethnic communal socializing in a secular setting. At a time when traditional modes of Jewishness were generally less forceful in establishing community— interwar Jewish youth were, as a group, considerably less likely to attend religious services than their Protestant and Catholic peers—summer camps offered a potent mixture of "American" leisure and ethnic connection.[23]

Working-class Brooklynites, living in neighborhoods such as Williamsburg and Brownsville, also attended summer camps.[24] Some of the poorest children were referred to camps by the Board of Child Welfare, the Jewish Family Welfare Society, the National Desertion Bureau, Domestic Relations Court, and even their local high schools.[25] But in leaving Manhattan, working-class and lower-middle-class Jewish Brooklynites had moved away from many of the neighborhood-based networks through which low-cost or free camps were traditionally made available. In 1936, surveying the effects of Jewish out-migration upon children's recreation, the Jewish Vacation Association noted that "As the Jewish community scatters and the agencies remain in their original locations, the number of those not served by any social-work organization is steadily increasing. The result is that a diminishing neighborhood like the Lower East Side is served by nearly all the agencies in the camp field, while the tremendous populations of Brooklyn and the Bronx, especially the former, are almost without camp facilities."[26] The borough had only one Jewish-identified Settlement House, the Hebrew Educational Society (HES) in Brownsville; unlike its Manhattan counterparts, the HES did not begin to run its own sleep-away camp until 1941.[27] By default, then, many Brooklyn families continued to participate in camps run by the same Manhattan-based organizations that had once served their parents, such as the Henry Street Settlement and the Educational Alliance.[28]

Back at the turn of the twentieth century, Brooklyn had represented a retreat from the bustle of the city, so much so that a number of Manhattan-based charitable organizations used the Brooklyn seashore as a convenient and inexpensive vacation spot.[29] But by the interwar years, the borough was increasingly developed. While it boasted the tree-lined, middle-class neighborhoods that Maurice Broder knew and loved, it also contained the urban world experienced by the children headed off to Camp Sussex, a kosher camp for undernourished and impoverished Jews. Their "wan cheeks," the *Brooklyn Examiner* explained, told of "the grimy city they had left behind."[30] As the newspaper described the scene, the Sussex campers assembled at Temple Petach Tikvah in Brownsville in 1929 were setting off from the "vortex of the blazing, sweltering city [to] the virgin hills and valleys of God's Great Outdoors."[31] What had once been a place for outdoor recreation had become, at least in part, a place from which to seek relief.

Even if less wealthy Brooklynites could not choose among many camping options, many consciously laid claim to social and religious community in their search for an appropriate camp. In the early 1930s, one Brooklyn father wrote to the 92nd Street YMHA in Manhattan hoping to secure a vacation for his thirteen-year-old son. His boy, he explained, had been active in the local YMCA for two years. This Christian organization was open to white boys of all creeds, and although Jewish membership was sometimes restricted, Jews could also attend YMCA camps. A small number did.[32] Still, where camping was concerned, this father made his parental preference clear: "I would like him to go to a Jewish (American) camp."[33] In the spring of 1938, a concerned older brother, Pincus B., wrote from Brooklyn to the YMHA's camp department on similar grounds. In making an appeal on behalf of his thirteen-year-old sibling, Pincus drew upon the Jewish tradition that at this age, boys entered into adulthood. As his letter explained, his brother "has never been out of city limits, and I thought it would be a good idea if he had a change of life before going into manhood."[34]

Not all Jewish parents chose Jewish-only camping environments. The emergence of nonsectarian youth organizations, including the Boy Scouts, Girl Scouts, and Camp Fire Girls, heralded new camping opportunities for their children. During the late 1920s, the Boy Scouts of America, a national organization for boys twelve years and older, was the single most popular camping option among Brooklynites. Even well-to-do families, who could afford private camps, often chose this less costly option because of their boys' prior involvement with the organization.[35] In 1924, the Brooklyn Jewish Chronicle, visiting the Brooklyn Boy Scout camp, observed that Jews and gentiles played and lived happily together: a sign, the paper proposed, not only of Jewish assimilation into American life but of the potential for camping to abet the emergence of a new and unprejudiced generation.[36] Yet scouting also provided opportunities for Jewish communal activity. More important than the question of *whether* Jews attended mixed camps was the question of *how* they did so. In Brownsville, thousands of Jewish boys and girls participated annually in scout troops hosted at the HES; in the 1930s, this settlement accommodated the Brownsville Boy Scout Council as well as the Girl Scouts, the Camp Fire Girls, and Young Judea, a Zionist youth group. At the Ocean Parkway Jewish Center, Temple Beth-El in Greenpoint, the Modern Hebrew School in Flatbush, and the Brooklyn Hebrew Orphan Asylum, urban children experienced scouting in the context of Jewish life.[37] The Brooklyn Council's Boy Scout Camp perpetuated these connections. The camp was ethnically diverse, but encouraged boys to come with their leaders and members of their local troop, and to live at camp as a tent group. And the Brooklyn Jewish Chronicle observed that families could opt for full or only partial integration into camp life, based on their degree of acculturation and religious observance. Some of the boys, the paper noted, camped in special troops with a kosher kitchen and dining room.[38]

Although Sabbath services were available to all campers, whether Jewish, Protestant, or Catholic, campers at the kosher units had a more focused Jewish cultural experience: daily services led by scout cantors, campfires where the boys sang Yiddish folk songs and Hebrew melodies, Friday night meals with white tablecloths and Shabbos candles, fasting on the morning of Tisha B'Ab (a holiday commemorating the destruction of the Temple in Jerusa-lem and the subsequent exile of the Jews), even the occasional bar mitzvah. The Boy Scout extension bureau of the United Synagogue (the central congregational organization for Conservative Judaism) was active in organizing Jewish activities both in the city and at camp. Arguing that "camp should be the place in which the Scout's Jewish training should find expression," this Manhattan-based organization provided rabbis for the New York kosher camping units, and published the Scout Menorah, free of charge for Jewish scouts, between 1928 and 1932.[39] The success of the kosher unit speaks to the number of families that hoped to integrate American and Jewish ritual; by 1940, when Jewish boys constituted 56 percent of the Brooklyn camp, their parents chose the kosher division more than three times as often as the regular one.[40]

In other words, Jewish children participating in a mixed camp continued to congregate together, mirroring the patterns of "concentrated dispersal" that had made for new Jewish neighborhoods. Just as most interwar Brooklyn Jews chose to live in areas with a significant Jewish presence, the majority sent their children to camp alongside other Jews. Sometimes, however, the desire to participate in nonsectarian activities necessitated distressing compromises. The camping needs of observant Jewish Girl Scouts were not served well by the Brooklyn Girl Scout Council. For one, visiting members of the Girl Scout National Staff often described the camp as poorly run. But more to the point, as some Jewish parents complained, the camp made no provision for kosher meals.[41] In 1937, the Council of Jewish Women requested that the Brooklyn Girl Scout Council set up a kosher kitchen, to be jointly funded by the two groups: "It was stated," the Brooklyn Council reported, "that 46% of the children at the camp are Jewish, and that 37% of them are orthodox Jewish children, and their parents object to their not having kosher food." The camp's leadership resisted a change that might segregate campers at meals and raise costs. But although some Orthodox parents protested, many continued to send their daughters back year after year.[42]

Jewish parents and their children had reason to prefer camps where they were not a small minority; where the percentage of Jews was lower, the camp environment might well be more hostile. At Camp Clearpool, run by the Madison Square Boys' Club in Carmel, New York, most of the campers were Irish and Italian boys.[43] Herb Grosswirth attended this camp in 1942, with a group from the Brownsville Boys' Club, including eighteen-year-old Jacob

"Doc" Baroff as their counselor. In Gerald Sorin's study of Brownsville boys, Grosswirth recalls that the other white children tormented his group and the two African-American boys in attendance, leading to a Jewish-black alliance: "It was at Camp Clearpool that I ran into anti-Semitism for the first time. We were called 'Baroff's Bagel Boys.' We took the two black kids into our bunk because no one else wanted them. They were called the 'Burnt Bagels.' However, we showed the gentiles what the Brownsville Bagel Boys could do: we finished first or second in every event they had."[44] Just as "concentrated dispersal" to city neighborhoods had created relatively sheltered spaces, all-Jewish camps, and those with a significant Jewish presence, shielded children from interethnic antagonism. As the *Scout Menorah* proclaimed of its Boy Scout camping efforts, "It is a home though away from home."[45]

Camping was a force that could both reinforce local identities and transcend them. Camp Che-Na-Wah, established in Minerva, New York, in 1922 by Eastern Parkway resident and public school teacher Cornelia Amster and her husband Sol, drew a significant number of its middle- and upper-class campers from the neighborhood.[46] At weekly campfires, the girls heard news about international floods, wars, and Hollywood gossip, but they also heard about the borough: a fire on Coney Island, or the Brooklyn Dodgers' eight-game lead.[47] And from 1926 onward, the girls' participation in an annual charity bazaar asserted their place in Brooklyn's wider Jewish community. Camping philanthropy gave material shape to the distinctions between Brooklyn Jews, providing middle- and upper-class children with practical experience in social leadership, but it also reaffirmed ethnic solidarity. In its first year, the Che-Na-Wah bazaar, attended by visiting parents and friends, raised $160 for the Brooklyn League of the Hebrew National Orphan Home. The camp newspaper commented that "we realize our good fortune in being here and the ill-fortune of those poor children who cannot leave the city in the summer."[48] In subsequent years, the girls supported a variety of other charities, the majority of them Brooklyn-based: the Pride of Judea Orphans Home, the Brooklyn Children's Fresh Air Camp Association, the Eastern District Maternity and Aid Society, and the Eastern Division of the Jewish Sanitorium for Incurables.[49] The camp's central philanthropic preoccupation was a local one, a declaration of its borough and ethnic roots.[50]

Camp Sussex was one of the organizations assisted by Camp Che-Na-Wah. From 1924 onward, 1,200 children

At Camp Che-Na-Wah, early 1920s. Photo from the Camp Che-Na-Wah Collection. Reprinted by permission of Ruth Wortman, owner and director.

each year had free three-week vacations at Sussex. In a sign of their extreme need, every camper received clothing, underwear, a raincoat, a sweater, even a toothbrush and toothpaste, as part of their camp equipment.[51] Other Sussex supporters included the *Brooklyn Jewish Chronicle*, which called on Jews to "take care of our own"; a local affiliate of B'nai B'rith; and the Camp Sussex Women's Committee, the members of which played cards in the borough to raise funds for the camp.[52] In 1924, quoting an unnamed visitor to the city, the *Chronicle* argued: "The future estate of Judaism depends upon the care and training of the children. If we neglect them, allowing thousands to mature with weak and undernourished bodies, then soon this will become the characteristic of the race."[53] Camping philanthropy, in other words, constituted ethnic uplift.

Che-Na-Wah girls ready for overnight hike, early 1920s. Photo from the Camp Che-Na-Wah Collection. Reprinted by permission of Ruth Wortman, owner and director.

rienced broader versions of local affiliates.[55] At Camp Cejwin, run by the Central Jewish Institute of the Upper East Side of Manhattan, Brooklynites from Borough Park and Flatbush found themselves in the company of children from similarly minded Bronx and Manhattan families.[56] These camps created new points of connection for the scattered urban families that supported them. For the Brooklyn boy who wrote to the 92nd Street YMHA, requesting a reunion of his Surprise Lake Camp tentmates, his new network of friends was an important legacy of the experience.[57]

Summer camp culture reflected the breadth of ways that Brooklyn parents "brought their children up as Jews." There were multiple visions of Brooklyn from which Jewish children left for summer vacations and different Brooklyns, seen through the lens of camp, to which they later returned. At Schroon Lake Camp, boys from Brooklyn, Manhattan, and Ohio, all with their own parochial allegiances, formed a new community together. Around their Adirondack campfire, where the group literally faced inward upon itself for reflection, discussion, and song, the provincialism of the campers came up against a wider world. For these children and their parents, the balance of nondenominational cultural practices and Jewish identity represented a successful negotiation of American life. As Broder's fellow camper Mike Hessberg related in 1923, "all of us decided that we had had a corking time, and we went home happy and contented, our only sorrow being that the season had ended. There was one consolation, however. That was—'Look at the time we'll have next year.'"[58]

As more and more Jews moved to Brooklyn, more and more went away to camp with the idea that this was "the best city in the world." But camps allowed children to transcend such local affiliations as well as to affirm them. They created the space for friendships surpassing individual neighborhoods; and even as they reflected local organizational structures, they offered the terms of a larger Jewish network based in pleasure and shared leisure experiences. Boys from the Willamsburg YMHA and the Brooklyn Hebrew Orphan Asylum attended the 92nd Street YMHA's Surprise Lake Camp, where they enjoyed their Saturday afternoon candy, meant "to encourage a true 'Oneg Shabbat' [Sabbath celebration] feeling," alongside boys from Manhattan and the Bronx.[54] The many Brooklynites who attended Camp Kinder Ring and Camp Boiberik expe-

NOTES

1. *Chronicle*, Schroon Lake Camp, 1924, 27, collection Schroon Lake Historical Museum (hereafter cited as SLHM).

2. On summer camps, see Abraham P. Gannes, "Camping," in *The Golden Heritage: A History of the Federation of Jewish Philanthropies of New York from 1917 to 1967* (Jewish Philanthropies of New York, 1969), 372–75; Eleanor Eells, *History of Organized Camping: The First 100 Years* (Martinsville, Ind.: American Camping Association, 1986); Jenna Weissman Joselit with Karen Mittleman, *A Worthy Use of Summer: Jewish Summer Camping in America* (Philadelphia: National Museum of American Jewish History, 1993); Leslie Paris, "Children's Nature: Summer Camps in New York State, 1919–1941" (Ph.D. diss., University of Michigan, 2000).

3. Isaac Moses (1847–1926), one of the charter members of the Central Conference of American Rabbis, was well known in Reform circles. The conference's *Union Prayer Book* of 1894 was based on his self-published 1892 manuscript. See *The Reform Advocate*, LXXIII, no. 23 (9 July 1927), SLHM.

4. Notebook inscribed "Schroon Lake Camp for Boys," 1923, SLHM.

5. See Andrew Heinze, *Adapting to Abundance: Jewish Immigrants, Mass*

Consumption, and the Search for American Identity (New York: Columbia University Press, 1990), 16.

6. Gerald Sorin, *The Nurturing Neighborhood: The Brownsville Boys Club and Jewish Community in Urban America, 1940–1990* (New York: New York University Press, 1990); Deborah Dash Moore, *At Home in America: Second Generation New York Jews* (New York: Columbia University Press, 1981).

7. C. Morris Horowitz and Lawrence J. Kaplan, *The Jewish Population of the New York Area, 1900–1975* (New York: Federation of Jewish Philanthropies of New York, 1959), 43–44.

8. Beth S. Wenger, *New York Jews and the Great Depression: Uncertain Promise* (New Haven: Yale University Press, 1996), 81.

9. In 1923, the number of Jews living in Brooklyn surpassed the number living in Manhattan by a margin of 740,000 to 706,000 (an additional 382,000 Jews lived in the Bronx, a smaller but significant center of Jewish out-migration from Manhattan). By 1940, only 270,000 Jews remained in Manhattan, 538,000 made their homes in the Bronx, and an additional 857,000 Jews resided in Brooklyn. See Moore, *At Home*, 23; Horowitz and Kaplan, *The Jewish Population*, 21–22.

10. As Brooklynite Samuel P. Abelow noted in his *History of Brooklyn Jewry* (Brooklyn: Scheba Publishing Co., 1937), 332, "many Jews are indifferent, and some are antagonistic to the entire question" of the laws of kashrut. On interwar Orthodox Jews, see Jenna Weissman Joselit, *New York's Jewish Jews: The Orthodox Community in the Interwar Years* (Bloomington: Indiana University Press, 1990); Jeffrey S. Gurock, *American Jewish Orthodoxy in Historical Perspective* (Hoboken: KTAV Publishing House, 1996).

11. Moore, *At Home*, 4.

12. Welfare Council of New York City, Research Bureau, *A Survey of Work for Boys in Brooklyn*, study no. 7 (New York: Welfare Council of New York City, 1931), 31.

13. Welfare Council of New York City, *A Survey of Work*, 306–9.

14. Abelow, *History of Brooklyn Jewry*, 330–31.

15. On Jewish consumerism, see Heinze, *Adapting to Abundance*.

16. On Jewish childhood, see Jenna Weissman Joselit, *The Wonders of America: Reinventing Jewish Culture, 1880–1950* (New York: Hill and Wang, 1994), especially "Yidishe Nachas" (ch. 2).

17. *Chronicle*, Schroon Lake Camp, 1936 1937 (1936 season), SLHM.

18. Joselit, "The Jewish Way of Play," in *A Worthy Use of Summer*, 15–28.

19. On schools and neighborhoods as places of ethnic interaction, see Deborah Dash Moore, "The Construction of Community: Jewish Migration and Ethnicity in the United States," in *The Jews of North America*, ed. Moses Rischin (Detroit: Wayne State University Press, 1987), ch. 6; Paula Fass, "Creating New Identities: Youth and Ethnicity in New York City High Schools in the 1930s and 1940s," in *Generations of Youth: Youth Cultures and History in Twentieth-Century America.*, ed. Joe Austin and Michael Nevin Willard (New York: New York University Press, 1998). In 1930, the membership of the Flatbush Boys' Club was 41.8 percent Jewish, 36.2 percent Catholic, and 8.1 percent Protestant, with an additional 13.9 percent of unknown religious or ethnic heritage. Welfare Council of New York City, *A Survey of Work*, 240.

20. Welfare Council of New York City, *A Survey of Work*, 31, 308.

21. *Brooklyn Examiner*, 1 May 1936, 8

22. In the 1917 brochure for Camp Severance, for example, the only clear indication of Jewishness was the list of supporters, which included a member of the East Harlem YMHA and the director of Camp Paradox, a Jewish camp for boys. *Camp Severance for Girls*, 1917, SLHM. In 1928, a card mailed to Camp Severance prospects referred to "the established policy of a limited and selected clientele," but made no direct mention of ethnic or religious particularity. Card dated December 1927, in Severance scrapbook, collection Adirondack Museum, Blue Mountain Lake.

23. Boys often stopped going to synagogue after they turned thirteen, the age of symbolic manhood in the religious community. Welfare Council of New York City, *A Survey of Work*, 20.

24. Brooklyn did not have Manhattan's extremes of poverty or wealth; in 1930, no Brooklyn Jewish neighborhood was as poor as Manhattan's Lower East Side, where the average income was $1,360 per year, nor were any as wealthy as the Upper West Side of Manhattan, with an average income of $8,700. The "second-generation" neighborhoods that supported private camps were relatively prosperous: median family income was $3,780 in Brighton Beach, $3,980 in Eastern Parkway, $4,040 in Borough Park, and $4,320 in Flatbush. But the median income of the Brooklyn neighborhoods settled by the immigrant generation remained fairly low: $2,000 in Williamsburg and $2,490 in Brownsville. Moore, *At Home*, 66.

25. "Agency Contacts of Camp Applicants" in "Report of Work Done for Camp Sussex 1937–38," *Jewish Vacation Association, Report 1935–40*, Dorot Jewish Division, New York Public Library (hereafter cited as Dorot).

26. Beginning in 1926, the organization provided a centralized camp placement service for social agency and charitable camp. "Report, Jewish Vacation Association, 1936," 6, in *Jewish Vacation Association, Report 1935–40*, Dorot.

27. The HES did, however, run a day camp from the early 1930s onward. On Camp H.E.S., located on Lake Tiorati in Harriman State Park, see *75th Anniversary of the Hebrew Educational Society 1899–1974*, Hebrew Educational Society, 1974, Dorot.

28. "Exhibit IV," in "The Jewish Vacation Association Inc. 1937–1938," *Jewish Vacation Association, Report 1935–40*, Dorot.

29. See, for instance, "History of the Fresh Air Work," folder 76 (Fresh Air folder), box 26, *Community Service Society Collection*, Rare Book and Manuscript Collection, Columbia University, New York.

30. *Brooklyn Examiner*, 4 July 1930, 1.

31. *Brooklyn Examiner*, 28 June 1929, 3, 16

32. According to a 1927 study, YMCA membership in New York City was 7.1 percent Jewish. At times the Jewish membership was restricted to keep the proportion low. E. Clark Worman, *History of the Brooklyn and Queens Young Men's Christian Association, 1853–1949.* (New York: Association Press, 1952), 200.

33. J. Isaacs, in "Surprise Lake Camp 1930–33 (4 files)," 92nd Street YMHA, New York (hereafter cited as YMHA).

34. Pincus B. to YMHA Camp Department, 26 May 1938, in "Camp Lehman, Applications, 1938," YMHA. That year, the YMHA's Camp Lehman operated free of charge to needy Jewish boys.

35. About twelve thousand borough boys participated in scouting in 1927; of the Brooklyn boys who attended social agency camps that year, about half attended Boy Scout camps, which, at about eight to ten dollars per week, were relatively affordable. Welfare Council of New York City, *A Survey of Work*, 13, 30.

36. *Brooklyn Jewish Chronicle*, 11 July 1924, 1.

37. Nationally, by 1936 almost 4 percent of Boy Scout troops were chartered by Jewish organizations. See Eighth Annual Report (BSA, 1917), collection Boy Scouts of America, and "Meeting of the Committee on Relationships," 14 January 1937, in American Jewish Archives, Frank Weil Collection, #48, as cited by Arnold M. Sleutelberg, *A Critical History of Organized Jewish Involvement in the Boy Scouts of America, 1926–1987: Based on Unpublished Archival Materials* (Rabbinic thesis, Hebrew Union College—Jewish Institute of Religion, New York, 1988), 1.

38. *Brooklyn Jewish Chronicle*, 11 July 1924, 1.

39. *Scout Menorah* II, no. 5 (May 1929), 3.

40. "Boy Scout Foundation of Greater New York, Brooklyn Council, Jewish Advisory Committee," 1/9/41, cited in Sleutelberg, *A Critical History of Organized Jewish Involvement*, 46.

41. In the period between 1929 and 1936, the Council Camp, at Wading River, Long Island, served from 144 to 510 girls per summer. Brooklyn Council History, prepared 8/19/36, Girl Scouts USA (hereafter cited as GSUSA).

42. Alice Conway Carney to Sibyl Gordon Newell, 15 December 1937, in Council materials, Council—Greater NYGSC—Outdoor/Camping materials 1936–1951, GSUSA.

43. "Surprise Lake Camp, Cold Springs, N.Y., Camp Counselors Training Course 1936," 13 July 1936, YMHA.

44. Sorin, *The Nurturing Neighborhood*, 48.

45. *Scout Menorah* I, no. 3 (May 1928), 3.

46. On Che-Na-Wah, see Porter Sargent, *Handbook of Summer Camps*, 8th ed. (Boston: P. Sargent, 1931), 421. Many private camps, at their inception, directly reflected their place and even their neighborhood of origin. Many Woodmere girls came up to the Adirondacks from Philadelphia, while the Idylwood boys traveled from Baltimore. Clusters of campers came from Washington Heights, or the Upper West Side, or Central Brooklyn. These patterns reflected the districts where camp directors and popular counselors lived or worked.

47. See Che-Na-Wah council log, 30 July 1931; 10 August 1933; August 1942, collection Che-Na-Wah (hereafter cited as CNW).

48. *Che-Na-Wit*, 21 and 31 August 1926, CNW.

49. "Bazaar" and "Bazaar 1930," CNW.

50. Camp philanthropy did not always flow back to the borough, or to city residents. In the 1930s, as conditions overseas became increasingly dire, the Che-Na-Wah girls raised money on behalf of European Jews, while Cejwin campers raised money for Jewish life both in America and Palestine.

51. Abelow, *History of Brooklyn Jewry*, 257–58; *Brooklyn Examiner*, 4 July 1930, 1.

52. *Brooklyn Jewish Chronicle*, 4 April 1924, 1 and 18 April 1924, 3; *Brooklyn Examiner*, 21 June 1929, 2.

53. *Brooklyn Jewish Chronicle*, 4 April 1924, 8.

54. "Surprise Lake Camp, Report, 38th Season, 1938," in "S.L.C., Reports Summer Camp 1905–1938," YMHA. Brooklyn became the best-represented borough at Surprise Lake Camp. In 1931 the largest group of affiliated campers, 261, came from the Williamsburg YMHA, while 37% of the campers came from the borough. See "Report, Summer Camp, June 29th to September 7th, 1931," and "Report, Summer Camp July 1st to September 5th, 1932," in "S.L.C., Reports Summer Camp 1905–1938," YMHA.

55. On Camp Boiberik, see Saul Goodman, ed., *Our First Fifty Years: The Sholem Aleichem Folk Institute* (New York: Sholem Aleichem Folk Institute, 1972). Sholem Aleichem had as its focus secular Jewish education and Yiddish culture.

56. On Cejwin recruiting in Brooklyn, see Joselit, "The Jewish Way of Play," endnote 7.

57. Irving Feinstein to Mr. Crysal [sic], 29 September 1938, in "Camp Lehman: Counselor Application 1938," YMHA.

58. *Chronicle, Schroon Lake Camp, 1923*, SLHM.

Blacks, Jews, and the Struggle to Integrate Brooklyn's Junior High School 258
A Cold War Story

ADINA BACK

If you mention Brooklyn, schools, blacks, and Jews in one breath, the image that surfaces in the minds of many is the 1968 struggle for community control in the Ocean Hill–Brownsville school district. Like many highly publicized events, the Ocean Hill–Brownsville struggle has generally been presented by the media and some of the key players as having come out of nowhere, an explosion without a history. But the Ocean Hill–Brownsville struggle had its roots in an earlier and less well-publicized history of struggles for equal education for African-American schoolchildren. In the 1950s, many black parents redirected their energies from documenting discrimination to organizing for integration. In so doing, they exposed a segregated northern school system. Paradoxically, their campaign revealed both the possibility that existed during this period to create a truly integrated system and the deep—ultimately intractable—resistance to that goal.

Charting these earlier struggles reveals a much bigger picture: the foundation of the current crisis in urban education lies in this concurrence of changing demographics and a transforming urban ecology, an emerging civil rights movement and the shaping of white ethnic identities and politics in the postwar era. The overall impact of McCarthyism on the battles for racial equality framed this period as did the anti-Communist purges of the labor movement and radical unions like the New York City Teachers Union. These earlier struggles also offer a map of the various intersections between African-Americans and American Jews that is helpful for evaluating the potent symbolism of Ocean Hill–Brownsville in the recounting of black-Jewish history.

The Ocean Hill–Brownsville conflict has come to symbolize, in popular and scholarly debate, the end of the supposed "grand alliance" between African-Americans and American Jews that emerged out of the civil rights movement. For many Jews the conflict sparks memories of anti-Semitism directed specifically at the United Federation of Teachers, the predominantly Jewish teachers' union. For many African-Americans, the conflict was about a racist and discriminatory school system in which the United Federation of Teachers was only one of the players and the ethnic identity of the city's teachers hardly the central issue. The mention of this incident in certain circles still provokes fierce emotions. However, just as historians are challenging the assumptions about a "grand alliance," so too must we question the symbolism of Ocean Hill–

Brownsville as pivotal in the changing relations between African-Americans and American Jews.[1]

Contemporary responses to the Ocean Hill–Brownsville conflict may reveal less about the event itself and more about current anxieties surrounding black-Jewish relations. The responses as well as the partisan reports that the event generated offer a polarized view of the relationship between African-Americans and American Jews that belies the complexity and heterogeneity of the communities and simplifies a far more complicated history of school integration battles.

This essay focuses specifically on the first battle to integrate a New York City public school on the heels of the 1954 *Brown v. Board of Education* Supreme Court decision. The various players in this effort illustrate the differences within African-American and Jewish communities. And this integration struggle offers a foundation for understanding the tensions emerging between some of these communities of blacks and Jews.

It was in 1955 that black parents and civil rights activists and their white (and largely Jewish) allies began their effort to integrate a new junior high school—JHS 258—in Bedford-Stuyvesant, Brooklyn's largest black neighborhood. With services declining as the black population increased, Bed-Stuy was becoming emblematic of many urban centers in the postwar period where federal and local policies were creating the structural foundation of racial identity and economic decline. The 1949 Federal Housing Act spurred the growth of suburbs and provided loans and affordable mortgages almost exclusively to white home buyers moving into segregated suburbs. Similarly, the "urban renewal" projects spearheaded by urban developers like New York City's Robert Moses under Title I of the Housing Act resulted in "Negro removal." By the mid-1950s, Moses had directed the demolition of hundreds of apartment buildings in the name of slum clearance, which resulted in the construction of middle-income housing and the displacement of at least 320,000 people. Those displaced were the city's poor. As Robert Caro (Robert Moses's biographer) notes, a remarkably high percentage of the displaced were African-American and Puerto Rican. Many fled to communities in Brooklyn like Brownsville, Bedford-Stuyvesant, and neighboring Crown Heights.

This disinvestment of blackness, the flip side of what George Lipsitz has characterized as the "possessive investment in whiteness,"[2] was not necessarily a new experience

for Bed Stuy's black parents. For years the community had complained about overcrowding and racial segregation in many of the district's public schools. For example, the 1938 report of the New York State Commission on the Condition of the Urban Colored Population charged the Board of Education with diluting the academic program at Girls High School, located in the middle of Bedford Stuyvesant, as the school's black population increased. And in the mid-1940s the School Council of Bed-Stuy and Williamsburg, a community group of parents and teachers, argued that children in those communities received inadequate education due to teacher shortages and the resulting reduced hours of instruction.[3] By the mid-1950s, outraged Bed-Stuy parents, who had for years sought to draw attention to the deterioration of their schools, were emboldened by the 1954 Supreme Court decision outlawing school segregation, and by the emerging civil rights movement in the South.

But the JHS 258 story is that of a lost opportunity. It was no accident that this test case for integration was happening in Brooklyn in the mid-1950s, when the borough's shifting ethnic boundaries could actually allow for school integration. During this decade, there was a window of opportunity to create an integrated school system that the demographic changes of the 1960s ultimately foreclosed.

The importance of this failed attempt is threefold. First, it offers insights into responses of white communities to civil rights challenges in the North. The Board of Education's resistance to implementing integration reflected both bureaucratic imperatives and a race-based ideology. At the simplest level, school administrators needed to protect their turf and defend their actions and policies. The institution's operating racial ideology is more difficult to untangle, as there was no consensus among the board's lay leaders and the superintendent of schools and his staff. For example, the schools superintendent masked his objection to integration proposals in his advocacy of the "neighborhood school" policy. At the same time, the board's lay leadership was far more likely to embrace the liberal racial ideology being advanced in the postwar period that sought to understand the black family in terms of behavioral pathology. The board's opposition, however, was also directly related to growing evidence of white flight and fears of white parents' protests.

The responses and identities of different groups of Jews complicate the white landscape. While major national

Jewish organizations supported this school integration effort, there was little response from Brooklyn's local Jewish communities. The Board of Education never forwarded a plan for integration to which the local communities might respond. However, the demographic shifts within the JHS 258 area and surrounding vicinity offer some insight into the area's changing Jewish communities. By the mid-1950s, Bedford-Stuyvesant had already lost most of its Jewish population. Neighboring Crown Heights, the area that integration activists proposed be integrated with the Bedford-Stuyvesant junior high school, also saw an overall decrease in its white population. However, while the neighborhood's Italian, eastern European Jewish, German, and Scandinavian residents were moving to the suburbs after World War II, the Lubavitch Hassidim, Orthodox Jews from eastern Europe, were expanding their community in Crown Heights. This insular community with its own infrastructure and educational institutions would not have been affected by any public school integration proposals. Finally, the active involvement of radical Jews (from Brooklyn and the city's other boroughs) in this school integration effort further complicates the meaning of Jewish involvement in the struggle for black civil rights, as these radicals did not necessarily identify primarily on the basis of ethnicity.

Second, this northern school desegregation conflict occurred as desegregation battles exploded in the South. In 1955, Autherine Lucy attempted to gain entry into the University of Alabama, and the Montgomery bus boycott began. These struggles inspired African-Americans in New York City. But they also revealed the tension within the civil rights organizations and between these organizations and their local membership about the extent to which northern struggles deserved institutional support.

Third, this fight for an integrated junior high school occurred within the Cold War climate of the 1950s. Fear of being stigmatized as "pink" for advocating racial unity severely disabled the efforts of progressive African-American parents and their white allies, many of whom were Jews associated with a variety of unions and with parent and civil rights organizations. The McCarthy attacks seriously impeded the radical New York City Teachers Union's support for the school integration struggle. Furthermore, opponents of integration used associations between JHS 258 activists and the Teachers Union to delegitimize their efforts.

The parents and civil rights activists framed their demands for an integrated school in direct response to the New York City Board of Education's recently adopted school integration policy. The resolution, announced on December 23, 1954, seven months after the landmark *Brown v. Board of Education* Supreme Court decision, stated

> . . . the Board of Education of the City of New York is determined to accept the challenge implicit in the language and spirit of the decision of the United States Supreme Court. . . . We believe that an effective method for obtaining these ends is to set up a Commission of the Board of Education charged with the responsibility of determining the facts and recommending whatever further action is necessary to come closer to the ideal, viz., the racially integrated school.[4]

In conjunction with the resolution, the Board of Education unanimously approved the establishment of a Commission on Integration that was charged with offering recommendations for integrating the city's public schools.

The board's resolution was a result of months of battles that predated the Supreme Court announcement. Dr. Kenneth Clark, the prominent black psychologist, had ignited these battles with his highly publicized demand that the Board of Education be held accountable for the inferior education it offered the city's African-American schoolchildren. At the Urban League's annual Brotherhood Month Dinner, Clark summarized the prior twenty-year history of education for New York City's black schoolchildren and characterized the educational situation as in a "stage of educational decline."[5] He claimed that the schools black children attended were the system's most overcrowded and poorly resourced. They also had the most inexperienced teachers. In a particularly incendiary assertion, he claimed that the high school zones had been gerrymandered purposely to exclude large numbers of black students from attending the best academic high schools. In spite of such provocative allegations, Clark's charge to the Board of Education was fairly mild: he simply called on the board to conduct a study of the conditions for blacks in the city's public schools.

High-level administrators within the Board of Education attacked Clark for months after he issued his call. The attacks ranged from outright rejection of Clark's characterization of the schools as segregated to attempts to discredit Clark himself. Many administrators refused to see the term "segregation" applied to a northern school system.[6] In addition, the board Red-baited Clark to discredit him. For example, one assistant superintendent attempted to link Clark with the Teachers Union, which was widely known as a left-leaning union. "You perhaps know," he wrote, "that he [Clark] and Judge Delany are current favorites of the Teachers Union and that the line they follow fits right in with their program of creating community dissension and distrust of the public school system."[7]

In the end, though, growing local and national attention to the issue of school segregation made it extremely difficult for the Board of Education to ignore Clark's charges. Locally, Clark was part of a new organization, the Intergroup Committee on New York's Public Schools, that was effectively gathering public support for its concerns. Concurrent to the formation of the Intergroup Committee, Mayor Robert Wagner, who also spoke at the Urban League's Brotherhood Month Dinner, promised that a new government agency, the Commission on Intergroup Relations, would also take up the issue of school integration on behalf of his office.[8] Nationally, the *Brown v. Board of Education* Supreme Court decision gave prominence not only to the issue of school desegregation but to Dr. Clark himself.

The Board of Education ultimately adopted the recommendation of its own public relations officer, who argued that embarking on a study would enable the Board of Education to "show good faith" with regard to the allegation of school segregation.[9] By the end of 1954, the board had endorsed a study and established a Commission on Integration, which was co-chaired by the outgoing and incoming presidents of the Board of Education.

How does all this background relate to the efforts of the Brooklyn parents who, a dozen years before Ocean Hill–Brownsville, attempted to integrate a school in their neighborhood? First, their efforts were premised on the self-declared mandate of the Board of Education's Commission on Integration to create racially integrated schools. They took to heart the words of the commission's co-chairs, that their school would be the "pilot project for integration,"[10] and they believed they would be the first test case of the commission's—and the board's commitment—to school integration.[11] But this background is also important for other reasons: the battles that led to the creation of the Board of Education's Commission on Integration reveal the Board's deep-seated ambivalence about school integration, and offers insights into why the parents' efforts to create this "pilot project for integration" ultimately failed.

Like public education administrators in other urban centers in the North and Midwest, New York City's educators were negotiating rocky terrain with regard to school integration. They rejected the premise of segregation as a northern problem, while also fearing that implementing school integration would only escalate the white flight that was already underway. The goal for black parents and advocates, however, was clear:"We urge the immediate integration of JHS No. 258. . . ."[12]

Six months after the board's declaration that it would end "racially homogeneous" schools in New York City, JHS 258 opened in Bedford-Stuyvesant in the fall of 1955 with a glaring 98 percent African-American student body.[13] For community and parent activists who for years had monitored and protested the state of education in Bed-Stuy, the opening of JHS 258 as a segregated school catalyzed a fight for desegregation.

The parents' argument was straightforward: they maintained that if a different zoning model was used, the site of the school on Halsey Street and Marcy Avenue placed it on the border between a black and a white neighborhood. Zoned for integration, the school could easily serve both white and black students in the area. The integration activists linked the desegregation of JHS 258 to another new school projected for construction that year, JHS 61. JHS 61 was slated to serve a primarily white area in neighboring Crown Heights. The twenty blocks between the two schools constituted an interracial area that could provide students for both schools. The activists suggested an alternative to the existing zoning pattern, which followed a "roughly radial pattern": they proposed instead a longitudinal pattern that would follow transportation lines and cut across the all-black, the interracial, and the all-white population areas. In that way, both JHS 258 and JHS 61 would be desegregated.[14]

Significantly, a multitude of groups supported this new zoning and integration plan. Civil rights leaders conducted the studies, tabulated the figures, wrote memos, organized rallies, and met repeatedly with Board of Education administrators and officials. Black parents provided the corps of grassroots activists who offered as evidence the poor education that their children received in the segregated schools. Finally, civil rights and civic organizations—a multiracial and interreligious set of groups—and radical organizations like the New York City Teachers Union also voiced their support.

Annie Stein, Winston Craig, and Reverend Milton Galamison led this campaign. This trio represented an ideological amalgamation of the interracialism promoted by the American Communist Party, the crusade against racial discrimination championed by the National Association for the Advancement of Colored People (NAACP), and a "Christian doctrine of social commitment."[15] Furthermore, the threesome itself was interracial. Annie Stein, the daughter of Russian Jewish immigrants, was a parent and longtime radical, with a notable history as a member of the American Communist Party and an organizer with the Women's Trade Union League and the Washington (D.C.) Committee for Consumer Protection. Her commitment to organizing for school desegregation when she and her family moved back to Brooklyn in the early 1950s stemmed from her political ideology as well as her participation in the struggle to desegregate Washington's eating facilities after World War II.[16]

In Brooklyn, Stein joined the Brooklyn branch of the NAACP and with Winston Craig, an African-American who was chair of the branch's Education Committee, spearheaded this particular integration fight. Stein's left-leaning reputation was in fact one reason that she and Winston Craig sought the assistance of Reverend Galamison, the minister of Siloam Presbyterian Church, one of Brooklyn's prominent black congregations in Bedford Stuyvesant. They needed to build a core of progressive leaders within the Brooklyn branch of the NAACP, a fairly conservative branch that was suspicious of Stein's radical past and concerned about her taking a leadership position within the organization.[17]

Galamison was an appropriate leader for Stein and Craig to approach. The reverend used his pulpit and his own theological interpretation of Christianity to fight against racial discrimination, and he welcomed Stein and Craig's request for assistance. They agreed to run the reverend for election to the Education Committee. He won that election and in December 1955 became the co-chair, with Winston Craig, of the Brooklyn branch's Education Committee.

Stein, Craig, and Galamison functioned as a triumvirate. Galamison was the undisputed public leader and spokesman. Craig, with deeper roots in the NAACP, organized within the organization and the African-American community. Stein, for her part, generated all the reports tabulating the racial composition of the schools in the Bedford-Stuyvesant area—reports that formed the foundation of the Education Committee's proposals for integration.[18]

Galamison, Craig, and Stein were strong and persistent leaders and aggressively pursued the Board of Education with demands that the board honor its promise to integrate the New York City schools. And they tried to hold the board accountable to the suggestion of its lay leadership that the segregation problems of JHS 258 could be resolved through a "pilot project" that would represent a new integration model. Black parents in the community supported the leaders. It was the parents, in fact, who had "stayed the course" for years. Their collective memory was fed by the efforts of the School Council of Bed-Stuy and Williamsburg, a community group of parents and teachers who had begun a decade earlier to complain about the inadequate education that children were receiving.[19] These were the parents who joined the NAACP Education Committee, provided the testimony, and organized and attended the meetings and rallies.

For example, parents and leaders filled Reverend Galamison's church on a hot June night in 1956 to protest the segregation of JHS 258 and to call for the integration of New York City's public schools. On the very same night, the Board of Education was holding a dedication ceremony for the new school just three blocks from the church. As JHS 258 students opened the dedication program by singing "Let's Break Bread Together," neighborhood parents committed to desegregating JHS 258 testified at the protest rally about the deficient education that their children were receiving in this segregated school. In spite of the school's new building, built of "the finest stone and steel," seven of the classrooms were unfinished, a large percentage of the teaching staff were on substitute lines, and of the forty-five teachers currently employed, thirty-three had requested to be transferred elsewhere.[20] Affirming their fundamental belief, based on experience, that segregated education was unequal education, the rally participants resolved that "none of the problems involved in the integration of Public Schools can be as serious as the problems created by segregation."[21] Furthermore, they challenged the popular defense that housing segregation was the cause of segregated schools, and they linked their struggle to a national and international movement for the rights of blacks:

> We affirm that we cannot afford to apologize for segregated education on the basis of housing and geographical racial distribution. The separationist policy of South Africa thrives on geographical distribution of population. If housing made justifiable criterion for segregated Public Schools, we place a new instrument in the hands of anti-integrationists of the South to bypass the Supreme Court decision.[22]

The southern struggles for desegregated education emerging at the same time gave greater meaning as well as strategic direction to the Brooklyn activists. But the attention to the southern battles was also a source of frustration for the borough's leaders. As Reverend Galamison noted, ". . . we are prone, due to our struggle in the South for full equality in a free society, to overlook our responsibility in Northern communities to see that no encroachments on our civil rights and liberties are allowed to exist."[23] The importance of the southern movement also made the leaders of the national office of the NAACP cautious in their support of this northern battle. The national office, in fact, disagreed with the Brooklyn branch about its strategic approach to rezoning JHS 258.

The national office had a vested interest in building public goodwill, and it was loath to jeopardize the support of white liberal allies in the North. As the national leadership warned, "If zoning is so conducted as to arouse substantial resistance in some part of the school community, and if the resistance should in fact have a violent outcome (or be susceptible to depiction as such) the consequences to the overall desegregation program, North as well as South, could be incalculably damaging."[24] Fears of "a violent outcome" were clearly linked to a recent New York Times article that quoted several members of the board saying, in private, "that if white children were forced to attend [JHS 258], violence among the parents might break out."[25] And concerns about violence were coupled with fears of white flight. Schools superintendent William Jansen had already noted that the new school year saw sixty white children move out of the district with only fifteen moving in.[26]

Within New York, the "private" comments of some board members outraged the leaders in the school integration movement. Dr. Clark explained to the president of the board that the anticipation of violence had been used in desegregation struggles in the South as an excuse to avoid challenging segregation. Clark was "shocked" that some New York City school officials, northern civic leaders, would promote the same fear tactics that had been used in the South.[27] The national office of the NAACP, however, did not align itself with these local leaders. It remained vigilant, and critical, of the Brooklyn branch's efforts. The national office communicated its concern about the branch's public and outspoken presence and political bedfellows within the context of the impact on the southern desegregation strategy. June Shagaloff, the national NAACP's education director, described how the national office was

often at odds not only with the Brooklyn branch but also with other local branches. "They [the national office] dragged their feet. They didn't like these issues [related to northern school zoning]. They had reservations that I thought were very conservative reservations.[28]

If support for this local northern school desegregation struggle reveals some of the differences within the African-American community, the nature of American Jewish support offers insights into the complex character of American Jewry in the postwar period. The community activists fighting to desegregate JHS 258 received support from mainstream Jewish organizations, a local rabbi, and radical Jewish teachers who were members of the New York City Teachers Union. The nature of their support differed, as did their identification as American Jews.

The nation's principal Jewish organizations, the American Jewish Committee, American Jewish Congress, and Anti-Defamation League of B'nai B'rith, registered their support for school integration in general and for the integration of JHS 258 in particular through the Intergroup Committee on New York's Public Schools, a coalition of union and religious, social welfare, parents, and civil rights organizations.[29] In the heat of the organizing campaign to integrate JHS 258, the Intergroup Committee voiced its support for the NAACP's efforts and attempted to establish clout with Board of Education leaders by demonstrating the extent and variety of its member agencies.

On the local level, the Brooklyn Branch of the NAACP found support within the organized Jewish community from Rabbi Eugene J. Sack, one of the borough's liberal rabbis. Rabbi Sack, the rabbi of Congregation Beth Elohim in Brooklyn's Park Slope neighborhood, was one of the invited speakers at the NAACP's June 1956 rally that drew over one thousand people. Sharing the platform with prominent civil rights leaders like Ella Baker and Edward Lewis of the Urban League, Rabbi Sacks participated in the rally cry to end segregation at JHS 258.[30]

What are we to make of Jewish institutional support for the integration of New York City schools in the 1950s, and in particular the case of JHS 258? For an organization like the American Jewish Congress (AJC), support for JHS 258 was part of a self-consciously articulated platform for black civil rights in the 1950s.[31] Much of AJC's rhetoric on the importance of Jewish involvement in the fight for civil rights focused on three beliefs. First, the congress saw American Jews foremost as Americans with a commitment to uphold the founding premise of the nation, equality, freedom, and democracy. As it explicitly stated,"The problem of achieving equal rights for Negroes is not a Negro problem or a Southern problem, but an American problem."[32]

Second, the congress reminded its constituents that it was in the self-interest of American Jewry to fight for the rights of other minorities. "No minority in the United States can advance its own rights," Shad Polier, the chairman of the congress's Commission on Law and Social Action (CLSA) claimed, "without at the same time aiding others to secure the rights guaranteed by the Constitution and American tradition."[33] Offering a concrete example of this, Will Maslow, the director of CLSA, described how a recent court case that challenged restrictive housing covenants benefited blacks and Jews as well as other minority groups. At AJC's annual convention in 1956, Israel Goldstein, the opening speaker, asserted that the very survival of Jews in America was linked directly to "the achievement of full eqality for the most underprivileged racial group. . . .[34]

Finally, AJC framed the responsibility of American Jews to defend the rights of African-Americans as a moral issue linked directly to the recent history of Nazi genocide and rooted in biblical and Talmudic texts that directed Jews to fight for social justice. Polier quoted a Talmudic sage, "Separate not thyself from the community," and referred to the section in the Passover Haggadah where the wicked son is described as the one who has withdrawn himself from the community, as evidence of American Jewry's moral responsibilities to be active participants in the struggles for civil rights.[35]

In this postwar period the American Jewish Congress was constructing an identity for itself—and American Jewry—in which it called on American Jews to be "courageous" and to support AJC's program for proposing laws and legislation that would protect and advance civil rights and liberties.[36] In taking this proactive position, the American Jewish Congress was responding to American Jewish leaders and citizens who preferred an "isolationist" standpoint, did not want to "take upon ourselves the additional burden of fighting for the Negro," and feared that engaging in these issues would open the community to anti-Semitic attacks.[37]

The legislative and political strategy of AJC's Commission on Law and Social Action (founded in 1945) also came out of a critique of the "good fellowship" approach to community relations that was at its height during World War II. One of the domestic responses to the war against fascism on the part of civic organizations ranging from parents' associations to fraternal, religious, and labor organizations was to promote intergroup gatherings as a way to combat prejudice and build tolerance. In a harsh assessment, Polier charged Jewish organizations and synagogues that embraced the "intergroup statesmanship" approach with avoiding controversy and conflict in an attempt to create a feel-good interaction: ". . . restraint, proper decorum and the promotion of good fellowship were thought to be a sufficient formula for minority group survival in the real world."[38]

Polier's attack was directed especially at the American Jewish Committee and the Anti-Defamation League (ADL). Though both organizations had signed onto the Intergroup Committee on New York's Public Schools, their attention was directed toward creating antiprejudice propaganda and programs in intergroup education. As historian Stuart Svonkin has documented, by the mid-1950s the ADL staff devoted more than half of its time to its "education for tolerance" campaign, which included teacher training institutes and the development of curricular materials.[39] Based on the work of prominent sociologists and psychologists of the period, this antiprejudice orientation was rooted in a model of prejudice that focused on individual pathology rather than systemic inequality. The American Jewish Congress criticized this "attitude modification approach" for being ineffective and not addressing structural inequality. Will Maslow put it bluntly when he said, "Integrated public housing, for example, will do more to break down Negro-white feelings of hostility, distrust and aversion than sermons, Brotherhood Weeks, and sessions with one's analyst."[40]

The support of AJC and the other mainstream Jewish organizations for school integration in New York City was part of a general postwar expansion of mutual efforts between black and Jewish organizations that related to the impact of the Nazi genocide. However, as Cheryl Greenberg has documented, the nature of the collaborations was limited, and differences emerged over strategies and tactics.[41] In the New York City battle, differences emerged primarily when it looked like Jewish schoolchildren might be directly affected. In other words, support for the JHS 258 struggle on the part of the national leadership of the mainstream Jewish organizations could be wholehearted as the reconfiguring of zoning boundaries that the JHS 258 school integration activists called for did not have a direct impact on Jewish neighborhoods and the public schools that Brooklyn's Jewish schoolchildren attended. However, when the Board of Education's Commission on Integration, in the midst of the JHS 258 battle, completed its report and offered recommendations for rezoning to encourage integration, the American Jewish Congress was quick to reassure its constituency that Jewish schoolchildren would not be rerouted to "inadequate and inferior schools" a long distance from their homes.[42]

If the postwar period represented a time of a broader outreach in perspective and action for mainstream Jewish organizations like the American Jewish Congress, by the late 1950s they would begin to pull back inward to more narrow conceptions of what it meant to protect the interests of their constituency—American Jewry. The New York City Teachers Union, however, never abandoned the broad social platform of economic and racial justice even when criticized by its own members saying that the union was not protecting the interests of New York City teachers.

The story of the struggle to integrate JHS 258 would not be complete without discussing the role of the New York City Teachers Union. In the 1950s, dozens of teachers' associations represented New York City's nearly forty thousand teachers. Organized on the basis of various identities, they ranged from reflecting teachers' geographical placement (for example, the Bronx Boro-wide Association of Teachers) to grade placement (for example, the High School Teachers Association) and racial and religious association (for example, the Negro Teachers Association and Brooklyn Catholic Teachers Association). While no one organization represented a majority of teachers, it was the Teachers Union (TU) and the Teachers Guild (TG) that functioned as unions with the explicit mandate of protecting and expanding the rights of the city's teachers. The Teachers Union was the radical union of teachers with members who belonged to the Communist Party or were "fellow travelers"; like its nemesis, the Teachers Guild, its leadership and membership were predominantly Jewish but secular.

The Teachers Union was the backbone of every effort to integrate New York City schools. Since the 1930s, one of the Teachers Union's primary commitments was to fight for equal rights for African-Americans. The Teachers Union called attention to the inferior facilities that prevailed in schools with predominantly African-American students. It published studies on bias in the textbooks used in the city's schools and created "Negro History Week" curricula. The union was especially devoted to

teaching in the so-called difficult schools, and it agitated to get more African-American teachers in the schools.[43]

In the mid-1950s, when the organizing focus shifted to school segregation, the Teachers Union already had its own proposal for integrating the New York City Schools. The JHS 258 integration activists relied on this proposal, in addition to the budgetary analyses that the TU presented annually at New York's capital budget hearings, in preparing their own position papers and public statements.[44]

The Teachers Union stood out as the organization of teachers that actively organized with the JHS 258 school integration activists. The Teachers Guild did not take on the JHS 258 battle, though it supported the spirit of school integration through its membership in the Intergroup Committee on New York's Public Schools. By the early winter of 1957, the Teachers Guild along with the other teachers' associations was turning its attention to the proposals generated by the Board of Education's Commission on Integration. In January 1957, the commission tested its various recommendations for facilitating school integration through a public hearing. The commission's proposal to rotate teachers as one way to ensure that more experienced teachers also serve in the city's "difficult schools" proved to be wildly controversial. Once again, the Teachers Union was the only teacher organization to offer full-hearted support for the rotation proposal and the entire school integration effort.

Yet how much the public position of the TU reflected the opinions and concerns of its full membership is open to debate. Even for the presumably socially conscious TU membership the teacher rotation proposal proved to be a hard sell. Essentially the leadership was attempting to convince teachers that the broader social agenda of integration could be served simultaneously with the narrower personal agenda of protecting and expanding teachers' rights. As TU members voiced their concerns about the proposal, the TU board rejected the James Madison High School chapter's request that the issue be submitted to a referendum of the membership. Divided in its loyalties to the community and to its union members, the Executive Board of the TU chose the community. As the TU's secretary explained, ". . . many Executive Board members felt that a campaign on the issue of reconsideration of the Union's position, especially at this point, would also be harmful to the entire movement for school integration."[45]

The Teachers Union's energetic involvement in the "entire movement for school integration" was undoubtedly an irritant to the Board of Education. Yet the union's impact was limited and, by the mid-1950s, quite diminished. Like many Communist and left-wing organizations of the time, the Teachers Union was essentially persecuted out of existence: many of its members were suspended, some were fired, and the union had to redirect much of its energy to their legal defense.[46]

The insidious and pervasive culture of McCarthyism had several ill effects on the desegregation efforts in general and the particular story of JHS 258. During this period when civil rights were beginning to expand nationally, civil liberties were being restricted. As historian Gerald Horne has noted, "The trick was to open space for blacks while closing it down for their traditional allies."[47] This was the case in New York as the aura of McCarthyism distanced the Teachers Union further and further from coalitions with organizations that in principle should have been its natural partners. For example, the Teachers Union was excluded from the Intergroup Committee on New York's Public Schools.[48] As Charles Cogen, the president of the Teachers Guild, reminded a fellow Intergroup Committee member, the committee had "deliberately not offered membership to the TU." As Cogen rhetorically asked: "Is not this an indication that the Intergroup Committee deemed it unwise to associate itself with Communist-front groups in order to protect the cause of Integration against the inevitable harm that comes from any relationship with totalitarian regimes?"[49] The TG's strong feelings about the TU certainly reflected the guild's deep wounds from its ideological and political battles with the TU that dated back to the mid-1930s. The Cold War atmosphere also gave the Teachers Guild moral authority in its ongoing competition with the TU for a leadership position among the city's teachers. Whether the TG's concerns came from a position of pure ideological differences or political self-interest, the guild articulated the fears of integration activists who understood the tenor of the times.[50]

And over the years, prominent leaders consciously chose to disassociate themselves from the TU for fear of disabling the integration movement. Recall that early on, one way that the Board of Education attempted to discredit Kenneth Clark was by linking him to the Teachers Union. Clark obviously understood the implications of that perceived association, and so, when the TU selected Clark in 1956 to receive its annual award, he felt compelled to decline the offer. As he explained to the TU leadership, he declined reluctantly but because he understood the political climate of the times: "The basic reason for not accepting this award is my belief shared by my friends and advisers that such acceptance would, in light of the present situation, create an unnecessary side issue which would be exploited way beyond its significance by those who are opposed to an orderly and effective desegregation of public schools in southern states and in New York City."[51] Other leaders also exercised caution in choosing their allies in this period of McCarthyism. For example, it was not until after Reverend Galamison left the Brooklyn branch of the NAACP in the late 1950s that he finally felt able to make his association with the Teachers Union public by accepting an invitation to address its annual meeting.[52]

The Cold War then had a dramatic and critical effect on these school battles. On a logistical level, the daily effort of combating accusations of Communist affiliation effectively distracted individuals and organizations from the work of desegregation. The impact of these accusations, however, was even more fundamental. The linking of Communism with school integration served to discredit the integration efforts and limit the possibilities of the desegregation movement.

Analyzing the significance of the fact that the majority of the Teachers Union activists were Jews is a tricky endeavor, as it relates in part to the complicated relationship between history and memory and to the equally thorny issue of who authorizes identity. In the union's written record, there is almost no reference to the ethnic composition of its members, though news items in the *New York Teachers News*, the union's newspaper, suggest the involvement of TU members in the Workmen's Circle and other secular Jewish organizations. In addition, during World War II the paper focused much attention on the war against fascism.

It was during the McCarthy period that TU members made the most explicit reference to their Jewishness and, in a sense, publicly claimed their Jewish identity. When TU teachers were subject to the Board of Education's investigations, the union noted that most of the teachers investigated were Jewish and charged that anti-Semitism infused the campaign against the TU. Investigated teachers received anti-Semitic hate mail that said Hitler was right and included statements like "Jews don't make good Americans."[53] TU members went so far as to invoke Jewish Talmudic law when the Board of Education passed an "Informer Resolution" in 1955 making refusal to reveal the identity of fellow teachers associated with the Communist

258   LIVING IN BROOKLYN

Party grounds for dismissal. References to Talmudic admonitions with respect to informers were directed personally against Saul Moskoff, the Board of Education's assistant corporation counsel who had been assigned to investigate Communist teachers. TU activist Mildred Grossman undoubtedly appreciated that observing Jewish law was of importance to Moskoff, a practicing Jew and leader in his community where he served as the first vice president of Congregation Agudas Israel. Therefore, she sent a letter to the members of his congregation in which she outlined the Talmud's condemnation of informers and included a copy of a resolution against the "Informer Resolution" adopted by the New York Board of Rabbis. Moskoff, anticipating this line of attack, had already lined up his own rabbis to offer their interpretation of Jewish law pertaining to the *mosor*, the informant.[54]

While the battle over Talmudic interpretation did not carry much weight in the court of law, it revealed the political divisions within the Jewish community during the McCarthy decade. Organizations like the Anti-Defamation League, American Jewish Congress, and American Jewish Committee shared the TU's fears that some of the McCarthy attacks were driven by anti-Semitism and were concerned about protecting civil liberties. However, only the American Jewish Congress actively opposed the Feinberg Law, which barred members of the Communist Party and affiliated organizations from working in the public schools, and filed an amicus brief against the "Informer Resolution."[55] And though AJC and the TU may have shared similar concerns about anti-Semitism, the protection of civil liberties, and academic freedom, AJC never supported the suspended TU teachers. Like the other mainstream Jewish groups, and most liberal organizations, AJC adopted anti-Communist campaigns and excluded Communist-affiliated organizations from participating in Jewish communal associations. These associations pursued this campaign for ideological reasons and pragmatic ones; they wanted to protect themselves against anti-Semitic charges of being soft on Communism.

Outside of the organized Jewish community other groups also made the connection between the TU's radical platform and Jewish composition. For example, the *New York Age*, one of the city's African-American newspapers, noted that it was not just radicals but Jews who were being suspended by the Board of Education during the school witch-hunts. A quote from the *New York Age* noted the following: "Two disturbing facts about the continued firing

and suspension of teachers in the Board of Education's drive against subversives are that the ax appears directed primarily at Jews and that most of these teachers have been active in fighting against discrimination and for school improvements among minority groups.[56]

For Teachers Union activists who forty years after the fact recounted through oral history interviews the stories of their involvement in the TU and their efforts on behalf of school integration, the fact of their Jewishness was both obvious and meaningful. As one TU activist described, "of course the union was full of Jews as we were the children of immigrant parents who had been members of unions like the garment workers union."[57] In other words, unionism had been modeled for them. However, as TU members described, their concerns about issues of racial equality were related as much to their radical politics as to their Jewish background.[58] These people's activism and convictions during this period were shaped then by multiple identities: they were Communist Party members or fellow travelers; they came from Jewish homes; and they identified as children of immigrants. They were part of a union that linked campaigns to combat anti-Semitism with battles for racial equality. Celia Lewis Zitron, one union leader whom the Board of Education dismissed for refusing to answer questions about membership in the Communist Party, countered accusations of disloyalty and subversion by explaining that these struggles against bigotry and discrimination were the rights and responsibilities of teachers. This intersection of radicalism, unionism, and Jewishness partly explains why Jewish teachers, organizing through the New York City Teachers Union, actively involved themselves in the school desegregation battles.

The repression and ultimate dissolution of the New York City Teachers Union had symbolic and real significance to the school integration battles that would continue into the mid-1960s. The loss of the TU represented the loss of white, Jewish allies who saw the goals of racial integration and equal education and teacher's rights as inextricably linked. And it paved the way for the school desegregation conflict to become further polarized between white and black voices. The story of JHS 258 represented a brief moment when blacks and Jews pursued a common goal, in some cases out of self-interest and in others out of a shared vision. After over two years, however, of working to make this school into a "pilot project" for a new model of integration—work that included conducting studies; presenting findings at hearings with the schools superintendent, Board of Education leaders, and members of the board's newly established Commission on Integration; and organizing meetings and rallies in the community—the student register for the school totaled 1,462 African-American students, 26 Puerto Rican students, and 9 white students.[59]

Even when the national office of the NAACP worked with the Brooklyn branch to exert pressure on candidates running for city and state offices, their efforts produced little but empty campaign promises. At the NAACP state convention leaders threatened Mayor Wagner ". . . that some 25,000 persons in the heavily Negro Bedford-Stuyvesant section 'will swing to the Republicans if this isn't cleaned up.'"[60] Though the NAACP claimed that the mayor responded with a promise that he would see that action was taken to integrate JHS 258 "tomorrow," in fact Wagner never exerted pressure on the Board of Education. Wagner left the issue in the hands of Frank Horne, the executive director of the Mayor's Commission on Intergroup Relations (COIR). Horne participated in many meetings with the Brooklyn branch activists and even offered an alternative proposal for integrating JHS 258 that would supposedly be less threatening to the community's white families.[61] In the final assessment, Horne and COIR had little influence on the mayor and the Board of Education. And the more provocative demands and protests of the local leaders yielded little response from the mayor's office.

What the local leaders and activists in this struggle finally understood was that the Board of Education had no intention of integrating JHS 258. While the integration activists may have initially been led to believe that some board leaders supported the effort to open JHS 258 as an integrated school, there proved to be little backing for this effort within the Board of Education administration. Schools Superintendent Jansen and his assistant superintendents fundamentally disagreed with the rezoning proposals that the integration leaders advanced. From their perspective, the school was practically inaccessible to non-Negro pupils.[62] The board's resistance to integrating JHS 258 reflected its fundamental opposition to rezoning schools in order to facilitate integration.

The Board of Education did not encounter opposition among the white residents in the area of JHS 61, the school that the integration activists proposed be integrated with JHS 258. The board never adopted a plan for integration to which local white families needed to respond. Yet the testimony of white parents at the Commission on Integration's public hearing, which happened amidst the efforts to integrate JHS 258, offered the board important information about the fears of the parents in the city's white working-class communities. Some couched their concerns in a race-blind rhetoric while others were explicitly racist; yet all who testified were unequivocal in their opposition to the commission's zoning proposal, which simply recommended that integration be added to the Board of Education's existing zoning criteria.[63] These families feared, perhaps rightfully so, that experiments in integration would be done at their expense. Certainly they knew that they did not have the economic options to be part of the large wave of white middle-class families who were fleeing the city for the suburbs. Nor did they have the resources to send their children to private schools as did the black and white middle class.[64]

Over the next ten years white working-class residents would become far more vocal and active in their opposition to the possibility of school integration. The Board of Education would continue to resist the efforts of parents and leaders—including some of the same people involved in the struggle to integrate JHS 258—engaged in a variety of tactics to integrate New York's public schools. By 1964, however, the school integration movement's window of opportunity was closing due to the increase in residential segregation in New York and the upsurge in "white flight" from the city. In 1964 there were more than two hundred segregated schools, a 400 percent increase since 1954.[65]

The outcome of this northern school integration effort can be understood most simply in relation to the deep-rooted, though often denied, race-based ideology that permeated New York's institutions and white communities. As a local case study of black-Jewish relations, this story suggests that the project of untangling the history of black-Jewish relations is a far more complicated endeavor that involves accounting for the heterogeneous nature of the Jewish community and exploring issues of identity, self-representation, and representation by others. The Jewish players in this effort illustrate that some, like the American Jewish Congress, identified almost exclusively on the basis of ethnicity and religion. During this period these Jewish leaders defined their self-interest in relation to integration and black civil rights. Self-interest would begin to shift within a few years as the leadership had to assure its constituents in Jewish neighborhoods that it did not support busing. Smaller groups, like the Teachers Union, were driven by political persuasion that may have (or not) been influenced by a Jewish background and identity. The support of radical Jewish teachers and the major Jewish civic organizations for school integration suggests that, at least for the moment, New York's Jews were falling outside of David Roediger's paradigm of a "pan-ethnic" ideology that was evolving in relation to race.[66]

Ultimately it was the Board of Education that failed the test of integrating JHS 258. In this failure, the board laid the foundation for a two-tiered, race-based school system in Brooklyn that would lead to the dramatic Ocean Hill–Brownsville confrontation of 1968. The polarization of black and Jewish voices that has come to epitomize the Ocean Hill–Brownsville struggle also had its roots in the failure to integrate JHS 258. The Teachers Union, with its unequivocal support of integration, lost the union election in 1960 to the newly formed United Federation of Teachers (UFT), and within a few years disbanded. Similar in ethnic composition to the Teachers Union, the UFT with its predominantly Jewish leadership and membership was more similar in outlook to organizations like the American Jewish Congress in relation to issues of racial integration. With a stellar record when it came to supporting school integration efforts in the South, the UFT's self-interest often came into conflict with the city's school integration activists. These conflicts would emerge full-blown in the Ocean Hill–Brownsville struggle. The failure of the integration efforts gave rise to the Ocean Hill–Brownsville community control experiment. The explosiveness of this event—fourteen years after the *Brown v. Board of Education* decision and after the New York City Board of Education set up its own Commission on Integration—that suggests that, in one sense, the Ocean Hill–Brownsville struggle marks the end, and not the beginning, of the story.

NOTES

This chapter was first published in *Journal of American Ethnic History* (Winter 2001).

Many thanks to Pennee Bender, Linda Gaal, Molly McGarry, Wendell Pritchett, and Daniel Walkowitz for their helpful comments on earlier versions of this essay.

1. The last decade has seen a flurry of new publications about the history of and current relations between African-Americans and American Jews including Paul Berman, ed., *Blacks and Jews: Alliances and Arguments* (New York: Delta, 1994); Emily Miller Budick, *Blacks and Jews in Literary Conversation* (New York: Cambridge University Press, 1998); Jack Greenberg, *Crusaders in the Courts: How a Dedicated Band of Lawyers Fought for the Civil Rights Movement* (New York: Basic Books, 1994); Michael Lerner and Cornel West, *Jews and Blacks: Let the Healing Begin* (New York: G. Putnam's Sons, 1995); Jack Salzman with Adina Back and Gretchen Sullivan Sorin, eds., *Bridges and Boundaries: African-Americans and American*

Jews (New York: George Braziller, 1992). The essays in *Struggles in the Promised Land* edited by Jack Salzman and Cornel West (New York: Oxford University Press, 1997) offer the most comprehensive and complex overview of the history to date. Within that volume, the article by Paul Buhle and Robin D.G. Kelley, "Allies of a Different Sort: Jews and Blacks in the American Left" is illustrative of historical interpretations that challenge popular conceptions about the relations between blacks and Jews and offers a reperiodization of that history through looking at different groups, radical blacks and Jews in this case.

2. George Lipsitz, "The Possessive Investment in Whiteness," *American Quarterly* 47 (September 1995): 369–87.

3. *New York Amsterdam News*, November 14,1945.

4. Preliminary Statement of the Board of Education Resolution of Action, December 23, 1954, Board of Education Papers, Special Collections, Milbank Memorial Library, Teachers College, Columbia University (hereafter referred to as B/E). S. 261, F.21

5. Speech by Kenneth B. Clark, Urban League of Greater New York, Negro History Week–Brotherhood Month Dinner, February 15, 1954, pp 1–2, United Parents Association Archives, Special Collections, Milbank Memorial Library, Teachers College, Columbia University (hereafter referred to as UPA).

6. Letter to Rose Shapiro [chair of the Public Education Association's Committee on Equality in Education] from Schools Superintendent William Jansen, January 18, 1955, B/E, S. 456, F. 3.

7. Letter to William Jansen from Clare C. Baldwin, Assistant Superintendent, May 12,1954, pp. 2–3,B/E, S. 456, F. 2C.

8. Remarks by Mayor Wagner at Dinner of the Urban League, February 15, 1954, New York City Municipal Archives, Robert F. Wagner Subject Files, Box 59, F. 685. February 2, 1956, Press Release on appointment of Dr. Frank S. Horn as executive director of the newly created Commission on Intergroup Relations, Wagner Subject Files, Box 76, F.1073.

9. Letter to William Jansen from Paul W. Aron, November 22, 1954, B/E, S. 456, F. 2c.

10. It was Arthur Levitt, one of the commission's co-chairs, who suggested that the segregation problems at JHS 258 could be resolved through "a pilot project" that would represent a new integration model. Letter to Reverend Shockley and Winston Craig of the NAACP from Col. Arthur Levitt, May 1, 1956, National Association for the Advancement of Colored People Papers, Collection of the Manuscript Division, Library of Congress (hereafter referred to as NAACP) NAACP III, A103.

11. "Suggested Plan for Desegregation of JHS 258 for the September 1956 School Year," Brooklyn Branch, NAACP. NAACP III, A103.

12. *New Amsterdam News*, June 30, 1956.

13. An Open Letter to Superintendent of Schools William Jansen from Milton A. Galamison, Co-Chairman Education Committee, Brooklyn Branch NAACP, November 1, 1956, NAACP III, A103.

14. Memorandum to the Board of Education of the City of New York from the Brooklyn Branch, NAACP, February 3, 1956, p.2, NAACP III, A103.

15. Clarence Taylor, *Knocking at Our Own Door: Milton A. Galamison and the Struggle to Integrate New York City Schools* (New York: Columbia University Press, 1997), 46.

16. To what extent Annie Stein identified as a Jew is open to speculation. Like many radical Jews of her generation, Stein, who died in 1982, seemed to operate more out of a political worldview than a religious or cultural one. Yet the fact that she was chair of the American Jewish Congress's Education Committee suggests that she claimed her Jewish background, whether for professionally pragmatic, politically

strategic, or culturally identified reasons. Résumé, Annie Stein Papers, Public Education Association (PEA).

17. Taylor, *Knocking at Our Own Door*, 55–60. June Shagaloff, then field representative with the NAACP Legal Defense and Education Fund, also refers to Red-baiting that went on in the Brooklyn branch of the NAACP (and the NAACP in general). Author's interview with June Shagaloff, September 20,1995.

18. "The Facts in Our Community," Report to the Members of the Executive Board, Brooklyn Branch NAACP, April 12, 1956, NAACP III, A103.

19. *New York Amsterdam News*, November 14,1945. Celia Lewis Zitron, *The New York City Teachers Union* (New York: Humanities Press, 1968), 92–93. June Shagaloff, who began working with the NAACP Legal Defense and Educational Fund under Thurgood Marshall in the early 1950s, described her amazement by and awe of parents who "stayed with it"—the school desegregation struggle—for years (author's interview).

20. "Integrate JHS 258 Now," June 2, 1956; "King's Diary," June 9 and June 23, 1956; "NAACP to Hold Rally Thursday," and "Segregation at JHS 258," June 16, 1956, *New York Amsterdam News*.

21. "King's Diary," *New York Amsterdam News*, June 30, 1956.

22. Ibid.

23. "NAACP Meeting on Bias Planned," *New York Amsterdam News*, June 9, 1956.

24. Memorandum to Roy Wilkins [head of the national NAACP] from his assistant, John Morsell, November 14, 1956, NAACP III, A103.

25. *New York Times*, November 2, 1956.

26. Letter to John Theobald, Deputy Mayor, from Superintendent Jansen, October 26, 1956, B/E, S. 261, B.1, F. 3.

27. Letter to President Silver from Kenneth B. Clark, November 2, 1956, B/E, S. 26l, B.1, F. 3. See also letter to President Silver from the Intergroup Committee on New York's Public Schools, November 14, 1956, NAACP III, A103.

28. Author's interview with June Shagaloff.

29. The Intergroup Committee was founded as a result of a conference that Kenneth Clark organized in April 1954. "Conference Recommendations," B/E, S. 456, F. 2c.

30. "Background on JHS 258" and "NAACP Rally," NAACP III, A103.

31. See Stuart Svonkin for a more comprehensive portrait of AJC's support (as well as that of the American Jewish Committee and the Anti-Defamation League) for black civil rights in this period. *Jews Against Prejudice: American Jews and the Fight for Civil Liberties* (New York: Columbia University Press, 1997).

32. "To End Inequality," *Congress Weekly*, October 24, 1955. This claim was made repeatedly in the pages of *Congress Weekly*, AJC's newspaper, generally in reference to a current battle for civil rights. The aforementioned quote was in reference to the recent murder of Emmett Till.

33. "Past Lessons and New Directions," *Congress Weekly*, April 16, 1956, p. 22.

34. "Social Change through Legal Action" and "Areas of Jewish Concern," *Congress Weekly*, January 10, 1955, and April 23, 1956.

35. "Past Lessons and New Directions" and "False Race Theories," *Congress Weekly*, April 16, 1956, p. 23, and October 15, 1956, p. 3. Press Release, "American Jewish Congress Leader Deplores Failure of Two National Jewish Agencies to Take Stand on Segregation," May 22, 1956, American Jewish Congress Archives, New York, N.Y.

36. In an editorial, the American Jewish Congress asserted, "Only a courageous American Jew can hope to preserve his joint heritage." *Congress Weekly*, April 16, 1956, p. 4.

37. "Past Lessons and New Directions" and "Areas of Jewish Concern," p. 30. Cheryl Greenberg offers examples of ADL's resistance during World War II to allying itself with African-American organizations and causes for fear of jeopardizing American Jewry's "already tenous position in America." Greenberg, "Negotiating Coalition: Black and Jewish Civil Rights Agencies in the Twentieth Century," in *Struggles in the Promised Land*, 158–59.

38. "Past Lessons and New Directions," p. 21.

39. Svonkin, *Jews against Prejudice*, 70. See chapters 2 and 3 for an expanded discussion of the American Jewish Committee and ADL's antiprejudice work. I have not found evidence of the materials that these organizations produced having made their way to the students or teachers at JHS 258. I have seen references, however, to these resources and "goodwill workshops" in Manhattan-based schools that saw large influxes of Puerto Rican students in the 1950s.

40. "Social Change through Legal Action," p. 12.

41. Greenberg, "Negotiating Coalition," 160–63. According to Michael Staub, by the mid-1960s a growing body of American Jewish leaders used Holocaust rhetoric to criticize the involvement of progressive Jews in the civil rights movement. See Michael Staub, "'Negroes Are Not Jews': Holocaust Consciousness, Black Civil Rights, and the Roots of Jewish Neoconservatism," *Radical History Review* 75 (fall 1999): 3–27.

42. "From Color Blind to Color Conscious," *Congress Weekly*, March 25, 1957, p. 9.

43. Author's interview with Anne R. Matlin (Teachers Union member, 1937–64), Manhattan, March 7, 1996; *Bias and Prejudice in Textbooks in Use in New York City Schools: An Indictment*, published by the Teachers Union, Local 555, UPW, 1949, Teachers Union of the City of New York Records, Labor-Management Documentation Center, Cornell University (hereafter referred to as TU Collection), 45–1; *A Survey of the Employment of Negro Teachers in New York City Schools*, conducted by the Teachers Union, Spring Term 1955, and *Program to Increase Number of Negro Teachers Employed in New York City Schools*, June 14, 1955; "Proposals for Special Steps to Improve the Staffing of So-Called 'Difficult' Schools," May 17, 1955, TU Collection, 45–5 and 76–6. For a summary of the union's "Negro History Week" curricula, see *New York Teacher News*, January 18, 1964, p. 3; interview with Alice Citron (TU teacher who spearheaded this work in the 1930s and 1940s), *Tamiment Oral History of the Left Collection*, January 6, 1981; and Zitron, *New York City Teachers Union*.

44. See, for example, "Program for Integration of Schools," December 1955, and letter from Rose Russell (TU legislative representative) to Annie Stein responding to Stein's request for the TU's school integration program, December 22, 1955, TU Collection, 45–6 and 44–16.

45. Letter to Albert Drachman, Madison Chapter, from Lawrence Lane, TU Executive Board Secretary, March 15, 1957; Letter from Fellow Member of the Madison TU Chapter, February 28, 1957; Letter from Les Speiser to Abe Lederman, February 18, 1957, TU Collection, 45–11, 44–14, 45–1.

46. "Negro History Week and the 8 Suspended Teachers," February 1952, TU Collection, 44–11; Murphy, *Blackboard Unions*, 184–95. While there is not yet a definitive study on the New York City Teachers Union and the relationship of its members to the Communist Party, Ellen Schrecker, in her exhaustive study of McCarthyism, concludes that most of the people called before the committees "had once been in or near the Communist Party." *Many Are the Crimes: McCarthyism in America* (Princeton: Princeton Univeristy Press, 1998), 4.

47. Gerald Horne, *Black Liberation/Red Scare: Ben Davis and the Communist Party* (Newark: University of Delaware Press, 1994), 13. Ellen Schrecker offers further documentation on the impact of McCarthyism

on the civil rights movement and the ways in which "Anticommunism proved invaluable to white supremacists." See *Many Are the Crimes*, 389–95.

48. Letter from Rose Russell to Hubert Delany (Intergroup Committee chairman), June 15, 1959, TU Collection 44–15. In the letter, Russell urged the Intergroup Committee to "break down the McCarthy 'ban.'"

49. Letter from Charles Cogen, President, Teachers Guild, to Edward Lewis, Executive Secretary, Urban League of the Greater New York, May 10, 1957, Teachers Guild, United Federation of Teachers Archives Collection, Robert F. Wagner Labor Archives, New York University (hereafter referred to as UFT-TG), UFT-TG, 1935–69, B. 5.

50. When black teachers founded the Negro Teachers Association (NTA) in 1956, they too understood that to establish its credibility the association had to situate itself in opposition to the TU. "Should we join the Teachers Union?" the NTA asked rhetorically. "As you know it is listed as subversive by the U.S. Attorney General. We are loyal Americans!" See "Negro Teacher Assn. Answers Mr. Granger," *New York Amsterdam News*, December 8, 1956.

51. Letter from Kenneth Clark to Rose Russell, January 27, 1956, Kenneth B. Clark Papers, the Collections of the Manuscript Division, the Library of Congress (hereafter referred to as the KBC Papers), B. 78, F: "B/E Commission on Integration, Subcommittee on Educational Standards and Curriculum, Correspondence, 1956."

52. Letter from Milton A. Galamison to Rose Russell, November 25, 1959, Milton A. Galamison Papers, Reel 33, State Historical Society of Wisconsin.

53. Quoted in Murphy, *Blackboard Unions*, 191.

54. Letter from Rabbi Benajmin Sharfman to Saul Moskoff, August 17, 1953, and Letter from Saul Moskoff to Rabbi Theodore Adams, President, Rabbinical Council of America, October 22,1953, B/E, S. 593, B.1, F. 5. Letter to Dr. Jansen from Saul Moskoff and Memorandum Re: New York Board of Rabbis, April 26, 1955; and Letter from Leonard Boudin (Mildred Grossman's attorney) to Saul Moskoff, April 28,1955, B/E, S. 593, B.1, F.5. I am grateful to filmmaker Sophie-Louise Ullman-Vidal for drawing my attention to these materials.

55. In 1949 New York State adopted the Feinberg Law, which required teachers to take a loyalty oath and gave permission to school superintendents to seek out Communists in schools. Brief Amicus Curiae of the New York Council American Jewish Congress, December 15, 1955; and Letter from Alexander Brooks (director of the American Jewish Congress's Commission on Law and Social Action) to Saul Moskoff, December 19,1955, B/E, S. 593, B. 1, F. 4. See Svonkin, *Jews against Prejudice*, chapters 5–7, for a discussion of the Jewish communal associations' anti-communist campaigns and liberal anti-communism.

56. *New York Age*, February 9, 1952.

57. Author's interview with Anne Filardo, November 2, 1995, Brooklyn, New York, and follow-up phone interview, November 3, 1998. The majority of teachers that Ruth Jacknow Markowitz interviewed were daughters of unionists. See Ruth Jacknow Markowitz, *My Daughter, the Teacher: Jewish Teachers in the New York City Schools* (New Brunswick, N.J.: Rutgers University Press, 1993), 151.

58. Author's interview with Henry Foner (phone interview), May 17, 1992, Queens, New York; and with Anne Matlin; interview with Alice Citron, *Tamiment Oral History of the Left Collection*; and oral history interviews included in "Dreamers and Fighters," a video documentary about the New York City Teachers Union produced by Sophie-Louise Ullman-Vidal (in progress).

59. Letter to William Jansen from Joseph Noethen, February 5, 1957, p. 4 B/E, S. 261, B.1, F.3.

60. "Brooklyn Pupils Shifted in Integration Program," *Herald Tribune*, October 30, 1956; and Robert Carter [of NAACP's National Legal Department], Report of Meeting with Brooklyn Branch Re: School Desegregation, September 30, 1956, NAACP III, A03.

61. Letters to Celia Sands from Frank S. Horne, August 13 and October 30, 1956, and letters to Charles Silver from Frank S. Horne, February 25 and March 28, 1957, B/E, S. 261, B. 1, F. 3.

62. Resolution Adopted by Board of Education, October 25, 1956, B/E, S. 261, B. 1, F. 7.

63. Commission on Integration Public Hearing, January 17, 1957, and Letters to Board of Education, B/E, S. 261, B. 2, F. 14, and B. 1, F. 9 and 10.

64. 1959 report confirmed these trends and documented that between 1950 and 1957 New York City lost a white population of 750,000 and gained a black and Puerto Rican population of 650,000. Apparently the biggest factor in the shift of white families related to the influx of black and Puerto Rican pupils into the city's schools. During this same period, the enrollment in the city's private and parochial schools had expanded dramatically. For example, one private school in Brooklyn had a 50 percent increase in students since 1954. Ninety percent of its student body was African-American. Similar trends were noted in Harlem's parochial schools. Quoted in "School Question Upsets Families," *New York Times*, September 20, 1959. Notably, even some of the black integration leaders, including Reverend Galamison, sent their children to private schools.

65. The 400 percent increase in segregated schools represented a jump from 52 to 201 racially segregated schools. It was Annie Stein who continued to provide statistical analysis for school integration activists. Analyzing the Board of Education's capital budget for 1965–71, she noted that it represented "an investment of $335,600,000 in new segregation" with over half of the 210 schools projected to be built in either all-white or all-black and Puerto Rican neighborhoods. See Annie Stein, "Containment and Control: A Look at the Record," in *Schools against Children*, ed. Annette T. Rubinstein (New York: Monthly Review Press, 1970), 28.

66. David Roediger argues that this "pan-ethnic" ideology made it possible for communities to be "self-consciously 'white ethnic,' but less self-consciously Greek, Polish or Italian at the same time." See "Whiteness and Ethnicity in the History of 'White Ethnics' in the United States," in *Toward the Abolition of Whiteness: Essays on Race, Politics and Working Class History* (London: Verso, 1994), 183.

A Tour of Jewish Coney Island Avenue

Text and Photos by

SEÁN GALVIN

Using an approximation of the model set forth by Allen J. Abel's 1995 study, *Flatbush Odyssey: Journey through the Heart of Brooklyn,* we[1] undertook a documentary study of Jewish Coney Island Avenue. This thoroughfare runs north-south from the base of Prospect Park at Park Circle to the Atlantic Ocean at Brighton Beach. Abel had conducted an exhaustive ethnographic study of the major avenue that essentially bisects the borough, including the myriad ethnic groups represented thereon. Our aim was to focus exclusively on signs and storefronts as markers of Jewish culture and identity on Coney Island Avenue. Why? The questions to hand were: Is there a recognizable Jewish presence on Coney Island Avenue to the untutored (read: non-Jewish) eye? Or are there manifest symbols of Jewish identity visible only to the "insider," one perhaps who understands Yiddish or Hebrew or Russian? Or, contrariwise, is Coney Island Avenue simply an endless sea of signs and storefronts indistinguishable from any other Brooklyn thoroughfare? The challenge, then, would be to capture, in a short series of images, those signs, whether apparent or hidden, of the continuing Jewish presence on one major artery in Brooklyn.

In a recent article, "Four Corners: When Shifting Groups of Immigrants Compete for the Same Turf, Even an Intersection Can Become Contested Ground," writer Nina Siegal chose a part of Coney Island Avenue as one of her "four corners" to study. Her thesis is simple:

> There is a saying among urban historians: You can always tell how a neighborhood is changing. The name of the outgoing ethnic group is on the funeral homes, and that of the incoming group is on the grocery stores. . . . The phenomenon, which sociologists call ethnic succession, is as old as the city itself and may be heightened in New York because of its size and the multiplicity of ethnic groups jostling for the same turf. A single street corner can become central to a group's identity. (Siegal 2000, 1)

This corner of her story directly concerns the Jews of Brooklyn. She tells how Yakov Semichan, the owner of a Russian Jewish barbershop, which has been at the corner of Glenwood Road and Coney Island Avenue for nine years, has seen his customer base slowly erode as the "Orthodox and Russian Jews whose synagogues and kosher restaurants once dominated the corner, have been departing for wealthier sections of Flatbush. Pakistani immigrants and businesses that catered to them were replacing

Talmud Torah of Flatbush, 1200 CIA (Avenues H and I). Synagogue-based Hebrew school, established 1925.

the former Jewish inhabitants" (Siegal 2000). Semichan struck a bold compromise after a second Pakistani barbershop opened across the street from him—he offered Shabbir Hussain, a Pakistani immigrant, one of the barber chairs in his shop, and "put a bright green sign in the window advertising, 'We speak Russian, English and Yiddish,' along with Mr. Hussain's name translated into Urdu, the Pakistani language" (Siegal 2000).

There are many ways of approaching an ethnographic study in a protean urban environment. Folklorist Barbara Kirshenblatt-Gimblett wrote a pioneering article titled "Times Square: A Pedestrian Perspective," as part of a 1989 conference celebrating "Times Square at the Crossroads of the World." She began by examining the different perspectives one may have of a place depending on the direction from which one approaches it, such as "the Broadway orientation, the 42nd Street orientation, the Midtown or West Side orientation," and so on, for Times Square (Kirshenblatt-Gimblett 1995, 170). So, too, with Coney Island Avenue (hereafter CIA). From the perspective of Prospect Park driving south, CIA looks very eclectically mixed—first

Golan Dry Fruit, 1348 CIA (corner Avenue J). Geography of Israel is mapped onto this predominantly Jewish neighborhood store.

some light industry, then commercial—some Asian, some Italian, some nondescript, some Jewish, then some Bangladeshi, and so forth, then stretches of mixed commercial at street level and residential above, then exclusively residential, before all or parts of the mix are repeated.

But, from the perspective of crossing CIA from Avenue J, the heart of Jewish Flatbush, or at Avenue M, the center

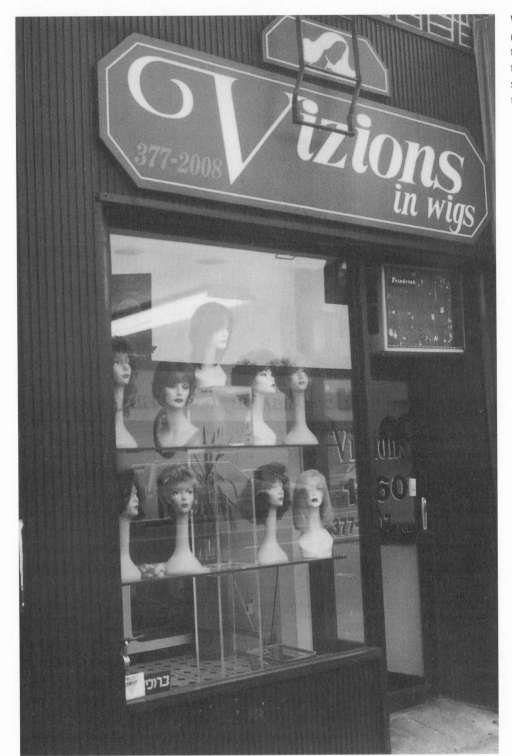

of Jewish Midwood, you might think CIA was almost exclusively Jewish-owned, Jewish-run, and Jewish-peopled. For example, from Fifteenth Street west of CIA on Avenue J, where the D and Q trains run overhead, going toward CIA, the storefronts were visibly, and almost exclusively, Jewish: "Natanya Fast Food & Pizza" (says "kosher" on the sign); "Kosher Bagel Hole"; "Garden of Eat-In Brooklyn's Finest Dairy Restaurant—Cholov Yisroel"; "Discount Store" (says "Shomer Shabat"); "Glatt Kosher Israeli and Middle Eastern Cuisine"; "Koolest Shoes by Fran" (Hebrew on awning); "China Glatt Kosher Chinese"; or "Avenue J Drugs" (sign in Hebrew). And, on the other side of CIA, the neigh-

"True Value" Esrogei, Moshe Friedman, 1400 CIA (Avenues J and K). As is typical on CIA, Moshe Friedman took advantage of the closing of the hardware store to hang his sign in preparation for Sukkos.

borhood is exclusively residential to Ocean Parkway with mezuzahs over doors, yarmulked children playing in yards, and residences with Hebrew nameplates on doors, to name just a few ostensible signs of Jewishness.

If you were to drive along any stretch of CIA on a Friday evening or Saturday during the day, then you would *feel* the Jewish presence by the long stretches of locked-up, closed-up, darkened storefronts alternating with the busy-bee, familiar weekend activities of other Brooklynites shopping for food, Bangladeshi men clustered on street corners talking and smoking, or nondescript couples walking the lots of the many car dealerships, angling for a deal. The Jewish-inhabited neighborhood presence would reveal itself only as you notice the single man or clusters of observant Jews walking to or from Sabbath services. And, as becomes abundantly clear from studying the types of commercial and religious establishments along these stretches of CIA, this Jewish "presence" is almost entirely composed of businesses or services that cater to the Orthodox Jewish community.

Over a two-year period (1998–2000) we saw storefronts that had existed for years, but that upon our return only weeks later were boarded up or had "Moved to [Wherever]" in the window with little else other than the sign overhead as proof they had once operated there. Park Circle is the very beginning of Coney Island Avenue. With direct acknowledgment of the aforementioned "Four Corners," we notice how the long-standing Riverside

Row of buildings, 1380 CIA (Avenues J and K). Note density of Jewish businesses in this short stretch of CIA.

Pentecostal Assembly of God, 1406 CIA (Avenues J and K). Missionary Pentecostal congregation masquerading as Jewish.

Eichler's Religious Articles & Books, 1401 CIA (Avenues J and K). Large, modern, high-tech Judaica center in heart of Jewish CIA.

Midwood Chapels (clock), 1625 CIA (corner Avenue M). The Hebrew letters in this clock indicate Jewish ritual time.

Memorial Chapels at Park Circle has morphed into an International Baptist Church congregation with little fanfare. On the side of the building that faces CIA, however, the sign reads "Iglesia Bautista Internacional," which offers a clue as to who the latest "newcomers" are to the neighborhood. In the same "Bangladeshi" neighborhood Siegal mentions, there has been a recent explosion of new food purveyors, telecommunications companies, and mom-and-pop shops in the course of the last nine months, which only emphasizes CIA's ever-changing composition and gives credence to the ongoing ethnic succession. Farther down, in the 1300 block of CIA, Bodek Kosher Products, Inc., has been replaced by yet another Jewish establishment. Or, in another example, the Garlick Funeral Home has moved twenty blocks north and the sign on the new establishment is written in Russian, indicating how the boundaries of this community have expanded northward. This type of business turnover, especially cases in which both the outgoing and incoming parties are Jewish, is a common occurrence along CIA, which points to a certain stability within the Jewish community at large.

A BRIEF HISTORY

Kirshenblatt-Gimblett also refers to the Times Square area as "various combinations of microregions [that] form

Row of buildings, 1431–33 CIA (Avenues J and K). Kosher Bagel Hole, the inevitable noshery; Bodek Kosher Products (1999), since replaced (2000) by another Jewish business—EASE/Tafkid.

Glatt Mart, 1205 Avenue M (E. 12th Street). Glatt Kosher has become the accepted standard in this neighborhood one block off CIA.

[right] "All Roads Lead to Midwood" mural (detail, side of Glatt Mart), 1205 Avenue M (at E. 12th Street). "This mural was made possible by the Midwood Development Corporation and in part by Glatt Mart. Special thanks go out to Noach Dear . . . June 25, 1998." The mural symbolizes the diversity of the people, food, and services available in this neighborhood.

[below] Lag b'Omer posters (Russian/Hebrew), 1800 CIA (corner Avenue N). Outreach to Russians in Midwood to join in celebration of festival in 1999.

various larger wholes" (1995, 171). Similarly, today's Coney Island Avenue crosses or forms the outer boundary of (1) the residential areas near Prospect Park, such as Albemarle, Kensington, and Parkville; (2) East Flatbush, including the neighborhoods of Prospect Park South, Ditmas Park West, and West Midwood; (3) Midwood; (4) Sheepshead Bay and the Kings Highway retail center, which borders on Homecrest; and (5) Brighton Beach. Brooklyn, the borough of neighborhoods, is technically composed of some ninety-nine distinctly bounded demarcations, but to be honest, it is mostly real estate agents who split hairs to these extremes. Someone giving directions along Coney Island Avenue would generally use the greater wholes of Flatbush, Midwood, Kings Highway, Sheepshead Bay, and Brighton as locators.

As we have said, Coney Island Avenue is by no means entirely Jewish-inhabited, or for that matter predominantly run by Jewish merchants, although historically, Jews have inhabited, or continue to live, work, and worship, along its entire length in varying degrees of density. That is to say, for long stretches of its six-mile length there are what appear to be a preponderance of Jewish-owned stores, intersticed by lengths of equally non-Jewish merchants. It is no accident, then, that the stretches of Jewish entrepreneurship correspond to the subsequent waves of Jewish immigrants from Eastern Europe, then from Russia, and, most recently, from Israel.

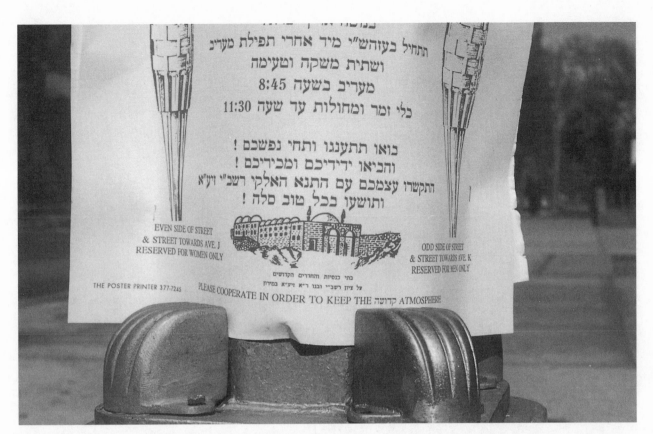

Detail of Lag b'Omer posters, 1800 CIA (corner Avenue N). Note how parking rules (e.g., "Even side of street & street towards Avenue J reserved for women only") mirror seating segregation in Orthodox synagogue.

The Kosher Gym, 1800 CIA (Avenues N and O). So what's kosher about a gym? Men and women surely exercise separately?

[above] Mekor Haseforim, 1987 CIA (Avenue P and Quentin Road). Sephardic Judaica store includes specialty items such as items for swanee engagement parties, for Syrian customers.

[left] Mekor Haseforim (close-up), 1987 CIA (Avenue P and Quentin Road). The passages from the Torah inside the tefillin and mezuzah must be ritually pure to maintain and ensure efficacy.

[below] The Torah Times, 1839 CIA (Avenues N and O). These kiosks are ubiquitous in New York City. There is a proliferation of specialized Jewish newspapers in this neighborhood—Torah Times is just one example.

Yablokoff Kingsway Memorial Chapel, 1978 CIA (Avenue P and Quentin Road). This is one of six Jewish memorial chapels on Coney Island Avenue.

The early development and origin of Coney Island Avenue may be quickly summarized by two studies:

> In 1823, the Coney Island Road and Bridge Company, a private enterprise . . . built the Coney Island Causeway, also known as the Shell Road. . . . In 1876, Andrew Culver acquired the interests and built his steam railroad along the Shell Road. The Coney Island Plank Road opened in 1850. The planks were removed in 1860, the road was turnpiked and a line of horse cars began operation. It was the principal road to the shore, and is the Coney Island Avenue of today. Later, open trolley cars operated by the Smith Street and Franklin Avenue lines, running down Coney Island Avenue and through Gravesend, yearly carried crowds to Coney Island. . . . (*Brooklyn Eagle*, as cited in Lines 1949, 5)

Another view, providing the history of the development of Coney Island, reveals that

> by the end of the 1870s, additional railroads had come to Coney Island—the New York and Sea Beach Railroad, the Brooklyn, Flatbush and Coney Island Railroad, which became today's Brighton Line, and the

"Irgun Shofar" (window of Fontana), 2086 CIA (Kings Highway and Avenue R). It is important for a kosher food establishment to include evidence of its supervising rabbi.

Prospect and Coney Island Railroad, which exists today as the Culver (F train) line running along McDonald Avenue. These lines not only ensured the future of Coney Island as a great resort, but also promoted the development of farmland along the rights-of-way. Concurrent with the development of these rail links to the Atlantic Ocean was the creation of the beachfront area around Coney Island itself. (Merlis 1995, 76)

What we learn, then, is that this relatively undeveloped area of Brooklyn, largely composed of farmland, became attractive first by right of the development of the Coney Island area as a resort for both tourists and local residents; and second, that this popularization led to the development of more rail lines, which in turn led to the change from farms to residential neighborhoods. Even before the Brooklyn Bridge or the other East River crossings were completed, there was ample evidence of the attraction of living in Brooklyn. Several ferries, one between Atlantic Street in Brooklyn and Whitehall Street in Manhattan, and another connecting Hamilton Avenue with the Battery, were running by 1846. "By 1860 the various East River ferries were carrying 33 million passengers a year (about 100,000 each working day), and by 1870 that patronage had increased to 50 million" (Manbeck, 1998, xxii). This trend was given more impetus with the incorporation of Flatbush into the City of Brooklyn in 1894. Then, the City of Brooklyn (Kings County) was consolidated into Greater New York in 1898. The opening of the Williamsburg Bridge in 1903, and the Manhattan Bridge in 1909, also opened the floodgates for Jewish immigrants who wanted to leave the perilously overcrowded Lower East Side of Manhattan. Williamsburg and Brownsville had received

Fontana Bella Kosher Italian/Sea Dolphin Kosher Seafood, 2086 CIA (Kings Highway and Avenue R). The Kings Highway shopping area, unlike the rest of CIA, is a mecca for full-service kosher restaurants. The closest area for similar services would be Avenue J and CIA.

Eppes Zis Bakery mural, Kings Highway CIA (corner Kings Highway and CIA). One of a series of multiethnic panels of a wall mural set on side of secular movie house. "Eppes Zis" means "Something Sweet." Note "typical New York" presence of graffiti.

Gourmet House Grocery, 929 Kings Highway (corner CIA). Brooklyn's Jews, like other New Yorkers, are always seeking new tastes.

Joey Glatt Kosher Palace, 936 Kings Highway (corner CIA). Big, bold Joey Glatt demonstrates Jewish confidence in the neighborhood.

Nathan's Glatt Kosher, 825 Kings Highway (corner E. 9th Street). A veritable Brooklyn institution in the heart of the Kings Highway/CIA area.

Nathan's Glatt Kosher (detail), 825 Kings Highway (corner E. 9th Street). "Nathan's Famous" has been taken to the next level to accommodate Brooklyn's Jewish population.

Bet Medrash—Chasidei David U'Moshe, 2200 block CIA (Avenues S and T). A small synagogue advertises upcoming kapores ritual.

Black Sea Bookstore, 3175 CIA (Brighton Beach Avenue). For over twenty years a Russian presence—where CIA meets Brighton Beach Avenue.

the lion's share of the previous wave of Jewish immigration, so it was natural that the next wave would be attracted to the less populous areas of Flatbush, Borough Park, and points farther south.

In 1908, the Interborough Rapid Transit (IRT), New York's first subway, connected to Brooklyn, opening the way for people to move to the newly constructed neighborhoods. Then, the Brooklyn Manhattan Transit (BMT) line opened to Brighton Beach in 1920, causing large-scale development in Sheepshead Bay (Manbeck 1998, xxiv). A little to the north, "CIA forms the western boundary of Flatbush, which is considered to be the heart of Brooklyn. Access to transportation suburbanized the northern parts of Flatbush, drawing middle- and upper-middle-class New Yorkers from Manhattan and Brownstone Brooklyn" (Freudenheim, 1999,161). Then, according to Brooklyn historian John Manbeck:

Between 1920 and 1940 Flatbush was filled with four and six-story apartment houses, both walk-ups and elevator buildings. The new availability of apartments attracted new residents to Flatbush. Many of the apartment dwellers were Jewish immigrants who had

Shorefront YM-YWHA, 3300 CIA (at the Atlantic Ocean). The Y is an important institution in Russian Jewish acculturation.

Rabbi Hecht's Esrogim Center (sign), 1110 Avenue I (corner CIA). Specialty center for lulav and esrog for the holiday of Sukkos.

moved from the Lower East Side or from the more crowded Brooklyn neighborhoods like Williamsburg and Brownsville. (1998, 118)

He continues:

After World War II much of the Jewish population of Flatbush was replaced by newer immigrants, many from the Caribbean, Pakistan, Afghanistan, Cambodia, Korea, Central America and the Soviet Union. . . . From 1970 to 1980 the neighborhood was transformed from eighty-five percent Caucasian to eighty percent non-Caucasian. Nearly all of these new arrivals lived in the apartment buildings of Flatbush. (1998, 119)

Perhaps the heart of Jewish Flatbush was depopulated during this decade, but CIA as a hub of Jewish business and commerce, particularly in Midwood and at the junction of Kings Highway, has retained its vitality. Many of the younger Jews have indeed moved to Long Island or to

New Jersey in the last generation or so, but they have maintained their connection to the neighborhood. They readily return to Flatbush or Midwood to visit family and friends for holidays, go shopping for bar and bat mitzvahs, or even for two loaves of Korn's kosher challah on Kings Highway, or ultimately, as the resident population ages, to attend a funeral in one of the seven or so memorial chapels along CIA.

THE PHOTOGRAPHS

To briefly summarize, Coney Island Avenue accurately reflects the patterns of ethnic succession that have historically shaped Brooklyn. Some groups prosper and dwindle; new groups take their place; others leave few lasting impressions. Yet the Jewish presence along CIA, although a scant 125 years in duration, has remained remarkably steadfast. The accompanying photographs are, in part, a reminder of the everyday life of the Brooklyn Jewish

Hecht's Religious Articles, 1265 CIA (Avenues H and I). "Oldest Judaica store in the United States."

community along CIA. We note bagel shops, fruit stands, wig stores, glatt kosher marts, newspaper kiosks, and exercise centers—all places where function takes precedence over form, and the changes of ownership or location are less important than the convenience they bring. Then there are photographs that pay tribute to the ritual Jewish life in Brooklyn, a legacy of the Jewish contribution to CIA—the buildings and institutions such as synagogues, memorial chapels, Judaica emporia, and funeral homes that form the backbone of a neighborhood. And finally are the markers of the celebratory life of the Jews who live, work, and worship on or along CIA—full-service kosher restaurants that display proof of rabbinical supervision, and posters for seasonal rituals, from slogn kappoeres and Lag b'Omer.

To return to our initial questions about the symbols of "Jewishness" along CIA, the answers are apparent. The signs and storefronts reveal a story that is written in English, Hebrew, Russian, and symbols recognizably Jewish to both "insider" and "outsider," just as Siegal points to the obvious signs of Pakastani, Bangaladeshi, or other Muslim shops along CIA between Glenwood and Avenue H. It all began with the introduction of the railroad, followed by the building of the bridges, which gave access to land ripe for development. Now the infrastructure is set,

and only time will tell what new developments will take place along this historic route through Brooklyn.

NOTES

1. The "we" of this article refers to my colleague and co-editor, Ilana Abramovitch. She spent many an afternoon and weekend driving with me up and down Coney Island Avenue documenting, surveying, and discussing possible points of interest to include.

REFERENCES CITED

Abel, Allen J. 1995. *Flatbush Odyssey: Journey through the Heart of Brooklyn.* Toronto: McClelland and Stewart.

Brooklyn Eagle. n.d. "Gravesend."

Freudenheim, Ellen. 1999. *Brooklyn! A Soup-to-Nuts Guide to Sights, Neighborhoods, and Restaurants.* New York: St. Martin's Press.

Kirshenblatt-Gimblett, Barbara. 1995. "Times Square: A Pedestrian Perspective," in Roger D. Abrahams, ed., *Fields of Folklore: Essays in Honor of Kenneth S. Goldstein,* pp. 169–83. Bloomington, Ind.: Trickster Press.

Lines, Ruth L. 1949. *The Story of Sheepshead Bay, Manhattan Beach and the Sheepshead Bay Library.* Brooklyn: Brooklyn Public Library.

Manbeck, John. 1998. *The Neighborhoods of Brooklyn.* New Haven and London: Yale University Press.

Merlis, Brian. 1995. *Brooklyn: The Way It Was.* Brooklyn: Israelowitz Publishing.

Siegal, Nina. 2000. "Four Corners." *New York Times,* July 30, sec. 14, p. 1.

Stiles, Henry R. 1884. *Civil, Political, Professional and Educational History and Commercial and Industrial Record of the County of Kings, and the City of Brooklyn, New York, from 1683 to 1884.* 2 vols. New York: W. W. Munsell and Company.

Dr. Alvin I. Schiff Talks about Jewish Education

TRYSA SHY

Dr. Alvin I. Schiff, a devoted leader in the world of New York Jewish education, has unique insight into the education of Brooklyn Jews. His work for the Board of Jewish Education of New York as Supervisor of the Department of Day Schools and Yeshivot from 1956 to 1965 and later as Executive Vice-President from 1970 to 1991 gave him a broad overview of Jewish studies in the borough. His experience as director of graduate Jewish education at Yeshiva University also helped him deepen his knowledge of local Jewish education. "You have to understand," says Dr. Schiff as our interview begins, "that Brooklyn is different from all other parts of New York, because, as Brooklyn developed [it] became the seat of right-wing Orthodoxy, of Ultra-Orthodoxy, and Hasidism." Schiff makes a strong point about the extraordinary concentration of Orthodox Jews in Brooklyn.

The Board of Jewish Education (BJE) provides Jewish educational resources and services to area schools and also serves as an avenue for the distribution of government-funded programs. Schiff mentions that the right-wing schools took advantage of the services the government made available, such as the school food program or the transportation program. They accepted some guidance in general studies, but as far as Jewish studies were concerned, they would not participate in community-sponsored educational services that work with other trends in Judaism. Schiff explains that the right-wing schools do not take supervision from anybody except their own rabbinic leaders (*roshei* yeshiva—heads of rabbinic seminaries) and/or Hasidic rebbes.

Schiff stepped back a bit to give some history of right-wing and ultra-Orthodox Jews. They are rigidly traditional, adhering with great care to the fundamental precepts of Judaism as expounded in the Talmud and Codes of Jewish Law, and they place great stress upon biblical and post-biblical scholarship.

Hasidism is an eighteenth-century movement founded in the Ukraine, essentially in opposition to the Lithuanian Jewish emphasis on knowledge. Hasidic founders and leaders placed fervent prayer, outward religious devotion, serving God with joy and happiness on an equal level with Torah scholarship and knowledge. In the United States, Hasidism stresses the importance of Jewish learning. Hasidim are clannish and zealously follow the dictates and authority of their group rebbes (rabbis). Most Hasidim in Brooklyn are immigrants from Hungary or progeny of Hungarian Jewish immigrants. Unlike modern or centrist Orthodox Jews, Ultra-Orthodox, right-wing, and Hasidic

Young Shaare Torah, located at 953 Coney Island Avenue, between Ditmas and Newkirk, houses its boys' yeshiva at this location. It has grown to include 250 youngsters from elementary through high school.

Jews are sectarian and reject exposure to secularism, especially to Western-style university studies.

"There was only one group of Hasidic schools to which the BJE would not give any support or services," Schiff explains, "and that was the Satmar, because they burnt the Israeli flag. They do not believe that we should be working for a Jewish State until the Messiah comes."

One of Schiff's achievements as Executive Vice President of the BJE was to make a deal in 1970 with the U.S. Department of Agriculture to provide surplus kosher food to schools, as an extension of an earlier arrangement with the U.S. government. The program was already in place for public schools and Catholic schools in New York. Schiff reasoned, "Well, if they could get surplus food, why don't the Jewish schools get it?" So, he made it happen, forging an agreement with Senator Hubert Humphrey and initiating a relationship with the Department of Agriculture.

Schiff also developed a more personal relationship with Brooklyn's Jewish schools. From 1956 to 1965, while working with the BJE, he trained teachers studying at the Teachers Institute for Men at Yeshiva University and the Teachers Institute for Women [now part of Stern College for Women] and supervised the practice-teaching programs for these institutions. Visiting the Modern Orthodox schools in the New York area, he would lead seminars for teachers and principals. Schiff felt a strong tie with one school in particular. He recalls, "The Shulamith School, founded in 1928, was the first day school for girls in the country. Its principal, Dr. Judith Lieberman, was an outstanding educator who stressed the importance of He-

The Young Israel Movement started in 1912 as part of the Orthodox youth synagogue-center movement. Young Israel of Flatbush, located at 1012 Avenue I, on the corner of Coney Island Avenue, continues its long and influential presence in the neighborhood.

braic—Ivrit B'ivrit—education, intensive Bible instruction and teaching of Zionism and Israel."

Schiff and Lieberman created an effective in-service program for teachers and student teachers alike. Dr. Schiff assigned Yeshiva University student teachers to work in classes at the Shulamith School. Schiff would visit the classes to monitor the progress of his practice teachers. On the days of these visits, Lieberman would have other teachers observe the classes and afterward would provide lunch for the teachers and student teachers involved. In these informal sessions, Schiff would guide discussions about the lessons he observed and about effective teaching in Jewish day schools. The program lasted nine years, and Schiff notes proudly, "It was outstanding." It produced knowledgeable new Jewish teachers, on the one hand, and helped to improve the instruction of veteran teachers, on the other."

Finally, I asked Dr. Schiff what he thought distin-

This billboard, located at 1200 Coney Island Avenue, is a representation of the Yeshiva of Flatbush building currently under construction. It was founded in 1926 by Joel Braveman, who retired from active principalship in 1964.

guishes Jews in Brooklyn from those in the rest of New York. "Brooklyn, like any other area, has people with varied interests; there are serious people and there are funny people; there are old people and there are young people; there are more religious and there are less religious (even though most of them happen to be more religious).

"An aspect of the uniqueness of Brooklyn is its Jewish density. Brooklyn is the home of hundreds of *shtiblach* (small synagogues) and *yeshivot* for boys and girls. There are about 65,000 yeshiva students in the Brooklyn area. There are many kosher eateries and lots of Jewish shopping. Now, Brooklyn is also home to thousands of Soviet Jewish immigrants.

"In the development of Brooklyn's Jewish community, Conservative and Reform Jews played an important role in Jewish life. In the early 1900s, there were several large Conservative synagogues (particularly in Flatbush, Midwood, and Crown Heights) and Reform Temples (in Bensonhurst and Crown Heights). During its transformation in the post–World War II years, many Conservative and Reform houses of worship closed down. There still are several such institutions in East Midwood, Park Slope, and Brooklyn Heights. However, there are few Jewish Day Schools under Conservative auspices. In their formative years, the Reform and Conservative synagogues sponsored large congregational schools. Currently there are a handful of supplementary Jewish school children in a few congregational educational institutions."

Rabbi Robert Kaplan Talks about Changing Institutions

JAN ROSENBERG

Bob Kaplan is like a giant balancing delicately on a tightrope. A very stocky six-foot-plus Orthodox rabbi, Kaplan brings a powerful Jewish presence to neighborhood conversations with New Yorkers—both Jews and non-Jews. As director of intergroup relations and community concerns for the Jewish Community Relations Council (JCRC) of New York, Kaplan helps diverse groups of city residents identify and promote their common interests. In the past few years he helped form the South East Queens and South Brooklyn Health Coalitions, organizational initiatives to balance the interests of frail, elderly Jews (a growing proportion of Brooklyn's Jewish residents) and new immigrants who work in health care.

Jews are a declining percentage of New York's population, and the internal differences among Jewish groups are more marked than they've been in half a century. The Jewish part of Brooklyn's population declined from 18 percent in 1980 to 16 percent in 1990, despite the arrival of large numbers of refugees from the former Soviet Union and immigrants from Israel. That's a far cry from the 42 percent of Brooklyn's population that Jews constituted in 1932. Among Brooklyn's Jewish population, a growing percentage are either Orthodox (about 20–25 percent), recent arrivals from the former Soviet Union (another 25 percent), or Israeli. For all three groups, specialized stores, services, and language (Yiddish is a primary language for many of the Orthodox) tie residents to one another and to their particular locations and distance them from other groups—imbuing these neighborhoods with meaning that's only a memory for most American Jews.

How will these very different Jewish populations interact with each other and with their non-Jewish neighbors? In what ways will the city's growing numbers of Latino, Caribbean, and Asian immigrants, young populations with very important internal differences, challenge or share power with the city's distinct Jewish populations? Rabbi Kaplan confronts these questions every day. One question Kaplan worries about involves "remnant" institutions, Jewish institutions that have remained in a neighborhood after most Jews have left. "You don't want Jews fleeing the city because they're no longer part and parcel of what's happening. We know what can happen . . . ," he says soberly, summoning a rush of memories of anti-Semitic fights over school control in Ocean Hill–Brownsville, the politics of racial division, and white flight.

Brooklyn's Canarsie exemplifies the demographic changes and institutional challenges facing the contemporary Jewish community. The neighborhood's population exploded from 30,000 in 1950 to 50,000 in 1960 to 80,000 in 1970; many of the newcomers were Jews. First residents and then institutions moved, mostly from small tenement apartments in increasingly black Brownsville and East New York, to white Canarsie's new houses and apartments.

Canarsie's Jewish (and non-Jewish) population peaked in the late 1960s. In 1969 the Hebrew Education Society (HES) opened its new center in Canarsie, complete with a swimming pool and gym, never anticipating that the neighborhood's recent Jewish migrants would leave as quickly as they had come. By the early 1990s the HES was in the red, barely surviving. Prodded by major Jewish institutions (UJA-Federation, JCRC, Met Council), Kaplan says, HES began to reorient itself to today's realities. Hiring a new director in 1996 eager to work with non-Jews as well as Jews, HES changed from a "closed shop" that only Jews could join to one open to the typical New York mix of neighborhood residents, including Latinos, African- and Caribbean-Americans, and Asians. Consequently the HES gym, pool, day care center, and camp programs began serving the diverse people who share the neighborhood with a variety of Jews—mainly Orthodox, from the former Soviet Union, and Israelis. "It's no longer an institution open only to Jews," Kaplan emphasizes. "They reach out further and wider, to Jews, including the Lubavitchers of Crown Heights, and to non-Jews. . . .They reach into Howard Beach, Mill Basin, the whole southern tier of Brooklyn." HES remains unmistakably, inclusively Jewish in terms of its programming, the holidays it observes (and ignores), and the food it allows into the building. The pool and gym, for example, designate single-sex-only times, and the candy machines have strictly kosher candy "so Orthodox parents don't have to worry if their kids buy a candy bar." By providing a venue in which a variety of Jews as well as non-Jews can interact with each other comfortably, HES hopes to anchor the Jewish families still there, ease the inevitable intergroup tensions, and model participation with the wider community. "All groups," says director Mark Arje, "want safe communities, good schools, and good transportation."

Even synagogues, Kaplan argues, have to adapt to new realities. For some, this might mean expanding beyond prayer and bar mitzvah teaching to develop more single-parent and bereavement groups, hire a social worker on the staff, and offer more "Basic Judaism" classes, for example. "In many communities we no longer have the population we used to. If you're basing yourself on Jews who pray, and most Jews don't pray formally, then you have a problem. You have to make yourself relevant. . . .These synagogues have to rethink themselves." And, of course, exciting, dynamic, charismatic religious leaders continue to attract people to their synagogues.

Rabbi "Yisroel" Weisman, for example, is an Orthodox rabbi whose post-Shabbat lectures in Sheepshead Bay regularly draw 1,500 people. "Crown Heights was the perfect example," he adds. "The rebbe held that community together when other Jews left."

New York City's political term limits are another of the "new realities" to which the city's diverse Jewish groups must adapt. The declining numbers of Jews in the city, coupled with a soon-to-be-elected class of new representatives, could mean "we're gonna lose out because what's going to be left behind in many Jewish communities in transition is the frail, elderly population, requiring more of the social service type system. . . . So if you no longer have the pharaoh . . . there are a lot of pharaohs who knew not Joseph coming into power . . . if you didn't build up ties with them along the road, because we weren't doing that, we never saw it coming. . . . that's really the basis for a lot of coalition work that I do today."

Many of Brooklyn's newly Orthodox neighborhoods, like the area around Nostrand Avenue and Avenue L, are awash with yeshivas, kosher butchers, pizza shops, and other specialized services and stores. But compared with the 1950s and 1960s, there's a noticeable lack of tension and conflict with non-Orthodox, mostly black coresidents. Kaplan explains: "In these types of neighborhoods it's okay that the public schools remain 'minority,' because the Orthodox don't utilize them. So the conflict that has decimated other Jewish and white ethnic communities across New York—public education and the race card—does not play out in the Orthodox community. Flatbush has obviated the problem. It's not Ocean Hill–Brownsville all over again." But he quickly continues, contradicting himself. "These tensions often lie right below the surface and can escalate quickly." It's Bob Kaplan's job to anticipate and help de-escalate the tensions.

Health care has offered the best opportunity so far to draw together the new groups that populate the city. Kaplan's efforts helped seed and sustain the South East Queens Health Coalition and, more recently, the South Brooklyn Health Coalition, eighty groups that work together to represent the interests of health care consumers (many of those elderly Jews mentioned previously) and providers, including many new immigrants. Child Health Plus, a state program for children of the working poor, acted as a catalyst for the Brooklyn group. Ten community-based groups (representing eleven different language and ethnic groups) hired staff to reach into their communities and sign up children who had no health insurance.

Another new challenge grows out of the changing demography of New York's Jews: inculcating a Jewish communal ethic among refugees from the former Soviet Union. Under the aegis of the JCRC Kaplan recently organized a group of successful, young, former Soviet Union Jews to meet regularly with the Jewish community's established business and political elites. The goal is to increase the level of participation of the new arrivals and to weave their concerns and perspectives into the woof and warp of established Jewish communal institutions.

Bob Kaplan has what textbooks call a "sociological imagination"; he loves to talk (and listen) to different kinds of people, to figure out what's important to them, tamp down the intergroup clashes, and help them try to achieve their goals. Reorienting an exclusively Jewish institution into a shared one, open to non-Jewish neighbors, exemplifies how institutions built for a growing Jewish population can be kept alive despite diminishing numbers.

Bob Kaplan embodies an older, venerable Jewish-American tradition that combines a universalist, cosmopolitan perspective with a strong individual Jewish identity. His life story adds an unexpected dimension to his work. Born forty-seven years ago, Kaplan ". . . grew up a typical Jewish kid in Brooklyn . . . in Canarsie, in a city housing project. My father was a civil servant. My mother was from a religious family and decided not to be religious anymore. I was sent to Hebrew school [but] had a major fight with the rabbi, and we both agreed it was not the place for me."

Though Hebrew school didn't turn out the way it was supposed to, Kaplan managed to keep one foot in the door of his Jewishness. Bob's close relationship with his Zionist, religious grandfather helped kindle his Jewish identity. At Tilden High School (1966–70), he joined a Jewish youth group. "When all the blacks were organizing black studies, I organized a Jewish studies course." Looking back, he says he wasn't really serious about his Jewishness, and was still exploring a dizzying variety of spiritual possibilities. During college in the early 1970s, he dug in deeper, read-ing a lot about Jewish history and learning Hebrew; at the same time, he was "turned on to the antiwar movement and radical hippieness . . . improving the world. I think that's ingrained in most Jews. . . . Jews have the "pintl Yid" that can get flared up. . . ." But as soon as he's said this, he remembers why it's also not true: "It's unfortunate; as generations go by people lose connections to the roots of what causes that; we lose it. . . ."

Part of Kaplan's personal and professional mission is to help nurture the Jewish institutions and sense of community (particularly among the non-Orthodox, whose connections to the Jewish world can dissolve so quickly) that sustain individual Jewish identity. Firsthand experience taught Bob Kaplan about spiritual yearnings and communal structures that entice and nurture young, secular Jews.

Like many people of his generation, Bob Kaplan sought spiritual fulfillment in a wide range of places. After graduating from Tilden High School he went to Israel with his Zionist youth group and lived "a hippie lifestyle" on a kibbutz. He returned to America "very deep in Eastern thought and meditation" and led a "profoundly spiritual lifestyle," finally landing on an ashram in Massachusetts. "I followed Baba Ram Das, and the whole deal. I chopped wood, ate vegetarian food, did hydroponic gardening. . . ." (And what about the woman who became your wife? I wondered, incredulous at the thought of two lifelong commitments following such a tangled path, in tandem.) ". . . when I went up there, she went too. But we got married in Brooklyn, by a rabbi, Reform, who was willing to talk to us."

The ashram turned out to be less than it seemed; the leaders were "in it for the money," and the Kaplans left, disillusioned, to travel across the country for a year before returning to the Bensonhurst neighborhood in Brooklyn ("we found a cheap apartment there") to have their first child.

Bob Kaplan became a successful manager in the furniture business, easy enough after managing the ashram. But spiritually, something was missing. He met a rabbi: "I decided to tell that rabbi everything I'd done in my whole life, all the hippie stuff, the whole nine yards. When I finished he looked at me and said, 'So what do you want to do now?'"

"I told him, 'I want to learn a little bit about Torah.'"

"How fast do you want to go?" he asked.

"I've been burned once before by this whole spiritual guru world and I'd like to take it real slow."

"He said, 'Good, anyone who jumps into a pool and doesn't know how to swim is gonna drown.'"

The retail furniture business, with its busy Saturdays, became less and less tenable. Studying Torah with his rabbi, Bob Kaplan left furniture for a new job with a multi-ethnic, congregation-based, Saul Alinsky–inspired energy cooperative that formed in the wake of the early 1970s oil shocks. (Coincidentally, I was also an early participant, representing Park Slope's Congregation Beth Elohim in the co-op's founding meetings in Brooklyn church basements.) When that closed, he signed on with an anticult group, helping "deprogram" young Jewish followers.

His next step followed naturally; Kaplan moved from anticult work to Hillel, working with disaffected, predominantly secular Jews, first at C. W. Post campus of Long Island University, then New York University, Brooklyn College, and finally as associate executive director of Hillel citywide. I'm sure he seemed as much at home there, reaching out to young spiritual wanderers, as he does in his current "calling."

Even as an Orthodox Jew, Rabbi Robert Kaplan continues to teach himself to swim. Although he follows Torah, eats kosher food, and keeps Shabbat, he admits that he still watches movies, listens to rock 'n' roll, wears jeans, and searches for spiritual fulfillment. His personal journey provides one model for the kind of sensitive, discerning adaptation that Brooklyn's new Jewish community (and communities) will have to make.

Radically Right
The Jewish Press

JAY EIDELMAN

If you happen to live in one of Brooklyn's more distinctly Jewish neighborhoods like Flatbush, Midwood, or Borough Park, you're probably familiar with *The Jewish Press*. Every Friday, *The Jewish Press* arrives at newsstands throughout Jewish neighborhoods in Greater New York City from its home on Third Avenue in the industrial Gowanus section of Brooklyn. Throughout New York Jewish neighborhoods, shoppers busy with their pre-Sabbath purchases come across the familiar black and white tabloid with the bold blue headline. For some in the Brooklyn Jewish community *The Press*, well known (some would say notorious) for its hard-line politics and often vicious attacks on critics, represents the worst kind of incendiary rag. But for many of its loyal readers, *The Press* is simply "the paper"—a source for news and guidance.

Billing itself as the "the largest independent Anglo-Jewish weekly newspaper," *The Jewish Press* offers a mix of politics and "Torah-true Judaism." *The Press* is best known for having given voice to the radically right political views of the late Rabbi Meir Kahane, who used the paper to develop his very particular interpretation of the Jewish concept of *ahavat yisrael* (the responsibility of one Jew for another). But even before Kahane began using *The Press* as his pulpit, the paper had a reputation for championing Jewish causes without regard to mainstream Jewish opinion. *The Press* was an early advocate for causes like Holocaust commemoration and freedom for Soviet Jewry, issues that were to become hallmarks of American Jewish identity.[1]

Regardless of the paper's political stance on any issue—and it is usually right of center if not downright right-wing—*The Jewish Press* unashamedly represents itself as Orthodox. Sometimes this can mean the Modern Orthodoxy of Yeshiva University and sometimes it can mean the Ultra-Orthodoxy of the *misnagdic* (non-Hasidic) yeshiva world. A Brooklyn visitor picking up *The Press* for the first time should not be surprised in finding serialized tales of famous rabbis in cartoon form alongside analyses of the latest happenings in Gracie Mansion or the Israeli Knesset. In addition to news and editorials, regular features include an eye on the Sephardi community, fashion, automotive, kosher food, health care, and women's news. Readers can seek answers to *halakhic* questions or write in to the Rebbetzin Jungreis, a popular feature mixing advice for the lovelorn with calls to live a kosher life.[2]

The Jewish Press was founded in 1960 by Rabbi Sholom Klass. Klass, who has since died, grew up in Williamsburg and was a graduate of Yeshiva Torah Vodaath (several members of the Klass family are still involved with the newspaper). Prior to the paper's founding, Klass was the copublisher of the now defunct *Brooklyn Daily*. Like all of Brooklyn's daily papers, the *Brooklyn Daily* eventually succumbed to increased competition and greater consolidation in the New York newspaper business. *The Press*, on the other hand, has thrived, growing its circulation steadily over the years by a rate of 2–3 percent per annum. To some degree this reflects the growth of Brooklyn's Orthodox communities, but it also reflects *The Press's* success in finding its niche, the right-wing segment of New York Orthodox Jews. The paper's readership, which was decidedly more diverse in the early years, has changed too.[3]

What makes *The Jewish Press* different from other local Jewish weeklies is the paper's old-fashioned style. In many ways *The Press* is much more like Yiddish papers of the turn of the century, such as the *Forverts* or the *Tog*. These papers offered news, but more than that, they offered readers an entrée into the unknown, sometimes forbidding, world that existed outside their community. This introduction was mediated through a strong editorial presence. Readers expected and enjoyed the passionate and partisan nature of their papers. They depended on their papers to provide them with direction and to voice opinions that mirrored their own beliefs. Most of all, readers expected their newspapers to entertain as well as inform. In certain cases, this helped integrate readers into American culture, as in the *Forverts's* famous column *A bintel brif*, which featured letters requesting advice on problems faced by the readership. Other times the newspapers stood guard, warning readers of the dangers they faced. So it is with *The Press*, whose distinct Orthodox perspective helps readers clearly demarcate the line between themselves and the rest of the Jewish community.[4]

The best-known period in the paper's history illustrates this important role. In 1958 Rabbi Baruch David Kahane, better known as Rabbi Meir Kahane, started writing for the *Brooklyn Daily* under the pen name of Michael King. Kahane, who would later found the Jewish Defense League (1969) and the Israeli political party Kach (soon after he moved to Israel in 1976), was the scion of an esteemed rabbinic family; his father was head of the Flatbush Board of Rabbis. In 1956 Kahane received his ordination from the Mirrer Yeshiva and completed his M.A. in international relations from Brooklyn College. He married and took a pulpit in Laurelton, Queens. When his synagogue switched its affiliation to the Conservative movement, the devoutly Orthodox Kahane lost his pulpit. Married with two children, Kahane turned to writing, among other things, to earn his living. One of his first jobs was as a sports reporter for the *Brooklyn Daily*. Later, as a member of *The Jewish Press's* editorial staff, Kahane would focus on Jewish political issues and become widely known for his aggressive stance on anti-Semitism and Israeli politics.[5]

The Kahane family had a long-standing connection with Zionism's right wing. Kahane's father was active in the Revisionist movement, and Meir had been a member of Betar, the Revisionist youth movement. A young Meir even had the opportunity to meet the Revisionist leader, Vladimir Ze'ev Jabotinsky, when he visited the Kahane family's Brooklyn home. But it was during the period around the Six Day War that Kahane's strident political stance coalesced. In the fall of 1967, as the press reported trouble brewing in the Middle East, Kahane feared the worst. He was not alone. Many Jews foresaw a second Holocaust should the Arabs attack. Israel's swift victory in the face of seemingly insurmountable odds only served to magnify the miracle of this deliverance.[6]

In the Soviet Union, where the Jewish community had long suffered from state-sponsored anti-Semitism, many younger Jews, encouraged by events in Israel, were desperately trying to recapture their Jewishness. Some hoped to immigrate to Israel but were refused permission to leave. Having rejected Mother Russia and the Soviet State, having allied themselves with "International Zionism," the State's enemy, these young Jews and their families now suffered the brunt of Soviet repression. Labeled refusniks, they lost their livelihoods and were forced to live under constant surveillance and fear of detention. Many of the refusniks spent time in Soviet prisons on trumped-up charges. Like the events surrounding the Six Day War, the plight of the refusniks focused American Jewish eyes on international Jewish causes.

At home, in the older Jewish neighborhoods of Brooklyn, antagonism between African-Americans and Jews was on the rise. Brownsville and other neighborhoods that had once had vibrant Jewish communities now held only aging remnants. Many of the older Jews who could not afford flight to the suburbs were all but abandoned in what was now seen as "foreign" territory. The so-called black-Jewish coalition that had been in place since the turn of the century was in the process of unraveling. Both sides were turning inward, focusing on their own agendas. Militancy was rising on both sides.

Kahane's editorial stance developed against this tumultuous background of change in American Jewish life. Using *The Jewish Press* as his platform, Kahane railed against the apathy of the "Jewish Establishment" toward his vision of Jewish interests. He attacked the "Establishment" for its unwillingness to act in face of what he perceived as Jewish oppression, for its devotion to liberal causes like civil rights, and for what he saw as its subservience to Jewish accommodationism and assimilation. The results of these policies, Kahane felt, endangered Jewish lives and weakened Jewish communities. What Kahane demanded above all was swift and direct action on behalf of suffering Jews. Anything less was, in his eyes, betrayal of *ahavat yisrael*, the special responsibility all Jews bear for each other.[7]

Typical of Kahane's brand of invective are his remarks regarding a 1970 riot in the Williamsburg section of Brooklyn. Similar to the Crown Heights riots of the 1990s, these riots, which pitted blacks against their Jewish neighbors, were touched off by a traffic accident in which a Jewish motorist struck a black child. The neighborhood erupted with violence. Some Jews looked on the riots as a pogrom and decided to fight. Politicians and Jewish leaders appealed for calm, but Kahane called on Jews to "forget the 'leaders . . .' [t]hey are irrelevant. . . ." What was relevant, however, was that "Jews came into a neighborhood to help other Jews . . . an alliance of Hasidim, ordinary Orthodox Jews, non-observant Jews, and totally alienated ones." According to Kahane, such an alliance was an unstoppable force that would "endure and overcome the timid pygmies who walk in the footsteps [of those] who attacked Moses and Samson for making things worse" (July 10, 1970).

Kahane's comments on Tishah-b'Ab (the Jewish fast day mourning the destruction of the Temples in Jerusalem and other catastrophes in Jewish history) demonstrate his conception of *ahavat yisrael* as "the unity and oneness of the Jewish people" (September 7, 1970, p. 30). His September 7, 1970, editorial goes on to admonish readers that "when Jew turns against Jew there can be no redemption," referring blatantly to Jewish liberals of all persuasions whom Kahane criticized for putting ideology ahead of kinship. "[W]hen Jews march for those who would destroy Jewishness . . . ," continued Kahane, "there can be no hope." What "must obsess" Jews, he concluded, was the love of their own kind and the impulse to aid Jews in distress (p. 30). For, as he wrote in an open letter to a Jewish prisoner on November 10 of 1972: "There is no hope or future for the Jews in Exile . . . the most 'golden' or pleasant exiles for the Jew must turn into a nightmare" (p. 22). Kahane's *Jewish Press* essays and editorials would later form the basis for his many books, including his now famous 1971 manifesto *Never Again!*[8]

While Meir Kahane may have added Revisionist militancy to *The Jewish Press*, he certainly did not invent its stance on religious issues or Jewish affairs. *The Jewish Press* has always been a strong voice for Brooklyn's Orthodox Jewish community, with a long editorial history pre-Kahane. What was changing by the 1960s was the nature of Brooklyn's Jewish community. The divide between the community's left and right wings was growing larger. Kahane's aggressive stance and fiery politics are reflections of the shift to the right in certain Orthodox circles.

Early in its history, even before the fevered pitch of the Kahane years, *The Jewish Press* saw itself as a strong advocate of Jewish rights and concerns. Following on the heels of the 1962 murder of a Brooklyn Jewish store owner, *The Press* ran an editorial demanding greater police protection for Jews (January 5, 1962, pp. 4–5). Anti-Jewish school bias in Britain and the opposition by New Jersey rabbis to Saturday openings at YMHAs (Young Men's Hebrew Association) received similarly strong editorial coverage (January 12, 1962, p. 4). And, in a move that would become a hallmark of the religious right, another editorial titled "The Korachs in Our Midst" reprimanded the *Press*'s opposition, calling them traitors (January 19, 1962, pp. 4–5).[9] In 1965, local Jewish community elements that opposed state aid to parochial schools were similarly rebuked (February 26, p. 4). In the 1970s *The Jewish Press* organized a charity to help Soviet Jews with money for kosher food and ritual objects called "*Al tidom:* We dare not be silent" (July 10, 1970, p. 20). The audience for these outspoken opinions was Brooklyn's growing Orthodox community. Yet, when we consider how much these opinions have come to reflect the American Jewish political agenda, it is clear that the ideas being put forward by *The Press* and its supporters have had a much broader impact. Said Rabbi Ronnie Greenwald, a political activist from Monsey, New York, *The Press* "became the voice . . .[and] protector of Orthodox Jewry." In political terms, support from *The Press* "was a sign that the Orthodox community was behind you."[10]

Controversial issues related to the State of Israel also found their way into *The Jewish Press* agenda early on. In a

1965 issue, *Press* editors called on the World Zionist Congress for stricter adherence to and reverence for Torah (the very same issue also called for an American *kehilla*—a corporate entity representing and regulating a Jewish community), while criticizing U.S. aid to Egypt. Chase National Bank, on the other hand, was congratulated for not conceding to Arab demands to boycott Israel (January 8, p. 4). Later that year the paper called on readers to boycott West Germany, claiming that Cairo controlled its foreign policy (February 26, p. 4). *The Press* could be counted on to promote the State of Israel and Orthodoxy at every opportunity.

Decades before Holocaust commemoration became commonplace in mainstream Jewish society, *The Press* insisted on it. Along with articles like "The Magnificent Danes" (January 5, 1962), which told the story of Danish resistance to the Nazis, came reprints of essays like Israel Gutman's "Teaching the Catastrophe" (January 1, 1965), an early work on Holocaust education. By the early 1970s *The Jewish Press* was running Arthur Morse's *While Six Million Died*. Morse's indictment of Western policy makers' failure to act on behalf of Jews trapped in Nazi-occupied Europe despite knowledge of Nazi atrocities was the first book of its kind.[11]

Contemporary readers of *The Jewish Press* would not be surprised to find any of the above articles or editorials in their paper. But they might be surprised to find that other articles seemingly out of character with *The Press*'s current Orthodox outlook used to populate its pages. In 1962, for instance, *The Press* ran a science fiction serial called "The Discovery of Our Century: A Novel about 1999," written by "Dr. S. Bullman Prominent Scientist and Philosopher." The mid-1960s also saw Ike Kaufman's *The American Jew in World War II* serialized in its pages. One 1965 column, titled "The Place of Religion in the State of Israel," and written by a self-declared Orthodox man, promoted separation of government and religion in Israel (January 1, 1965).

If the paper's voice was not always as decidedly conservative as currently evidenced, neither were its readers. So it was not unusual in the 1960s to see advertisements in *The Jewish Press* for center-left Zionist groups like *Hadassah*. Letters to the editor from the 1960s reveal readers' disagreements with the paper's staunch Orthodox stance. For instance, when *The Press* deemed it inappropriate for Jews to send Christmas cards to Christian acquaintances, one

The spirit of Meir Kahane lives on in this poster for the Kahane Website. Photo courtesy of Seán Galvin.

reader complained about the closed-mindedness and unneighborliness of the editors' judgment. One can hardly imagine a contemporary reader sending such a letter to *The Press* (or seeing it in print).

By 1972 *The Jewish Press* had begun to resemble more closely the paper now available on newsstands. Not only did the paper feature Meir Kahane's strong rhetoric, but *The Press* now had ample resources available to it by way of the revitalization of Israel's political and religious right. Each edition now included columns by Menachem Begin and Menachem Porush, respectively the leaders of Israel's Herut Party and National Religious Party. The "Who is a Jew?" question (what criteria would be applied to determining who was Jewish according to Israeli law) also received coverage. As Menachem Porush commented, "It is indeed regrettable that the Knesset has become insensitive to the threat which the obstacles pose for our unity and uniqueness as a nation" (October 5, 1973). *The Press* was now decidedly in the camp of the Israeli religious right.[12]

The 1970s also witnessed the final break between Orthodoxy and the Conservative movement sparked by the Conservative decision to count women in a minyan (prayer quorum). This decision was called by Sholom Klass *chilul hashem* (blasphemy), while Irene Klass wrote: "unfortunately the Conservatives' move does not come as a shock. They have a long disturbing record of betraying Torah Judaism" (September 28, 1972, p. 16). With Conservative Jews thus dismissed as outside the bounds of *halakhic* Judaism, *The Press* further winnowed its readership.

The United States as a whole had moved further to the right politically during the Nixon regime, and *The Press* reflected that shift as well. During the Watergate scandal *The Press* supported the president as a great friend of Israel. In an editorial headlined "Nixon Support for Israel Exceeded Truman, Eisenhower, Kennedy, and Johnson," *The Press*'s editors wrote: "Now is not the time to question the reliability of the President of the United States . . . we urge every American to support President Nixon" (October 19, 1973, p. 5).

Reaction to the Yom Kippur War completes the picture of *The Press*'s transformation. *Press* editors saw the war in light of previous calamities; the casualties were seen as martyrs. "Like the Six Million who were destroyed in the holocaust [sic]," they wrote, "the blood drenched soil of Sinai will never dry . . . The brave Israeli youths who ran from synagogue to battle for the preservation of our home shall never be forgotten." (October 19, 1973, p. 5). Israel's progress in the war was described in religious language: "As our L-rd inscribed our fate in the Book of Life, He was interrupted by the bursting of a shell. He did not stop writing until the last prayer was said. It was only then that He turned His wrath on the violators of our sacred day, Yom Kippur, and gave the Israeli forces the power and courage to engage the enemy" (p. 18). Again, though contemporary Jewish observers might not have admitted it, *The Press* was expressing the gut reaction of many American Jews at that time. In bringing together Jewish politics with religious imagery and belief, *The Press* had found a powerful focus that continues to resonate with certain segments in Brooklyn's Orthodox community.

By 1973, then, *The Jewish Press* was a very different paper from the one founded in the 1960s. These changes came hand in hand with changes in political outlook amongst Brooklyn Jews during the 1960s and 1970s. For the most part, this was a period of retrenchment for right-wing politics both here and abroad, in Israel. Like Meir Kahane's Jewish Defense League, *The Jewish Press* reflected that retrenchment, as did the change in the paper's readership during the same period.

Since 1973, *The Jewish Press* has maintained its staunch Jewish conservatism. In terms of American politics, this has meant supporting candidates whose foreign affairs agendas demonstrated support for the State of Israel and whose domestic politics favored Jewish religious communities. Ronald Reagan, who, prior to his election in 1980, had a weekly column in *The Jewish Press*, received ringing endorsements, as did Senator Alphonse D'Amato. In local Brooklyn politics, however, it was often Democrats who were supported. In 1992, anger over the Bush administration's attempts to pressure Israel, the lack of clemency shown to the convicted Israeli spy Jonathan Pollard, and Patrick Buchanan's exclusionary rhetoric at the Republican National Convention shifted *The Jewish Press*'s support to the Democrats. The paper's stance on religious issues and Israeli politics has been more single-minded. It has routinely thrown its support behind the Israeli right while constantly criticizing Jews who choose paths other than "Torah-true" Judaism.

NOTES

1. Alternatively, *The Jewish Press* bills itself as "the largest orthodox Anglo-Jewish weekly newspaper"; see http://www.thejewishpress.com. According to *Bacon's New York Publicity Outlets* (Hightstown, N.J.: Bacon's Information, 1999), *The Jewish Press* has a circulation 101,000. By comparison, *The Jewish Week* has a circulation of 94,100, and the *Forward* has a circulation of 25,000. The Yiddish-language *Der Yid*, also published in Brooklyn, has a circulation of 51,000.

2. For a compendium of responsa written by Rabbi Sholom Klass, the late founder and publisher of *The Jewish Press*, see *Responsa of Modern Judaism: A Compilation of Questions and Answers on Past and Present Day Halacha as Presented in the Jewish Press* (Brooklyn, N.Y.: The Jewish Press, 1992).

3. Rabbi Sholom Klass died in January 2000; he was eighty-three. See Steve Lipman, "Rabbi Sholom Klass, 83," in *The Jewish Week* (January 21, 2000). For a discussion of newspaper consolidation in New York City, see *The Encyclopedia of the City of New York*, Kenneth Jackson, ed. (New York: Columbia University Press, 1997).

4. On the Yiddish press, see Irving Howe, *World of Our Fathers* (New York: Harcourt Brace Jovanovich, 1976), 518–51. The *Forverts* column *A bintel brif* is available in two edited volumes; see *A Bintel Brief*, Isaac Metzger, ed. (Garden City, N.Y.: Doubleday, 1971–81).

5. On Kahane and his impact on Jewish affairs, see Keith Elliot Greenberg, "The Children of Kahane," in *Brooklyn Bridge*, September 1998, pp. 56–63. See also http://www.kach.org.

6. On Kahane's early life, see Robert I. Friedman, *The False Prophet:*

Rabbi Meir Kahane: From FBI Informant to Knesset Member (Brooklyn, N.Y.: Lawrence Hill Books, 1990).

7. On Kahane's political views, see Meir Kahane, *Never Again! A Program for Survival* (Los Angeles: Nash Publishers, 1971), and *Uncomfortable Questions for Comfortable Jews* (Secaucus, N.J.: L. Stuart, 1987). See also Friedman, *The False Prophet*, and Yair Kotler, *Heil Kahane* (New York: Adama Books, 1986).

8. Other Kahane works include *Time to Go Home* (Los Angeles: Nash Publishers, 1972), *Our Challenge: The Chosen Land* (Radnor, Pa.: Chilton Book Co., 1974), *The Story of the Jewish Defense League* (Radnor, Pa.: Chilton Book Co., 1975), *They Must Go* (New York: Grosset and Dunlap, 1981), and *Uncomfortable Questions for Comfortable Jews*.

9. Korach rebelled against Moses, according to chapter 16 of the biblical book Numbers.

10. Greenwald quoted in Lipman, "Rabbi Sholom Klass."

11. Arthur Morse, *While Six Million Died* (New York: Random House, 1968).

12. On the rise of the right in Israel, see Ehud Sprinzak, *The Ascendancy of Israel's Radical Right* (New York: Oxford University Press, 1991).

Leaving Brooklyn
Returning to Brooklyn

Former Jews of Brooklyn enjoying south Florida sunshine.
Photo by Sam Erickson, 946 Lorimer Street, Brooklyn, N.Y.

"Across the Great Divide"
Alfred Kazin and Daniel Fuchs

ROY GOLDBLATT

The central spans of the three bridges connecting Brooklyn with Manhattan range from 1,470 to 1,600 feet, probably making the width of the East River below them no more than half a mile. Completed in 1881, Brooklyn Bridge has always been viewed as an engineering wonder; it has always been a symbol, of the power, the importance, the greatness of the United States and New York. It also formed the central image of unification in America, bringing things and people together, for example, recently arrived European, Jewish immigrants, and assimilating, Americanizing, them. The viability of this image needs to be investigated. Did the bridges truly deliver the Brooklyn poor to Manhattan, to America, or were the murky waters of the East River a barrier that was insurmountable to them?

Brooklyn is a physical location depicted in the writings of two significant Jewish writers, the critic Alfred Kazin and the novelist-screenwriter Daniel Fuchs, and the borough had a psychological effect on each of them, or in Fuchs's case on the characters he created. The historical period they portray is basically the same, the early 1930s. Kazin returns to Brownsville in 1951, sometimes looking back nostalgically, in his autobiographical work *A Walker in the City*. Fuchs's Brooklyn is at the opposite end of the borough, his Williamsburg fictionalized in three novels written between 1934 and 1937 during summer breaks from teaching as a permanent substitute at PS 225 in Brighton Beach and before answering Hollywood's call in 1937. These works later came to be known collectively as the *Williamsburg Trilogy*. Brooklyn, for both, represented a veritable imprisonment, a trap from which the individual had to be "sprung." The methods of escape they themselves used were the same: education, the traditional, honorable means available to the immigrant in New York—the degree from City College. While Kazin places all the hopes of his youth in crossing the river, in the civilization epitomized by Manhattan, beyond Brooklyn Bridge, Fuchs allows few hopes to his characters; they rarely leave the confines of Williamsburg or Neptune (read Brighton) Beach in *Low Company*, the last of the Brooklyn novels.

As transportation systems improved and with the opening of the Manhattan and Williamsburg Bridges, Jews on the Lower East Side started to cross the East River in increasing numbers to settle in Williamsburg on the Brooklyn side of the river and farther out in what seemed to be the more rural surroundings of East New York, Brownsville and New Lots at the other end of the borough. Irving Howe notes Brownsville being regarded as "a pastoral village in which 'Jews could live as in the old country, without any rush or excessive worries. Jews there didn't work on the Sabbath, and they went to shul three times a day,'" and then reports a newspaper story praising this area, which, unlike the East Side, would ". . . never have tenements. The houses are three stories, apartments have four or five rooms, with a bathtub and other conveniences, and a yard for the kids" (Howe 131–32). But were these seemingly wide-open spaces really little more than a receptacle to catch the spill from the East Side? To the immigrants these areas could also serve as a new Pale, a hopeless restriction enforced by an alien language where street names are meaningless and only landmarks are recognizable. Kazin's memories in *A Walker in the City* are also far from elegiac. His Brownsville was not New York, but a foreign city, a prison at the end of the world, the city's back door, a place of rubbish, filth and emptiness. It was the "margin of the city, the last place, . . . filled with 'monument works' where they cut and stored tombstones' . . . nearer the ocean . . . but our front on the ocean was Canarsie—in those days the great refuse dump.

Canarsie was the place where they opened the sluice gates to let the city's muck out into the ocean" (Kazin 10–11). In essence it was the ass-end of New York, just about as far as one could get from the culture and life the metropolis symbolized. The yards the newspaper promised turned out to be encircled by tenements, where the walls of the houses were barriers beyond which was the city; escaping, getting beyond them—the preposition *beyond* in its recurrence becomes a key word—was paramount.

Kazin's attempts at escape clearly embody the belief in education, industry, and self-improvement that the American society of Benjamin Franklin and Horatio Alger marketed as the quickest and perhaps sole manner of escape open to its immigrant working class. It is a road upon which the individual sets out alone. Despite the fact that *A Walker in the City* is Kazin's own reflections on his boyhood, he permits us only occasional references to friends; rarely are they mentioned by name. Perhaps this represents the competitive and individual nature of his quest for higher education, and individuality a means of subconsciously dissociating himself from eastern European Jewry, hastening his assimilation.

Consider the image of the school and its richness: the stage of the assembly hall is dominated by the words—in gold—KNOWLEDGE IS POWER; there is a photograph of Theodore Roosevelt; a great silk American flag with a staff crowned by a gilt eagle. "There was the other land, crowned by the severe and questioning face of Theodore Roosevelt, . . . *staring and staring through me as if he were uncertain whether he really approved of me*" (25–26, emphasis mine). Kazin was continuously returning to the president as a figure to be emulated. The classroom was a battlefield, the teacher dividing his troops into Army and Navy forces competing in the weekly Friday morning civics test (27). For Kazin the battle was crucial; individual averages were calculated weekly; those scoring 90 percent or more were honored by their names appearing on a blue honor roll. Its importance was obvious to him: "Every time I entered that room for a test, I looked for my name on the blue chart as if the sight of it would decide my happiness for all time" (28). This academic success coupled with character— something the immigrant Other never had, something that had to be trained in them, and defined by the Jewish immigrants as demonstrative obedience—was both an oppressive phenomenon to him as well as something to be held in awe. Mobility, advancement through education, and the ticket out of Brownsville were promise held out not only to the child but to his parents as well. . . . Character and proper English were the "sickening invocation of 'Americanism'—the word itself accusing us of everything we apparently were not." Making a good impression on the powers-to-be encouraged their assistance; a bad one more or less represented cutting one's own throat. Failure offered the ominous vision of a falling out of the daily race, being kept back in the working class forever—and in Brooklyn (19–22). Though Kazin notes the traditional sports open to poor Brooklyn slum-dwellers, handball, punchball, stickball—each requiring no equipment other than a cheap ball and broomstick—education and competition seem to leave little time for them. They are secondary, even during the summer vacation when Kazin spends most of his time walking to the library, borrowing books to aid his intellectual advance. References to baseball are rare. Perhaps Ebbets Field was at the wrong end of Prospect Park; the other end of the park was the cultural end: the Brooklyn Museum and the Botanical Gardens. That was the Eastern Parkway end: Allrightnik's Row, a world apart from Brownsville.

These two cultural institutions were oases—halfway across Brooklyn to New York—beyond which were the Metropolitan and Natural History Museums up by Central Park. Beyond the filth, the stink, the entrapment of Brownsville was the true America, the real world. It is with perfect irony that Kazin remembers his father coming home with a copy of the *World*, printed in the shadow of Brooklyn Bridge, on the Manhattan side, of course: bringing "the outside straight into our house with each day's copy of the *New York World*. The bridge somehow stood for freedom, the *World* for [a] rangy kindness and fraternalism and ease" (53). And is it of any less significance that the paintings his class was taken to see were American: post–Civil War pictures of New York—"skaters in Central Park, . . . a gay crowd moving round and round Union Square Park; horse cars charging between brownstones of lower Fifth Avenue at dusk" (95). "They," the educational authorities, the agents of assimilation, took him out of Brownsville, to see such paintings and those of nineteenth-century farmscapes of America and woodlands, and instilled a desire to return, to come back to those places, beyond Brooklyn Bridge. This is a boy whose Brownsville is but an enclosure, no woodland, whose city is all other than New York, than America.

The direction of Kazin's walks were always west, out of Brownsville, toward the river, the bridge, the city, toward America. These walks occurred in his final summer before setting out for City College of New York. They were for the most part to the new library and through American districts populated by non-Jews. His odyssey took him through sections—Italian, German, and finally Irish neighborhoods—populated by groups who had been in the city and the country for increasingly longer periods of time, as he closed on New York. His walks became longer, anything to escape, to be away longer from Brownsville, as he was able to contrast his city with theirs. The Italian streets rose into the hills, "all the trolley car lines flew apart into wild plunging crossroads—the way to anywhere, it seemed to me then." These crossroads contained tree-lined traffic islands, calling up a completely different image from the leaky steps that "led down to the public toilets below, instantly proclaiming the end of Brownsville (166). The clutter and noise of Brownsville yielded to a second change in landscape, of a different order: "wide, clean, still, every block lined with trees . . . the names of the streets, Macdougal, Hull, Somers, made me humble with admiration. . . . Every image I had of peace, of quiet shaded streets in some old small-town America, I had seen dreaming over the ads in the *Saturday Evening Post*. . . ." (169). Only half an hour closer to New York and Kazin found himself in nineteenth-century America—where they lived—clearly a place without Jews, or at least a place the Jews had not yet reached!

Alfred Kazin's confidence in his individual ability to cross the East River, his knowledge of escaping Brooklyn to Manhattan's City College, certainly has no parallels in Daniel Fuchs's three Brooklyn novels of the 1930s—*Summer in Williamsburg* (SW 1934), *Homage to Blenholt* (HB 1936), and *Low Company* (LC 1937). Whereas Kazin, in the course of *A Walker in the City*, presents his reader with glimpses of his increasing excursions outside the confines of his Brownsville block, Chester Street, which culminate in the summer-night hopes described above, Fuchs becomes more "withdrawn," allowing his characters fewer and fewer departures. The buoyant optimism of Kazin has turned to dark pessimism in Fuchs's Williamsburg and Neptune (Brighton) Beach.

Rather than Kazin's reminiscences of a single individual, Fuchs's novels relate the stories of the community. In the first two novels the narrative chiefly centers around incidents and circumstances involving a single individual, Philip Hayman in *Summer in Williamsburg* and Max Balkan in *Homage to Blenholt*, and his relations to the larger group. In *Low Company* there is no main character, but rather a selection of six, whose stories and interactions taken together comprise a collective narrative. Thematically, in respect to entrapment, escape, and the unrelenting summer heat, there are great similarities between Kazin and Fuchs. The end result, however, is not: people rarely get out of Williamsburg or Neptune Beach, and if and when they do, it is often in a box—if there are enough of the remains to place in the coffin. Kazin is able to ignore, or at least chooses to leave undepicted, the violence that comes with the unbearable summer temperature; Fuchs cannot. His Brooklyn is hell. His landscape is strewn with bodies: suicides fished out of the river, a head removed from the oven in the kitchen, the ashes of the men immolated in their tenement, a storekeeper murdered in a Brooklyn subway station. Even those who survive are dead: the idea man and the scholar who are condemned to their delicatessen counter, the gangster hiding like a rat in a hole from the syndicate in an Eastern Parkway apartment.

Summer in Williamsburg opens with a suicide, Sussman, who took the gas, and Philip Hayman, a young college student, trying to make sense of it. "Certain men are the sum of a million infinitesimal phenomena and experiences," he is told, and to discover the reason he must make sense of Williamsburg; "you must pick Williamsburg to pieces until you have them all spread out on your table before you, a dictionary of Williamsburg" (SW 12).

This Fuchs proceeds to do and, unlike Kazin understanding Brownsville in contrast to inner Brooklyn and New York, in doing so he need not leave the area.

The physical aspects of the area are plainly no better than those of Brownsville. At the opposite end of Brooklyn, directly across the river via the Williamsburg Bridge from the Lower East Side, it is more impoverished and lacks the "green qualities" noted of Brownsville. Fuchs depicts deserted streets on a summer Sunday, their inhabitants jamming the subways for the beaches or else seeking the dark coolness of the movie houses. But Coney Island or the other Brooklyn "beach resorts" provide no relief from this ugliness, as Fuchs notes in this description of Neptune Beach, and his view of what life there is built on, in *Low Company*:

> The sidewalks were broken in all those places where the blocks caved in, and he [Spitzbergen] had to be careful, avoiding puddles. Everything in Neptune Beach was sand. It was a misery. No matter how hard the street cleaners worked, shoveling the sand in mounds along the gutters, more blew in from the beach. On a rainy day you walked in black gritty mud. Nothing was solid, neither the pavements nor the foundations of the buildings. As the sands gave, the sidewalks broke and the houses on their pole foundations never stopped settling. . . . (LC 28)

In contrast to the Brooklyn sections described in his fiction, Fuchs provides the following description of Flatbush in "The Williamsburg Bridge Plaza," a reminiscence (he is accompanying his father, a newsstand-candy-stand-owner, who is delivering Christmas chocolates) originally published in 1971 in *The New York Times*:

> . . . a section of Brooklyn just a few miles away from us in Williamsburg but like a place in another country. Flatbush then was a kind of village. I saw the blaze of lights, the Christmas decorations, the gleaming, well-stocked butcher shops, the ruddy faces of the tradespeople as they dealt with lady customers—all of it was new to me, remote and seeming unreal. (*Apathetic Bookie Joint* 268)

As in Kazin, the journey out of the Jewish slum permits an entry into another world, the true America, with its lights, brightness, plenty, its calm; the American reality unreal to the ghetto Jew. In fact, an extremely striking similarity between the two is their use of the Yom Kippur prayer of Kol Nidre. In *A Walker in the City* Kazin describes the scene in the synagogue, each man bitterly repenting his sins of the previous year in a "kind of purifying ecstasy, for they were summing up the whole earthly life of Brownsville" (102). Fuchs employs the chant as the epigram to *Low Company*, the darkest and most hopeless of the Brooklyn novels, a work in which human feeling seems to have almost completely disappeared. Perhaps the transgressions noted in Kol Nidre require the Brooklyn Jews' banishment to the slums, almost as if their sins demand eternal penance through "incarceration." Like Moses, it appears that they are only to see the Promised Land, not reach it.

Escape in Fuchs is always temporary. For ghetto-dwellers—women and children—the exodus into America could take the form of a few weeks at a Catskill boarding-house. The Catskills also provide a more durable escape, financial gain to the likes of Papravel, Philip Hayman's gangster uncle, a key player in a war between rival Brooklyn bus companies whisking the poor off to the mountains. The Brooklyn gangster—be it Papravel, Blenholt, the deceased commissioner of sewers revered by Max Balkan as a Tamburlaine in *Homage to Blenholt*, or Shubunka, the ghetto Gatsby of *Low Company*—is emblematic of one of the Fuchsian alternatives to the call of honest, moral education presented by Kazin. Though successful in *Summer in Williamsburg*, Fuchs rejects dishonesty, corruption, and business in his last novel of the 1930s as a suitable tool for rising out of Brooklyn. While both Papravel and Shubunka proclaim themselves honest businessmen—in the spirit of Rockefeller and Morgan—the Yankee ingenuity, entrepreneurship, and self-reliance these ghetto Jews cloak themselves in can no longer compete with modern-day monopolistic capitalism.

The second Fuchsian alternative is that provided by old Label Balkan, a former performer on the Yiddish stage now reduced to carrying a sandwich sign for a cosmetologist through the Williamsburg streets. He relates the following to Max, his luftmensch son:

> ". . . two kinds of work there is, honest and not honest. Standing in a stationery store all day, pressing in a shop, cutting fur—that's honest work and it's no good." Mr B ran from this, it made him sick and he became an actor. "The other kind is ganavish, . . . You know what ganavish means, Max? To make a living not honestly, by tricks, by schemes, not with the hands.

Gamblers, actors, poets, artists. That is good. It is easy, you can have a good time playing, but you need luck. Luck and tricks." "Sometimes," he said, "the craziest tricksters and schemers are the biggest successes, I don't know what it is." (HB 231–32)

If Kazin physically escapes from Brownsville on foot, Fuchs's characters get only as far as the movies or may never even have to leave the house or the cash register, where they escape through romantic novels, the precursors of today's Harlequins. Along with the beauty parlor, they chiefly provide sanctuary to women, who, due to the job shortage of the Depression and traditional attitudes that they need only marry and stay at home, had nowhere else to go. They permit the illusions necessary for Ruth and Rita in *Homage to Blenholt* to rid themselves of the painful drudgery and dreariness of Brooklyn and imagine a better America. These locales take them away from the everyday routine of worrying about whether their men will ever achieve the modicum of success needed for marriage and a home. At the movies, Hollywood, America's dream factory created by eastern European Jews similar to them, feeds them on fantasies of Gable, Cooper, and Crosby instead of Max and Munves; in the beauty parlors their imaginations are filled with the Garbos, Dietrichs, Crawfords, and Harlows they wish they could be as they doze off during their manicures.

Fuchsian escape is just fleeting, for the men as well. The dream of success foisted on the ghetto poor by men such as Louis Mayer, the Warner brothers, and the rest of the Hollywood moguls, to become Horatio Alger–type success stories, is the aspiration of Max Balkan, a Williamsburg inventor. He is the dream incarnate, a wholehearted believer in the success ethic and the virtues of honesty, ambition, industry, thrift, and sacrifice sold to America's immigrants. Fuchs brutally spares nothing in exposing the inanity of his luftmensch, listing his ideas: radios in the subways to entertain riders, soft-drink stands selling chicken soup, self-sustaining parachutes (to make everyone a luftmensch?), and bottled onion juice. Unfortunately

Max is always a step behind, a moment too late—a constant also-ran. And when Max takes the fall, he goes down hard. The gambling winnings of a friend provide the necessary capital for him and his crony Munves (a linguistic scholar representing the Fuchsian rejection of education as the surefire lane to success) to marry and open a delicatessen. Fuchs is cruelly ironic. Max's unsuccessful attempt to escape Williamsburg and its poverty, to achieve the freedom and benefits of the "ganavish life," is crushing: being kept back in the working class forever—an even more devastating condemnation to Brooklyn.

So, was Brooklyn Bridge a force connecting Jews in Brooklyn to New York and America, or was the East River an insurmountable barrier? That certainly depends on whose perspective we take. The Brownsville and Williamsburg working class of the 1930s may have occasionally crossed the bridge to visit friends and relatives, or to work, but it did not raise their standard of living, did not really bring them any closer to the American mainstream. Their hopes were placed in their children—in Kazin and Fuchs. And they did get out of Brooklyn. Kazin became an academic, a *macher*, and lived on the Upper West Side, the old Allrightnik's Row, until he died in June 1998. Fuchs got fed up being a schoolteacher writing in his spare time who sold only two thousand copies of some wonderful fiction; he followed Horace Greeley's advice and went west. He won an Oscar for the best screenplay of 1955, *Love Me or Leave Me*. He wrote to survive and never really made any big money; he died in 1993.

WORKS CITED

Fuchs, Daniel. *The Apathetic Bookie Joint*. New York: Methuen, 1979.

———. *The Williamsburg Trilogy*. New York: Avon Books, 1972. (Reprint of *Summer in Williamsburg*, first published 1934; *Homage to Blenholt*, first published 1936; and *Low Company*, first published 1937).

Howe, Irving. *World of Our Fathers*. New York: Harcourt Brace Jovanovich, 1976.

Kazin, Alfred. *A Walker in the City*. New York: Harcourt, Brace and World, 1951.

Approximations Made with Line

An Interview with Phillip Lopate

SUZAN SHERMAN

Despite Phillip Lopate's literary success, he has never forgotten his origins. Raised in a Jewish working-class family from Williamsburg, Lopate as a boy sang in the Silbermintz Hebrew choir and was even slated to become the boy cantor in an Orthodox synagogue. Yet his curiosity for the very different world of Manhattan was irresistible. Lopate left Brooklyn to attend Columbia University and later achieved great acclaim for his numerous books. These include several essay collections (*Bachelorhood, Against Joie de Vivre, Portrait of My Body,* and *Totally, Tenderly, Tragically: Essays and Criticism from a Lifelong Love Affair with the Movies*), books he has edited (*The Art of the Personal Essay*), *Writing New York: A Literary Anthology,* and *The Art of the Essay*), and the novels *The Rug Merchant* and *Confessions of Summer.* But Phillip Lopate is perhaps best known and loved for his essays. These portraits of minute moments in his own life are the gems sifted from daily living. In "Shaving a Beard" Lopate discovers, "As I cut away the clumps of darkness, a moon rises out of my face." And in "Confessions of a Shusher" Lopate reveals that when going to a movie, "I can live with the kickers, the candy unwrappers, the baldies, etc., but I draw the line at prattlers." In reading his words there is an immediate sense of warmth and intimacy, as if Lopate were whispering his ruminations into the reader's ear. Each page reveals more of him.

So when I first met with Phillip Lopate in a Greenwich Village café, I felt as though I already knew him. Having read his books, I knew many of his ticks, peculiarities, and revelations, as well as his likes, dislikes. I knew his sense of humor. Lopate moved back to Brooklyn six years ago, and lives in Carroll Gardens with his wife and daughter. We discussed how being raised as a Brooklyn Jew has influenced who he is and the work he does.

Suzan Sherman: Though you are not particularly observant in a religious sense, what is your present attachment to your religious identity and what has it meant to you in the past?

Phillip Lopate: I grew up in Williamsburg, in a very religious neighborhood. My parents, though they were not observant, still considered themselves Jewish. We had Passover, we lit the candles on Hanukkah, and there may have even been a time when my mother lit the candles on Friday night, but I don't think so. In fact, there was a certain testiness in our relationship to the more Orthodox Jews in the neighborhood. I remember one time when my mother was leaving a supermarket on a

From left: *sister Betty Anne Lopate, brother Leonard Lopate, and Phillip Lopate. Photo courtesy of Phillip Lopate.*

Saturday and these Jewish kids outside kept saying to her, "Shabbas goy! Shabbas goy!" So my mother said, "Get out of here! I work all week, when else am I going to do shopping?" So the Jewish kids who were more religious would make fun of us, and on the way home from Hebrew school the Irish kids would beat us up.

And yet it seemed perfectly appropriate that we would live in a Jewish neighborhood. All the shops were kosher; the delicatessens, the butchers. In those days Williamsburg was not just Hasidic, there was much more variety, there were people like my parents who were basically secular. It was a Jewish ghetto, and there wasn't this sense that everybody had to be strictly observant. But every time people like my parents moved out, the Hasidim took over the apartments. What you have now is a much more monolithic community.

I was born in 1943 and by 1947 we were living on Broadway in Williamsburg. I wasn't even aware that there was such a thing as Conservative or Reform Jews. Everybody was Orthodox; either you were nonobservant Orthodox or observant Orthodox. So when my parents sent me to Hebrew school it was an Orthodox one. It was one of those wild Hebrew schools you read about where some scholar has reluctantly been put in charge of kids who are screaming and throwing chalk, throwing erasers. He had absolutely no feeling for working with young people at all. A lot of my Hebrew school teachers were these kinds of very unworldly, luftmensch types who basically wrung their hands and said, "what did I do to deserve having to work with children?"

My brother, who is three years older than I am, I remember he had gotten wind of this Hebrew choir which was basically made up of Yeshiva boys. He and I liked to sing, we both had good voices, so he got me

into it and we each made something like twenty-five dollars a year. So there was that as an incentive. It was called the Silbermintz choir, and it was the second largest Hebrew choir in New York at the time. It was so large that on the High Holidays they would split us into several groups; one of us would go to Kings Highway in Brooklyn, another to the Grand Concourse in the Bronx, and another someplace in Manhattan. And when the whole choir was assembled we'd sing with some famous cantors like Charles Vigoda and David Koussevitsky in Saturday night concerts. So I grew up steeped in the sound of liturgical Judaism, loving the archaic sound of the music. It wasn't hard for me to identify as a Jew growing up in Brooklyn.

Suzan Sherman: I understand that there's a Conservative synagogue in Brooklyn which you're particularly fond of now. Is this the Kane Street Synagogue?

Phillip Lopate: Yeah. I would probably go to an Orthodox synagogue if I was still a bachelor because it's what I grew up with. But because I'm married to a woman who would take offense at being seated separate from the men, we go to a Conservative synagogue. When I was on my own I would go to services on the Lower East Side, and even though I didn't really understand the Hebrew, I would be steeped in the memories and the sounds, and those old men. I still feel a certain loyalty towards Orthodox Judaism even though I go to a Conservative synagogue.

Suzan Sherman: Were you bar mitzvahed?

Phillip Lopate: Of course. Not only was I bar mitzvahed, I performed the whole service. I didn't just do the Haftorah; I did what the cantor usually does. Because I was in the Fort Greene Jewish Center and they didn't have the money to hire a cantor. In fact there was some talk in the congregation that maybe they should use me as a kind of boy cantor. So in a way I was slated to move in that direction. And I remember somebody in the synagogue said to me that if I became a cantor I could be a chaplain in the army. I wouldn't have to go into battle, I could hang back and I'd be safer that way, you know?

But then I started to rebel, and question the stories in the Bible. I had had a big argument about Sodom and Gomorrah, and whether or not God should have destroyed the kids and the babies because they didn't have a chance. Basically I was beginning to question, but before then I would go to synagogue and my parents wouldn't. They said, "We would go if we had more energy but we can't, so why don't you go?" They didn't even go to High Holiday services. I wasn't alone in being most religious when I was about ten, eleven, twelve. This is often the period when kids need a sense of certainty, they don't want ambiguity. And I would see the famous rabbi who was passing through, who was giving a sermon at the Williamsburg synagogue. The whole place would be filled with people. And the sense of occasion was very clear to me, even if he was talking in Yiddish and I didn't understand it. At the time it didn't bother me that I didn't understand because I didn't think I was entitled to understand everything. The point was that I was watching the way the community operated, that was what was interesting to me. The guys would be pulling on their tallises to make their points, and the kids would be running around in the back. It was like a medieval fair.

Suzan Sherman: Theater.

Phillip Lopate: It was theater, exactly. I appreciated it as theater.

Suzan Sherman: Were your parents first-generation Americans?

Phillip Lopate: Both my grandfathers had come over, so my parents were first-generation born in America, that's right.

Suzan Sherman: Did they speak Yiddish?

Phillip Lopate: They spoke Yiddish in the house, but they didn't teach it to us. They spoke it as a secret language.

Suzan Sherman: That's how it was with my family too. Do you ever go back to Williamsburg to visit?

Phillip Lopate: Sometimes. We lived on Broadway near Marcy Avenue, in the area that abutted what is now the Hasidic neighborhood. I was not near the part where all the art bars are now, though we would go down there and play. Before my wife and I got married she was living in Williamsburg; she's a painter and was living in a loft there. So when I visited her I would get all nostalgic and she hated it, she would say it's so dirty. It's so incredibly toxic, the Williamsburg Bridge is filled with asbestos and lead. I don't go back that often anymore. The Williamsburg I grew up with, the Williamsburg which was much more tolerant, is gone now. I remember going back to the house I used to live in with my sister, and these kids were sitting on the brownstone steps with their *pais* and yarmulkes and they looked at us in a very hostile manner, like, how dare you come into our neighborhood. And my sister

said, "What are you looking at us like that for? We were here long before you."

Suzan Sherman: I wonder what it was like for you after you and your wife got married and moved back to Brooklyn, back to the borough you grew up in. What does Brooklyn signify for you as compared to life in Manhattan?

Phillip Lopate: Well it definitely felt like a diminution of vitality; it was like going into a decompression chamber. Suddenly there was nobody out on the streets Saturday night. Of course a lot of that has changed because unknowingly we moved into a neighborhood which has gone through a tremendous transformation.

Smith Street and Court Street have become very hip, now it's like an extension of the East Village. But none of that was there when we moved in five and a half, six years ago. We couldn't find the amount of space we needed in Manhattan for less than a million dollars, so we bought a house in Brooklyn, and it ended up being a very smart thing to have done. At first it felt like one of those dreams where you're back in elementary school and you thought you'd already graduated. One of those discouraging dreams where you thought you had risen above your situation. But it's certainly a better place for raising a child.

Suzan Sherman: I used to live in Brooklyn, and my relatives couldn't believe I wanted to because everyone had grown up in a tenement in Brooklyn. They had escaped, and didn't understand why I wanted to go back.

Phillip Lopate: I remember going out with this girl in high school and her great ambition in life was to move out of Williamsburg. And here we are coming back to these areas. I think it's the right thing to do. Certainly Jewish Brooklyn is not as powerful as it once was. There's a lot of solid, middle-class Jewish neighborhoods around the areas of Kings Highway and near Brighton Beach.

Suzan Sherman: But Jewish Brooklyn is generally very religious now—Williamsburg and Borough Park. If people can afford to, they move away to Long Island, the Five Towns.

Phillip Lopate: What's missing from Brooklyn now is something that impressed me quite a bit when I was a kid—what you might call working-class Jewish culture. Clearly a lot of the people, working-class Jews like my parents, pulled themselves up and moved out to the suburbs. But there was such vitality in the working-class Jewish culture. My father was someone who worked in a factory, and when he came home he read books. Self-education was taken very seriously. There was an excitement about culture and ideas which was an allowable dessert for people who did not have much money.

Suzan Sherman: I'm curious to hear more about your experiences as an undergraduate at Columbia and how it contrasted from your working-class upbringing. In your essay "Terror of Mentors" you mention as an aside that while at Columbia you mistrusted the academic setting.

Phillip Lopate: Columbia was a completely different world. I had grown up in a Jewish ghetto, I'd only known ghetto life, and then when I got to Columbia there was this indirectness and code of behavior I was unfamiliar with. Instead of saying, "Get out of my face or I'll kill you," they would just freeze you out. I remembered submitting an article to the campus newspaper, and they rejected it but wouldn't tell me why. It wasn't gentlemanly to go into it, you know. And in the first weeks of class they had speech tests where they asked me to read a passage, and when I did they said, "Mr. Lopate, you have regionalisms." And I said, "Whadda ya expect?" I talked with a Brooklyn accent.

Suzan Sherman: Did you resent that or feel ashamed?

Phillip Lopate: I felt a bit of both. I resented it, but I also began to mumble. And one time I was on a date and this woman said, "Are you from Czechoslovakia?" Because I was ashamed of my accent. Columbia had had an anti-Semitic exclusionary policy at one time, and one of my teachers, Lionel Trilling, was the first Jewish professor in the English Department. Even though he never denied he was Jewish he had developed a whole Anglican appearance, his accent and this kind of tweedy, Mid-Atlantic gentleman's style—God knows where he cobbled it together from. But I didn't want to do that. The year I went to Columbia—I was the class of 1964—they had decided to admit students strictly on merit and test scores. It was an experiment by a guy named David Dudley, the head of admissions. Anyway, they called it Dudley's folly because there were so many Jews from the New York area in the class that they decided to never do that again.

One of my experiences was meeting other Jews at Columbia from different backgrounds. One of my best friends from Columbia was Jewish and lived on Park Avenue; he'd had a much more privileged upbringing. I remember the first time I ever even fathomed that there were Jews with money, and the whole notion of a JAP, for instance, seemed so exotic to me. I mentioned it in one of my essays, "The Invisible Woman." They seemed like creatures from another world. They could whine and their fathers would get them something, while we were not encouraged to complain at all. When I see how children are raised now, including my own daughter, I'm amazed. Because we were supposed to suffer in silence, not complain. If something bothered you, you dealt with it. You didn't expect your parents to remove every discomfort. My experience was much more like I had grown up in Poland or something.

Suzan Sherman: Columbia was a whole other world, even though it wasn't that far from where you grew up. Just over the bridge.

Phillip Lopate: Exactly. I was definitely part of the generation that used their brains to get ahead. I got a Regents' scholarship, and my parents urged me to go to Brooklyn College and cash in my scholarship so I'd have a little money. They couldn't imagine the Ivy League. They wanted their children to go to college, but assumed we would all go to city universities. The reason I applied to Columbia was because my parents almost said don't. In some ways their experience of the world was too narrow, and it was up to me to go beyond it. But in another way my parents were right; Columbia was a very difficult adjustment for me. It would have been much easier if I had gone to Brooklyn or to City College, but I wanted to see something else. I was the valedictorian of my high school, so if anybody could get into an Ivy League school it was going to be me. I had a reason to dream that way. When I left that world I didn't retain a single friendship from high school, and often I wish I had. I used to fantasize about placing an ad, saying would so-and-so please contact me.

Suzan Sherman: Has anyone contacted you since seeing your books?

Phillip Lopate: Yeah, one or two people have contacted me, but certainly none of the boys who stayed in the neighborhood. There was a feeling that I wasn't one of them, that I was different. I was moving on, and they were staying.

Suzan Sherman: Tell me a bit about what I imagine was a huge amount of research that went into editing the anthology *Writing New York*. Did you have any help?

Phillip Lopate: I had some help from the Library of America, but basically I would draw up lists and try to get my hands on as much writing as I could find. I started out with a fairly rich knowledge of some of New York literature, but then there were gaps. I had a year to do the whole thing.

Suzan Sherman: A year? That's all?

Phillip Lopate: Yeah, I just dived in. And because it was saturation reading I ended up getting an almost three-dimensional sense of how writers connected to each other. I got a sense of a living history. It was a wonderful opportunity, even though I would have liked two more years to work on it.

Suzan Sherman: And maybe three volumes.

Phillip Lopate: At the beginning they had wanted me to do a five-hundred-page volume. Before I had even begun the project I said, I think this is going to need a thousand pages. They said no, we want to price it not that expensive, we want it five hundred pages. So I said, OK, we'll see. And I kept throwing material at them, every time I found good stuff. So in the end, in the last two months, they began to realize it had to be a thousand pages. But by that time I was thinking. . . .

Suzan Sherman: Fifteen hundred!

Phillip Lopate: Fifteen hundred would really do a good job. I knew that with a thousand pages there were some people I was leaving out, but with fifteen hundred pages it could have been unassailable. In any case I'm pleased with what came out. I think there's a lot of flavor.

Suzan Sherman: There are three essays which you've written over the years which stand out for me as almost frighteningly personal and true. As I was reading them I thought, how did he have the guts to write this, how did he have the bravery to see a living person with such dimension. One of the essays was about the film critic Pauline Kael, one was about your father, and the other was about the writer Donald Barthelme. When you were in the process of writing about these people, did you ever feel any . . . trepidation?

Phillip Lopate: Terror.

Suzan Sherman: You did feel terror.

Phillip Lopate: I think one of the reasons I wrote about them is because I felt butterflies in my stomach, I felt terror. And a strong sense of taboo. I was going against, I was violating something. And that emotion convinces me that there's something strong there that I should continue to work with. It's harder to write where you, you're just grinding it out without a strong emotional connection. One emotional connection I can

have to something is squeamishness. The Barthelme piece took me six months, just to get those thirty pages.

Suzan Sherman: Was it the fear that also kept you from writing it?

Phillip Lopate: The fear was to try to get enough balance so that I could say what about Barthelme I was critical of. Sometimes if I feel the urge to be critical then I forget the other part of me that's not critical. I had to will myself into a more objective space, I had to be wiser than I normally feel.

The essay on my father is very close to my heart. My father was in very bad shape at the time. He was dying, and I basically wrote it before he died.

Suzan Sherman: Before it could become sentimental.

Phillip Lopate: Yeah. I didn't want to write it after he died. It was a strange kind of like pre-elegy, pre-obituary, and I'm very glad I did it. When he died I had a real feeling of calm and acceptance about it because I'd gone through it in the writing. But in another way it was a piece that flew in the face of my family. It helped me resolve my feelings toward my father, but my family thought it too nice a portrait.

Suzan Sherman: When did they first read it?

Phillip Lopate: When the book came out.

Suzan Sherman: So it's not only your fear in the process of writing it, but once it's published you have to deal with the responses of the people involved. Which is more frightening for you?

Phillip Lopate: I'm not that afraid of dealing with the people.

Suzan Sherman: Your portraits of people remind me of Giacometti drawings. Do you know Giacometti?

Phillip Lopate: I love Giacometti drawings. I often think about them, and the way he would do all of these approximations using line. I really feel that I can't always get at a person in one gesture, so I put one thing next to the other and hope that it all adds up to something complex. In some ways it connects back to Judaism, and a reverence for the fathers. I have this idea that you can be more truly reverent not only by saying flattering things about the deceased, or in the case of my father, Pauline Kael, or Donald Barthelme, but by attempting to be as honest as you can. I hope when I die people will come forward and speak honestly about me, and not just say all kinds of flatteries. I once spoke to my friend Max Apple about feeling like I wasn't a good Jew. He keeps kosher, and he said, "No Phillip, you question, and that's part of the Jewish tradition. You're one of those questioners." So I feel a closeness to Judaism, I feel close to the intellectual side of it, the idea of examining the text, trying to understand the forty-nine levels of the Talmud. And I do feel reverential toward tradition.

When you look at someone like Pauline Kael, another Jewish thinker, you might say she had these strengths and these narrownesses, and she always tried to use the narrowness and pretend they were assets. I felt I had an understanding of where she was strong and where she was less strong. She hated that piece I wrote on her. She could not understand it. She was used to the idea that people either loved her or hated her. She didn't understand the attempt to be objective. It was an insult.

Suzan Sherman: To her it was as if you were lukewarm.

Phillip Lopate: Lukewarm, exactly. Tepid. I want to do another piece that makes me squeamish, about the photographer friend of mine, Rudy Berkhardt, who killed himself. It's another surrogate father piece; I want to try to understand the life. And to understand something about bohemia and art-making, what is expected of us as artists and as people on this earth.

Suzan Sherman: Although you grew up in a household with a father who was depressed, you are amazingly expansive. I wonder how you do it, how you've circumvented repeating your father's dynamic.

Phillip Lopate: Well, for one thing, my mother was an actress and was much more extroverted, though she had her bouts of depression. There's a certain stubbornness in me that likes sanity, and a lot of it has to do with my relationship to work. As long as I have my work I don't have to get depressed; it roots me. And then there's a kind of stoicism in me, I don't expect every moment to be wonderfully happy. It seems like a paradox that I wrote *Against Joie de Vivre*, but on the other hand I have a lot of upbeat energy. It's partly due to the fact that if you don't try to be happy, then you don't have to feel ashamed when you're not, and you can have more energy for other things. So there's a certain amount of the proper use of pessimism. What I've really always aspired to is a kind of worldliness which is neither optimism or pessimism, but is more like, oh well, that's the way people are, it can't be helped.

But depression still frightens me a little bit to be around. My father was a prototype of defeat and withdrawal. It was like a black hole in a way, and to think about him and go into it still feels scary. But then there was his other side which was this worker side, this stoical side, that always showed up and did the job. And that's a part of him that I really valued.

Suzan Sherman: That's the relationship to your writing.

Phillip Lopate: This Sunday I have a piece in the Arts & Leisure section of the *Times* on Frederick Weissman, documentary filmmaker. I really like his work. Weissman is symbolic of the way I want to go through life which is beyond positive and negative. He turns the camera on, you're on a terminal ward, and he says, This is it. Take it in. Face it. Be in it. This is the world. We're in it, just look at it. So that's where I'd like to go, I'd like meet things head on.

Cyber-Spirituality
An Interview with Binyamin Jolkovsky

ILANA ABRAMOVITCH

Brooklyn is Brooklyn. But Brooklyn is also more than its physical boundaries. Though contained physically within its municipal borders, Brooklyn's larger geography is global, embracing the people and ideas, the music and the mystique it launches out into the larger world. Brooklyn buzz has frequently extended beyond its borders, but now its reach is farther and quicker. In the early twentieth century, Brooklyn sent radio waves out into the larger world. The early twenty-first century features thriving Brooklyn-based and Brooklyn-themed Internet sites that can be accessed anywhere. Brooklyn exists in the space between those who converse about it worldwide.

According to Yosef I. Abramowitz, founder of JewishFamily.com and Jskyway.com, a distance learning network for day schools, "The best our community can do is understand the Internet and harness the dynamics that the information revolution is about to unleash—not only ride the wave, but guide it. . . . . Judaism is about to metamorphose. . . . It will become populist, unconstrained geographically, unfettered by denominations, and personalized."

The JewishWorldReview.com, a Brooklyn-based Web magazine, can truly claim global status. By early 2000, it boasted 25,000 regular daily readers in all corners of the world. A digest of reports from Jewish newspapers in Europe, Australia, and the United States, the *Jewish World Review* has become such a high-profile showcase for talent that many writers literally beg to come on board, according to Binyamin Jolkovsky, site founder, designer, all-round maverick, and Web maven.

While the JWR provides information and entertainment, its true mission is spiritual—the creation of a community of like-minded people. Originally aimed at an audience of Jews who were on the road to being lost for Judaism, Jolkovsky's site became popular with a much wider audience. Now, he invites readers of all backgrounds to make up his community: "where religion, politics and culture meet." This, of course, covers a lot of territory, but, as ever, has quite specific meanings.

Previously, working as a journalist, Jolkovsky's heart was in Jewish journalism. An Orthodox Jew, Jolkovsky was concerned with why so many Jews abandon Judaism. The answers he received told him that many found Judaism to be obsessed with paranoia, the Holocaust, with the negative. He felt that the warmth of the grandparents' generation, the emotional glue, seemed lost.

Jolkovsky decided to use his talent to produce something bright and fresh that would attract unaffiliated Jews to the Jewish world. He wanted a site that would appeal to Generation X, his own media-savvy generation. Looking around at five or six thousand other Jewish sites, Jolkovsky found most of them wanting. (As of August 2000 there are ten thousand Jewish Web sites.) Many were not sophisticated. Others seemed to him only tangentially Jewish, sticking to superficial topics, such as stars who happen to be born Jewish. Jolkovsky knew something else was needed to attract serious people. He wanted something slick, yet with substance, something that would be a success. He created the *Jewish World Review*, and "people ate it up."

Jolkovsky has created an audience for his brand of Jewish renewal. He is aware of the tremendous power he potentially wields. "There is no way I could otherwise get radio hosts and senators to pay attention if I wrote a letter." And they do read his Web magazine.

The Jewish World Review comes out five times a week, ghosted by a not-for-profit organization. It's free, though people are asked to make donations. A medley of columns about politics, Judaism, and lifestyle pieces, it includes cartoons, children's stories. "I want to make people think," Jolkovsky said. "I'll run anyone who causes people to stop and think about the society around them."

Jolkovsky is extraordinarily devoted to his magazine. He gets sick two or three times a year from sheer exhaustion; he regularly sleeps two to three hours a night. Yosef Abramowitz says, "There is a generational gap between most of the decision-makers in Jewish life and Jews who use the Web on a daily basis.''

According to Jolkovsky, readers don't come for information alone. Some like the feeling of community; others are looking for help. When a woman in Singapore wanted to find an Orthodox synagogue in Amsterdam, or a Midwestern reader had a yen for Brooklyn bagels, each turned to Mr. Jolkovsky, and he delivered in the latter case, sending a dozen bagels by overnight express.

Newspapers often seek him out to explain events in the tightly knit Orthodox world. The *New York Post* calls him when a story breaks in his community. Jolkovsky, who lives in Boro Park, Brooklyn, the largest concentration of Jews outside Jerusalem, likes to be a liaison between the mainstream media and the Orthodox world. Jolkovsky is pluralistic and inclusive, but he is still coming from an Orthodox, right-wing perspective. The writers for the *Review*, on the whole, come from conservative viewpoints. Regular writers include Charles Krauthammer, Dr. Laura, and George Will.

Jewish World Review uses a contemporary medium to propagate ancient teachings. Jonathan Rosen, author of *The Talmud and the Internet: A Journey between Worlds*, finds affinities between two seemingly distant worlds. "Both the Talmud and the Internet inspire a community of users, who join in a dialogue across space and time. Both are complex and nosy with a sense of ongoing arguments and interruption. And both are partly born out of loss—the Talmud out of the 'Jewish need to pack civilization into words and wander out into the world' after the Temple was destroyed; the Internet out of the loss of books as objects."

Thoroughly Modern Orthodox
An Interview with Rina Goldberg

ILANA ABRAMOVITCH

Her voluminous red mane aglow as she bounds down the office corridor, Brooklyn-bred Rina Goldberg is the picture of dynamism. But Rina is no ordinary product of the Brooklyn neighborhoods. At twenty-four, she is the assistant to the director of the Museum of Jewish Heritage—A Living Memorial to the Holocaust in New York City. She is also a graduate of Barnard College, the former head of her high school's girls' basketball team, and a devout member of the Modern Orthodox community. Devout yet also progressive.

For those unfamiliar with its world, a shorthand image of Orthodox Jewry is the "exotic" picture of a Hasidic man. In the New York area, this visual image is perhaps the most easily identifiable of a group of Jews who are somehow different, part of a self-segregating group. In actuality, there are many varieties of Orthodoxy, while women and men within it move in distinct domains. Many Jews, as well as non-Jews, are ignorant of its diversity and of the large differences in customs and halachic (Jewish law) interpretations.

Rina would strike any observer as a fashionably dressed woman, whether in trousers or a skirt. Her attire is modest, but not strikingly different from that of many New Yorkers. In this, as a Modern Orthodox community member, she differs from her counterparts in other sectors of the Orthodox world. Other Orthodox women will not wear trousers. Their skirts are always long, and their sleeves cover below the elbow. After marriage, many Orthodox women expect to shave their heads and wear a *sheitel* (wig), hat, or headscarf. Not Rina. She is, furthermore, an avid sports fan, takes modern dance classes, is a voluminous reader of fiction, and fan of music and movies. Despite her obvious attractiveness and bright bubbliness, she has no immediate plans to marry, nor are her parents applying any pressure. Not very much, anyhow.

The Orthodox make up approximately 10 percent of America's Jews and are growing. The Modern Orthodox world distinguishes itself from the Ultra-Orthodox and the yeshivish wings of American Orthodoxy in its interpretation of ritual observance and degree of accommodation to secular life. Each group differs in customs, community social structure, and patterns of leadership.

Rina explains some of the differences: Modern Orthodox Jews scrupulously maintain traditions, are Shomer Shabbat and kashrut (strictly observant of Sabbath and dietary laws), but function expansively in American secular society. There is no sense of animosity with the outside world. In contrast, the yeshivish engage with American society in a hands-off way. They won't watch most movies, carefully monitor their kids' leisure activities, and avoid the modern world in many of its guises. The Hasidim engage even less with the outside world.

"My family embraces feminism. Within Orthodoxy. It's hard, because we live in American society where you are considered equal, and then, within religion, the equality is different, and it's hard to understand. Strides are being made in Orthodoxy and within my family, too. My parents sent me to schools where girls learn Talmud, and there is no ceiling on what we could learn and what we could ask, because we were girls.

"Both my sister and I had bat mitzvahs, although we did not do any Torah reading. Family and friends gathered, and we gave a d'var torah (biblical interpretation) after the Torah portion was read. That shows some of American society's influence on my family."

Modern Orthodoxy has been transformed and energized by feminism, with the appearance of women's study groups, prayer groups, and interest in remedying the problems of agunot (women unable to obtain a ritual divorce). A report of the American Jewish Committee by Brandeis University sociologist Sylvia Barack Fishman cites the high level of Jewish education for women to be the major area of transformation. Although the number of women's prayer groups is relatively small, the report states that their visibility has been greatly enhanced by those who oppose and demonize them. Despite the respectful attitude toward halacha displayed by the Orthodox women's innovations and their absolute lack of interest in becoming rabbis, right-wing rabbis have strongly criticized Orthodox feminism.

Rina's family is among the innovators. "My sister did a few progressive things for her wedding. The biggest thing was that she had a verbal acceptance of the ring. In traditional weddings, the bride is completely silent. The most important part of the ceremony is when the groom gives the bride the ring and says: 'Here I am betrothed to you with this ring, according to the law of Moses and Israel.'

"He puts the ring on her finger, and she closes her hand and rabbinically that is considered acceptance. My sister could not abide by that, being completely silent. Not just being silent but feeling silenced. So, she did a verbal acceptance in Hebrew of the ring: 'And here I am accepting the ring.' That was the biggest issue, the hardest-fought one: That's what people were talking about later. She did not make up the phrase or invent the ritual. She found ha-

lachic sources for it, and discussed it with other people, including rabbis. I think a friend of hers did it in Israel. It was completely halachic. There was another innovation in the ketubbah [marriage contract]. Normally, it includes the names of the bride and groom's fathers. My sister wanted her mother's name on it, too.

"There was more! Traditionally someone gives a d'var torah about the couple under the huppah [wedding canopy]; it's usually a big rabbi. My sister invited a woman friend who is a great scholar, and another female friend to recite a ninth-century blessing. So, she had two of her friends standing for her. You see, a lot of witnesses are needed at weddings. It's halachic. They ensure that the ring was bought and owned by groom, witnesses for this, witnesses for that. My sister felt she wanted some of her own 'witnesses,' so she asked two friends. These innovations were quite big. There has been a lot of word-of-mouth reaction to her, to me. People are afraid of change. Feminism is a scary thing. People saw it as a challenge to tradition."

Rina grew up in Midwood/Flatbush—the same neighborhood in which her mother was raised. Three generations of the family have been involved with their synagogue, the Kingsway Jewish Center. Very involved, in fact, as leaders, in this multipurpose synagogue center, an Orthodox shul with a pool. The neighborhood was one in which Jewish and non-Jewish children played together on the street, although because of the laws of kashrut, never ate at each other's homes. Attending the Yeshiva of Flatbush, one of the prime Hebrew day schools in New York, from prekindergarten through high school, Rina was involved with other Jews like herself. While she had some contact with a few non-Jews in her neighborhood, it took until college for her to mingle with Jews of other streams, even to know about committed Jews of different backgrounds.

"Some friends became more Orthodox; it happened around the year in Israel. It has become the thing to do for the Modern Orthodox to spend a year in Israel focusing on Jewish studies in a yeshiva-like setting. Some people become more Orthodox. Some of it sticks, some not. My female friends are still in touch. I feel it more from my male friends; some stopped talking to me. Talking to women is prohibited according to some rabbis. One male friend was still talking to me. I asked him about this: 'What customs do you ascribe to?' He wanted to be friends with me. 'If you believe in something, you should not compromise.' He said: 'Well, that means I won't talk to you.' A few months later, a letter arrived: 'I miss your friendship, but I cannot talk to you anymore.' I see him at events, and we talk for five minutes. I walk away being sad. Other friends just stopped talking. I respect those choices. I do not feel rebellion against restrictions."

Rina is proud of her Brooklyn grit: "When people find out you are from Brooklyn, they say: 'Oh, Brooklyn?!' There is a kind of tough image of Brooklyn." She takes satisfaction in having grown up in a place where on your lunch hour at school you could choose between kosher pizza, kosher Chinese, the kosher bakery, and kosher delight. "It's very specific to Brooklyn. Nowhere else has the number of shops, the variety."

She has nonetheless decided that she will not return to Brooklyn to live. As nurturing as the neighborhood has been to her, it's changed. "I would not go back to settle in my old neighborhood. It's completely 'Brooklyn Jewish,' a more religious but, from my point of view, very materialist culture. "Everyone has custom *sheitels* [wigs]. You always have to be dressed. It's disturbing to me. It's not just in Brooklyn. There are different tones in the 'Five Towns,' Queens, etc. Brooklyn's tone is more religious, a pious tone.

"My shul remains the same. Some religious wars are going on. Some younger members wanted the *mechitzah* [separation between men and women] to be higher. The schools seem to be influencing the kids. There were big fights over this, and some people left when we did not put it as high as they wanted. My synagogue is still strongly Modern Orthodox. On the other hand, more Hasidic elements are around, with white socks and streimels [wide fur-trimmed hats] on Shabbat. They are building their own synagogues. A *shtibl* on every block to fit their needs. Seems the antithesis of community. Although as, they say: two Jews, three synagogues. What kind of community is it where everyone just leaves to make a new one? Of course, everyone should have a place that is comfortable.

"In my parents' friends' families, the kids have left for Queens, Jersey, the Five Towns. My parents stayed but won't stay forever. When they get older they will go to Israel. Certainly not Brooklyn. My parents are not the majority in the neighborhood anymore. When your friends, people like you, are not there anymore, you do not feel at home." As Brooklyn Jewry grows more right-wing, other elements are slowly leaving.

Rina has a community in Manhattan of thoughtful and lively Modern Orthodox young people. While she may have left Brooklyn behind, she remains rooted in the sense of community it brought her and firm in her religious affiliation. "Orthodoxy is how I grew up, and I do not think I have to leave it in order to be happy with myself and religion and God. We have problems. But I have found other people who share similar ideas. It is still frustrating, but we bond together."

Danny Kaye
Brooklyn Tummler

JOSEPH DORINSON

Jewish comics enjoy a high profile in American culture. Many emerged from poverty and pain. And a disproportionate number emerged from Brooklyn, New York. In their pursuit of *parnoseh* (payoff) and *fargenign* (bliss minus the Volkswagen), they traveled from vaudeville to movies, from burlesque to television, or around the world in eighty jokes. In releasing their stored-up aggression, they provided comic relief *shvitzing* (some like it hot) and *shpritzing* (some prefer a cool spray). While diverting mainstream Americans with stereotype, dialect, caricature, satire, and parody, they earned money and *yichus* (status) beyond the wildest dreams of Tevye, the hairy dairyman.

Post-Depression Jewish comedians started in the local candy store, once the hub of urban culture. Nervous, restless, loud; egged on by their upwardly mobile parents and inflated with too many egg creams (have I got a recipe for you!), they summered in the city, excelled in self-mockery: pricking the pretensions of their parents to high culture. They grappled with *kunst* (culture) in the candy store. Like their parents, they became masters of the needle trade. Capitalization on verbal wit, parody, needling the opposition prepared these immigrant children for public performance. Some achieved professional status either as stand-up comics or sit-down writers of comedy. Others tummeled to the top.

The candy store yielded to the Borscht Belt. At White Roe, for example, in the Catskills there emerged an enormous talent: David Kaminsky, known later as Danny Kaye. Born in Brooklyn's East New York section in 1913, he was the youngest of three sons. His mother, Clara, doted on him and smother-loved him with Yiddish phrases. His parents encouraged the young Dovidl to perform. Funny faces in the school year endeared him to Lou Eisen (later Lou Reed), who was Danny's first partner in comedy. Their antics drove teachers crazy and propelled Danny to an early exit from Thomas Jefferson High School at age sixteen.

Danny's mother had died shortly after his bar mitzvah. This loss plus the onset of the Great Depression pushed the restless youth off the education track. Danny hung out at the local candy store, where he could receive phone calls. One evening as Lou and Danny were singing in front of their favorite store, a Borscht Belt regular heard them and was impressed. He secured their services for White Roe Lake Hotel, near Liberty, New York. A tummeling they would go. A tummler is Yiddish for "fool or noisemaker who does anything and everything to entertain the customers so that they won't squawk about their rooms or food."

Lou and Danny tummeled at Sunday night concerts, weeknight masquerades, campfires, games, and plays (usually on Friday nights). They also tummeled during the day, especially when it rained. From this activity, they earned seventy-five dollars a summer plus room and board. Inspired by Fishel (Phil) Goldfarb, they combined British diction with Yiddish fiction and intonation—"dot noble beast, dot marwellos stelyin, dot fency stead." From Kaminsky and Eisen they metamorphosed into Kaye and Reed. Kaye perfected his trademark talents: conducting orchestras, dancing, singing, pratfalling, and acting.

Conducting orchestras became a staple. He would arrive onstage looking disheveled, in one hand a telephone book, in the other several batons. He banged the batons quickly. They broke. The orchestra refused to follow his lead. He dropped his arms; the orchestra played. A saxophone player blew a wrong note. Kaye pounced off the podium to inspect the sheet music. He flicked a dropping and looked skyward at the offending bird (reprieved later as a funny bit in a Mel Brooks movie), mockingly. Returning to the podium, he tripped, scattering the music of a violin player. He adjusted the stand higher, and the violinist rose in response. Another sour note brought Kaye to the offender. He grabbed the instrument, played it, badly, and bopped the musician over the head. In wiping the perspiration from his forehead, the handkerchief turned into an endless sheet of music. I recall one riff on early television where Danny began to fence with a violinist, baton to bow. Laughter rolled like thunder as the coda featured "Stars and Stripes Forever." As Kaye bowed, the orchestra played. He spun around; they stopped. After many repetitions, Kaye collapsed in exhaustion as audiences roared with delight.

The country's depression deepened. "Dr. New Deal" entered with promises of "Happy Days." Kaye didn't derive any immediate benefits. Like Snow White, he drifted. In 1933, he decided to go on a tour with his girlfriend dancer Kathleen Young (the first of several gorgeous gentile women in his love life) and her partner, Dave Mack. They called themselves The Three Terpsichoreans. Dividing sixty dollars a week they headed for the Far East in 1934 as part of a larger review called La Vie Paree. One night in Osaka, a tremendous typhoon cut off the electricity while Danny was about to perform. He called for two flashlights, which he turned on his own face. And he began to sing and talk nonsense. Panic yielded to fascination, fear to laughter. The double-talk communicated uni-

versally. Unable to speak oriental languages, Kaye developed his own: double-talk with a

Git-gat giddle
With a geet-ga-zay.

This Yiddish-flavored nonsense evoked laughter everywhere. Verbal slapstick evoked mock Russian, German, Italian, French. A homeless Jew found comfort in a zone of funny ambiguity. Audiences connected with this new comic language heavily salted with Yiddish inflection. They appreciated this Desperanto.

When Danny returned in 1935, he joined the vast army of unemployed. His former honey, the dancer, departed for her home base in the Midwest. Danny headed back to the Catskills, where White Roe signed him to a thousand-dollar contract. Teamed with Phil Goldfarb, he discovered a new comic voice coupled with a unique style, blending old and new. Next, he moved to the President Hotel, where he teamed up with Lillian Lux and Alex Olshanetsky to sing Yiddish songs, serve as emcee, and promote Yiddish entertainment. He also met Benay Venuta, who got him a "gig" as a comic's stooge in a Manhattan club, Casa Manana, after Labor Day. Sandwiched between long periods of unemployment, Kaye went to London, where audiences did not respond well to his novelty songs. Ousted from his booking, he returned, defeated and depressed.

An opportunity in 1939 changed his life. *Sunday Night Varieties*, directed by recent émigré Max Liebman, was in need of talent. Kaye auditioned; so did Sylvia Fine. Though the play closed after opening night, Max moved the fledgling team of Kaye and Fine to Camp Tamiment. There, they merged their talents and, later, their lives.

Sylvia Fine was born August 29, 1913. Her parents were middle-class, her father a dentist for whom Danny briefly worked as a teenager. Sylvia was an intellectual, a musician, a *macher* (a person of influence) in school. She had talent, personality, and wit. Unlike Danny, the dropout, Sylvia graduated from Thomas Jefferson High School with honors and went on to Hunter College, where she also excelled. Socially conscious and politically aware, Sylvia inclined to the left.

Max Liebman, a fine talent scout, hired Sylvia for Camp Tamiment. A haven for Jewish left-wing vacationers, Tamiment offered cottages with kitchens for rent—a higher class of *kochalayn*. A variety show on Friday and a major revue on Saturday served as entertainment magnets. Whereas vaudeville followed a strict formula of eight acts ritually ordered and working-class oriented, revues labored for and aspired to sophistication in sketch comedy. They appealed to middle-class people. Kaye left tummeling behind.

Fine partnered, accompanied, and encouraged Kaye. At the end of a successful summer, Liebman decided to take the revue to Broadway while demanding 10 percent of his performers' future earnings for the next four years.

The *Straw Hat Review* opened on September 29, 1939, with Alfred Drake, Imogene Coca, and Danny Kaye, in featured roles. Greeted with mixed reviews, the show lasted eleven weeks. After watching a former flame, Rosie Kaye, get married in Florida, the lonely and the restless Danny—without much fanfare—proposed to Sylvia Fine. She accepted. In a civil ceremony, January 3, 1940, they tied the knot. A *mariage de raison*, it smacked of a Faustian bargain—mutually convenient and eventually loveless.

Kaye ventured into a nightclub, a dark inferno conjured up by Dante, and emerged a bright, shining star. A twelve-minute act, fashioned by Fine and Liebman, featured Tamiment material: Stanislavsky, Pavlova, Otchi Tchnorniya, "Minnie the Moocher." He reprised the orchestra shtick and led a spontaneous eruption of a participatory "conga." He took the act to Chicago's Gay Paree. With the assistance of Kitty Carlisle, Fine encouraged Kaye to try out "Anatole of Paris"—a send-up of a fey designer.

> Voilà, a chapeau
> At sixty bucks a throw.

Chicago noticed.

So did Moss Hart and Max Gordon. They plotted a Kaye debut in their Broadway show, *Lady in the Dark*. Perhaps a projection of Moss Hart's ambiguity, Danny played an effeminate fashion photographer. He stopped the show with a thrust into Russian culture: "Tchaikowsky." This breathless effusion showed Kaye's penchant for pastiche, heavily layered with Russian-Jewish sensibility. Listen:

> There's Malichevsky, Rubinstein, Arenstein and
>   Tchaikowsky
> Sapelnikoff, Dmitrieff, Tscherepnin, Kryjanowsky . . .
> Stravinsky, Rymskykorsakoff, Mussorgsky and
>   Gretchaninoff;
> And Glazonouff and Caesar Cui, Kalinikoff and
>   Rachmaninoff.

As the swishy photographer, Danny stopped the show and almost stole it from veteran star Gertrude Lawrence. This sensational debut led to an offer Kaye could not refuse.

He jumped ships, rather shows—to Cole Porter's *Let's Face It*, which opened on October 29, 1941. Now, in a starring role at double his previous salary, he gained national recognition. Kaye put scat into skit, fusing black and Jewish experience. "Git gat gittle, giddle-de tommy, riddle de biddle de roop, da-reep, fa-san, skeedle de woo-da, fiddle de wada, reep?" Thus, Danny mimicked a would-be (chocolate?) soldier who pleads bad ears, flat feet, ulcers, and decayed teeth in pursuit of deferment. "Shad-ap?" the sergeant bellows; case closed. Rosamond Gilder penned an ecstatic review describing Danny as "a khaki playboy with an immortal comic mask, infinitely malleable, wide-mouthed, large-eyed, broad in the ear, with hands as eloquent and precise as his torrential speech."

Such positive reaction led to a movie contract. Mogul Sam Goldwyn, master of the malaprop, earned Neal Gabler's praise as one of the principal Jews "who invented Hollywood." He also invented the movie persona of Danny Kaye. Initially, he tried to anglicize Kaye. Signing Kaye to a contract—not an oral agreement, which he "insisted is not worth the paper it is printed on"—Goldwyn wanted Kaye to bob his nose. Danny refused. They compromised. Kaye dyed his rusty hair blond, refusing to follow Milton Berle, "who cut off his nose to spite his race . . . a thing of beauty and a goy forever." Kaye went west on February 27, 1943, to co-star in the tailor-made movie *Up in Arms*.

Recycled from a Broadway comedy, *The Nervous Wreck*, *Up in Arms* conveys Kaye as a hypochondriacal hero in spite of himself. Was this a veiled attempt to depict the Jewish character as fearful of military combat? There is a long tradition in Jewish folklore of antimilitarism harking back to the European experience. The schlemiel-schlimazel duality has been amply documented. Invariably the schlimazel drops the buttered bread. So does the schlemiel, with a difference: the buttered side up.

I saw the film with my parents in 1944 when it opened at Radio City Music Hall. Along with other enthusiasts, we contributed to the box office gross of $3.34 million. We chortled at his "Melody in Four F," reprised from *Let's Face It*, and the concluding "Jive Number." Taking pride in the success of our ethnic landsman (fellow Jew), we eagerly awaited his future films.

We did not have to wait too long, for *Wonder Man* was released in 1945 as World War II was ending on a happy note. The United States had emerged as the premier world power. We had fused the moral vision of Woodrow Wilson and the realpolitik of Theodore Roosevelt. Despite our imminent victory, Americans faced an uncertain future, fraught with anxiety. Even before the hot war ended, the cold war had begun. In this context of almost schizoid dimensions, manic energy coupled with Hamletic indecision, *Wonder Man* appeared. Written by Don Hartman and Mel Shavelson, the script called for Danny to play twin brothers, one an arrogant entertainer with ties to the mob, the other a nerdy scholar.

The nerd thwarts his brother's murderer and gets the hometown beauty, Virginia Mayo. Kaye spoofs exotic dancing in "Bali Boogie," concert music in "Otchi Tchorniya," opera in the "Opera Number." Unlike the Marx Brothers's destructive assault on high culture, however, Kaye showed great musical gifts. He wanted to belong to this cultural elite. *Time* marched onto the Kaye bandwagon. Profiling the prolific Danny, a writer for the magazine enthused over his "high baritone, with a two octave range. He can impersonate an Irish tenor, mimic a coloratura soprano . . . or plead like a Slavic gypsy singer with a basso profundo and schmaltz."

On the silver screen, Kaye impersonated a Brooklyn type in *The Kid from Brooklyn*, 1946; a day-dreamer in *Walter Mitty*, 1947; and a classical musician who converts to jazz in *A Song Is Born*, 1948. A child was born to Sylvia and Danny Kaye in 1946. Instead of bringing the family closer as in the lyric ". . . baby makes three," Danny grew distant. He went off to tour minus the two other Kayes, hardly a blue heaven above. Eve Arden, a lover of five years, trailed along. Without Sylvia, Kaye failed in his last film, *A Song Is Born*. No one could write for him like Sylvia. A free fall at the box office ended the Goldwyn relationship. The master of malaprop dropped him like a hot tomato.

In search of a new self, Kaye headed for London's Palladium. Starting on February 2, 1948, he took England by storm, something even Hitler could not do. He strode onto the stage and sang "Anatole . . . ," "Minnie . . . ," and in cockney "I've Got a Loverly Bunch of Coconuts." Then he did the orchestra bit followed by a dance to "Ballin' the Jack." He then pulled an Al Jolson—descending into the audience to bum a cigarette and to engage in chitchat. He related the Osaka incident. After a five-minute hiatus, he gathered steam for a triumphant conclusion of the fifty-five-minute act culminating in the ritualistic invocation: "God save the King!" The cool Kaye had connected with his hot audience. One psychiatrist likened the process to a transformation into hysterical children. Elizabeth and Philip, once and future monarchs, became part of Kaye's retinue. They were

joined by Britain's royalty of theatre: Lawrence Olivier and Vivian Leigh. Later, King George and Queen Mary visited the theatre and sat with the commoners. Their younger daughter, Margaret, was quite taken with the American entertainer. They became fast friends, perhaps even lovers. Kaye had come a long way from Brooklyn. He had crested. He could now prove Thomas Wolfe wrong. He went home, again. To Sylvia and Deena.

Danny returned to a new movie venture and trouble in paradise. The House Un-American Activities Committee tried to ferret out communists long before a junior senator from Wisconsin added his name to an infamous witch-hunt and a new "Red Scare." Starting under Martin Dies and continuing under J. Parnell Thomas, the committee cast a wide net for Hollywood "pinkos." In 1947, one of the "Jews who invented Hollywood," Jack Warner, volunteered as the committee's first "friendly" witness. Ultimately, twenty-four "friendly" witnesses were summoned including Robert Taylor, Robert Montgomery, Adolphe Menjou, Gary Cooper, Walt Disney, and Ronald Reagan, all goyim except for Warner. Eleven "unfriendlies" prepared to testify. The first, Bertolt Brecht, denied communist affiliation under oath. He fled the country; then there were ten: Alvah Bessie, Herbert Bieberman, Lester Cole, Edward Dmytrik, Ring Lardner, Jr., Albert Maltz, Sam Ornitz, Adrian Scott, Dalton Trumbo, and their leader, John Howard Lawson.

Waiting in the wings, a support group calling themselves the "Committee for the First Amendment" wanted to testify. They included Edward G. Robinson, Humphrey Bogart, Lauren Bacall, John Garfield, Gregory Peck, John Huston, and Danny Kaye. They inclined toward the left but wanted to stay on the high, middle ground. Also waiting in the wings ready to fly into action were "tail gunner" Senator Joe McCarthy and his minions. The always liberal Sylvia Fine and her husband had signed a petition in 1947 denouncing HUAC. Subsequently, they were linked with Frederic March, Olivia deHavilland, and Edward G. Robinson as "swimming pool pinks."

Kaye was slated to film the life of Harry Lauder, a legendary Scottish entertainer, for Warner Brothers. However, Jack Warner, eager to please the less than grand inquisitors, scotched the project. Kaye withdrew from the anti-HUAC movement. He wasn't really "yellow." He just preferred the color of money. Mollified, Warner signed Kaye to do *The Inspector General*. Loosely modeled after the Gogol masterpiece, Kaye turned it into a tour de farce. He played Farfel, an illiterate vagabond who is mistaken for the inspector general. If Danny harbored ill will toward the grand inquisitors who questioned his patriotism, he could channel the fury into this movie: corruption runs riot in society, which the innocent Farfel (Yiddish for a tiny noodle) exposes and exploits simultaneously. In the movie's most ambitious song, "Soliloquy for Three Heads," Kaye sings four-part harmony in four different dialects: Russian, German, English, and his own with a touch of the Ink Spots thrown in for good measure. When my students viewed this film in a class that I teach on humor, they sat on their hands so to speak. As Fibber's Molly used to say: "T'aint funny, McGhee." My students' reaction reflected the poor box office that the movie generated. Yet, when Kaye and Fine went to London, they were greeted like royalty.

Danny Kaye was a frequent flyer. He flew to Korea with Frank Sinatra to entertain the troops. Psychologically, he descended into periodic depressions and ascended to new heights of creativity. His colleagues noticed "something strange" about him. He portrayed a moody if brilliant Dane in *Hans Christian Andersen*. A weak story line was elevated by the magnificent music and lyrics of Frank Loesser and the abundantly talented Danny Kaye. "Thumbelina," "The Ugly Duckling," "Wonderful Copenhagen," and "Anywhere I Wander" resonated throughout the country, perhaps the world. Only the dour Danes were not amused with the fictional treatment of their culture hero, spinner of fairy tales. To placate the people of Denmark, Kaye flew to the country that spawned Andersen. He won friends, influenced people, quieted critics, and mesmerized children. And the picture grossed $6 million. Kaye had everything: fame, fortune, adulation. But he could not rest or gain nourishment from his own cultural roots.

Kaye rejected his Jewish past. One observes this thrust toward assimilation in words, music, and movies. He warned a young Alan King, eager for encouragement, that his act was too Jewish. The kid from Brooklyn became a citizen of the world. He parlayed his love for children, desire for service, and enormous talent into a parallel career as spokesman for UNICEF. The UN, headed at that time by Dag Hammarskjöld, sent Kaye all over the world. He publicized the plight of poor children through film. He raised enormous sums of money, thereby fulfilling ancient Jewish imperatives of *zedakah* (charity).

Kaye's film career also flourished, no doubt fueled by favorable publicity attendant on his benevolence on behalf of children. Luckily, he decided to form his own production company with Norman Panama and Melvin Frank. Their first vehicle, *Knock on Wood*, mounted in conjunction with Paramount Pictures, produced a critical success and a large capital gain for Kaye. Again, he plays a "double" who as ventriloquist dabbles in psychotherapy, love (with his "shrink," Mai Zetterling), spying, mistaken identity, and murder mystery. Sucked into espionage, Kaye cannot convince the authorities that an English gentleman is the true spy. He flees danger with various disguises. Thrust into a ballet, by turns, Danny is klutzy and elegant, manic and depressive, like his two dummies—not unlike his real self. In this film, he performs several classic shticks: as Irish roustabout in a pub, as a nebbishy hide-about under the table.

In that same year, 1954, Kaye teamed up with Bing Crosby, Rosemary Clooney, and former Goldwyn sidekick Vera Ellen for an ultragoyish movie, *White Christmas*, with songs by Irving Berlin, another Jewish genius who had bleached his material if not his hair in pursuit of profit and prestige. Despite an inane plot and patriotic pabulum involving a retired officer, the movie ranked number one at the box office that year with a gross of $12 million.

Kaye's next film, *The Court Jester*, in 1956 coincided with President Eisenhower's reelection. Defeated twice by Ike, whose affability was celebrated in song by Irving Berlin, Adlai Stevenson confessed that, like the boy who stubbed his toe in the dark, "He was too old to cry but it hurt too much to laugh." Richard M. Nixon could afford to laugh, because he was almost dumped from the Republican ticket. Having been censured by his peers in the Senate and thwarted by enlightened Supreme Court decisions, Joe McCarthy cried in his scotch as his ambitions faded with his liver. Mickey Mantle won the "triple crown" in 1956. Don Larsen, also no mean drinker, pitched the only perfect game in baseball's annual classic, the World Series, as the New York Yankees defeated their crosstown rivals, the Brooklyn Dodgers *alova sholem* (bless the departed), four games to three. Danny Kaye was an avid baseball fan, passionately devoted to his beloved Brooklyn Dodgers who broke the *shneid* by beating the Yankees in the previous World Series.

The Court Jester was a winner too on all fronts except at the box office, a cause for that distinctively Jewish combination of laughter and tears. The picture, shot at Paramount Studios, featured a stellar cast headed by Danny Kaye and supported by Basil Rathbone, Angela Lansbury, Mildred Natwick, Glynis Johns, and Cecil Parker. A satiric send-up of misty medievalism, the movie parodies the romanticized English past. In glittering Technicolor, the picture purveys castle and court, jester and joust. We witness a wicked king, a sinister minister, and a long litany of names with "G" strings: Giacomo—"king of jesters and jester to kings"—Griselda, the witch, Gwendolyn, the princess, and "the grimly, grizzly, gruesome Griswold"—the satanic suitor.

A carnival jester of considerable talent (suggesting the future Art Carney), Kaye as Giacomo becomes embroiled in a plot to restore the good king while playing the bad king's fool. Empowered by the good witch Griselda with a hypnotic trance, Kaye is transformed into instant heroism by a finger snap. That same gesture, the snap, causes Kaye to revert to cowardice. The film's most dramatic moment is also the funniest—it's a song that involves Kaye's signature wordplay, madly rhyming chalices, palaces, pestles, vessels, flagons, and dragons.

Such true comedy evoked gales of laughter. At a cost of $4 million and a gross of $2.2 million, however, it proved that unlike modern crime, comedy did not pay. Although Kaye continued to make movies in the 1950s—*Merry Andrew* for MGM in 1958, *Me and the Colonel* for Columbia in 1958, and *The Five Pennies* for Paramount in 1959—the winds of change propelled him into a different medium in the 1960s, namely, television.

Despite a few dazzling bits, reminiscent of vintage Kaye, Danny's venture into television 1963–67 was a disaster. He had aged prematurely. His persona seemed invested in sentimental goo, cutesy-poo, and Peter Panish infantilism. He gave freer vent to snobbery and arrogance at the same time that he yearned for love. A clue to Kaye's divided soul—mirrored in all those split characters he played over the years—can be found in an Ed Murrow–Fred Friendly special, "The Secret Life of Danny Kaye," which aired on CBS in late 1956. The program showed a glittering surface, perhaps facade: Kaye as comic, humanitarian, bon vivant, children's advocate, family man. It was this latter pose that elicited a skeptical response from critic Marie Torre. She zeroed in on Kaye's mood swings, his distance from wife Sylvia, and monumental ego bordering on hubris, that tragic flaw that precipitates a fall from high places either as Oedipus Rex or Humpty-Dumpty.

In the twilight of their careers, comedians or entertainers-"lite" sometimes venture into serious drama. Ed Wynn, Bert Lahr, even Fred Astaire spring to mind. Danny Kaye made a fugitive attempt in *Me and the Colonel*,

based on a Broadway play by Franz Werfel and S. N. Behrman. Perhaps trying to reconnect with his Jewish roots and aspiring to high culture, Kaye assayed the role of a Jewish businessman in flight from the Nazis as they prepare to capture Paris in 1940. Often cast as the "good" German in Cold War Hollywood, Curt Jurgens plays the anti-Semitic Polish colonel hired to help Kaye, the Jewish refugee, escape. In this film, Kaye sought to escape comedy, assimilation, alienation. It was the first of several attempts to reconnect with the Jewish experience, which ultimately found fruition late in Kaye's career when he played a Holocaust survivor. "Skokie," 1981, a docudrama based on an actual confrontation between Jewish survivors and neo-Nazi demonstrators, aired on CBS November 17, 1981. Confronting the constitutional parameters of free speech, the drama raised compelling issues and provided a forum for Danny Kaye's reconciliation with Judaism.

Why did Danny Kaye with all his *meilehs* (virtues)—talent, charm, energy, charisma, ambition, genius—fall short of greatness? For British critic Raymond Durgnat, Kaye represents the chronic underachiever:

> Danny Kaye, like Cantor and Hope, made many comedies for Goldwyn; he had the widest range of the three, and his career is all the more disappointing. His face is at once handsome, sensitive, and infinitely transformable, and he combines a straight romantic appeal with wild plunges into frenetic parody. . . . But his fancy was rarely free, and outside his git-gat-gabble musical numbers, he was hampered by a milky goodwill which . . . smothered his comic attack. . . . Kaye deteriorated into a charmer whose screen heart is as wide as Cinemascope and as sickly sweet as candyfloss.

This became painfully evident in the television years, 1963–67. Invariably, with a child perched on his knee, like Kolya that little gypsy, he would bill and coo, regressing into syrupy childhood. The plea for love remains a constant among Jewish comic entertainers. So does the quest for something more. Kaye became a gourmet Chinese cook, a licensed airplane pilot, a baseball franchise owner, a symphony orchestra conductor, a goodwill ambassador to the world: many characters in search of identity. Larger than life, sports broadcaster Vin Scully observed, Kaye was ". . . a lot of person . . . a group photo."

A group of all-stars gathered at the Kennedy Center in Washington, D.C., to receive honors from President Reagan in 1984. Danny Kaye joined Lena Horne, Isaac Stern, Arthur Miller, Gian Carlo Menotti for this happy event. Film clips of *Hans Christian Andersen* and *The Secret Life of Walter Mitty* highlighted Kaye's creativity. Students from the United Nations School in New York serenaded Danny as he writhed in pain from arthritis.

Kaye was honored as "King of Brooklyn." Though close to death, he continued to jest, perhaps realizing the wisdom of his wife's one-liner: "A jester unemployed is nobody's fool." Joking, unfortunately, could not defer the Moloch Hamoves (Angel of Death) indefinitely. Drained by an incurable case of hepatitis, not AIDS as malicious rumor had it, Kaye succumbed on March 3, 1987. One year later, the United Nations paid tribute to the kid from Brooklyn. On screen, the jester laughed, sang, and danced. He comforted blind children. Old friends remembered. UN Secretary General Perez de Cuellar cited Kaye as the man who "heightened global awareness of the plight of unfortunate children throughout the world." Douglas Fairbanks, Jr., conveyed Kaye's secret with children: he "made them feel they were real people." Liv Ullmann, Peter Ustinov, and Harry Belafonte sang his praises. Roberta Peters sang. Eighty children representing twenty-two nations at the UN School also sang:

Danny Kaye, you gave us laughter.
We'll remember you ever after.
You made us sing, and with your song
You kept us laughing all day long.
You flew to lots and lots of places
And made such funny, funny faces.
You were a clown in every town.
You made us giggle endlessly.
You never left us friendlessly.
Thank you! Merci! Danke!
Danny Kaye.

The Doctor and the Comedian

JOYCE ANTLER

My father always wanted to be a doctor. His strong motivation came at least in part from the death of his two-year-old brother, Meyer, from appendicitis, due to a doctor's misdiagnosis. Born in 1912 to poor, working-class eastern European immigrants living in the East New York section of Brooklyn, my father made his way through PS 149, graduating from Thomas Jefferson High School in 1928, and from New York University in 1932. Locked out of medical schools in the United States because of anti-Semitism, he started medical school at the University of Göttingen in Germany the following year. But when a decree came down that all foreign students had to practice in Germany after graduation, he immediately transferred to medical school in Bern, Switzerland. He began a private practice on Carroll Street in Crown Heights at the end of the 1930s; in 1942, he and my mother purchased a home on Argyle Road in Flatbush and relocated his practice to our home. It was a large, noisy, friendly office, with dozens of patients usually sitting in our living room, which served as the office waiting room, several afternoons and evenings a week. We ate in the adjacent dining room, usually very late, since mealtimes happened only after the last patient was seen and were often interrupted by new arrivals. The family atmosphere of the office was enhanced by the fact that my mother was Dad's office assistant, much better at plying the waiting patients with tea and *rugaleh* than at filing charts. In the 1950s, when many of Dad's patients became part of the Jewish migration to Long Island, he refused to join them (how could he leave the patients who remained behind?) but opened a second office in Hewlett. Later, some of the patients moved farther away, to Florida, and so did some of the doctors, but this time my father refused to follow. By the late 1960s, however, he had added another affiliation to his list of hospitals and clinics: with others, he developed a clinic with mainly Spanish-speaking clients in Fort Greene. He was proudly learning Spanish when he passed away, suddenly, at age sixty, in 1972. Over five hundred mourners came to his funeral, many of them lifelong patients who had named their children Leo, or Lee, after their beloved physician. My father was not a rich man when he died; many of his patients had bartered goods for the services he provided them, and a good number had never received any bills due to my mother's erratic billing practices. Money, in any event, was never his primary concern; the care of his patients was so overriding that he never took an out-of-town vacation, fearful of not being there if one of his many hundreds of patients needed him.

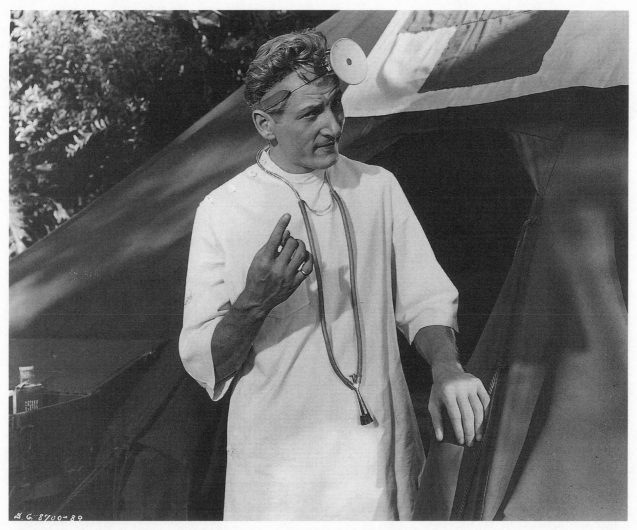

Danny Kaye in Up in Arms. *Photo courtesy of Film Stills Archive, The Museum of Modern Art.*

It was his pacing up and down the living room floor, late at night, anxious over some patient's illness, that convinced me that whatever else I might be when I grew up, I would never become a doctor.

Though my father's calling was clear from the time he was six, it might have been otherwise. Like other mothers on Barbey Street, my *baleboste* grandmother believed in the importance of music lessons, and she managed to provide lessons for her Leo. My father's first teacher was Mark Warnow, son of the owner of a local music store who went on to become a musical director at NBC. But my father was so talented that a more advanced teacher was recommended, and he soon was being taught by a German violinist who had once taught Heifetz. The teacher, who predicted a concert career for my father, insisted that his wondrous talent was being wasted on the "junk violin" that he was playing. Somehow my grandmother managed

to scrape together the money to buy a better violin, though $150 was an unheard sum in 1919 for the family of an often seasonally employed milliner. My grandmother did what she could to help the family survive economically, sewing neckties at night, and she certainly helped along her son's future in whatever way she could. Once she tore up a satin flower girl dress that had been made by a cousin for one of her daughters because Leo "needed a handkerchief." And her tall, handsome brother never had to carry anything, remembers his younger sister Dina, since his slender hands had to be preserved. Dina was the one designated to bring in the heavy blocks of ice the family used for refrigeration.

My father played not only the violin but the guitar, banjo, and viola. By the age of fourteen he had started a band—Charlie Katz played the sax, Milt Levinson the drums, Sam Glasser the piano, Danny Glasser the alto sax, Irv Shorten the trumpet, and my father the fiddle.

*Leon Kessler in medical school, leader of the Leo Cass Orchestra,
ca. 1934–35.*

Though the boys were teenagers, they were so good that they began to get gigs, playing at weddings and bar mitzvahs, even at Simchas Torah temple celebrations, and Leo was soon contributing to the family's living expenses. Even Leo's young sister benefited; young children were so enamored of the band that they loved to come up to the Kesslers' front porch and kneel on the bench that overlooked the front room of the downstairs apartment where the band rehearsed. The older boys, with their clowning, their klezmer music, jazz, and band medleys, were an inspiration for the neighborhood kids, who were willing to give Dina the penny apiece she charged for watching the rehearsals.

Soon my father's band, "Leo Cass and Orchestra," was playing places like Brown's in the Catskills and in many small resort towns like Big Indian, Ferndale, Fallsburg, and Monticello. By the time he was sixteen, my father's band (he called it his "fraternity") was a well-established Catskills entertainment. So it was no surprise that a Brooklyn friend of my father's, a very funny, skinny cutup named David Daniel Kominsky, wanted to work in the Catskills with the band. In Brooklyn, Danny Kaye, as he would be

known, who was about a year and a half younger than my dad, had sometimes traveled with the band, going to its gigs with an empty music case so that he would be fed along with the musicians. My father, who was also a very funny man, loved Kaye's new idea, and so Danny spent his first summer at the Catskills as the emcee for the Leo Cass Orchestra. Of course, Kaye was a tremendous success, and for the next few summers he worked as a "tummler" at various Catskill resorts with Lou Eisen, another neighborhood boy (who became a chiropodist). For some of the time, Kaye played in Livingston Manor, the small town, in fact, where my mother grew up (her father, a Jew from Kiev, having impulsively bought land there hoping to open a dairy farm). Mother left Livingston Manor when she was sixteen, moving in next door to my father on Barbey Street. The boldness and creativity of the Brooklyn boys were something new, and she enjoyed meeting them. Although she had a few dates with a number of them, including the irrepressible David Kominsky, it was my father with whom she instantly fell in love, and they became sweethearts.

My father's band would last throughout his college years; his earnings as bandleader supported his attendance at a private university. Of course, as an immigrant son, my father was always thrifty; often he would tell me how he used to walk across the bridge to Manhattan to save the nickel subway fare. After he died, we found the letters he wrote to my mother from medical school, expressing shock and displeasure that she had spent money on the movies or dinner when they had been trying to save money for their marriage, and equally important, for a microscope for him. Perhaps my father would have done better, financially, as a performer than a doctor, at least the kind of patient-oriented family doctor he became, but he passionately loved his work as a physician. In many ways, he performed his role as a doctor the way I imagined he performed on the stage as bandleader. Like Danny Kaye, he was full of antics—role-playing, storytelling, jokes, and funny monologues. My sister and I used to make house calls with him, and often we came along when he visited patients at the Home for Incurable Diseases and other hospitals. They loved my father because he always paid attention to each of them, but also because he was a show-business ham who knew well before "Patch" Adams did that humor was a powerful weapon in curing the sick.

With his oversize personality, my father was a "larger-than-life" doctor the way that Danny Kaye was a larger-than-life performer. They were similar in many ways. Of course, Kaye's talent was extraordinary, and although his rise in show business was relatively swift, there were moments in the early years when he felt like giving up and becoming what he always wanted to be—a doctor. Some of his biographers wrote that with his fine hands, he often thought of becoming a surgeon. Others noted that he admired doctors because of the humanitarian work they performed. Later, of course, Kaye would become known for his own humanitarian efforts on behalf of children, especially through UNESCO.

In 1953, when I was ten, my father took me to see Danny Kaye at the Palace, a performance that had sold out its extended run. My father sent a note backstage, and after the show we went to visit the actor. "You made it!" Kaye exclaimed to my father. "You became a doctor!" I have every reason to believe that he meant it.

That so many immigrant sons of this generation became doctors, while so many others became comedians, is not, in fact, suprising. The Jewish tradition of humor has always been powerful (my father, in fact, comes from generations of *badkhanim*—storytellers and clowns who performed at communal events). Humor served immigrants and their offspring well, helping them to cope with the vagaries of the new, often bewildering or hostile conditions, and allowing them a field of endeavor without rigid entrance requirements in which they could excel. The Jews' versatility of performance, their characteristic role-playing, code switching, mockery, imitation, and parody can be seen in the nonsense patter, bantering, and dialect songs that performers like Danny Kaye and Sid Caesar honed to perfection. Like other Jewish performers, Kaye also perfected a kind of schlemiel character, but one that highlighted the character's usually sly wit and benevolent intentions.

Was Kaye's characteristic zaniness, the goodwill and sound values he projected, a product of Brooklyn? I think it was. In his 1946 movie, *The Kid from Brooklyn*, a Goldwyn-produced musical, Kaye plays a naive, bumbling milkman who becomes a star prizefighter because of his nimble "ducking" movements. His success causes him momentarily to forget his roots, and he becomes arrogant and obnoxious. In the end, however, he remembers his humble background and goes back to being the "Kid from Brooklyn," smart, successful, and funny, but always respectful of the ordinary men and women from whom he came. There is something in this scenario that rings true to Kaye, no matter the disappointments and idiosyncrasies of his own career, and to the careers of men (and some women) like my father, who remembered from whence they came after they had moved solidly into their middle-class professions.

My father loved to sit down at the piano and play the "Minnie the Moocher" song that Danny Kaye parodied so well. He did other Kaye routines, and more that were his own. I regret that my children never met him, nor knew of the "shtick" to which he often treated his family and lucky patients. That my older daughter, Lauren, has become a comedy performer, specializing in improv, seems a natural extension of the family heritage that she never knew. She is, in fact, the seventh in the line of our family's *badkhantes*. It seems natural, too, that having been brought up in Brookline (Massachusetts), she now resides in Brooklyn.

Almanac

BY ANNE KADET

Scenes From a Superstar's Childhood

FOLLOWING IN THE FOOTSTEPS OF BROOKLYN'S MOST FAMOUS DAUGHTER

ASKED ABOUT HER CHILDhood, Barbra Streisand once told a friend, "Brooklyn was baseball, boredom and bad breath." But though Barbra (she dropped the middle 'a' when she left Brooklyn) has shunned the borough, her old home still holds a lot of memories for her.

Any tour of Streisand Land ought to begin where Barbara Joan Streisand made her debut, at the Jewish Hospital of Brooklyn (located at 555 Prospect Place), on April 24, 1942.

Her first home, an elegant brick-and-limestone apartment building at 457 Schenectady Avenue, is located just south of Empire Boulevard in Wingate. But the Streisands weren't there long.

Streisand's father, Manny Streisand,

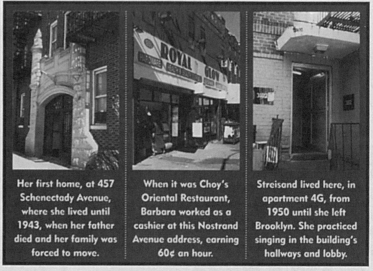

Her first home, at 457 Schenectady Avenue, where she lived until 1943, when her father died and her family was forced to move.

When it was Choy's Oriental Restaurant, Barbara worked as a cashier at this Nostrand Avenue address, earning 60¢ an hour.

Streisand lived here, in apartment 4G, from 1950 until she left Brooklyn. She practiced singing in the building's hallways and lobby.

an English teacher at George Westinghouse High School, died in 1943, following a mysterious head injury he received while working upstate as a summer camp counselor. He is buried in Mt. Hebron Cemetery in Queens.

Diana Streisand and her two children, Sheldon, born in 1932, and baby Barbara, moved into her parents' three-room Williamsburg apartment at 365 Pulaski Street. The family lived on the top floor of the drab brick tenement, and Barbara shared a bed with her mother. She would later regale reporters with horror stories about this period, insisting that a hot-water bottle covered with a doll's sweater had served as her only toy.

In 1950, Streisand's mother had an affair with Louis Kind, a married man. When Diana got pregnant, Kind moved the Streisand family to Flatbush and waited until his divorce was final before joining them. Streisand's final Brooklyn residence, unit 4G in a huge, sterile-looking apartment building at 3102 Newkirk Avenue near the corner of Nostrand, was within walking distance of Loews Kings Theater on Flatbush Avenue, where Streisand spent her adolescent weekends salivating over Marlon Brando. She attended P.S. 89, played in the apartment's courtyard and

shopped on Nostrand Avenue.

By 13, she had enrolled in Erasmus Hall High School and was a cashier at Choy's Oriental Restaurant, at 1850 Nostrand Avenue. The restaurant has since been converted into Royal Glow, a bargain store, but at the time, it was a den of exotica in the neighborhood, and for Barbara, who took to wearing kimonos and learning Chinese, it was a home away from home. At Erasmus, she sang in the choir, and legend has it that the young Neil Diamond sang in the same chorus with her for a short period of time.

Louis Kind, her indifferent stepfather, deserted the family in 1957. By that time, the ambitious 15-year-old was already making regular trips into Manhattan to take acting lessons and work in a small theater. "I always wanted to be out of what I was in," she later told a reporter. "Out of Brooklyn. I had to get out."

Upon graduating from high school, in January of 1959, she moved in with her acting teacher's Manhattan family. The Duchess of Brooklyn never looked back. ∎

Almanac by Anne Kadet, from Brooklyn Bridge.

"That's Entertainment!"

DAVID SPANER

The twentieth century's entertainment world would be unrecognizable without the contribution of the Jews of Brooklyn.

It would be a world without Bogie and Bacall, Martin and Lewis, Abbott and Costello. There would be none of Harry Houdini's magic, no Gershwin melodies. It would be a drearier world, without the Three Stooges' slapstick, Danny Kaye's Walter Mitty, Mel Brooks's *Blazing Saddles*, Woody Allen's *Annie Hall*, Phil Silvers's Sergeant Bilko, or Jerry Seinfeld's Seinfeld.

There would be no productions of *Death of a Salesman* (Arthur Miller), no *Porgy and Bess* (George Gershwin), no *Born Yesterday* (Garson Kanin), no *Guys and Dolls* (Abe Burrows), no *Singin' in the Rain* (Betty Comden), no *Man Who Came to Dinner* (Moss Hart). There would be no Beastie Boys or Bowery Boys or Funny Girls.

Barbra Streisand, whose portrayal of fellow Brooklynite Funny Girl Fanny Brice won her an Oscar, didn't have to take the subway to Carnegie Hall to find great acoustics when she was growing up in Flatbush. "I remember singing in the hallways of my Brooklyn apartment," she recalled, "and there was this great echo sound in the hallway and I thought, 'Oh, that's pleasant. That doesn't sound bad.'"

The first Jewish born-in-Brooklyn performer to make a name for herself was Josephine Marcus. She left Brooklyn as a child when her family moved to San Francisco, and at the age of eighteen ran away from home to join the Wild West, performing with the touring Pauline Markham Theatre Company. In Tombstone, Arizona, she met her husband-to-be Wyatt Earp, and the rest is history. For forty years, Wyatt and his Jewish wife, Josephine, traveled the West in search of adventure.

A selection of other Brooklyn-born Jews who have entertained beyond the borough:

Comedians Buddy Hackett, Jerry Lewis, Bud Abbott, Fanny Brice, Jerry Seinfeld, the Three Stooges (Moe, Curly, and Shemp Howard), the Ritz Brothers, Danny Kaye, Mel Brooks, Woody Allen, Phil Silvers, David Frye, Alan King, Sandy Baron, Marty Ingels, Gabe Kaplan, Joan Rivers, Jack Carter, Sam Levenson, Morty Gunty, Jan Murry, Andrew Dice Clay, Phil Foster, Arnold Stang, Lenny Bruce, Joey Adams, Henny Youngman, Stanley Myron Handleman, Irwin Corey, Jerry Stiller, Adam Sandler, Jon Stewart
Composers George and Ira Gershwin, Aaron Copland, Arthur Schwartz, Allan and Marilyn Bergman, Betty Comden, Jimmy Haskell, Mitch Leigh, and Hal David

Singer-songwriters Carole King, Neil Diamond, Neil Sedaka, and Leslie Gore

Singers Barbra Streisand, Helen Forrest, Abbe Lane, Julie Budd, Barry Manilow, Lainie Kazan, and Steve Lawrence; musicians Buddy Rich, Si Zentner, Peter Nero, and Herbie Mann

Opera stars Robert Merrill, Mimi Benzell, Beverly Sills, and Richard Tucker

Vaudevillians Lou Clayton and Gus Van and Joe Schenck

Folkies Arlo Guthrie, Oscar Brand, Ramblin' Jack Elliot

Choreographer Michael Kidd

Television personalities Larry King, Lawrence Spivak, Geraldo Rivera, Al Michaels, Howard Cosell, Alan Funt, Clifton Fadiman, Judge Judy Sheindlin, Marv Albert, and Carl Sagan

Producer-directors Herbert Ross, Joseph Papp, Billy Rose, Paul Mazursky, James Brooks, Ralph Bakashi, Irving Thalberg

Actors Billy Halop and Bernard Punsley (the Bowery Boys), Lauren (*To Have and Have Not*) Bacall, Shelley (*A Place in the Sun*) Winters, Richard (*The Goodbye Girl*)

Dreyfuss, Alan (*The Russians Are Coming*) Arkin, Gene (*Bat Masterson*) Barry, Jeff (*Broken Arrow*) Chandler, Dane (*Moonrise*) Clark, John (*Dynasty*) Forsythe, Martin (*Mission Impossible*) Landau, Lilyan (*New York Nights*) Tashman, Ricardo (*Torrent*) Cortez, Michael (*Mighty Aphrodite*) Rapaport, Eli (*The Misfits*) Wallach, Jessica (*Play Misty for Me*) Walters, Harvey (*The Piano*) Keitel, Elliot (*M*A*S*H**) Gould, Steve (*Diner*) Guttenberg, Herschel (*Arnie*) Bernardi, Harvey (*Torch Song Trilogy*) Fierstein, Jack (*Save the Tiger*) Guilford, Robert (*Stalag 17*) Strauss, Harvey (*Bikini Beach*) Lembeck, Vic (*Alice Doesn't Live Here Any More*) Tayback, David (*Rhoda*) Groh, Marvin (*Meet Millie*) Kaplan, Warren (*The Wackiest Ship in the Army*) Berlinger, Fyvush (*Picket Fences*) Finkel, Bernie (*Love Boat*) Kopell, Stanley (*Falcon Crest*) Ralph Ross, Herb (*The Good Guys*) Edelman, Didi (*The Practice*) Conn, Al (*The Munsters*) Lewis, Donny (*Happy Days*) Most, Zero (*The Front*) Mostel, Rhea (*Cheers*) Perlman, Leah (*The King of Queens*) Remini, Michael (*FM*) Brandon, Debra (*Will and Grace*) Messing, Jennifer (*Requiem for a Dream*) Connolly, Dan (*Dick*) Hedeya.

"Play Ball!"
Jewish Athletes from Brooklyn

DAVID SPANER

Brooklyn is the capital of the Republic of Baseball.

The game lives deep in the heart of Brooklyn, in the kind of visceral way that football belongs in Texas, basketball in Indiana, hockey in Montreal. "Like most of my friends," recalled Brooklyn's Marvin Miler, who grew up to play a major role in baseball as executive director of the players' association, "I could recite the vital statistics of every Dodger and most of their competition too." The borough's Jewish residents, like pretty much everyone in Brooklyn, loved their Dodgers. Abe Stark, a Brooklyn Jew with a clothing store on Pitkin Avenue, placed a famous ad on the right-field fence at the Dodgers' Ebetts Field: "Hit sign, win suit."

Brooklyn fans had little use for the rival New York Yankees and New York Giants, but Sid Gordon, a two-time National League all-star raised in Brooklyn, was revered in his home borough despite playing for the Giants in the 1940s and 1950s. When a Sid Gordon Day was held at Ebbets Field, the slugging outfielder received a new Chrysler, then hit two homers against Brooklyn, where, he said, "If 30,000 fans were in the stands, I knew 25,000 of them."

For a few glorious baseball seasons in the 1960s, Brooklyn's Sandy Koufax may have been the most unhittable pitcher in the history of the game. Koufax had been a basketball star at Lafayette High, leading the Jewish Community House on Bay Parkway to a national championship, then winning a hoops scholarship to the University of Cincinnati. He turned to baseball and pitched briefly for the Dodgers in Brooklyn, then followed the team to Los Angeles. Koufax filled stadiums everywhere he played, combining an overwhelming fastball and dazzling curve to win five straight earned-run-average titles and lead the majors in strikeouts four times.

"You don't have to be Jewish to love Sandy," read a popular bumper sticker.

There were other Jewish ballplayers from Brooklyn. Some were in the big leagues briefly, such as Cy Block, Hy Cohen, Conrad Cardinal, Jacob Pike, Larry Yellen, Bill Starr, Herb Karpel, and Hal Schacker. Several had more substantial careers such as Harry Eisenstat, Cal Abrams, Joe Ginsberg, Saul Rogovin, and Lipman Pike.

Pike was a noted slugger and base runner who played on the Brooklyn Atlantics in the National Association, then joined the National League when it was founded in 1876. He led the NA or NL in home runs four times. Rogovin led the American League in earned run average in 1951.

Blanche Scacter also grew up in Brooklyn and played ball in the 1940s in the first women's professional league, the All-American Girls Professional Baseball League.

Off the field, the Jews of Booklyn played a role in one of the pivotal events in American race relations when they stood up and cheered for Jackie Robinson as he became a Dodger and desegregated baseball in 1947. The racial tolerance of the Dodgers' huge Jewish fan base helped make the borough a relatively friendly place for Robinson to break major league baseball's color line.

Brooklyn was more than baseball. It was a sports town, and droves of young Jewish athletes came from the playgrounds and Hebrew "Y"s, representing their high schools and Jewish organizations. Many of them were second-generation Jews for whom sports was an entry into American culture.

Moe Goldman was one of the early Jews from Brooklyn to make his mark on basketball. He was a college all-American who went on to win the Most Valuable Player award in the NBA precursor, the American Basketball League. Red Holzman was an NBA all-star player who coached the New York Knicks to two championships. Don Forman was a college all-American who played in the NBA. Max Posnack, Hy Gotkin, Harry Boykoff, and Sid Tannenbaum were Jefferson High hoopsters who became college all-Americans. Boykoff and Tannenbaum also played in the NBA. Another Jefferson alumnus, Max Zaslofsky, was one of the NBA's first stars. Zaslofsky led the league in scoring in 1948 and was a five-time all-star. Basketball hall-of-famer Red Auerbach coached the National Basketball Association's Celtics from 1950 to 1966, winning nine league championships. Auerbach was all-Brooklyn when he played for Eastern District High School.

Brooklyn-born Larry Brown won an Olympic gold medal in 1964, was a three-time all-star in the American Basketball Association, and has had a great coaching career in college basketball and the NBA. Nancy Lieberman was an Olympic silver medalist and national college player of the year in the 1979 and 1980. Layfayette High's Rudy LaRusso became a five-time NBA all-star, once scoring fifty points in a game.

Jewish Brooklyn produced two world middleweight boxing champions, Solly Krieger (1938–39) and Al McCoy (1914–17). It also produced boxing hall-of-famer Charley Goldman, a tough bantamweight who became one of pugilism's all-time great trainers, working with five world titlists including heavyweight champion Rocky Marciano. Many other world title contenders came out of Brooklyn's Jewish neighborhoods, including Bernie Friedkin, brothers Miltie and Ruby Kessler, Artie Levine, Herbie Krono-witz, Al "Bummy" Davis, and Abe Simon. Heavyweight Simon knocked out Jersey Joe Walcott in six rounds en route to two losing title fights with Joe Louis.

Football hall-of-famer Sid Luckman graduated from Erasmus Hall High to all-America status at Columbia University, then became a legendary Chicago Bears quarterback. His Bears won four NFL championships, and Luckman was an all-pro nine seasons. He won the NFL's Most Valuable Player award in 1943 when he set a league record by tossing seven touchdown passes in a single game. Lyle Alzado was a five-time all-NFL defensive end in the 1970s and 1980s. NFL quarterback Allie Sherman become more famous behind the bench, named the league's coach of the year in 1963 and 1964. Al Davis has been coach, general manager, and owner of the Oakland Raiders.

The borough also produced jockeys Walter Miller and Walter Blum. Miller won the national riding championship in 1906 and 1907 and was the first jockey to surpass 300 wins in a year. Blum won American riding championships in 1963 and 1964 and was the sixth U.S. jockey to ride 4,000 winners. Miller and Blum are members of the National Horse Racing Hall of Fame.

Brooklyn's Marty Glickman was a track star named to the 1936 U.S. Olympic team. Glickman and another Jewish runner, Sam Stoller of Cincinnati, were pulled from the U.S. relay team just before it raced at the Berlin Games. They lost a chance for medals in a controversial move many considered an attempt to appease Hitler. Glickman returned home to become a renowned broadcaster and is a member of the American Sportscasters Hall of Fame.

Other great Brooklyn Jewish athletes include handball's Victor Hershkowitz, who won forty national and international titles; tennis star Herb Flam, who was ranked among the top ten in the world four times between 1951 and 1957; and bowler Mark Roth, a member of the Professional Bowlers Association Hall of Fame and four-time PBA player of the year.

As the twentieth century ended, Brooklyn was still producing Jewish athletes. Brooklyn-born Wayne Rosenthal, Steve Rosenberg, and Keith Glauber played major league baseball in the 1990s. Another Brooklyn product, Mike Zimmerman, was a college all-American who made it to the top of baseball's minor leagues. His father, Jerry, is living proof that some things in Brooklyn haven't changed.

"He's a die-hard Brooklyn Dodger fan," Mike said. "One day I brought a Yankees hat into the house and he threw it out."

On Wisconsin

FRED CIPOREN

"Sure you're going," said his father, "and I'll tell you why—because the whole world is coming in New York, so you're going to Visconsin." When Solomon told his parents he was going to the University of Wisconsin they did not believe him. "Such ah smart guy you are that Brooklyn College isn't good enough for you. When your father is dead, that's when you could go starve in who knows where." Solomon's mother, a very short woman with a great bosom and poor health, said, "Solomon, what would you do if God forbid you got sick, who would even come in to you to see maybe you need something?"

When Solomon's intention was repeated a week later his mother called her sister Adele. "Nu Adele, Solomon wants to go in ah school that's so far it's already outside from New Jersey. Irving tried to talk to him and it doesn't do any good." "Don't let him go," said Adele. "What kind of a college could they have that's already in ah school inside New Jersey? Let him go better already in ah school inside New Jersey." At least in Jersey she felt her husband Eddie could get in his car and drive then, "to look, to see what it is there." Such troubles, thought Adele, to raise children, and when they grow up all they have is ideas. Who, she thought to herself, does such things? And where such ideas come from, she hardly knew. "Oy America," Adele sighed.

Well thank God, thought Adele, her daughter Irene had better sense. "Irene," she called out. "Your cousin Solomon wants to go in Visconsin ah school that's outside even from New Jersey." Irene had big bones, according to her mother, and didn't have to diet. "Ma, Wisconsin it outside of Chicago, not New Jersey." "My God," said Adele, "outside from Chicago—who knows even where is Chicago." Now she called her sister back. "Esther, what are you talking, you talk, talk, and you don't know even what you are talking, what are you talking outside of New Jersey, Irene says that Visconsin isn't even in Chicago." "Oy vey!" said Esther, and she made her sister promise not to tell Irving. So when Adele got off the phone she turned to her daughter and warned her. "Don't say a woid to Uncle Irving, Aunt Esther doesn't want he should find out where is Visconsin or he'll get aggravated." "Ma," said Irene, "it's on all the maps. Uncle Irving is sure to find out." "He won't find out if you'll be quiet. Your uncle doesn't read maps, he reads the *Forwards*, and when he goes someplace he asks someone where he is going. So if Uncle Irving gets aggravated I'll know you opened your mouth."

Solomon's mother understood that it was sometimes

necessary to make a long trip. Hadn't she come to America from Russia, and doesn't she even now walk all the way to Belmont Avenue pulling her shopping cart to save money? These were necessary, important trips, undertaken because no alternative presented itself. But to go to Wisconsin when Brooklyn College is within reach of the IRT Flatbush Avenue line, that she couldn't understand. She would puzzle over things that were crystal clear to her, but when explained to her children brought forth only smiles or outbursts.

She could not understand why her middle son was now contemplating a trip so far from the warmth and love it was her duty and pleasure to provide.

One morning she rushed into Solomon's room and woke him. "Your father's father came to me in a dream," she said. "Ma, what do you mean he came to you?" asked her son. "You mean you had a dream about him." "You'll teach your kids," she said, "not me. He came to me while I was asleep. He was wearing his brown coat and he won't take it off even after he sat down in the kitchen. I asked him if he wanted tea. You must be cold to come from such a long way, I said. But he waved his hand, the one with the twisted finger, to say no. 'Tateh, its good to see,' I said. 'Why did you come?' Then he stood up with the same hand he waved no tea, he bangs on the table. All of a sudden he says in ah very loud voice, 'Loss ihm nicht gain ah sei veit.' [Don't let him go so far.] 'What should I do?' I cried. 'Look for a way,' he said, and he walked out."

Since the dream was a communication from the family patriarch, Mrs. Kallenstein called her sister immediately. "Adele, Irving's tateh came to me in a dream." "Yeah," said Adele, "what does he think?" "Solomon shouldn't go in Wisconsin." "So what does Irving say?" asked Adele. "He is giving me plenty aggravation also," replied Mrs. Kallenstein. "He just bought a brown jacket to go with his navy blue pants. Gray goes good with blue, brown goes only with brown. How many times I told him he shouldn't go in ah store without me and he still goes."

Solomon knew that Wisconsin was far from Brooklyn. But to his family, distance, time, and height were measured solely by subjective experience. A 120-mile trip to the old bungalow colony Mr. Kallenstein bought to avoid the expected post–World War II depression took eight hours and three weeks preparation. "To your mother," Solomon's father pointed out, "every time she goes in the car she is going to America."

Solomon lived all his life in the Brownsville section of Brooklyn. And when someone wanted to compare distances or convey the idea of distance, they would say, "it is as far as from here to Canarsie." Then Canarsie was a sparsely populated, predominately Italian neighborhood in South Brooklyn. Canarsie meant far. Solomon first heard how far Canarsie was from his grandmother, when she related her courtship with her second husband. Her first husband, Solomon's maternal grandfather, was killed in Europe like everyone else. When she came to America she met her present husband, who was loved by all the grandchildren and called "Zada." "Nu, when I met your zada he wanted to show me a good time. For ah good time you could go in Coney Island." "How did you go to Coney Island?" Solomon asked. "Anybody you ask would tell you Coney Island is far. It musta be that Coney Island is farer even from Canarsie. Being dat it was so far, we get on a bus and went to the last stop. Nu, you think your zada went in ah school once? There are smarter men then your zada, good he is good, fine he is fine, and in a lot of ways you can't beat him, but he is not so smart. Nu, I never saw Coney Island, not even when we get off at the last stop." "But why didn't you ask if the bus went to Coney Island?" "We don't ask because your zada doesn't like to show he doesn't know. And because we knew Coney Island is so far we thought it musta be at the last stop. In America you can't find ah Jewish bus driver. They goyim drive the buses and the Jews make out they know where they are going."

"Solomon, you know when you said you were going to Wisconsin, it was like the house fell on my head," Mrs. Kallenstein wept. "Ah mother doesn't like to see a child should go away. But in America it looks to be that everyone feels entitled to move and go someplace else. In Europe where everything was terrible people stayed in one place and suffered. In America where it's good already, everybody goes away to find a way to suffer." Mr. Kallenstein, like a chorus, repeated, "Listen to your mother," as his wife talked. His father would have said more, for his heart was not yet empty, but his throat was choked. His mother approached a tall slender woman who was bidding her daughter farewell as she entered the Chicago-bound bus. "Nu, what can I do, my middle son is going to Wisconsin."

"He'll be fine," said the tall woman. "You'll see him during Christmas." Up to that point Christmas never meant a thing to Mrs. Kallenstein.

So Solomon was surprised when his mother kissed him and whispered how he shouldn't forget to come home on Christmas.

Knish Reminiscence

LAURA SILVER

Bland black lettering stands in place of the scripted neon that once proclaimed Mrs. Stahl's Knishes. The dulled orange counter that ran the length of the shop is gone. There's no indication of the continued availability of cherry lime rickeys. And, as if to compound the retreat of Mrs. Stahl's into the back right corner of the shop: no onion pletzels today.

The pletzel is a flat latke wanna-be, a rectangular tongue of onion-strewn dough: hot, thin, salt-tickled, and just greasy enough to assert its presence with a translucent brown-bag smudge. Cyrillic letters are skewed pictograms on the five-foot-high Plexiglas knish menu. Semiforeign characters represent the steady cast of ingredients: cherry cheese, spinach-potato, mushroom. The current-day incarnation of Mrs. Stahl plucks one steaming kasha from the metal knish repository. She bags it for me and chatters in Spanish. I take a plastic white knife to the tawny knish, douse both halves in mustard, and order a hot tea. This is the only place that makes me sentimental about Styrofoam. Without Gramma, Mrs. Stahl's is elevated from pit stop to destination.

I rummage for money and find none. My wallet is at home. The knish woman shows no signs of recognition or pity. For two years I have kept myself from Mrs. Stahl's and Brighton Beach. There's no reason she should recognize me or note my reappearance. I go to the car, scrounge up $2.20 for my snack, resign to return soon for the neat, pleated metal trays of cocktail knishes. My Atlanta cousins are dying for another shipment.

Today the wind coaxes me past the blank excavation of Brighton Baths. The gray sky tucks itself into my pocket. A black-hatted Jew walks toward me. I am convinced he will stop to reveal a cabalistic message from Gramma. She dreaded the day they would dismantle the baths. Just as well, I think, as I approach the boardwalk; just as well she is not here to witness it: the new development would have ruined her view. My second birthday without her and I decide, impromptu, to buck past the Brooklyn landmarks I have eschewed in grief and weakness.

The Prospect Expressway dumps me onto Ocean Parkway. Alone, I rekindle my traditional birthday pilgrimage. Today, place will be person. I count on Brighton to assuage my restlessness and indecision. Each cross street screams a story.

Church Avenue: her husband's used car lot—appropriately converted to an incomplete church across from the stables. Rugby Road: the dim apartment above the alley-

WORLD'S BEST
EST. 1935
KNISHES

Mrs. Stahl's ®
Baked, Not Fried
ВОСТОЧНЫЙ ПИР
ШАШЛЫКИ · САМСА · МАНТЫ · ПЛОВ
MEDITTERENIAN FOOD
SHISH KEBAB · SALADS · TEA · COFFEE

FREE DELIVERY

1001

Mrs. Stahl's, before [below left] and after [above]. Photos courtesy of
Seán Galvin.
[below right] Fritzie Silver, by the sea at Brighton Beach. Photo © Laura
Silver, 1996.

way, where, before there were trees, she holed herself up with perpetually packed cardboard boxes and cigarettes; where no visitors were allowed; where she fought with Al, or ignored him in the kitchen he infused with a Sunday smell of lox, eggs, and onions.

Avenue M: the Caravelle Diner, only acceptable eatery for Aunt Sid and Aunt Rose (this double title necessary to prevent insult to either one). The sisters piled their dining room three layers thick with heirloom furniture and urged cases of matzo on Gramma before and after Passover, until their deaths.

Eleven ninety-nine Ocean Avenue, apartment 1L, phone GE4–3868, where she wooed Caribbean neighbors with stuffed cabbage and applesauce pinked from peels. The bus shelter right in front of the building where she was pushed to a broken hip and her first stay at Maimonides Hospital. (I raced home from Massachusetts.)

Avenue U Chinese restaurant we shuttled her to every second or third weekend in the 1980s. Gramma and I would split the egg rolls, but she always gave me her tough, bubbled skin.

The Coney Island Avenue funeral home we filled with friends and tardy, insistent relatives is on the verge of demise. Today, the Ocean Parkway foliage seems to peak; golden leaves stream from trees against my windshield. The street must be as it was for the funeral. Jenn and Sarah got there early, so sat on a bench to bask in the Brooklyn autumn. I was as if color-blind. Today, I imagine that the dark oak paneling of Schwartz Brothers chapel has been peeled away, that light floods the somber den and congregation room, thwarting the tentative movements of a flat-faced funeral director who spoke only in the third person past tense.

It is easier to be on the beach than I expected. My favorite jetty is dotted with afternoon lovers. I balance myself on a rock surrounded with ocean thunder and residual foam. Again, the black-hatted Jew. Again, his silence. A seagull stares at me from the crest of a wave. Bald-legged Russian women wade along the hard sand. The tea is milky and sweet, the knish warm and grainy. Kasha was Gramma's favorite too. There were always several in her freezer. Now, I allow myself to thaw. I look up at the building where she lived, find the window that was hers, and realize I don't need a cryptic black-hatted messenger to invoke her presence.

Flatbush Memories in the Florida Sun

PETER DUFFY

The sprawling suburban expanses of Broward County, Florida, have little in common with Linden Boulevard in East New York or Church Avenue in Flatbush. The palm tree–filled landscape is marked by winding culs-de-sac, man-made lakes without names, and scores of planned condominium communities full of tanned and relaxed retirees. The sun is hot, the golf is plentiful, and dinner is served early. It may not look like it, but the borough is everywhere. "There are so many Brooklynites," says one woman, "it's a joke."

Ray Halper, a stocky, talkative World War II veteran living in the Kings Point development in Tamarac, Florida, can't stop thinking about his hometown. The main feature of his sunny two-bedroom, 1,500-square-foot apartment, which overlooks a lake in the rear, is a large wall dedicated to memories of his Flatbush childhood. He has hung framed pictures of streetcars, old Brooklyn Dodgers pennants, and pieces of Coney Island memorabilia. Halper knows more about Kings County history than most of his 5,300 fellow condo-dwellers. At least that's what everybody says.

Halper's a charter member and vice president of the Brooklyn club at Kings Point, which is located about twenty miles northwest of Fort Lauderdale. The club, which has more than 600 members, was formed a year and half ago by Paul M. Kahn, who lived in Crown Heights, Canarsie, and other neighborhoods before moving to Oceanside, Long Island, in 1976, and Florida in 1994. Kahn kept running into Brooklynites at the pool, on the tennis courts, at dinner, and he decided it was about time they all got together.

"Originally Kings Point didn't want it," he explains. "They said, 'What's the big deal about Brooklyn?' They said, 'If we make a place for you, we gotta have a Bronx club, a Detroit club.' I said, 'So what's wrong with that?' I said, 'Let me explain to you something. If you didn't come from Brooklyn, you don't know what the difference is. People from Brooklyn have a nostalgia that nobody else has, a mystique that nobody else has.'"

When he started the Kings Point Club, Kahn knew little about the other Brooklyn clubs that had popped up at many of the adult communities in Broward County, which surrounds Fort Lauderdale. The 600-member Brooklyn club at the 9,800-resident Wynmoor development in Coconut Creek has been in existence for sixteen years. "It has always been the largest and most popular club within the development," says Toba Bimby, who is editor of the club's monthly newsletter. The Brooklyn club at the approximately 15,000-resident Century Village in Pembroke Pines, which has been active for eleven years, has about 125 members, but that's largely because the community's Brooklyn population still clings to neighborhood rivalries: There is a separate Coney Island club that draws membership from former residents of the neighborhoods of Brighton Beach, Sea Gate, Sheepshead Bay, Manhattan Beach, and Coney Island.

The Brooklyn clubs are singular in their celebration of the old borough. Talk often turns to the Dodgers, favorite restaurants on Pitkin Avenue, weekend strolls on Eastern Parkway, and days spent at Steeplechase Park in Coney Island. Kings Point's Kahn sometimes posts signs with the names of neighborhoods or high schools and asks members to gather near the one that corresponds with their past. Century Village's club members arrange the tables so that conversations can easily be started, and club president Muriel Judkowitz's first question to new arrivals is always, "What neighborhood are you from?" "Invariably someone will say, 'Oh, I come from there too,'" says Jean Barusch, club secretary. "And then, 'Where did you live? Did you go to this school or that school?'"

Marilyn Grossman, the entertainment chairperson of the Kings Point club, organizes Brooklyn-themed events, including a klezmer, knishes, and egg creams night; a '50s night with hula hoop and bubblegum contests; and a Brooklyn day with bottled chocolate egg creams and pretzels. Evelyn Miller and Lillian Rubine of the Wynmoor club coordinate group trips to locations all over the globe. The former Brooklynites have visited the Greek Islands, Turkey, Russia, and other exotic spots. They're thinking about going to Australia and New Zealand next. The Century Village club takes sight-seeing boat rides along the Florida coast, attends dinner-theater performances, and makes excursions to the Gulfstream Race Track, which hosted a Brooklyn Day in February. Judkowitz and some other club members had their pictures taken with a winning jockey.

The Kings Point and Wynmoor clubs are dominated by Jewish retirees, many originally from East New York and Brownsville. The Century Village club has a greater degree of diversity, with Jews, Italians, Poles, and a few Hispanics making up its membership. Some of the retirees moved directly from Brooklyn to Florida, but a large percentage made their homes, sometimes for decades, in Long Island, New Jersey, or upstate New York, part of the white flight from the inner cities to the suburbs. The former Brooklynites like Florida for its sunny weather, lack of stressful responsibilities, and early-bird specials. "The biggest thing in Florida is the early-bird special," says Kahn. "You have to be willing to eat early."

"We have an enormous Jewish community in Broward County, and a large number are from New York and Brooklyn," says William Marina, a professor of history at Florida Atlantic University. Marina notes that the country's Jewish population, which is mostly Democratic, gave Governor Lawton Chiles the margin of victory in his narrow race against Republican Jeb Bush in 1994. "They turned the election," he says.

Many of the Brooklynites followed friends to the developments, which offer residents a wide variety of services. Condo owners pay monthly (or yearly) fees for the upkeep of lawns, lakes, pools, golf courses, condominium buildings, and other communal facilities. They are offered reduced rates for entertainment, free transportation within the complex (Kings Point and Century Village have buses that look strikingly like old Brooklyn trolley cars), and a security apparatus that prevents unauthorized guests from trespassing on the property. When someone arrives at the front gate of Century Village—where a posted sign warns, "This is a patrolled community"—a security guard calls the host's condo to ensure that the guest's presence is indeed requested. Once the visitor is allowed to enter, the next task is finding the particular "neighborhood" or "village"—a series of condominium buildings with names like Buckingham, Ivanhoe, or Cambridge—where the resident lives. Century Village has 140 separate condo buildings (spread across 724 acres of land), all of which look very much alike, so the job isn't easy.

Former Brooklynites say they enjoy the safety, convenience, and comfort of their surroundings, even if they lack, say, the unpredictability of their hometown. "There's nothing not to like," says Barusch of Century Village. "There's the clubhouse and all the activities, and the different clubs you can join if you want to." Adds her husband, Martin, "There are different kinds of shows. Anything you need. You don't even have to go out of the village. And there are plenty of bathrooms all over the place. That's important. You're laughing, but that's important."

Unlike most, the plainspoken Mildred Beacher, who grew up in Borough Park, Sheepshead Bay, and other neighborhoods, isn't quite sold on the Florida ideal. The condo she shares with husband Irving was purchased by her oldest son as a fiftieth-wedding-anniversary gift, and when Irving suffered a heart attack, the couple decided it was time to move to a more relaxed environment. But that doesn't mean she's happy about it. "I miss everything," she says. "My dream is to live in the city." If she hadn't found the Brooklyn club, she says she might've returned to New York.

"I found people that come from my own town," she says of the ex-Brooklynites. "They are not clannish. They are not snobbish. They are people that you can love. When you meet someone and they say they are from Brooklyn, you got friends right away."

The Beachers met during World War II, when Mildred, at the suggestion of one of Irving's relatives, started writing to the decorated (and lonely) airman stationed in the Pacific. In 1953, eight years after the couple married, they moved to Far Rockaway, Queens, although they visited Brooklyn as often as three times a week. Mildred, who speaks with deliberate emphasis on each word, has an easy grasp of Brooklyn history, which comes from lived experience rather than book study, she says.

With a wide smile, she remembers taking the trolley to visit her grandmother in Williamsburg, stopping by her uncle's bar near the Brooklyn Navy Yard, and spending part of her honeymoon at the Hotel St. George. She mentions businesses on Flatbush Avenue and in passing notes how the old Fox Theater was located next to the Brass Rail Restaurant. Irving strenuously objects, arguing that the theater was across the street from the Paramount. "No, it wasn't," she says, rising to the challenge. "For all the tea in China, I'll fight you on that."

The Brooklyn club is different from any other club, Mildred says, because it is friendly and welcoming, even offering membership to non-Brooklynites. A few members of the Bronx club have even been spotted hanging around the Brooklynites.

"These people don't belong in Florida," she says of club members. "They belong in Brooklyn."

The most common experience of Brooklynites in Florida is finding old friends they haven't seen in forty or fifty years. Hy Grossman found five ushers and the best man from his wedding after his wife, Marilyn, placed an ad in a local newspaper looking for people who used to hang out at the Two C's Luncheonette in East Flatbush. The ad brought phone calls from men who spent time at a candy store nearby called the Cozy Corner, but Marilyn politely told them that, no, she was looking for a different group of people. When the phone calls from the wedding party

finally came, the Grossmans were overjoyed ("One guy lives a golf shot away from here!" says Hy), but not entirely surprised.

"I'll tell you one thing, a standard thing down here, you gotta watch your mouth," says Hy. "Because you meet people that know people that know people."

Most retirees carry Brooklyn with them in the way they talk ("They say I have a Brooklyn accent," says Kahn. "We don't talk 'Toity-Toid Street.' That's the old Brooklyn accent of the longshoremen") and in the food they eat. There is an ongoing dispute over whether you can get a decent bagel in Florida, with some arguing that Brooklyn water is required to make a good bagel and others saying that if you look hard enough you can find an eatable one. A business called Bagelmania, not far from Kings Point, reportedly offers serviceable versions of the New York specialty. "I miss kosher delicatessens," says Irving Beacher of Brighton Beach. "I'd love a good hot pastrami sandwich. You can't get one here. They don't make a decent rye bread."

Judkowitz argues for members of her club the Brooklyn of the past is more than just distant memories of the Dodgers and trolley cars. It is something far more concrete. The closeness and camaraderie that the retirees remember from their days in the halls of Tilden High School or on the ball fields of Prospect Park are present in the air-conditioned condominiums and gently sloping golf course of south Florida. "I think the Brooklyn spirit is here," she says. "It's like an extended family. There's a neighborliness. That pretty much parallels what we had in Brooklyn."

Judkowitz's fourth-floor apartment overlooks the first tee of the Flamingo Golf Club at Century Village, and when her two sons come to visit she likes to watch them make their drives up the fairway. A retired statistician for the State of New York, she runs the Brooklyn club with a close attention to detail and a warm regard for her membership, although she must cope with the occasional "kvetchers." "I treat them exactly as I do my children," she smiles. Originally from Borough Park, Judkowitz was thirty-five years old when she moved to Queens with her husband, a bank auditor.

Sitting at her kitchen table after one of Florida's typical, fleeting midafternoon rainstorms, she reminisces about her grandfather's butcher shop, Shulman's, on Fort Hamilton Parkway in Borough Park, where as a small child she would pluck the feathers of the chickens that would eventually be sold to customers. Her grandfather was a tall, heavyset man with a gray beard who was strictly Orthodox and who loved having children running around the place. Judkowitz remembers him opening the shop right after dark on Saturday for a couple hours of post-Sabbath business. "There are some things you never forget," she says.

"I am very content where I am," Judkowitz adds. "In fact, when I do go up north to visit—I have a son who lives in New Jersey—it would be very easy for me to get in the car and take a ride to Brooklyn if I wanted to. But I just haven't had that desire. You know the old saying, 'You can't go home again'? I think it's true."

NOTE

This chapter was first published in an expanded version in *Brooklyn Bridge* (October 1998). It is published here with the permission of *Brooklyn Bridge*.

Are We There Yet?
One Family's Brooklyn Diaspora

SPIDER KEDELSKY

There's no one left in Brooklyn.

Well, of course there are people left in Brooklyn. Lots of them. But no one is left from my family. It's a curious thing, because Brooklyn offered us, like so many immigrant and next-generation families, security and opportunity—the chance to become America. Yet none of us stayed.

My maternal grandparents, Rifka and Barney Malamud, and my mother, Betty, all came from the Ukraine, from the shtetl of Sovron. Barney came to America first, his wife and child several years later.

After a brief sojourn on the Lower East Side, they settled in Bay Ridge, Brooklyn, where he opened a grocery store. They arrived in Brooklyn because, as my aunt Chaya says, her father was an "impetuous grocer" and had taken the train from Manhattan to the last stop, which happened to be in Bay Ridge, looking for a site for a new store.

They were one of the few Jewish families in a neighborhood of Scandinavians. Bay Ridge is where the Verrazano Narrows Bridge starts—it ends, of course, on Staten Island, where my best friend Harvey Abrams and I would go on long bike rides before the bridge was built, taking the ferry to get there and back.

Well, there was Mom and her parents. Then came sister Chaya, ten years Mom's junior. She lives in Israel now with her husband of forever, Mordy, also from Brooklyn. He was a Seabee in the Pacific in World War II and I've always loved the story about him bringing a beautiful carved canoe prow home from New Guinea after the war. He stored it at the apartment of his soon to be in-laws and one day came over and asked, "Hey, where's that canoe prow?"

Rifka had thrown it out because she said it smelled bad! I collect tribal art, have for years, so I know what that canoe prow would be worth today, but if you're from the Ukraine and Bay Ridge, what do you know from New Guinea?

So anyway, Mom and Chaya grow up, they and parents move a few more times, open other stores, and Mom, who said she was always a bit of a wild child—hard to believe if you ask me—meets Sidney Silver from East Flatbush, Brooklyn. Very good dancer, drugstore cowboy, high school dropout, funny and charming. After a whirlwind romance they elope. My brother Martin came first, then me in 1943 on Pearl Harbor Day, right in the middle of the war.

We lived in lots of places growing up, but the first I can remember was a two-family house on East Fifth Street in very middle-class Flatbush. Big trees lined the street. It's in the driveway of that house the famous family picture was

My mother, Betty, and her mother, Rifka, in the Ukraine, ca. 1914. Mom's father, Barney, may already have left for Palestine.

Our "famous" family photo taken in the alleyway of the East Fifth Street house.

taken of my jaunty dad standing next to me and my brother, both of us in our spiffy collarless sports jackets and saddle shoes.

So like I was saying, there's nobody left in Brooklyn. I think it probably first started with Mordy and Chaya. You see, all of us used to live pretty close to Rifka and Barney, who were always Bobby and Zaydy, near-Yiddish for Grandmother and Grandfather. I didn't even know they had proper names until I was in my teens.

One day I came into Bobby's apartment on East Thirteenth Street off Kings Highway, across the street from where Zaydy had his final grocery store, and around the corner from the Triangle Theater, one of four movie houses in an eight- or nine-block stretch of the "Highway." There's Bobby sitting with legs delicately crossed, a cigarette artfully dangling from two fingers, with wrist bent like a Vogue fashion model, her long hair completely undone. To top it all off, she's reading not her usual yiddush newspaper but the *New York Times*!

Who the hell is this urban sophisticate? I ask myself.

Not my cookie-baking, *Forvitz* reading, hair up in a bun all the time, broken English, never seen her with a cigarette before in my life grandmother. Turns out she was pretty well educated in Russia for a shtetl girl and a bit of a political firebrand—Zionist socialist type. But who knew then?

So anyway, the first break in the united Brooklyn Jewish heartland family bond is Mordy and Chaya. They have a baby, Ranan, who now lives in Bonicia, California, and the three of them move to the far edges of the earth—to a place in South Brooklyn called Beachhaven. A development of five-story apartment houses, it seemed an awfully long way from us. Though my parents moved several times depending on which way the economic winds were blowing, we always stayed in the central corridor of Brooklyn, always a close walk, car or subway ride to Bobby and Zaydy.

Mordy and Chaya had made a huge leap in distance, to be followed several years later by an even more incredible one—out to a house in Levittown on Long Island. Talk about shifting paradigms! If I took a walk I would invariably get lost because, unlike Brooklyn, all the houses looked exactly the same. I could never remember if theirs was on Ash Lane or Angel Lane, these streets being one block apart. In that little house, which grew in physical size over time, were added Dina then Beth as sisters to Ranan, both of whom now live in Seattle.

Oh, before I forget and get too far on this family odyssey, there is the Israel thing. My grandparents and their daughters were ardent Zionists, and the dream of return played strong in their lives. Zaydy left the Ukraine first to avoid being drafted into the czar's army, a cruel fate for a young Jewish fellow from the boondocks. He got to the Promised Land, but was eventually rousted out by the Ottoman Turks who, as allies to Germany, were expelling Russian nationals during World War I. He wound up in the port of Piraeus, Greece, with other Jewish pioneers, all eventually brought to New York on a ship supposedly chartered by Henry Morgenthau, later to be FDR's treasury secretary.

In New York, Zaydy started out by selling herring from a pushcart under the Williamsburg Bridge. His parents and Bobby's, who also planned to make *aliyah* (emigrate) to Palestine, never made it out of Russia. One set was murdered in a pogrom in Sovron, the other died of hunger.

Our family remained ardent American Zionists, and after Israel was established Chaya and Mordy went to live there, helping to establish Kibbutz Sasa on a beautiful hill in the Galilee. Mom and Dad, Mart and I arrived a year or so later in 1949.

We stayed for a while, but my folks couldn't make a go of it and returned to Brooklyn. Upon retirement they moved back there, this time staying for six years more. Mom now lives in Seattle, as do brother Martin and I. Chaya and Mordy also came back from that first foray to the Promised Land so Mordy could get an engineering degree at the University of Missouri. About a decade ago they moved back to Israel and now live in Har Halutz, atop another beautiful hill in the Galilee.

Relativity of place and time is particularly acute in a child, and in some ways Levittown, Long Island, where Mordy and Chaya bought their first house, seemed as distant from my small Brooklyn world as did Israel. I can remember standing on the outdoor platform of the Kings Highway train station in Brooklyn as a boy and if I leaned out far enough, and the day was clear, I could see the Empire State Building standing tall in that near yet far kingdom called "The City." Travel to see relatives in the Bronx was almost as exotic as a trip to Brazil, where "Bomba the

Mom (foreground) and me with the mukhtar of a nearby village. Why Martin is running away behind us will forever remain a mystery. Kibbutz Sasa, Israel, 1949.

Jungle Boy" (hero of my favorite boy's book) frolicked among the pumas and anacondas.

I was the complete Brooklyn product in allegiance and education, and there was much the borough could offer. I was a rabid Dodgers fan and was there for Pee Wee Reese Night and the time the Duke (Snider) hit three home runs and then a double that just missed going over the right field fence by about a foot.

Ebbets Field, the Dodgers' beautiful bandbox of a stadium, was right in the middle of a neighborhood near Prospect Park, always only a few subway stops from whatever apartment I was living in at the time. It was near the Bond Bread factory, where kids could take a tour and get miniature loaves to take home with them, and even now when I smell fresh bread baking I think of baseball and Brooklyn.

I swam indoors at the St. George Hotel's beautiful tiled pool in the winter and at Brighton Beach in the summer. I

Brother Martin and I in front of the greenhouse at the Brooklyn Botanical Garden, 1948.

No wonder the Dodgers left Brooklyn! Neighbor Johnny Gamarana (catching) and me in the front yard of 417 Canton Avenue near Ocean Parkway and the Parade Grounds.

frolicked on the meadows of Prospect Park (Olmstead's greatest pastoral creation), loved the Egyptian art at the Brooklyn Museum, shopped with my mother "downtown," and still cherish the beauty and tranquillity of days spent in the Botanic Garden. Years later I read a book about the great garden of the world and was shocked to see "my" gardens featured along with the great ones of Europe. Who'da thunk?

My closest friends were Jews, but I knew and was on good terms with Irish and Italian kids. Sometimes relations with these "others" could be adversarial, such as when battles were fought with the boys from St. Brendan's over accusations of Christ-killing. I can remember these same fellows talking loudly about food, particularly products of a porcine nature, as they paraded past the Kings Highway Jewish Center on Yom Kippur.

However, the sweetest words I heard as a youth were those uttered by the toughest goy of all, Frankie Pizzelli,

after I annihilated Louie Quagriello in a school yard fight, much to everyone's shock, most of all my own. Looking me up and down the next day he said, "I heard you beat up Louie yesterday. Not bad . . . for a Jew!" A qualified compliment to be sure, but coming from Pizzelli, the scourge of the universe in duck's ass haircut, tight jeans, and pointy black shoes, it was comparable to being notified of having won a Nobel prize.

I went to PS 130 and 238 and James Madison High School and then got an excellent and free education at Brooklyn College. I took the bus up and down Ocean Avenue from my parents' house to get there. My best friends in high school were the same in college. My fraternity, Zeta Beta Tau, was a Jewish one, and almost all of us lived with our parents into our early twenties. After college, and the 1960s onslaught of sex, drugs, and rock 'n' roll, I took up residence in Park Slope, a gracious neighborhood of beautiful brownstones in several of which I had apartments,

Me, Spider, as a bellhop at the Nevele Country Club in the Catskills in 1959. I parked guests' cars, but with no driving experience this ended when I planted a new Thunderbird into the side of an equally new Cadillac.

the last with six and a half rooms for eighty-two dollars a month.

I became an elementary school teacher, first in Crown Heights and then at the brand-new Intermediate School 320 directly across the street from where fabled Ebbets Field had stood only a few short years before, now home to low-income high-rise apartments. I met and associated with black and Puerto Rican people for the first time and became involved with the anti–Vietnam War movement and radical teacher politics. It was 1968.

After the teaching day I indulged my first passion, dancing, and spent many, many hours at the Brooklyn Academy of Music, which had become a center of contemporary American dance. At the end of that school year I left teaching to pursue performance as a full-time career. I later moved into Manhattan, and a year after left to live and dance in California.

My family was not unlike any number of Jewish ones who found in Brooklyn a stop along the way after arrival in America. Like Bobby and Zaydy, many set up on the Lower East Side first. Brooklyn was inviting for a next move. It was less crowded, with trees and houses, beaches, and many different neighborhoods—some ethnic enclaves, others more mixed. There were grand institutions and avenues befitting what was once America's fourth-largest city. It was a place families could start spinning out lives that were before only dreams.

My world in Brooklyn was of tribe and of clan. We could be family and Jews, Zionists and Americans all at the same time. It was not until my college years that I began to think of myself as "white," a description reserved to that point for Christians in some other America.

I asked Mom recently what she liked about living in Brooklyn, and right off she said that she "felt safe" among so many Jews. Although she and Bobby and Zaydy were always wary of what I came to call "the footsteps," the truth was that no drunken Ukrainian villagers or Cossacks ever rampaged through Flatbush.

Chaya on the other hand, ten years younger and born in America, loved Brooklyn because it "was a great place for ambitious kids—I always felt the horizons were limitless." As for Judaism, "for us it wasn't God, it was history, holidays, homeland, a clan."Although she, Mom, and their parents always had one eye on a return to the Promised Land, they had in a way already found it in Brooklyn.

My brother, the self-proclaimed existentialist who rejected the supposed hypocrisy of religion at an early age, claims he never thinks about Brooklyn. Prodded by me, he does say that it was "too crazy" growing up there, and that he would have preferred being raised in Middle America somewhere—by Ozzie and Harriet I presume. This probably explains his one great youthful deviance—living in Brooklyn, yet being a fan of the New York Giants baseball team.

A man immune to sentiment (I inherited both our shares), it was after only a few minutes of talk about the "Old Country" that he began reminiscing with me about the crisp hot dogs and greasy fries at Nathan's in Coney Island, and the unbelievably delicious vanilla custard with chocolate sauce at A&S, the big department store in downtown Brooklyn. The stomach, it seems, has a long memory.

We both now live in Seattle, as does Mom, and while my brother may not think about Brooklyn, I do. In this predominantly white and gentile corner of America, I miss not

At "Tap II—A Celebration of Black Tap Dance" with some of the greats. Left to right: Foster Johnson, Sandman Simms, me, Harold and Fayard Nicholas. Royce Hall, Los Angeles, 1979.

having more Jews around me, feel estranged from my history; and I grow nostalgic. It has become a small matter of pride to tell people that I'm from—not the East Coast, not New York—but Brooklyn. It lends an aura (or so I imagine) of hipness and sharpness, not to mention eccentricity, that you can't earn if you're from Los Angeles, Chicago, or Tacoma.

I was taking a swing dance class recently and did a double-time step, the one basic to what we called the Lindy in my youth. It being a triple-time class, the instructor came over and asked if I used to watch *American Bandstand* on TV. I said that I had not. He then asked me where I had grown up. "Brooklyn," I said. "Ah," he said, and nodded. I was treated with a certain respect and deference thereafter. Brooklyn can do that for a man.

Before I came to Seattle, and after a long stay in California, I returned to the East in 1983, living first in Amherst, Massachusetts, and then Washington, D.C. This gave me ample opportunity to travel to New York City, and on several occasions to visit old haunts in Brooklyn.

Park Slope, always a genteel and elegant area, was now "hot" and fully yuppified. Cheap apartments were but a faded memory. A rich and vibrant cultural stew of Caribbeans now lived in Flatbush, and Russian Jews had revitalized a decaying Brighton Beach. The grand movie houses were gone, shuttered or turned to new use. None remained on my favorite stretch of Kings Highway.

But much appeared the same. I visited Madison High School, still that big ugly lump of a building on staunchly middle-class Bedford Avenue, and was thrilled to see the "athletes' wall of fame" with my name on it just where I remembered it hanging in the boys' gym. Puffed up, I pointed this out to a student standing nearby. He responded with a look of disbelief, apparently assuming that someone immortalized in 1961 should now be long dead.

The Brooklyn Museum was wonderful and hipper, the Academy of Music had prospered, the Grand Army Plaza Library, that WPA-built wonder, remained a storehouse of knowledge and opportunity for new Americans. The nearby greenhouse in the Botanic Garden was still the charming place I visited as a boy to fantasize about Amazonian jungles years before I actually traveled to them.

I saw many of my old friends and attended high school and college reunions. No one that I spoke to lived in

Three great chiefs of aboriginal Australia and one boy from Brooklyn, on tour, Berkeley, Calif., 1981. Left to right: Maurice Jupurrula Luther, Nandjiwarra Anagula, moi, Clive Karwoppa Yukaporta.

Well, I'm not sure we're there yet, but at least we're in Seattle in the year 2000. Left to right: Brother Mart, me, Mom, my wife, Joan Zegree.

Brooklyn anymore. Like my own family, they had moved on to Manhattan, to Queens, to the "Island," to other cities, states, even countries. We had created our own lives and families, and it all made sense. We Jews had made assimilation a high priority. We took the opportunities America offered and drank them in.

Like our parents and grandparents before us, allegiance was not owed to any one place but to each other, our history, ideas, and dreams. Brooklyn had been a haven. It allowed us to feel secure, to grow, to learn, and to prosper. Having done so, my generation joined the great mobile American way of becoming and moved on, even if it was just across the river or out the Brooklyn-Queens Expressway.

But the heart has its ways, and Brooklyn takes on a glow seen from afar—in both years and miles. As well traveled as I am, and of all the strange and wonderful places I have been, Brooklyn is . . . well, still Brooklyn. It will always be home of the Dodgers, Cohen's Candy Store, Brighton Beach Baths, Steeplechase Amusement Park, the Triangle Theater, Bobby and Zaydy, and the most beautiful bridge ever built.

Just as I was completing this chapter, Dennis Mandell, a sweet and generous man, passed away in Manhattan. A college fraternity brother, I had stayed in contact with him over the years. I flew back to New York for his funeral, went to the burial, and sat shiva with his family.

At the cemetery as we put our dear friend into the earth I looked around at faces no longer young. I realized our coming together was not only to honor Dennis but also to celebrate our shared youth and the bonds formed in Brooklyn over thirty-five years earlier. The entire day was extraordinarily rich and evocative, and I was surprised at the comfort I felt among men and women I had not seen for years. Fellow mariners, we had started the great voyage into adulthood together and would always embrace each other if only for that shared experience.

That day reminded me of another a decade or so earlier. After a period of great professional turmoil in my life I found myself back in Brooklyn visiting my old neighborhood off Kings Highway. It was a bright Indian-summer day. I had no idea what my future was to be. After a long walk I was sitting in my car, the heat of the radiant sun warming my face and body. I leaned my seat back and closed my eyes. Slowly the pain of recent events drained away, and I was suffused with a profound sense of relaxation and serenity. For those few, precious moments I was at peace. Memory, like a blade, had cut through life's sorrows. I had come home.

Time Line of Selected Jewish Brooklyn Events or People

Seán Galvin

This time line is meant to reference some of the major chronological events in the lives of Jewish Brooklyn. It is in no way exhaustive, drawing largely from events mentioned in the body of *Jews of Brooklyn*. We also acknowledge the use of these invaluable sources of information: the time lines in Manbeck (1998), Snyder-Grenier (1996), and Kaufman (1999); events featured in Abelow (1937), Horowitz and Kaplan (1959), Postal and Koppman (1978), and various other sources for demographics; as well as the many contributors to JoB.

1600s

Dutch form five towns in what is now known as Brooklyn: Breucklen (Brooklyn), 1646; New Amersfoort (Flatlands), 1647; Midwout (Flatbush), 1652; New Utrecht, 1657; Boswijck (Bushwick), 1661.

1645

Lady Deborah Moody, an Englishwoman in search of a place where she and her Anabaptist followers can worship in peace, founds Gravesend.

1654

Beginning of first period of Jewish immigration. Spanish and Portuguese Jews continue to arrive in NYC until last decade of eighteenth century.

1660s

Asser Levy purchases substantial amounts of land in Bruecklen.

1787

Erasmus Hall Academy receives a state charter, making it the first public school in the country.

1800

New York is largest Jewish community in North America.

1815

Beginning of second period of Jewish immigration into NYC, starting with Jews from Germany, Austria, and Bohemia and continuing for at least fifty years, although German-Jewish immigration continues until 1910.

1816

Village of Brooklyn is incorporated within Town of Brooklyn.

1823

Coney Island Road & Bridge Co. builds Coney Island Causeway, also known as Shell Road, opening way for development of Coney Island.

1827

Village of Williamsburg is incorporated within Town of Bushwick.

1834

City of Brooklyn is incorporated (formerly town).

1837

Arrival of Adolph Baker, first known Jewish settler in Williamsburg.

1848

Congregation Kahal Kodesh Beth Elohim is formed in Village of Williamsburg; first Jewish cemetery in Brooklyn, Union Fields in Cypress Hills, is opened by members of K. K. Beth Elohim congregation.

1850

Coney Island Plank Road (later Coney Island Avenue), a toll road, opens; Samuel Liebman's brewery (later Rheingold) is established.

1851

City of Williamsburg is chartered; first kosher slaughterhouse is established on Bushwick Avenue by Ernest Nathan.

1852

Town of New Lots (formerly part of Town of Flatbush) is organized.

1854

City of Williamsburg and Town of Bushwick are annexed by City of Brooklyn, to be known collectively as the Eastern District.

1855

Consolidated City of Brooklyn is established, merging City of Brooklyn with City of Williamsburg and Town of Bushwick.

1856

Congregation Baith Israel is founded in City of Brooklyn (first in Brooklyn); Philip Licht founds Eagle Fireworks Co., in Williamsburg. Eagle later makes signal rockets for Union Army during Civil War.

1861

Secessionists from congregation Beth Israel create a second Beth Elohim (now known as Garfield Place Temple), Brooklyn's first Reform congregation.

1865

Charles S. Brown buys land he names Brown's Village (later Brownsville); Abraham Abraham and Joseph Weschler found dry goods emporium that later becomes Abraham & Straus, Brooklyn's largest department store (the A&S name was adopted in 1893 when Isidore and Nathan Straus, who built Macy's, joined the firm).

1867

Prospect Park opens, designed by Frederick Law Olmstead and Calvert Vaux.

1868

Hebrew Benevolent Society (later [1909], Brooklyn Federation of Jewish Philanthropies) is organized in Williamsburg; Eastern Parkway, world's first six-lane parkway, is completed.

1870s

Third period of Jewish immigration, in which eastern Europeans, primarily from Russia-Poland but also includes Austria-Hungary, Rumania, and other Balkan countries, becomes significant. (By 1881, the first tidal wave of immigration from Russia and Poland would sweep into the United States, bringing more than two million Jews on its crest; continuing to 1914, it would entirely engulf previous Jewish settlements.) Brighton Beach area is developed by William Engemann as alternative to "Sodom by the Sea" Coney Island (but he excludes Jews from his Brighton Beach Hotel).

1874

Charles Feltman introduces "frankfurter" at Coney Island.

1876

Ocean Parkway, a toll parkway designed by Olmstead and Vaux, opens for travel between Prospect Park and Coney Island.

1878

Brooklyn Hebrew Orphan Asylum is formed.

1883

Brooklyn Bridge is completed.

1889

YMHA, Hebrew Free School Association, and Aguilar Free Public Library merge to from Hebrew Institute (later, Educational Alliance), the pioneering Jewish settlement.

1890s

Brownsville's Jewish population reaches 4,000.

1893
Shaare Zion School is founded in Brooklyn, first "National Hebrew School" in America.

1894
Israel Fisher becomes first Jew elected to Congress from Brooklyn.

1895
Founding of the Jewish Hospital, an outgrowth of the Hebrew Hospital Dispensary, Brooklyn's oldest Jewish medical institution.

1897
Sabbath and holiday services are first instituted at Educational Alliance; Brooklyn Public Library is formed; Brooklyn Institute of Arts and Science (later, Brooklyn Museum of Art) opens on Eastern Parkway.

1898
City of Brooklyn (Kings County) is consolidated into Greater New York.

1899
Hebrew Education Society (HES) is founded with aid of the Baron de Hirsch Fund; Brooklyn Children's Museum, the world's first museum for children, opens.

1901
HES's weekday afternoon Hebrew school opens; in 1902 the Reform-oriented Sabbath school opens.

1903
Williamsburg Bridge opens; Shaarey Zion School is established in Williamsburg, first evidence of a Zionist presence in Brooklyn; first attempts at establishing an American branch of Mizrachi (which would founder two years later).

1906
Jewish Hospital (now Interfaith Medical Center) opens in Bedford-Stuyvesant; National Hebrew School is established in Brooklyn by Ephraim Kaplan using "Ivrith b'Ivrith" natural method curriculum for girls only.

1904–8
Peak period of Jewish immigration (640,000 enter the United States).

1907
Brighton Beach Baths open.

1908
Baith Israel merges with Talmud Torah Anshei Emes, Kane Street; Brooklyn IRT, New York's first subway, is connected to Brooklyn.

1909
Manhattan Bridge opens; Clara Lemlich Shavelson, garment union activist, gives speech that begins Uprising of the 30,000—largest women's strike to date.

1910
Birth of *Bruklin-Bronzvil Post*, "largest Yiddish weekly in Brooklyn."

1912
The Young Israel movement started as part of the Orthodox youth synagogue-center movement. "Young Israel of Flatbush," located at 1012 Avenue J, corner of Coney Island Avenue, continues its long and influential presence in the neighborhood.

1913
Ebbets Field stadium for Brooklyn Dodgers opens.

1914
National-Radical folk shul founded in Brownsville; Brooklyn Public Library opens Brownsville Children's Library, the first children's library in America.

1915
Fourth period of Jewish immigration to NYC begins. (Covering 1915 to the 1960s, it would reach significant proportions in the 1930s, during the Hitlerian period, and immediately following World War II, from 1946 onward. Between 1915 and 1924, the rate of Jewish immigration to NYC would exceed 50,000 per year. The impact of the quota system would first be felt in 1922.)

1916
Nathan Handwerker opens a food stand pioneering the nickel hot dog at a choice location between the new boardwalk and subway terminal. (Nathan's would become an institution, and "Make mine Nathan's" a national slogan); Margaret Sanger opens world's first birth control clinic in Brownsville; Abraham J. Shiplacoff first Socialist elected to N.Y. State Assembly (from Brownsville).

1917
Max Kufeld becomes principal of Etz Hayim in new Jewish community of Boro Park, a Jewish public day school, "first Hebraic all-day school"; Balfour Declaration announces British government's support for Zionism.

1918
December, First American Zionist Congress is held in Philadelphia.

1919
Jewish Communal Center of Brooklyn is formed, first of many "Jewish centers"; First Syrian Jewish synagogue is established in Brooklyn (Williamsburg).

1920
Subway arrives at Coney Island; Brownsville's Jewish population is 250,000.

1921
Founding of Brooklyn Jewish Center (Conservative), under Rabbi Israel Levinthal; Congregation K. K. Beth Elohim and Temple Israel merge to form Union Temple; Yeshiva of Flatbush opens.

1923
Largest number of Jewish people live in Brooklyn: its Jewish population (740,000) exceeds Manhattan's (706,000) for first time.

1924
Immigration Act of 1924 restricts eastern and southern European immigration.

1925
Eastern Parkway has a Jewish population of 47,570, or 48.8 percent of the neighborhood's total; next-door Brownsville is 95 percent Jewish with 169,906 population, highest concentration in NYC.

1928
Hebrew Alliance of Brighton by the Sea, Inc., is completed—Brighton Beach's first synagogue.

1929
Enduro's Sandwich Shop is opened by Harry Rosen at Flatbush and DeKalb Avenues (would be known as Junior's Restaurant after 1950).

1930
Brooklyn population, 2,560,401, is most populous in NYC, with 850,000 Jews.

1930s
Sidney Franklin [né Frumkin], first Jewish matador from Brooklyn, gains international fame and friendship with Ernest Hemingway.

1933
Over 1,350 boys are studying in Torah Vodaath–style elementary schools in Brooklyn.

1936
IND subway opens in Brooklyn.

1937
Jewish population of Brooklyn, at 947,765, is 37 percent of borough's total population; first Bais Yaacov school (Orthodox girls' school) in America opens in Williamsburg.

1940s
Brooklyn becomes "4th largest city in America," home to nearly one million Jews, "the largest Jewish community of any city in the history of the world" (Kaufman 1999).

1940
Brownsville Boys Club is established when Board of Education of NYC rules that boys over fourteen can no longer use after-school centers. Brownsville is still 80 percent Jewish.

1941
Rabbi Joseph Isaac Schneerson, a direct descendant of the founder of Hasidism, establishes Lubavitcher world headquarters on Eastern Parkway in Crown Heights; Circumferential Highway (Belt Parkway) opens.

1947
Jackie Robinson signs with Brooklyn Dodgers to become first African-American to play in Major leagues.

1948
Founding of State of Israel.

1950
Brooklyn's population peaks at 2,738,175, of which 920,000 are Jewish; Brooklyn Battery Tunnel opens.

1954
Brown v. Board of Education, Supreme Court decision outlawing school segregation.

1955
Brooklyn Eagle shuts down after 114 years.

1957
Brooklyn Dodgers, after winning their last game at Ebbets Field against Pittsburgh Pirates, move to Los Angeles.

1958
Brooklyn's Jewish population at 854,000.

1963
Brooklyn's Jewish population has declined to 765,000.

1964

Verrazano Narrows Bridge opens.

1967

Warbasse Apartment Houses are opened by Amalgamated Clothing Workers' Union in Brighton Beach, allowing thousands of Jewish retirees to flood neighborhood; Six Day War in Israel.

1968

Ocean Hill–Brownsville teachers' strike.

1969

Rabbi Meir Kahane founds Jewish Defense League and Israeli party Kach.

1972

East New York YM-YWHA, area's major Jewish institution, moves to Queens.

1973

New York elects first Jewish mayor, Abe Beame of Brownsville; Yom Kippur War in Israel.

1974

Yaffa Eliach founds Center for Holocaust Studies, Documentation and Research in Brooklyn, housed at the Yeshiva of Flatbush.

1975–80

Soviet Jewish émigrés (40,000, second wave) arrive in Brighton Beach.

1976

Jewish population of Brooklyn at 514,000, 42 percent of NYC's total Jewish population; 75,000 Jews in Canarsie alone.

1977

Howard Golden is elected borough president.

1985

Brighton Beach: estimates of general population 74,400 (Jewish 46,400, or 62%); Borough Park: estimates of general population 203,000 (Jewish 63,400, or 31%); Flatbush: estimates of general population 219,500 (Jewish 101,900, or 46%). Dedication of Sheepshead Bay Holocaust Memorial Park by Mayor Edward Koch.

1990

Brooklyn is still most populous borough of NYC, with 2,300,664 inhabitants; Center for Holocaust Studies, Documentation and Research in Brooklyn merges with Museum of Jewish Heritage—A Living Memorial to the Holocaust in Manhattan.

1991

Three days of riots in Crown Heights as a result of accidental killing of black child, Gavin Cato, by rebbe's chauffeur. Australian scholar Yankel Rosenbaum is killed by a black mob.

1992

President Assad lifts travel restrictions on Jews in Syria (with a resulting wave of as many as 3,500 immigrants to Brooklyn); collapse of Soviet Union; Soviet Jews come en masse to United States.

1994

Death of Menachem Schneerson, Grand Rabbi of Lubavitch community, whose world headquarters is located in Crown Heights.

1999

Controversial killing of Gidone (Gary) Busch in Borough Park by NYC policemen.

2000

Death of Grand Rabbi Shlomo Halberstam, a Holocaust survivor who nurtured postwar rebirth of Bobov Hasidic sect in Brooklyn; Chabad Lubavitch, first Jewish organization with its own Website, organizes educational networks for nearly one million children, through more than 2,500 Jewish institutions worldwide.

2001

Scheduled opening in Crown Heights of first Jewish Children's Museum.

Selected Bibliography and Recommended Reading

Brooklyn—Jewish

Abelow, Samuel P. 1937. *History of Brooklyn Jewry*. Brooklyn: Scheba Publishers.

Anti-Semitism in America, 1878–1939. 1977. New York: Arno Press. See chapter 2, a reprint of "Coney Island and the Jews: A History of the Development and Success of this Famous Seaside Resort, Together with a Full Account of the Recent Jewish Controversy" (New York: G. W. Carelton & Co., 1879).

Belcove-Shalin, Janet. 1988. "Becoming More of an Eskimo: Fieldwork among the Hasidim of Boro Park," in Kugelmass, Jack, ed., *Between Two Worlds: Ethnographic Essays on American Jewry*, pp. 77–102.

Belcove-Shalin, Janet, ed. 1995. *New World Hasidim: Ethnograpic Studies of Hasidic Jews in America*. New York: SUNY Press.

Braunstein, Susan L., and Jena Joselit Weissman, eds. 1990. *Getting Comfortable In New York: The American Jewish Home, 1880–1950*. New York: The Jewish Museum.

Cohen, Richard. 1988. *Tough Jews*. New York: Simon & Schuster.

Cohn, Michael, ed. 1963. *The Hasidic Community in Williamsburg, Brooklyn*. A report prepared by the Anthropology Workshop of the Brooklyn Children's Museum. Occasional Paper in Cultural History #4. New York: Brooklyn Children's Museum.

———. 1964. *Crown Heights and Williamsburg: A Comparison of Two Hasidic Communities in Brooklyn, NY*. New York: Brooklyn Children's Museum Cultural Anthropology Workshop.

Costabel, Eva Deutsch. 1988. *The Jews of New Amsterdam*. New York: Athaneum.

Eisenberg, Robert. 1995. *Boychiks in the Hood: Travels in the Hasidic Underground*. San Francisco: Harper San Francisco.

Friedman, Murray. 1955. *What Went Wrong? The Creation and Collapse of the Black-Jewish Alliance*. New York.

Frommer, Myrna Katz, and Harvey Frommer. 1993. *It Happened in Brooklyn: An Oral History of Growing Up in the Borough in the 1940s, '50s, and '60s*. New York: Harcourt Press.

Fuchs, Daniel. 1972 [1937]. *Williamsburg Trilogy: Summer in Williamsburg, Homage to Blenholt, and Low Company*. New York: Equinox/Avon.

Grinstein, Hyman B. 1945. *Rise of the Jewish Community of NY: 1654–1860*. Philadephia: The Jewish Publication Society.

Gurock, Jeffrey S., and Marc Lee Raphael, eds. 1995. *An Inventory of Promises: Essays on American Jewish History in Honor of Moses Rischin*. Brooklyn: Carlson Publishing, Inc.

Harris, Lis. 1895. *Holy Days: The World of a Hasidic Family*. New York: MacMillan.

Hoffman, Edward. 1991. *Despite All Odds: The Story of Lubavitch*. New York: Simon & Schuster.

Horowitz, C. Morris, and Lawrence J. Kaplan. 1959. *The Jewish Population of the NY Area: 1900–1975*. New York: Federation of Jewish Philanthropies of NY.

The Jewish Population of Greater NY: A Profile. 1984. New York: Federation of Jewish Philanthropies of New York.

The Jews of NYC 1654–1926: A Record of Cooperation and Service. 1927. New York: The Jewish Tribune.

Joselit, Jenna Weissman. 1990. *New York's Jewish Jews: The Orthodox Comunity in the Interwar Years*. Bloomington: Indiana University Press.

———. 1994. *The Wonders of America: Reinventing Jewish Culture, 1880–1950*. New York: Hill and Wang.

Kaufman, David. 1999. *Shul with a Pool: The "Synagogue-Center" in American Jewish History*. Hanover and London: University Press of New England and Brandeis University Press.

Kazin, Alfred. 1951. *A Walker in the City*. New York: Harcourt Brace.

Kessner, Thomas. 1977. *The Golden Door: Italian and Jewish Immigration Mobility in New York City, 1880–1915*. New York: Oxford University Press.

Kipust, Dr. Philip J. 1988. *I Remember Boro Park: Volume I, 1976–1987*. Brooklyn: Boro Park Historical Society, Ltd.

———. 1996. *I Remember Boro Park: Volume II, 1988–1955*. Brooklyn: Boro Park Historical Society, Ltd.

Kirshenblatt-Gimblett, Barbara. 1998. "Objects of Ethnography," in K-6,B *Destination Culture: Tourism, Museums, and Heritage*. Berkeley: University of California Press, pp. 17–78.

———. 1991. "Confusing Pleasures," 203–48.

Koskoff, Ellen. 1987. "The Sound of a Woman's Voice: Gender and Music in a New York Hasidic Community," in *Women and Music in Cross Cultural Perspective*, pp. 213–23. New York: Greenwood Press.

Kranzler, George. 1961. *Williamsburg: A Jewish Community in Transition*. New York: Feldheim Books.

———. 1972. *The Face of Faith: An American Hasidic Community*. Baltimore: Baltimore Hebrew College Press.

———. 1995. *Hasidic Williamsburg: A Contemporary American Hasidic Community*. Northvale, N.J.: Jason Aronson, Inc.

Kugelmass, Jack, ed. 1988. *Between Two Worlds: Ethnographic Essays on American Jewry*. Ithaca, N.Y.: Cornell University Press.

Landesman, Alter F. 1971 [1969]. *Brownsville: The Birth, Development and Passing of a Jewish Community in NY*. 2nd ed. New York: Block Publishing Co.

Markowitz, Fran. 1993. *A Community in Spite of Itself: Soviet Jewish Émigrés in New York*. Washington, D.C., and London: Smithsonian Institution Press.

Markowitz, Ruth Jacknow. 1993. *My Daughter, the Teacher: Jewish Teachers in the New York City Schools*. New Brunswick, N.J.: Rutgers University Press.

Mayer, Egon. 1979. *From Suburbs to Shtetl: The Jews of Boro Park*. Philadelphia: Temple University Press.

Mintz, Jerome P. 1968. *Legends of the Hasidim: An Introduction to Hasidic Culture and Oral Traditions in the New World*. Chicago: University of Chicago Press.

Moore, Deborah Dash. 1981. *At Home in America: Second Generation New York Jews*. New York: Columbia University Press.

Postal, Bernard, and Lionel Koppman. 1978 [1954]. *Jewish Landmarks of New York: A Travel Guide and History*. New York: Fleet Press.

Rieder, Jonathan. 1985. *Canarsie: The Jews and Italians of Brooklyn against Liberalism*. Cambridge: Harvard University Press.

Rischin, Moses. 1977. *The Promised City: New York Jews, 1870–1914*. Cambridge: Harvard University Press.

Rose, Ernestine. 1917. *Bridging the Gulf: Work with the Russian Jews and Other Newcomers*. New York: Immigrant Publishing Society.

Rosen, Marvin, and Walter Rosen, with Beth Allen. 1999. *Welcome to Junior's Restaurant, with Receipes and Memories from Its Favorite Restaurant*. New York: William Morrow.

Rosenblum, D. 1979. *Relatives*. New York: Dial Press.

Roth, Henry. 1934. *Call It Sleep*. New York: Robert O. Ballou.

Rothchild, Sylvia. 1981. *Voices from the Holocaust*. New York: New American Library.

———. 1985. *A Special Legacy: An Oral History of Soviet Jewish Émigrés in the United States*. New York: Simon and Schuster.

Rubin, Israel. 1972. *Satmar: An Island in the City*. Chicago: Quadrangle Books.

Sanders, Ronald. 1972. *Reflections on a Teapot: The Personal History of a Time*. New York: Harper & Row.

Schindler, Pesach. 1990. *Hasidic Responses to the Holocaust in Light of Hasidic Thought*. Hoboken, N.J.: Ktav Press.

Schwartz, Lyne Sharon. 1989. *Leaving Brooklyn*. Boston: Houghton Mifflin.

Sexton, Andrea Wyatt, and Alice L. Powers, eds. 1994. *The Brooklyn Reader: Thirty Writers Celebrate America's Favorite Borough*. New York: Crown Trade Paperback.

Shokeid, Moshe. 1988. *Children of Circumstances: Israeli Emigrants in New York*. Anthropology of Contemporary Issues. Ithaca, N.Y.: Cornell University Press.

Smith, Anna Deavere. 1993. *Faces in the Mirror: Crown Heights, Brooklyn, and Other Identities*. New York: Anchor/Doubleday.

Smith, Betty. 1943. *A Tree Grows in Brooklyn*. New York: Harper & Row.

Solomon, Polly. 1962. *The Hasidic Community of Williamsburg*. New York: The Free Press of Glencoe, Inc.

Sorin, Gerald. 1990. *The Nurturing Neighborhood: The Brownsville Boys Club and Jewish Community in Urban America, 1940–1990*. New York: New York University Press.

Storm, Yale. 1993. *The Hasidim of Brooklyn: A Photo Essay*. Northvale, N.J.: Jason Aronson, Inc.

Sutton, Joseph A. D. 1979. *Magic Carpet: Aleppo in Flatbush*. New York: Thayer-Jacoby.

———. 1988. *Aleppo Chronicles: The Story of the Unique Sephardeem of the Near East in Their Own Words*. New York: Thayer-Jacoby.

Warshaw, Mal. 1976. *Tradition: Orthodox Jewish Life in America*. New York: Schocken Books.

Wenger, Beth. 1996. *New York Jews and the Great Depression: Uncertain Promise*. New Haven, Conn.: Yale University Press.

Wexelstein, Leon. 1925. *Building Up Greater Brooklyn, with Sketches of Men Instrumental in Brooklyn's Amazing Development*. Brooklyn Biographical Society.

Ph.D. and Masters Theses on Jewish Subjects

Belcove-Shalin, Janet Sera. 1989. "A Quest for Wholeness: The Hasidim of Boro Park." Ph.D. diss. [anthropology], Cornell University, UMI Microfilms.

Drucker, Erna. 1984. "Jewish Settlers in New Amsterdam and Early New York, 1654–1825: A Selected Annotated Guide to Source Materials." MLS thesis, Queens College.

Epstein, Shifra. 1979. "The Celebration of Contemporary Purim in the Bobover Hasidic Community." Ph.D. diss., University of Texas, UMI Microfilms.

Halpert, Max. 1958. "The Jews of Brownsville, 1880–1925: Demographic, Economic Socio-Cultural Study." D.H.L. diss., Yeshiva University.

Harris, Zevi H. 1956. "Trends in Jewish Education for Girls In New York City." Ph.D. diss., Yeshiva University.

Kamen, Robert Mark. 1975. "Growing Up Hasidic: Education and Socialization in Bobover Hasidic Community." Ph.D. diss., University of Pennsylvania.

Levy, Sydelle Brooks. 1973. "Ethnic Boundedness and the Institutionalization of Charisma: A Study of the Lubavitcher Hasidim." Ph.D. diss., CUNY, UMI Microfilms.

Morris, Bonnie Jean. 1989. "Women of Valor: Female Religious Activism and Identity in the Lubavitcher Community of Brooklyn, 1955–1987." Ph.D. diss. [history], SUNY Binghamton, UMI Microfilms.

Rubin, Israel. 1965. "Contemporary Satmar: A Study in Social Control and Change." Ph.D. diss. [sociology], University of Pittsburgh, UMI Microfilms.

Brooklyn—General Interest

Abel, Allen J. 1995. *Flatbush Odyssey: Journey through the Heart of Brooklyn*. Toronto: McClelland and Stewart.

Alleman, Richard. 1988. *The Movie Lovers' Guide to New York*. New York: Perennial Library.

Binder, Frederick M. 1995. *All the Nations under Heaven: An Ethnic and Racial History of New York City*. New York: Columbia University Press.

Brooklyn Rediscovery. 1984. *Brooklyn Almanac: Illustrations, Facts, Figures, People, Buildings, Books*, ed. Margaret Latimer. New York: Brooklyn Educational and Cultural Alliance.

Carton, Bernice. 1988. *Beyond the Brooklyn Bridge*. Santa Fe, N. Mex: Sunstone Press.

Daly, Margaret. 1997. *Brooklyn Eats: The Guide to Brookyln Restaurants*. New York: Brooklyn Chamber of Commerce.

Dolkart, Andrew S. 1990. *This Is Brooklyn: A Guide to the Borough's Historic Districts and Landmarks*. Photos by Tony Velez. Brooklyn: Fund for the Borough of Brooklyn.

Everdell, William R., and Malcolm Mackay. 1973. *Rowboats to Rapid Transit—a History of Brooklyn Heights*. Brooklyn: Brooklyn Heights Association.

Fischler, Stan. 1997. *The Subway: A Trip through Time on New York's Rapid Transit*. New York: H&M Productions II.

Fisher, Edmund D. 1902. *Flatbush Past and Present*. Brooklyn: Midwood Club.

Glueck, Grace, and Paul Gardner. 1991. *Brooklyn: People and Places, Past and Present*. New York: Harry N. Abrams.

Hood, Clifton. 1993. *722 Miles: The Building of the Subways and How They Transformed New York*. New York: Simon & Schuster.

Jackson, Kenneth T. 1995. *The Encyclopedia of New York City*. New Haven, Conn.: Yale University Press.

Lancaster, Clay. 1961. *Old Brooklyn Heights: New York's First Suburb, Including Detailed Analysis of 61 Century-Old Houses*. Rutland, Vt.: Charles E. Tuttle.

Latimer, Margaret. 1983. *Two Cities: New York and Brooklyn: The Year the Great Bridge Opened*. Brooklyn: Brooklyn Educational and Cultural Alliance.

——. 1984. *Brooklyn Rediscovery*. New York: Brooklyn Educational and Cultural Alliance.

Lines, Ruth L. 1949. *The Story of Sheepshead Bay, Manhattan Beach and the Sheepshead Bay Library*. Brooklyn: Brooklyn Public Library.

Manbeck, John, ed. 1998. *The Neighborhoods of Brooklyn*. Introduction by Kenneth T. Jackson. New Haven, Conn.: Yale University Press.

McCullough, David W. 1972. *The Great Bridge: The Epic Story of the Building of the Brooklyn Bridge*. New York: Simon & Schuster.

——. 1983. *Brooklyn . . . and How It Got That Way*. New York: The Dial Press.

Merlis, Brian. 1995. *Brooklyn: The Way It Was*. Brooklyn: Israelowitz Publishing.

Miller, Ruth Seiden. 1979. *Brooklyn, USA: The Fourth Largest City in America*. Brooklyn: Brooklyn College Press.

Monti, Ralph. 1991. *I Remember Brooklyn: Memories from Famous Sons and Daughters*. New York: Birch Lane Press.

Prince, Carl E. 1996. *Brooklyn's Dodgers: The Bums, the Boroughs, and the Best of Baseball, 1947–1957*. New York: Oxford University Press.

Rosten, Norman. 1986. *Neighborhood Tales*. New York: Geo. Braziller, Inc.

Snyder-Grenier, Ellen M. 1996. *Brooklyn! An Illustrated History*. Philadelphia: Temple University Press, for the Brooklyn Historical Society.

Stiles, Henry R. 1867–70. *History of the City of Brooklyn*. 3 vols. Brooklyn: Published by subscription.

——. 1884. *The Civil, Political, Professional and Ecclesiastical History and Commercial and Industrial Record of the County of Kings, and the City of Brooklyn, New York, from 1663 to 1884*. 2 vols. New York: W. W. Munsell.

Weld, Ralph Foster, 1950. *Brooklyn Is America*. New York: Columbia University Press.

Willensky, Eliot. 1986. *When Brooklyn Was the World, 1920–57*. New York: Harmony.

Younger, William Lee. 1978. *Old Brooklyn in Early Photographs, 1865–1929: 157 Prints from the Collection of the Long Island Historical Society*. New York: Dover.

Contributors

Ilana Abramovitch received her Ph.D. in performance studies at New York University, where she conducted research in Jewish folklore and ethnography. She has written and lectured on the cultural politics of U.S. immigration in the early twentieth century. Abramovitch is Manager of Curriculum at New York's Museum of Jewish Heritage—A Living Memorial to the Holocaust, has consulted on numerous Jewish arts festivals, and was Director of Folk Arts Programs at the Brooklyn Arts Council. She has lived in Brooklyn since 1986.

Joyce Antler is the Samuel Lane Professor of American Jewish History and Culture at Brandeis University. Her books include *The Journey Home: How Jewish Women Shaped Modern America; Talking Back: Images of Jewish Women in American Popular Culture; and America and I: Short Stories by American Jewish Writers.*

Adina Back lives in Brooklyn, works in Brooklyn, and teaches a course on Brooklyn history. She is Assistant Professor in the History and Library Departments at Brooklyn College, CUNY, where she also directs a minor in archival studies and community documentation.

Fred Ciporen is Vice President and Group Publisher of *Publisher's Weekly, Library Journal,* and *School Library Journal.*

Joseph Dorinson is Professor of History at Long Island University. He also teaches at St. Francis College of Brooklyn. A noted authority in the field of popular culture, Dorinson's research specialties span sports history, Russian immigration, Brooklyn and Jewish history, and World War II movies and music. Among his publications are *Jackie Robinson: Race, Sports and the American Dream,* published by M.E. Sharpe, 1999 (paper edition), and a book on Paul Robeson (edited with William Pencak), McFarland Publishers.

Dr. Jay Eidelman is a historian at the Museum of Jewish Heritage—a Living Memorial to the Holocaust in New York City. Originally from Montréal, Canada, he now lives in Prospect Heights, Brooklyn, with his wife.

Walter Zev Feldman is a leading researcher in both Ottoman Turkish and Jewish music and a performer on the klezmer dulcimer cimbal *(tsimbl).* He is author of *Music of the Ottoman Court: Makam, Composition and the Early Ottoman Instrumental Repertoire* (Berlin: VWB Publishers, 1996) and both the "Ottoman Music" and "Klezmer Music" articles for the *New Grove Dictionary of Music and Musicians.* For many years the Coordinator for Turkic Language Programs in the Department of Asian and Near Eastern Studies at the University of Pennsylvania, Feldman lectures frequently on Jewish, Turkish, and Burkharan music and is currently compiling material for a monograph on klezmer music. Together with Steven Greenman he founded the ensemble Khevrisa. Their CD *Khevrisa: European Klezmer Music* came out on Smithsonian-Folkways in spring 2000.

Carole Belle Ford, who grew up in Brownsville, is Professor Emerita at Empire State College, the State University of New York's alternative college. She has a master's degree in minority and immigration history from SUNY, New Paltz, and a doctorate from Teachers College, Columbia University. Her book, *The Girls: Jewish Women of Brownsville, Brooklyn, 1940–1995,* was published in 2000 by SUNY Press. Like most other retired people she knows, she continues to work part-time—at Empire State College and on a new book.

Seán Galvin is Project Director, Liberty Partnership Program, LaGuardia Community College, CUNY. He received his Ph.D. from the Folklore Institute, Bloomington, Indiana. He worked on the Global Jukebox Project for the Association for Cultural Equity, Hunter College, and has been writer, filmmaker, and grant writer for numerous projects having to do with art, folklore, and community life in Brooklyn. He has served as Director of Folk Arts Programs at the Brooklyn Arts Council.

Ilana Goldberg received her B.A. from the Hebrew University in Bible and Assyriology, and her M.A. in anthropology from New York University, where she studied ethnographic film. Her latest work in progress is a film about an alternative public high school in New York City.

Roy Goldblatt has returned to his roots. Having lived in Finland since 1973, where he is lecturer at the University of Joensuu (the easternmost university/academic outpost in the European Union), he now spends a number of weeks a year teaching in Poland, the venue where his grandmothers began schlepping to America.

Henry Goldschmidt is a Brooklyn native, and Brooklyn nationalist, who received his Ph.D. in cultural anthropology from the University of California at Santa Cruz. His doctoral dissertation explores the intersections of race and religion in the construction of black-Jewish difference in Crown Heights. He would like to thank the Social Science Research Council, the Lucius N. Littauer Foundation, and the National Foundation for Jewish Culture for their generous support of his research.

Jillian Gould received her M.A. in performance studies at New York University. She currently works for the Eldridge Street Project, which is restoring the landmark Eldridge Street Synagogue on the Lower East Side. She lives in Brooklyn.

New York City–born Paul S. Green covered World War II for the military newspaper *Stars and Stripes* in North Africa, Italy, France, and Germany. After spending ten years on the U.S. Senate staff in Washington, D.C., he freelances as a journalist and author. He is author of *From the Streets of Brooklyn to the War in Europe* (Council Oaks Books, 1999), from which his essay is excerpted.

Laura Greenberg studied English literature and music at Brooklyn College, Manhattan School of Music, City College, and Columbia University. She teaches music at CUNY's John Jay College. Her compositions have been recorded and performed in the United States and abroad. Her memoir, *Memorizing Time,* recounts the Brooklyn childhood of a young musician.

Judith R. Greenwald, an attorney, has been a member of Baith Israel Anshei Emes for over thirty-three years. Currently the congregation's Archivist and Historian, she has also served as Journal Committee Chair, Recording Secretary, Vice President, and President.

Jeffrey S. Gurock is Libby M. Klaperman Professor of American Jewish History at Yeshiva University. He is presently completing a history of Jewish religious life in America between the two world wars.

Miriam Gottdank Isaacs was born in a displaced persons camp in Germany to eastern European parents. She lived in Brooklyn from 1960 to 1967, attending Erasmus Hall High School and Brooklyn College. Trained as a linguist, she teaches Yiddish language and literature at the University of Maryland. Her research has been on the languages of Hasidim and the Yiddish publications in refugee camps.

Eve Jochnowitz is a graduate student at New York University.

George Jochnowitz is Professor Emeritus of Linguistics at the College of Staten Island, CUNY. He is especially interested in dialects, in particular, the languages of the Jews of Italy and southern France.

Spider Kedelsky has spent his entire working life involved with the performing arts. As an artist he received three National Endowment for the Arts Choreography Fellowships, and as a teacher he served as Director of the dance program at Amherst College, Artist-in-Residence at the University of North Carolina, and elementary schoolteacher in Brooklyn public schools. He was the founder-director of the Los Angeles International Dance Festival and produced or curated special programs and events including the landmark 1981 tour of America, "Aboriginal Artists of Australia," and "The Dance and Music of Africa" at Jacob's Pillow Dance Festival as well as various programs honoring Latino, African-American, and Asian dance and music traditions. Spider now lives on a houseboat in Seattle, Washington, with his wife Joan Zegree, is the program director of Town Hall Seattle, a community cultural center, and also works as an arts consultant.

Mark Kligman is an Associate Professor of Jewish Musicology at Hebrew Union College, Jewish Institute of Religion, where he teaches primarily in the School of Sacred Music in the New York School. His research interests include the interconnection of music and Jewish cultural life among Sephardic and Orthodox Jews in Brooklyn.

Jack Kugelmass is Director of the Jewish Studies Program and Professor in the Interdisciplinary Humanities Program at Arizona State University in Tempe. He is the author of, among other books, *The Miracle of Intervale Avenue: The Story of a Jewish Congregation in the South Bronx* (New York: Columbia University Press, 1996) and co-author of *From a Ruined Garden: The Memorial Books of Polish Jewry* (Bloomington: Indiana University Press, 1998). He is currently completing a book on the public culture of American Jewry. He is also the editor of *City & Society*, the journal of the Society for Urban, National, Transnational and Global Anthropology.

Zachary Levin is a New York–based freelance writer who has written for *New York Press*, *Brooklyn Bridge*, and the *Denver Quarterly*. He has also written for various Websites, such as DrDrew.com, Rx.com, PraxisPost.com, and BigWords.com. His articles can be found at his Website: ZacharyLevin.com. He is currently at work on a collection of short stories based on his experiences as a tree worker in Connecticut and a deckhand on a New York Harbor sanitation tug.

Laura Mass grew up in Manhattan but now resides happily in Brooklyn. She works at The Jewish Museum.

Louis Menashe was Charles S. Baylis Professor of History and head of the department of social sciences at Brooklyn's Polytechnic University before his retirement. He continues to teach Russian history and film there.

Mark Naison is Professor of African-American Studies and History at Fordham University and directs its Urban Studies Program. He is the author of *Communists in Harlem During the Depression* and of numerous articles on popular culture, labor, and African-American history. His most recent writing project is a memoir titled *Whiteboy: Reflections of a Life between Racial Boundaries*, from which his chapter is excerpted, which will be published by Temple University Press in 2002.

Roberta Newman was Curator of Photographs and Films at YIVO Institute for Jewish Research in 1988–92. She has served as a researcher on many documentary films and exhibitions and is the Senior Content Producer of the DVD-ROM version of "Heritage: Civilization and the Jews." She is now YIVO's Director of New Media.

Annelise Orleck is the author of *Soviet-Jewish Americans* (1999) and *Common Sense and a Little Fire: Working Class Women's Politics in the U.S.* (1995). She is also co-editor of *The Politics of Motherhood: Activists Voices from Left to Right* (1997).

Leslie Paris is Assistant Professor of History at St. Mary's University in Halifax, Nova Scotia. This article is drawn from her dissertation, titled "Children's Nature: Summer Camps in New York State, 1919–1941," which she completed at the University of Michigan in 2000. Her scholarly interests include American culture, childhood, and gender relations. Both her parents were born in Brooklyn.

Lori Robinson is a nice Jewish grrl (not a typo) who lives on the Upper West Side, writes, sings, and tells a good joke. Her writing can occasionally be seen at *www.wemedia.com* as well as other, more obscure publications. She has many friends who live in Brooklyn, many of them Jews.

Robert A. Rockaway teaches in the Department of Jewish History at Tel Aviv University. His most recent book is *But—He was Good to his Mother: The Lives and Crimes of Jewish Gangsters*.

Alan Rosen lectures in the English Department at Bar-Ilan University. He publishes on early modern drama and on Holocaust literature. He is the author of *Displacing the End*, the editor of *Celebrating Elie Wiesel*, and is writing a book on the Holocaust and multilingualism.

Jan Rosenberg was born in Peoria, Illinois. She has lived with her husband, Fred Siegel, and two sons, Harry and Jake, in Brooklyn for more than twenty years. She is a sociologist at Long Island University's Brooklyn campus.

Henry Sapoznik is the author of *Klezmer! Jewish Music from Old World to Our World* (Schirmer Books) and is co-producing a series with David Isay on the history of Yiddish radio for National Public Radio.

Suzan Sherman is an editor at BOMB magazine. Her fiction and nonfiction have appeared in BOMB, The Mississippi Review (online), Bookforum, and Poets and Writers. She has been awarded writing residencies at The Edward Albee Foundation, The Cottages at Hedgebrook, The Ragdale Foundation, and The Virginia Center for the Creative Arts. She is presently completing a collection of short stories titled My Hidden Children.

Trysa Shy is in her senior year at Brandeis University. She lives in Port Washington, N.Y., and plans to pursue a career in Jewish education.

Writer and photographer Laura Silver is a third-generation Brooklynite who doesn't want anyone to know she was born in the borough of Queens.

Renata Singer is a writer and editor who lives in Melbourne, Australia, and New York City. Her published books include Goodbye and Hello and True Stories from the Land of Divorce. The Front of the Family, her first novel, was published by Bruce Sims Publishing in February 2001.

Peter Sokolow has lived in Brooklyn for fifty-nine of his sixty years. He has been an active performing musician since 1956, when his career began in the catering halls of his home borough. Mr. Sokolow is well known in commercial "club date" music, Jewish music, and in traditional jazz circles, as a pianist/keyboardist, vocalist, and bandleader. He has performed with many klezmer and jazz greats, has recorded extensively, and concertized across North America and Europe. He has appeared in numerous radio and TV documentaries and his films, among them The Chosen, A Tickle in the Heart, In the Fiddler's House, and Fiddler on the Roof.

Gerald Sorin is Director of Jewish Studies at SUNY, New Paltz, and the author of more than one hundred publications. His latest book is Tradition Transformed: The Jewish Experience in America, and he is currently working on a biography of Irving Howe.

Daniel Soyer is Assistant Professor of History at Fordham University. His book, Jewish Immigrant Associations and American Identity in New York, 1880–1939 (Cambridge: Harvard University Press, 1997) was co-winner of the Saul Viener Prize of the American Jewish Historical Society for the best book in the field.

David Spaner has worked as a feature writer, reporter, and editor for numerous publications. His writing has also appeared in such books as Total Baseball and Jewish Women in America: An Historical Encyclopedia. He is currently a movie critic at the Vancouver Province newspaper.

Michael Taub is Professor of Jewish Studies at Purchase College. Taub is the author of Modern Israeli Drama and Israeli Holocaust Drama, and co-editor of Contemporary Jewish-American Writers. As an undergraduate he went to Brooklyn College and lived in East Flatbush and Boro Park, two Brooklyn neighborhoods.

Aviva Weintraub is Director of Media and Public Programs at The Jewish Museum in New York. She writes and lectures on Yiddish and Jewish culture, film, and performance art.

Walter Zenner is Professor of Anthropology at the University of Albany. His forty years of research on Jews from Syria in Brooklyn culminates in A Global Community: The Jews from Aleppo, Syria (Detroit: Wayne State University Press, 2000).